APPROPRIATE
Christianity

CHARLES H. KRAFT, ED.

DEDICATED TO DEAN S. GILLILAND

WILLIAM CAREY
LIBRARY
publisher

Cover design: Amanda Valloza

Book design: Corinne Kershaw

Published by William Carey Library
1605 E. Elizabeth Street
Pasadena, California 91104
www. missionbooks.org

William Carey Library is a Ministry of the U.S. Center for World Mission, Pasadena, California.

Library of Congress Cataloguing-in-Publication Data

Appropriate Christianity / Charles H. Kraft, ed.
     p. cm.
  Includes bibliographical references and indexes.
  ISBN 0-87808-358-8 (alk. paper)
1. Missions--Theory. 2. Christianity and culture. I. Kraft, Charles H. II. Title.

BV2063.A67 2005
266'.001--dc22

2005049425

Printed in the United States of America

Contents

gratis

132118

Culture + Contextualization

APPROPRIATE
Christianity

Contents

Dedicated to Dr. Dean S. Gilliland

Dedication

This book is affectionately dedicated to Dr. Dean S. Gilliland, the first and, to my knowledge, still the only professor on a seminary faculty with the term Contextualization in his official title. He was brought onto the faculty of the School of World Mission (now School of Intercultural Studies), Fuller Seminary in 1977 at about the time Evangelical missiologists began to feel comfortable with the term "contextualization" to designate what we had previously called "indigenization." He joined a faculty already committed to incarnational mission and became our point man in developing our emphasis on teaching and research concerning contextualized theology.

Dr. Gilliland is a graduate of Houghton College (B.A. 1950), Evangelical Theological Seminary (Naperville, IL, B.D. 1954), Princeton Theological Seminary (Th.M. 1960), and Hartford Seminary Foundation (Ph.D. 1971). His doctoral dissertation was a study of the interactions between Islam and African religions in Northern Nigeria and was published under the title of *African Religion Meets Islam* (1986).

He is married to Lois (since 1951) and together they have raised four sons and a daughter and are the proud grandparents of four. When not engaged in academic work, Dean loves to sing, to the great delight of all who hear his lovely tenor voice. He is also fond of driving his 1930 Ford Model A sedan and he is an accomplished storyteller.

Dr. Gilliland was commissioned for missionary service with The Evangelical United Brethren Board of Missions in 1955 after seven years of pastoral work and spent the years from 1955 to 1976 in various capacities as a missionary in Nigeria. During much of that time he taught in and principled two Bible schools (1956-63) and the Theological College of Northern Nigeria (1970-76). He attained fluency in the Hausa language and did much of his teaching and interacting with students in that medium rather than in English.

It was with great sadness that he and Lois found it necessary to leave Nigeria in 1976, but the Lord had another place for Dean to serve—in Fuller's School of World Mission. So he moved his family to California to take up what would be his career for the next quarter of a century.

Upon his arrival at Fuller in 1976, Dean joined Arthur Glasser, and later Chuck Van Engen, teaching courses in the biblical theology of mission. His approach to contextualization drew heavily on Paul's ministry among the Gentiles as did the book he published in 1983, *Pauline Theology and Mission Practice*. Of special relevance to this project is his 1989 volume, *The Word Among Us*, a valuable contribution to contextualization studies and still a useful textbook for courses on contextualization. The world of missiology is grateful for these and other books and articles that have proceeded from his computer. I have included Dr. Gilliland's *curriculum vitae* as an appendix to this volume as an indication of his accomplishments while active with us at Fuller.

Outside of Fuller, but not unrelated to our mission, Dean has always been in demand as an interpreter for mission to the wide variety of churches represented by the student body of Fuller and within his own Denomination (United Methodist). As with other members of the SIS faculty, he has traveled widely to teach mission courses in Europe, Asia and Africa. He was Chairman of the Board of Zwemer Institute for Muslim Studies during a strategic seven-year period (1992-1999). For years he has been active in the American Society of Missiology and was President of ASM in 1995. He was an early member of the Board of Mission Society (Norcross, GA), Board Chairman for Global Mission, Inc. (Pasadena, CA) and consultant to Medics International Care, Inc. (Broken Arrow, OK) and Missions, International (Nashville, TN).

Now, as he winds down this career, we (I speak here for our whole faculty) want to express our deep appreciation to Dean for who he is to us and for what he has contributed to our lives, to Missiology and to those he taught and mentored. We have valued his classroom teaching and the careful way he has gone about mentoring students working toward masters and doctoral degrees. He has also become an informal pastor to many of these students, especially those from Africa, and has deeply affected them spiritually.

But to focus on Dean as an academic is but to give half of the story.

Dean is an absolute delight to have as a friend and colleague. We know him as the person who, more than any of the rest of us, livens up our faculty meetings and constantly reminds us that what we are doing is *fun* as well as significant. His stories and marvelous sense of humor will long be remembered by all of us and are deeply missed now that he doesn't come to our meetings regularly. We faculty, as well as countless students, are all different because Dean Gilliland has come to the School of World Mission.

And Lois, too, though not an official part of our faculty has blessed us all in the frequent informal times we have had with faculty and spouses. She also has just completed a significant career—hers as a counselor with a specialization in assisting the children of Missionaries. There are many of her counselees and their parents who call her "Blessed" for the ministry she has had among them. She is usually quiet among us and supportive of Dean as he tells stories she has heard a hundred times. She has been supportive also in the background as Dean has carried out his academic duties. Thank you Lois for all you have meant both to Dean and to the rest of us.

We love you Dean and Lois and miss you. May this volume be for you a token of our deep appreciation for who you are and what you have meant to us.

Charles H. Kraft

Introduction

A book of this size and scope is not easy to put together. There were delays and emails going back and forth concerning revisions. Dealing with the busy schedules of many of us provided many challenges. So, we heave a sigh of relief as we send the manuscript off to the publisher.

And the relief is accompanied with excitement. Not only are we relieved to see the book get into print but we are excited about the quality of the book's contents. For, though there are many contributers, each coming from his or her own perspective, the quality is uniformly high. So, what you have in your hands is, we believe, truly a new and valuable contribution to the literature on contextualization.

We have focused on "appropriate" as the word that best serves to label what we intend to highlight (see Chapter 1). There has been a lot of inappropriateness in the introduction of Christianity to peoples around the world. And because of this inappropriateness, the Gospel has been interpreted in distorted ways (e.g. as Western religion rather than as a faith that can be at home in any culture-see Chapter 6). This ought not to be and we hope the present volume can be another useful step toward the correcting of such distortions.

This book is meant to be a textbook, so it covers a lot of ground. Whether one is looking for history (Chapters 2, 3) or definition (Chapters 1, 4) or theory (Section II) or breaking new ground (nearly every chapter), it is all here. And the chapters are written by practitioners who, though we are also theoreticians, have put our theories to the test in real life situations.

There is plenty here for every student and practitioner of contextualization. The introductory student will find in this book a broad and stimulating view of the subject. Yet the experienced scholar will find him/herself challenged by the many fresh perspectives here exhibited. And those practitioners who do not consider themselves either students or scholars will find many helpful insights to enable them to do their job more appropriately.

Problems are addressed honestly, whether they stem from history (Chapters 2, 3), or from the fact that our best scholarly insights are often ignored on the field (Chapter 5), or from avoiding or ignoring important aspects of the subject such as:

- Whether we are dealing with a Religion or a Faith-Chapter 6
- The Hebraic Covenant as a model-Chapter 9
- The relationship of contextualization to hermeneutics-Chapters 12-14

The experienced will find new theory on just about every page. In one of my contributions, I have tried to provide a threefold grid on which to hang our approaches (Chapter 7) and, later in the book, illustrated how to handle the two of these areas that have been most neglected (Chapters 19-22). There is also methodology, especially in Chapters 8, 11-14. Chapter 8 by Hiebert and Tienou in which the authors see parallels between various types of theologizing and the American legal system, is one of my favorites. And we seldom see treatments of the important place of music in contextualization (Chapter 18). The application of Travis' C1-6 typology is well worth the two chapters (23, 24) we have devoted to it. We don't have all the answers yet but there are enough suggestions here to enable us to move toward some new ones.

We have dedicated the book to Dr. Gilliland. The book is not, however, a festschrift. For one thing, a festschrift is a surprise. For another, the chapters of a festschrift are written to the person being honored. Only one of these chapters falls into that category (Chapter 4). In a book like this that is dedicated to a person, we honor him by writing new approaches to the subject he has given his life to. And then we have asked the one honored to write the final chapter, surveying the preceding chapters and breaking new ground of his own. For Chapter 28 is a breakthrough chapter, introducing the concept of the Incarnation as a matrix rather than simply a model. The models, then, all fit into the much broader matrix of Jesus' Incarnation.

So, we have here a textbook that is intended to cover and expand our view of contextualization and also to break new ground. There are many authors but a singleness of purpose-to enhance the spread of the Good News of Jesus Christ to the ends of the earth as effectively as possible.

Acknowledgements

I have not done this book without help. Obviously, the many authors have worked to write and rewrite their chapters. I feel that every author has done an exceptional job and I want to thank each of them for their contributions. I also want to thank them for being patient in waiting for their chapters to be published. The book has been a long time in coming.

There are others who deserve commendation as well. The work of getting the manuscript into final shape is tedious and demanding, especially when dealing with the different writing styles, the sometimes technical content and the sometimes complicated figures. For their faithful and untiring efforts in this regard, I want to thank Corinne Kershaw and Judi Brodeen who certainly deserve more than I was able to pay them. I bless you both for your help.

So, we offer this book in the hope that God will use it to inform and instruct both the inexperienced and those who are experienced in taking the Gospel of Jesus Christ to the ends of the earth. Our prayer is that the book will help many to communicate that message in such a way that the peoples of this planet will receive it as Good News. Considering all that our God has done to bring mankind back to Himself, we should commit ourselves to seeing to it that the good news of salvation is not perceived as bad news about a people's culture. That's what appropriate contextualization is all about.

South Pasadena, CA

January 2005

List of Contributors

Dr. Jonathan S. Campbell co-leads a team who encourages indigenous movements of Christ-centered spiritual communities among neo-pagans in the Pacific Northwest and beyond. Before launching a management consulting firm, Jonathan served as church planter strategist in Los Angeles for the North American Mission Board (SBC). He has also served as adjunct faculty of Fuller Seminary, Golden Gate Baptist Theological Seminary, and Mars Hill Graduate School. Jonathan and Jennifer live with their four children on Bainbridge Island, Washington.

Paul H. DeNeui is a doctoral candidate at Fuller Theological Seminary and a missionary with the Evangelical Covenant Church of America serving in Thailand since 1987. While continuing in his missionary status he will join the faculty of North Park Theological Seminary in Chicago as Associate Professor of Missions in the fall of 2005.

Dr. Robert L. Gallagher is Assistant Professor of Intercultural Studies at Wheaton College Graduate School where he teaches courses in history and theology of mission as well as leadership studies. He served for many years as an executive pastor in Australia and a theological educator in Papua New Guinea and the South Pacific.

Dr. Eddie Gibbs holds the McGavran Chair of Church Growth in the School of Intercultural Studies, Fuller Seminary, where he has taught for twenty years. Before coming to Fuller, he served a Church of England parish, then went to Chile as a missionary and later served as Home Secretary with the South American Missionary Society, then worked with the British and Foreign Bible Society and the Billy Graham Evangelistic Association.

Dr. Paul G. Hiebert was brought up in India where he also served as a missionary. He taught Anthropology and South Asian Studies at Kansas State University, the University of Washington, and Fuller Seminary before moving to Trinity Evangelical Divinity School where he has been chair of the Department of Mission and Evangelism and continues as Professor of Mission and Anthropology.

Dr. Frecia C. Johnson served with her husband in Kazakhstan where he was engaged in business and they planted a church together. She has been an Adjunct Instructor in the School of Intercultural Studies, Fuller Seminary.

Dr. Roberta R. King is Associate Professor of Communication and Ethnomusicology in the School of Intercultural Studies, Fuller Theological Seminary. Based at Daystar University in Kenya for twenty-two years, she served as Professor and administrator, and also led worship at Nairobi Baptist Church. Dr. King traveled annually as a missionary-ethnomusicologist with CBInternational in eleven African nations and parts of Asia.

Dr. Charles H. Kraft has served as a missionary in Nigeria, taught African languages and linguistics at Michigan State University and UCLA for ten years and Anthropology and Intercultural Communication in the School of Intercultural Studies, Fuller Seminary for the past 35 years. He travels widely and has pioneered in the field of Contextualization. He also is widely used in a ministry of inner healing.

Dr. Sherwood G. Lingenfelter is Provost and Senior Vice President of Fuller Seminary, and Professor of Anthropology in the School of Intercultural Studies. Before coming to Fuller he held teaching positions at State University of New York and Biola University where he also served as Provost for eleven years. He has served as an International Consultant to SIL International since 1977.

Dr. Paul E. Pierson is Dean Emeritus and Emeritus Professor of History and Latin American Studies in the School of Intercultural Studies, Fuller Seminary. He served as a missionary and professor with the United Presbyterian Church (USA) in Brazil and Portugal from > 1955-1973.

Shawn Redford has served among the Maasai tribe in Kenya, and is currently completing a Ph.D. in Intercultural Studies at Fuller's School of Intercultural Studies under Chuck Van Engen. Shawn is also Van Engen's Teaching Assistant and an Adjunct Instructor, teaching Van Engen's Biblical Theology of Mission course while Chuck is on sabbatical.

Dr. Katie Rawson is the International Student Ministry Area Director for InterVarsity Christian Fellowship in the Carolinas and Virginia. She first became involved with international students while studying in France, has ministered among internationals at North Carolina State >University and UCLA, and did her doctoral dissertation on conversion patterns among East Asian students in the United States.

List of Contributors

Dr. Wilbert R. Shenk was a missionary in Indonesia, and is presently Professor of History and Contemporary Culture at Fuller Seminary, School of Intercultural Studies. Previously, he has served as director of the Mission Training Center, Associated Mennonite Biblical Seminaries, Elkhart, Indiana and vice-president of Overseas Ministries, Mennonite Board of Missions.

Dr. Tite Tienou serves as Academic Dean at Trinity Evangelical Divinity School. He is also Chair of the Department of Mission and Evangelism and Professor of Theology of Mission. He was born and has ministered in West Africa. His M.A. and Ph.D. were earned at Fuller School of World Mission under the direction of Dr. Gilliland.

John and Anna Travis, along with their two children, have lived in a tight-knit Asian Muslim neighborhood for nearly 20 years. They are involved in contextualized sharing of the good news, Bible translation and the ministry of prayer for inner healing. They have also helped train field workers in a number of Asian, Middle Eastern and North African countries. Both are pursuing graduate degrees – John is a Ph.D. candidate.

Dr. Charles Van Engen was born and raised in Mexico, where from 1973-1985 he also served the National Presbyterian Church of Mexico in theological education, evangelism, youth ministries and refugee relief. He is presently Professor of Theology of Mission and Latin American Studies at Fuller Seminary's School of Intercultural Studies.

Dr. Darrell Whiteman is Dean of the E. Stanley Jones School of World Mission and Evangelism and Professor of Cultural Anthropology at Asbury Theological Seminary, Wilmore, Kentucky. He has had mission and research experience in Central Africa, Solomon Islands, and Papua New Guinea, has been the editor of Missiology (1989-2003) and presently serves as president of the International Association for Mission Studies.

Part I

Introduction

Chapter 1

Why Appropriate?

Charles H. Kraft

As can be seen from the historical overview in the following chapter, it was orthodox for years to speak of *indigeneity* as the ideal toward which we strive. Those who discussed and advocated indigeneity, even in its most formal sense, were sincerely striving for a type of Christianity for their converts that would be both maximally meaningful within their cultural contexts and maximally faithful to the Scriptures. We do well, even when we see flaws in their conceptualizations and applications, to honor their intent.

Likewise, with those who saw the flaws in the older concept and came to advocate what seem to be more enlightened understandings under labels such as *contextualization, localization, inculturation, Incarnation* or even my *dynamic equivalence* (1979a). Over the years, there have been quite a number of helpful discussions of the concept of contextualization.[1] We have been helped greatly by them and by current experiments with contextualization.[2] I believe, however, that there is much more to be said and done in this area.

First, a Change of Terminology

Perhaps terminology is not a major problem. It is not difficult to read those who write of inculturation or of localization and simply convert that term in our minds to our preferred term. But, since meaning is in the minds of people, we need to recognize that there will be a variety of understandings of any of the terms we use. And the more technical the term, the less likely non-specialists are to hold to similar understandings of it.

I recently participated in a large meeting to discuss the topic of contextualization. About two-thirds of the way through the week we began to realize that we were not all speaking the same language. So it became necessary to appoint a small committee to develop a definition of what *contextualization* means. Another committee was appointed to define what we mean by *Gospel*.

Perhaps things like that occur because we have become too technical. If our concept is simple, and this one is (even though its implementation is often

---

[1] See the bibliography for a listing of the more significant of these.

[2] See, for example, Chapters 23 and 24.

quite complex), let's keep the terminology simple. For example, not everyone is aware of the fact that contextualization means doing whatever is necessary to make sure Christianity is expressed in ways that are appropriate to the context of the receiving group. They may or may not realize that the *context* part of the word refers to the context of the *receptors*. And they may or may not realize that, at least when evangelicals use the word, they are specifically assuming that the messages conveyed and the expressions that result will be true to biblical Christianity.

Some, in fact, misunderstand us to be referring to a new kind of theology when we talk of the contextualization of theology. One theology professor at a distinguished seminary, thinking that we are advocating some new and different kind of theology, asked in my presence, "What is the difference between Systematic Theology and Contextual Theology?" And then, when we answered him, he had a difficult time understanding that what we mean is the way God went about doing things in the Bible. It had never occurred to him that contextualization was God's way of dealing with theological truth in relation to human culture and language and that, therefore, it ought to be a part of the teaching of his subject, theology.

With this in mind, let me suggest that we move to a less technical and perhaps more vague word. This is the word we use when defining what we mean by contextualization, as I did above. It is the word *appropriate*. When people ask us what our word means, we say, *appropriate to the cultural context* and we may or may not remember to say, *and also to the Bible*. Since what we all seek is *appropriate Christianity*—a Christian expression that is appropriate both to a given social context and to the Scriptures—why not just say that our ideal is appropriateness in both directions.

Appropriate at Both Ends

One problem with terms such as contextualization (and the other terms listed above) is that, besides being too technical, they don't automatically signify accountability to Scripture. These terms come from a valid concern for the relationship between the Gospel and the receiving culture. They represent the period in missiological thinking when we were emerging from the naive assumption that communicating Christianity is largely a matter of exchanging our *Christian* culture for their *pagan* culture. To overcome that fallacy, we began to focus on the receiving culture while simply assuming that we knew how to be appropriate to the Bible in message and method.

Since questions continually arise concerning what we are recommending at both the cultural and the scriptural ends of our task, then, I suggest we move to a term that takes us beyond the single focus of the terms we have been using. The term *appropriate* does just that, since it necessarily raises the question, "Appropriate to what?" And our answer will be twofold since our subject is twofold: Gospel on one side and culture on the other. *Appropriate Christianity* will, therefore, be a Christianity that is appropriate to the *Scriptures*, on the one hand, and appropriate to the *people* in a given cultural context, on the other.

Where the term contextualization has helped us is with regard to the inculturating of Christianity at the receptors' end. It assumes we know what we are doing at the Scripture end. But we can't use the word contextualization at the Scripture end except to point out that Scripture illustrates how God approached people in their cultural contexts in this way. We can only say, as Darrell Whiteman has said, that *good contextualization* will offend people (1997:3). What he means is that a properly scriptural set of meanings that are properly contextualized, when measured against the sociocultural norms of the receptor society, will not be agreeable to everyone in that society. But no similar measure is in focus for the scripturalness of the meanings to be conveyed. We simply assume, though we know we shouldn't, that everybody knows and agrees on what constitutes scripturalness.

With the term *appropriate* we seek to keep ourselves alert to the fact that we need a measure on either side of the equation. A diagram might help (note the arrows):

	Scripture	Culture and Society
Contextualization (focused on the culture end)	|———————————▶|	
Appropriate (focused on both ends)	|◀———————————▶|	

Figure 1.1 Appropriate Contextualization at Both Ends

Appropriate to Scripture

As noted above, I feel we have focused so much on appropriateness at the culture end that we may have neglected the Scripture end of our discussion. Several authors have written about this end of the process. Often, however, it has been more in a spirit of alarm than of helpfulness that they have written [e.g., Bruce Nicholls (1979), Morris Inch (1982), and David J. Hesselgrave and Edward Rommen (1989)]. More helpful, at least in outlining the approach we must take, has been the work of Paul G. Hiebert, especially in his article on what he calls "Critical Contextualization" (1984).

For one thing, it is high time we began to deal with the contextualization of the whole of Christianity, not just theology. Theology is important, but we err if we only deal with truth, knowledge, and information about our faith. As noted below and presented throughout this volume, any adequate and appropriate treatment of Christianity needs to deal also with the contextualization of allegiance or commitment. For allegiance to Christ is the basis for all we do that makes us Christian.

In addition, Jesus was very much into spiritual power. And, in spite of the neglect of this area in Evangelicalism, if we are to be truly biblical, we must deal with this area, especially since it is this power that brings freedom. So, this topic will be regularly referred to as well throughout this volume in an attempt to deal with a more complete Christianity than that presented in treatments of the contextualization of Christian theology alone.

In 1991 I published an article that focused on three encounters in Christianity: *allegiance, truth, and power* (1991b). Ours is a faith that has encounter at the core of it. It is not simply an "add on" to whatever a people already believes. And, as I pointed out in that article, it involves encounter in at least three areas. These areas of encounter I now see as representing three *crucial dimensions* of biblical Christianity. And these three crucial dimensions form a major part of the framework of this book. I will introduce them here and deal with them in more detail in Chapter 7.

The dimensions may be labeled *relationship, understanding,* and *freedom.* Each proceeds from one of the encounters mentioned above. *Allegiance* is the basis for relationship, *truth* for understanding and *power* for freedom. But these are dimensions, not separable entities. We cannot have Christian allegiance without some truth and enough power to allow freedom from our enemy, Satan. Nor can we experience God's truth without saving allegiance and, again, the freeing power of the Holy Spirit. Furthermore, the power we experience must be the true power of God, a power available to us only on the basis of our allegiance to Jesus Christ. It must never be the power of the counterfeiter, Satan.

If these dimensions are indeed crucial, each will be an area in which those members of a society who are serious about Christianity will confront their sociocultural ideals and behavior with the claims of Christ. I, therefore, suggest here that *appropriate to Scripture* should be understood to involve appropriateness in at least these three dimensions, two of which (relationship and freedom) have not been prominent, if mentioned at all, in the literature on contextualization.[3]

Much of the discussion on contextualization seems to assume that the contextualization of the truth (theology) dimension is to be our major concern. Among numerous treatments of the contextualizing of theology, some may have mentioned thinking *about* one or both of these other dimensions of Christianity. The actual contextualization of relationship and freedom in appropriate ways, however, is seldom if ever referred to, at least in the literature I'm acquainted with.

---

[3] See the chart in Chapter 7 for a summary of what each dimension includes.

Our concern here, however, is the contextualization of Christianity, not just of Christian theology, though theological contextualization is an important part of the whole. But, since our relationship with Christ is foundational, shouldn't we also be dealing with the contextualization of that relationship? We should not treat it as simply a byproduct of knowledge and truth.[4] Nor should we ignore the importance Jesus placed on the exercise of spiritual power in the communication of Christianity. So, we speak of contextualization of spiritual power as well.[5]

Appropriate Treatment of Truth

Though more has been done in the area of contextualization of theology than in other areas, we need to question whether we have done enough. Have all of the nooks and crannies of this area been dealt with? For example, have we done enough with the judgment dimension of the use of Scripture? Have we held *God's TRUTH* up against cultural *truths* enough? Though we may have a fair idea of what the scriptural ideals are, have we adequately worked out the process by means of which we can attain such goals? In seeking to remedy this lack, I have suggested in my book *Christianity in Culture* (1979a) that God is willing to start at subideal places and move people toward more ideal understandings and practices. Have we done enough with what might be termed *how to move appropriately toward God's ideals?*

This question points us toward what may be the greatest lack in theological thinking and instruction, both in cross-cultural contexts and at home: "How do we go about the process of theologizing?" Several years ago, Daniel von Allmen wrote a seminal article entitled "The Birth of Theology"(1975) that is, I believe, still one of the clearest statements of the process by means of which theological thinking was developed during and after the New Testament period. Appropriate approaches to the truth and knowledge dimension of Christianity need to include biblically-based treatments of the process of theologizing that can be taught in Western and nonWestern theological institutions.

Appropriate at the Meaning Level

Let's be clear, though, that it is appropriateness of *meaning*, not simply of *form*, that we are advocating. But, as I point out below and in Chapter 10, since meanings are in people, not in structures, our focus must be on people, not culture. So the question must be, "Do the meanings these people are attaching to the forms they are using correspond to the meanings God seems to have intended as indicated by the Scriptures?" That is, are these meanings scripturally appropriate?

---

[4] See Chapters 19 and 20.

[5] See Chapters 21 and 22.

And here we are squarely into the problems of interpretation. "Scriptural by whose interpretation?," we may ask. "By the interpretation of the people themselves, not by that of outsiders," we should answer. A cross-cultural approach to hermeneutics thus becomes a pressing concern.[6]

Years ago, Alan Tippett had it right when he said that appropriate Christianity has come into existence when the meanings in the minds of the "indigenous people" have them seeing "the Lord as their own, not a foreign Christ" (1973:158). Several years earlier, William A. Smalley also focused on meaning when he pointed to the fact that an appropriate church functions directly "under the guidance of the Holy Spirit [to] meet the needs and fulfill the meanings of that society and not of any outside group" (1958:55-56). My own 1978 statement, likewise, points to the fact that appropriate Christianity "would preserve the essential meanings and functions [that] the New Testament predicated of the church, but would seek to express these in forms . . . appropriate to the local culture" (1978:330).

So we are looking for appropriateness in the minds and hearts of those who receive scriptural messages and who attempt to structure their responses in their own cultural patterns. The forms employed, then, need to focus primarily on the meanings that people, both inside and outside the churches will attach to them. When outsiders look at church structures, are they attracted to them or repulsed by them? The meanings intended by the advocates could be Scriptural but the onlookers could perceive them either way, depending on the forms used.

Since it is the receptors who will interpret the forms and attach meanings to them, we must concern ourselves primarily with whether the meanings in their minds are Scriptural or not. How will they interpret the forms used?

Appropriate Relationship

And what have we done about these other two dimensions? What does a biblically and socioculturally appropriate expression of commitment (allegiance) to and relationship with God through Christ look like for any given person or group in any given society? Is the formal, seemingly nominal relationship to the Church practiced by many in societies that consider themselves *Christian*, from State Church Europe to the South Pacific, an appropriate expression of Christian allegiance? What about the highly individualistic American evangelical Protestant version? Or the all-encompassing, total dedication of Japanese Pentecostals? And if any of these should be considered culturally appropriate, are they scripturally appropriate?[7]

An Old Testament example of cultural appropriateness may illustrate what I have in mind here. God chose to define the relationship between Himself and the Jewish people in terms of socioculturally appropriate covenants. A covenant

---

[6] See Chapter 14.

[7] See Chapters 19 and 20 for more on this topic.

was a well-known type of agreement in Semitic societies involving the highest type of commitment. This was a two-way commitment, involving obligations on both sides, with the understanding that if one party to the agreement broke the agreement, the other was free of its obligations.

We learn about God's desire to be culturally appropriate from the fact that He chose this cultural form. Culturally appropriate? Very much so. Covenants, and the processes of making and keeping them, were well understood by the parties concerned. So God chose this culturally appropriate pattern for defining His relationship to the Jewish people and for enabling them to define their relationship to Him.

During the course of His relationship with Israel, however, we learn a very important fact about the character of God. This is that He chooses to patiently honor His agreements with humans for a long time after human beings have broken theirs with Him. For, even though the terms of a covenant allowed either party freedom from the covenant as soon as the other broke it, God did not exercise His right to be free from the covenant for a long, long time in spite of Israel's repeated unfaithfulness. And some of His covenants He has vowed to fulfill in the future anyway. What in today's societies are the culturally appropriate relationship structures that parallel Jewish covenants?[8]

In asking about culturally appropriate commitments and the relationships flowing from them, we must distinguish between the ideal a people have for their commitments and relationships and the actual ways in which these are carried out in the society. Insight into cultural behavior worldwide indicates that actual behavior in every aspect of life will often be found to be subideal. What we recommend as culturally appropriate, however, needs to be at the ideal level, no matter how infrequently such an ideal occurs in real life, since this is what the members of the society learn to aim at.

Appropriate Expressions of Spiritual Power

With regard to spiritual power, the usual situation worldwide is that the enemy's power is not even contested. And when it is, that confrontation usually takes an imported form (as with Pentecostal missionaries in certain African Indigenous Churches) or it emulates shamanistic practices (as with some Korean Prayer Mountain deliverance practices). The latter is a worse scenario in that the *ministers* beat the people in an attempt to rid them of demons.

When spiritual power issues are not addressed, large segments of believers—many of whom have a genuine relationship with Christ—remain captive to the enemy in various degrees. People who call themselves Christians faithfully attend church on Sundays but also seek the help of healers and diviners who operate under satanic power when they need healing, guidance, or any other power-related assistance. Although Jesus has promised that His power

---

[8] See Chapter 9 for more on this topic.

will accompany His followers (Jn. 14:12), many of them find no spiritual power in Christianity.

Given Jesus' promise, I assume that some sort of exercise of spiritual power is scripturally appropriate. But what would culturally appropriate spiritual warfare look like in any given society? For one thing, it would look like a challenge to whatever satanic systems are in operation. It would look enough like those systems to be recognizable as challenging them in appropriate ways.

The advocates of Christianity need to learn to operate in the power of the Holy Spirit like Jesus did as he ministered with spiritual power in terms of the sociocultural realities of His time. In the same manner, Christian advocates today need to work in spiritual power within their own sociocultural realities in order to free people from Satan's grip and demonstrate that God is alive, active, and using His power to communicate His love to them. The way such power is exercised would also be appropriate to the way God's power is manifested throughout Scripture.[9]

Appropriate to People

The terms contextualization, localization, inculturation, and especially the earlier term indigenization, fix our focus on culture rather than on people. Culture, in spite of the regular misuse of the term as a label for people, is a structural thing. And, though the cultural forms employed for Christian purposes are very important, especially since people attach meanings to them, our primary concern has to be for the *people* who are observing, using and interpreting them.

People and culture are quite different. For example, people *do* things, culture doesn't do anything. Culture is like a script, memorized by the actors, but not necessarily followed by them in every detail. There are times when any actor forgets the lines he or she memorized. There are times when one actor makes a mistake and the other actor has to improvise. Or some of the set may fall down, forcing all of the actors to scurry around seeking a solution that was not anticipated by the script-writer. In short, the behavior of actors illustrates quite well the ways in which personal cultural behavior relates to the cultural scripts we have been taught. Or, to use another analogy, culture is like a system of roads. The roads *don't go* anywhere, they simply lie there to be used by people. It is people who go places on (or off) the roads.

The point is, it is *people* who perform the activities we call cultural. Culture itself does not behave, people behave. So our adaptations of Scripture need to be thought of as people-centered, not culture-centered. The technical word we use for people is *society*. A society is a group of people who habitually

---

[9] See Chapters 20 and 21 for more on this topic.

behave according to cultural patterns but who may change them at any time and in the process develop new habits to go along with the new patterns.

So, we want a Christianity that is appropriate to the *people,* and their experience with God. This Christianity may or may not conform to the cultural patterns the people have inherited from their forebears. Indeed, they may be tired of at least some of those patterns and gladly adopt others. In any event, whether the people are seeking change or not, this appropriateness will commonly involve some, perhaps many, changes in the cultural structuring in terms of which they live their lives.

For some people, for example, it may be appropriate—and they even may desire—to become more westernized while they grow in their Christian experience. We outsiders may look at their churches and decry the fact that they are drifting away from their traditional culture. But, again, much of the life and behavior of the nonChristians around them, especially those living in urban centers, doesn't look very traditional either. Our question, then, should be, "What is appropriate for these people, given the sociocultural realities of life around them?"

I'm afraid in our conceptualizing of what contextualization means some of us may have unwittingly fallen into the fallacy of what has been called *salvage anthropology*—an attempt at preserving the older way of life whether or not the people want it. Foreigners (especially Westerners) usually focus more on cultural structures than on people, and thus they are liable to lose sight of the more dynamic aspects of appropriate contextualization. Structures tend to be static. People are dynamic.

And yet, some people are not caught up in modernizing as some others are. There are sizeable traditional populations in most of the societies of our world. What is appropriate for traditional peoples will be quite different from what is appropriate for the westernizing segment of their own societies. It is inappropriate to offer people only the choice of adopting a Western variety of Christianity. I wonder if this isn't a major problem with the nonChristian majority in Korea. While we rejoice in the fact that somewhere between twenty-five and thirty percent of the Korean population has turned to Christ, could it be that it will take a more traditional approach to Christianity to attract the other three-quarters of the population? And what about Japan, where Western Christianity has so far failed miserably to attract and keep adherents, even though polls show that Jesus has a very high reputation among Japanese?

On the other hand, when we offer only a traditional variety of Christianity to people who want to become more westernized, it is likewise inappropriate. There are places where the rural, more traditional form of Christianity practiced in the villages is totally inappropriate for the highly schooled, city-dwelling youth who grew up there and got schooled out of sync with their families. And yet, the imported Western Christianity of most city churches may be just as inappropriate to them as well. An appropriate alternative is in order.

We are trying to ask the basic questions concerning appropriateness to cultural structuring and to the people enmeshed in that structuring. We believe that God wants His Church incarnated in the cultural way of life of every society (people group). Just as Jesus totally participated in first century Palestinian life, not as a foreigner but as a native son, so contemporary Christian communities should not be living like foreigners in their own lands, speaking their language with a foreign (usually Western) accent, performing foreign-looking rituals at strange times and in strange-looking places.

Much has been written concerning the need for inculturation of theology and structures. And we will add to that here. But, as I contend above, I believe we have been hurt by an overemphasis on the theological and structural concerns at the expense of the concern for persons. The appropriateness of cultural structuring, though very important, must always be secondary to appropriateness at the social (group and individual) level.

To this end we present two chapters discussing the C1-C6 analysis of church culture (Chapters 23 and 24). These chapters deal with Muslim and Buddhist societies. I regret that we do not have a third chapter dealing with Hindu society, especially since Herbert Hoefer's book *Churchless Christianity* (2001) suggests that there are many in India who fall into the most unWestern C4-C6 categories. Though each of the proposed levels involves a culturally distinct approach to Christianity, each is appropriate to some group within the societies in view, and each is inappropriate to most of those in groups other than their own. And none of them should be imposed on any population as the only valid form of Christianity, though the more westernized of these types have regularly been so imposed.

Could Appropriateness Be Measured?

An argument (though perhaps not a strong one) in favor of using the term *appropriate* instead of contextualized is that we may more easily think of measuring it. Things can be more appropriate or less appropriate either scripturally or socioculturally. The following diagram may help:

	More Appropriate	Less Appropriate
Scripturally	←	→
Socioculturally	←	→

Figure 1.2 Appropriateness Measurement

As we have emphasized, we need to be concerned about practicing appropriateness at both the scriptural and the sociocultural ends of whatever we are dealing with. But as soon as we decide to speak of appropriateness, we raise the possibility of *more* or *less* in either area.

We may cite, for example, the many situations in which Christians go to native shamans to seek healing. We would have to say that such a practice, while *culturally* appropriate, is not *scripturally* appropriate. On the other hand, we frequently observe Christians meeting regularly on Sunday mornings for worship in foreign-looking meeting places. We can say that their practice of meeting regularly is scripturally appropriate, but that the foreignness of the place (and, often, of the time as well) make their meetings culturally inappropriate.

An example of appropriateness at both ends of the spectrum comes from the experience of Bible translators Wayne and Sally Dye (1976) in Papua New Guinea. The rather isolated Behinemo people (both Christians and nonChristians) met regularly on Sunday mornings to hear the latest translated portion of the Scriptures. At the end, their tribal leaders led them in discussions concerning the meaning and application of the passage read. This appears to have been appropriate both to the Scriptures and to the social setting at that time. Whether that approach is still appropriate after nearly three decades is another question.

Counterexamples?

In studying and advocating culturally appropriate Christianity, we dare not neglect the many churches in the world that appear to be counterexamples. In considering them, then, we can begin to look critically at our theories. We need to study what is really going on in the churches around the world even if they don't confirm our theories. Though we do not focus on this topic in the chapters that follow, we need to ask, Where are the studies of counterexamples?

Such studies would look at many of the largest, apparently most *successful* churches (e.g., in Korea, the Philippines, Singapore, Nigeria) that appear to be poorly contextualized. We will need to ask, Are there factors that override cultural fit? If so, what are they? Are we missing something in our commitment to our theory?

A start toward dealing with the counterexamples would be to look at the relationship of spiritual power to the growth of these large, uncontextualized churches. I venture to suggest that most of them are healing churches, churches that regularly pray for healing and deliverance. Though these churches may be very Western in most features and even in some cases quite anti-traditional culture, they would be speaking to a major felt need of most of the peoples of the world by involving themselves in demonstrating the power of God to heal and deliver. Perhaps the exercise of spiritual power is more important to people than cultural appropriateness. Should this be true, we ought to be aware of it.

But some of these churches are apparently not into spiritual power. They are just Western. Can their growth be attributed solely to the desire of their members to westernize? Or are there other factors we should know about?

I'll leave this subject here, not because it is not important but because we know so few of the answers we need to get to know if we are to write intelligently about the subject of counterexamples.

Appropriate Theory and Practice

In the chapters that follow a number of us who have been practicing, thinking about, and teaching contextualization will attempt to deal with appropriate theory and practice for the pursuit of appropriate Christianity. We will attempt to deal with a number of issues related to this topic. This includes the relationship and power dimensions mentioned above, and also questions of timing, leadership, epistemology, renewal, contextualizing for Western societies and the like. It is our hope that the chapters in this book will help those who, like us, are striving towards appropriate *expressions* of Christianity among the peoples of the world. We further hope that our debate will be all the more fruitful as we correct and stimulate one another in our common pursuit of our God-given tasks.

Chapter 2

The Development of Contextualization Theory in Euroamerican Missiology

Charles H. Kraft

The term *contextualization* has not had a long history as the preferred label for the ideal toward which we evangelicals strive as we communicate the Gospel to the peoples of the world. It wasn't until the late 1970s that it displaced *indigenization* as the label of choice. What follows is a brief history organized into seven "stages" of how this came about, followed by a list of what I see as unresolved issues in contextualization studies.

Stage I: Cultural Encounter

In the earliest days of the modern missionary era (roughly since William Carey went to India in 1792), the basic concept European and American missionaries carried with them may be labeled cultural encounter. Taking the Gospel to nonWestern peoples was assumed to be an encounter between the "Christian" culture of Euroamerica and the "pagan" cultures of the nonWestern world. The cultures of nonWestern peoples (and especially their religions) were seen as evil and needing to be stamped out if the Gospel was to be effective. In their place, the early missionaries felt called to substitute a purified form of our Western approach to Christianity to replace the forms of their religion.

Though both Protestant and Catholic missionaries approached mission with this encounter mentality, they differed with respect to the brand of European culture they imposed. Protestants imported austere northern European customs surrounding organizational and doctrinal concerns while Catholics imported the more expressive customs of southern Europe within which were packaged a great concern for ancient ritual and allegiance to Rome.

Both streams of missionaries recognized the presence and activity of Satan in nonWestern societies (though they largely ignored it in their own) and proceeded to fight his evil influence. They erroneously assumed, however, that the enemy's presence invalidated just about every aspect of nonWestern cultures as potential vehicles of God's love and grace. So they sought to defeat the enemy through converting so-called *pagan* peoples to Western ways they assumed were Christian. The problem as they saw it was that nonWestern peoples were so blinded they couldn't think straight. So they needed to be taught how to think before they, the missionaries, could expect any results from their witness. Their watchword thus became *civilize in order to Christianize*.

Speaking of the background out of which these early missionaries came, historian Wilbert R. Shenk states,

> The seventeenth-century New England Puritan missionaries largely set the course for modern missions. They defined their task as preaching the gospel so that Native Americans would be converted and receive personal salvation. But early in their missionary experience these New Englanders concluded that Indian converts could only be Christians if they were "civilized." The model by which they measured their converts was English Puritan civilization. These missionaries felt compassion and responsibility for their converts. They gathered these new Christians into churches for nurture and discipline and set up programs to transform Christian Indians into English Puritans. From this emerged the slogan, "Civilization and Christianity," which was shorthand for saying that native peoples and their cultures had to be made over in the likeness of European culture. They assumed that European culture was synonymous with Christian culture. Therefore, to be a Christian required that the convert adopt European culture. All other cultures were "heathen" and depraved. Christianization was the same as civilization (1980:35-36).

The missionaries considered Western institutions such as schools, hospitals and churches as the means to the end of getting nonWesterners to think like Euro-Americans and, in the process, to become truly Christian. The assumption they worked on was similar to that of one of my missionary colleagues who said to me (in about 1958) regarding the Nigerian Church, "We have had 2,000 years of experience with Christianity. We have a right to tell them what to do."

In addition, Western missionaries tended to assume that producing Christianity in nonWestern lands was totally their responsibility with little or no participation by the receiving peoples in the process. In their eyes, the natives were like children, needing constant instruction, direction and supervision as they moved along the road toward civilization.

Stage II: Three Selfs (Formal Indigeneity)

Toward the middle of the nineteenth century, even without the benefit of formal anthropological training, various missionaries began to develop an awareness of their own ethnocentrism and domination. The writings of Henry Venn in the 1840s and Rufus Anderson[1] on the *Three Selfs* (self-support, self-governance, self-propagation) were an attempt to change things, though mostly

---

[1] For a list of the work and works of Rufus Anderson, cf. *To Advance the Gospel: Selections From The Writings Of Rufus Anderson*, R. Pierce Beaver, ed. (1967:39-44).

at the superficial form level. The central idea was to allow the nationals to be in charge of their own churches.[2]

From 1856-1893 John Nevius was rigorously applying Three-Selfs principles in China. He put the principles in writing sometime in the mid-1880s and helped implement them in Korea after 1890 as the famous "Nevius Plan."

As early as 1879, William M. Taylor's *Pauline Methods of Missionary Work* sparked an interest in revisiting the apostolic missionary enterprise as a model for the Christian Church. W. M. Taylor was a precursor of Roland Allen who, a generation later, published his *Missionary Methods: St Paul's or Ours?* (1912) and *The Spontaneous Expansion of the Church* (1927). Sidney Clark's *The Indigenous Church* (1928) espoused a similar approach.

Three-Selfs theory was considered enlightened missiology for nearly a century. Alan Tippett, in pointing to Venn's contribution to missiological theory, says,

> over a century the missionary world has had this basic theory of mission before it. Because God spoke to the missionary world through Venn's writings we have no one to blame but ourselves for our preference for paternalistic and foreign missions and the problems that have emerged from our policy (1973:155).

On the Roman Catholic side, the tendency was to speak of *accommodation,* since their polity requires the continuation of a given ecclesiastical system which, though it may be modified, is intended to always be an import. Though they admit that the model may be locally modified, it is always an import. Even with certain accommodations to the surrounding culture, their ideal is a kind of *form indigeneity*, requiring the introduction of certain cultural forms in areas such as worship, the Mass and baptism.

Up to this point, both Protestants and Catholics had usually assumed that missionaries were to take an existing system to the ends of the earth. And, though, there would be inevitable accommodations and adjustments of that system, be it Methodist, Presbyterian, Baptist, or Roman Catholic, few questioned that the governance, doctrines, ceremonies, teaching structures, and just about all else were to be imported.

During this period enlightened missionaries began to advocate and, to a certain extent, implement the change from foreigners running the system to nationals running the system. But it was still a foreign system they were operating. The indigeneity was, therefore, with few exceptions, simply a matter of the forms of Christianity in the hands of nationals but the meanings were still largely foreign.

---

[2] Whether or not the national leaders exerted enough actual power in the *control* of their churches was another matter. The important aspect was the *impression* of self-governance that the elevation of selected indigenes into *positions* of leadership provided.

Stage III: Early Impact of Anthropology

In the 1940s and 1950s, with roots going back as far as the turn of the century in Europe (especially among Roman Catholics) and the 1920s and 30s in America, the findings of anthropology were starting to be felt in missiological thinking. Missionary training institutions began to teach anthropology as a way of sensitizing outbound missionaries to the cultures of the peoples with whom they were going to work.

Among the first missionary training institutions to introduce anthropology courses were the Kennedy School of Missions at Hartford Seminary Foundation (late 1920s, early 1930s), Wheaton College and Wycliffe Bible Translators[3] (both dating back into the 1930s), the Jaffray School of Missions at Nyack, NY, and the Toronto and Meadville language and culture summer programs run by the American Bible Society (early 1950s).

A very influential source of anthropological insight among Evangelical[4] missionaries and missiologists during the 1950s and 1960s was the bimonthly journal *Practical Anthropology*. This publication, started in 1953 by Robert Taylor, then professor of anthropology at Wheaton College, aimed at getting the anthropological message out to missionaries. It limped along during the last half of 1953 and all of 1954 until the American Bible Society Translations Department (under the leadership of Secretary for Translations, Eugene Nida) took over with William Smalley being appointed as editor in 1955. The publication influenced a whole generation of missionaries through the perceptive writings of Smalley, Nida, William Reyburn, Jacob Loewen and others. In 1973, *PA* was absorbed into *Missiology,* the journal of the newly established American Society of Missiology.

The popularizing of anthropological and communicational insights related to missionary work owes a great deal to Eugene Nida whose personal influence began to have great impact in the 1940s. Nida's spell-binding lecturing and writing style served to awaken the missionary community to cultural realities and their influence on the work of the Gospel around the world. Two of his books, *Customs and Cultures* (1954) and *Message and Mission* (1960), were especially helpful and constitute obligatory reading for missiologists/missionaries even today.

The significance of anthropological input for the discussion of contextualization cannot be overemphasized. Up until the 1960s and 1970s,

---

[3] The case of WBT was a little different in that the organization emphasized the *linguistic* side of what was then one area of specialization, viz., *linguistic anthropology*. It took Wycliffe quite a few years to make the study of *cultural* anthropology a major component of their training programs for Bible translators (1980s onwards).

[4] A number of Catholic cross-cultural workers also received a good deal of help from the articles in *PA*. Though the contributors to *PA* were largely Evangelicals, their focus was on contextualizing the biblical message not on advocating a particular brand of Evangelicalism.

anthropology was virtually the only field of study that focused on the validity of nonWestern cultures. Though the most effective missionaries learned to respect the cultures of the peoples among whom they worked, it was only as we began to incorporate the insights of anthropology into missionary thinking that we gained a theoretical perspective from which to counter our natural ethnocentrism. This perspective enabled us to improve our understandings in at least three crucial areas: the implications for life and witness of the cultural involvements of the people we seek to reach, the implications of our own involvement in culture and our ability to probe and penetrate in new ways the cultural dimensions of the biblical revelation.

Not all anthropological teaching was relevant to the task of Christian witnesses. We had to learn to temper anthropology's commitment to a nearly absolute relativism with the biblical truths concerning a Creator who sustains the universe and who offers an answer for the sin problem that underlies the cultural difficulties anthropologists can only describe. But by applying anthropological insight to the biblical revelation, we learned that the Creator interacts with humans *within* the cultural worlds they (we) have created. This insight, then, enables us to make sense of the times when God worked differently in the Old Testament than in the New because he was adapting his approach to the culture of the people he was working with. We began to understand biblical texts like 1 Corinthians 9:19-22, in which Paul states his commitment to adapt culturally in order to witness effectively, as an articulation of God's own approach to humans through culture. The development of such insights into the relationships between God, culture and human beings helped us move into deeper understandings of how to handle the Christian witness in a world of richly diverse cultures.

Stage IV: Beyond "Form Indigeneity"

The publication of William Smalley's "Cultural Implications of an Indigenous Church" in *Practical Anthropology* (1958) was a major breakthrough in our thinking about indigeneity and contextualization. To this point, the assumption of most of those who wrote on the subject seemed to be that if we simply turn our institutions (e.g., churches, schools, medical facilities and development projects) over to nationals to govern, support and propagate, all would go well. But Smalley challenged this assumption. He noted that in his mission and in many others that had committed themselves to three-self indigeneity, the nationals running things were doing their jobs in what was often an uncritical commitment to *Western* principles. Given this fact, Smalley asked whether a church run by nationals but according to Western patterns was truly indigenous. He concluded that an "indigeneity" solely at the form level was no indigeneity at all, even when the nationals were operating the system. Smalley proceeded, then, to define a truly indigenous church as

> a group of believers who live out their life, including their socialized
> Christian activity, in the patterns of the local society, and for whom

any transformation of that society comes out of their felt needs under the guidance of the Holy Spirit and the Scriptures. . . . An indigenous church is precisely one in which the changes which take place under the guidance of the Holy Spirit meet the needs and fulfill the meanings of that society and not of any outside group (1958:55-56).

The business of Christianity, Smalley asserts, whether in matters pertaining to church structures, doctrinal formulations, the way we live or any other part of our biblical faith, is to follow the leading of the Holy Spirit according to patterns that are meaningful to those inside any given society. Patterns and institutions imported from outside, no matter how meaningful they might be to the missionaries or how long they have been in force, cannot be seen as indigenous, even if they are run by nationals.

In the late 1950s, we evangelical Protestants who were struggling to understand the relationship between Christianity and culture had little awareness of what was going on in Roman Catholic circles. But even with the limitations of the Roman Catholic approach noted above, their voices were not totally silent during this period, especially after Vatican II. Characteristic of the best of Roman Catholic thinking was Louis Luzbetak's *The Church in Cultures* (published in 1963, revised and expanded in 1988). Luzbetak, an anthropologically trained missioner who worked in Papua New Guinea, demonstrated in his book that he was very much in touch with both Roman Catholic and informed Protestant thinking on this subject, including all that was published in *Practical Anthropology.*

The 1970s were an important time in the history of contextualization theory and practice. The mood of the times in missiological discussions was that we should be advocating an approach to the relationship between Christianity and culture that was more dynamic than the form indigeneity concept. Seeking to advance our thinking along this vein, Alan Tippett of Fuller's School of World Mission (now School of Intercultural Studies) wrote "Indigenous Principles in Mission Today" in a book called *Verdict Theology in Missionary Theory* (1973). In this chapter, Tippett dealt with quantitative, qualitative and organic church growth and suggested that we should focus on the *quality of selfhood* when discussing whether a church was truly indigenous or not. He suggested that we looked for a dynamic, indigenous quality in six areas: self-image, self-function, self-determination, self-support, self-propagation and self-giving. Tippett stated,

When the indigenous people of a community think of the Lord as their own, not a foreign Christ; when they do things as unto the Lord meeting the cultural needs around them, worshipping in patterns they understand; when their congregations function in participation in a body, which is structurally indigenous; then you have an *indigenous* Church (1973:158).

In my 1978 Willowbank paper on dynamic equivalence churches, I expressed the concern we were feeling in that decade over the use of the word indigenous. I said,

> Strictly speaking, "indigeneity" is not necessarily the most appropriate label for the ideal toward which we strive. A church *totally* indigenous in appearance, function, and meaning would be no different from the rest of the culture. Christianity, because it comes into a culture from the outside, is inevitably intrusive to a certain degree. There is "no such thing as an absolutely indigenous church in any culture," observes Smalley ("What Are Indigenous Churches Like?" *Practical Anthropology*, 1959, Vol. 6, p. 137). Nevertheless, we will employ the term "indigenous church" (as Smalley does) to signify an expression of Christianity that is both culturally authentic and genuinely Christian (Kraft 1980:214)

Then, as a further indication of our dissatisfaction with the term *indigenous*, I and my co-editor Tom Wisley decided to name our collection of readings on the subject *Readings in Dynamic Indigeneity* (Kraft and Wisley, eds. 1979). By 1979, some of the more open evangelical thinkers started using the term *contextualization*. It was, however, still very suspect to the more conservative, including the group that was helping fund our book. We, therefore, had several serious discussions concerning the name and concluded that the evangelical groups we sought to reach would probably reject our book if we used the new term. Thus our title and the following words in the Introduction:

> Two recent articles (Coe 1973; Taber 1979) have raised the issue of the terminology that we use to label the subject matter of this volume. Both of these authors suggest that the older term "indigenization" connotes a static view of what is desirable for the church while "contextualization" connotes a more dynamic concept. They have a point.
>
> We believe, however, that the crucial distinction that these authors are bringing to our attention lies deeper than any mere surface level change from one term to the other. Which label one prefers is secondary to how one conceives of the process. While it may be true, as Coe and Taber contend, that most of those employing the older term, indigenization, had an inadequate, more static view of the way Christianity is to become a part of a new culture, it is by no means true that most of those now speaking of contextualization hold a very different view. The problem, as we see it, lies in whether the process is conceived of as basically a matter of 1) preformulation, transfer and modification within the receiving culture of a given system or 2) the creation within the receiving culture of something new which is the result of fertilization from outside but may bear little formal resemblance to the source culture system.

It is the latter concept that we recommend in this volume, whatever the label attached. Our aim is to bring about "dynamic equivalence" to God's processes made explicit in the Scriptures . . . We have no disaffection for the term contextualization. Indeed, we use it freely, especially with reference to theologizing (Kraft and Wisley, eds. 1979:xix-xx).

Stage V: Transition to Contextualization

Prior to the above publication, in a World Council of Churches consultation, Shoki Coe formally introduced the term *contextualization*. His presentation was published in 1973 in *Theological Education* and reprinted undert the title "Contextualizing Theology" by Gerald Anderson and Thomas Stransky in *Mission Trends* No. 3 (1976). In that article Coe said,

> indigenization tends to be used in the sense of responding to the Gospel in terms of traditional culture. Therefore, it is in danger of being past-oriented. Furthermore, the impression has been given that it is only applicable to Asia and Africa, for elsewhere it was felt that the danger lay in over-indigenization, an uncritical accommodation such as expressed by the culture faiths, the American Way of Life, etc. But the most important factor, especially since the last war, has been the new phenomenon of radical change. The new context is not that of static culture, but the search for the new, which at the same time has involved the culture itself. . . .

> So in using the word *contextualization,* we try to convey all that is implied in the familiar term *indigenization,* yet seek to press beyond for a more dynamic concept which is open to change and which is also future-oriented (Coe 1976:20-21).

As noted above, the fact that the term surfaced in World Council circles gave many evangelicals, especially those at the more conservative end of the spectrum, great problems. An early, though grudging acceptance came from Bruce Nicholls in his 1979 book, *Contextualization: A Theology of Gospel and Culture*. Nicholls started by presenting so many cautions about the term and the concept that one was led to believe he was against both. But by the end of the volume he turned positive and accepting. Bruce Fleming, however, in the publication of his thesis done at Trinity Evangelical Divinity School, entitled *Contextualization of Theology: An Evangelical Assessment* (1980) made no such accommodation to the term. Fleming critically evaluated the origination and development of the concept within ecumenical circles, taking a negative stance toward the term but accepting most of the concept under his proposed label *context-indigenization*.

Among the significant events of the 1970s was the publication of several specific attempts at contextualization of theology by representatives from the Two-Thirds World. Many of these were from a liberal theological perspective and, therefore, increased the suspicions of the more conservative evangelicals in the U.S. (e.g., Nicholls, Hesselgrave) that the whole exercise was a threat to biblical Christianity. And, I believe, much of their reticence was justified. These were the days when Liberation Theology, especially in Latin America, and Black Theology[5] in the U.S. were gaining popularity.

The reticence of North American Evangelicals was especially understandable in reaction to liberation theologians who often seemed more concerned about what they defined as liberation than about being faithful to Scripture. For example, though we may sympathize with their desire to be free of domination by Euroamerican theological thinking, we cannot endorse the way the Bible is treated by such Latin American theologians as Gustavo Gutierrez (in *A Theology of Liberation*, 1973) or Juan Segundo (in *The Liberation of Theology*, 1975, Spanish; 1976, English). Likewise with such Asians as C. S. [Choan-Seng] Song in *Third-Eye Theology* (1979) and at least some of the authors in Gerald Anderson's collection *Asian Voices in Christian Theology* (1976).

Yet some of those authors and Japanese theologian Kosuke Koyama bear careful reading even if one disagrees with their interpretations.[6] So do works by John Mbiti from Africa.[7] More cautious voices from Africa were those of John Pobee in *Toward an African Theology* (1979) and Kwame Bediako (1992).

A particularly sharp reaction against theological contextualization in Africa came from Byang Kato who served for several years, before his untimely death, as the leader of the Association of Evangelicals of Africa and Madagascar. Kato was a conservative Nigerian who studied theology at Dallas Theological Seminary and published his doctoral dissertation in 1975 under the title, *Theological Pitfalls in Africa.* At the time of his death (in 1976), however, he was beginning to recognize some validity to the motivations behind the contextualization movement and rumor has it that in one of his last (unpublished) presentations, he was fairly positive toward the need for contextualization. Perhaps it was this recognition that led him to apologize to John Mbiti shortly before his death for some of the criticisms he had published in the above book.[8]

In the U.S., Carl Armerding edited a largely negative Evangelical reaction to Liberation Theology, entitled *Evangelicals and Liberation* (1977). It included essays by Harvie Conn, Steven Knapp, Kenneth Hamilton, and Clark Pinnock.

In spite of such reactions on the part of some conservative evangelicals, the climate began to change during the mid and late 1970s. As we began to take seriously the broadening of the concept beyond the earlier discussions surrounding indigeneity, first the more open and then the more conservative

---

[5] See, for example, James Cone, *Black Theology and Black Power*, 1969.

[6] See, for example Koyama's insightful *Waterbuffalo Theology*, 1974.

[7] See *New Testament Eschatology in an African Background,* 1971.

[8] See Kraft 1978a.

evangelical missiologists among us began to overcome our prejudices toward the ecumenical origins of the term and to find both the term and the discussion useful and instructive. We have never condoned the way some seem to dilute the authority of the Scriptures (e.g., Song, Segundo) as they propose new approaches to contextualization, though we join them in seeing the value and necessity of the process of contextualization.

Stage VI: Evangelical Acceptance of the Concept of Contextualization

Though Evangelicals had considered *indigeneity* the ideal for decades, we now abandoned that word in favor of the new term and the broader concept it was intended to signify. At the School of World Mission, Fuller Seminary, we initiated what was probably the first professorial position with the term contextualization in its name when we appointed Dean S. Gilliland to be an Assistant Professor of the Contextualization of Theology in 1977.

Typical of the new mood were the several events important to this discussion that happened in 1978. First, the entire January 1978 issue of *Evangelical Missions Quarterly* was devoted to the topic. In the lead article, "Contextualization: Is It Only a New Word for Indigenization?" James Buswell suggested that the issues we are dealing with require a broader perspective than that encompassed by the word indigenization. He then suggested we use the term *inculturation* when dealing with the witness dimension of Christianity, *indigenization* when it is the contextualization of the church and its leadership in view, and either *contextualization* or my term *ethnotheology* for the production of appropriate theology. This article was followed by F. Ross Kinsler's article, "Mission and Context: The Current Debate About Contextualization." Pushing beyond the controversy over the term contextualization, Kinsler pointed out that we need to recognize that our discussion has to get to deeper issues such as 1) the very nature of the Gospel, 2) the question of syncretism, 3) tradition and renewal, and 4) the apparent conflict between biblical theology and contextual theologies.

In "Contextualization: A New Dimension for Cross-Cultural Hermeneutic" Conn (1978) suggests we develop a *contextual hermeneutic* that addresses two important questions to the church:

> How are the divine demands of the gospel of the kingdom communicated in cultural thought forms meaningful to the real issues and needs of the person and [his/her] society in that point of cultural time? [and] How shall the [servant] of God, as a member of the body of Christ and the fellowship of the Spirit, respond meaningfully and with integrity to the Scriptures addressing [his/her] culture so that [he/she] may live a full-orbed kingdom lifestyle in covenant obedience with the covenant community?" (1978:43).

In my article entitled, "The Contextualization of Theology," I tried to demonstrate that contextualization is a *biblical* process, results in theologies none of which are absolute and is a risky enterprise. My concluding statement was as follows:

> What is the contextualization of theology? That is what happens whenever the given gospel, the message of Christ, is reinterpreted in new cultural contexts in ways equivalent to the ways in which Paul and the other Apostles interpreted it from Aramaic into Greek thought patterns. Contextualization of theology must be biblically based if it is to be Christian. It may take place in a number of different ways—such as sermons, hymns, poems, discussions, art, and many other ways. Contextualizing Christian theology is risky, but is not as likely to lead to syncretism as is the preservation of antique forms of theologizing and the importation of these forms into contexts in which they are not appropriate. No theology is an absolute representation of the mind of God. Appropriate contextualizations, produced by Spirit-led interpreters of God's word, enable them to present the Christian message within a biblically allowed range of variation in such a way that today's peoples will respond to Christ as those in the first century did (Kraft 1978:36).

Then, from January 6-13, 1978, under the auspices of the Lausanne Theology and Education Group, the Willowbank Consultation on Gospel and Culture was convened. Though the subject of the consultation was wider than the topic of contextualization, extending to such things as the definition of culture, the nature of inspiration, the normative nature of Scripture, culture and the communication of the Gospel, conversion, the church in culture and even Christian ethics and lifestyle, the concern for contextualization was evident throughout.

Insight into the Willowbank scholars' view of contextualization comes to the fore when the matter of understanding God's Word for today is discussed in the Report of the Consultation. The Report states that a contextual approach to understanding the Bible

> takes seriously the cultural context of the contemporary readers as well as of the biblical text, and recognizes that a dialogue must develop between the two.
>
> It is the need for this dynamic interplay between text and interpreters which we wish to emphasize. Today's readers cannot come to the text in a personal vacuum, and should not try to. Instead, they should come with an awareness of concerns stemming from their cultural background, personal situation, and responsibility to others. These concerns will influence the questions which are put to the Scriptures. . . . We find that our culturally conditioned presuppositions are being challenged and our questions corrected. . . .
>
> In this process of interaction our knowledge of God and our response to his will are continuously being deepened. The more we come to know him, the greater our responsibility becomes to obey

him in our own situation, and the more we respond obediently, the more he makes himself known.

It is this continuous growth in knowledge, love and obedience which is the purpose and profit of the 'contextual' approach. Out of the context in which his word was originally given, we hear God speaking to us in our contemporary context, and we find it a transforming experience. This process is a kind of upward spiral in which Scripture remains always central and normative (Coote and Stott, eds. 1980:317).

In dealing with the church in culture, the Report suggests that the criticisms of models of indigeneity were not so much applicable to "the ideal itself, but [to] . . . the way it has often been applied." Nevertheless, "a more radical concept of indigenous church life needs to be developed, by which each church may discover and express its selfhood as the body of Christ within its own culture" (Coote and Stott, eds. 1980:329).

The Report then recommends the dynamic equivalence model for contextualizing churches—an issue I had discussed in the paper I presented at the consultation, saying

Just as a 'dynamic equivalence' translation . . . seeks to convey to contemporary readers meanings equivalent to those conveyed to the original readers, by using appropriate cultural forms, so would a 'dynamic equivalence' church. It would look in its culture as a good Bible translation looks in its language. It would preserve the essential meanings and functions which the New Testament predicated of the church, but would seek to express these in forms equivalent to the originals but appropriate to the local culture (Coote and Stott, eds. 1980:330).

Three more significant publications of 1978 came from Charles Taber. The lead article in the first (January) issue of the (unfortunately, short-lived) journal *Gospel in Context,* edited by Taber himself, was entitled, "Is There More Than One Way to Do Theology?" (1978a) He argued that, although all theologies are to be subject to Scripture, they are also to be conditioned by the culture in which they function. Also in January of that year, Taber published "The Limits of Indigenization in Theology" in *Missiology* (1978b). Stephen Bevans and Norman Thomas (1991) say of that article,

A seminal article outlining six propositions regarding the doing of theology in context and seven criteria for measuring indigenous theology, noting that as far as form and methodology go, there are no a priori limits which can be imposed on Christian theology (1991:108).

In that same year, Taber contributed a chapter to *The Gospel and Islam* (McCurry, ed. 1979), entitled, "Contextualization: Indigenization and/or Transformation." (Taber 1979) In that chapter, Taber helpfully (though sometimes more hopefully than realistically) contrasted contextualization with indigenization in six ways, contending that

> Indigenization . . . was a step in the right direction, but it did not go far enough, especially if we are to take seriously the 20th century context. Contextualization extends and corrects indigenization in the following directions.

> 1. Indigenization tended to focus exclusively on the cultural dimension of human experience . . . Contextualization recognizes the importance of this dimension but insists that the human context to which the gospel is addressed also includes social, political, and economic questions: wealth and poverty, power and powerlessness, privilege and oppression. . . .

> 2. Indigenization tended to define culture in rather static, traditional terms. The various aspects of culture are "given," and they sit there while the gospel works around them. There was insufficient appreciation for the flexibility and changeableness of culture. . . .

> 3. Indigenization tended to think of sociocultural systems as closed and self-contained; the type of society was the small tribal group, isolated by distance and jungle from outside influences. . . . Today groups and societies relate to each other, trade with each other, fight each other, and defeat and exploit each other within a vast politico-economic system which operates on a global scale. Our model must take into account this global system and its differential impact on the various groups, societies, and nations of the earth. . . .

> 4. Indigenization was almost by definition something that happened 'out there' on the mission field; it had nothing to say about how the gospel related to the missionary's society and culture on its own home turf; it merely said that the missionary's culture was not for export. In fact, indigenization tended to take a rather too uncritical and optimistic view of *each* given culture in its home setting, and to see evil only in the imposition of an alien culture on groups in the 'mission field.'. . . But contextualization insists on two additional insights: that the demonic as well as the divine is manifest in all societies and cultures, and that the same processes of cultural confrontation and/or syncretism plague churches in the West as in any other place, and must be faced with the same attitudes and means.

> 5. Indigenization, on the whole, tended to deal with relatively superficial questions such as the 'expression' of a gospel which was conceived to be 'the same' in all contexts. Contextualization argues that there is indeed a sense in which the gospel is 'the same' all over the world; but that universal dimension is much more remote from

the surface level of verbal and symbolic expression than was previously acknowledged. . . .

6. . . . [T]hough indigenization was intended to place responsibility, authority, and initiative in the hands of national Christians, it usually did so in only a part of the total missionary enterprise: the work of the local church. More complex operations, such as hospitals and major schools, were without question designed, financed, and controlled from the outside. Seldom . . . was the more fundamental question asked, whether the very concept behind these efforts was itself sound. . . .

Contextualization, then, is an attempt to capitalize on the achievements of indigenization, to correct its errors and biases, and fill in its gaps. It is the effort to understand and take seriously the specific context of each human group and person on its own terms and in all its dimensions—cultural, religious, social, political, economic—and to discern what the gospel says to people in that context. . . . Contextualization takes very seriously the example of Jesus in the sensitive and careful way he offered each person a gospel tailored to his or her own context . . . (Taber 1979:144-146).

Then, in 1979, my book *Christianity in Culture* appeared. In that book I attempted to advance what we now would call contextualization theory by suggesting that new insights into Bible translation theory be looked at as a model for how Christianity as a whole should look in any given culture. Specifically, I suggested that the Bible translators' ideal of *dynamic equivalence* be the model for all other aspects of Christianity as well.

As J. B. Phillips said, the first rule of translation is a translation should not sound like a translation but, rather, like an original work in the receiving language (1960:vii). By analogy, I suggested that churches ought not to look like imports but, rather, like original works in their own cultures. I then applied this principle to several aspects of Christianity, suggesting how we might achieve dynamic equivalence transculturation (e.g., preaching), dynamic equivalence theologizing, dynamic equivalence conversion, dynamic equivalence cultural transformation, dynamic equivalence leadership principles and the like.[9]

In the section of *Christianity in Culture* in which I discuss dynamic equivalence theologizing, I was greatly helped by an article written by Daniel von Allmen entitled "The Birth of Theology" (1975) in which the author

---

[9] In "Signs of Progress in Contextual Methodology" (1981), Louis Luzbetak (who called my *Christianity in Culture* "a landmark in missiological theory") suggested that my book and the work of Robert Schreiter (published as *Constructing Local Theologies* in 1985) were signs of hope in the process of understanding and working toward truly contextualized Christianity.

parallels Pauline contextualization with contemporary contextualization. As I have written, von Allmen

> sees all theologies . . . including Pauline theology, as the result of "contextualization" done by certain people within a group to meet the needs of that group. Missionaries, translators, and those who "sang the work that God had done for them" ([von Allmen] 1975:41) provided the raw materials for theologizing in the early churches. These consisted of expressions of need, translations and transculturations (including preaching) of the message in Greek, and partial preliminary formulations in culturally appropriate fashion (Kraft and Wisley, eds. 1979:295).

A key point made by von Allmen is that a proper theology is not simply some sort of adaptation or contextualization of an existing theology. He says,

> Any authentic theology must start ever anew from the focal point of the faith, which is the confession of the Lord Jesus Christ who died and was raised for us; and it must be built or re-built (whether in Africa or in Europe) in a way which is both faithful to the inner thrust of the Christian revelation and also in harmony with the mentality of the person who formulates it. There is no short cut to be found by simply adapting an existing theology to contemporary or local taste (von Allmen 1975:50).

Stage VII: Since 1980

Contextualization studies have increased greatly, among both Protestants and Roman Catholics, since 1980. In Bevans and Norman Thomas' helpful bibliography of contextualization studies, published in the January 1991 issue of *Missiology*, thirty-two significant studies are listed. Of these, twenty-five have been written in the 1980s, with only three of the seven earlier studies published before 1978. Twelve of the twenty-five studies are from Roman Catholic perspectives, including an eleven-volume collection of papers presented at a conference on inculturation held in Jerusalem in 1981 (Crollius 1984).

In a valuable attempt to respond to and go beyond my book, *Christianity in Culture,* Harvie M. Conn published *Eternal Word and Changing Worlds* in 1984. In preparation for that book, Conn, who has solid theological and missionary credentials, worked hard to educate himself anthropologically. Thus, he was able to wed theological and anthropological insights in a very helpful way to provide evaluation of old approaches and suggestions for new approaches to theologizing and theological education.

1984 also saw the publication of Hiebert's seminal article "Critical Contextualization," in which he articulated what many of us had assumed but not stated so clearly: that Christians need to critically assess the *scriptural validity* as well as the *cultural appropriateness* of each Christian practice. A dangerous and unbiblical extreme is to consider anything that is indigenous as automatically worthy of incorporation into Christianity. The biblical authors were not uncritical of cultural practices. Neither should we be. Our drive toward relevance should not obscure the fact that we are to be tethered to the Bible.

In 1985, Robert Schreiter published his experiment with a semiotic approach to contextualization entitled, *Constructing Local Theologies*. In this work he presents an insightful but very complex approach to producing local theologies and shows a preference for the term *localization* in place of contextualization.

The 1989 publication of David Hesselgrave and Edward Rommen's *Contextualization*, provides an indication of how the more conservative wing of Christian thinkers were receiving several of the above explorations. This book contains, for example, a very harsh reaction against myself and several others.

On the Roman Catholic side, Louis Luzbetak's revised and enlarged *The Church and Cultures* (1988) is in reality an introduction to missiology within which he has enfolded his earlier anthropology text. It thus updates and expands his helpful understandings of contextualization.

At least four other valuable Roman Catholic contributions appeared during this time period. Eugene Hill's article on "Inculturation" in *The New Dictionary of Theology* (1987) surveys the subject and argues that Jesus' Incarnation demands contemporary inculturation. Aylward Shorter's, *Toward a Theology of Inculturation* (1988) provides a valuable overview of Roman Catholic theological thinking on the subject. J. Peter Schineller's *A Handbook of Inculturation* (1990) is an introduction to the theology and practice of contextualization for the non-specialist. Another guide for practitioners is Gerald A. Arbuckle's, *Earthing the Gospel: An Inculturation Handbook for the Pastoral Worker* (1990). These works demonstrate to the evangelical world both the centrality of the Bible and a sound concern for cultural appropriateness in the thinking of Roman Catholic missiologists.

In *The Word Among Us*, edited by Dean S. Gilliland (1989), the faculty of Fuller's School of Intercultural Studies provide statements on a wide variety of contextualization issues. In a statement of evangelical commitment to our subject, Gilliland says,

> The conviction behind this volume is that contextualization, biblically based and Holy Spirit-led, is a requirement for evangelical missions today. Contextualization is incarnational. The Word which became flesh dwells among us. It clarifies for each nation or people the meaning of the confession, "Jesus is Lord." It liberates the church in every place to hear what the Spirit is saying. Contextual theology will open up the way for communication of the gospel in ways that allow the hearer to understand and accept. It gives both freedom and facility for believers to build up one another in the faith. Contextualization clarifies what the Christian witness is in sinful society and shows what obedience to the gospel requires. These are

the components of a theology for mission that meets the needs of today's world (1989:3).

A very useful book entitled *Models of Contextual Theology* was published in 1992 by Bevans. The author contends that enough contextualization studies have now been done to enable us to categorize and classify them. So he attempts to take stock of and organize the various approaches by lumping them into five categories or models he calls: Translation Model, Anthropological Model, Praxis Model, Synthetic Model, and Transcendental Model. The book, though not without the kind of limitations one would expect of such a large venture, is an excellent attempt to organize and synthesize both Protestant and Roman Catholic approaches.

Emblematic of the importance missiologists attach to this subject, contextualization is one of the most frequent topics appearing in missiological journals. Various issues of *Missiology* have either been devoted to contextualization or contain significant articles on the subject. The January 1991 issue, entitled "Contextualization in Mission," and the January 1997 issue, entitled "Contextualizing the Gospel," are completely devoted to this subject. Each contains several useful articles and the former contributes an excellent bibliography by Bevans and Norman Thomas. Other missiological journals such as *Evangelical Missions Quarterly, The International Bulletin of Missionary Research* and *International Review of Mission* have also featured numerous articles on contextualization.[10]

Remaining Issues

This is where we have come from. And what has been accomplished, at least in the area of conceptualization, is impressive, especially in the theological area. Still, we have much to learn. Each attempt to construct a localized, "ethnic" theology must still be seen as experimental. We still have a lot do in terms of conceptualizing, and implementing, what might be called *structural contextualization*—such as culturally appropriate models of church governance, leadership training, ceremony, communication and the like. There have, however, been impressive breakthroughs in the area of the contextualization of worship, especially in music.[11]

In general, though, the implementation of these ideas has lagged far behind their conceptualization. Churches that were once under the domination of missionaries and Western patterns have largely replaced the missionaries with national leaders who keep the same foreign structures and use the same

---

[10] Recently, Darrell Whiteman, former editor of the journal *Missiology,* has weighed in with an important essay entitled, "Contextualization: The Theory, the Gap, the Challenge" (1997).

[11] See Chapter 10.

approaches they learned from the Westerners. It is as if the nationals are simply filling in for foreign workers who have gone on a long vacation.

So there is much still to do, both in conceptualizing and especially in applying what we think we know. In concluding this chapter, I would like to point to six important areas of unfinished business in contextualization.

1. The first, and I believe by far the most important problem is, as Darrell Whiteman (1997) put it: How to get what we think we know academically across to field missionaries, to entrenched church leaders and to the administrators of missionary-sending organizations. The place where most research breaks down is at the point of implementation. Many of the things we missiologists teach and write have been known to us for decades but are either unknown to or ignored by one or more of the above groups.

National church leaders have often been trained well in Western ways and have a considerable emotional investment in keeping their present positions. They have, therefore, no desire to change their ways, even if they privately admit that contextualized approaches might be better. Field missionaries, for their part, often have neither read the studies nor have they understood the issues behind the calls for contextualization. Furthermore, they may feel threatened in their positions and prestige if things are done in ways they do not fully understand. The administrators of missionary-sending organizations, then, are often hamstrung either by ignorance or by feeling the continual press of administrative duties—or, as in Whiteman's illustration, by boards to whom denominational expansion is more important than inculturated Christianity.[12]

2. A second issue—in some ways similar to the first—is: How to solve the problem of missionaries who know enough to work in culturally sensitive ways but who do not do it. Many who go out as cross-cultural witnesses have read and received good instruction in the theory of contextualization but tend to dominate and to impose foreign patterns on their converts once they get to the field. Or, when they enter a Western/westernized mission situation, they fall into the familiar patterns and fail to work to improve the situation.[13]

---

[12] Back in the late sixties and early seventies, we at Fuller's School of World Mission conducted several Church Growth Seminars in various places for people in positions to implement change in missionary organizations. We felt at that time that our message had gotten across to many mission administrators and practitioners. It is, however, disappointing to see so little change even among the missionary organizations we felt had been listening to us. I believe we would do well now to institute Contextualization Seminars both at home and abroad for church leaders, missionaries and administrators to get this message across.

[13] Some have suggested that the primary culprit may be culture stress (often called "culture shock"). They note that people under culture stress tend to revert to familiar patterns, even if they know better. An important part of this reactionary stance may be the personal insecurity and, often, outright fear experienced by people attempting to function in a cultural world not their own. Or, the problem may simply be laziness or a feeling that things can't be changed. Some might even feel that the people want things to be foreign since they don't complain, though such an attitude may simply be the result of the people never having experienced anything different and, therefore, being unable to imagine another

3. A major problem, hardly mentioned in the literature, is the fact that there are important differences in the contextualization issues faced by each generation of converts. In the first generation of a people's Christian commitment, when everything is new and they are just coming out of their preChristian allegiance, the major issues seem to be *separation* and *contrast*. People are rightly concerned over which of their previous ways to modify, which to reject and how to demonstrate their new faith in contrast to the life of those around them who have not converted.

We cannot expect that new Christians will be able to contextualize their newly acquired faith in appropriate ways at all levels. There are a multitude of details involved in changing their way of life and especially their worldview to fit their new faith. And the converts should not be criticized if they adopt what will eventually be seen as too much foreignness in the first generation. There may be much adaptation, to be sure, but also much remaining to be done.

A major problem stemming from this incomplete contextualization in the first generation is the fact that first generation practices tend to get "set in cement" and not worked on in succeeding generations. Many churches in mission lands are today saddled with a disturbing number of inappropriate cultural forms adopted by the first generation of Christians and simply handed down from generation to generation as if they were ordained by God.

The first generation problem is, of course, quite different for those who have entered Christianity through a people movement. When large groups adopt the Christian faith with their preChristian ways largely intact, they may change their behavior and worldview less than they should rather than more than they should in the first generation. Either way, there is much contextualizing to be done in succeeding generations.

Perhaps most of what we seek by way of developing appropriate cultural expressions of biblical faith should be dealt with in the second, third or following generations, rather than in the first. We need to look carefully at our subject in relation to the specific problems of each generation.[14] In addition, we need to learn how to instill in each generation of new believers what might be labeled a "spirit of openness to continual adjustment and change," lest they simply pass on from generation to generation patterns that are culturally and personally dysfunctional.

4. A fourth area of concern is the matter of the contextualization of relationship. We have made progress with theorizing concerning contextualizing theology and structures but have largely ignored what is scripturally the most important dimension of Christianity, that that involves allegiance/commitment to God, leading to a lasting relationship with Him. The need for conversions that lead to a relationship with God has frequently been mentioned, and I have suggested (1979a) that we need to encourage conversions that are dynamically

---

approach.

[14] See Chapter 8 for more on this problem.

equivalent to those advocated in the New Testament. But discussions of culturally and biblically appropriate commitment and relationships have seldom appeared. I suspect that there are cultural differences, perhaps large ones, from society to society in the expression and experiencing of allegiance and relationship that go beyond our theorizing concerning conversion.

My feeling is that we have dealt too narrowly with our subject. We have probed the contextualization of many of the important *cognitive* issues and, to a lesser extent, some structural factors. But our central concern for experiencing (not just theorizing about) commitment to God and fellow Christians has been neglected in contextualization studies.[15]

5. I would, likewise, question whether we have adequately dealt with issues of spiritual power in contextualization. Given the fact that most of the world is heavily into spiritual power, where are the discussions concerning biblically and culturally appropriate expressions of healing, deliverance, prayer, dedication, visions, dreams, concepts of the territoriality of spirits, angels, demons and the like? Shouldn't we be discussing the contextualizing of spiritual warfare? What are the scriptural principles applicable to every cultural situation and what are the cultural variables in this important area?

6. Lastly, we need to look critically at our theories of contextualization in relation to counter examples that seem to challenge some of our findings. Why, for example, does it look like many of the largest, apparently most "successful" churches (e.g., in Korea, the Philippines, Singapore, large parts of Africa) are poorly contextualized? Are there factors that override cultural fit? If so, what are they? Are we missing something in our commitment to our theory? Could it even be that our theory is wrong? [16]

These and other issues are still on the table, even after we have gleaned all we can from this impressive history. May God give us the necessary ingredients both to study and to implement what he has shown us and continues to show us in this important area of life and witness.

---

[15] See Chapter 11 for more on this subject.

[16] See Chapter 10 for more on this topic.

Chapter 3

The Missionary Encounter with Culture since the Seventeenth Century

Wilbert R. Shenk

From the time of the first apostles (Ac. 15; 1 Cor. 7-9) the missionary has had to continually wrestle with the Gospel-culture nexus. In 601 A.D., while en route to England from France, Pope Gregory the Great wrote to Mellitus with advice for Bishop Augustine of Canterbury as to how he should deal with the "case of the Angli: to wit, that the temples of idols in that nation should not be destroyed, but that the idols themselves that are in them should be." Gregory urged that structures be cleansed and transformed so they might be used for "the service of the true God" (Hillgarth, ed. 1969:152). Gregory argued that when the people saw that these familiar structures could be brought into the service of God they would be confirmed in their newfound faith.

The way the missionary has conceptualized and theorized the culture problematic has invariably reflected the missionary's cultural background. The missionary had no choice but to filter experience and observation through the only grid available: the missionary's own culture. However, for several reasons the shape of the "Gospel and culture" question has continued to change. First, the experience in cross-cultural missions has kept turning up new challenges. Simply to mention the names of Bartolemé de Las Casas (1484-1566) and Matteo Ricci (1552-1610) is to call up images of missionaries in the sixteenth century who struggled heroically against the uniformly negative reaction of the *sending* church to their efforts to make sense of the Gospel for people who had never before heard it by using linguistic and cultural resources drawn from their own culture. A second reason is that continually broadening cultural contacts enlarged the historical framework within which past experiences could be compared and evaluated. The third reason has been the formulation, starting in the nineteenth century, of theories of culture to assist in the systematic study of cultures.

This chapter is a historical study of the way the culture-Gospel problematic has been conceptualized and theorized in the several stages of the Protestant cross-cultural missionary experience from the rise of Protestant missions in the 1600s through the twentieth century. This 350-year period divides readily into three phases. Each historical phase will be approached through the lens of the prevailing understanding of culture: 1) 1640-1850, pre-critical phase; 2) 1850-1970, indigenization; and 3) 1970 to the present, contextualization. We will follow the change in missionary outlook from the time when all missionary action proceeded from the assumption that the first task of the missionary was to "civilize" people in order that they might become Christians, to the late twentieth century when earnest Christians in Asia, Africa, and Latin America were calling all missionaries to employ contextually appropriate concepts and methods. This challenge is intensified by the concern to get rid of a methodology that has consistently produced dependence on outside resources—both financial and leadership—in favor of an approach based on interdependence in relationship.

Pre-Critical: 1640-1850

By 1600 the Protestant European nations had set out on the course established by the Spanish and Portuguese a century earlier: sending expeditions to explore other continents for the purpose of creating strategically located entrepôts. But it was also understood that Europeans, whether Roman Catholic or Protestant, represented Christendom and carried their religion with them. Preaching at Whitechapel (London) on April 20, 1609, William Symonds said: "Shame it is that the Jesuites and Friers, that accompany every ship, should be so diligent to destroy souls, and wee not seeke the tender lambes, nor bind up that which is broken" (O. E. Winslow, 1968:80). Two days earlier Robert Gay had proclaimed: "Farre be it from the hearts of the English, they should give any cause to the world, to say that they sought the wealth of that Countrie above or before the glorie of God and the propagation of his Kingdome" (Ibid). This view drew no dissent. Religion, culture, and politics were of one piece. The Massachusetts Bay Colony charter granted by the British crown in 1629 stipulated that one of its purposes was to "wynn and incite the natives... to the knowledge and obedience of the onlie true God and Savior of mankinde, and the Christian faythe" (Ibid:82). In 1630 a group of Puritans led by John Winthrop got control of the Massachusetts Bay Company and began promoting the migration of Puritans to New England where they would establish a Christian commonwealth, a purified Christendom. Out of this settlement came the first mission to the Native Americans. The Puritan missions to North American indigenous peoples, molded in part by the need to fulfill the legal requirement of the Company charter, defined the model for Protestant missions for at least two centuries.

John Eliot (1604-1690) is the representative figure of this first stage. He was born and reared in that part of Essex, England that has been called the "hotbed of Puritan sentiment" at a time of political tumult (Ibid, 22). Thomas Hooker, a Puritan divine who employed Eliot as a teacher, a year or so after Eliot's graduation from Cambridge in 1622, fled to Holland in 1630 to escape imprisonment. In 1631 Eliot sailed on the *Lyon* for Boston, thus joining what would become a large migration of Puritans to New England. Upon arrival,

Eliot became interim pastor of the Boston church. When John Wilson returned to Boston the following year, Eliot moved to Roxbury, five miles to the West, as founding pastor of the church there. He served this church until his death in 1690. By all accounts, John Eliot was a devout and conscientious pastor. He was committed to Puritanism that was at the center of political and religious reform in Great Britain, especially 1620-1650, and that was extending its influence to the New World. Puritanism was imbued with a strong sense of its elected purpose in God's plan to establish the ideal Christian commonwealth in the New World. With regard to the native peoples, the operative assumption was that the Indians lacked a civilization (Bowden and Ronda, eds. 1980:3-4).

As one of the earliest, widely publicized, and long-serving Protestant cross-cultural missionaries in the seventeenth century, Eliot perforce played a major role in defining the model of mission and culture, a construct that would prevail well into the nineteenth century. The basic assumption was that *civilization* must precede *Christianization.* Of course, civilization meant Western culture, but to the Puritan mind Western culture could not be separated from Christianity. Historical Christendom was the manifestation of a culture that had been Christianized and the goal was to reproduce this religio-cultural synthesis in every other culture.

Development of the social sciences was still two centuries away. Linguistics, anthropology, and sociology would emerge and be established only in the nineteenth century on foundations laid, in part, by missionaries who after 1800 were being dispersed in increasing numbers throughout the world. Until that happened, the means were not at hand to carry out comparative studies of cultures. Instead, each people viewed their particular culture as the standard by which other peoples were to be judged. One's own culture was "civilized" while others were primitive, inferior, or barbarian. This is the pre-critical view. The conceptualization of culture as a field of study and the tools required for the comparative study of cultures lay in the future.

Eliot made his first attempt to preach in Algonquian in 1646 and quickly discovered his incompetence in that tongue. At age 42 he set out to master the language. This required that the Algonquian language be reduced to writing and grammars and dictionaries created. Only then could the Scriptures be translated into Algonquian. Historians regard Eliot's work as a translator to be his enduring contribution.

Whatever concessions Eliot made by learning the language, however, were offset by his strict adherence to Puritan theology and church order. One of the procedures he introduced was to have Indians converts "make confessions" to their fellow Indians, the elders of the Roxbury church, and to the official representatives of the Congregational churches of the region. These confessions were comprehensive examinations of candidates' theological views. "Eliot's Indian converts," concludes Sidney Rooy, "were more than converts to the Christian faith; they were Anglicized Puritans. Though Eliot saw the Indians to be on the lowest rung of the ladder of civility, at the same time he saw them as educable and redeemable through the grace and Spirit of God" (Rooy 1965:170). To foster the civilizing process Eliot sought to institute a permanent quarantine that would protect Christian Indians from traditional Indian culture by establishing "praying towns," villages where these indigenous Christians could live as "civilized" people separated from Indian culture.

John Eliot lived in the dawning years of the Enlightenment and this intellectual environment was not one that would encourage the missionary to adapt to the culture of non-European people. Indeed, this intellectual climate was increasingly hostile to any compromise with nonWestern cultures. From the time of René Descartes (1596-1650). the Western intellectual quest was for a universal rationality that was independent of a particular cultural context. Rationality was the foundation on which the modern intellectual house was constructed.

Modernity emerged as a multifaceted and dynamic movement that was gaining momentum. It was bent on repudiating all things traditional. Only in this way could a burdensome past be replaced by a culture attuned to universal "laws of nature" and scientific knowledge. Increasingly, education was regarded as an indispensable motor propelling forward this ceaseless search for knowledge. Over the next several centuries all branches of learning would aspire to become "scientific" in their approach. These developments reinforced the attitude of the superiority of Western culture. The Enlightenment was Western but it was based on the assumption that this program was destined to be universal. Modern knowledge would benefit all of humankind. The Jesuit experiments in cultural adaptation in India and China in the sixteenth and early seventeenth centuries were forgotten (Clooney 1990; Ross 1994). Since peoples everywhere needed the benefits of modern knowledge as well as the Christian message, the role of the missionary was clear. The missionary's duty was to promote "civilization" together with the Christian faith. Indeed, the two were held to be interlocking. In the pre-critical phase mission could best be described as a process of *replication*.

Indigenization (1850-1970): The Failure of an Ideal

The modern missionary movement that emerged after 1792 bore all the marks of the Enlightenment worldview, including its characteristic self-confidence as to its superiority. Traditional peoples were regarded as disadvantaged and they could only make progress by becoming modern and Western. Enlightenment science, knowledge, and epistemology held the key to human progress. Advocates of Christian missions readily yoked the "blessings" of Christianization with progressive modern civilization.

This new phase of Christian missions coincided with a far-reaching intellectual development, namely, the formulation of the idea of culture.[1] In the

---

[1] For an overview of the intellectual currents flowing into the formulation of the

early years of the nineteenth century the founders of the disciplines of sociology and anthropology were grappling with the concept of culture. As late as 1948 it was observed that the "culture concept of the anthropologists and sociologists is coming to be regarded as the foundation stone of the social sciences."[2] In other words, this foundational conceptual development gradually worked its way into the wider intellectual process so that, in time, the *modern* concept of culture became as important in explanatory terms as "such categories as gravity in physics, disease in medicine, evolution in biology" (Ibid.). Even though a measure of agreement as to the term itself was reached late in the day, by the mid-twentieth century the notion of "culture" was incorporated into most academic disciplines as an essential component of discourse (Ibid:4-8).

At first sight it appears that these developments had little direct bearing on the developing theory of missions. In fact, missions and the emerging social sciences alike had to grapple with two basic questions: 1) What distinguishes the human species from animals? and 2) How do we speak about the unity and diversity of humankind (Hiebert 1978)? Of course, their approaches to answering these questions were quite different, and at times brought anthropologists and missionaries into conflict.

The modern missions movement was a fruit of the eighteenth-century Evangelical Revival but it also gained impetus from the awakened conscience of British evangelicals later in that century concerning the evils of slavery. Key leaders in the anti-slavery movement were also involved in the founding of the new mission societies that began springing up in the 1790s. Christian missions were answering the dominical command: "Therefore go and make disciples of all nations" (Mt. 28:19a, NIV). There was no question that the Christian mission was addressed to all humankind because every individual was a sinner but each one was of equal worth before God; and they were also committed to ending the trafficking in human lives, a cause that continued to influence mission thought and practice until the 1850s.

The first two missionaries appointed by the Church Missionary Society went to Freetown, Sierra Leone in 1804, a strategic center of the growing anti-slavery campaign. The instructions that Josiah Pratt, CMS secretary, gave to Melchior Renner and Peter Hartwig on the eve of their departure for Freetown, anticipated the complex and ambiguous situation they would face:

> You will take all prudent occasions of weaning the Native chiefs from this traffic, by depicting its criminality, the miseries which it occasions to Africa, and the obstacles which it opposes to a more profitable and generous intercourse with the European nations. But while you do this, you will cultivate kindness of spirit towards those persons who are connected with this trade. You will make all due

---

concept of culture, see Taber 1991:36-43.

[2] Stuart Chase cited in Kroeber and Kluckhohn 1952:3.

allowances for their habits, their prejudices, and their view of interest (Stock 1899, I:84-85).

Pratt exhorted the missionaries to confront those engaged in the slave trade in a way that focused on this particular practice—activity he regarded as criminal—without attacking the culture and dignity of the persons involved.

In spite of such evident respect for people of other cultures, the prevailing viewpoint was still pre-critical and would remain so for several more decades. However, the fund of information was growing. Patterned on such works as Captain James Cook's *Journals* based on his expeditions to the South Pacific between 1768 and 1779, missionary pioneers in the early nineteenth century published many volumes such as John Campbell's *Travels in South Africa* (1822) and *Maritime Discovery and Christian Missions* (1840), and Robert Moffat's *Missionary Labours and Scenes in Southern Africa* (1842).[3] These books provided readers with extensive observations about peoples in other parts of the world, including religious practices, cultural customs, language, and living conditions, as well as geography, flora, and fauna. The missionaries developed the model for fieldwork that anthropologists would follow, adapt, and elaborate on later.

Moffat's *Missionary Labours* went through four printings within three years, making him the foremost British missionary of the day. Under commission from the London Missionary Society, Moffat (1795-1883) went to Southern Africa in 1817 where he settled among the Tswana and almost immediately began translating the Bible into Tswana. From his base at Kuruman he traveled widely exploring and establishing relationships with the chiefs and their people. Notwithstanding his great achievement as a Bible translator and long residence in Southern Africa, "he never gained a deep understanding of African culture" (Ross 1998:464-465). For example, Moffat devotes one chapter in *Missionary Labours* to the role of the rainmaker in Southern Africa. While he shows sensitivity and sympathy for the people, his Enlightenment worldview causes him to dismiss these beliefs and practices as mere superstition rather than probing their meaning.

Because of their commitment to Bible translation, preaching, and teaching, missionaries early recognized the importance of language study and linguistic research. Sigismund W. Kölle, a German-born missionary serving with the Church Missionary Society in Sierra Leone, carried out an unusual project (Stock 1899, II:102-03). Well-trained in the Semitic languages, he taught Hebrew and Greek in Fourah Bay College, 1847-53. With encouragement from CMS secretary Henry Venn, Kölle carried out comparative studies of West African languages. Taking advantage of the presence of people from diverse backgrounds in Freetown, Kölle collected some 300 words and phrases from

---

[3] For a comprehensive listing of missions literature available in 1860 see Appendix IV, "Modern Works on Christian Missions," *Conference on Missions* (1860).

150 West African languages and dialects and published this volume as *Polyglotta Africana* in 1853. The French Institute awarded Kölle the Volney Prize for 1853 in recognition of his contribution to linguistic science.

If we ask what role the theme of "culture" played in the extensive discussion concerning missionary methods and strategies among mission thinkers in the early nineteenth century, we have to say that it is conspicuous by its absence. Instead, the discussion was framed in terms of the pre-critical model and assumptions. R. Pierce Beaver aptly characterized the prevailing outlook in the early nineteenth century: "'Evangelization' and 'civilization' had been the key words in American missionary methods—and in Protestant missions as a whole" (Beaver, ed. 1967:13). The mission task could be summarized in two words: *Civilization* and *Christianization*—code for Christendom. In 1800 mission leaders were still arguing about which one took precedence over the other in terms of process—civilization as precursor to Christianity or Christianity as the foundation of civilization—but all agreed the two were intertwined and could not be separated. By the 1820s the balance was shifting to the side of Christianization on grounds this would engender the desire for "civilization," i.e., Western culture. This view was a staple of the missionary books of the day.

After more than twenty years of experience in Southern Africa, Robert Moffat asserted in *Missionary Labours*: "Much has been said about civilizing savages, before attempting to evangelize them. This is a theory which has obtained an extensive prevalence among the wise men of this world; but we have never yet seen a practical demonstration of its truth" (Moffat 1969:502). He reiterates the importance of conversion as the foundation on which moral and cultural change can be carried out. African culture is depicted as depraved and Western civilization as the ideal and norm.

Yet Moffat's view was not to be the last word. For several reasons doubts concerning the moral superiority of Western civilization were growing. First, wherever missionaries went European merchants, colonial civil servants, and military contingents were bound to be present also. Invariably, the missionaries found themselves being embarrassed by the less than exemplary moral conduct of their compatriots. Instead, the ideals of *Christian* civilization upheld by the missionaries were shamelessly compromised by the conduct and lifestyles of their fellow Westerners. Second, after a generation of attempting to establish churches in nonWestern cultures according to Western standards, even a cursory evaluation showed that these churches lacked vitality. It was sometimes said that these churches looked more like "cut flowers" than vigorous plants rooted in the soil. Evidently something vital was missing from the process by which churches were being established. Third, a widespread economic depression in 1840-41 drove home the point that an enterprise dependent on external resources was seriously at risk in the event funds from abroad were cut off.

Henry Venn became Honorary Clerical Secretary of the Church Missionary Society in 1841 during this period of financial crisis. He soon began to argue that CMS ought to introduce a policy that encouraged the mission-founded churches in Africa or India to be *self-financing* as early as possible. This was the first step in his formulation of a new theory of mission. Venn then proceeded to work out a plan that was introduced in 1846 as the Native Pastorate Organization in Sierra Leone that would lead to the independence of that church from the mission within a period of twenty years (cf. Hanciles 2001, 2002). And Venn was not alone in this quest. Rufus Anderson, his American counterpart, was contemplating similar policies in relation to the missions of the American Board of Commissioners for Foreign Missions (Beaver, ed. 1967:31-36; cf. Harris 1999).

By 1850 the views of Venn and R. Anderson were attracting growing support among mission leaders. They emphasized that the "grand aim" of missions was the establishment of *indigenous* churches and the discipling of converts in the Christian faith. It continued to be assumed that a *Christian* culture must be developed but it had to be related to the indigenous culture. The work of the foreign missionary agency should result in a church that was fully self-reliant, expressed in terms of being *self-governing, self-financing,* and *self-propagating.*

The intellectual ferment and attempt to reformulate understandings is reflected in this statement that Henry Venn addressed to his missionaries in 1856: "The principle that men must be civilized in order to embrace Christianity is untenable; for civilization, though favorable to the development of Christianity, so far from being essential for its initiation, is, on the contrary, the consequence, not the forerunner, of the gospel" (Venn 1856:153). Perhaps Venn's most remarkable statement in this regard is his instructions to outgoing missionaries in 1868 where he spoke about the importance of "national distinctions." He noted that the typical approach to missionary motivation had been to appeal to the universal mandate as given in the Great Commission. But his long experience and continual reflection on the missionary process had led him to the "idea of 'nationality' in the mode and progress of the world's evangelization" (Venn 1868:316). Venn presciently anticipated the growing racism that lay ahead. He set forth five statements for consideration: 1) Study the national character of the people among whom you labour, and show the utmost respect for national peculiarities. 2) Race distinctions will probably rise in intensity with the progress of the Mission. 3) Let a native church be organized as a national institution; and avail yourselves of national habits, of Christian headmen, of a church council similar to the Indian Panchayat; let every member feel himself doubly bound to his country by this social as well as religious society. 4) As the native church assumes a national character it will ultimately supersede the denominational distinctions which are now introduced by foreign Missionary Societies. 5) The proper position of a Missionary is one external to the native church (Venn 1868:316-318). Venn's view that all cultures are equal vis-à-vis the Gospel was too radical for most of his contemporaries.

After 1850 the disciplines of anthropology and sociology began to emerge as academic fields. The revolutionary new idea just being introduced was the theory of evolution and social scientists quickly adopted this theory of human origins as they set about their interpretation of particular cultures. The logical next question was how to determine the point in the evolutionary process when the human creature emerged out of precedent forms of life (cf. Kuper 1988). Are all groups of people fully human or are they ranged along the evolutionary continuum from the least developed to the fully developed? The debates among anthropologists around this issue came to a head in 1863 when a schism took place in the British Ethnological Society. The rift was healed a decade later after most anthropologists had embraced a view of the essential unity of humankind. But the idea of "scientific racism" that would shortly be joined to theories of imperialism had taken root (Curtin 1960).

The conceptual change in mission theory formulated by Rufus Anderson and Henry Venn, and generally supported by other mission thinkers, did not win the day. It was one thing to promulgate new theory and quite another matter to turn theory into committed practice. Mission secretaries typically met stiff resistance to their proposed policy changes on the part of their field missionaries. Since mission secretaries rarely visited their missionaries on site, it was virtually impossible to enforce policies. While it became fashionable to affirm the "indigenous church" ideal of Venn and R. Anderson, the Puritan model of *replication* remained firmly in place.[4]

In view of this, John L. Nevius (1829-1893) offers a remarkable case study (Chao 1988; Hunt 1994). Nevius served with the Presbyterian Mission in China from 1854 until his death there in 1893. He summed up his ideas on missionary strategy in a series of articles he wrote for the *Chinese Recorder* in 1886 and subsequently published as a book, *Methods of Missionary Work* (1886).[5] Although there is substantial overlap between the Venn-Anderson formulation and Nevius' plan, he worked out his approach some ten years later and, apparently, he arrived at his ideas largely on his own. While Venn and R. Anderson might be accused of being armchair theorists, Nevius could not be dismissed on these grounds since he propounded his ideas of the "indigenous church" based on his sustained missionary experience in China. He was exemplary in terms of devotion to the cause and self-sacrifice. Indeed, we can say that Nevius' experience amply vindicated Venn's and R. Anderson's theory.

In addition to emphasizing the three "selfs"—self-supporting, self-governing, self-propagating—the Nevius plan called for the missionary to engage personally in "wide itineration," systematic and sustained Bible study

---

[4] C. P. Williams (1990) is a study of the way the CMS gradually repudiated in practice Venn's principles so that by 1900 it had effectively abandoned the "indigenous church" ideal.

[5] Republished in 1899 as *Planting and Development of Missionary Churches* (Nevius 1899).

and training of all believers at appropriate levels, and readiness to assist the people in times of physical need. Nevius was openly critical of what he called the "Old Plan" and offered his scheme as the "New Plan." In response, missionary colleagues in China largely rejected his ideas; but the budding missions in Korea enthusiastically embraced his principles and made them foundational to the development of the church in that land.

Against the background of the Boxer Rebellion in China in 1900, Roland Allen (1868-1947) wrote *Missionary Methods: St. Paul's or Ours?* (1912). He had observed this uprising firsthand, while helping care for victims. He noted, in particular, the way Chinese Christians were taunted by their countrymen as "foreigners." In his book R. Allen paid tribute to the impressive work of missions throughout the world, but he drew attention to "three very disquieting symptoms" (R. Allen 1962:141-142). 1) Mission Christianity remains "exotic." 2) These missions are dependent on foreign resources. 3) "Mission" Christianity looks the same the world over, by which R. Allen meant that, because mission-founded churches had in common dependence on a patron outside their own culture, they manifested passivity and a slavish concern to please their sponsors. He spent the rest of his life writing and speaking against the modern mission system that consistently produced these results. He was convinced that the New Testament furnished the only sound model of mission in its emphasis on the power of the Holy Spirit to transform people into the living body of Christ in each local context. He criticized modern missions for the way they instilled dependence on themselves rather than on the Holy Spirit.

The R. Anderson, Venn, Nevius, and R. Allen critiques of the modern mission model implicitly rejected the pre-critical attitude and mechanical replication. *They called for a critical approach based on the principle that each culture be approached in its own terms.* However, between 1850 and 1950 there was no discernible theoretical development with regard to the mission-culture nexus. Periodically, an apologist for missions would write a new book reiterating the importance of the "indigenous church"; but, in spite of the gathering forces of nationalism in one country after another, imperialism and visions of open-ended human progress defined the *zeitgeist*.

It is a matter of historical interest that in the late nineteenth century several scholars attempted to show the natural affinity between sociology and missions. This was the apologetic purpose of James S. Dennis in his monumental three-volume work, *Christian Missions and Social Progress* (1897). He held that since "Christian missions have already produced social results which are manifest, and that society in the nonChristian world at the present time is conscious of a new and powerful factor which is working positive and revolutionary changes in the direction of a higher civilization" (1897, I:31), sociology should see missions as an engine of social change. Dennis asserted that missions are a spiritual enterprise, but he reflected the influence of the ideal of evolutionary progress. His study showed what Western missions had done for other peoples and overlooked indigenous contributions to the process he was celebrating. In this Dennis reflected the dominant perspective of his day, the hegemony of Western culture (cf. Axenfeld 1910). Neither sociologists nor anthropologists regarded missions sympathetically during most of the twentieth century.

Until 1900 John Nevius was the rare—if not the only—*modern* missionary who tried to make *indigenization,* rather than replication, the foundation of church development. Historical records contain few examples where a mission founded on the replication model was later successfully reformed according to the indigenization model. In the twentieth century many more missions and missionaries would attempt to follow indigenous principles; but it appears that virtually all the examples of missionaries who based their work on the indigenization model were associated with new missions rather than established ones. In this regard the outstanding example is the Pentecostal movement that emerged in the twentieth century. Pentecostals took Roland Allen seriously and developed a missionary approach based on the idea of the Holy Spirit as the primary agent of mission (McGee 1986:97; cf. Hodges 1953).

Others also adopted indigenous church principles from the outset. John Ritchie (1878-1952), born in humble circumstances and with only a Bible school education, went from Scotland to Peru in 1906 (G. S. McIntosh 1995:26-30). "A man out of season," he refused to fit into the prescribed categories. He married a Peruvian wife, identified with the struggles of the indigenous people, and used his gifts of publicist to champion religious liberty and translation of the Scriptures into Quechua. Ritchie's enduring legacy is the Iglesia Evangélica Peruana comprised of more than 1600 congregations that grew from the witness he initiated. Ritchie made sure from the outset that this church would never experience dependency on foreign resources. His book, *Indigenous Church Principles in Theory and in Practice* (1946), sets forth his vision of church development.

The first steps to develop missionary anthropology were taken in the 1940s. Kenneth L. Pike and Eugene A. Nida, trained in anthropology and linguistics and working in Bible translation, led the way in revolutionizing the relationship between missionaries and academic anthropology and linguistics. In 1953 the journal *Practical Anthropology* was established and, for the next nineteen years, served as a forum for the discussion of culture, linguistics, missionary methods, and theology from the standpoint of the field missionary. These writings increasingly exposed the limitations of the indigenization model.

Representative of these seminal contributions was William A. Smalley's essay, "Cultural Implications of an Indigenous Church" (Smalley 1958) which showed that the three "selfs" in reality are "projections of our American value system" and these have rendered "indigenous" theory inoperative. By contrast, according to Smalley, an *indigenous* church is "a group of believers who live out their life, including their socialized Christian activity, in the patterns of the local society, and for whom any transformation of that society comes out of their felt needs under the guidance of the Holy Spirit and the Scriptures." Using critical tools of cultural analysis the missionary anthropologist could examine the deep-level assumptions that define each culture and show the barriers that impede intercultural communication.

Since 1970: Contextualization

By the 1960s missions were in crisis. The crisis was multifaceted: after four centuries Western colonialism was ending and both colonies and mission-founded churches were demanding independence; the institutional forms of modern missions were aging and becoming dysfunctional in the new era; tensions between rich and poor nations were rising; critics like Donald McGavran called missions to concentrate their efforts on church growth as their main concern while others urged missions to shift their energies and resources to programs that promoted "humanization" and opposed such social evils as racism. Amid the many discussions of the "crisis of missions" one issue received constructive attention and that was theological education starting in 1956.

A key figure in these deliberations about the future of theological education was Shoki Coe, principal of Tainan Theological College, Taiwan (Wheeler 2002). Coe left Taiwan in 1965 and became director of the Theological Education Fund. He had long been preoccupied with the observation that "in trying to improve the levels of our theological education we are in fact *uncritically repeating* and *imitating* the particular pattern which we happened to inherit" (italics in original) [C. H. Hwang 1962]. Coe was convinced that "a new missionary situation" confronted the church everywhere. What kind of leadership was needed to prepare the church to participate in the *"Missio Dei*, directed to the world?" Effective theological education, Coe insisted,

> should be defined in terms of that kind of theological training which leads to a real encounter between the student and the Gospel in terms of his own forms of thought and culture, and to a living dialogue between the church and its environment. The aim should be to use resources so as to help teachers and students to a deeper understanding of the Gospel in the context of the particular cultural and religious setting of the Church, so that the Church may come to a deeper understanding of itself as a missionary community sent into the world and to a more effectual encounter within the life of the society (1973:236).

This line of investigation led to a deep questioning of the inherited patterns of thought concerning the relationship between Gospel and culture and the way this was reflected in institutionalized theological education. For the theological educator the great exemplar was the Apostle Paul who said: "I am again in travail until Christ be formed in you" (Gal. 4:19). Theological education, said Coe, must foster three things. 1) *Christian Formation*: "I live, but no longer I, but Christ lives in me" (Gal. 2:20). 2) *Theological Formation*: "I think, but not

I, but the mind of Christ thinks through me" (Phil. 2:5) [Ibid, 239].
3) *Ministerial Formation*: "I work, but not I, but the Ministry of Christ works through me" (Ibid). If the goal of theological education is *formation*, then where and how is this to be cultivated? "It was in struggling with this question… that we came upon the two words *contextuality* and *contextualization* as the way towards reform in theological education" (Ibid). Coe argued that this conceptual development was required if "indigenization in theological education" is to be realized. There could be no question as to its importance since "indigenization is a missiological necessity when the Gospel moves from one cultural soil to another" (Ibid:240) and theological education must prepare the church for its role in the *Missio Dei*: "Contextuality, therefore, I believe, is that critical assessment of what makes the context really significant in the light of the *Missio Dei*. It is the missiological discernment of the signs of the times" (Ibid:241). Thus, Coe argued for a critical contextualization (cf. Hiebert 1984). He warned against allowing the "local" to dictate the terms of Gospel-and-culture engagement. In the Incarnation we see the tension that must be maintained between the universal and the particular. Coe warned about "over-indigenization, an uncritical accommodation such as expressed by the culture faiths, the American Way of life"—that the faithful church, wherever it finds itself, must always guard against.

What began as an initiative to rethink and reform theological education quickly became the organizing theme of mission theory, theology of mission, and missiology. It moved far beyond questions of educational philosophy and methodology. Indeed, a new agenda was set that drew on the tools of anthropology, linguistics, biblical theology, and missiology in relation to all phases of the Christian mission. "Contextualization" stimulated some of the most creative work in mission studies during the 1970s and 1980s. It posed in fresh terms an essential missiological issue: how missionaries, as outsiders, can engage particular cultural contexts with the same seriousness that God modeled in the sending of Jesus Christ into the world in a particular time, to a particular people, and a particular culture in order that the universal meaning of his salvific love and intention might be demonstrated.

The significance of this new paradigm can be readily illustrated through one of the key ideas in contextualization theory. Drawing on principles of communication and the evolving theory of Bible translation, Eugene A. Nida introduced the concept of "dynamic equivalence" as the way to achieve a translation that was faithful to the message of the text in its original linguistic-cultural context but communicated with equal impact on the reader today from an entirely different language and culture (Conn 1984:184). Charles H. Kraft worked out the most comprehensive theory of contextualization in *Christianity in Culture* (1979a) by applying the concept of dynamic equivalence to the range of activities involved in the development of the church in diverse cultures, including conversion, discipleship, ecclesiology, leadership, revelation, theologizing, and translation.

Conclusion

Culture and mission remain inseparable.   Mission is always directed to people in their particular contexts, i.e., their cultures, and must be communicated in the language of the people.   The way culture is understood, studied, and conceptualized has changed greatly over the past four centuries. In the seventeenth century the missionary, as a representative of Christendom with its authoritative religious-cultural synthesis, assumed no concessions were to be made to the host culture and the Christian message could not be separated from this synthesis.   But this missionary approach that tried mechanically to reproduce Christendom outside the West was, at best, frustrated and is generally regarded as having failed. Widespread missionary reluctance in the nineteenth century to cede control to the Holy Spirit and the emerging local church thwarted efforts to apply indigenization theory.   In the twentieth century a range of new approaches were followed and the resources of missionary anthropology and linguistics were deployed in the service of a missiology dedicated to appropriate contextualization.   Nonetheless, missionary practice continued to present a mixed picture.   At the end of the twentieth century one did not have to look far to find examples of missionaries energetically working to *replicate* Christendom in other cultures.   Others professed to be committed to indigenization theory and policies as they went about church planting and program development. A third group has been at work applying, clarifying, and deepening the theory of appropriate contextualization as it relates to all aspects of the life of the faithful church in diverse cultural contexts.

Chapter 4

The Function of Appropriate Contextualization in Mission

Darrell L. Whiteman

The dedication of this book to Dean Gilliland is appropriate for many reasons, but primarily because of his significant contributions to the field of missiology in general and contextualization in particular. For example his edited book, *The Word Among Us* (1989), is a landmark contribution, and his studies on Pauline theology (1983) advanced our understanding of New Testament contextualization considerably. The two themes of his life, Incarnation and contextualization, are ones that have driven my passion in mission as well, and will be the prominent themes in this chapter.

A few years ago as editor of *Missiology* I received an unsolicited article that was very critical of the dynamic equivalence translation approach as a model for contextualization and ministry among Muslims. I thought we should publish the article even though I disagreed with it, because it captured well the fears and suspicions that many people in mission have about contextualization. But I wasn't going to publish the article without a significant rebuttal, and so I called on my friend Dean Gilliland. In a most winsome way, Gilliland wrote a devastating critique of the arguments raised in opposition to the translation model of ministry among Muslims. In that article, he anticipated the development of the concept of appropriate Christianity when he said, "The real point before us is how best to lead men and women to seek salvation in Jesus. Contextualization is, first of all, concerned with communicating by *appropriate* and understandable means that salvation is in Jesus only" (2000b:330, emphasis added).

In responding to the argument that Islamic religious and cultural structures are inherently evil, and therefore automatically condemn Muslims, Gilliland argued passionately,

> Structures bind people, but structures do not condemn people. In responding to the message of Jesus, some do not, cannot, leave the structure. Some leave almost instantaneously with miraculous freedom while others require time, often much time, to do so. If we could speak of missiological axioms, this would be one of the first to learn: Whether making a clean break with Islamic culture or not, the church must faithfully embrace and encourage Muslim believers in

their journey wherever it may take them. I was slow in learning this, but knowing it now, I will never surrender it (2000b:331).

Gilliland's missiological axiom will be our starting point in this chapter as I discuss the role of contextualization in mission, and pursue cultural relevance in tension with biblical integrity. There is perhaps no better starting point than the debate of the Jerusalem Council as recorded in Acts 15. This was the first and most important crisis in the young church. The issue was this, Could Gentiles follow Jesus in their faith without first having to adopt Jewish culture in their practice? Such an idea was anathema to the Judaizers who argued that if the Gentiles were to be saved they must become culturally Jews and obey the Law of Moses. Peter stood up and objected vehemently,

> My friends, you know that a long time ago God chose me from among you to preach the Good News to the Gentiles, so that they could hear and believe. And God, who knows the thoughts of everyone, showed his approval of the Gentiles by giving the Holy Spirit to them, just as he had to us. He made no difference between us and them; he forgave their sins because they believed. So then, why do you now want to put God to the test by laying a load on the backs of the believers which neither our ancestors nor we ourselves were able to carry? No! We believe and are saved by the grace of the Lord Jesus, just as they are (Ac. 15:7-11).

Although the Jerusalem church was the center of gravity for early Christianity, it would not be long before most Christians would not be Jews. This decision of the Jerusalem Council allowed Christianity to break out of its Jewish cultural mode and to flourish in the Gentile world. Appropriate Christianity would now change forms as it spread from one cultural context to another. The problem has always been that those who take the Gospel to a nonChristian people take it with all kinds of deep assumptions about what following Jesus must look like, and frequently they hold up themselves and their church as a mirror for the new converts. I would therefore argue that contextualization is a critical dimension for mission today.

Unlike the "Death of God" movement in theology, contextualization is no mere missiological fad that will fade when another "hot topic" catches our attention. Concern over issues of contextualization have been a part of the Christian church from its inception, even though the vocabulary of contextualization dates back only to the early 1970s. It is a perennial challenge—one Christians have faced every time they have communicated the Gospel across language and cultural boundaries. The church has struggled with this problem through the ages as it has evolved from one era to another. Essentially, contextualization is concerned with how the Gospel and culture relate to one another across geographical space and down through time.

Gilliland (1989a) has reminded us in the opening chapter of *The Word Among Us* that contextualization and Incarnation are closely related. In the same way that Jesus emptied himself and identified with first-century Romanoccupied, Palestinian Jewish culture (Phil. 2:6-8) we must also empty ourselves of our cultural biases and identify with the people among whom we live and serve. We must go in a spirit of humility, ready to listen and to learn. God did not become a generic man in the Incarnation. God became Jesus the Jew, shaped by Jewish culture, speaking Aramaic with the low-prestige accent spoken around Galilee, unaware of the germ theory of disease or the heliocentric view of the universe. God was willing to constrict himself to the narrow confines of this Jewish culture and language at this point in time in order to communicate to humanity something about himself. The Incarnation as a model for cross-cultural ministry reminds us that the Gospel must be contextualized, and that Christianity should be communicated and practiced in appropriate ways in different cultural settings. The theme of the Philippians passage (2:5-8) is "have the mind of Christ." So we are invited to imitate Christ. After emptying himself of the power and prestige of being God's son, he took the form of a slave, he became like a human being, he appeared in human form, he humbled himself, and became obedient to the point of death. These five phrases tell us what it means to have the mind of Christ. They are important aspects of the contextualization process.

Contextualization captures in method and perspective the challenge of relating the Gospel to culture. In this sense the concern of contextualization is ancient—going back to the early church as it struggled to break loose from its Jewish cultural trappings and enter the Greco-Roman world of the Gentiles. On the other hand, contextualization is something new. Ever since the word emerged in the 1970s, there has been almost an explosion of writing, thinking, and talking about contextualization.[1] One of the most important texts that has stimulated discussion on contextualization, especially for evangelicals, is Charles Kraft's masterpiece *Christianity in Culture* (1979).

Contextualization is part of an evolving stream of thought that relates the Gospel and church to a local context. In the past we have used words such as adaptation, accommodation, and indigenization to describe this relationship between Gospel, church, and culture, but "contextualization" introduced in 1971 and a companion term "inculturation" that emerged in the literature in 1974, are deeper, more dynamic, and more adequate terms to describe what we are about in mission today.[2] I believe we are making some progress in our understanding

---

[1] See for example, Charles R. Taber, "Contextualization" (1983); Harvie M. Conn, "Contextualization: Where Do We Begin?" (1977); Robert J. Schreiter, *Constructing Local Theologies* (1985); Stephen B. Bevans, *Models of Contextual Theology* (2002); Justin S. Ukpong, "What is Contextualization?" (1987b), and "Contextualization: A Historical Survey" (1987a). For a conservative evangelical perspective see Bruce C. E. Fleming, *Contextualization of Theology: An Evangelical Assessment* (1980); and David J. Hesselgrave and Edward Rommen, *Contextualization: Meanings, Methods and Models* (1989).

[2] The term inculturation in Roman Catholic circles first appeared in item 12 in the Final Statement of the First Plenary Assembly of the Federation of Asian Bishops' Conference (Taipei, 22-27 April 1974) where the Asian bishops noted, "The local church is

of the relationship between Gospel, church, and culture, but we have a long way to go in everyday practice.

Contextualization is not something we pursue motivated by an agenda of pragmatic efficiency.[3] Rather, it must be followed because of our faithfulness to God who sent God's son as a servant to die so that we all may live. Jesus came "just as we are" so that we could respond with "Just as I am" (Rynkiewich 2004). As Peter Schineller (1990:3) says, "We have the obligation to search continually for ways in which the good news can be more deeply lived, celebrated, and shared."

In this brief essay I will discuss three functions of contextualization in mission today. I will then look at the gap that exists between theory and practice of contextualization, and then I will discuss two areas of resistance to contextualization. We will conclude with three challenges and a discussion of appropriate Christianity as perhaps the next stage in our conceptual thinking

Let me first proceed with an illustration from out of my classroom. One of our students at Asbury Seminary, studying with us from Thailand said to me, "Now that I have been studying contextualization and have discovered how the Gospel relates to culture, I am realizing that I can be both Christian and Thai." On a sabbatical in Southeast Asia I probed the question of how the Gospel was being proclaimed and lived out in a contextualized manner, and frankly, I was disappointed in what I saw. In Thailand I heard over and over again, "To be Thai is to be Buddhist." The notion that one could be both Thai and Christian was an oxymoron to many. However, this student went on to confide, "It always seemed strange to me that after I converted to Christianity out of Buddhism I became so aggressive, and was forced to turn my back on my Buddhist family, and denounce my Thai culture. Now I realize through the insights of contextualization that I can practice a cherished value of meekness, affirm most of my Thai culture, and follow Jesus in the Thai way." Contextualization was the key that unlocked the door in her understanding that had kept Christianity locked up in a Westernized room. But now, with this new insight, a burst of sunshine has come into her room of confusion which had been created by Buddhist teaching on meekness, a profound love and respect for her family, and also a deep love for God as revealed in Jesus Christ. She has now finished her dissertation entitled "The Way of Meekness: Being Christian and Thai in the

---

a church incarnate in a people, a church indigenous and inculturated." (1976:332) The Society of Jesus (Jesuits) at their 32nd General Congregation in late 1974 to early 1975 focused on fostering the task of the inculturation of Christianity. For a history of the term see Gerald A. Arbuckle, "Inculturation and Evangelisation: Realism or Romanticism" (1985); Ary A. Roest-Crollius, S.J., "What is so new about inculturation?" (1978), and also his article on inculturation in the Dizionario di missiologia (1993). See also Peter Schineller, S.J., *A Handbook on Inculturation* (1990). The fullest treatment of the term to date is Aylward Shorter, *Toward a Theology of Inculturation* (1988).

[3] For a discussion of contextualization as a method in contrast to church growth strategy see Charles R. Taber, "Contextualization" (1983).

Thai Way," and returned to Thailand where she and her husband are introducing a revolutionary approach to evangelism and discipleship. It is a significant breakthrough where after 150 years of Protestant presence in Thailand less than one percent of Thais are Christian.

Three Functions of Contextualization in Mission

We practice contextualization in mission in order to 1) Communicate the Gospel, 2) Critique culture and 3) Create community. Unless our communication of the Gospel is contextualized it will fall on deaf ears, and will not be culturally relevant. Secondly, the Gospel that is communicated must also critique human beings within their culture. Human culture is a gift of God's grace, but it also reflects the fallenness of humanity. And thirdly, through contextualization a wider community of understanding the Gospel is created when we discover the perceptions and practices of the Gospel in cultures other than our own.

The story of my Thai student sets the stage for discussing the first function of contextualization in mission that focuses on communication:

Contextualization and Communication

We contextualize so the Gospel will be heard. Contextualization attempts to communicate the Gospel in word and deed and to establish the church in ways that make sense to people within their local cultural context, presenting Christianity in such a way that it meets people's deepest needs and penetrates their worldview, thus allowing them to follow Christ and remain within their own culture.

This function seems at first to be self-evident, but it is clear we have not always done mission in this mode. Why then this sudden burst of energy and excitement, at least in the academy, about this notion of contextualization? I believe the answer lies partly in the post-colonial discovery that much of our understanding and practice of faith has been shaped by our own culture and context, and that we have often assumed that our culturally conditioned interpretation of the Gospel *was* the Gospel. We are now beginning to realize that we have often confused the two, and have inadvertently equated the American Dream with the Kingdom of God.

As we have become more critical in a postmodern world, we have discovered how urgent is the task of contextualization everywhere in the world, including, or should I say, especially, in North America. An example of good contextualization is the Willow Creek Community Church in suburban Chicago, Illinois that discovered the need to contextualize the Gospel and their church in order to reach a particular subculture of American society in this Midwest location.[4] Their church has now become a place to feel at home for these

---

[4] See George Hunter's discussion of the Willow Creek Community Church in *Church*

people. But perhaps a warning is appropriate at this point. A church should not be a place where people feel so much at home that no one else is welcomed. Some churches have become so much at home in their culture that they have lost their prophetic voice. I'll discuss this problem more in the second function of contextualization.

My concern over why the mission of the church so often required people to abandon their culture is the main reason I trained as an anthropologist in preparation for cross-cultural ministry. I initially expected my research and ministry in Melanesia to help primarily expatriate missionaries understand the complex and diverse Melanesian cultural context. But it did not take me long to discover that when I talked about contextualization with Melanesians they became very excited about the possibility of being Christian *and* Melanesian, without first having to become Australian, German, American, or whatever the cultural origin of the mission with whom they identified.

I remember while on a furlough assignment sharing with churches in the United States about my mission work in Melanesia and driving home the idea that my work was not to encourage Melanesian Christians to become like Americans, but rather to enable Melanesians to become better Melanesians by becoming Christian. This was a brand new idea for many congregations with whom I spoke. I remember the enthusiasm of one elderly parishioner when she asked, "Did you invent this way of missionary work? I've never heard anyone talk like this." "No," I replied, "I can't take credit for it. It's not my invention." Being a good Methodist, she figured this must have been John Wesley's invention. And although he was certainly on target, credit for this approach to mission must go back to the early church as it broke free from its Jewish cultural trappings and made the important decision at the Jerusalem Council that one could follow Christ without first becoming culturally a Jew (Ac. 15). Present-day discussions of contextualization are getting us back in touch with this principle, for at nearly every era of the church's history, Christians have had to relearn this important principle. This is why Andrew Walls (1982:98) has noted that, "No group of Christians has therefore any right to impose in the name of Christ upon another group of Christians a set of assumptions about life determined by another time and place."

Contextualization is a fine balancing act between necessary involvement in the culture, being in the situation, and also maintaining an outside, critical perspective that is also needed. In anthropology, we would call this holding in tension emic and etic perspectives—the insider's deep understanding with the outsider's critique. This brings us naturally to the second function of contextualization I want to discuss.

---

for the Unchurched (1996).

The second function of contextualization in mission is the function of critique. We contextualize so the Gospel will be felt. The biblical critique of culture is often offensive to people. We need to be sure we are offending people for the right reasons, not the wrong ones. Good contextualization enables the church to offend people for the right reasons. Bad contextualization, or the lack of it altogether, offends them for the wrong reasons. What do I mean by this? I mean that when the Gospel is presented in word and deed, and the fellowship of believers we call the church is organized along appropriate cultural patterns, then people will more likely be confronted with the offense of the Gospel, exposing their own sinfulness and the tendency toward evil oppressive structures and behavior patterns within their culture. It could certainly be argued that the genius of the Wesleyan revival in 18th-century England occurred precisely because through preaching, music, and social organization in a society undergoing rapid and significant social and economic change, John and Charles Wesley contextualized Christianity so well that the power of the Gospel transformed personal lives and reformed a nation.[5] The Wesleyan form of Christianity was more appropriate for the majority of people in this rapidly changing society.

Andrew Walls said it so clearly years ago in contrasting the indigenizing and the pilgrim principles, which we must always strive to hold in balance. He notes:

> Along with the indigenising principle which makes his faith a place to feel at home, the Christian inherits the pilgrim principle, which whispers to him that he has no abiding city and warns him that to be faithful to Christ will put him out of step with his society; for that society never existed, in East or West, ancient time or modern, which could absorb the word of Christ painlessly into its system. Jesus within Jewish culture, Paul within Hellenistic culture, take it for granted that there will be rubs and frictions—not from the adoption of a new culture, but from the transformation of the mind towards that of Christ (1982:98-99).

Unfortunately, when Christianity is not contextualized or is contextualized poorly, then people are culturally offended, turned off from inquiring more about who Jesus is, and/or view missionaries and their small band of converts with suspicion and as cultural misfits and aliens. When people are offended for the wrong reasons, the garment of Christianity gets stamped with the label "Made in America and Proud of It," and so it is easily dismissed as a "foreign religion" and hence irrelevant to their culture. When this happens potential converts never experience the offense of the Gospel because they have first

---

[5] See J. Wesley Bready's classic study, *England: Before and After Wesley; The Evangelical Revival and Social Reform* (1938). Cf. Leon O. Hynson, *To Reform the Nation* (1984).

endured the cultural offense of the missionary or Westernized Christians. Contextualization need not prohibit the prophetic role in mission as some fear it will. Paul Hiebert's (1984) landmark article on "Critical Contextualization" is a wonderful tool for applying this prophetic dimension and critiquing function of contextualization.

Creating Community

We now come to a third function of contextualization in mission. We contextualize so the Gospel will be internalized and society transformed. I see this third function as the need to develop contextualized expressions of the Gospel so that the Gospel itself will be understood in ways the universal church has neither experienced nor understood before, thus expanding our understanding of the Kingdom of God. In this sense contextualization is a form of mission in reverse, where we will learn from other cultures how to be more Christian in our own context.

This is an important function of contextualization in mission because it connects the particular with the universal. The challenge is creating a community that is both Christian and true to its own cultural heritage. Contextualization can bring about transformation of the local community, which then opens the way for that community's place in global Christianity. Peter Schineller (1990:72) argues, "Every local Christian community must maintain its links with other communities in the present around the world, and with communities of the past, through an understanding of Christian tradition."

I have experienced this many times where two Christians from very different cultures have much more in common than do their respective cultures. This is because the common bond that unites them and bridges the chasm created by language and cultural differences is the Holy Spirit who knows no boundaries of race, class, gender, or social location.

Encounters with Christians from other cultural contexts expand our understanding of God, for no longer are we satisfied with our own limited perception and experience. For example, I learned very little about the church functioning as a community and body of believers growing up in the United States where faith is so privatized and individualized. I had to learn this important biblical principle of the community nature of the church by living with Christians in a Melanesian village. Contextualization, therefore, forces us to have a wider loyalty that

> corresponds to an enlarged and more adequate view of God as the God of all persons, male and female and as a God who especially hears the cry of the poor. God can no longer simply be the god of myself, my family, my community, my nation; such a god is ultimately an idol or false god, one made according to my narrow and limited image and perspective (Schineller 1990:72).

In this sense the anthropologists are correct—human beings have a tendency to create God in their own image, but we must always counter this with the biblical view that God has created all human beings in God's image. Stretching our understanding of God through contextualization will enable us to gain insights from around the world, which we need to inform each other and certainly the church in North America. From Asia we can learn more about the mystery and transcendence of God; from Oceania we can recover the notion of the body of Christ as community; from Africa we can discover the nature of celebration and the healing power of the church; and from Latin America we are learning about the role of the church in the work for justice.

John V. Taylor in his well known book *The Primal Vision* (1963) reflecting on his study of the growth of the church in Buganda, helps us realize the value of learning from and listening to other voices of Christian faith, when he notes,

> The question is, rather, whether in Buganda, and elsewhere in Africa, the Church will be enabled by God's grace to discover a new synthesis between a saving Gospel and a total, unbroken unity of society. For there are many who feel that the spiritual sickness of the West, which reveals itself in the divorce of the sacred from the secular, of the cerebral from the instinctive, and in the loneliness and homelessness of individualism, may be healed through a recovery of the wisdom which Africa as not yet thrown away. The world church awaits something new out of Africa. The church in Buganda, and in many other parts of the continent, by obedient response to God's calling, for all its sinfulness and bewilderment, may yet become the agent through whom the Holy Spirit will teach his people everywhere how to be in Christ without ceasing to be involved in mankind (1963:108).

When I think about this function of contextualization expanding the universal church's understanding of God, I am reminded of the picture we are given in Revelation 7:9 of people from every ethnolinguistic group surrounding the throne of God, not worshipping God in English, or even English as a second language, but in their own language shaped by their own worldview and culture. We can count on hearing about 8,000 languages. The view we get of the kingdom is a multicultural view, not one of ethnic uniformity. One of the things we admire best about the Gospel is its ability to speak within the worldview of every culture. And this to me is the empirical proof of its authenticity.

Perhaps one of the most important functions of contextualization in mission is to remind us that we do not have a privileged position when it comes to understanding and practicing Christianity. It cannot be the exclusive property of any one culture, for it refuses to be culture bound, and continually bursts free from the chains of bondage to cultural tradition. Kosuke Koyama (1977) reminded us that there is *No Handle on the Cross*, and Lamin Sanneh (1989) has persuasively argued that Christianity demands to be translated from one cultural context to another.

In his recent book, *The Next Christendom: The Coming of Global Christianity,* Philip Jenkins (2002) reminds us that the explosive southward expansion of Christianity in Africa, Asia, and Latin America in the last century is creating many new and vibrant forms of Christianity that are appropriate to their context. We in the West who have been slow to understand this movement have much to learn from this global church. Becoming aware of the diversity and growth of Christianity in the Southern hemisphere, Jenkins says, is like "Seeing Christianity again for the first time" (2002:211).

Having considered these three functions of contextualization in mission—to communicate, to critique, and to create community (in this case a global Christian community)—I want to turn now to discuss the gap that exists between our theory of contextualization and its practice.

The Gap between Our Talk about Contextualization and Our Actual Practice of It

There is a huge gap between theory and practice when it comes to contextualization. Most missionaries have good intentions and mean well. They want to communicate the gospel and plant churches in ways that are culturally relevant. But like the Judaizers in Acts, they want to make sure that their new converts follow the same form of Christianity that they practice back home. They see their work as replication more than contextualization. An illustration of this gap between what missionaries practice and what we teach about contextualization comes from a conversation I once had over breakfast with the president of a large Protestant denominational mission board in the United States. In our conversation he said, "I have come to realize that the cutting edge of missiology and our most urgent need in mission today is contextualization. Unless we present the gospel locally in ways that connect to peoples' language, culture, and worldview, we will fail in our efforts at world evangelization." I nodded in hearty agreement, cheered him on, and affirmed his insight. I said that this approach to cross-cultural ministry represented the best thinking in missiology today and was clearly anchored in the biblical model of our Lord in the Incarnation. But then this mission executive went on to say, "The problem I face in trying to move our mission and our missionaries toward a more contextualized approach is that I am held accountable to a board of trustees and they don't understand anything about contextualization. They are interested only in extending our denomination across the face of the globe, sincerely believing that this is the best way to win the world for Christ." He was obviously stuck between a theological rock and an ecclesiastical hard place. I urged him to push ahead in leading his mission and training his missionaries to become more contextualized in their approach. With confidence I boldly stated that if his mission chose the contextualization route, in the end they would have more churches planted and connected to their denomination than if they continued in their present non-contextualized approach. I warned him, however, that these churches wouldn't resemble the churches his board of trustee members were use to attending every Sunday. In fact they would be very different because their cultural context was different.

This conversation illustrates the fact that there still remains an enormous gulf between the models of contextualization that we missiologists discuss and teach in our seminary classes, and the practice of contextualized mission by North American and European missionaries, both Protestant and Roman Catholic, as well as Orthodox. Contextualization and denominational extension are two very different agendas, but if most of us are committed intellectually to the former, we frequently draw our paycheck from the later, and herein lies the problem. It must also be noted that this is not just a problem for Western missionaries. For example, Korean missionaries, as well as other nonWestern missionaries, have the same struggle of disentangling their culture from their understanding and practice of Christianity.[6]

Another illustration of this tension between contextualization and denominational extension comes from my mission work in Melanesia. I was asked to lead a week-long workshop on Melanesian culture and religion for a Catholic mission working in the Southern Highlands of Papua New Guinea. They wanted to pioneer a new pastoral approach called Basic Christian Communities. As we know, this concept originated in Latin America, and for this Catholic Order it had spread to Tanzania, and was now being brought to Papua New Guinea. As an anthropologist, I led them through the process of understanding the social structures, economic patterns, values, and worldviews of Melanesian communities. We had a wonderful week together as we got deeper into understanding things Melanesian. Then I came to the final session. I recalled how we had discussed in great detail the nature of basic Melanesian communities, and I suggested that if they would begin their new pastoral approach in this Melanesian context, and let it take on a Melanesian face, and be expressed in Melanesian ways, and infuse this Melanesian world with gospel values, then their pastoral plan would be successful. These basic Christian communities would be both Melanesian and Christian. "But," I warned them, "if you approach these communities with a pre-packaged plan of what the church should look like, and lay that heavy burden on the backs of these Melanesian communities, I fear your approach will fail, because it will not be rooted in Melanesian soil."

A veteran missioner at the back of the room jumped up, and with anger in his voice, said "Now you have gone too far. We are here first as (and he named his Order) and there are certain distinctive features of our Catholic Order on

---

[6] Two recent doctoral dissertations attempt to close the gap between theory and practice. See Tereso C. Casino, "The Text in Context: An Evangelical Approach to the Foundations of Contextualization" (1996); Hyun Mo Lee, "A Missiological Appraisal of the Korean Church in Light of Theological Contextualization" (1992).

which we must insist.   We cannot forfeit those in order to adapt to the Melanesian context."

My heart sank and my blood pressure rose. After pouring myself out for a week to help them understand how these communities could be both Christian and Melanesian, they still didn't get it. They were fearful that contextualization would lead to at best a weak church or at worst to syncretism. In fact, it is just the opposite. When we fail to contextualize, we run a much greater risk of establishing weak churches whose members will turn to nonChristian syncretistic explanations, follow non-biblical lifestyles, and engage in magical rituals.   This is because a non-contextualized Christianity seldom engages people at the level of their deepest needs and aspirations, and so we end up with what Jesuit Jaime Bulatao in the Philippines calls a "split-level" Christianity.[7] When this happens, Christianity appears to provide answers to some of life's questions such as one's ultimate destiny, eternal salvation, etc., but the concerns of everyday life such as why tragedy strikes, why one's garden dries up, etc., do not receive a Christian answer, so people return to animistic explanations for dealing with everyday problems.

But the news on the contextualization front is not all bad. In fact, there is a lot of good news. We *have* made some progress.[8] Where has it been? In worship styles? In church social organization and structures? In contextual theology? We can celebrate the incremental progress that has occurred over the past thirty years, but there is still a gap—and at times an enormous gap— between our scholarly books and articles on models of contextualization that we write to one another, and the actual practice around the world, where in far too many corners of the globe, Christianity is still identified as a Western religion and where for various reasons people have missed the universal appeal of Jesus.

There are of course notable exceptions where contextualization is taking place, but they tend to occur in churches where Western missionaries or Western-trained national church leaders are not in control. In fact, if we look around the world to see what has happened in the past thirty years since the concepts of contextualization and inculturation came into missiological discourse, we will discover that some of the arguments about contextualization may have passed us by as the Christian church's center of gravity has shifted from the North and West to the South and East as Walbert Bühlmann (1978) predicted a generation ago in his *The Coming of the Third Church*. This is also the clear message in Philip Jenkins' (2002) recent book, *The Next*

---

[7] Jaime Bulatao, S.J., *Split-Level Christianity* (1966).

[8] Discussion of inculturation (contextualization) at the grassroots level in South Africa has been the subject of articles and letters in *Challenge: Church and People* (Institute for Contextual Theology 1991-?). See No.26 (November 1994), No.28 (February/March 1995), No.30 (June/July 1995), No.32 (October/November 1995), No.34 (February /March 1996). A very practical guide to contextualization (inculturation) is Gerald A. Arbuckle, *Earthing the Gospel: An Inculturation Handbook for Pastoral Workers* (1990). See also Peter Schineller, S.J., *Handbook on Inculturation* (1990).

Christendom: The Coming of Global Christianity. Like the early Jewish Christians discovered, as the center of Christianity moved out of Jerusalem into the Gentile world, we are waking up to learn that we are no longer the center of Christianity in the world. This is going to require that we take a humble posture of a learner from the indigenous churches, and that we enter into partnerships as true partners and not domineering partners. It means we must encourage and learn from the self-theologizing that will inevitably occur as the church in the South grows among the poor.

A notable exception to this lack of contextualization are some of the African Independent Churches, or what are now sometimes called African Initiated Churches (Allan Anderson 2001a, 2001b).[9] The documentary film, *Rise Up and Walk*, profiles five of these churches that do not belong to any denomination, and it knocks the theological and ecclesiastical socks off my students every time I show it. Ecclesiastical hegemony—a carry over from colonial and political domination, and a close cousin of economic domination and globalization today—is one of the major obstacles to contextualization. Let me illustrate what I mean.

A few years ago we initiated a Ph.D. program in intercultural studies in the E. Stanley Jones School of World Mission and Evangelism at Asbury Seminary. One of my colleagues in the School of Theology was complaining that our E. Stanley Jones School did not need a Ph.D. program in intercultural studies because the nonWestern church leaders who would be attracted to our program would be people who already understand their culture and context. He mused, "What could they possibly learn from a Ph.D. in intercultural studies that they don't already know because they were born into a nonWestern context? What they really need," he argued, "is a Ph.D. in systematic theology and biblical studies so that they could return to their countries and teach and preach the truth" (which of course to him comes wrapped in a Methodist/Wesleyan/Holiness package). Little does my systematic theologian colleague at Asbury realize, that until nonWestern Christians learn how to exegete their own cultural context as well as they exegete the biblical text, no number of Ph.D. students trained in standard Western theological studies will automatically enable and encourage church leaders to plant and grow indigenous, contextualized, churches of appropriate Christianity.

This discussion of the gap between theory and practice of contextualization leads us to our next considerations, Where are the obstacles to contextualization, and what are the points of resistance?

---

[9] See David Barrett, *Schism & Renewal in Africa* (1968); Harold Turner *History of an African Independent Church: Church of the Lord (Aladura)* 2 Vols. (1967) and *Bibliography of New Religious Movements in Primal Societies: Volume I: Black Africa* (1977); and M. L. Daneel, *Old and New in Southern Shona Independent Churches* 2 Vols. (1971-1988).

Obstacles and Points of Resistance to Contextualization

I will limit my discussion to two primary sources that are thwarting contextualization. One source of resistance comes from the mission-sending organizations themselves. I have often observed the enthusiasm with which missionary candidates train for cross-cultural ministry. It is thrilling to see them acquire skills to begin distinguishing the universal gospel from their parochial culture. They come to realize the value of their cross-cultural training, and the need to express the gospel in ways that are appropriate to the local context of their host's society. But then they arrive in their host country and are sometimes surprised, and certainly disappointed, when they soon discover that their mission sending organization is very intent on reproducing the church "over there" to look like the church back home. I have observed this problem in an independent "faith" mission, a denominational mission board and a Catholic mission order. In other words, we are all guilty.

So, the first point of resistance to contextualization often comes from mission executives and denominational leaders who are frequently not thinking missiologically about these issues. They nevertheless hold positions of power and influence that shape the patterns of mission work.

The second source of resistance to contextualization, and sometimes the dominant one, comes from the leaders of the very churches the missions created several generations previously. This resistance can certainly catch new missionaries by surprise. They wonder, "Why would these church leaders be so hesitant and cautious about connecting the gospel to their own context in ways that are both relevant and challenging?" I believe the primary cause, but not the only one, is that they have a vested interest in preserving what they learned and the power they have obtained. They have learned a non-contextualized Christianity from their missionary teachers and have adopted it at a formal, behavioral level, but it still has not yet penetrated the deeper levels of their worldview. It has not connected with their social structure or addressed the critical questions arising from their political and economic situations. When this happens, after several generations it is not unusual for the church to be plagued with nominalism. But of course there is security in familiar ways of doing things, and so any newfangled talk about contextualization can be both frightening and threatening, especially to those persons who are in positions of power.

I believe the only way through this hegemonic maze is to discover the tools and perspectives of contextualization and then with a spirit of true humility, mission boards, missionaries, and national church leaders must discover why contextualization is such a threat. It may be the case that the concept of appropriate Christianity will be less threatening. We must work at closing the gap between our discussions about contextualization and the training of cross-cultural witnesses and church leaders, and their actual practice of contextualization around the world.

Why, for example, does Christianity continue to be viewed as a foreign religion in much of Asia and Southeast Asia? The answer? Because it frequently is. For example, in China before 1949 there were about 10,000 missionaries and 1.5 million Christians. A common phrase uttered by Chinese people at the time was, "One more Christian, one less Chinese." Or, "Gain a convert, loose a citizen." A common, if not implicit, perception by both missionaries and Chinese was that one could not follow Christ without becoming Westernized in the process. This is the old Judaizer problem in a new guise. Mao Tse-tung then came to power in 1949 and the Western missionaries were forced to leave China. And of course many mission leaders thought the church would now die without their presence. But of course it didn't. In fact, it has flourished with a conservative estimate of 40-50 million Christians today. When I visited leaders of three underground church movements in China in November, 2002, they all said that there were over 100 million Christians in China today. Now what is the missiological lesson to be learned here? Kick out the missionaries and the church grows? Perhaps, but I do not think so. The lesson to be learned is that the Chinese discovered that the gospel could be contextualized in their own contemporary Chinese experience, as oppressive as it often was under Mao. They discovered they could follow Jesus and remain Chinese. In other words, they discovered the important principle hammered out in the Jerusalem Council as recorded in Acts 15. Gentiles did not have to become Jews culturally in order to follow Christ. And Chinese do not have to become Westernized, acquiring white, middle class values to be Christian. One of the most precious items out of China that I have held in my hands is a two-inch thick Chinese hymnal printed on thin rice paper, containing 1000 hymns— all created during the turbulent period following 1949. It is a beautiful symbol and vivid reminder of the importance and fruit of contextualization. There are now appropriate forms of Christianity in China and this is contributing to the impressive growth of the church.

Conclusion

Let me now bring this discussion to a close. Although we can see the obvious need for contextualization, the actual practice of it is not easy. Blinded by our own ethnocentrism and ecclesiastical hegemony we find it is very difficult to cultivate the art of listening and learning from those different from ourselves. But in a spirit of humility this is a fundamental requirement for contextualization.

The challenge that contextualization brings to us is how do we carry out the Great Commission and live out the Great Commandment in a world of cultural diversity with a gospel that is both truly Christian in content and culturally appropriate in form.

One who knows only one culture, knows no culture (Augsburger 1986:18). There is a wonderful Kikuyu proverb from Kenya that captures the blinding ethnocentricism that comes from knowing only one culture. It says, "He who does not travel, believes his mother is the world's best cook." Without an understanding of how Christianity must be expressed in ways appropriate to the cultural context, it is too easy to conclude that Christianity in my own culture is the proper form for all cultures, at all times. In other words, we practice mission as replication, not contextualization. When this happens not only will we loose our ability to communicate the gospel effectively across cultural barriers, we may also succumb to our own culture and equate our cultural values with the gospel, believing our values and institutions are divinely ordered. For example, in 1805 the Elkhorn Baptists in Kentucky announced that, "This Association judges it improper for ministers, churches, or Associations to meddle with emancipation from slavery or any other political subjects and as such we advise ministers and churches to have nothing to do therewith in their religious capacities" (quoted in Eighmy 1987:4).

The goal of contextualization is not just to have churches relate to their culture, for we can see the damage that is done when churches relate so well to their culture that they are barely distinguishable from it. This is the old Christendom model that is now a spent force. The goal is to connect the gospel to the culture in such a way that the gospel brings transformation to individuals and society. If the gospel over identifies with the culture then we end up with syncretism and biblical integrity is sacrificed. If the gospel is disconnected from the culture then biblical integrity may be maintained but cultural relevance is lost, and the gospel has no impact on the society. The goal of contextualization is appropriate Christianity that maintains the critical balance between cultural relevance and biblical integrity. To do this we must have a deep appreciation for cultural differences and multiple expressions of Christian faith. We must proceed in mission with a spirit of humility, always listening to the other, and ready to learn and be surprised by what God is doing in the world. Complete reliance on the Holy Spirit is necessary as we proceed.

I have identified three functions of contextualization in mission that I believe will facilitate the development of appropriate Christianity:

1. Contextualization helps us communicate the gospel in such a way that people will understand in their own terms from their own worldview, so that people feel that Christ has come to give them the abundant life they have been searching for. Contextualization will fulfill, not destroy a people's culture.

2. Contextualization enables us to critique culture in such a way that the offence of the gospel convicts people of personal and corporate sin, thus we offend people for the right reasons, not the wrong ones.

3. Contextualization helps build community in two ways. It transforms the local community and it connects us to the larger global community. In this way it enlarges our understanding of how Christianity shapes people and their cultures. It expands our understanding of the gospel and the Kingdom of God.

I have noted the two major sources of resistance to contextualization are mission agencies and Western trained church leaders. The common denominator in both of these groups is ethnocentricism and a confusion of cultural forms with biblical meanings. We have so much to learn from Christians in the nonWestern world as global Christianity takes on many cultural expressions and expands, especially in the southern hemisphere.

There are some important missiological implications of this discussion on the role of contextualization in mission. As Christianity becomes more contextualized we can anticipate growth in understanding what it means to have the mind of Christ, more effective discipleship, greater quantitative growth in the church, and an increase in the cultural diversity of the church. The term used in this book has been "Appropriate Christianity." This term may turn out to be more suitable, more appropriate, in the long run. It may not carry the negative stigma that some associate with the term contextualization, for fear that contextualization might lead to syncretism. There is much more research and practice to be done in this area in order to discover the many different ways that Christianity can be appropriately lived and expressed in various cultures.

Finally, I want to suggest that contextualization in mission, at its best, leaves us with three challenges:

1. Contextualization critiques, changes, and transforms the context—this is the *prophetic* challenge.

2. Contextualization expands our understanding of the gospel because we now see the gospel through a different cultural lens—this is the *hermeneutic* challenge.

3. Contextualization changes the missionaries because they will not be the same once they become part of the body of Christ in a context that is different from their own—this is the *personal* and *communal* challenge.

In our discussion and practice of contextualization we must take our cues from the Incarnation. In the same way that Jesus emptied himself and dwelt among us, we must be willing to do likewise as we enter another culture with the gospel. We must go in a spirit of humility, ready to listen and to learn. The Incarnation is our model for contextualization, for as J. D. Gordon once said, "Jesus is God spelled out in language human beings can understand." and I would add, "in every culture, in every language, in every context."

Chapter 5

Why Isn't Contextualization Implemented?

Charles H. Kraft

In Darrell Whiteman's 1997 article and its follow-up, Chapter 4 in this volume, the question is raised as to why what we've been teaching for several decades is often not implemented even by those who know enough to do so. It is easy to assume that once missionaries and national church leaders know what to do, they will do it. Unfortunately, such is often not the case.

Though we have much to learn and each attempt to construct an appropriate Christianity must still be seen as experimental, we have made considerable progress in theorizing what we believe ought to be done, at least in the theological area. In other areas such as church governance, though with "national" rather than foreign leadership, church leaders and their missionary partners seem less able to implement culturally appropriate models. With regard to worship, in many places we find impressive experiments in contextualization, especially in the use of traditional music. But a survey of the history shows that much remains to be done, both in conceptualizing and in applying what we think we know.

But even with the progress that has been made, a major problem is the lack of application of the insights already arrived at. There are at least two sources of difficulty when those involved with planting and growing churches deal with contextualization. There are problems from the outsiders' point of view and problems that insiders face. We will look first at outsider problems, then at those of the insiders.

Outsider Problems

What I'm calling "outsider problems" are those faced by cross-cultural workers who should be concerned about receptor-oriented approaches to the propagation of Christianity. As we see below, some of these are trained but not involved in contextualization. Others are not trained and don't know that they should be contextualizers.

A Broader Concept of Contextualization

The first hindrance to contextualization I'd like to mention is something we'd like to help rectify in this book—*a broader approach to contextualization.*

We've always talked of contextualization of theology (i.e., contextualization of knowledge) but it is probable that most people, even including most pastors, are not very interested in theological knowledge. Though from an academic point of view we can contend that theology covers all that needs to be done, it is unlikely that most people perceive it that way. They are more likely to be interested in things that are more easily seen to affect day-by-day behavior such as relational things or spiritual power things or worship or patterns of communication—things that the average person or even the average pastor may not see as theological.

I am convinced that the primary questions in the minds of most of the people of the world who either have turned to Christ or are considering that possibility are not questions concerning knowledge. People are more practical and their concerns more "down to earth" than to be interested in the usual theoretical presentations of theology. They want to learn how to deal with the practical problems of life—things like how to handle difficult relationships, how to heal or prevent sickness or how to assure good fortune.

In fact, most of their questions relate to perceived needs for spiritual power. The fact that those who deal with the contextualization of Christianity don't ordinarily deal with this issue, then, dampens interest in discussions of how Christianity can be expressed in culturally appropriate ways. One reaction to this deficiency is seen in the fact that many of the breakaway movements from Western Christianity make spiritual power issues central. They see such power exemplified in Scripture but not in the traditional churches. So they break away in order to be more appropriate to Scripture as well as to the concerns of their people.

In addition to people's concern for power is their major concern for relationships. Though we who attempt to communicate Christianity frequently talk about commitment to Christ, love, faithfulness, fellowship, the fruits of the Spirit, intimacy with Christ (e.g., Jn. 15), forgiveness, repentance, reconciliation, obedience, and other components of the relationship dimension of Christianity, there is often very little attention given to how these are to be expressed and experienced in culturally appropriate ways. Treatment of these issues tends, following the lead of the West, to be reduced to rules rather than adapted to the sociocultural life of the people into whose context they have been introduced. This often leaves people to continue their traditional relational patterns with little or no biblical Christian influence.

Behind such a deficiency lies the Western evangelical Christian disdain for focusing on experience rather than on doctrine. The intellectualization of evangelical Christianity has been pitted against the experiencing of Christian truth to the detriment of much emphasis on the latter. We tend to act as if it is sufficient for people claiming to follow Christ to have one experience—conversion—but from then on to focus on intellectual knowledge of the doctrines of the faith. It is recommended that they express their faith in culturally appropriate ways, but often we can offer them little assistance in this area.

Contextualization that is appropriate to the Bible and to culture should, I believe, focus as much on relationship and spiritual power as it does on knowledge. Most of the nonWestern peoples to whom the gospel has been taken are strongly relational and strongly concerned for spiritual power. It is very important, then, if we claim to be biblically and culturally appropriate to strongly emphasize these areas so prominent in the Bible and in their cultures.

Lack of Implementation

The second problem is one mentioned by Whiteman (Chapter 4): How to get what we think we know academically across to field missionaries, to entrenched church leaders and to the administrators of missionary-sending organizations. The place where most research breaks down is at the point of implementation. Many of the things we missiologists teach and write have been known to us for decades but are either unknown to, or ignored by, one or more of the above groups.

National church leaders have often been trained well in Western ways and have a considerable emotional investment in keeping their present positions. They have, therefore, no interest in changing, even if they privately admit the suggested new way might be better. I remember discussions with the Nigerian church leaders I worked with in which they were quick to admit that changes in the direction of contextualization would be good. The discussions, however, tended to come to naught when these leaders admitted that they were not willing to risk their leadership positions (and salaries) to advocate changes that they felt would turn the higher church leaders against them. As it turned out, some of these leaders did make changes but then had to look for different employment. One of them worked his way up into a significant position of leadership from which he could make some changes but even then found that, except in his home area, the majority of leaders would not implement the changes.

Field missionaries, for their part, often have neither read the studies nor understood the issues behind the calls for contextualization. They often see themselves as simply encouragers of the nationals as they carry on with what they have always done. Or, on the other hand, they may feel they need to take over situations they don't fully understand because things don't seem to be going as they do at home. It can be a scary thing for those who have learned to lead churches in their home countries to be asked to put aside what they have learned and to learn new, culturally-appropriate approaches to church and ministry. Change can be especially scary for missionaries if they don't have the tools to really understand how churches should relate to the cultural context in which they operate. Not understanding what's going on around us makes us feel ignorant in spite of all the schooling we may have had.

It is the custom in America for missionaries to have completed college or Bible school as a precondition for being accepted by a mission board. But it is unlikely that in those schools they would have learned much about culture in relation to Christian faith. And if they have learned anything in this area, it is unlikely that they have dealt more than superficially with the extent to which contextualization occurred in the Bible and, therefore, should be advocated in today's cultural contexts. The fact that missionaries have attended advanced educational institutions, however, often misleads them into thinking that they understand cultural things better than they do. Thus, they may feel more certain than they ought about their decisions with regard to the interactions between culture and Christianity.

The administrators of missionary-sending organizations, then, are often negative to what seem to them to be new ideas. Often those in charge of mission boards have had very little or no cross-cultural experience themselves, having been appointed from the ranks of the sending churches for their administrative abilities or their denominational loyalties. Their concern for the realities of administration, then, often hinder any desire to expand their vision of what ought to be done. In addition, as in Whiteman's illustration, many mission administrators are accountable to denominations and boards for whom denominational expansion is more important than inculturated Christianity.

Many administrators, however, have spent considerable time expanding their understandings of what Christian mission ought to be. Thus, they find themselves ahead of their field people theoretically. But often they find it difficult to make the kind of changes enlightened theory demands because of the conservatism of field missionaries or, more often, of the national leaders of the churches. These have usually been strongly indoctrinated in noncontextual forms of Christianity and are not about to change.

Back in the late sixties and early seventies, we at Fuller's School of World Mission conducted several Church Growth Seminars in various places for people in positions to implement change in missionary organizations. These seminars seemed to have a positive effect on the thinking of many of those who attended, though they tended to attract more field missionaries than administrators. Unfortunately, such seminars, though strong on the need for church planting, were less strong on the cultural implications of planting truly contextualized churches. I believe we would do well to institute Contextualization Seminars both at home and abroad for church leaders, missionaries and administrators to get this message across.

Knowing But Not Doing

A third issue is: How to solve the problem of missionaries who know enough to work in culturally sensitive ways but who do not do it. Many who go out as cross-cultural witnesses have read and received good instruction in the theory and practice of contextualization but, in spite of this fact, tend to dominate and to impose foreign patterns on their converts.

A major reason for this is *insecurity*. Many who volunteer for missionary work are personally insecure. In standing for Christ in their schools and even in their churches and then in volunteering for missionary service, they may have felt unaccepted by others and not quite sure of who they are and whether they have committed themselves to the right thing. The insecurities arising from such experience frequently lead missionaries to "lord it over" those they work with in an effort to convince themselves that they are capable of doing what they are assigned to do. Perhaps without realizing it, and without noting the differences between what they are doing and what they believe ought to be done, such missionaries dominate their people and impose their ideas in very destructive ways.

Often the people with whom such cross-cultural witnesses are working are quite compliant, not wanting to be impolite to the foreigners. Thus, they may be quite willing to go along with the domination of an insecure missionary. In addition, since a typical attitude is that Christianity is a foreign thing anyway, the receiving people may not even be aware that there might be a better way than the way they are being taught.

Another type of insecurity plagues missionaries who would like to contextualize but feel threatened by those over them who might not agree with what they are doing. Many a missionary who believed what we are teaching has "knuckled under" to senior missionaries who do not believe in working *with* rather than *against* the culture. I can speak from experience on this issue, having confronted our mission leaders over certain cultural issues and been forced to stay home and to seek another career. Many junior missionaries, knowing that this kind of thing has happened to others, are fearful lest it happen to them and, therefore, do not push for changes they believe to be for the better.

Whether or not they are insecure, missionaries, especially if they are new, may simply *fall into the familiar Western patterns* and fail to work to improve the situation. They may lack seniority or feel they have no right to suggest new ideas in a context dominated by senior missionaries and/or senior national leaders. If there is to be change, some feel, let the senior people suggest it and bring it about. For the program is theirs, not mine. Maybe, if I get to be a senior missionary, then I can suggest changes.

I suspect that, for many, the primary culprit is *culture stress* (often incorrectly referred to as "culture shock"). It can be observed that people under the stress of working cross-culturally tend to revert to familiar patterns, even if they know better. The off-balancedness of working in another cultural context can create a high degree of insecurity and fear even among those who are quite secure in their home context.

In defense of inaction, some point out that the people want things to be foreign since the foreignness gives them more prestige. In many parts of the world there are churches that have been started without foreign support (e.g., African Independent Churches) that have little prestige compared to the ones started by missions. So the nationals resist efforts to contextualize, even in some cases, committing themselves to Western patterns to an even greater extent than the missionaries had. But even if prestige is not the main motivation, many resist contextualization simply as a result of the fact that they have never experienced or observed any approach to Christianity other than a Western approach and think that's the way things ought to be. They may not be able to even imagine another approach.

A more acceptable attitude that hinders contextualization is the feeling that if we as outside advocates seek to introduce new ideas, we are likely to *come across as manipulating and dominating* or at least interfering in something that belongs to the people, not to us. Many missionaries feel that the people have been pushed around quite a lot in the past so they are reluctant to become pushy again, even in an attempt to introduce better ideas. Whether for this reason or for some other reason, many missionaries allow themselves to be isolated in Bible school teaching positions, teaching Bible in Western academic ways. In such positions they are often unable to really get close to the people to find out what their life is all about. Indeed, many in such teaching positions are so totally unprepared to study the cultural situation that they wouldn't be able to find out much even if they spent time with the people.

Or, the problem may simply be *laziness*, an unwillingness to step out simply because it will be too much work. Or there may be the feeling that it's too late for things to be changed.

Whatever the reasons, this is a major problem and has been for some time. Perhaps the kind of seminars suggested above would provide a way of tackling this problem.

Lack of Training

A fourth outsider hindrance to the implementation of appropriate contextualization is the fact that most missionaries and national church leaders have had no training at all dealing with the cultural aspects of their task. The feeling in many of the sending churches, both in North America and in the two-thirds world (e.g., Korea, Nigeria) is that commitment to Christ and enthusiasm are enough to qualify people for missionary service, whether or not the missionaries have much understanding of their task. In North America it has often been felt that working in other societies doesn't require the same level of expertise that working in the home churches does. I'm afraid this attitude is prominent in nonWestern sending churches as well.

Though most mission agencies in the West ordinarily require university-level or at least Bible school training for those they send out, that training usually involves very little that helps people to work in another society. In fact, traditional college and Bible school curricula have usually been counterproductive in assisting people in understanding and working in other cultural contexts. Typically, Bible schools and Christian colleges have been strong on preparing their students in biblical understanding, at least from a

Western perspective. This is commendable, though it often tends to lock students into *absolutized Western interpretations* that obscure in the students' minds the possibility that other, more culturally relevant interpretations are possible. Little or no attention is given in Christian institutions to the need for cultural relevance, much less how to go about working toward it.

In the non- (often anti-) Christian institutions attended by some missionary candidates, then, a politically correct valuing of and tolerating other people's ways of life has become extreme. In these places, openness to other people's ways has devolved into an *absolutizing of relativism* and tolerance. We are taught to believe that people of other societies are okay no matter what they believe and do and we are wrong if we criticize or try to change anything in their way of life. Caught between such teaching and the dogmatism of conservative Christian interpretations of Scripture, many young missionaries find themselves hard put to figure out what a balanced approach might be.

Behind the problem of lack of training, at least in the West, is the fact that when Western missions started there was virtually no training in cultural issues available. The tradition of mission boards sending out people without cultural training once established, then, was pretty well "set in cement" before modern training institutions came into existence. Pastors, likewise, have often been ignorant concerning the need for those they advise and send out to engage in cultural studies. There usually were no such studies in the institutions in which the pastors trained, even though many of these institutions claimed to be training missionaries as well as pastors. So the pastors often fail to properly advise missionary candidates in this area.

Though things may have changed for the better in many contexts, I look back on my own quest to find the proper kind of training for pioneer missionary work and marvel at how close I came to following poor advice given by those who sincerely wanted to help me. I remember being advised at the Christian college I attended to major in Bible or history or even Greek as the best preparation for work in Africa. It seemed like a chance conversation, then, with a prospective missionary that led me to go into anthropology. Fortunately, unlike most Christian institutions to this day, the college I attended had a struggling anthropology department.

In my 35 years of teaching experience in an institution committed to providing top-notch training for missionaries and two-thirds world church leaders, then, I have noticed another major problem. Many who take our classes just don't seem to "get it." This may be because they have come before they have had enough life experience for the material we present to "connect" with and bring about change in long-held attitudes and presuppositions. Or it may be because of the persistence of biases toward certain interpretations of Scripture and/or Christian witness. I have had students, for example, who strongly resisted my claim that we need cultural and communicational insight to go along with a high level of commitment to the guiding activity of the Holy Spirit. They believe that the Holy Spirit is all we need and the fact that many missionaries have done a poor job of presenting the gospel in cross-cultural contexts is to be explained by their lack of listening to the Holy Spirit. They just don't accept my contention that if we learn to do a better job of communicating, the Holy Spirit will be able to do His job more effectively.

Non-Contextual Churches Often Seem More Successful

A fifth reason why contextualization is not as widely implemented as we could wish is the fact that there are many non-contextualized, very Western-looking churches that are large and growing. As we look at the churches of the world, it becomes clear that many of the largest, apparently most "successful" churches (e.g., in Korea, the Philippines, Singapore, some parts of Africa) are poorly contextualized. This fact discourages would-be church planters who might plant contextualized churches if it were obvious that churches that grow contextually grow bigger. Instead, they tend to imitate what is working without regard to whether or not the churches they plant are culturally appropriate.

Or, to look at this factor another way: perhaps churches that look non-contextual are in reality contextualized, but to a westernizing segment of the population rather than to the traditional majority. In Korea, for example, though we rejoice that about a quarter of the population has turned to Christ, they have largely turned to Western-style churches probably at least partly for cultural reasons. I feel there is nothing wrong with churches that are culturally appropriate to westernizing people, as long as people are not given the impression that Western expressions of Christian faith are the only ones acceptable to God. Unfortunately, that is the impression that many come away with.

Such a situation raises several questions for me. One is, If Korean Christianity was more culturally Korean, would more of the traditional populace be attracted? I'm afraid that a major part of the Christian message as perceived by Koreans is that one must express Christian allegiance in Western ways. Traditional Korean ways of expression are not acceptable to the Christian God.

That impression might be overcome if there were, in addition to the Western-style churches, churches that are culturally appropriate for traditional peoples. Might it be, for example that the majority of the population of Korea that is now rejecting Christianity would be more open to the gospel if their traditional cultural ways were in evidence in some of the churches? Given the fact that part of the society is quite Westernized, there is still a part that is quite traditional. Shouldn't there, then, be at least two kinds of churches—one kind that is culturally appropriate to westernizing people but another that is culturally appropriate to traditional people? In many parts of Africa, the African Independent Church movement has provided just such churches as an alternative to the Western-style churches brought by the missionaries.

To turn to another possible reason for non-contextualization, Could it be that there are factors in Christian experience that override cultural fit? That is, are there things in non-contextual churches that are seen by their adherents as more important than cultural appropriateness? I suspect there are. Among them would be the desire on the part of many to identify with the West. Those who have attended Western schools, for example, are often proud of their westernized ways. Many of these find their ways to the cities of Asia and Africa where a semi-Western way of life is in vogue or at least considered prestigious. If a church is a part of the life of these semi-westernized people, then, it is more likely to be one that assists them in their quest to be seen as Westernized.

Another quality of many successful non-contextual churches is an emphasis on healing and deliverance. Probably the majority of the large non-contextual churches are Pentecostal or charismatic with issues of spiritual power in focus both in Sunday worship and in their small group activity. Since a concern for spiritual power is high on the list of most people's felt needs, the cultural relevance of such a focus would seem to outweigh in people's minds the irrelevance of much of the rest of what goes on in these churches.

However great may be our commitment to cultural appropriateness, we dare not simply ignore the "success" of non-contextualized churches. For the success of non-contextualized churches diminishes motivation to plant churches that are more appropriate to the culture of the people. This is especially true if such churches do offer something that meets a felt need such as the prestige of Western forms or an emphasis on spiritual power.

Insider Problems

In addition to the considerable number of problems faced by cross-cultural witnesses coming from outside the societies they work in, there are a number of problems faced by insiders who seek to contextualize.

Expectations and Reputation

Whether we like it or not, Christianity has *a long-standing reputation of being Western* and even requiring a Western cultural orientation. This is regrettable for historical reasons as well as because it hinders present appropriateness. For historically, the origin of Christianity was not Western but Middle Eastern.

This perception partners with another perception to hinder serious attempts at developing culturally appropriate forms different from those of the Western source countries. That second perception is that Christianity is a religion and as a religion belongs to a particular culture, major elements of that culture being required if the religion is to be practiced correctly.

It is not widely understood either outside of or even inside of Christianity that our faith is intended to be different from the religions in its relationship to the culture of the people who practice it. Whereas religions such as Islam, Buddhism and Hinduism require a sizeable chunk of the culture in which they were developed, Christianity rightly understood does not. Jesus came to bring life (Jn. 10:10), not a religion. It is people who have reduced our faith to a religion and exported it as if it is simply a competitor with the religions. And so, those receiving our message tend to interpret Christianity as if it was simply another religion—a culturally-encapsulated religion—rather than a faith that can be expressed in terms of any culture.

But Christianity correctly understood is commitment- and meaning-based, not form-based. A commitment to Jesus Christ and the meanings associated with that commitment can, therefore, be practiced in a wide variety of cultural forms. This is what contextualization is all about. And this is an important feature of Christianity that is often misunderstood by advocates as well as potential receptors.

Still another part of the reputation of Christianity worldwide is that it is more a matter of thinking than of practicality. For many, our faith has little to do with the issues of real life such as how to gain protection from evil spirits, how to gain and keep physical health and how to maintain good family relationships. Instead, Christianity is often seen as a breaker-up of families. And when the issue is a need for spiritual power and protection, even Christians need to keep on good terms with a shaman, priest or medicine man/woman since, in spite of biblical promises, Christian pastors can only recommend secular approaches to healing and protection.

A Christianity that is appropriate both to the Bible and to the receiving culture will confront these misperceptions and, hopefully, get them changed.

Traditions Die Hard

Any discussion of this topic needs to take into account the fact that the situations most cross-cultural workers are working in nowadays are seldom pioneer situations. Thus, we who teach contextualization are dealing primarily with those whose major concern will have to be on how to bring about change in already existing situations rather than on how to plant culturally appropriate churches.

Typically, then, those who learn what contextualization is all about find themselves working with churches that are quite committed to their Western approach to Christianity. This has become their tradition and they are not open to changing it.

The leaders of many such churches may never have seen culturally appropriate Christianity and probably lack the ability to imagine it. And if they can imagine such an approach, they are unlikely to want to risk what they are familiar with in hopes of gaining greater cultural appropriateness. For many, the risk of losing their position may be very real since their colleagues, committed to preserving the "sacred" tradition, may turn against them and oust them from their parishes.

We need to learn, then, not only the principles of cultural appropriateness, but the principles of effective communication. And this needs to be coupled with patience and prayer plus a readiness to make the right kind of suggestions if asked to.

Fear of Syncretism

A major hindrance to many, especially those who have received theological instruction is the fear that they might open the door to an aberrant form of Christianity. They see Latin American "christo-paganism" and shy away from what is called Christian but is not really. Fearing that if they deviate from the Western Christianity that they have received they are in danger of people carrying things too far, they fall back on the familiar and do nothing to change it, no matter how much misunderstanding there might be in the community of unbelievers concerning the real meanings of Christianity.

There are, however, at least two roads to syncretism: an approach that is too nativistic and an approach that is too dominated by foreignness. With respect to the latter, it is easy to miss the fact that Western Christianity is quite syncretistic when it is very intellectualized, organized according to foreign patterns, weak on the Holy Spirit and spiritual power, strong on Western forms of communication (e.g., preaching) and Western worship patterns and imposed on nonWestern peoples as if it were Scriptural. It is often easier to conclude that a form of Christian expression is syncretistic when it looks too much like the receiving culture than it when it looks "normal," that is, Western.

But Western patterns are often farther from the Bible than nonWestern patterns. And the amount of miscommunication of what the gospel really is can be great when people get the impression that ours is a religion rather than a faith[1] and that, therefore, foreign forms are a requirement. To give that impression is surely syncretistic and heretical. I call this "communicational heresy."

But, what about the concept of syncretism? Is this something that can be avoided or is it a factor of human limitations and sinfulness? I vote for the latter and suggest that there is no way to avoid it. Wherever there are imperfect understandings made by imperfect people, there will be syncretism. That syncretism exists in all churches is not the problem. Helping people to move from where they are to more ideal expressions of Christian faith is what we need to address ourselves to.

As long as we fear something that is inevitable, however, we are in bondage. I remember the words of one field missionary who was studying with us, "Until I stopped worrying about syncretism, I could not properly think about contextualization." Our advice to national leaders (and to missionaries), then, is to stop fearing syncretism. Deal with it in its various forms as a starting point, whether it has come from the receiving society or from the source society and help people to move toward more ideal expressions of their faith.

---

[1] See Chapter 6.

Insecurity

I have spoken above about the insecurity factor in missionaries. Nationals can feel at least as insecure as missionaries. They may be in positions that can easily be taken away from them if they don't conform to the expectations of those in authority over them. So, if they experiment with approaches that their superiors consider threatening, they may have to look for new employment, just as some of us former missionaries have had to.

I came to a new understanding on this issue one day when discussing with a prominent Nigerian leader the change I believed we ought to make with regard to baptizing believing polygamists. He had been cured of leprosy but the disease had taken parts of his fingers and left him with hands that could no longer wield a hoe for farming. At one point in the discussion, he looked at me and said, "I would gladly baptize believing polygamists. But if I did, what could I do with these hands?" His meaning was clear to me: if he did what I recommended, he would lose his position as a pastor and would have to go back to farming. But his hands were so damaged that they would not let him succeed at farming and his family would suffer because of the stand he took.

He was insecure because a new stand might cause him his job. So he retreated from a position that was easy for me as an outsider to recommend and, in fact, was a position that he believed in for fear of the consequences. This same leader had earlier chosen not to approve of church-sponsored square dancing out of the same fear. When I challenged the mission leaders on these issues, I was forced to stay home but was able to find other employment. He may not have been able to do the same if he had followed my lead.

Believing that All Converts Have to "Pay the Price"

One group of nationals that is most against contextualization is made up of people who have paid a high social price in becoming Christians. In parts of the world where Islam or Hinduism are the majority religion, those who come to Christ are often banished from their families and lose all of their social privileges. Their lives may even be in danger and, if they are unmarried, they may have difficulty attracting or arranging for a spouse.

When such people are asked to allow others to become Christians without going through the hardships they have had to endure, they often object strenuously. They look on contextualized Christianity as an easy and invalid way of coming into the church and, if they are in power, will often fight against any changes in that direction. They assume that a contextualized church has lowered the standards. "Everyone who comes to Christ must pay the price as we have," they contend. They are, therefore, unwilling to consider contextualization if it means that people can become Christians without some or all of the social rejection they have experienced.

Conclusion

In spite of the fact that missiologists have been speaking and writing about contextualization for decades, there seems to be little real implementation of the concept. We can point to the house churches of northeast Thailand planted by missionaries supported by the Evangelical Covenant Church as a shining example. Or the movement of Muslims to Christ, mosque by mosque in Bangladesh. Or many of the thousands of African Independent Churches.

Beyond these and a few others, though, non-contextualization seems to be more the norm than the exception in worldwide Christianity. We can thank God for all that He is doing in these churches, however, even while regretting that Westernization is all too often a part of the Christian message as perceived by the followers of Christ. It is my prayer that these chapters will help some to overcome their reticence to attempt to truly incarnate the gospel in whatever society they may be working in.

Part II

Appropriate Theory

Chapter 6

Is Christianity a Religion or a Faith?

Charles H. Kraft

One of the major areas of concern in contextualization is the matter of how Christianity should be compared with the religions of the world. When we talk of appropriate Christianity, are we talking about one religion among the many religions of the world? Or are we talking about something that by its very nature is of a different sort? That is, is biblical Christianity a religion or is it something else, something deeper? Or, better, was Christianity intended by God to be a religion in competition with the religions of the world? Or was it intended to be something else and, if so, what?

Given, whatever Christianity was intended to be, people have made a religion out of it. So, at one level, Christianity is a religion. This is necessary, since all human behavior will be expressed in cultural forms and religion is an organization of cultural forms. My question, however, is, Does God intend Christianity to be simply a set of cultural forms that we can call a religion or did He intend something more?

If ours is simply a religion, we can speak of *adaptation* when we take it to other peoples. We can see so-called "Christian" forms (i.e., the cultural forms used in the practice of Christianity in the home country) introduced into the cultures of the world with slight modifications to accommodate to the receiving culture. But we cannot speak of *contextualization*. For contextualization is the expression of Christian *meanings and commitment or allegiance* in truly traditional cultural forms that may remain the same or may be adapted but in which the major change will be in the meanings conveyed and the commitment/allegiance chosen rather than in the forms themselves.

We may picture a religion as a box that can be taken intact from one place to another and, though the corners may be rounded and perhaps other changes can be made to adapt it to the new setting, it is still easily recognizable as a structure that has come from another culture.

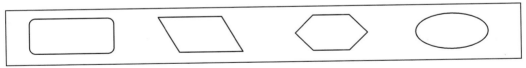

Figure 6.1 Schematic of Religion

A faith, on the other hand, is more like an arrow that is aimed at a particular society, is allowed to enter the culture and then pricks people at various points to elicit a response to God, not simply a response (i.e., acceptance or rejection) to a cultural structure (the religion box) that has its origin in another place, time or society.

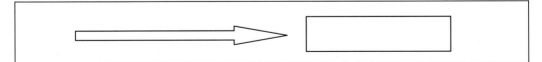

Figure 6.2 Schematic of Faith

Jesus said He came to bring life (Jn. 10:10). Does this mean He came to add one more religion to the list of the religions of the world? Or does it mean He was bringing something that differs from the religions and that, therefore, can be conveyed even through traditional cultural forms, including those cultural forms that are identified with the religion of the people who use them?

Religion Defined

If we are going to answer this question properly, we need to define what we mean by religion. For, not all mean the same thing when they use that term. Some would define religion as the collection of basic assumptions in terms of which a people live their lives (i.e., what I would call worldview) plus the rituals they use to express those assumptions. If that definition is accepted, the religion of most of the members of Western societies (including a large number of those who call themselves Christians) would be something called "secular humanism" or, perhaps, "scientism." This is a non- or even anti-supernaturalistic perspective that exalts humans and human thinking above anything claimed to be a revelation from a supernatural being. Such a perspective, then, would function within Western societies in a way very similar to the way supernaturalistic beliefs and practices serve within most nonWestern societies.

If we choose to go in this direction, we can speak of scientists as the priests of Western religion and the various rituals of scientific and/or educational activity as the rituals of that religion. A university education, then, would be seen as a religious rite of passage for our youth. And the activities that most people would label religious activities would be seen as the concern of a subset of our population who happen to believe in God.

With this approach, then, we can justify the widespread competition between Western cultural perspectives and those of traditional peoples around the world as proper from a religious point of view. We could, like many of the early Western missionaries, choose as our motto, "Civilize (i.e., Westernize) in order to evangelize." We who have given our lives to the cross-cultural communication of biblical Christianity could then dispense with the whole concept of contextualization and continue, in the name of religion, the conversion of the peoples of the world to Western ways.

Or, like many, we could see religion as the beliefs concerning supernatural beings and powers and the behavior and rituals associated with those beliefs. This definition would nicely cover the beliefs and practices of most of the peoples of the world plus the minority of Westerners who take their relationship with God seriously. It would see religion as embodied in a culture, whether as the core of that culture or as something more peripheral, and as requiring the learning of some important aspects of the originating culture if one converts to it.

As Christians, then, we would see our beliefs and practices as basically in competition with the beliefs and practices of nonChristians and seek to convert them to the cultural forms of our religion on the assumption that these forms, our religion, are the best of the competing religious options available. This is, in fact, what has ordinarily been aimed at by Christian witnesses down through history. Christianity has been identifiable by the cultural forms in which it has been encapsulated and it is those forms that are carried from society to society as the religion spreads. Taking the Christian religion to the peoples of other societies, then, involves the taking of our religious forms and adapting them to the culture of the receiving peoples.

A third approach is, however, the one that is basic to any consideration of contextualization. This approach is the one recommended by the Apostle Paul in Acts 15 as not requiring that Gentiles be converted to Jewish custom in order to follow Jesus. Paul had learned this approach by watching God give the Holy Spirit to Gentile converts on the basis of their faith alone, in spite of the fact that they had made no attempt to convert to Jewish culture. Though the early Christians set out to win people on the basis of approach number two above, the Holy Spirit broke their rule and endorsed Gentile cultures as adequate vehicles for Gentile interaction with God. The culture in which Jesus met His followers was not to be the cultural norm for the expression of Christianity.

The focus, then, was to be on the relationship between the converts and God rather than on the cultural forms in terms of which that relationship is expressed. It became clear to those who agreed with Paul that what God wants is not a certain set of cultural forms but a faith response that can be expressed in a multiplicity of cultural forms. The battle for the Christians of the early centuries of our faith, then, was to be over whether one worshipped Caesar, calling him Lord, or whether one worshipped Jesus as Lord—not over whether one practiced the religious forms followed by the Jewish Christians.

But down through the centuries, those who have come to Christ have tended to "domesticate" their Christianity. Just as the early Jewish Christians who disagreed with Paul required Gentiles to accept Christ in a Jewish cultural package, so Romans and Germans and Americans have pressured those who convert to Christ to also convert to the culture of those who bring the message. Thus, our faith has come to be known as primarily a cultural thing, a religion wrapped in the cultural forms of the group in power. And from about the fourth century on it has been seen largely as a European cultural thing—captured by our European ancestors and domesticated in cultures very different from that in which the faith was originally planted. Converts to Christianity, then, are seen as those who have abandoned their own cultural religion and chosen to adopt the religion and, usually, many of the forms of European culture. Often such converts are regarded as traitors to their own people and their ways.

If ours is simply a "form religion," as approach number two above assumes, it can be *adapted but not contextualized*, it can be *in competition with other forms of religion* but not flow through those forms because by definition it seeks to replace those forms. But biblical Christianity is not simply a set of cultural forms. Cultural Christianity, however, is. And we get tangled up in our discussions because it is often not clear whether we are speaking of essential, biblical Christianity or of the traditional religion of Western societies that is also called Christianity. In one of my books (1979a) I have attempted to make this distinction by spelling biblical Christianity with a capital C and cultural christianity with a small c.

I would define religion, then, as a cultural thing, a surface-level expression of deep-level (worldview) understandings of the beings or structures or ideas we deem worthy of worship and the rituals and beliefs developed to worship them. At the deep, worldview level, most of the peoples of the world assume the existence and activity of a large number of invisible spiritual beings and powers. Their responses to these beings and powers, then, are what their religion is all about. And much of their cultural life is spent in dealing with this area. So we would say that they are a very religious people. In other societies (e.g., the West), many claim to not believe in supernatural beings or in other things considered religious. In their cultural lives, then, there is very little if any activity ordinarily labeled "religious," though their activities in other areas (e.g., science, sports, career) might rival in function if not in form the dedication of the most ardent religionists.

I would, then, call religion a form thing, the expression through cultural forms of deep-level (worldview) assumptions and meanings. Religious forms are culture-specific and, if the religion has been borrowed from another cultural context, it requires certain of the forms of that other culture to be borrowed. Islam, for example, requires certain forms of prayer, a specific pilgrimage, an untranslatable Arabic book, even clothing styles. Likewise Judaism, Hinduism, Buddhism and culture christianity. These are religions.

Essential biblical Christianity, however, requires none of the original cultural forms. That's how it can be "captured" by the West and be considered Western even though its origin is not Western. *Essential Christianity is an allegiance, a relationship, from which flow a series of meanings that are intended to be expressed through the cultural forms of any culture.* These forms are intended, then, to be chosen for their appropriateness to convey proper biblical meanings in the receptors' contexts.

I believe Christianity is intended to be "a faith," not a set of cultural forms and therefore different in essence from the religions. Religions, because they are cultural things, can be *adapted* to new cultures. Adaptation is an external thing resulting in smaller or larger changes in the forms of the religion. Christianity, however, can be *contextualized*, a process in which appropriate meanings may be carried by quite different forms in various cultures.

Unfortunately, due to the interference of culture christianity, we have not seen all the variety that is possible. Like a religion, the usual form of initiation into Christianity is a first century cultural form involving water and the consolidation ceremony called Communion usually involves the original drink, wine (though many churches have contextualized this to grape juice) and bread (often contextualized to our kind of bread rather than unleavened, Jewish bread). True contextualization for many peoples would employ a form of initiation similar to that of their tradition and staple items of their diet for the Communion service. It would also employ their methods of communication rather than culture christianity's preaching forms and their forms of worship and music rather than Western forms to express these important meanings.

Religion or a Faith?

A way that I have found very helpful to deal with this subject is to ask two questions, What characterizes a religion? and then, What is the essence of biblical Christianity?

I believe the answer to be the distinction between religion or, rather, *a religion* and a faith. What I mean by "a faith" is a commitment to someone or something, supported by a set of deep worldview-level assumptions. For most of the world, such a faith involves commitment to a God, gods or spirits. In the West, the majority of people both outside and inside of the church seem to have opted for a commitment to human achievement, especially scientific, economic or political achievement supported by human scientific, economic or political structures that serve as the real religion of Westerners, called "scientific humanism."

A religion, then, is a set of cultural forms in terms of which a faith is expressed. These cultural forms are at surface-level in any given cultural structuring, as opposed to the worldview-level forms of a faith, though they are designed to express the worldview-level understandings of the faith. The practicing of the religious forms, further, may or may not involve a deep-level commitment to a God, gods or spirits. The forms may be seen as valuable in and of themselves and, indeed, may be the object of a people's commitment. That is, a people may, in their religious life, in reality be pledging allegiance to the religious forms themselves rather than to any being or thing that exists beyond the forms.

Inherent in this analysis is the distinction between people and structures set forth in my book, *Anthropology for Christian Witness* (1996). That analysis emphasized the fact that cultural structuring and human beings are quite different things. And, even though human beings live by cultural patterns, we are not determined by them. One important implication of the consistent recognition of this distinction is to note that the thing that keeps us following cultural patterns is not the patterns themselves but the fact that we have, along with our learning of the patterns, developed *habits* of following them. The customs themselves have no power to keep us following them. What keeps us following the patterns or customs is something inside of us, not something inside of the customs themselves—human habit. So, in analyzing religious behavior, we need to look at both the cultural patterns and the human activity in relation to those patterns.

Another important implication of this analysis is to note that a major part of human activity in relation to culture is *commitment*. And commitment, like the learning of our customs and the habits of following them is something we learn as we grow up. In childhood, we not only learn our customs and develop the habits that keep us following those customs but we, mostly unconsciously, make a commitment to them. And we practice that commitment habitually as well.

Our commitment, then, is certainly to the culture itself, to the customs that distinguish us from others. But it also involves commitments to *beings*, both beings within our society such as family members and beings outside of the society such as spirits and gods. Our commitment to the people we love, then, is quite a different thing from our commitment to our customs. Likewise, if we commit ourselves to God, gods or spirits, beings that are not culture-bound, these commitments are of a different order than our commitment to the culture or our commitment to some of the people who share our culture with us.

People can, of course, commit themselves to ideas as well as to beings. In such a case, the commitment is to something inside the culture. It is not to beings such as family who are not in the culture but are a part of the society that uses the culture. Nor is it a commitment to someone outside the culture such as God, a god or a spirit.

The point is, we have in the world both religions and faiths or commitments. Religions are structure. Faiths are personal/group commitments. These are two very different things. A faith commitment is the first step whereas the expression of that faith in cultural structures, called religion, is a second step. The most obvious part of this two step process is, however, the cultural expression called religion. This fact confuses some people, especially if the term "religious faith" is used to distinguish the religious type of faith from, say, faith in a government, in an economic system, in a family, in oneself or the like. To make the point that there is a difference between these two things, let's look at ten of the contrasts between them. The various points are discussed below.

RELIGION (STRUCTURAL)	A FAITH (PERSONAL)
1. Structural, Cultural/Worldview	1. Personal/Group/Social
2. Rituals, Rules	2. Relationship
3. Beliefs	3. Commitment/Allegiance
4. Perform	4. Obey
5. Adapt	5. Contextualize
6. Borrow/Accept/Imitate (e.g., worship forms)	6. Create/Grow (e.g., new cultural forms)
7. "One size fits all"	7. Cultural varieties of expression
8. Like a tree, must be transplanted	8. Like a seed that gets planted
9. Like a loaf of bread that gets passed on	9. Like yeast that gets put into raw dough
10. An Institution	10. A Fellowship

Figure 6.3 Ten Contrasts between Religion and Faith

Ten Contrasts

These ten contrasts are crucial in distinguishing religion from a faith. The differences are as follows:

1. Religion, being a cultural thing is structural. It involves religious beliefs and behavior grounded in a cultural worldview. A faith, however, is a personal thing, experienced by people, usually in groups, often as a whole society who make commitments to a being (e.g., God, a god, a spirit, an ancestor, a living human) or thing (e.g., an idol, an idea such as Communism, a structure). This difference is the basic one, opening the way for each of the others.

Though, as discussed below, a faith, like every human commitment, is expressed culturally, it is not the same as the cultural expression. And it is the cultural expression of a faith that I will use the label "religion" to designate, not the faith itself, though popularly this distinction is often not made.

2. A religion is centered around a certain kind and number of rituals accompanied by rules and regulations for ritual behavior and for everyday behavior as well. A faith, on the other hand, is centered around a relationship, usually with one or more supernatural beings, based on a person's commitment to that being or, alternatively, a commitment to an idea, an idol, a structure or a living being. Though the relationship is primary, a faith is usually ritualized, even if it is just a commitment to an idea (e.g., Communism, evolution).

Rituals conducted in worship of God, gods or other beings with which people have established a relationship are well-known. There are, however, also academic, economic and political rituals performed by those with a religion-like commitment to certain ideas and theories.

3. A religion involves a set of intellectual beliefs. These are worldview-level assumptions on the basis of which the religion is practiced and lived. A faith, however, is a commitment, an allegiance to someone or something. There are beliefs underlying the allegiance, to be sure, and these assumptions are also worldview-level. But the allegiance itself is not simply an intellectual thing, it is a matter of a person's will to commit oneself to that something or someone outside of oneself. Commitment, therefore, is a person thing, not a structure thing. It is the act of a person, not of cultural structure in spite of the fact that it results in cultural behavior, as do all commitments.

At this point we need to reiterate that the thing committed to may be any part of the culture, including the religion itself if not to supernatural beings or even in addition to a commitment to supernatural beings. This fact may confuse some people if they fail to understand the difference I am making between structural things such as religion and the personal thing called allegiance or commitment. Since people are entirely immersed in culture, however, they will automatically express whatever allegiances they have in cultural ways.

I have said "allegiances," in the plural. To this point I have been speaking of an allegiance or commitment as if people have only one. In reality, though, each person has many allegiances. And the allegiances that are directed toward supernatural beings or religious structures may not even be at the top of the list. For many of the peoples of the world (including the Jews of Jesus' day), for example, allegiance to family is their primary allegiance. All other commitments or loyalties are secondary to that one. What Jesus intends, however, is that our allegiance to Him be primary with all other allegiances, including family, secondary to that.

4. The essence of a religion lies in the performance of the beliefs and behaviors in terms of which that religion is expected to be expressed. The essence of a faith, especially if it is to a personal being, is obedience. If we worship God or gods or spirits, the object is to obey Him/them according to the worldview guidelines that accompany that faith. If we worship a human, we are to obey that person. If our faith is to an academic discipline or some other system of ideas, we are to obey those things specified by the underlying worldview assumptions of that system.

With worldview assumptions underlying both religion and a faith, then, we cannot avoid the structural, cultural requirements for expressing either. But, again, a religion and a faith need to be separated analytically if we are ever to fully understand contextualization.

5. A religion, being a cultural thing, when taken from the originating people to the people of another society can be adapted to that culture. The rituals, beliefs and other customs of that religion can be moved. But, since a religion is already a cultural system, when it is moved to another people will have to be adjusted to those people and their culture. But such adjustment is not contextualization, it is adaptation.

A faith, on the other hand, since it is rooted in personal devotion to beings or ideas, can be expressed in any cultural forms. It does not require as a precondition that the cultural forms in which it was first expressed be carried to another people. The personal relationship between God and Abraham, for example, could have been expressed in other cultural forms if Abraham had been immersed in some other culture. As it was, though, he responded to God in terms of rituals and behaviors that characterized his life before he and God made their covenant. That same faith relationship between a human being and God, then, became the experience of many people within Western societies who express that faith quite differently than Abraham expressed it.

But this possibility was not in the minds of the majority of Jewish Christians in the early years of Christianity. For they saw our faith as a religion, encased in and wedded to Jewish cultural forms, perhaps allowing for some adaptation by Gentile converts but certainly not to be contextualized in Gentile culture. But God had other ideas. In the events recorded in Acts 10, God attempted to blast Peter out of his ethnocentric view of what Christianity was to be. In Acts 15, then, Paul and Barnabas reported on how God had broken the rules of the Jewish church and given the Holy Spirit to uncircumcised Gentiles on the basis of faith alone, without cultural conversion. Thus God showed that He was in favor of contextualization, not simply adaptation.

6. With a religion, to follow it properly, one accepts, imitates and learns certain cultural forms brought in from the source culture. To become a Muslim, one has to learn to pray in a certain way and in a certain direction. To become a Buddhist, one has to learn to use incense and clap your hands to awaken the spirits when one goes to a temple. Though certain Christians may prefer certain postures for prayer, there is no cultural requirement. Jewish Christians may prefer to stand, many prefer to kneel or sit. The crucial thing is not the posture (a cultural thing) but the attitude (a personal thing).

Thus, a faith can be expressed creatively in a variety of cultural forms, and people can grow in that faith whether or not they follow the cultural forms meaningful to someone else. Though one Christian may prefer a given posture for prayer and a given musical and communication style, another can be just as committed to God and prefer other postures and styles. One person, in fact, may prefer different styles in different settings because the important things for a faith are allegiance and meanings, not cultural forms.

7. A religion typically is a single entity. Thus, one size, one set of forms is to be carried wherever the religion is taken. A faith, however, is flexible and takes on the cultural form of the receiving people. Thus, if a faith is properly contextualized, there will be endless variety in the ways in which it is expressed. There should, I believe, be as much difference between the forms in which true Christianity is expressed as there are in the forms of the various cultures of the world. The creativity discussed under point 6 is to be a major feature of properly contextualized Christianity.

8. A religion is like a tree that springs up in one place and then is taken, half grown, to another. It has been nurtured where it was planted with water and nutrients available there and needs a certain amount of such water and nutrients to continue to live in the new context. A seed, on the other hand, is planted where it is to grow and lives for the rest of its life on the water and nutrients of that place.

Unfortunately, though Christianity once came to our Gentile ancestors as a seed, it has often been transplanted as a European religion rather than planted like a seed. Thus, much of the world has gotten the wrong impression of our faith, thinking that they must accept a Western package, a Western transplant if they are to be acceptable to God. But, as Jesus said, our faith is intended to be a seed, even a very small seed, that sprouts in the soil of the receiving people, being nourished on their water and nutrients. It then is to grow tall and vital becoming a refuge for the birds of the air (Lk. 13:19).

9. To refer to another picture that Jesus drew, our faith is to be like yeast, not like the loaf of bread that the yeast has permeated (Lk. 13:21). A religion, though, is like the loaf. It has already grown to its full size and then may be taken from one place to another fully formed.

But yeast, like a faith, is small, and may even go unnoticed. Someone inserts it into the dough of a culture and it grows there, spreading throughout the culture and influencing every part. This is what contextualization is all about.

10. A religion is soon institutionalized, leading to all kinds of problems for those who seek true Christianity. For the fellowship that the Christ Way is intended to be can easily be submerged in the concerns of an institution. Note, for example, what happens in the second, third and following generations of a church or school as it becomes more and more an institution with its primary concern becoming self-preservation. If looked at in terms of its actual function rather than in terms of someone's ideal, many churches and especially training institutions have come to exist mainly to perpetuate themselves.

It is a very sad thing when the actual function of a training institution becomes to train a few people who will fill the teaching positions in that school or others like it with or without much concern for serving the needs of the churches they are supposedly training people for. But this is what most of our seminaries and Bible colleges have become. People learn what they do. And what students in these institutions do is to learn how to conduct classes, buying and selling information, often at the expense of the development of their faith.

Christian churches and training institutions are, however, intended by God to be centered in relationships with God and with others. Note Jesus' statement of the two greatest commandments (Mt. 22:36-40). Fellowship rather than institutionalization should, therefore, be the primary concern of these entities if we are to be true to our calling. The tendency for a faith to become institutionalized is probably the reason why it seems necessary for each church or training institution to experience a faith-renewal movement every generation if the proper relationship with God is to be maintained.

Recombination Theory

Years ago, an anthropologist named Homer Barnett wrote and excellent book on culture change entitled *Innovation, the Basis for Culture Change* (1953). One of the concepts he suggested is called "recombination theory." This concept is intended to assist us in understanding one of the things that may happen when people adopt another society's custom or when we seek to introduce a custom into another culture.

The theory says that when we seek to introduce a custom into another culture, we may divide that custom into its form and its function. We then do the same thing with the custom we would like to displace in another culture. With this done, we can assist the receiving people to combine Form 1 in their culture with Function 2 in the donor culture or vice versa.

The way this would work with a religion can be charted as follows:

Religion 1 of Culture 1	Religion 2 of Culture 2
Forms 1	Forms 2
Faith Commitment 1	Faith Commitment 2

Figure 6.4 Recombination Theory – Religion and Culture

Note that each of the cultures has its "religion," consisting of forms plus faith commitment. If, for example, we look at Islam and Christianity, we would see Muslim forms and Muslim faith in one column, with so-called Christian forms and Christian faith in the other column. If we sought to contextualize one of these "religions" in the opposite culture, we would seek to combine "Forms 1" with "Faith Commitment 2," or "Forms 2" with "Faith Commitment 1." If "religion 1" is Islam and "religion 2" is Christianity, our diagram would look like this:

Islam	Christianity
1. Muslim Cultural Forms	2. "Christian" Cultural Forms
1. Muslim Faith Commitment	2. Christian Faith Commitment

Figure 6.5 Recombination Theory – Islam and Christianity

If we wish to contextualize Christianity in Muslim cultural forms, then, the recombination would look like this:

Christianity Contextualized in Muslim Cultural Forms
1. Muslim Cultural Forms
2. Christian Faith Commitment

Figure 6.6 Recombination Theory – Contextualized Christianity

Note that the opposite combination—Christian cultural forms and Muslim faith—cannot be done if one is to be an orthodox Muslim, since Islam requires certain cultural forms to be brought over into the receiving culture. I believe, though, that many Western converts to Islam are attempting to contextualize Islamic faith by committing themselves to the God and religion of Islam without adopting the cultural practices required of the orthodox.

Culture Christianity Is Merely a Religion

In popular parlance, Christianity is regularly classified as a "religion." It has beliefs, a faith-allegiance to a supernatural Being, rituals, places of worship, a holy book, a priesthood and many other characteristics that parallel the characteristics of the religions of the world. We can find all of these things in Hinduism, Buddhism, Islam, Animism, etc.

People have taken the teachings of the Bible and worked out a belief system that is supported by Christian leaders and taught to the adherents of the faith. That faith, then, is expressed in personal and group rituals in homes and churches. So are the world's other faiths. Each faith is based on worldview assumptions and personal and group commitments.

When looked at from this point of view, Christianity sure looks like a religion. But is this the way it ought to be seen? Contextualizers need to ask and answer this question. For if ours is simply one of the religions of the world, our relationship with the other religions is a competitive relationship and our aim should be to replace those religions with ours.

As mentioned, culturally naïve missionaries often saw Christianity in this light. They saw their task, then, as introducing people to Christian beliefs and practices in the hope that they would convert from their false beliefs and practices and embrace Christianity. And along with conversion to Christ (the faith commitment), the usual expectation was that the converts would embrace the Western cultural packaging in terms of which the missionaries expressed their Christianity. To assure this, the missionaries set up Western schools to teach children how to live "Christian" (i.e., Western Christian) lives. There were additional, and better, reasons for the schools. But winning children to Christ and training them to live as Christians were often articulated as goals of the schools.

When, then, the receiving people were impressed (even intimidated) by the culture of the missionaries, many came to the schools and converted both to the faith of the missionaries and to as much of their culture as possible. Thus, large numbers of the peoples of Korea, Africa, the South Pacific, Latin America and other areas converted to Christ and to Western culture at the same time. In places like China, India, Japan, Thailand and the Muslim world, however, if anything the missionaries brought was accepted, it was more likely to be the perceived benefits of the schools and the culture they taught rather than the missionaries' faith. For, though the faith came in Western packaging, it was easy for people to see that the schooling did not depend on the acceptance of the faith. They could take the one without having to take the other. It was, though, not so easy in many parts of the world for people to accept the faith without the cultural packaging. Literacy, for example, was often a requirement for baptism.

So, for many of the peoples of the world, Christianity is simply a religion, a cultural thing with or without the faith that is intended to be central to biblical Christianity.

A Christian Worldview?

It is common for Western Christians, especially conservative Evangelicals, to speak of *a* or *the* Christian worldview. These have learned that the term worldview is to be applied to the basic assumptions of a people and have come to label the basic assumptions of Christianity as worldview assumptions. So far so good.

But what these people are generally referring to when they speak of a "Christian worldview" is a set of doctrinal assumptions that are important to Christianity—things taught in the Bible that Christians need to give assent to if they are to be truly Christian. These assumptions, then, are to contrast with humanistic assumptions or the underlying assumptions of nonChristian religions. And, once again, Christianity is put in competition with the religions of the world.

The problem here is that the concept of worldview, as defined by anthropologists, those whose expertise is in dealing with culture and worldview, is much broader than this popular usage of the term. For anthropologists, a worldview is the deep level of culture[1] and includes assumptions concerning time, space and classification as well as concerning persons and power. Though Christian assumptions deal a lot with these latter two aspects of worldview, a so-called "Christian" worldview has little to say about changes required by Christian faith in assumptions concerning time, space and classification. What is apparent to Christian anthropologists, the experts on the subject of worldview, is that the relatively few worldview assumptions focused on by those who use the term "Christian worldview" should not be treated as if they are the whole of

---

[1] See Kraft 1996.

a person's worldview. For, though these few things are truly significant, they do not come near comprising a total worldview.

Instead, such a focus gives the misimpression that Christianity offers a total worldview that is in competition with the cultural worldviews of the peoples of the world. This view, then, would assume that Christians are to be radically different from the nonChristians in their society in a much larger number of assumptions than is necessary. This would be competition allowing only for adaptation, not contextualization. Given, we are to differ radically in a few crucial areas. But, as mentioned above, the number of areas is comparatively small. Most of a people's worldview assumptions require little if any change when they convert to Christianity. This is what allows for contextualization within a culture rather than replacement of it.

If, then, Christianity is to be seen as a religion in competition with religions, ours is a worldview in competition with other worldviews. And our job is to convert people from their worldviews to ours. There can, in such a case, be some adaptation but no real contextualization of our faith. I believe, though, that there is a better way.

A Matter of Meanings

It is, I believe, crucial that we see the essence of true Christianity in the area of meaning and allegiance (both person things) rather than in the forms (cultural things) through which meaning and allegiance are expressed. Our faith is a matter of relationship with a living God and a living Christ and the rituals we perform can vary widely in form as long as the meanings are there. We can worship in a wide variety of ways and even on different days as long as our worship is "in spirit and in truth" (Jn. 4:23-24). We can pray in any posture as long as our motivation is right. We can even interpret the meanings of various doctrines differently as long as our allegiance is to the one Christ.

As mentioned, in the religions certain cultural forms are required, usually those that originated in the source culture or, as with Christianity, in the Western cultures that have become its primary home. Whether these cultural forms be a certain posture for prayer or a specific language or certain rituals or special artifacts, without them the religion cannot function properly. To practice a religion one has to learn what these forms are and how to use them properly. To practice Christianity appropriately, however, one has only to learn what the supracultural meanings of Scripture are and to set them to whatever cultural forms one feels are appropriate to convey those meanings.

For religion is a facet of culture. And, just as the non-religious forms of a culture are available for the expression of Christian faith, so the religious forms of that culture can also be used—on condition that the satanic power in them is broken and the meanings are Christian. Almost any cultural forms can be captured for Christ.

The tragedy of requiring Western rather than traditional forms to be used in Christianity is twofold: that the foreign forms will not be assigned the proper meanings and that Christianity will devolve into simply being seen as a religion. This misunderstanding, then, produces a pull back toward the meanings of the traditional religion. And Christianity devolves into merely a competing religion rather than a faith that is intended to capture the cultural forms once used to express that other faith.

Conclusion

It is my conclusion, then, that true biblical Christianity neither is nor was intended to be a religion in the sense of that cultural structuring that is ordinarily in view as people talk about the religions of the world. It is intended to be, rather, a faith, a commitment to God through Jesus Christ, which, though it must be expressed culturally, can be expressed through any cultural system. Unlike religions, then, Christianity can and should be contextualized, not simply adapted as is required of cultural religions when they are taken from one society to another.

Chapter 7

Contextualization in Three Crucial Dimensions

Charles H. Kraft

It is obvious from what has already been said that much has been written on contextualization, including such synonyms as *localization, inculturation,* and *indigenization.* In spite of all this attention, however, I feel that we have dealt too narrowly with our subject. Our bibliographies show that most of our studies have focused on the important *cognitive* and *structural* dimensions of our subject. But where are treatments of the more *experiential* side of Christian life and practice—theology as it is lived, not just as it is thought about?

Given the fact that the Bible's primary concern is our relationship to God, a relationship that starts with commitment or allegiance to Him, Where are the contextualization studies dealing with this issue? What are the culturally appropriate varieties of commitment and relationship to God through Jesus Christ? And, since spiritual power is high on the list of concerns for most of the peoples of the world, where are the contextualization studies in this area? Doesn't the Bible have a lot to say about this subject? And might there not be culturally appropriate differences in the ways God's authority and power are to be exercised from society to society?

In 1991 and 1992[1] I published articles dealing with three encounters that are crucial to the experience and communication of the gospel of Jesus Christ. I labeled these encounters: *Allegiance* (or Commitment), *Truth,* and *Power.* As I have pondered these encounters, I have come to the conclusion that these areas are even more important than I had realized.

In my articles, I pointed out that each of these encounters leads to a very important dimension of Christian experience: *relationship, understanding,* and *freedom.* Each of these areas is a crucial dimension of the God-connected life. I now believe the areas of encounter are pointing to *the three crucial dimensions* of Christian experience and witness. If they are this important, then, we need to theorize concerning contextualization in each of these areas, rather than simply

---

[1] Cf. "What Kind of Encounters Do We Need In Our Christian Witness?" (1991b), and "Allegiance, Truth and Power Encounters in Christian Witness" (1992a).

dealing with the truth (knowledge) area. We may diagram these dimensions as follows:

| ALLEGIANCE COMMITMENT —— Leading to ➝ RELATIONSHIP |
| TRUTH/KNOWLEDGE ———— Leading to ➝ UNDERSTANDING |
| POWER (SPIRITUAL) ———— Leading to ➝ FREEDOM |

Figure 7.1 Dimensions of the God-Connected Life

What I Mean By *Dimensions*

A *dimension* is an aspect of Christianity that, though closely interrelated with the other dimensions, is quite distinct in its content and, therefore, needs to be defined and treated as a distinct entity. We can focus on this distinctness in several ways. One way is to look at the distinctness of the human problems in view under each category.

Knowledge, for example, is the appropriate antidote for ignorance and/or error. Spiritual power is what is needed when the problem is satanic captivity, harassment or temptation. Allegiance/commitment to Jesus Christ, then, is what is needed to replace any other allegiance that a person has made primary in his/her life. We can't, however, *fight* a wrong primary allegiance with either knowledge or power. We can only fight one allegiance with another allegiance. Likewise, we cannot fight error or ignorance with either an allegiance or with power. These must be fought with knowledge and truth. So also with power. We cannot fight power with knowledge or truth, only with power. In other words, we *fight* allegiance with allegiance, truth with truth, and power with power.

There are those in the evangelical community who are *cult watchers*. Though they know a lot about cults, they seem to poorly understand *power*. They, therefore, are very good at exposing the errors of the cults, but can do nothing with their power. In fact, some of them, in their lack of understanding of power, actively condemn legitimate Christian power ministries along with the cult groups.

Another way of distinguishing these dimensions is to look at the differences in the content of each dimension. Though I will go into greater detail below, I here present an overview of these differences. In the relationship dimension we find things like love, the fruits of the Spirit, faith, repentance, prayer, fellowship, intimacy with Christ and all of the other things in Christian experience that factor into our relationships with God and other humans.

These aspects of life, then, are quite different in experience from the things we deal with in our thinking behavior. Though we can think about, talk about, and teach about relationships, none of these knowledge aspects of the subject is the same as *participating in a relationship*. Indeed, many who demonstrate a considerable expertise in thinking about relationships don't seem to do well in relating to others. Similarly, working in spiritual power is quite distinct from thinking about it. It is also quite distinct from relating.

In the truth-understanding dimension are all of the cognitive aspects of Christianity. Doctrinal and theological tenets such as our understandings of God, Jesus, the Holy Spirit, humanity, sin, redemption, faith, Satan and demons, the Church, the Kingdom of God and all the rest of the things we believe fall into this category. So do the things we understand concerning the allegiance-relationship and power-freedom dimensions. This dimension is the easiest of the three to deal with since it largely involves the mere transmitting of *information*. And transmitting truth, though it is better done when people are free from satanic power and linked together in solid relationships, is not as complicated as either relating or dealing with spiritual power.

The spiritual power dimension, then, involves working in the power of the Holy Spirit to bless, heal (both physically and emotionally), cast out demons and challenge territorial spirits. As with relationships, it involves *doing* something, not just thinking and talking about it. Jesus taught and demonstrated that we are at war with a powerful enemy but that we have authority and power to defeat him (Lk. 9:1). The exercise of that power, under the direction of the Holy Spirit, constitutes a dimension distinct from the other two but working in conjunction with them, since the power we use must come from the true Source of power and the authority to work in that power from our relationship with Him.

The Problem

In the aforementioned articles, I focused on the fact that most Euroamerican Evangelicals have known virtually nothing of the spiritual power dimension of Christianity. Unfortunately, in certain circles, at least, there is also a tendency to degrade or ignore the experiential, relationship dimension as well.[2]

Church historians tell us that whenever there is renewal the experiential component comes into focus in a major way. This focus tends to be maintained in pietistic and Pentecostal groups, though often allowed to dim in "more respectable" evangelical circles except perhaps at conversion and revival times. In mainline liberal groups, then, experiential emphases tend to be discouraged or even castigated. The conversions involved in renewal movements, pietism or the like, of course, bring new people into the Church on the basis of new relationships to God and the Christian community. And these new people need training if they are to move toward maturity.

The training we offer, however, tends to move the focus from growing in the allegiance-relationship dimension to acquiring knowledge in the understanding (cognitive) dimension. Unfortunately, this change of focus often does great damage through leading to neglect of the much more important process of growth in Divine-human and human-human relationships. Whether

---

[2] See Kraft 2002.

in pre-membership classes in our churches or in the classrooms of our Bible schools, Christian colleges and seminaries, people are weaned away from the centrality of their relational experience with God into an emphasis on learning information *about* the faith. This is one of the main reasons why many people "lose their faith" (that is, their closeness to Christ) in Christian colleges and seminaries. And because people lose their faith in academic institutions, many Christians, especially those at the more conservative end of the spectrum and those who value the relational-experiential dimension most highly, have become anti-academic.

When the emphasis is on the truth/knowledge dimension, the focus becomes *knowledge about* Christian things, including the relational and the freedom dimensions, rather than *experience of* these things. The result is that many people who are well trained in Christian institutions can discourse very learnedly even about subjects such as relationship and spiritual power—subjects with which they have had little or no experience.

Evangelicals who come from this knowledge-oriented stance tend to make statements against emphasizing experience, as if it were something to be afraid of, not to be trusted and, therefore, avoided. This has led to the experiential/relational dimension functioning largely underground. For example, even though all knowledge is grounded in experience and all interpretation pervasively affected by experience, many evangelical knowledge brokers perpetuate the fantasy that what they are teaching is objective Truth unadulterated by their subjective interpretations. Whether they admit it or not, however, all of what they teach as *objective* truth is strongly conditioned by their or someone else's experientially-influenced interpretations. And both their experience and their interpretations are conditioned, perhaps quite unconsciously, by the kind of relationship they have with God and their fellow human beings.

The fact is, then, that all we know is totally conditioned by both our conscious and our unconscious interpretation of our experience and our relationships. When someone teaches theology, for example, the real quality of what he/she teaches is dependent on the nature of his/her relational experience with the God whose Truth he/she claims to proclaim. A distant relationship with God, the Source of theology, or with the subject being dealt with (e.g., pastoring, deliverance) yields a mere theoretical knowledge of those subjects that at least reduces, if not destroys the relevance of what is being taught.

Needed: Balance

I am not contending that relationship and experience should be emphasized more than understanding, though, given the fact that there is no salvation without that relationship, we must give it proper priority. That relationship saves, whether or not we have a lot of knowledge to go with it. My plea is for balance, a balance that goes three ways. The academic nature of what we call theology and the classroom context in which we teach have, however, led us to largely ignore two of these dimensions.

Jesus called the twelve to *be with him* and only then to communicate and engage in power ministry (Mk. 3:14). His teaching of Truth was, I believe, intended to serve these relational and ministry ends, not to be an end in itself. I have recently read and responded to two articles critical of some of what I am doing because, the authors contend, my theology may have some flaws in it. The impression I am left with is that these authors feel that what God really wants in this world is correct theology, whether or not people get helped. I think, though, Jack Deere was on the right track when he titled his chapter in the book *Power Encounters among Christians in the Western World,* "Being Right Isn't Enough."(1988) By this he meant to indicate his repentance for seeking *right* theology over participating with God to bring freedom to those whom God loves.

My encounter articles point to an imbalance among evangelicals in our neglect of the power-freedom dimension of biblical Christianity. The additional neglect of the allegiance-relationship dimension may, however, makes the situation even worse than I suggested, at least among the academically inclined. We may even have done injustice to the relational dimension out of fear of anything that is not easily explainable in rational categories.

We have recommended allegiance-relationship experience as the way to salvation. But, at least in academic circles, we have often downplayed the validity of interpretations of Scripture and life based on experience. Instead, we go full tilt for the knowledge-understanding dimension as if that were the most important. But even in this knowledge-truth dimension we go off the track because our understanding of knowledge and truth has been Western Enlightenment rather than scriptural. When we think of knowledge, for example, our *interpretational reflex* is to think of intellectual, theoretical knowledge. This kind of knowledge and truth is not, however, what the scriptural authors had in mind. The knowledge/truth spoken of in Scripture is *experiential truth,* not intellectual, theoretical truth/knowledge. If we are to be true to the original Greek (and the Hebrew worldview behind it), then, John 8:32 should be translated: "You will *experience* [not know in a theoretical sense] the truth and the truth will set you free."

People die spiritually in seminaries and Bible colleges (not to mention churches) because the relational dimension that is so foundational to Christian experience is submerged, ignored, even spoken against in our quest for *knowledge about* whatever subject we are investigating. Sometimes those subjects are relational things like conversion, spiritual growth, prayer, love, the fruit of the Spirit, faith and any of the other aspects of Christianity that belong to this dimension. But knowledge *about* is quite a different thing from actually *experiencing* these aspects of allegiance-relationship. And the focus on knowledge about, plus the time and energy required in our schools and churches to learn information, mitigates against the practice of the very things we are learning about.

In order to further define what I see in these dimensions, I offer the following discussion.

The Allegiance/Commitment-Relationship Dimension

The first and most important of the three dimensions is what I call the *relationship* dimension. This is the dimension the other two dimensions are intended to support. We may picture this fact as seen below in Figure 7.2.

This dimension begins with an initial allegiance/commitment to Christ that we often refer to as conversion and issues in a continual growth in commitment and intimacy with Christ. The dynamic of this dimension is growth, a process that involves change in the direction of Christlikeness on the part of the convert and movement into closer and closer relationships with Christ and with His people. As we grow, we are to become more and more conformed to the image of Christ, becoming more and more like Him to whom we have committed ourselves.

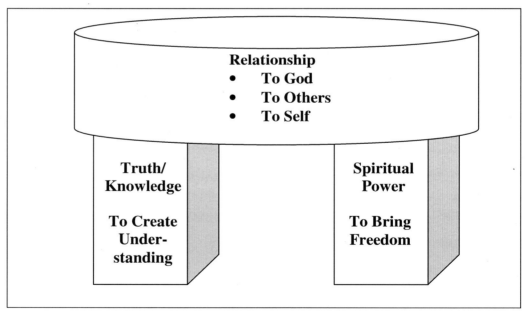

Figure 7.2 Relationship Dimension Supported by the Other Two Dimensions

Our allegiance to Christ and the ensuing relationship is to replace any other allegiance/relationship that is primary in one's life. All other allegiances are to be secondary to this one. In His own family-oriented society, Jesus spoke in no uncertain terms of the need to put Him first saying, "Whoever comes to me cannot be my disciple unless he loves me more than he loves his father and his mother, his wife and his children, his brothers and his sisters, and himself as well" (Lk. 14:26). In this way, Jesus commanded those for whom allegiance to family was supreme to put family second and Himself first.

The allegiance-relationship dimension is quite distinct from the other two dimensions. For example, no one becomes a Christian simply through knowledge or power. As James says, even demons have enough understanding to cause them to tremble in fear (Jas. 2:19). They have all the knowledge they need but none of the relationship required for salvation. Yet we are often taught to witness primarily by increasing the person's knowledge, as if that knowledge is going to bring him/her into the Kingdom. This is a radically different dimension from the knowledge dimension, though related to it. Besides, we can't simply *click into* a relationship on the basis of what we know.

The problem we face, though, is how to cultivate and pass on this relationship. As Christians, we need to be constantly attentive to growing "in the grace and [experiential] knowledge of our Lord and Savior Jesus Christ" (2 Pet. 3:18). For me, since I have learned well to read the Bible mainly for information, this has involved changing certain habits in order to learn to read the Scriptures relationally. I have been teaching myself to experience the events of Scripture as I read them.

The thing that propelled me in that direction, however, is something we will discuss below under the power-freedom dimension. I began to experience the presence of Jesus in ministry. I began doing some of the *works* Jesus promised we would do in John 14:12, His works of power and of love. Participating with Jesus in doing the kinds of things He did while on earth, then, has driven me ever closer to Him in the *abiding in Him* relationship He spoke about in John 15.

Leading others into a relationship with Christ, then, is a major challenge. It is much easier to contribute information to them than to bring them into Jesus' family. But, though many are able to establish a relationship on their own once they have heard the message, as a general principle *it takes a relationship to bring about a relationship*. This is why certain groups advocate *friendship evangelism*, a way of bringing people to Christ that involves the witness first in establishing a friendship relationship with potential converts.

I remember helping a young woman who had been seeing a Christian psychologist for some time. I had learned that this psychologist had gone way out of her way to help this young woman, going to be with her at all hours of the night, even driving some distance to rescue her when she had run away. I asked the client what her relationship was with Jesus Christ. She replied that she probably didn't have one and went on to describe her deep disappointment at the way she had been treated in various churches.

Wondering what to do, I ventured the question, "Would you accept [your therapist's] Jesus?" Her face brightened as she said, "Yes, I'll accept *that* Jesus." And she did. Her relationship with the Christian therapist enabled this very damaged woman to experience genuine love. This experience, then, made it easy to lead her into a relationship with the Source of that love.

The following chart summarizes my understanding of the allegiance-relationship dimension:

The Allegiance Dimension
Primary Concern: *Relationship*
1. This is the most important of the three dimensions 2. Starts with conversion—a commitment to Christ—to establish a saving relationship with God through Jesus Christ 3. Aim is to replace any other allegiance/relationship as primary—all other allegiances are to be secondary to this one 4. It continues as growth in one's relationship with Christ and with others expressed as loving God with one's whole heart and one's neighbor as oneself 5. It includes all that the Bible teaches on subjects like love, faith(fulness), fellowship, the fruits of the Spirit, intimacy with Christ (e.g., Jn.15), forgiveness, repentance, reconciliation, obedience 6. True intimacy and relationship should not be confused with *knowledge about* intimacy and relationship 7. All other allegiances are to be countered with commitment to Christ 8. Under this dimension, the church is to be experienced as *family* 9. Witness to one's personal experience is key to communicating this dimension 10. Theology is experienced in worship and submission to God (Rom. 12:2)

Figure 7.3 Allegiance Dimension

The Truth/Knowledge-Understanding Dimension

This is the dimension most familiar to us. Jesus spent a high proportion of His time and energy in the teaching of truth. He wanted people to understand as much as possible about His Father, Himself and all that the relationships between God and humans and between humans and other humans should involve. He punctuated His teaching with regular power encounters and appeals for allegiance. He regularly *demonstrated,* not just talked about, both the allegiance-relational and the power-freedom dimensions as a part of His teaching of truth.

One of the crucial aspects of Jesus' method was to enfold His teaching of truth in a relational context—discipleship. He chose twelve people to teach by example in the context of the day-in, day-out activities of living together and ministering to people in love and power. He used His freedom-giving power to minister relational love to others within a discipling relationship with His closest followers (including more disciples than the twelve plus several women). But He wrapped all of this in a truth teaching context. His was a balanced approach to *doing* and *thinking about the doing.* He never allowed His ministry to become a merely *thinking about* ministry.

Unlike Jesus, though, we in our Bible schools, colleges, seminaries and churches tend to focus strongly on *knowledge about* some aspect of Christian life rather than on actually experiencing that aspect. We hope, often vainly, that people who hear about repentance and converting to Christ will come to repent and convert. We hope that people who hear about faithfulness or intimacy or love or reconciliation or grace or any of the other relational aspects of Christian life will, through hearing about them, grow in their experience of them. We also hope that those who hear about the freedom we can receive and impart to others through the use of the authority and power Jesus has given us will go ahead and use that authority and power. Unfortunately, there is often little or no transfer from *knowledge about* to *experience of* in many of these areas because we don't have the holistic balance Jesus had.

Nevertheless, we continue to fill people's minds with information, knowledge and truth to the point of intellectual indigestion because our training techniques seldom include actually doing what we are talking about. With one notable exception. In Christian training institutions focused on producing pastors, there are usually courses designed to train people to preach in which the students actually have to produce and deliver sermons. Well and good. They actually learn how to do something by doing it. Yet what they learn is seldom more than how to present information about Christian topics. If they are to learn anything about how to interact with people relationally to bring about healthy relationships with God and humans, they have to learn these things elsewhere. And if they are to learn how to operate in God's power to bring the freedom their people crave, they have to learn this outside of the curricula of the schools supposedly established to train them to do pastoral work.

Ideally, then, we should be teaching truth as Jesus did to combat ignorance and error. We should know, however, that whenever the Scripture speaks of knowledge and truth, it is referring to *experiential* knowledge and truth, not merely the *intellectual* byproducts of these factors. And we should be led in teaching truth by the Holy Spirit who, incidentally is also the Producer of the relational fruits of the Spirit and the Giver of the power-oriented gifts of the Spirit. That is, He is in charge of all three of these crucial dimensions.

The Truth Dimension
Primary concern: *Understanding*
1. This dimension involves teaching led by the Holy Spirit (Jn. 16:13) 2. Scripturally both truth and knowledge are experiential, not simply cognitive 3. Truth provides antidotes for ignorance and error 4. Though spiritual truth is pervasively relational and experiential (Jn. 8:32), there is also a cognitive and informational dimension 5. This dimension embodies truth and knowledge of all aspects of Christian experience 6. We are to learn in this dimension about the contents of the other two dimensions 7. We are expected to grow in this knowledge dimension as in all other dimensions of Christian experience 8. Satanic and human lies are to be countered with God's truths 9. Under this dimension, the church is to be experienced as a teaching place (discipleship, mentoring, classroom) 10. Theology is both cognitive and experiential

Figure 7.4 Truth Dimension

The Power-Freedom Dimension

Jesus said He came to set captives free (Lk. 4:18). In making such a statement, He implied both that there is one who has captured many people and that people need the freedom God offers. People need freedom so badly that He, Jesus, came to earth to offer this freedom. He then demonstrated throughout His ministry what He meant by this statement.

We read in Philippians 2:5-8 that Jesus laid aside His divinity and worked totally as a human being in the power of the Holy Spirit while He was on earth. He did nothing to indicate to the world, including the people of His hometown, Nazareth, that He was, in fact, God incarnate until after His baptism. Then, functioning wholly as a human being under the leading of the Father (Jn. 5:19) and the power of the Holy Spirit (Lk. 4:14), He began to set people free from captivity to the enemy as evidenced by sickness, lameness, blindness, demonization and the like. Jesus worked in the authority and power given Him by the Father, never once using His own divinity while on earth.

Jesus did all this to demonstrate God's love (a relational thing), to teach us what God and the Christian life are all about (knowledge/truth things) and to free people from Satan (a power thing). Thus He showed us how we should go about our lives as participants in the Kingdom of God that Jesus planted in the middle of Satan's kingdom. He gave to us the same Holy Spirit under Whom He worked, saying that whoever has faith in Him will do the same things He did, and more (Jn. 14:12). Since today, as in Jesus' day, the enemy is doing power things, Jesus gave us His authority and power (Lk. 9:1) to carry on the freedom-giving activities of Kingdom builders.

When Jesus left, He gave us power in His name. We, then, are to operate in His authority to bring about the same ends He came to bring. We are to focus on bringing people into a relationship with God as Jesus did. But we are to recognize, as He did, that many are in captivity and, therefore, in need of freedom from the hold of the enemy. Only when they are freed will they be able to understand the gospel and, building on that understanding, to commit themselves to Christ.

This is the dimension that Westerners and the westernized understand the least. Many in the West fail to see either the extent of the satanic blinding (mentioned in 2 Cor. 4:4) or the possibility of breaking through that blinding by using the power Jesus gave us. If we are to imitate Jesus, though, our ministries should be filled with instances of healing and deliverance as well as authoritative praying and teaching. The evangelists of Argentina have been demonstrating the effectiveness of an approach to evangelism that starts with breaking the enemy's power over people before witness takes place.

After witness and conversion, then, many Christians are still captive to emotional hurts and demons. How different our churches would be if classes leading to church membership employed the power of God to heal and "clean up" the new converts before they joined the church. God's power is available both at the start and throughout a Christian's life to bring healing and deliverance.

Many Christian leaders ignore the fact that their followers remain captives, even after conversion. They consciously or unconsciously heap blame on their constituents by teaching that all hurts are to be gone when we convert. Others attempt to rectify this situation by throwing knowledge about spiritual warfare at converts. But the power of Satan cannot be countered merely by knowledge and truth. Knowledge and truth are very important in their place, but power can only be fought with power. So those Christians still under the power of Satan, wielded through wounds of the past and demonization, will get little or no help from sound teaching on spiritual warfare if they do not experience the application of God's healing and delivering power to their specific problems.

Power Dimension
Primary concern: *Freedom*
1. The power in focus here is spiritual power (not e.g., political, personal, etc.) 2. This dimension recognizes that humans are held captive by Satan 3. Jesus worked in the power of the Holy Spirit to set captives free (Lk. 4:18-19)—He did nothing under the power of His own divinity (Phil. 2:5-8) 4. Jesus passed this power on to His followers (Lk. 9:1; Jn. 14:12; Ac. 1:4-8) 5. Satanic power must be defeated with God's power (it cannot be defeated simply with truth or a correct allegiance, though these help) 6. Under this dimension, the church is experienced as both a hospital where wounds are healed, thus freeing people, and an army that attacks the enemy, defeating him both at ground level and at cosmic level 7. Awareness of the power dimensions of Christianity needs to be taught both cognitively and, especially, experientially (as Jesus did) 8. Theology is experienced as victory in warfare resulting in freedom to relate and think

Figure 7.5 Power Dimension

Ways in Which the Dimensions Function Together

All three dimensions are present in every activity of God in the human sphere. If a given interaction with humans is from God, it will involve the power and love of the true God in operation. Any teaching of God's truth, furthermore, will involve the power of God with the aim of bringing about growth in relationship with God. In contrast, whenever the enemy's power is active, it is a counterfeit power rather than a true power, and is designed to lead people into a wrong allegiance.

I have spoken above of the frequent need for God's power to be in operation before people can understand enough to pledge allegiance to Jesus Christ. It is the power of God engaged through prayer, then, that enables us to grow stronger in our commitment to Christ and in our knowledge of His truth. Likewise, it is prayer-power that enables us to minister to others the truth that leads to Christian commitment.

As indicated above, I suggest a threefold approach to bringing people into church membership. What is usually done is simply to increase the potential member's knowledge and to make sure that he/she has experienced a conversion to Christ. These ought to happen, but much more needs to be done for most people if they are to experience freedom through the healing and delivering power of Christ and to grow in their relationship with Christ.

I have no statistics to prove it, but if my experience in ministering to hundreds of hurting Christians is a secure indication, I suspect that a high percentage of church members (and church leaders) are in great need of healing from deep emotional hurts and even demons. Such a condition is crippling our churches. An approach to these problems that focuses as much on spiritual freedom and relationship as it usually does on truth and knowledge could revolutionize Christian experience and expression.

Contextualization in Three Dimensions

How does all of this relate to an appropriate contextualization of Christianity? First of all, it should make clear to us that we are to deal with contextualization in three dimensions, not just one. It has been our habit to speak of the contextualization of theology. How about the contextualization of a peoples' relationship with God? Or the contextualization of the experience of spiritual power and the freedom that issues from the correct use of the correct power? These are subjects for encounters. They are also subjects for contextualization.

With regard to contextualization of relational experience, we should not be content with simply communicating *knowledge about* an experience with God. What should that experience look like in other cultural contexts? And how is it brought about (not simply how is it described)?

There have been some discussions of conversion in cross-cultural contexts. We have learned that in many societies, conversion needs to take place in people movements, rather than *one by one against the stream* (McGavran). Well and good. These studies need to be included in discussions of contextualization. In addition to what we have done on conversion, however, we need to pay more attention to the dynamics of relational growth in various sociocultural contexts.

Jesus taught through discipleship. First of all, He demonstrated relationship by practicing it, both with His Father and with His disciples. In this context, then, He demonstrated how to work in authority and power to set people free. And He coupled His demonstrations with the teaching of truth, designed to explain experience and undergird further experience.

We should contextualize incarnational relationship, ministry and teaching. We make this difficult for ourselves by being attached to a school-based approach to teaching and an intellect focused approach to theologizing.

Do we know how to contextualize all three of these dimensions? I doubt it. We will need more experimentation as we seek to contextualize our ministries in appropriate ways.

How Do We Contextualize Non-Cognitive Elements of Biblical Christianity?

It is clear that most of the current discussions of contextualization relate to how we contextualize in the cognitive dimension. On occasion we speak of contextualizing church structures. This gets us a bit beyond the purely cognitive into the realm of thinking about *doing* certain of the necessary things. When we think about allegiance/relationship or power/freedom, likewise, we are getting a bit away from the purely intellectual aspects of theologizing. But we are still in our heads rather than into experiencing what Christianity is all about.

Turning to thinking about actually contextualizing in these other two dimensions, the question we need to ask is: What are biblically, culturally and personally appropriate expressions or contextualizations of The Allegiance/Commitment leading to Relationship Dimension.

It is likely that there will be culturally different ways of expressing allegiance and commitment. In many societies *loyalty*, a form of allegiance, is very important. Should not the ways in which loyalty is expressed in family, clan, tribe, nation in each society be studied as possible models for the expression of commitment to God and His people?

Biblically we must teach the importance of Christians living out the fruits of the Spirit (Gal. 5:22-23) in every society. What, though, are culturally appropriate ways of expressing love, joy, peace, patience, kindness, goodness, faithfulness, humility, and self-control? Surely there will be differences, perhaps great differences, in cultural behavior attached to these qualities. Cultural uniqueness in expressing these qualities, then, should be expected and encouraged in contextualized Christianity.

I have mentioned above that some study has been done of people movement conversion. Undoubtedly, there are a variety of culturally appropriate ways of expressing such a major change. What are they and how can people be encouraged to convert in their own ways and then to develop culturally appropriate rituals to signify such change? The Early Church, in adopting baptism, chose a culturally appropriate form, currently in use in several religious contexts to signify the change in allegiance we call conversion. It would seem appropriate that a truly contextualized church in one culture would develop different initiation rituals than one in another culture. Likewise, it would be appropriate for the members of a church in one culture to differ along cultural lines from those in another culture in their conversion experience.

The way people in different societies experience growth in their relationships with God and with other believers will also differ. There will be differences in their forms of repentance, forgiveness, and reconciliation. Differences will likewise be found in their forms of prayer, fellowship, "familyness" and the way people express their obedience and faithfulness to God and to their Christian brothers and sisters.

All of these issues and many more fit into this allegiance-relationship dimension. Cultural differences need to be discussed. But more than that, relational factors need to be experienced.

What, then, are biblically, culturally, and personally appropriate expressions or contextualizations of The Spiritual Power Leading to Freedom Dimension?

It is likely that there will be culturally different ways of expressing spiritual power and also of experiencing freedom from demonic oppression. As important as this area is to the peoples of most societies, we can expect a wide variety of approaches. What are they and can any of them be models for the expression of God's power?

We may expect appropriate cultural differences in approaches to power encounter. In the beginnings of Christianity in the South Pacific, power encounters often involved the challenging of the traditional gods by their priests or chiefs who had converted to Christ. These were initiated by cultural insiders, the converted priests or chiefs, perhaps under the influence of the missionaries (Tippett 1971). The power encounter initiated by Elijah against the Prophets of Baal resulted from a command by God to a cultural insider. In the case of Moses challenging Pharaoh, the encounter was commanded by God and was carried out by a partially inside advocate on behalf of cultural outsiders. In the temptations of Jesus, it was Satan who initiated the encounter. In most of Jesus' healings and casting out of demons, the Lord initiated the encounter at the request of the affected persons. What are the various kinds of culturally relevant approaches to power encounters in today's societies?

Many societies already have those who heal and deal with demons and, therefore, well-defined expectations concerning how they will go about bringing healing. In some societies, for example, a healer is expected, under the guidance of the spirit under which he/she works, to tell the client what is wrong without any input from the client. If the healer has to ask, he/she is considered a charlatan. What do this custom and others suggest concerning the ways a healing and deliverance ministry ought to be conducted in such societies?

And what about the personnel who operate in spiritual power? Most societies have well-defined expectations concerning the life and behavior of healers. In some societies the shamans and priests are expected to be virtual recluses or ascetics, in some they may be required to go into ecstasy or trance as they perform their rites of healing. What do such customs suggest concerning culturally appropriate contextualizations of spiritual power?

Bible translators have worked a bit on discovering the words and phrases to use concerning spiritual power. A major problem in many societies is that there are too many words for spirit, all of them referring to capricious entities that are more likely to be harmful than helpful. A "holy" Spirit is, therefore, an oxymoron to such people.

And what about culturally appropriate ways of dealing with the gifts of the Spirit? Are tongues intended by God to be the same for all peoples? What about prophecy, preaching, healing, encouragement, hospitality, words of knowledge and wisdom, etc?

What varieties might there be in dealing with deep inner wounds? Given that many peoples are quite reluctant to share their deepest feelings and hurts, are there other, more culturally appropriate ways of doing deep-level healing and deliverance?

How should the Church as hospital function in culturally appropriate ways in various societies? And what about the Church as army? Each of these truths concerning the nature of the Church needs to be expressed in ways that are true to the Scriptures but also recognizable by the people as appropriate expressions of the scriptural injunctions. For example, we learn in Revelation 1-3 that local churches are to overcome the enemy. How is this best done in society after society?

A further consideration, related to the whole of our subject is the question: How do the three encounters get contextualized?

Questions in Three Dimensions

A consideration of contextualization in three dimensions leads us to a series of questions, some of which we seek to deal with in this volume, others of which will have to await future studies and applications. These are questions that can be used by researchers and practitioners who seek to broaden their approach to working toward appropriate Christianity.

The first series of questions to ask relates to the Allegiance-Relationship Dimension.

1. With regard to allegiance, What would be appropriate expressions of allegiance in a given society? Who is to be approached when decisions such as those leading to change of religious allegiance are to be considered? Further, What are the decision making patterns in this society? How in this society ought an allegiance encounter to take place?

2. With regard to relationship, How are human relationships expressed in this society and what do those patterns suggest concerning how Christians in this society ought to relate to God and to other Christians?

3. With regard to growth, How are children socialized in this society and what do such patterns suggest concerning the ways in which people should grow spiritually in this society?

4. With regard to the fruits of the Spirit, What are the ways in which the people in this society express the human counterparts of love, joy and the rest of the fruits of the Spirit and what do such expressions suggest concerning the appropriate expressions of the Spirit-led manifestations of these attitudes?

5. With regard to such things as faithfulness, trust, forgiveness, reconciliation, and the like, How are these appropriately expressed in this society and how should Christians adapt and "capture" such customs for Christ?

Another series of questions can be asked to uncover some of the areas not much dealt with in the Truth-Understanding Dimension.

1. With regard to the introduction of knowledge, How is new knowledge appropriately introduced in a given society? Who should be approached with new knowledge? There are structures for the introduction of new knowledge in most societies and the reputation of what is brought in often depends on how it is introduced and who introduces it.

2. With regard to dealing with truth, What would appropriate truth encounters look like in this society? Are distinctions made between absolute truths and relative truths? What about distinctions between truth and fact, truth and error, knowledge and ignorance?

3. With regard to ignorance and error, How are they treated traditionally and what does this suggest for dealing with Christian truths and for training structures?

4. With regard to training, What kind of training structures are appropriate? Are the people being misled by Western schooling and, if so, what can be done to make training of Christian leaders more appropriate?

Some of the following kinds of questions can be asked to pave the way toward appropriate dealing with spiritual power.

1. With regard to power encounters, What would appropriate power encounters look like in a given society? What kinds of things are recognized by the people as power encounters?

2. Who are the right power brokers to challenge? How much of such challenges should be done in secret and how much openly?

3. When those with spiritual power (whether human or invisible) are challenged, How is it appropriately done? Should such confrontations be staged or should we simply wait for them to happen?

4. What is assumed when one power defeats another? Will people assume they should follow the more powerful god? Or will they simply continue with their old allegiance?

5. When healing from God through prayer is offered, Are there people of status who need to receive prayer before it is considered legitimate to help others?

6. Where are the places of power and how can they be challenged appropriately? Can they be captured and used for the true God or should they be destroyed?

7. What are the times of power and how should they be appropriately challenged? Can these be captured?

These are some of the questions that flow from the above consideration of a three-dimensional approach to contextualization. In the chapters that follow we will attempt to show more of how this can be done.

Let's learn to contextualize in all three dimensions.

Chapter 8

From Systematic and Biblical to Missional Theology

Tite Tiénou and Paul G. Hiebert

In recent years, missiologists have increasingly drawn on the insights of the human sciences to inform their work. One key question keeps arising: how can mission practice keep from becoming captive to the sciences, and how can the scientific findings be integrated into missiology while keeping solid theological foundations? This problem of relating theology to science is not unique to missions. It underlies much of the discussion surrounding the inclusion of psychology in training ministers and Christian counselors, the integration of medical sciences and Christian healing, and the use of modern business sciences in the administration of churches and church institutions. Despite these discussions, a big chasm often exists between theology and the sciences.

At a deep level, the problem of integrating theology and the sciences is a worldview issue. It is due, in part, to our definitions and perceptions of what constitutes "theology" and the "sciences." We will examine these and suggest avenues for a rapprochement between these two critical bodies of knowledge and the research traditions that underlie them.

Research Traditions

Larry Laudan (1977) refers to the sciences as "research traditions"— bodies of knowledge shared by communities of scholars seeking to understand the truth in their fields. Each research tradition is determined by: 1) the critical questions it seeks to answer, 2) the body of data it examines and 3) the methods it accepts as valid means of discovering answers (Figure 8.1).

Each research tradition is embedded in a worldview—the fundamental assumptions it makes about reality. Different answers or "theories" are offered to the key questions, and competing ones are debated until one or the other emerges as accepted doctrine, reigning until it is further questioned. For example, physics, as a research tradition, is the study of the building blocks of the material world that it assumes to be real. It examines material objects using experiments, electron microscopes, ion chambers and other means to find answers to questions such as, What are the basic components of matter? What are the major physical forces? And how do these interact?

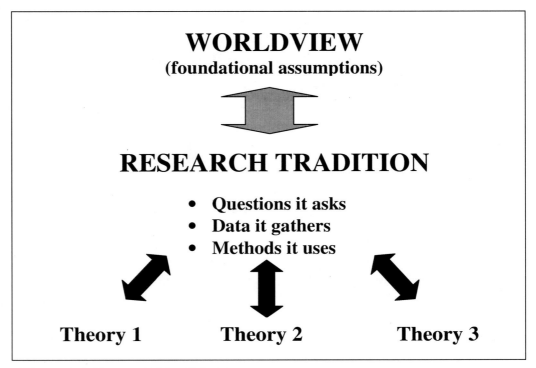

Figure 8.1 Research Traditions

Theology, too, is a research tradition. It is a body of knowledge debated by a community of scholars seeking to answer certain critical questions. On the Theories level there are debates over Calvinism and Arminianism; pre-millennial, post-millennial, and amillennial eschatologies; and orthodoxy, liberalism and neo-orthodoxy. These are true arguments because the different proponents are seeking to answer the same questions using accepted methods. In other words, theology is a research tradition not because it has arrived at one universally agreed upon answer, but because those in the field are seeking to answer the same questions using the same methods of inquiry and examining the same data.

Ways of Doing Theology

If theology is a research tradition, how does this change our perception of it as a discipline, and its relationship to the sciences? Before answering this, we need to clarify what we mean by "theology." We are assuming here that Scripture is divine revelation given to us by God, not simply a human document recording our human search for God. Theology, then, is our attempt to understand that revelation in our historical and cultural contexts (Figure 8.2).

As Millard Erickson notes, it is a second level activity (1983-1985). It is important, therefore, that we study Scripture carefully so that our theologies are biblically informed. We must remember, however, that all our theologies are shaped by our cultures and worldviews. We must remember, too, that there are great gulfs between biblical times and our times, between universal theories and the particulars of everyday life, and between synchronic theologies that examine the unchanging structure of reality and diachronic theologies that study cosmic history. It is important in any theological reflection to work to bridge these differences.

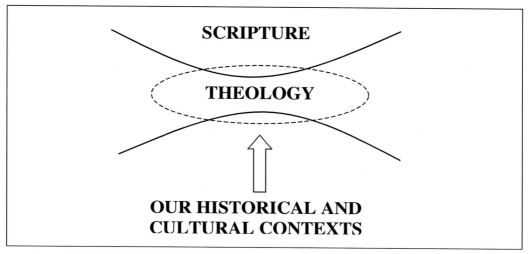

Figure 8.2 The Nature of Theology

Theology, like the sciences, is divided into different research traditions, each seeking to answer specific questions, making certain assumptions, and using different methods of research (Figure 8.3). We will examine two of these types briefly.[1]

Philosophical Theology

One approach to the study of Scripture is to use the assumptions, questions and methods of philosophy. In the West this led to Systematic Theology, which emerged in the twelfth century with the reintroduction of Greek logic from the universities of the Middle East and Spain (Finger 1985:28-21). At first, Systematic Theology was seen as the "queen of the sciences," but over time it became simply one discipline among others in theological education–alongside

---

[1] We will not examine the tropological theology of Eastern Orthodoxy that is done in the context of worship, and stresses the mystical, sacramental and iconic nature of truth. The key question it addresses is, How can we comprehend complex, transcendent truths about God and reality that lie beyond words, logic and human reason? It uses non-discursive signs and tropes such as icons, metaphors, types and parables to communicate transcendent truth.

biblical exegesis, hermeneutics, history, missions and other disciplines (Young 1998:78-79).

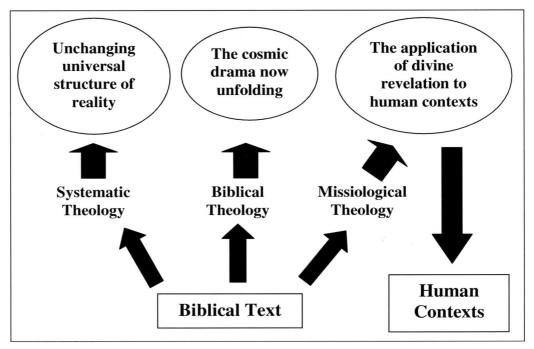

Figure 8.3 Types of Theology

The central question Systematic Theology seeks to answer is, What are the unchanging universals of reality? This research tradition assumes that there are basic, unchanging realities, and that, if these are known, we can understand the fundamental structure of reality.[2] It also assumes that ultimate truth can be known by means of human reason, and that that truth is ahistorical and acultural in nature. That is, such truth is for everyone everywhere. It uses the abstract, digital, algorithmic logic, legal categories, and rhetoric of Greek philosophy, which are propositional in nature. It rejects all internal contradictions and fuzziness in categories and thought.[3] Its goal is to construct a single systematic understanding of ultimate truth (a Grand Unified Theory) that is comprehensive,

---

[2] This is rooted in the Newtonian assumption that everything is composed of basic building blocks and put together as a machine. This view leads to determinism and an engineering approach to reality based on technological solutions. It also leads to the division of the sciences into disconnected disciplines, creating a division of labor and a gap between experts and laity.

[3] An algorithm is a formal logical process which, if carried out correctly, produces the right answer. Algorithmic logic is sometimes called "machine" logic because it is the basis on which calculators and computers work, and can be done faster and more accurately by these than by humans. (For an introduction to fuzzy categories and fuzzy logic see Hiebert 1994:107-136).

logically consistent and conceptually coherent.[4] To arrive at objective truth, Systematic Theology, like the modern sciences, separates cognition from feelings and values, because the latter are thought to introduce subjectivity into the process.

The strength of Systematic Theology is in its examination of the fundamental elements and categories in Scripture. It gives us a standard with which to test our knowledge, and helps us to understand reality from God's perspective as revealed to us in Scripture.

But Systematic Theology has its limitations. Because it focuses on a synchronic analysis of the ultimate structure of reality, it loses sight of the cosmic drama or plot in the Scriptures, and the place of history and historical events in that drama. It cannot adequately deal with change, and must see changes in God's attitudes and responses as surface phenomena, not intrinsic to God's ultimate nature.

Because Systematic Theology focuses on universals and an ascent to knowledge through contemplation divorced from everyday life, it does not tell us how to deal with the beliefs and practices found in different societies, or the change and flux in the historical and sociocultural contexts of human events. Its focus on abstraction and rational coherence has often turned it into an intellectual exercise remote from life's everyday issues. It has also led to a distinction between "pure" and "applied" theologies and has relegated the latter to a position of lesser importance, because they deal with the subjective and changing messiness of human lives.

Western philosophical theology is also in danger of becoming captive to the methods of Greek logic.[5] In the West, the search for a comprehensive system based on digital sets and algorithmic logic implies that humans can grasp

---

[4] Peter Lombard founded systematic theology when he sought to disengage key theological questions from their original biblical contexts and to arrange them in a logical sequence of their own that would provide a comprehensive, coherent and synthetically consistent account of all the major issues of Christian faith and demonstrate the rational credibility of Christian faith (Finger 1985:19). Lombard's *Scentences*, written in the 1140s, provided the form of much of later Medieval and Reformation Theology (Evans, McGrath, and Gallway 1986:71, 132).

[5] For discussions about doing theology from nonWestern perspectives, see Taber 1978a and 1978b, Schreiter 1985, Stults 1989, Dyrness 1992 and A. B. Spencer and W. D. Spencer 1998. One issue philosophical theology must wrestle with is the fact that different peoples use different logics—each of which is perfectly logical and internally consistent, but differs from the others in the assumptions it makes. For example, much of modern logic is based on digital sets, all things can be sorted into different discrete, non-overlapping categories. In number theory, this sees numbers as intervals. This is true of Euclidian geometry and Cantorian algebra. Other logics, such as Indian logic and calculus, see numbers as ratios—as infinite continua from one point to another (Zadeh 1965). Greek logic is abstract and analytical. Other logics are concrete and functional. Can we do philosophical theology using different logics, and, if so, what are the strengths and weaknesses of each of these logics?

the fullness of truth with clarity. It leaves little room for the ambiguities of life, the mysteries that transcend human comprehension, and the wisdom that can deal with the contradictions and paradoxes of a rapidly changing world.

Systematic Theology too often has a weak sense of mission. Thomas Finger notes, "Systematic theology arose as a branch of academic study pursued in universities and not primarily as a task of the church involved in the world at large" (1985:20-21). Missiology is not a category in Systematic Theology, and Systematic Theology is not the driving force behind missions.[6] Missiology is commonly treated as merely a subcategory of "Practical" Theology.

Finally, Systematic Theology was itself a product and reflection of Western intellectual history. Calvin, Luther and their successors appealed not only to *sole scriptura*, but logic, legal categories, rhetoric and other methods available to them to shape their theologies. In so doing, they allowed scholasticism in at the back door. G. Ebeling notes,

> What was the relation of the systematic method here [in the post-Reformation] to the exegetical method? Ultimately it was the same as in the medieval scholasticism. There, too, exegesis of holy scripture went on not only within systematic theology, but also separately alongside of it, yet so that the possibility of a tension between exegesis and systematic theology was a priori excluded. Exegesis was enclosed within the frontiers fixed by systematic theology (1963:82-83).

Systematic theologians need to examine the cultural and historical contexts in which they formulate their theologies to discern the biases that these might introduce into their understanding of Scripture. All theologies are human creations seeking to understand divine revelation, and all theologies are embedded in worldviews that shape the way they see things. There are no culture-free and history-free theologies. We all read Scripture from the perspectives of our particular contexts. This does not mean we can know no truth. It does mean that we must never equate our theology with Scripture, and that we need to work in hermeneutical communities to check our personal and cultural biases.

Philosophical theologies are now being done by committed evangelical theologians in a variety of societies around the world. And these different human contexts raise different questions that require theological reflection. Donald Stultz writes,

> The time is also past when Western theologians had all the "definitive answers." Asian theologians now bear the responsibility and willingly accept it. The latter have discovered that Western

---

[6] Few trained as theologians go into missions, and many schools with strong departments of theology have no department or vision of missions. On the other hand, missionaries, of necessity, must become theologians.

definitive answers do not automatically fit the Asian situation and often answer questions not asked in Asia (1989:23).

Different societies also use different logics which, if applied to theology, would produce differences in philosophical theologies. African theologians often use extrinsic relational sets and concrete functional logic rather than intrinsic digital categories and abstract analytical logic. Indian theologians use analogical categories and "fuzzy" logic.[7] Each of these logics helps us gain new insights into the Scriptures, and forces us to examine the logical systems used in formulating systematic theologies.

In addition to the need for different philosophical theologies, there is a great need for philosophical theologians to develop systematic theologies in which mission is central, and not a footnote. The central theme of Scripture is the story of God on a mission, creating his eternal Kingdom, and bringing sinners back into that Kingdom.

Biblical Theology

A second theological research tradition that emerged in the West was Biblical Theology. Reacting to the scholasticism of post-Reformation theologians, Johann Gabler advocated a new way of doing theology. He saw theology as a practical science, and stressed experience and the illumination of the Spirit (Evans, McGrath, and Galloway 1986:170-71). His central question was, "What did the biblical passages mean at the time of those writing them, and what lessons can we learn from them today?" In so doing he advocated a return to the Bible as history, and an emphasis on the unfolding of the cosmic story.

Biblical Theology examines the narrative nature of Scripture. It assumes that the heart of revelation is historical in character—that there is a real world with a real history of change over time that is "going somewhere," and that has meaning because it has a "plot" and culminates in God's eternal reign.[8] Biblical Theology argues that this view of truth as cosmic story is fundamental to the Hebrew worldview, and to an understanding of Scripture. To describe ultimate reality, the Jews told and reenacted in rituals the acts of God in their lives. Wolfhart Pannenberg reminds us that God is not only the ground of all existence, but all of history is a revelation of His existence and reign (1968).

Biblical Theology uses the questions, methods, and assumptions of modern historiography.[9] It uses the temporal logic of antecedent and consequent

---

[7] See Hiebert 1999.

[8] We use the term "plot" here in the way Paul speaks of the "mystery" now revealed to us (Rom. 16:25, Eph. 1:9, 3:3, 6:19, Col. 1:26). This is to say that there is real history, that it is moving in a direction and not changing randomly, and that behind it is a "plot" or drama—a cosmic story that gives it meaning because it is "going somewhere." For us it is the story of God creating a perfect world, redeeming the lost who turn in faith to him, and restoring creation to perfection in which all will bow before Christ the Lord.

[9] For G. Vos, Biblical Theology is the "History of Special Revelation" (1948:23).

causality, and accepts teleological explanations in which God and humans act on the basis of intentions. Biblical Theology is important because it gives us the diachronic dimension of a biblical worldview. It gives meaning to life by helping us see the cosmic story in which human history and our biographies are embedded.

But, like Systematic Theology, Biblical Theology has its limits. It focuses on diachronic meaning, leaving the unchanging structure of reality in our peripheral vision. It focuses on past biblical history, not on present events. It looks at the universal story, not the particular lives of individuals and communities outside the biblical narrative. It does not directly help us apply biblical truth to the problems we face in specific cultures and persons today. If we are not careful, it can become a study unto itself with little relevance to us today. We must focus on the cosmic story, but we need to remember that God speaks to us through Scripture in the context of concrete settings of human and personal history. We must keep in mind that our stories as individuals and as the church are part of that cosmic story.

Biblical Theology is essential to our understanding of Scripture, but like Systematic Theology, God's mission in the world, particularly as it relates to us today, is not a central theme in its analysis. It has not been a strong motivating force leading people and churches into missions.

Missional Theology

To communicate the gospel in human contexts, we need a third way of doing theology—a way of thinking biblically about God's mission in the world here and now.

Missionaries, by the very nature of their task, must become theologians. Mission, Martin Kähler wrote almost a century ago, "is the mother of theology" (cited and translated by David Bosch 1991). Theology began as an accompanying manifestation of Christian missions. It was not originally a luxury of a world-dominating church. David Bosch notes, "Paul was the first Christian theologian precisely because he was the first Christian missionary" (1991:124). Elwood points out, "Asian theology cannot afford to be purely academic and philosophical, but rather it is valid only if it is produced not primarily in between piles of books, but in the 'field' where it is put to the test every day" (1980:75). Theology cannot be seen as valid simply because scholars, working primarily in ivory towers, have produced piles of books on the subject. It must be validated in real life.

The question arises, How do mission theologians do theology, and how is this different from other ways of doing theology?

For mission theologians the central question is: "What is God's Word to humans in their particular situations?" Mission theologians assume that God is a

---

Biblical Theology is historical, Systematic Theology is logical.

missionary God, that mission is the central theme in God's acts on earth, and that all Christians are to be a part of this mission. They also assume that all humans live in different historical and sociocultural settings, and that the gospel must be made known to them in the particularity of these contexts. Eugene Peterson writes,

> This is the gospel focus: *you* are the man; *you* are the woman. The gospel is never about everybody else; it is always about you, about me. The gospel is never truth in general; it's always a truth in specific. The gospel is never a commentary on ideas or culture or conditions; it's always about actual persons, actual pains, actual troubles, actual sin; you, me; who you are and what you've done; who I am and what I've done (1997:185).

The task of the mission theologian is to translate and communicate the gospel in the language and culture of real people in the particularity of their lives, so that it may transform them, their societies and their cultures into what God intends for them to be. Missional Theology seeks to build the bridge between biblical revelation and human contexts. It seeks to bridge the gap between orthodoxy and orthopraxy—between truth, love, and obedience.

An Analogy to Modern Legal Systems

The logic of Missional Theology is that used in modern common law, particularly as this has been developed in the United States.[10] In the United States there are three levels of law: Constitutional Law, Statutory Law, and Case Law (Figure 8.4; see Romantz and Vinson 1998).

The Constitution is the unchanging foundation on which the legal system is built. *Constitutional Law* examines Statutory and Case laws to see if any violate the Constitution. If they do, they are declared invalid.

Statutory laws are laws passed by legitimate government bodies such as Congress, state governments and government agencies. They seek to interpret constitutional principles in a changing world. For example, federal agencies determine what is private property with the introduction of new technologies and information (e.g., music, video and books put out over the internet).

Case or common laws are the legal guidelines that emerge out of legal rulings in precedent cases on specific issues. Judges are bound by the principle

---

[10] The use of common law as a model draws on a western paradigm. Like all human models, including those of philosophy and history, this has its limitations and weaknesses. In other societies, there are other ways of handling the problems of everyday life, such as *panchayats* in India, and *palavers* in West Africa. All these seek to apply moral principles to specific situations using different logics embedded in the broader method of "wisdom." The relevance of these methods for doing missional theology needs to be studied. Most of them lack a set of eternal absolutes that determine ultimate truth and morality. Consequently these are determined by social consensus, not divine revelation that shows us Truth and Morality as God sees them, and has revealed them to us.

of *stare decisis* which requires courts to make their judgments in accord with the legal findings by judges in the past on similar cases, except where such precedents can be shown to be unconstitutional (Romantz and Vinson 1998:7-9).

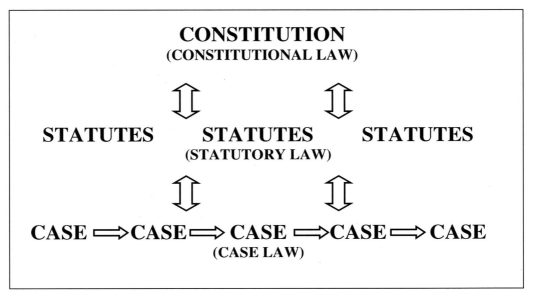

Figure 8.4 Modern Legal System

In relation to Missional Theology, Systematic Theology plays the role of Constitutional Law. It helps us understand the ultimate realities in which all reflections regarding human contexts and specific human cases must take place. It is important to remember that, though Systematic Theology is in the position of Constitutional Law, it is not like the American Constitution in that it is not the ultimate authority—Scripture is. Systematic Theology is *our understanding* of unchanging universals (not the universals themselves), based on our study and interpretation of Scripture. It does not carry the authority of biblical revelation. It is, however, our best understanding of the unchanging universals found in divine revelation, even as we constantly test it against Scripture to determine its truthfulness.

Biblical Theology, and church creeds and confessions serve the function of Statutory Law. They show how the universal principles revealed in Scripture have been manifest in history and interpreted by God's people in an ever changing world. Both Systematic and Biblical Theology are the reflections of the Church in its attempt to understand divine revelation.

Missional Theology uses the methods of modern law. It draws on Systematic and Biblical Theologies to understand God's message to humans, and seeks to apply these in the infinitely diverse and particular situations of human life. It also draws on precedent cases in the life of the church—on how other Christians have ruled in similar situations.

Because Missional Theology is based on systems,[11] not linear logic, the missional theologian begins either with questions emerging out of Scripture or out of human contexts. Each leads to the other in a hermeneutical spiral of understanding and transformation.

Steps in Missional Theology

The first step in Missional Theology is *phenomenology*. Like common law, Missional Theology begins by a careful study of the specific case at hand—the participants, the events and the sociocultural and historical context. As missionaries must study the participants, events, and sociocultural and historical context using empirical analysis and reason to organize our findings. This provides us with our own understanding of the problem in which we seek to understand the world as the people whom we serve understand it. We must also seek to discover the categories, logic and culture of the people involved, for these have deeply informed their behavior.

These "emic" analyses help us see the world as the participants in the cases see it. They do not, however, provide us a comprehensive understanding of human realities, nor a bridge for intercultural communication. So missional theologians must go further and, by comparing different cultures, provide a metacultural "etic" grid that enables them to translate between cultures. In these ways missional theologians are able to employ the methods of the human sciences and history, among others, to enable them to develop broader generalizations and theories about humans and their cultures and histories than would be possible if they were limited to systematic and biblical theological methods.

The second step in Missional Theology is *ontology*. Having studied the case, missional theologians, like the judge in modern law, examines Constitutional, (i.e., Systematic Theology), Statutory (i.e., Biblical Theology and Church History), and Case (i.e., precedent cases) laws as these apply to the case at hand. We turn to Scripture to throw light on the problems people face in specific human settings. We examine Scriptures, using the questions, categories, assumptions and logic we bring with us. In the process, however, we must take another critical step, namely, we must examine and change our own questions, categories, assumptions, and logic in the light of biblical revelation.

Missional theologians then evaluate the human situation (the case) in the light of biblical truth and the history of how the Church has interpreted that truth in previous specific situations. From this platform, then, missional theologians can make decisions on the issues under investigation, developing and determining a course of action based on these reflections.[12]

---

[11] For a discussion of systems theory see W. Richard Scott (1987).

[12] For a full discussion of this process see "Critical Contextualization" (Hiebert 1984). For an application of it to issues raised in folk religions see *Understanding Folk Religion* (Hiebert, Shaw and Tiènou 1999).

The final step is *missiology*. The analogy to common law is not perfect. Missional theologians must go beyond the role of modern judges. We are part of the Church, the community of people we judge. We must seek to help the Church and its people move from where they are to where God wants them to be. This is a process of transformation that includes individuals, and corporate social and cultural systems. We cannot expect people to simply abandon their old ways and adopt new ones. They can only move from where they are by an ongoing process of transformation.

One strength of Missional Theology is its focus on mission. It takes humans seriously, in the particularity of their histories and their sociocultural contexts. It recognizes that as humans we all live in and are shaped by particular cultural and historical contexts, and we can only begin with our existing systems of thought.

Missional Theology seeks to build a bridge between philosophical and historical theologies on the one hand and humans in their particular contexts one the other, between theory and application on the one hand and beliefs, feelings and morals on the other. It defines faith not simply as mental affirmations of truth, nor as positive experiences of God, but as beliefs and feelings that lead to response, relationship, and obedience to the call of God. It sees ministry as a way of doing theology and as a form of worship.

One danger is that missional theologians can make experience, not biblical revelation, the foundation for determining truth and holiness. It is important, therefore, that they consciously reflect on and alter their questions, assumptions, methods and theories in the light of revelation. This reflection needs to be done by the community of theologians—including systematic, biblical and topological theologians, because they can help correct one another's biases. Similarly, this hermeneutical community should involve theologians from different cultures to correct cultural biases.

Complementarity

How do these theologies relate to one another? The Enlightenment project sought to build one Grand Unified Theory (GUT) that integrated all knowledge into one comprehensive system. Today we know that that is not possible. Our human minds are finite and cannot comprehend even the full measure of truth about nature, let alone of an infinite God. Moreover, Kurt Gödel (1992) has pointed out the limits of human knowledge systems, saying that they can be characterized by two, but not all three, of the following: 1) powerful [able to explain many things]; 2) logically consistent [have no internal contradictions], and 3) self-contained [needing no explanations external to the system].

Today, there is a growing awareness of "complementarity" as a way of relating different but overlapping understandings of reality (Hiebert 1999:84-85). Just as an architect makes different blueprints for the same building—structural, electrical, plumbing and so on, and as planners use different maps to map a city—roads, population density, zoning and the like, so we as humans need to look at reality from different perspectives and through different lenses. Different theologies throw different light on the nature of God, and His works and revelation.

We need Systematic Theology to help us understand the questions, assumptions, categories, and logic found in Scripture regarding the structure of reality, using the logical methods of Greek and other cultural philosophies. We need Biblical Theology to help us understand the cosmic story unfolding in Scripture, the "mystery" now revealed to us. We need Iconic Theology in order to transform our theologizing into worship. We need Missional Theology to communicate the transforming gospel into the particular contexts in which humans find themselves. In all these we need to make God and His mission the central unifying theme of our reflections and our lives.

Illustrative Cases

Two cases can help us understand Missional Theology and the methods it uses. The first is from Scripture, the second a hypothetical case from modern missions, but one that draws on thousands of real cases.

Acts Fifteen

The first major case in the early church is recorded in Acts 15. The problem of neglecting the Hellenist widows was handled by an administrative decision made by a council of the twelve apostles (Ac. 6:1-2). Now a new problem arose that called into question the very identity of the church, and threatened to split it apart. The crisis arose in Antioch, and the church sent Barnabas, Paul and others to present the case to the apostles and elders, who met together to consider the matter (Ac. 15:6). The question was clear: Did Gentiles have to be circumcised and become practicing Jews before they were admitted into the Church?

First the council gathered information from different witnesses on the events leading up to the crisis. The facts were clear. After persecution set in at Jerusalem, Philip went to preach to the Samaritans (Ac. 8:4-25), and many were healed and believed. When the apostles heard about this they sent Peter and John to investigate. They reported back that the Holy Spirit had indeed come and that these could legitimately be seen as new believers. Some may have argued that the Samaritans were half Jews, and that God was gracious in letting them back into the fold.

But Philip, claiming to be led by the Holy Spirit, baptized an Ethiopian (Ac. 8:26-40). Some may have argued that the Ethiopian was a "God Seeker" who had come from Jerusalem where he was probably looking into becoming a Jew through the prescribed process. But he was a eunuch, and eunuchs were not allowed into the temple. He resolved the problem by leaving the scene and not disturbing the status quo in the church.

Then Peter witnessed to Cornelius (Ac. 10), a godly man, but fully a Gentile. This raised the anger of circumcised believers who criticized Peter when he came to Jerusalem, and he explained himself to them. What could they say? Peter was one of the Apostles, and who were they to challenge him?

But then, some unnamed people began to witness to the Hellenists in Antioch, and many Hellenists and Gentiles turned to the Lord and began to meet in fellowship together (Ac. 11:19-21). The elders sent Barnabas to investigate, and he decided, on the spot, that God indeed was bringing Gentiles into the church. In fact, Barnabas and Paul had gone out on a mission journey and openly invited Gentiles to follow Christ and join the Church without requiring them to become Jews. Now the matter had come to a head, and a decisive decision was needed to resolve the problem.

There was little disagreement about the facts in the case. There was, however, much disagreement on what should be done. All the parties involved argued their briefs before the council, seeking to persuade the elders that they were right (Ac. 15:7). After Peter gave his closing statement, the assembly asked Barnabas and Paul to retell the central facts surrounding the issue. Then James announced the verdict. After citing Scripture to lay the foundation for theological reflections on the matter, he decided that a Scriptural interpretation of the facts justified the admission of Gentiles into the church, and that without becoming Jews by circumcision and keeping the law. He then issued instructions on implementing the findings, and urged Gentile converts, for the sake of maintaining unity, to abstain from behavior that was an unnecessary offense to the Jewish Christians. This was not a new law, but an exercise of their freedom in Christ to show love to their fellow Christians.

James and the elders, in fact, were doing Missional Theology. They began by studying the facts in the case, and hearing arguments from various factions in the church. Then James used theological reflection to reach a decision and pass judgment based on the situation at hand.

A Case of Polygamy

A second case can add to our understanding of the methods of Missional Theology. It is from Africa, but the same questions arise around the world. What should the Church do with polygamy, whether one husband with many wives, or (rarely) one woman with many husbands?

We cite a case in which the facts are clear. Amadu is the chief of the village. When the missionaries came, they asked him for permission to stay, and, out of hospitality, he allowed them to do so. After three years of ministry, a small church of believers was formed, made up of two singles and five young couples, all monogamous. Having heard the gospel and seen its effects on new believers, Amadu came and wanted to be baptized into the church, along with his five wives. What should the church and missionaries do?

If we turn first to Systematic Theology for an answer, we are in danger of passing judgment on situations we do not understand, and, therefore, of falling into a blind legalism. If, on the other hand, we turn to Biblical Theology, the answer is more ambiguous. All the heroes of the Old Testament were polygamists, and there is no divine sanction of their actions. If, however, we start with a careful study of the culture and the real life issues involved, we can come to an answer that is biblically based and culturally sensitive.

We first need to examine the reasons for Amadu having five wives. The first was arranged by his family, because as the to-be chief the matter is a political and social matter. The first wife had no children, so Amadu took a second wife. It is imperative that a chief have an heir, and a man's greatness is measured, in part, by having many descendants who remember and honor him. Amadu inherited two wives when his brother died. Each society must make provision for widows and orphans, and one worldwide custom is for a man to take care of his deceased brother's wives and children. This gives him the right to cohabit with them, but, more important, it provides them with food, shelter, companionship, offspring, parenting and role models. In his old age, as a renowned chief, Amadu took a young wife to help at home, and to add to his prestige.

Second, we need to look at the theological and sociocultural issues involved in the case. A few of these are:

- Are traditional marriages true marriages, or should Christians be remarried with Christian rites?

- Is polygamy [in this case polygyny] sin?

- Is divorce sin?

- Which is the greater sin–polygamy or divorce [if traditional marriages are true marriages and we ask Amadu to "put away" all but one wife, we teach monogamy but also divorce]?

- If we ask Amadu to put away all but one wife, which one should he keep–the first, the mother of his children, the ones of those he inherited, the youngest?

- If we ask Amadu to put away some wives and children, what will become of them [often they become prostitutes or are sold into slavery]?

- Can the Church baptize the wives of a polygamist [they are all monogamous, but if we do so the church will be made up largely of women and, in addition, we will often be baptizing the guilty ones, since in many societies it is the wives who push their husbands to marry more wives]?

- How should the Church deal with the sins people commit before they become Christians?

- What must change at conversion, and what can be changed through discipling over time?

- What are the evangelistic consequences of our decision [forcing men to put away wives has been a great hindrance to the growth of the church]?

• If Amadu is baptized with his wives, can he be a leader in the church [1 Tim. 3:2, 12]?

• Can a leader who is widowed remarry? [Paul's instructions are that a leader is to be "a one woman man." In the Greek context, this is likely a prohibition of digamy—remarriage of a widower, since polygamy was never practiced in Greek society].

• Who should make the decision [the missionary, the young church, the mission board]?

• What should the missionaries do if their mission board has given them specific instructions not to baptize polygamists [they may be fired if they disobey]?

The next step is to study Scripture for principles that determine our judgments. Here we should begin by studying how the character of God himself informs our judgment. God is a covenant keeper, so Amadu should honor the covenants he made, even though he made these before he became a Christian. God is compassionate, so the decision must take into account the wives and children who are the real victims if they are sent away. God is concerned that none should perish, so the judgment must be such that the door to forgiveness and salvation is open to all.

We should then examine specific issues that arise in this case in the light of our theological reflections. There is no question that monogamy is God's ideal, but is polygamy a sin, and, if so, what do we do with nonChristians who come with several wives, and how do we avoid making Amadu sin by divorcing wives to whom he is legitimately married so that he can be monogamous? After extended biblical studies, theologians such as Karl Barth find no compelling certainty that polygamy is a sin. The Old Testament makes no issue of it, and the instructions in the New Testament are for leaders in the church. On the other hand, divorce is condemned in both the Old and New Testaments.

There are other issues that must be decided. If we ask Amadu to put away all but one of his wives, what should Amadu or the Church do for those sent away? Is it realistic for Amadu to continue to support them–including his own children, and not to treat them as wives? They will be looked down upon, and gossiped about. The young ones can have no children and will be condemned by a society in which women are honored for their children. And what will the church do with widows when the traditional solution has been rejected? Each of these, and many more issues, need extended theological reflections.

We need also to look at how polygamy has been viewed throughout history. In the Old Testament little is said about it. In the New Testament Paul makes reference to "one-wifeness" (likely digamy, not polygamy) only with regard to elders. The Church in the West followed Greek morality and condemned polygamy outright. In modern mission history, Protestant missionaries from the West have traditionally required polygamists to put away all but one of their wives. For example, in 1888 the Lambeth Conference of the Anglican Church resolved that:

It is the opinion of this Conference that persons living in polygamy be not admitted to baptism, but that they be accepted as candidates and kept under Christian instruction until such time as they shall be in a position to accept the law of Christ.

The wives of polygamists may, in the opinion of this Conference, be admitted in some cases to baptism, but it must be left to the local authorities of the church to decide under what circumstances they be baptized (Society for the Propagation of the Gospel in Foreign Parts 1888).

In recent years many missions and churches have taken a different view, and now will baptize Amadu and his wives on their confession of faith, and on Amadu's willingness to affirm monogamy in the Church. Some will not allow Amadu to be a pastor, though he will, inevitably, have great influence in the Church.

After we evaluate the case in the light of the findings of Systematic Theology, Biblical Theology and Church History, and of the ways other mission agencies have handled such cases in that and other parts of the world, we need to formulate principles that inform the case, make a decision, and provide ways in which to carry out the judgment and deal with its consequences.

We will not pass a final judgment on the case here. Our purpose is to illustrate the methods of Missional Theology. What is clear is that a careful study of both Scripture and specific cases can help us apply biblical teachings to the realities of everyday life. It makes theology live for us, because theology is no longer an abstract understanding of truth, but a map for living our lives.

Missional theology is at the heart of the church's call to live in the world, but not to be of it, and to bear witness to God's transforming power in individuals and societies. It cannot be reduced to an academic exercise. It must be the everyday ongoing process by which we as followers of Jesus Christ shine as lights in the world that needs that light so desperately.

Chapter 9

The Hebraic Covenant as a Model for Contextualization

Robert L. Gallagher

Introduction

It was a hot Australian summer afternoon and the communion service had just begun. The minister was preaching about the Last Supper and I had just finished handing out the small cups of grape juice. Glancing over the congregation I saw the usual scenario for a Sunday afternoon. Along the back rows of the church the teenagers were passing notes and candy; over on the right side the young parents were sitting (close to the rest rooms), and their babies were crying and crawling around; in the middle of the auditorium the older folk were nodding and swaying and at the front brother John was fast asleep. Then the voice of the pastor interrupted my thoughts: The gospel according to Saint Luke records these significant words from the narrative of the Last Supper: "In the same way, after the supper he took the cup, saying, 'This cup is the new covenant in my blood, which is poured out for you,'" and then his voice trailed off as I began to ponder.

Were these really significant words? Luke certainly made it clear that the main concern of Jesus at this time was to announce the new covenant. It was a matter of utmost importance in this last gathering with his disciples before the crucifixion. But for all its poignancy, Jesus never once paused to define what he meant by the phrase "the new covenant in my blood." Not one of the disciples even interrupted him to ask, "Master, what do you mean by these words 'new covenant'?" That afternoon I asked the question not only for myself but also for all those in my church who found communion so irrelevant. Surely Jesus had used the phrase, "new covenant," confidant that it would be understood since the concept was known in ancient Hebraic culture. Therefore, if we, the modern audience, are to comprehend the full meaning of this term, we need to understand its historical roots and what it meant to the people of Israel.

Thesis of the Chapter

In this presentation I will introduce the idea of covenant to shed light on what it meant to Jesus and His disciples at the Last Supper. Jesus was highly relational and the Last Supper was a typical relational event at the end of His ministry. It was, then, an event to be celebrated in remembrance but also as a foreshadowing of the sharing of meals in the coming Kingdom. The remembrance, however, was not only of Jesus' death but, since it was celebrated at Passover time, a remembrance of the whole covenant relationship between God and His people.

In what follows, I will consider the ritual forms and their meanings used by the Jews to remember and reinforce their covenant relationship with God. My thesis is that God has placed within the Hebraic covenant his message of relational love for Israel. This inculturated covenant was also used as a mission vehicle to communicate God's love for the nations and serves as a scriptural model for contextualization. Even though this idea underwent development within Israel's history, it was a concept that was "woven into the fabric of her faith from the beginning" (Bright 1953:27).

If we are to see this custom as a possible model for contextualization, we need to investigate the earlier period of the Old Testament where the notion of covenant took shape. This chapter will attempt to answer the following questions:

• What were the various forms and meanings of the Hebraic covenantal ritual?

• How did the Hebrew people use them?

• How did God use the ritual to develop relationships with the nations?

• Finally, do these ceremonial acts of covenant have any relevance to the contemporary church and its mission?

• In other words, does the Hebraic covenant offer a biblical model for contemporary contextualization?

Definition of Terms

Before I consider these questions, I need to establish definitions for some of the terms used in this chapter. First, the Israelite idea of "covenant" (*berît*) centers on an "arrangement between two parties involving mutual obligations" (Elwell 1988:530). With respect to covenants between God and humanity in Scripture, Wayne Grudem gives the following definition: "A covenant is an unchangeable, divinely imposed legal agreement between God and man that stipulates the conditions of their relationship" (1994:515). John Walton further explains that, "In the Old Testament the term *berît* is used to refer to international treaties (Josh. 9:6; 1 Kgs. 15:19), clan alliances (Gen. 14:13), personal agreements (Gen. 31:44), legal contracts (Jer. 34:8-10), and loyalty agreements (1 Sam. 20:14-17), including marriage agreements (Mal. 2:14)" (1994:14). The versatility and functionality of *berît* in the Old Testament suggests that the practice of covenant making was not only a regular occurrence but it was an integral part of community life.

Second, the expressions "form" and "meaning" will be based on Kraft's definitions. The forms of a culture are the static parts. They are the structural elements within the cultural pattern that, when used by persons, serve various functions and are given meaning by those people. The meaning of a cultural form is what a given person or persons attach to it, how they interpret the form (Kraft 1996:135-137). Third, the process of communication depends on senders and receivers of messages agreeing on the essential meanings of the forms they use to convey those messages. God's intent in using a covenant, a familiar cultural form, is to convey to Israel a message that Israel will correctly interpret as relational. What God intended His people to do with that message, then, is the "mission."

Finally, it is important to note that this chapter focuses on God's contextualization of His relationship with His people through covenant. Although contextualization is a modern term (Gilliland 2000a:225), the concept and practice of the term has been evident throughout Christian history. Contextualization may be seen as the transformation of elements within a culture to convey new meanings. This transformation or adaptation may be made with a variety of cultural elements including the doctrinal, social, experiential, mythical, ethical, and ritual dimensions. In the case of the covenant treaty between God and his people, God used a ritual to define his relationship with Israel. He transformed the legal treaty form of covenant and used it as an instrument to explain his relationship with Israel.

Scope of the Subject

As I begin this quest for missiological understanding, I am aware of a number of broader issues that need to be clarified. First, since this paper will be working mainly from the Book of Genesis, it should be pointed out that the main purpose of Genesis was to describe the earlier relationship between God and humanity and in particular, the connection of God with the family of Abraham (Fee and D. Stuart 2002:24-27). To communicate this understanding, the concept of covenant served as a major theme with mission to the other nations as a subtheme. Cross-cultural interaction between God's people and the surrounding peoples was a mission motif that was sprinkled throughout Genesis.

Second, when we speak of mission in the Old Testament we need to remove our New Testament theological lenses and view the biblical intersection of God's people with the Gentiles in their historical context. Hebraic mission is certainly not manifested in the style of Matthew 28:19-20. However, where God's people do relate with the other nations His Spirit is active. In different historical contexts Israel used various means to communicate the sovereignty of their God. Many times these encounters were seemingly without intention on the part of the children of Yahweh, and we do not always see the full fruit of their witness, as in the case of Nebuchadnezzar (Dan. 1-4). The final result of the encounter between God's people and the Gentiles in the Old Testament is seldom recorded. Yet there seems to be evidence that a progressive awareness of the power of Yahweh had often taken place that led to a fuller revelation and submission on the part of the Gentiles. Perhaps Melchizedek king of Salem

(Gen. 14:18-20), Achish king of Gath (1 Sam. 29:6) and Ittai the Gittite (2 Sam. 15:21) were such testimonies.

Third, the love that God has for every people and nation did not begin after Jesus' resurrection. From the beginning of time, God's desire was that all humanity would be reconciled through faith (Eph. 1:4-6). God's reaching out to humanity is throughout the Hebraic Scriptures as well as the records of the early church. The methodology God used to draw the separated towards Himself is of special interest to this paper. I hope to show that the Hebraic covenant is God's model for such an action of love.

Fourth, Paul recognized in Galatians 3:8-9 that "the Scripture foresaw that God would justify the Gentiles by faith, and announced the gospel in advance to Abraham: 'All nations will be blessed through you.' So those who have faith are blessed along with Abraham, the man of faith." In quoting Genesis 12:3b Paul was using this phrase as the Old Testament's summary of the gospel of Christ to prove that the Gentiles belonged to the Kingdom of God. The question I would ask is: Did the Abrahamic covenantal blessing of Genesis 12 actually take place in his lifetime? To put it another way, Is there biblical evidence that the peoples of the earth were blessed through the life of Abraham? I believe that through the covenant ritual with other nations there is biblical proof that Abraham was a dispenser of God's goodness and thus foreshadowed the blessings of the gospel of Jesus Christ (Gen. 12:3a).

Lastly, I have not attempted to provide an exhaustive study of every type of biblical covenant. An examination of covenant shows that there existed in Israel different forms of secular covenant. Also, although the most frequent term for covenant is *berît*, it is not the exclusive word. This is to say that the idea of covenant in Hebrew thought is complex and flexible in nature, and the limited scope of this chapter risks pushing the Old Testament concept into one essential covenant doctrine. The danger of oversimplifying the history of the idea needs to be kept in mind throughout this work. Thus, I begin this chapter with a brief explanation of the nature of the Hebraic covenant. Then the following sections will show the influence of covenant on the Israelites through Abraham, Moses and Christ and how this functions as a model for contextualization. In the last part I will apply this theological understanding to contemporary situations with special emphasis on Australia and the Pacific region.

Nature of the Hebraic Covenant

In considering the nature of the Hebraic covenant, I shall discuss the historical perspective, the forms and meanings of the ritual, and the missiological message and mission behind the ceremony.

In fairness to the reader it must be said that there is a wide divergence of opinion regarding the origins of ancient covenant tradition. Some scholars have suggested that the notion was borrowed from the realm of law and given a special theological application. In the ancient Semitic world, covenants between groups were the legal agreements that made peaceful community relations a possibility. Covenant making was an ordinary affair of daily life. In this nomadic society, whoever was not a relative or friend was considered an enemy. A non-relative was admitted into the family or society circle by means of a pact, and this was a frequent occurrence (Kalluveettil 1982:15).

Near Eastern Covenants

The scholarship of G. Ernest Wright (1950:55) and George E. Mendenhall (1954:50) claimed that Old Testament covenant relationships were borrowed from the traditions of ancient Semitic civil law. These early investigations are foundational to our understanding, as is the work of E. W. Nicholson (1982:79) and Delbert R. Hillers (1969:27) who claimed that the origin of the concept was to be found in Arabic and Greek literature. Although the Hebrew covenant forms are somewhat parallel to a number of non-biblical texts, their foundations must be sought in the very nature of Israel's relationship with her God. Thus, the reader needs to carefully note the use of the word "assumed" in the following quote from G. E. Wright.

> It has been assumed that a considerable proportion of Israel's allegedly unique contributions to religion were not of her own discovery. She borrowed from many sources and her uniqueness consisted in the alterations and improvements that she imposed upon what was borrowed (1950:15).

This view ignores the existence of a commonality of ideas for the peoples of the Noahic world and also the initiative of God in revealing himself to the nations. When God sought to communicate with the Hebrew people, He employed their linguistic and cultural forms in spite of their limitations. "This appears to account for the fact that God chose to work with Hebrews in terms of a culturally known covenant relationship" (Kraft 1979a:114) since this was the closest concept to the God-human relationship that He desired to convey.

In understanding the way God used the forms of Hebraic covenant to express His relationship with Israel, it is helpful to review the forms of covenantal ritual practiced in the Near Eastern world. In the last century, archeological research has brought to light various political manuscripts dating from the 14th century B.C. Of these manuscripts, the treaty documents from the Hittite empire have been of particular value to biblical scholars. Archaeologists have found that six components typically outline Hittite treaties between a suzerain (overlord) and his dependent vassal (servant). The contract between the two parties guaranteed the vassal protection and benefits if the vassal was loyal to the suzerain by keeping the conditions stipulated in the covenant. When the stipulations were violated, the suzerain was required by the covenant agreement to punish the vassal.

The six elements of the covenantal format may be summarized as follows:

1)   a preamble that identified the suzerain or overlord by titles and ancestry;

2)   a historical prologue, which described the past relationship between suzerain and vassal, emphasizing the suzerain's beneficence;

3)   the stipulations assumed by both parties, but especially the obligations of the vassal toward the suzerain;

4)   provision for the deposit—usually in the temple—of the vassal's deity and periodic reading of the treaty document;

5)   a list of gods as witnesses, by whom both parties, especially the vassal, swore allegiance to the treaty;

6)   the sanctions that are the list of curses and blessings accruing to the vassal for success or failure in complying with the treaty's stipulations (Mendenhall 1954:61; Tucker 1965:487-503; McKenzie 2000:32).

This structural outline for political treaties is found intact in certain biblical covenants. The prime example is the Mosaic covenant first recorded in Exodus 20-Leviticus 27 with additions in Numbers and its reiteration as found in Deuteronomy. The structural parallel between the Hittite treaties and the Mosaic covenant is almost exact except for the fifth step in which heaven and earth are summoned as witnesses instead of the gods. While there has been much debate about the historical and theological significance of the parallel, there is one clear conclusion—Israel was not alone in her covenantal tradition. This establishes the historicity of the covenant agreement and proves that the ritual was not restricted to the nation of Israel.

The universal nature of covenant is further witnessed in the extent of its influence in the Near Eastern world. Gary A. Herion and Mendenhall explain that, "the large number of international treaties preserved in texts from all over the Ancient Near Eastern world is dramatic witness to the importance of covenants in ancient social and political life" (Herion and Mendenhall 1992:1180). They go on to say that, "as instruments for the creation and regulation of relationships between different social groups, they seem to have been universal in the ancient world." Covenants were essential for the political and social welfare of nations throughout the ancient Near East. Likewise, they appear to be both commonplace and routine in matters of national and international politics. It is from this culture of treaties and covenants that the nation of Israel emerges, similar to its surrounding neighbors yet, at the same time, distinct.

It is clear that covenant played a large role in Israel's history. The first reference to *berît* in the Old Testament is found in Genesis 6:18 when God established a covenant with Noah before the construction of the ark. From this first covenant God continued to make covenant agreements with Abraham (Gen. 15:18), Isaac (Gen. 26:3-5), Jacob (Gen. 28:13-22), Israel (Ex. 19:5), Levi (Mal. 2:4-10), Phinehas (Num. 25:11-13) and David (Ps. 89:3, 28, 34). In each case it is God, the suzerain, who initiated the covenant process. Dennis J. McCarthy stated: "The idea that God alone grants the covenant and that covenant is essentially his grace may well be retained. The people do not earn it. The almighty Yahweh imposes it" (1972:3). The fact that these covenants were divinely initiated indicates that God desired to be united with his people. It is likewise significant that God used the traditional treaty form of covenant as a means to describe his relationship with Israel.

In addition to the covenantal relationship Israel had with God, the practice of covenant making was evident on many social levels. Covenants existed throughout Hebrew history between leaders and their people: Joshua (Josh. 24:1-28), Jehoiada (2 Kg. 11:17), Hezekiah (2 Chron. 29:10), Josiah (2 Kg. 23:3) and Ezra (Ezra 10:3). Similarly, covenants also existed between leaders such as Abraham and Abimelech (Gen. 21:27-32), Laban and Jacob (Gen. 31:43-55), David and his elders (2 Sam. 5:1-3), Ahab and Ben-Hadad (1 Kg. 20:34) and friends such as David and Jonathan (1 Sam. 18:3). Although other legal treaties were made between individuals, not all of them were identified with the term *berît*. From the list of covenants recorded in Hebrew Scripture, it is apparent that the covenant tradition was widespread and used with regularity. The covenant relationship was not to be taken lightly but instead was a serious step towards political, or social, or personal unity between two individuals or groups.

Forms and Meanings

The question of what rituals constituted a *berît* is difficult to answer since the details of covenant were so well known that they might not have been fully recorded in Scripture. Despite the many challenges due to this lack of detail, the essence of the covenant relationship that God made with humanity is found in the promise, "I will be their God, and they will be my people" (Jer. 31:33; 2 Cor. 6:16). The full meaning of the ancient Hebraic covenant can be determined only indirectly (von Rad 1961:181).

In spite of these limitations there is evidence of regularity in the Hebraic covenant forms. The uniqueness of the Hebrew focus on covenantal ritual

> reveals an idea of covenant which was somewhat different from
> that exemplified in the treaty [format]. The manifest power and
> glory of Yahweh and the ceremonies affecting that union are the
> things that ground and confirm alliance more than history, oath,

threat and promise. It was an idea of covenant in which the ritual looms larger than the verbal (McCarthy 1978:256).

A number of the following elements will nearly always be found in the ritual. Yet it may not align directly with the ancient Near Eastern covenantal elements already mentioned, since the ceremony was not culturally rigid. Rather there was considerable variation in the order of the elements, and occasionally one or another of the elements may be missing, whether by design or by accident it is difficult to determine. For ease of description the following hypothetical covenant-making ceremony will assume continuity between the various elements.

1. Invitation for Covenant. A covenant was a contract in the sense of a binding agreement between two or more parties. The characteristic phase *krt berît* means to "cut covenant." The cutting of a covenant joined together the lives of the parties, an association symbolized by the mystical force released in the shedding of sacrificial blood. For the Hebrews, blood was the source of life and as such was reserved for God (Lev. 17:11). The invitation to enter into a pact was not done lightly. It was a matter to be considered solemnly before accepting the call to cut covenant together (Amos 3:3).

2. Exchange of Coat and Belt. The idea that "I am yours and you are mine" underscored the declaration of a covenant. The act of accepting the other person as oneself reflected the basic concept. In other words, it was an attempt to extend the bond of blood beyond the family sphere. One of the symbols used to depict this intimate union of two people becoming as one soul is the exchange of the robe and belt with its attached weapons. When Jonathan made a covenant with David in 1 Samuel 18:1, 3-4 the Scripture says:

> After David had finished talking with Saul, Jonathan became one in spirit with David, and he loved him as himself. . . . And Jonathan made a covenant with David because he loved him as himself. Jonathan took off the robe he was wearing and gave it to David, along with his tunic, and even his sword, his bow and his belt.

The exchange of the coat represented the giving of oneself to the other person so that the message conveyed was: "All I am and all I have now belongs to you. I am no longer living only for myself. I give myself to you as you give yourself completely to me." Likewise, the exchange of the weapons was an extension of this declaration. The symbolic message was: "Since we are united together, if any person or group threatens your existence, then I am legally bound to come to your assistance to protect you, as you are for me."

3. Animals Split. After the belt and coat were exchanged, the two covenant-making parties would split animals in half and, with the blood strewn on the ground, would walk between the pieces of meat. This part of the ritual described an act of self-imprecation: "As the blood of the sacrificial victims had been spilt, so likewise will the blood of those who break their obligation to this covenant be spilt." They expressed thereby a curse upon themselves and their covenant partner (Jer. 34:17ff.). "In covenant-making ceremonies, animals were often slaughtered and cut to pieces or dismembered as symbols of what would happen to the covenant partner who violated the covenant agreement" (McKenzie 2000:17).

4. Conditions of the Covenant. When the partners to the covenant had walked through the halved animals they faced each other in preparation for the oath. This functioned as a safeguard to the covenant and bound the parties to the pact. The mutual vows were the conditions of the covenant agreement and as such were not to be violated.

5. Blood Brothers. After the oaths had been exchanged the partners would then incise their arms or legs and join the parts together symbolizing the infusion of one's life with the other. Figuratively their life flow was united as one as their bloods were intermingled.

6. Names Exchanged. As an act of acknowledging they were blood brothers, each participant received a part of the other's name. This represented the giving of a portion of their person to the other. This is illustrated in Genesis 28:13a when God identified himself to Jacob as "the God of your father Abraham and the God of Isaac." At this point God had made covenant agreements with both Abraham and Isaac and had become their God and they his people. After God covenanted with Jacob, God is then called the "God of Jacob" (Ex. 3:6).

7. Curses and Blessings. Next, they listed the blessings that the covenant would be provide. For instance, concerning Israel's covenant with God, Moses listed the blessings in Deuteronomy 28. He began with these words: "If you fully obey the LORD your God and carefully follow all his commands I give you today, the LORD your God will set you high above all the nations on earth. All these blessings will come upon you and accompany you if you obey the LORD your God." Then followed the list of curses caused by breaking the covenant: "However, if you do not obey the LORD your God and do not carefully follow all his commands and decrees I am giving you today, all these curses will come upon you and overtake you" (Deut. 28:15).

8. Covenant Meal. Having completed the above sections of the covenant contract, the blood brothers would then sit down to have a covenant meal. This meal was more than a sign of accepting the fact of the contract. Eating together had a profound meaning for the ancient Semites since it was a symbol and confirmation of fellowship and mutual social obligations. By this very act the participants were tied to one another by a bond of friendship. They became brothers since only family ate together. The covenant meal was "a sign that the weaker is taken into the family of the stronger, a reassuring gesture on the part of the superior toward the inferior and not a pledge by the latter" (McCarthy 1978:254). With implications often stronger than friendship, the covenant meal created a quasi-kinship relationship between the two treaty participants.

9. Memorial Planted. The covenant meal completed, the two men would plant a memorial to serve as a reminder to them and future generations that they had cut covenant together. This memorial could be a pile of rocks (Gen. 28:18; 31:52), or pillars (Gen. 31:52; 35:14), or a flock of sheep (Gen. 21:30), or circumcision (Gen. 17:11), or a stand of trees (Gen. 21:33), or even a gift for the occasion (Gen. 21:27).

10. Descendants Blessed. Finally, all the members of the clan, the children and kin people who had been represented by the head of their house were also recipients of the covenant. They enjoyed all the privileges and responsibilities of the tribe's covenant (1 Sam. 19; 2 Sam. 9).

Message and Mission

All of the above ten phases of the covenant-making ceremony may not always be present in a particular pact. Various combinations of these acts could constitute a covenant agreement and did not have to have the same significance or function. It was not a static concept but a dynamic process within varying contexts.

In Genesis there appears to be a correlation between God's love for the nations and covenant making. After Yahweh made a covenant with Abram in Genesis 15, there are three situations where covenants are cut between two parties. Genesis 21 discusses the covenant between Abraham and Abimelech; Genesis 26 has the covenant of Isaac and Abimelech; and in Genesis 31, Jacob and Laban made a pact. In each of these situations a Hebrew person forms a treaty with a non-Hebrew. It would seem that when this occurred there was more involved than just an economic and political dimension. In such an agreement there was also a spiritual component that God used to contextualize his relational message in an appropriate manner for the receptors.

1. Abraham and Abimelech. The ruler Abimelech clearly recognized God's blessing on Abraham's life and because of that desired to enter into covenant with this man of God. In Genesis 21:22b-23 he said to Abraham: "God is with you in everything you do. Now swear to me here before God that you will not deal falsely with me or my children or my descendants. Show to me and the country where you are living as an alien the same kindness I have shown to you." Abimelech invited Abraham to form a covenant based on a religious framework. His motive may be inspired by economic gain, yet God used Abraham's prosperity, Abimelech's ambition and the covenant ceremony to make himself known to this Gentile king.

Before the covenant was made with Abraham, the Philistine observed from a distance the prosperity of the Hebrew's life both materially and spiritually. Through the pact Abimelech would experience the God of Abraham in a more intimate way because he was connected to Yahweh through his blood brother. The covenant forms and meanings were conveyed to him, as may be seen by the relic in verse 29 when Abimelech asked the meaning of the seven ewe lambs.

Abraham's God was now connected to the Gentile since a legal agreement was made for Yahweh's protection (Gen. 21:23).

2. Isaac and Abimelech. Abimelech must have prospered because of this relationship since after Abraham died the king approached Isaac to renew the contract. In Genesis 26:28-29 it is recorded that Abimelech with his advisors said: "We saw clearly that the LORD was with you; so we said, 'There ought to be a sworn agreement between us'—between us and you. Let us make a treaty with you that you will do us no harm, just as we did not molest you but always treated you well and sent you away in peace. And now you are blessed by the LORD." So Isaac performed a set of covenantal forms and the agreement was made. Just prior to Isaac coming to Abimelech's land, God renewed the covenant he made with Abraham. In the midst of reconfirming the blessings and promises to Isaac, the Lord reiterated that a part of the covenant agreement was the blessing that "through your offspring all nations on earth will be blessed" (Gen. 26:4b). Surely King Abimelech of Gerar is fruit of that promise and the covenant-making process a vehicle that God used to channel his message of love.

3. Jacob and Laban. The last of the covenant trilogy is the agreement between Jacob and Laban. The contract that God had made with Abraham and renewed with Isaac is once again renewed with Jacob in Genesis 28. In the midst of the *berît* there is a repetition of the promise that "all peoples on earth will be blessed through you and your offspring" (Gen. 28:14). Towards the end of Jacob's stay with Laban, his father-in-law confessed that he was materially blessed because of God's hand on Jacob and he does not want him to go because of it (Gen. 30:27, 30). When he realized that nothing was going to stop Jacob returning to his homeland, Laban does the next best thing to ensure that Yahweh's blessing will remain on his life. He said to Jacob, "come now, let's make a covenant, you and I, and let it serve as a witness between us" (Gen. 31:44). God accommodated the weaknesses of both these men and used the covenantal forms to impart a message of love to Laban. The God of Abraham, Isaac and Jacob is a vital part of this pact as may be seen in Genesis 31:49, 50, 53.

To summarize, the above non-Israelite rulers had witnessed the prosperity of the Hebrews and therefore initiated all three covenant agreements with Abraham, Isaac and Jacob. In spite of tainted motives, they came to be connected with the Hebrew patriarchs and their God. I believe that Yahweh used the covenant rituals and their meanings to draw these men closer to him even though they were still perhaps entwined in their Gentile worship. The Lord's message of care and concern is conveyed through the covenantal rituals by the blessings they received as a result of entering the agreement. Furthermore, God's people had a mission to bring blessing to "all peoples on the earth" (Gen. 12:3) and one of the ways the Lord did this was through the patriarchs of Israel making covenant agreements with the other nations. It would seem that in all three cases God's people reluctantly undertook this mission since in each instance the initiative came from the Gentile leaders.

Extent of the Impact

To further expand my thesis I would like to view three major covenantal events in the Bible and correlate them with the different elements of the ceremony previously listed. The events discussed will be the covenant God made with Abraham and his family; the covenant God made with Israel at Mount Sinai; and finally, the covenant the Messiah made at Calvary for the church. The missiological implications of each event will also be considered.

God's Covenant with Abraham

The story of Abraham began with his call by God to leave his country and family (Gen. 12:1-3; Ac. 7:2-3). Abraham was seventy-five years old (Gen. 12:4), was originally from Ur of the Chaldeans, was married to Sarah who was barren, was a descendent of Shem and was living with his nephew Lot and his family. There is no indication in the Bible as to whether Abraham knew God before the Lord spoke to him. Abraham first appeared on the biblical scene as a man from a foreign land whose former relationship with God is unknown. However, he is identified by the narrator as a descendant of Noah, a man who was righteous before God and who was in covenant with him. It is this godly heritage that perhaps explains God's identification with Abraham and his descendants.

1. Invitation for Covenant. Although the word *berît* is not used in Genesis 12:1-3, it is clear that God made a promissory agreement with Abraham in this first encounter. While he was commanded to "leave your country, your people and your father's household and go to the land I will show you" (12:1), it is only Abraham's obedience that is required of him. This initial command can be seen as an invitation to covenant. By means of his response, Abraham can choose whether or not to enter into a treaty relationship with God. Once Abraham agreed through his obedience, God's involvement in the relationship was more comprehensive. God promised to: 1) make Abraham into a great nation, 2) bless him, 3) make his name great, 4) make him a blessing (v.2) and 5) bless all peoples on the earth through him (v. 3). This list of God's abundant blessings upon Abraham was equivalent to the promissory blessings given during a covenant ceremony. While Genesis 12 may not be the sealing of the covenant agreement (Gen. 15:18), it is certainly the beginning of God's covenant with Abraham.

2. Exchange of Coat and Belt. The symbolism implied in the exchange of the coat and belt between Jonathan and David was evident in Yahweh's covenant with Abraham when God answered him and said, "I am your shield, your very great reward" (Gen. 15:1b). Here God promised that he would protect Abraham from his enemies and that God would bless him.

3. Animals Split. Abraham was not content with mere words so "God himself entered a communal relationship with Abraham under the forms which among men guarantee the greater contractual security" (von Rad 1961:181). God used the cultural ritual whereby two people cut covenant together to reinforce His message of love and promise to Abraham (Gen. 15:8). Once the animals were cut in half (v. 10), Abraham fell into a deep sleep and God Himself walked between the bloody pieces confirming what He had promised. "When the sun had set and darkness had fallen, a smoking firepot with a blazing torch appeared and passed between the pieces. On that day the LORD made a covenant with Abraham" (Gen. 15:17-18a). The passing of Yahweh between the pieces was an act of deepest condescension.

4. Missiological Implications. During the sleep of Abraham, the Lord prophesied what would happen to the nation that would come from Abraham's body. In the midst of making a covenant with Abraham, God spoke of slavery and punishment. After 400 hundred years of bondage in Egypt, Israel would be released and return to the land of their covenant promise. The historical account in Exodus of the fruition of this prophecy states that it was because God "remembered his covenant with Abraham, with Isaac and with Jacob" (Ex. 2:24; 6:5) that He delivered His people. God achieved this through the ten miracles that were progressively severe in their intensity towards the Egyptian gods, and ever-increasing in their geographic influence. Through the ten plagues, God's gracious presence and sovereign power was not only manifested to Israel, but also to Egypt and the other nations (Ex. 5:2; 7:5, 17; 10:6).

With the covenant Yahweh made with Abraham in Genesis 15, God had prophetically declared that He would use this agreement to proclaim His message to Egypt and the nations. In Exodus 9:13b-16 God communicated to Pharaoh the reason why He demonstrated His might.

> Let my people go, so that they may worship me, or this time I will send the full force of my plagues against you and against your officials and your people, so you may know that there is no one like me in all the earth. For by now I could have stretched out my hand and struck you and your people with a plague that would have wiped you off the earth. But I have raised you up for this very purpose, that I might show you my power and that my name might be proclaimed in all the earth.

As a result of God's covenantal obligation to protect His people Israel in Egypt, God demonstrated His power and also allowed an opportunity for the Egyptian king and his nation to repent and enter a relationship with the living God.

God's Covenant with Israel

God's purpose in manifesting such a powerful deliverance for Israel was to bring His people to Mount Sinai to worship Him (Ex. 3:12). There He said, "I will take you as my own people, and I will be your God. Then you will know that I am the LORD your God, who brought you out from under the yoke of the

Egyptians" (Ex. 6:7). John Bright explains that the covenant with Israel "created a bond between God and people which was based in gracious and saving actions of the Deity already performed, and it laid upon the recipient (Israel) the binding obligation to obey the divine commandments under threat of the severest penalties in the event of failure to do so" (Bright 1976:28). Exodus 19-24 reveals the following cultural forms that were used when Yahweh cut covenant with the nation of Israel.

1. Invitation for Covenant. God invited the people of Israel to a covenantal relationship based on the agreement He had made with the family of Abraham. They agreed, and in Exodus 19 God prepared His people to meet their awesome covenant Partner. The key Scripture in understanding this passage is found in Exodus 19:5-6 where God said that if Israel will obey Him and keep the covenant then they would be a special people. "Now if you obey me fully and keep my covenant, then out of all nations you will be my treasured possession. Although the whole earth is mine, you will be for me a kingdom of priests and a holy nation."

2. Conditions of the Covenant. After the meeting of the covenant parties, God set forth the covenantal terms from Exodus 20:22 to 23:33. Here the civil, social and religious regulations of the contract are established before final ratification in Exodus 24.

3. Blood Brothers. Once the people of God agreed for the second time concerning the conditions of the pact (Ex. 19:8; 24:3), Yahweh then sealed the terms by cutting covenant with the nation of Israel (Childs 1974:505). God does this by having Moses sprinkle the blood of sacrificial bulls on an altar at the foot of Sinai that figuratively represented Him. Moses also sprinkled the blood on twelve stone pillars representing the twelve tribes of Israel. Israel is now consecrated as God's holy people. McCarthy says of this ritual: "Here Yahweh and the people share in some sort the same blood and hence the same life; they are members of one family" (1978:255).

4. Covenant Meal. Israel was now officially Yahweh's "kingdom of priests and a holy nation" and the leaders of Israel no longer had the same restrictions imposed on their access to Him as in Exodus 19. They then went up and saw "the God of Israel." No longer just the God of Abraham, Isaac and Jacob who had been in covenant with God, but, from this time on, the God that belonged also to the nation of Israel. Here on the mountain they ate and drank with God in a covenantal meal.

> Moses and Aaron, Nadab and Abihu, and the seventy elders of Israel went up and saw the God of Israel. Under his feet was something like a pavement made of sapphire, clear as the sky itself. But God did not raise his hand against these leaders of the Israelites; they saw God, and they ate and drank (Ex. 24:9-11).

5. Missiological Implications. It was God's intention that the Israelite nation see themselves as "a kingdom of priests"; a people who would go before God on behalf of the nations and then go before the nations on behalf of God. It was impractical for all the people to serve as priests, so God chose approximately a tenth to represent the nation in their duties before Him. God's desire to use this covenant nation to share His message may be seen in the reinstatement of the broken Sinaitic covenant. In Exodus 34:10 Yahweh said that He was making a covenant with Moses and Israel and told Moses: "I am making a covenant with you. Before all your people I will do wonders never before done in any nation in all the world. The people you live among will see how awesome is the work that I, the LORD, will do for you."

Here again is the correlation of covenant with God's message to the nations and the mission of His people. It is through the children of Israel, God's priests, that Yahweh desired to reveal Himself to the nations of Canaan as the all-powerful God of gods. If they will obey Him and keep His covenant, then God's people will influence the nations to change their allegiance to the living God.

This last section of the chapter shows that the solemn commissioning of Israel as "a holy nation and a royal priesthood" at Mount Sinai was to allow God's people to function among the nations in the same manner as a priest would in Israelite society. The covenant gave the nation not only status, but also an obligation to be obedient to God's will for mission. William W. Klein supports this notion when he suggests a missional purpose in the election of Israel.

> God's love alone stands as the motive for his choice of the people of Israel to be his own. Never do the biblical writers describe election as a reward. It does not come in response to any attribute or action of Israel. His election did not give Israel a privileged position among the nations so she might gloat. Rather, God chose Israel to serve him and reflect his character and ways to other nations—"that they may proclaim [his] praise" (Isa. 43:21). In this sense God's election of Israel parallels his election of individuals—he has called her into existence to serve him in the world. Thus Israel's election does not mean God has rejected the other nations. Rather, election creates for Israel the task of representing God among the nations so salvation might come to them (1990:43).

God's Covenant with the Church

The history of Israel was strewn with broken promises as the prophets repeatedly called the people to honor their Sinaitic agreement. So from within the old covenant God planted a seed (Jer. 31:31-34; Ez. 36:24-28) that finally flowered in the coming of the new covenant through Jesus Christ.

It is not the blood of animals sacrificed and split into half that constituted an element in this new covenantal contract. Instead it is the blood of God Himself in the form of His Son that is spilt on Calvary's cross. Here Christ became the sacrifice and cut covenant with God on our behalf that we may be in eternal relationship with Him. Jesus said in John 6:53-58:

I tell you the truth, unless you eat the flesh of the Son of Man and drink his blood, you have no life in you. Whoever eats my flesh and drinks my blood has eternal life, and I will raise him up at the last day. For my flesh is real food and my blood is real drink. Whoever eats my flesh and drinks my blood remains in me, and I in him. Just as the living Father sent me and I live because of the Father, so the one who feeds on me will live because of me. This is the bread that came down from heaven. Your forefathers ate manna and died, but he who feeds on this bread will live forever.

This figuratively spoke of becoming a blood brother with Christ through faith in Him by the indwelling power of the Holy Spirit. As we receive the Holy Spirit, the life of Christ enters our being and we are dynamically unified with Him (Jn. 14:20; Gal. 2:20; Phil. 4:12-13).

Many of the Old Testament covenantal forms and their meanings are present in the Messiah's sacrifice. They were shadows of what Jesus would do at Calvary. Through His shed blood Christ became the Head of a new family, and as believers we are members of that universal family. He was our representative for this new covenant, and we are the beneficiaries by faith in Jesus (1 Pet. 2:9-10). The blessings of this covenant are listed in Hebrews 8:10-12.

Missiological Implications. One of the gifts that God our covenant Partner gave the believer was the seal of the Holy Spirit (Eph. 1:13). It is the Spirit of God that enabled this new covenant to extend beyond the Hebraic ethnic boundaries to include all peoples (Ac. 2:17-21; Heb. 8:11). This new covenant that Christ cut for all those who believe in Him was the fulfillment of the promise given to Abraham "that God would justify the Gentiles by faith" (Gal. 3:8). Paul explained in Galatians that the expression "all nations will be blessed through you [Abraham]" found in Genesis 12:3 was an advance announcement of this gospel.

The ultimate mission of God that "the earth will be filled with the knowledge of the glory of the LORD, as the waters cover the sea" (Hab. 2:14) has been underway since Pentecost in Acts 2. God's message to the nations was not accomplished by Israel, His "kingdom of priests," so God has instigated a new Israel, composed of Jews and Gentiles saved through faith. Paul stated that "his [God's] purpose was to create in himself one new man out of the two, thus making peace, and in this one body to reconcile both of them to God through the cross, by which he put to death their hostility" (Eph. 2:15b-16). It is the church brought into existence through the cross of the new covenant that God has used through history to achieve the expansion of the Kingdom of God among the nations. The covenant forms of Christ and their corresponding meanings are continuing to be implemented to bring every person under his Lordship (Phil. 2:10-11).

In the last section of this paper I will describe how these findings affect our participation in God's mission. Australia will be considered first, followed by the Pacific Rim and finally the church's mission in the world.

Australia

The covenant concepts I have shared were especially helpful with my pastoral ministry in Australia. When conducting pre-wedding interviews and during the actual ceremony, I emphasized the aspect of marriage recorded in Malachi 2:14-15. Israel was asking why God was ignoring their religious activity and the reply came:

> It is because the LORD is acting as the witness between you and the wife of your youth, because you have broken faith with her, though she is your partner, the wife of your marriage covenant. Has not the LORD made them one? In flesh and spirit they are his. And why one? Because he was seeking godly offspring. So guard yourself in your spirit, and do not break faith with the wife of your youth.

God sees marriage as a lifetime commitment whereby two people become united as one life. God described the marriage bond as a covenant (Ezek. 16:8; Prov. 2:17) and as such, He hated divorce. I encouraged this view of marriage as an antidote to the spirit of the world that had infiltrated the Western church. When a couple stood before God and the witnesses, holding hands and saying their vows to each other, they were entering into a covenant agreement. The exchange of wedding rings then served as a witness, or a sign, of the covenant that would remind them of their contract that day.

An understanding of biblical covenant is most helpful in strengthening a Christian's understanding of the unity of Scripture. In teaching the Bible I have used the scarlet thread of covenant to show how God progressively unfolded His revelation of the coming Messiah and the Kingdom of God. From Genesis 3:15, 9:8-17, 12:1-3, 49:8-12 and on through the biblical record (2 Sam. 7:11-16), the covenant of God with His people was a motif that unified both the Old and New Testaments.

Pacific Rim

Teaching opportunities came to me in the early eighties in Papua New Guinea and the Solomon Islands, and of the many topics taught, the theme of the blood covenant has been one of the most beneficial to the Melanesian church. In Papua New Guinea, these concepts of covenant have had particular significance. For instance, the students of the Bethel Bible College in Port Moresby came from most provinces of the nation and as far as the Fijian Islands and India. In class discussions on this theme the students have many times indicated that various aspects of the Hebraic ritual of covenant are practiced in their villages today. Whether in buying land, or in marriage arrangements, or in settling a dispute, covenantal forms of blood rites and gift exchange are a vital part of the ceremonies.

Garry Roche in his article "Moka and Covenant," tells of the Melpa people of Papua New Guinea using the traditional Moka ceremony as a highly organized process of exchange (1989:165). He then elaborated on this subject, not to show the many similarities between covenant and Moka, but to explore whether Moka itself can be used in analogy to describe the relationship between God and his people. Once again we find the Melchizedekian factor that Don Richardson spoke of in his books *Eternity in Their Hearts* (1981) and *Peace Child* (1974): that God has enculturated the gospel story in many societies. Roche concluded that Moka helps to illustrate that God invites us into a partnership, working for the salvific transformation of the world (1989:180). I would suggest that since all peoples of the earth came from the family of Noah, the steps of cutting covenant were passed down from one generation to another and from one people group to another. Over time the different forms of covenant were changed or neglected so that today we only see remnants of the original format. The Moka ceremony of the Melpa is one such ceremony.

Other Nations

In many other people groups, evidence of biblical covenantal elements may be witnessed and used as a contextual bridge for God's message of love. In traditional Africa, formal oath taking by two individuals or groups of people is a means of establishing and maintaining good human relationships. This is achieved by blood being either shed or exchanged. These oaths bind people together mystically because in them is the union of one life with another by drinking or transfusion of blood. Like the Hebraic people, they believe that blood is life and the commingling of the blood of two persons is equivalent to the joining of their lives and personalities. They are thus indivisibly united (Nabofa 1985:398).

In parts of Nigeria it is common for a husband and a wife to enter into a blood covenant to cement their relationship. Other peoples of the same nation ensure political stability between diverse groups by cutting covenant together. In Morocco, people who desire reconciliation share a common meal after which they symbolically join hands. A friendship covenant in Taiwan is made by drinking simultaneously from the same cup while putting their arms around each other's necks (Arulefela 1977; Ruganda 1973).

In fact, my research uncovered many different people groups that have similar covenant forms and meanings as the ancient Hebrews. Agreements between two parties often have combinations of these rites: sacrifices, common meals, feasts, name exchange, shedding of blood, curses and blessings, and memorials planted. These pacts communicate the same meaning to the groups as was seen in this study of the children of Israel; namely, bonding together for mutual sharing, protection and commitment.

All in all, it may be proposed that what is evidenced in many societies of the world is the surviving traces of the ancient covenant practices of biblical times. From Africa and Asia to Australia, these remnants of a by-gone epoch still speak a contextualized message from God through their cultural forms. For those who have ears to hear, these forms still serve God's mission to reveal His invisible qualities—His eternal power and divine nature (Rom. 1:18-23).

Conclusion: Proclaim Until He Comes

This chapter has provided some of the answers to the questions established in the introduction. The various forms of the Hebraic covenantal ritual and their respective meanings have been described as well as how they were used in the Bible by God to communicate His message of relationship to Israel and the surrounding nations. In the second part of this study, the chapter also drew attention to the specific missiological implications for participation in God's mission and made suggestions for the church's mission in the world.

The use of the Hebraic covenant ceremony by God to communicate His message of love to Israel and the nations was merely noted from the books of Genesis and Exodus. Further study needs to be made in the Pentateuch and other Old Testament literature. Also, the correlation between the work of Christ's redemption and the concept of covenant was briefly discussed and warrants greater attention. Lastly, there is an obvious need to have a stronger appreciation of the cultural significance of the times. Further work in this area will surely bring greater insight.

The Bible gives us the basis for the covenant relationship between God and His people. This was true with ancient Israel as it is for the contemporary church. Nevertheless, the obligations of fulfilling God's mission using our covenant agreement through Christ as a springboard, needs greater clarity through scholarly work. Perhaps in this regard, the signs of the new covenant, of both baptism and the Lord's Supper, need closer study (Col. 2:11-12; Rom. 6:3-4; and 1 Cor. 11:25).

The importance of covenant for a proper understanding of the Communion Service needs to be adequately explored. The fact of being in a covenantal partnership with God is an aspect of Christian spirituality that could be developed using the covenantal meal of the Communion Service. As the Apostle Paul stated in 1 Corinthians 11:23-26:

> For I received from the Lord what I also passed on to you: The Lord Jesus, on the night he was betrayed, took bread, and when he had given thanks, he broke it and said, "This is my body, which is for you; do this in remembrance of me." In the same way, after supper he took the cup saying, "This cup is the new covenant in my blood; do this, whenever you drink it, in remembrance of me." For whenever you eat this bread and drink this cup, you proclaim the Lord's death until he comes.

Since the time of that hot Australian summer afternoon when the words "the new covenant in my blood" began to challenge my thinking, I have taken a number of opportunities in celebrating communion to consider the Christians' new covenant. Symbolically we eat the body and drink the blood of Christ in a ceremony as old as Melchizedek. In doing so we identify Jesus as our covenant partner and we accept all the associated benefits and obligations of such a covenant arrangement. Yet I told my church only part of the story. There are other requirements that need to be applied. Not only should we look back at the cross and remember the covenant sacrifice, but we should also look to the future and continue to "proclaim the Lord's death until he comes." The proclaiming of the covenantal relationship we have with God through faith in Jesus needs to be constant; and one way to do so is through actively participating in the covenantal meal of communion. God is still using the forms and meanings of the Hebraic covenant to share the gospel with the whole world.

Chapter 10

Meaning Equivalence Contextualization

Charles H. Kraft

For the last several years, it has been commonplace to speak of contextualization, localization, or inculturation as the ideal toward which we strive in the planting and nurturing of Christian churches. By this we mean that it is important for people to receive and express Christianity in culturally appropriate ways.

Our discussions of this topic, however, have all too often tended to focus on finding the appropriate cultural *forms* through which to express either theological truths or structural necessities. Well and good. Finding the proper forms is absolutely crucial to the conveying of the proper meanings. The wrong cultural forms in the receiving society result in the wrong meanings in the minds of the people.

But it is because of our concern for meanings that we must be so concerned about the forms. The forms are not important for their own sakes. They are important for the sake of the meanings. When, for example, the form of a church building, or the music or rituals used therein are interpreted by the people of a given society as foreign and not their own, we say that the wrong forms are being used. But this is not because there is anything inherently wrong with those forms. Indeed, they may be just the right forms in another sociocultural context. The problem is that the use of those forms signal certain meanings that are theologically wrong since they are not what the Scriptures show to be God's intent.

Cultural Forms (Or Customs)

Culture is made up of what we call "cultural forms." Forms are the customs, the ideas, the patterns and structures in which we live and move and have our being. In language, words, sentences, and paragraphs are cultural forms. Beyond language, material objects such as chairs, pencils, cars, and dishes are cultural forms. So are non-material items such as ceremonies, ideas, and beliefs.

Cultural forms are used by the people of a society in the living of their lives. We often refer to them popularly as customs. We may speak, then, of forms or customs that are linguistic, religious, political, economic, family, educational, etc. We may even speak of deep-level, largely subconscious worldview assumptions as cultural forms.

Forms, then, are the vehicles of culture and worldview. By definition, every custom, whether visible or invisible, is a cultural form. The forms are the basic elements of culture. Cultural forms are what people use to live their lives. How we use each cultural form, then, provides the basis on which people interpret what we are doing.

Any given form can be the vehicle of more than one meaning. For example, an automobile may mean such things as transportation from one place to another, status for those who buy expensive cars to show off their prosperity, trouble and expense when it needs fixing, freedom from dependence on other people and other means of transportation, coming of age for young people just getting their licenses, danger to those crossing the street and perhaps several other things. A form we call "wedding ceremony" can mean different things to the bride, the groom, the bride's parents, the attendants, the musicians, the pastor, the janitor and those in the audience. The same musical forms can mean one thing to the members of the younger generation and quite another thing to their elders.

People choose the language forms they use on the basis of the meanings those forms will convey to those they are talking to. I am attempting to be careful as I write to use just the right language forms to enable you, the reader, to understand what I mean.

The Input of Communication Theory

A major assist in understanding the dynamics of contextualization comes from the field of communication theory. It is axiomatic that the response we seek from the receptors of gospel communication will be based on the receptors' interpretation of the life and messages coming from those seeking to communicate Christianity. If we are to guide that interpretation so that our receptors understand and work toward appropriate contextualization, we need ourselves to understand the process of communication and to be able to use the principles effectively.

There are two primary areas of understanding to be gleaned from communication theory. They concern receptors and meaning. What follows is a listing of several important principles relating to each of these areas.[1]

Receptors

1. *Receptors are parts of reference groups.* Receptors (like all humans) are never alone, even when they are "by themselves." Whether one lives in an individualistic society like we Americans do or in a strongly group oriented

---

[1] For more detail, see my books *Communication Theory for Christian Witness* (1991a) or *Communicating Jesus' Way* (1999).

society like those of most of the Two-Thirds World, we always consider the reactions of others when we make decisions. Whenever an appeal is made to people to consider a change of opinion or behavior, their basic question is, What will the people in my group think?

All humans are related to reference groups whose opinions strongly affect the choices they make. Any change a person contemplates and/or carries out is, therefore, made in relation to the person's perception of the desires of such a group. If the person feels his/her reference group is likely to react negatively to a given decision, it is probable that the person will turn away from that decision. Or the person may make the decision, later discover that his/her group is against it, and go back on the decision.

2. *Receptors are committed to their group and to the values of that group.* When approaches are made to people to make changes in their attitudes and/or behavior, it cannot be assumed that they are not already committed to competing attitudes and/or behavior. People do not operate in a vacuum. People not only exist in groups, they are committed to those groups and for what they stand for. This is a deep-level commitment. And people often feel they are being asked to be disloyal to family and society when approached with the challenge to make a total commitment to Jesus Christ.

People are usually more open to changes that appeal to their own self-interest. If a new commitment can be presented in such a way that the receptors feel their positions in life will be improved if they make that change, they are likely to be more open to it—that is, if it isn't perceived to cost them too much socially. Christianity, of course, offers quite a number of good things that can appeal to receptors' self-interest if presented rightly. Many people are looking for such Christian benefits as a more meaningful life, peace, forgiveness, freedom from fear, release from physical, emotional or spiritual captivities and the like, not to mention eternal life. To effectively appeal for people to give up previous commitments to gain these benefits is one of the greatest challenges of the Christian communicator.

3. If Christian appeals are to be attractive they need to be addressed to the *felt needs* of the receptors. An important thing to recognize, though, is that human beings never seem to be fully satisfied with whatever their state in life. And no sociocultural system seems to adequately provide for every need felt by the people within that system. Those left over problems, therefore, provide fertile ground for any communicator prepared to discover and provide answers for them. Like Jesus, we are to allow receptors to articulate their need (e.g., the rich young man of Mt. 19:16–22, blind Bartimaeus in Mk. 10:46–52, and the Samaritan woman of Jn. 4). We then can deal with whatever the receptors are conscious of and thus gain their permission to deal with the deeper needs that may be on our agenda.

The appeal to needs perceived by receptors is a crucial dimension of effective communication. We cannot, however, assume that those we seek to reach understand life in exactly the same way we understand it. We need, therefore, to do whatever research is necessary to discover where our receptors are and what they perceive their needs to be before we attempt to speak to them. Only when we have a fair idea of what they see to be their unanswered problems, should we seek to discover how to apply Scriptural answers to them. Merely applying even Scriptural answers to questions they are not asking seldom works well.

4. *Receptors are always interpreting.* And everything about the communicational situation gets interpreted. The communicators' words are, of course, interpreted. But so are their tone of voice, gestures, use of space, general appearance and the like. Interpretation is clearly one of the most important, though least conscious, of the activities of receptors. And most of it is based on what the receptors have learned through past experience, rather than on their experience in the present situation.

5. These interpretations feed directly into the most important of the receptors' activities, that of *constructing the meanings* that result from the communicational interaction (see below on meanings). It is messages, not meanings, that are transmitted from person to person. These messages are usually in linguistic form. The meanings, then, exist only in the hearts and minds of people. Contemporary communicologists see communicators with meanings in their minds that they would like to transmit to receptors. Communicators take these meanings and formulate them into messages that they then transmit to receptors. Receptors listen to the messages and construct within their minds sets of meanings that may or may not correspond with the meanings intended by the communicator.

6. Receptors, then, either *grant or withhold permission* for any given message to enter what might be termed the receptor's "communicational space." Receptors may be pictured as encased in a kind of bubble which only they can give permission to enter. When someone wants to transact or negotiate some form of communication, then, he/she needs to gain permission for the interaction from the one who can control access to that bubble. The transactional nature of communication requires that each participant gain the permission of the other in order to either initiate or continue the interaction. The attitude of the participants toward each other is, of course, crucial to the nature of the interaction. Permission may, for example, be more readily given to persons of higher prestige than oneself, to persons whom one trusts, to those in authority over oneself, to those with greater expertise than oneself, to those whose favor one seeks, to those whom one perceives as interested in oneself and the like.

Whether or not a receptor grants permission for a message to enter also relates to what may be termed the "range of tolerance" of that receptor for the particular type of message presented and/or for the person presenting the message. A communicator needs to give high priority to the winning of the permission of his/her receptors. Once permission is gained, however, it is not certain that it will be retained until the end of the communication. For receptors evaluate as the interaction continues and sometimes take back permission once granted before the event is over. Sometimes such withdrawal can be read in the receptors' behavior as feedback.

7. Closely related to the activity of giving permission is that of *evaluating the message*. In any communicational interaction the participants evaluate each component of that experience. The communicator, the message, and the receptors are all evaluated and so is the total situation in relation to similar experiences the participants have had in the past and whatever expectations they have concerning the future. From this evaluation the participants construct an overall impression of the situation, an impression that has much to do with how they interpret what goes on in that situation.

8. Another closely related kind of activity in which receptors are engaged is the matter of *selectivity*. People are selective in the kinds of things they allow themselves to be exposed to. If they fear something, it is unlikely that they will allow themselves to be exposed to it unless they are forced to. If they allow themselves to be exposed to something, however, and then find that it is disagreeable, they can refuse to pay attention.

Even if people are paying attention, though, they may or may not perceive what is being communicated in the way the communicator intends. People tend to perceive messages in such a way that they confirm already held positions, whether or not the communicator intended them that way. This is usually done unconsciously and relates to their overall evaluation of the situation and the various components of it. It also relates strongly to their past experiences and their perception of how the new information relates to what they already know.

9. Receiving communication is a risky business. Receptors are, therefore, continually *seeking to maintain their equilibrium* in the face of such actual or imagined risk. Whenever people expose themselves to communication they are risking the possibility that they might have to change some aspect of their lives. People ordinarily seek at all costs to maintain their present equilibrium, to protect themselves from assimilating anything that is perceived to possibly upset their psychological balance.

Receptors and Contextualization

All of these principles apply to our task of advocating appropriate Christianity. The commitment of people to their reference groups is a major obstacle to any group such as Christian witnesses who seeks to get them to change their allegiance. Allegiance to family is probably the major commitment of most of the peoples of the world. But Jesus demands that He be our primary allegiance (Mt. 10:37-38). Getting this fact across in a winsome way to people who are exhibiting all of the above characteristics of receptors, then, is an incredible challenge.

We need, therefore, to discover a people's felt needs and present our messages in such a way that they will interpret what we say and do as relating to those needs. The messages they hear, however, will be those that they construct, largely from the materials in their own minds, with or without much understanding of where we are coming from. For example, the ready reception of schools by many of the peoples of East Africa is reported to have been based on their perception that schooling would give them spiritual power. They assumed that the power of the Europeans was spiritual power and that the way to obtain this power was through attending school. This misinterpretation resulted, of course, in a felt need for schools, a need that the missionaries were quick to take advantage of. What neither the missionaries nor the East Africans anticipated was the pervasive secularization that came with the schools.

Contextualizers need to be constantly aware of the process of interpretation that is going on with receptors and the fact that they will interpret from their own point of view, whether or not that is even close to our intent. When there is a wide cultural gap between those who bring the gospel and those who receive it, then, we can assume that the potential for misinterpretation is great. I found it a challenge, for example, to deal with Noah and his ark and, for that matter, the fact that we had come to Nigeria in a large ship with northern Nigerians. For the largest watercraft they had ever seen was a canoe! The story of how God got all those animals onto one canoe proved to be an enormous test of the Nigerians' faith.

A more serious problem exists in Japan where the Japanese word *kami* is used for God. This is the word for any spirit. In the animistic perspective of the Japanese, such spirits are powerful, capricious, and dangerous, requiring constant vigilance and appeasement to keep them happy. The same spirits may be good at one time, especially if they are kept happy, but bad at another time, especially if displeased or neglected. Given, then, that Japanese people, whether nonChristian or Christian will attach their own meanings to this term, is it any wonder that there is in Japan widespread misunderstanding of the Christian God and how people should behave in relation to Him?

A major part of our job as contextualizers is, then, to do whatever we can to help people to arrive at meanings that are as close as possible to the Scriptures by which we seek to be guided. This will, however, involve a process of redefinition of terms that are chosen as labels for elements of Christian faith. For those Japanese who are able to redefine *kami* in a scriptural direction, for example, that cultural form will be adequate to symbolize the biblical meaning. I'm afraid, though, that the preChristian associations of that term may greatly interfere with the understandings of those who use the term to refer to the Christian God.

A major problem is, however, that if the word *kami* is not used, what term should be used? It is usually a poor choice to borrow a term from another language. In Hausa, for example, the word *ekklesia* has been borrowed from Greek to designate the Christian church. Had one of the Hausa words for a gathering or a fellowship been used, the people would be able to understand such groupings as normal. As it is, the taint of foreignness is always on the church because of its foreign name. Insiders may in time overcome that taint.

But those outside the church will tend to regard that term as an intrusion into their society rather than an understandable expression of certain members of the society.

With regard to the word for church in Hausa, the choice of *ekklesia* is regrettable since there are other possibilities from within the language. With *kami*, however, Japanese Christians feel there is no better alternative. So their choice is to work toward transforming the meaning of the word. They want to "capture" that word for Christ as the first century Christians did with *kurios*, the Greek word for Lord. *Kurios* was used as the title of Caesar, signifying his deity. The Christians chose this word to apply to Jesus and were killed when they refused to use it to refer to Caesar.

God wants His people to capture customs also. Throughout the Old Testament we see God using customs of worship and sacrifice that were also used by pagans. When God and Abraham began working together, the message to Abraham was, "From now on use your culture for Me." So God was worshipped in "high places," just as pagan gods were. And blood sacrifices were offered to Yahweh, just as they were by pagans to their gods. Indeed, God even reintroduced the ritual of circumcision that was practiced by the surrounding people but had apparently lapsed in Abraham's culture. But, though the universal meaning of the custom was initiation into the tribe, God gave it an additional meaning—commitment to Him.

In contemporary Japan, I have suggested that the Christians experiment with the development of Christian shrines. People go to shrines when they seek blessing, protection, healing and supernatural answers to specific requests. Shrines are known as places of power and people go to them at any time of the day (not just on Sundays). Given their concern for spiritual power, Japanese are unlikely to go to churches when they feel the need for power since churches don't look like places of power. And anyway, they usually are not open except at specified times during the week. A shrine in which people met Christians who would pray with them concerning their needs would soon gain a reputation as a good place to go for help. It would also provide a good first step into Christian groupings (hopefully contextualized) in which people could grow in understanding and commitment to Christ.

One of the most important dynamics of contextualization[2] is the capturing of such terms and customs to invest them with new meanings that serve the purposes of Christianity. If such terms and customs are to undergo the transformation required for this to happen, the Christian community must put constant pressure on its people to use the terms and customs with Christian meanings. If such pressure is not put on the users of the terms and customs, the meanings will continue to be traditional, with little or no Christian significance.

---

[2] See Chapter 11.

Our respondents will be selective, often unconsciously, of what they allow themselves to be exposed to, and they will evaluate everything they hear and see—again in terms of their past experiences with similar activities. When they see Christian churches that look foreign and Christian people who behave strangely, they will be open or closed to them on the basis of their general attitude toward that foreignness. And they either will or will not grant permission to those who represent Christianity to enter into their "communicational space." Unless they feel that the foreign organization will meet some of the needs they feel, they are most likely to attempt to maintain their equilibrium by staying as close as possible to their previous understandings and involvements. That is, there must be something that attracts them to the foreign organization for them to risk the possibility of change and perhaps social disequilibrium.

In order to cope with the challenges of new appeals, people often build walls around themselves in such a way that they can shed anything they hear that would put pressure on them to change their lifestyle. They can refuse to take seriously whatever they choose to ignore or they may pick and choose the things that require the least change. Effective contextualization takes all these communicational things into account both in the introductory stages of gospel presentation and in the continuing experience of the growth of the Christian movement.

Meanings

There has been a great deal of discussion down through the years concerning meaning. Some have claimed that meanings are simply contained in the linguistic and cultural forms people use to convey them. It is, however, obvious that different people regularly assign different meanings to the same cultural forms. And, if we expose people of widely different cultures to the same forms, the interpretations differ widely. Meanings, then, are the result of interpretation.

Meanings are the interpretation of cultural forms. They are assigned by people and in a sense "flow" through the forms as people interpret them. Whenever people use cultural forms in the presence of others, meanings are attached to them first by the person(s) who originate the forms and then by those who hear or observe them.

Meanings lie within people, not in either the external world or in the symbols we use to describe that world. Meaning is a personal thing, internal to persons rather than either a part of the world outside or of the symbols people use. Meanings, being personal, are attached by people to message symbols according to cultural rules in their minds.

This fact is well stated by David Berlo when he says:

Meanings are in people, [they are] covert responses, contained within the human organism. Meanings . . . are personal, our own property. We learn meanings, we add to them, we distort them, forget them, change them. We cannot find them. They are in us, not in messages. Fortunately, we usually find other people who have meanings that are similar to ours. To the extent that people have similar meanings, they can communicate. If they have no similarities in meaning between them, they cannot communicate (1960:175).

Communication does not consist of the transmission of meaning. Meaning does not inhere in linguistic and other cultural forms. Meanings are, rather, attached to those forms by the people who use them. For meanings are not *contained* in forms, though they are *conveyed* by them. Meanings are in people. It is people who attach meanings to the linguistic, religious, political, economic and other forms of culture they use. Meaning is, therefore, a function of personal interpretation on the basis of social agreements rather than something inherent in the forms themselves.

Meanings are not transmittable, not transferable. Only messages are transmittable, and meanings are not in the message, they are in the message-users. Meaning is the result of interpretation. And interpretation is the subjective interaction of one or more persons with a situation. What that situation means to the person is what he/she comes away with from that situation. And persons attach their meanings independently of each other, though ordinarily in keeping with habits they have learned to share with other members of their community.

But forms and meanings always come together in real life. Only as we analyze the communication process do we distinguish between the two. There are no forms that people don't attach meaning to—no forms without meanings as long as there are people around to interpret them. And there is no communication or understanding of meanings without cultural forms—no meanings conveyed in human life except through cultural forms.

The forms that are used are, therefore, extremely important to the communication process. They need to be the forms that the receptors will interpret as meaning what the communicator intended. If, therefore, a message generated by one group is to be effectively presented to another group, the forms/symbols used to convey that message need to be those "owned" by the receiving group, whether or not they are the same as those preferred by the generating group. For meanings are attached on the basis of group agreements developed from the shared life experience of the group.

These facts result in several implications of relevance to the process of contextualization:

1. The first is that in every communicational situation we can point to at least *two separate "realities" or views of reality*. The first may be labeled *Objective (or "capital R") Reality.* This is the Reality that God alone is able to see and know in an undistorted way. This Reality includes all that actually

exists and happens in the world. It includes all that goes on both external to and internal to the participants in a communicational interaction.

Each participant in a communicational situation, then, has *his/her own perception of the Reality* of that situation. The communicator sees in terms of what may be labeled the communicator's reality. Receptors, however, understand in terms of their reality. The receptors' reality, though, is likely to be different from that of the communicator—less different if they are a part of the same culture, more different if their cultures are different. And communicational interactants act and react in terms of their *perceived* reality, rather than according to the objective Reality of the situation. Both communicator and receptor, then, respond not to what is actually said or done, but to what each perceives to have been said or done. The materials with which each is working to construct meaning, therefore, lie not in the objective details of the interaction, but in their subjective interpretations of the situation.

Meanings, then, "are the internal responses that people make to stimuli" (Berlo 1960:184) based on their perception of the stimuli from within their own realities. On the basis of these meanings both the reality from which communicators respond and the reality to which receptors respond are constructed.

2. A second implication of this view is the *importance to the process of communication of the personal relationship between the participants*. The personal nature of the assignment of meaning requires that we give at least as much attention to the relationships between the participants. The dynamics of the relationship between the communicators and the receptors provide them with crucial information concerning how to interpret what is really meant by what each says and does.

It is crucial that we keep ourselves continually aware of this factor. It is too easy to focus on the words we speak and to ignore the relational aspect of communication unless something goes radically wrong. When the relationship between the interactants is healthy, they may be quite unconscious of the part that relational healthiness plays in their ability to communicate effectively. If, however, the relationship is "sick," the interactants will be constantly hindered in their attempts to effectively convey content to each other.

Jesus, of course, based His whole ministry on the personal relationships He had with a fairly small group of followers. It was His life involvement with them that enabled His messages to get across at such a deep level. His example confirms a major insight of those who have studied communication theory. It also provides for us the right example for us to imitate.

3. A third implication of this view is that *those with similar perceptions of similar experiences are most likely to construct similar meanings*. It is not enough to have similar experiences. Persons must perceive them similarly if they are to come out with similar meanings.

The fact that people live in cultural groups within which they conduct most of their interpersonal interactions leads to the members of each group agreeing that given symbols are to be interpreted in the same way. This raises to a very high level the predictability of similar interpretations and responses to similar stimuli on the part of the members of any given group.

4. The personalness of communication results in the fact that *meanings are more felt than reasoned.* The immediate response of people to any given situation is more likely to be emotional than rational. If, however, they think over the event, they may revise their earlier reaction on the basis of a more rational consideration. First impressions based on feeling are, however, very difficult to shake, even when considered rationally.

5. A further implication derives from the nature of the Christian message. For *this message is far more than a verbal message—it is a "person message."* God specializes in messages that are personal rather than simply informational. Information messages such as those about scientific facts, the world news or weather don't require good behavior on the part of the communicator to make them valid. God's messages, however, require a high degree of personal involvement. For in this kind of message, the person who brings the message is a major part of the message he/she brings.

✝ God Himself is the message, and we are to respond to a person to properly attach meaning to that message. At the purely human level, we do the same thing with messages of love, care, concern, sympathy and the like—we respond not simply to words but to the person who does the deed. Such messages are only effectively conveyed by life rubbing against life. The ultimate Christian message, then, is a person. And anything that reduces that message to mere words stimulates in the receptor meanings unworthy of the message. Our message is a message of life and only life can properly convey it. Thus, only if that message is actually conveyed by life can it be properly understood.

Meaning Equivalence Christianity

Years ago (1979a), I suggested the concept of "dynamic equivalence" used in Bible translation as a useful label for what we intend by the term "contextualization." An alternate term for dynamic equivalence would be "meaning equivalence."

The idea is that what people do in response to Christ today should carry the same meanings as the ideals presented in the Scriptures. Not that those ideals are always readily deduced. As some of my critics have pointed out, the Bible does not always show us how even the Early Churches worked out their Christian experience. We do, however, know some of the ideals. And it is these meanings that a Christianity that is appropriate to Scripture and to culture will attempt to exhibit.

We know, for example, such things as that Jesus Christ is to be the center of Christian life for each person, whether we are alone, at home or at church.

We are to be committed to Him and to strive to be like Him. We are to love God with all our heart, soul, mind and strength and our neighbors as ourselves (Mt. 22:37). We also know that Christians are to meet together in groups for fellowship, prayer and Bible study. The New Testament shows that Christian fellowship groups were organized and that they believed certain cardinal doctrines concerning God, Jesus (Phil. 2), sin (Rom. 3:23; 6:23), salvation (Jn. 3:16; Ac. 16:31), etc.

From many of the things the Apostle Paul and other New Testament writers mentioned, we know a lot of specifics concerning the kind of behavior Christians are expected to exhibit. We know that Christian groups are to stand for righteousness and to discipline their members who willfully turn from righteousness. We are to exhibit the fruits of the Spirit (Gal. 5:19), we are to do the works that Jesus did (Jn. 14:12), we are to live dependent on Jesus as He was dependent on the Father, and so on. The ideals are fairly clear.

The problems lie in how these ideals are to be appropriately expressed in any given society. What, for example, is an appropriate expression of love—an expression that insiders will interpret as love. Mission history is full of attempts by outsiders to show love that were interpreted as something else by the insiders. In our area, for example, our mission was deeply involved in attempting to show love through schools, medical clinics, and hospitals. These efforts, however, were largely understood by the cultural insiders as ways to make money (clinics and hospitals) or converts to Euro-American culture (schools). And the fact that schools were the primary ways of recruiting people for the churches led people to assume that one couldn't become a Christian unless he/she went to school or at least learned to read.

One medical effort of the mission did, however, seem to get love across. The mission in the early years started a leprosarium, a place where lepers came to live. At the leprosarium people in great need, a need that traditional medicine was unable to meet, received loving treatment from doctors and nurses and soon became part of a meaningful community, even across language and culture barriers. The way they were treated in the leprosarium contrasted markedly with the way they had been treated at home and the message of God's love came across loud and clear. Though the church at the leprosarium was only partly contextualized, it seemed to be less dominated by the missionaries than the other churches in the area.

The difference between the leprosarium and the other mission stations seemed to center around the fact that important needs were being met—both medical needs and social needs—and the fact that more time was invested in those who lived there. A Christian community was brought into existence and in that community many grew spiritually to such an extent that in the early 1950s when, due to the advent of new medicine, most of them were released from the community, many went back to their tribal areas and become important witnesses for Christ.

Christian meanings seem to have gotten across better in the leprosarium than elsewhere in the mission area. These meanings also got across better wherever the missionary or Nigerian pastor spent a lot of time with the people. We have said that meanings are *in* people. Christian meanings are also *through* people. So, when the advocates of Christianity are personal, the meanings are more likely to get across than otherwise. The key to contextualization, then, as the key to communication, is the person(s) who relate(s) to the receptors.

Meaning equivalence contextualization, then, is first a relational thing before it is anything else. In 1 John 1:1-3 we get a glimpse of the impact Jesus, as a person, had on His followers. The experience of the Apostles was so intimate that John speaks of "handling" Jesus and implies that this closeness with the Master has left them radically changed and anxious to pass on the messages they have received from Him.

But Jesus was brought up in the culture in which He worked. We who come from outside need to learn the culture in which we work, or at least enough of it to be able to show love in ways appropriate to the insiders' frame of reference. Personal concern may, however, be more easily demonstrated than many of the other things we try to get across, since people are more alike than our cultures (Goldschmidt 1966:134). We may be able to tap into our basic humanbeingness to get across such concern if we take the trouble to try to do things in their way rather than in ours.

On one occasion I was discussing with a group of young cross-cultural witnesses working in inner city Los Angeles the fact that they were not getting across to an old woman they wanted to win to Christ. They had been trying to get her to come to their meetings. They had witnessed to her various times as they passed by her home on their way to their various engagements. But all she seemed to want to do was to sit on her porch and rock in her rocking chair. I asked the group if any of them had thought of sitting and rocking with her. They hadn't. They were too intent on bringing her into their orbit so they could talk to her on their terms. Considering the validity of her life and her ways of behaving and thinking, however, set this group to thinking differently—relationally rather than informationally. As someone has said, she didn't care how much they knew until she knew how much they cared.

Meaning equivalence Christianity will be rooted in relationships meaningful to the people we seek to reach.

Contextualization Is a Matter of Negotiation

It is clear, then, that whatever the cultural and linguistic forms used in the presentation of Christianity, it is the receptors who will attach the meanings. The meanings they attach to the various messages we bring can, however, be influenced to some extent, at least within an inner circle of friends. Meanings can be negotiated.

We do this all the time. Someone says something we don't quite understand and we ask for that person to repeat or to illustrate the point. As the point is worked through again, we may or may not get it. If we do, we may turn to something else. If we don't, we ask for more clarification. In this way we conduct a transaction that hopefully will result in a fairly good understanding of what the person is saying.

Such negotiation is not very effective when the means of communication is monologue. It is greatly increased when the interaction is give and take, question and answer, statement and explanation. And this kind of interaction is best when it takes place in small groups. I believe this is why Jesus worked primarily with twelve. And even when there was a larger group, He permitted questions and negotiated with His audiences.

The discipleship group around an advocate of any new message serves several purposes. The twelve got to spend more time with Jesus and, therefore, got to interact with Him more than others and, presumably, got to understand Him better. They could, therefore, interpret Him to those who did not get to spend so much time with Him. The fact that they were in contact with these others, then, enabled them to be able to communicate to Jesus what these others were thinking. See, for example, their statement in response to Jesus' query concerning what others were saying about Him (Mt. 16:13-16).

In negotiating for the meanings of Christian witness, then, it is important for the advocates to have a group of close friends who will be able to function in the communication process as Jesus' disciples did. I was privileged to have five such men. We did all kinds of things together and got to know and respect each other very well. They learned a lot about what I was thinking and I learned a lot about what their life was all about. We trusted each other and they, not I, led the church. They and I negotiated to achieve understandings of how to apply Scripture in their context. And they negotiated with their own people to implement those understandings both inside and outside of the church. What went on in the churches, then, and in the individual lives of the Christians served as a means of negotiation for certain meanings with the society at large.

Conclusion

The aim of contextualization is to see expressed in the lives of the receptors the meanings taught in Scripture. If we are to participate effectively in bringing about that kind of Christianity, it is important for us to learn as much as possible about receptor-oriented communication. And, having learned the principles, with the Holy Spirit guiding, we need to apply them in a relational manner, as Jesus did. The primary vehicle of meaning equivalence Christianity is the Christian advocate. The method is negotiation, grounded in respect for the receiving people and their way of life.

Chapter 11

Dynamics of Contextualization

Charles H. Kraft

In 1979 I published a book on contextualization entitled *Christianity in Culture* (1979a). One of the concepts I discussed in that book was the importance of the pressure put on by a community of believers to the process of cultural transformation. Specifically, once a person or group makes a commitment to Christ, they are expected to embark on a process of change in the direction of greater Christlikeness. That process is not an easy one. It ordinarily requires guidance so that people will know what the goal is and how to get there and pressure to keep them working in the right direction against their natural tendency to resist change.

It is from this perspective that I want to discuss the dynamics of contextualization. It is well and good that we discuss, as we have, the nature of Appropriate Contextualization and its various facets. But an important question is, How do we get there? Does movement toward local expressions of Christianity just happen without effort? If people are left alone with nothing but the Bible to guide them, are they likely to develop culturally and biblically appropriate forms of Christian expression?

Unfortunately, the answer to each of these last two questions is, "No." The answer to the first, How do we get there?, is more complex. And it is to the various facets of the answer to that question that I wish to direct our attention in this chapter.

The Goal

It is not necessarily obvious to people who are newly Christian what the goal of their new faith commitment is. Very few individuals who come to Christ and the groups of believers who form the churches seem to understand that the ideal for a church is that they be

> a group of believers who live out their life, including their socialized
> Christian activity, in the patterns of the local society, and for whom
> any transformation of that society comes out of their felt needs under
> the guidance of the Holy Spirit and the Scriptures. . . . An
> [appropriate] church is precisely one in which the changes which
> take place under the guidance of the Holy Spirit meet the needs and

169

fulfill the meanings of that society and not of any outside group (Smalley 1958:55-56).

Nor do they see that it is only

> When the indigenous people of a community think of the Lord as their own, not a foreign Christ; when they do things as unto the Lord meeting the cultural needs around them, worshipping in patterns they understand; when their congregations function in participation in a body, which is structurally indigenous; then you have an *[appropriate]* Church (Tippett 1973:158).

Though we may seek for "an expression of Christianity that is both culturally authentic and genuinely Christian" (Kraft 1980:214), for many, the goal in their minds may be nothing more than achieving new and more powerful friends, or the benefits of schooling, or the chance to perhaps travel overseas. For others, it may be some other personal or social attraction. But even if the motivation for coming to Christ is more or less pure, converts may be puzzled as to what comes next.

As we know, the Christian community may be living far below any ideal for the Christian life that we find in Scripture. And new converts may not even know they are supposed to live up to Scriptural ideals, especially if they, like seventy percent of the world, cannot read. Christians may not be more moral, more honest or more admirable than nonChristians, and they may not know they are supposed to be. In addition, they may be more westernized, which may be a plus or a minus to those considering turning to Christianity.

Such characteristics, however, may not be entirely the fault of the Christians themselves. The local Christians may simply be ignorant of the need for change that is so prominent in Scripture. For they may know little of what the Scriptures teach. They may be illiterate or not functionally literate in an area where the missionaries focused on reading rather than hearing (e.g., via cassettes) the Bible. The missionaries may have conducted literacy campaigns but been unaware of the fact that most literacy campaigns fail to bring people to a position in which they are able to get new information from reading.

Furthermore, what they have learned concerning the need for change may have focused more on changes of custom in the direction of certain Western practices than on learning to express Scriptural ideals in their own cultural context. They may have been presented with Christianity as religion or from their own perspective interpreted the new message that way, rather than learning that it is a faith relationship with God that can be expressed in their own way. They then assumed that all they needed to do was to adopt and adapt a new set of religious customs.

If the confusion is to be overcome, then, we must be clear concerning what a Christian in any society should be aiming for. What is the goal toward which Christians are to move? We have stated the goal of cultural appropriateness above. This is an appropriateness in *meaning* and *commitment*. No cultural forms in use for Christian purposes are appropriate if people attribute to them the wrong meanings or fail to get into the right relationship with God.[1]

Appropriateness to the Scriptures, then, means appropriate Scriptural meanings in the receptors' minds with appropriate responses to those meanings. The ideals presented in Scripture are, therefore, important goals for a people to understand and to express in life. Things like righteousness, truthfulness, kindness, compassion, humility, love and the rest of the fruits of the Spirit (Gal. 5:22-23) immediately come to mind—all expressed in ways appropriate to the culture. I would add ministering in the love and power of Jesus. Most of these are manifested in observable behavior. Other, not so easily observable things should be added, however. Among these are closeness to Jesus, prayerfulness, the ability to resist temptation and a God-approved thought life. All of these add up to being like Jesus, the perfect example of what humankind was intended to be—again expressed in culturally appropriate ways.

The ideals seem clear in the abstract. But questions arise when we recognize that Christianity is meant to be contextualized and ask how these ideals should look in a culture quite different from that of the persons who brought the message. For each society will have its own definitions of righteousness, love and all the rest of the visible behaviors. And there may be differences between peoples when it comes to some of the invisible behaviors as well.

A start toward an appropriate goal may, however, be made by attempting to imagine what Jesus' behavior might look like in any given society. How would He show righteousness, love, compassion, etc., in culturally appropriate ways in society X? And how would He express prayerfulness and closeness to the Father in that society? And how would Jesus avoid the trap that both missionaries and nationals ordinarily fall into of borrowing behavioral patterns from a foreign culture?

The goal, then, is clear. But the implementation is a challenge, in terms of our aim to see produced a contextually appropriate Christianity.

The Uniqueness of Christianity

As discussed in Chapter 6, biblical Christian faith is unique, especially when compared with the religions of the world. For, as mentioned above, it is a matter of meanings, not of cultural forms. Religions are locked into certain cultural forms. They come in cultural containers. If one is to be an orthodox Muslim, for example, there are certain ways of worship, modes of dress and memorization of the Koran in Arabic that are required—all of which are parts of the culture of origin of Islam. Likewise with Hinduism, Judaism, Buddhism, Shinto and all the rest.

---

[1] See Chapter 6 on whether or not Christianity is a religion and Chapter 9 on meaning equivalence Christianity for more on this subject.

Animism, the faith of probably three-quarters of the peoples of the world—including most of the adherents of the above-named religions—may be an exception to the above rule. The reason is that this is Satan's cleverest counterfeit of Christianity and is, therefore, adaptable to—contextualized in—any culture just as Christianity is supposed to be.

Biblical Christianity (as opposed to the religion called Christianity) is not intended to be merely a religion. Jesus said, "I am come that they might have *life* (Jn. 10:10, emphasis added). And this life, according to the Apostle Paul is to be expressed in Jewish culture by Jews and in Gentile culture by Gentiles (1 Cor. 9:19-21). The intended cultural container for Christianity, then, is not that in which our faith was born but that in which those who receive it live. Ours is a "receptor-oriented" faith, made up of meanings and life-expressions that are intended to be detached from its cultural source when embraced by those of societies other than the Jewish society in which it was born.

For this reason we talk about contextualization rather than adaptation. Religions can be adapted to a certain extent to the receptors' culture. But, in addition to the adapted forms, the religions of the world (except for animism) always require cultural forms that originated in the source culture. Christianity, however, is made up of commitments and meanings that can and should be expressed in cultural forms that bear no such stigma of foreignness. The fact that many cultural expressions of Christianity have failed in this regard is unfortunate. This fact, then, produces an agenda for Christian leaders who understand that if Christianity is to be appropriate in any given society it should be expressed in cultural forms as different from those of another cultural expression of Christianity as the overall forms of that culture differ from those of the culture in question.

Some may object to this characterization of the uniqueness of Christianity vis-à-vis the culture in which it is expressed. They might contend that such elements of Christianity as worship, church and the sacraments are givens that need to be expressed in all cultures as they were in the New Testament. I would contend in response that each of these things and all else in Christianity are to be planted in every society as *meanings*, not as forms. That is, our faith is to involve us in worship, but how worship of the true God is appropriately expressed in any given society can and should be quite different. It should be easily identifiable by cultural insiders as worship.

We can point to Japanese Christianity for an example of the ignoring of this principle. One traditional form of worship in Japan (perhaps not the only one), is to go to a shrine to honor the god (*kami*) of that shrine by pouring water over a stone representation of that god (plus perhaps doing additional things) and asking it for a blessing. Unlike Western Christians who worship only at set times, Japanese are accustomed to performing such rites to seek spiritual power at shrines at any time of day and well into the night (the shrines I observed closed from about 11:00 pm to about 7:00 am). A culturally appropriate form of Christian worship—one that would be easily interpretable by nonChristian

Japanese as meaning worship—would involve the use of places and rituals similar to the shrine places and practices. We would not, of course, bathe idols. But establishing places that look to Japanese like they are places where one can meet God (the word *kami* is used for the Christian God as well as for pagan spirits) would go a long way toward communicating to Japanese that God wants to enter their culture rather than simply to convert them to American cultural worship forms.

As with worship, so with church. The groupings called church in the New Testament were appropriate to each of the cultures in which they functioned—synagogue-type churches in Jewish culture, house churches in Gentile cultures. American churches are often quite different in many ways from New Testament churches, as they should be. The structuring of the church in other societies should, like worship and all the other structuring involved in Christian expression, also be easily understood by the receptors (nonChristians as well as Christians) as serving the biblical function intended by God. These functions should be culturally appropriate and, therefore, enable the receptors to readily attach the proper meanings to them without the need of learning what these things signify in the culture of the foreigners who brought the Christian message.

With regard to the sacraments, I would contend (contrary to some opinions) that for Christianity to be appropriate in a culture in which rice and *sake* are the typical food and drink for special occasions, these should be used in communion services. And the way initiation is regularly done in any given society should provide the model for the initiation into Christianity that we call baptism. If people want to borrow the traditional baptismal and communion forms in order to demonstrate their solidarity with the worldwide Christian community, okay. But this is not required and may mark Christian faith in that society as foreign, especially if the foreign elements make up a large part of the ceremony. If used, then, these "historically Christian forms" should be practiced as parts of larger traditional events so that people understand the significance and importance of the ceremonies.

For in many societies initiation ceremonies are quite elaborate. Thus, if entrance into Christianity is to be seen as important, the initiation ceremony needs to be elaborate. An elaborate ceremony, then, opens up the possibility of performing most of the ceremony in a culturally appropriate way but including the foreign baptismal custom as a small part of that ritual. A people could do something very much like their own cultural tradition for initiation and fellowship that is both understandable and meaningful to cultural insiders with the forms of worldwide Christian tradition added. When the percentage of foreign elements in a mostly traditional ceremony is small, the people of a given society would ordinarily have little problem recognizing the whole ceremony as theirs. That would be appropriate Christian ritual.

The point is that *Christian expression is to be translated culturally as well as linguistically*. Just as we expect the words of a good Bible translation to be easily interpretable by the receptors, so the other forms—the cultural forms—in terms of which our faith is expressed should be such that the receptors assign the correct meanings to them. This is the Apostle Paul's intent when he uses Jewish cultural forms to appeal to Jews with a message that is intended to convey God's meanings through their familiar forms. It is also his intent when he uses Gentile cultural forms to express that message in ways that enable Gentiles to correctly interpret God's meanings (1 Cor. 9:19-22).

The Process

In *Christianity in Culture* I presented a number of models to help us think through the various aspects of theologizing in relation to culture. One of those models is what I have called "Point Plus Process." This model simply labels the fact that God starts with people where they are and then seeks to partner with them to move them toward Christlikeness. Once again, though, it is culturally appropriate Christlikeness that we seek.

In working with people who have recently chosen Christ, it is important to help them understand that, though God accepts them as they are, He has no intention of leaving them that way. Though it is not Jesus' intent to take them out of their familiar cultural life, they are to be changed within that cultural context. Change is built into true Christianity with the goal of Christlikeness firmly in view.

God has no problem accepting a selfish person who, even perhaps from selfish motivation, comes to Him through Jesus. But it is God's intent to work with that person toward selflessness. God will, likewise, accept people deep in habitual sin. But it is His intent to work with and empower such people to gain victory over both the sin and the habits. He regularly partners with unloving people to make them loving, with proud people to make them humble, with liars to make them truthful, with uncompassionate people to develop compassion in them. And none of this with the additional requirement that they adopt the customs of another people.

Likewise, God has no problem with accepting people who at the start are not loving toward other people groups. An important part of the movement toward maturity of such people (probably all of us) is, however, that they learn that God loves all of us, even our enemies, and that we are to love everyone also. We are taught in Scripture to love even our enemies (Lk. 6:27-36). This is the ideal toward which we all are to work. Few there be, though, who are already practicing such love when they come to Christ.

A basic principle of God's interaction with humans has been codified in what has been termed "the Homogeneous Unit Principle." This principle, simply stated, is that God accepts people groups as they are, with all of their idiosyncrasies and subChristian practices when they turn to Him in faith. Where God starts with a people is not, however, where He intends to end with them. At the start, He accepts and endorses their homogeneity, their groupness, ignoring for the time being their exclusiveness and even animosity toward other people groups. But an important part of their growth in Christianity is to be the recognition that even enemies who belong to Jesus are their brothers and sisters and are, therefore, to be accepted as "us" rather than "them."

So, when we talk of people growing in their Christian experience, we are talking about the process of change that God expects of them. Where He starts is not where He intends to end. The start is the beginning point of a process during which a convert moves toward Christian maturity.

Motivation to Change

A problem in all of this is the fact that people tend to be culturally conservative and unwilling to expend the energy required to change habits and customs. They are not, therefore, usually seeking to change, unless it is obvious that there is some major benefit to be gained. The economic principle of gain minus cost is often key in the thinking of those considering change. That is, if they count the cost of the change (e.g., the possibility that their family might turn against them) and subtract that from the anticipated benefit (e.g., eternity with God in heaven), and decide that the latter gain is more valuable than the former cost, they may be willing to make the change—if they are willing to expend the necessary energy.

Since it is habit that keeps people following their customs, it is habits that have to be changed. And changing habits is hard work, even if a person or group is highly motivated. Such change, then, is even more difficult if the goals are clear. If people are highly motivated to make the recommended changes, there can be great success. If, however, their motivation is not high and/or the goals not clear, the process of change may not go very far.

A place where agents of change often fail is in the setting of clear goals. Many American converts, for example, are welcomed into the Kingdom when they first decide for Christ but not realistically informed as to what awaits them in their journey with Christ in the years to come. They may be taught that there is something called "Christian maturity" toward which they should strive. But just what that amounts to may be quite vague. In cross-cultural situations, then, the closest thing to defining the goals toward which people are to strive may be the impression people receive that they should imitate Westerners. Such external things as learning to read, having only one wife, earning a salary and living like Euroamericans may (whether consciously or unconsciously) be considered requirements for spiritual growth.

The challenge for contextualizers, then, is to discover what the goals should be in any given society and to make them clear to the Christian populace. For the marks of spiritual maturity in one society should not automatically be considered normative for those of another society. And, in any event, the focus needs to be where Jesus put it—on internal motivation rather than simply on external behavior, though the latter should be in view as well.

If, in the process of change, we can assume that the goals are clear, great attention needs to be given to developing and increasing the motivation so that the process will go the full distance. Something as difficult as changing habits needs strong motivation to see it through.

Perhaps the two major factors in increasing the motivation necessary for permanent change are what might be termed things that "push" and things that "pull." People can be motivated toward or away from change through group pressure. Such pressure is a kind of external push factor when it is used to bring about change. Another external push factor for many is the presence of rules and/or laws. People can also be motivated toward or away from change by internal push factors such as the fear of failure in living up to the rules or fear of not keeping in good standing with the society.

Push factors that come from outside a society are likely to be less effective than those coming from within a society. Or, if outside pressure is effective, it often results in a negative reaction and a reversal of whatever change has been made once the outside force leaves. That is, outside push factors such as missionary rules may bring about fairly quick change that gets reversed once the missionaries are no longer in control. In our area of northern Nigeria the teachers in mission schools were required to be monogamous by the mission. Several of them took additional wives, however, after the government took over the schools.

In addition to push factors, there are things that pull or entice people to change. The desire to become like some admired person would be a pull factor. So would the desire of a group to become like another group. Unlike push factors, pull factors coming from outside the society can remain powerful even after those who introduced them have left.

Dissatisfaction with what already exists provides what is possibly the greatest push factor. When things are not working, people often develop high motivation for change, if they know of or can imagine a better approach. When needs, especially needs considered basic, are not being met by a person's or group's present cultural involvement in a given area, such persons or groups are often (not always) more open to possible change than otherwise. We are told that when the early missionaries arrived in Hawaii they entered a situation in which the traditional gods were felt to have died. This resulted in a cultural void that provided the people with a push toward consideration of the new faith.

That kind of push when combined with the pull of something that appears to be a good way out of a problem produces a strong impetus toward change. The Hawaiians were wide open to the message of the missionaries to make that initial change into Christianity with both a motivational push and a pull toward change.

As I have written in other chapters, a major area of pull in most societies is the promise of greater spiritual power. Perhaps the greatest quest for the majority of the world's peoples is the quest for enough spiritual power to make the living of life more bearable. Thus, the introduction of a Christianity that demonstrates more power and better power (i.e., without the negative consequences of traditional options) can provide a strong pull in a Christward direction. For many people their traditional understandings of and approaches to spiritual power are felt to be oppressive. This opens up for Christians the opportunity of pointing people to the power wrapped in love that Jesus demonstrated and commissions His followers to provide.

The possibility of being in relationships with the members of an attractive group can also be highly motivating, bringing with it the desire to change to fit into that group. Such a pull is a horizontal relational pull. A desire to be pleasing to God provides a kind of vertical relational pull. Such a pull may center around gratefulness for what God has done for us, motivating us to obey His commands not out of obligation but out of love and a strong desire to please the One who has done so much for us. When the horizontal pull of an attractive group is combined with the vertical pull of gratefulness to God, the impact on motivation is great.

A major pull for Christians is to be like Jesus or like someone who follows Jesus closely. The Apostle Paul recognized his own responsibility in this area by inviting people to follow him as he followed Jesus (1 Cor. 11:1). For those deeply committed to Jesus, the pull of Christlikeness can be a powerful motivating factor. We are instructed in Romans 12:1-2 to work with God to transform our whole lives into a long term act of worship. Such a commitment makes the pull of Christlikeness effective. There may, however, be challenges if the person being imitated is of a different culture than those seeking to imitate him or her. Cross-cultural witnesses need to be aware of this fact and continually use as their ideal model how Jesus and they themselves would live if they were a part of the receiving society.

The greatest challenges in this area come from the attempts to motivate groups who have just begun to change to continue to press on toward Christian maturity. The temptations to quit once the hard work begins are many. While highly motivated individuals usually succeed, the task of keeping the press and pull in the direction of Christlikeness on whole churches is fraught with difficulties and the danger that groups of new converts will be drawn back into their preChristian understandings and behavior a real threat. For worldview assumptions can have what might be called a "bungee cord" influence on people who may be moving in the right direction but have not completely replaced their previous assumptions. As with Gideon in the Old Testament (Jud. 7-9) and the people of Judah every time a wicked king followed a good king, people who at one time decide for Christ, at a later time may revert to their previous worldview if the pressure to keep moving in the right direction is relaxed.

The Church is God's instrument to keep the right kind of pressure for change on those who convert. It is often the case, however, that any given church body is not itself pulled or pushed enough in the right direction to provide the proper motivation for its members. We see in Latin American

Christianity the results of a movement toward Christianity that did not involve the right kind and amount of motivation to move people into orthodoxy.

In this case, it is a fact that the Christianity that came from Spain and Portugal had already been "paganized" before it was brought to the New World. That is, such things as worship of Mary and the Saints were already a part of the version of Christianity introduced in the Americas. This syncretized form of Christianity, then, was accepted by the people as little more than an overlay on their preChristian worldview and loyalties. The result is what we call "Christo-paganism"—a system of loyalties and practices that have "Christian" names (e.g., the names of European saints) and employ certain Christian symbols (e.g., the crucifix) but that perpetuate most of the pagan beliefs and practices they were intended to replace (e.g., the names of the saints and of God and Mary really represent preChristian deities). Though there were changes on the part of the converts, there was and is not the push or the pull to move the adherents into true Christianity.

The Need for Pressure

The conservatism of people contemplating change leads to the need for something to apply pressure for change. As mentioned, high motivation toward seeking to become Christlike is probably the best form of pressure, since motivation-induced pressure comes from inside of people. It is important, then, to seek ways to nurture and increase such motivation. This is to be a major function of the Church.

Jesus admonished us to seek first His Kingdom and righteousness (Mt. 6:33). The Church, the Christian community, should apply pressure on its members to aim at that goal, a relational goal. Jesus also indicated that it is in the keeping of His commandments that we show love toward Him (Jn. 14:21). This too is relational. The Christian community is the vehicle, established by God, that is charged both with informing us of what those commandments are and with pressuring us to keep them. Our growth, however, is to be in the relationship with the command giver, not merely in the impersonal keeping of the rules as if it is the rules, not the relationship, that are central.

When, then, the activity of the Church devolves to merely providing a weekly lecture (sermon), the amount of pressure for relational growth is usually not enough to bring about the appropriate kind, amount and speed of change. For, communication experts tell us that lectures are seldom effective in bringing about change in people unless the people are already highly motivated to change. And when, as is common around the world, the lectures are more likely to center around intellectual issues rather than the kinds of things that could motivate people to grow in their relationship, their ineffectiveness is magnified.

Jesus lectured from time to time. It is instructive to note, though, that He spoke pictorially rather than intellectually, and almost always with a relationship to God and/or people in focus. His use of stories that can be pictured corresponds with insights underlined in research into how our memories work (see Schacter 1996). That research shows that our ability to remember pictures and stories is much greater than our ability to remember statements, doctrines and intellectual propositions.

However, though Jesus used the best way to communicate verbally, His primary communication was relational and experiential, primarily with the disciples but also with others with whom He interacted. What He said was much less important in His ministry than what He demonstrated of God, what He demonstrated concerning how humans ought to live and behave and His relational way of teaching His followers. He pressured His followers to change by leading them relationally, setting an example for them and then empowering them with the Holy Spirit and leaving the Kingdom in their hands.

An additional important aspect of the press and pull Jesus was able to exert was the fact that He offered the thing most people were most attracted to—spiritual power. The essence of His ministry and the thing He focused on concerning God the Father was, of course, love—a relational thing. However, He used His power to show His love, combining an emphasis on relationship with a use of spiritual power. Spiritual power provided a motivational draw for the people of Jesus' day. It does the same for the people of our day. Relationship, then, with the example He set for His followers, provided powerful motivation for those with Him to become like their Master. These facts should reinforce our interest in the contextualization of relationship and spiritual power in addition to our emphasis on contextualizing knowledge/truth.

As pointed out in Chapter 7, the relational dimension of the Church pictures the Church as a family. A healthy family grows together, each person encouraging and helping the others to become all they are meant to become. The spiritual power dimension of the Church, then, pictures the Church as first a hospital, bringing healing to people, and then an army, fighting the enemy and taking "territory" from him. Working with Jesus in power, then, both motivates by bringing healing and by the renewing power of experiencing great results when we work with Jesus to set captives free. Each of these dimensions, then, can play an important part in helping to keep the pressure on for change.

Reevaluate Each Generation

In Chapter 15, I write of the need for the Christian community to reevaluate and adjust their relationship to the culture each generation. The dynamic of such reevaluation and adjustment can be an important factor in keeping the pressure on for change, especially if the guiding principle is that the community experience growth toward maturity.

The process of looking at the forms in use and asking questions about their relevance at least every generation is an enlivening and motivation-building process. The changes that are made during and after such a process, then, can result in greater attractiveness of Christianity to the nonChristian population and a corresponding influx of new converts. Such evangelistic success would be a great encouragement to the Christian community and could stimulate them to spiritual growth as they enfold and teach the new converts.

Having said this, it is unfortunate that we have to note that churches ordinarily do not reevaluate each generation and, therefore, do not take advantage of this dynamic. Christians seem, rather, to largely carry on from generation to generation whatever practices were developed in the earliest generations without asking whether these practices are appropriate to the present generation. In so doing, then, the Christian community tends to move into nominalism and spiritual deadness.

Worse yet, if the first generation simply imitated the cultural forms of the advocates who brought them the gospel, it is these uncontextual forms that get carried down from generation to generation. And, as I point out in Chapter 15, a nationalistic reaction, usually by the third generation, against both the forms and the meanings of what is experienced as a foreign Christianity often results in a serious decline in both the membership of the churches and their vitality.

Ways of Keeping the Pressure On

There are various ways in which the Christian community can keep the pressure on themselves for growth. Scripture study and memorization should be a major concern, since it is Scripture that provides the clearest goals and guidelines. An interesting confirmation of this fact is that research concerning African Independent Churches that split off from mission churches showed a significant difference between the orthodoxy of those churches that centered their life and ministries on the Bible and those that did not (see Barrett 1968). Those that made the Bible central moved toward greater orthodoxy. Those that did not make the Bible central moved away from orthodoxy.

Bible study in small groups is, of course, more effective in this regard than simply listening to sermons. When the church is made up largely of non-literates or minimally literate people, the use of taped reading or dramatization of Scripture is an important method. Whether the people are literate or nonliterate, singing Scripture and scriptural themes can be perhaps the most effective way of getting Scripture into the hearts of people. Chapter 18 deals with the value of appropriate music for such a purpose.

In taking the gospel to the Behinemo people of Papua New Guinea, Wycliffe translators Wayne and Sally Dye developed a contextualized approach that served well to keep the pressure on. Having learned the language and started translation of the Bible, they carefully chose for translation those portions they deemed to be most relevant to their people. As the Dyes translated these portions, then, they presented them to the tribal leaders for discussion among the leaders in village gatherings on Sunday mornings. These discussions became the Behinemo church services. Though at first the leaders had made no profession of faith in Christ, the aim of the discussions was to determine how these words from God would be applied to their lives and the lives of their followers. In this way, the pressure was generated by sincere people with the encouragement of the missionaries for personal and cultural change (Dye 1976).

In all situations, prayer should be a major part of the process. Invoking the help of the Holy Spirit to keep the pressure on for change should be rule number one. All discussion, all use of Scripture, all singing and worship, even lecturing should be bathed in prayer and openness for God to show the group what changes need to be made and when. Every Christian ministry should have people with the gift of intercession active in supporting the ministry in intercessory prayer.

Conclusion

The aim of this chapter is to alert us to at least some of the dynamics of contextualization. Christianity is not meant by God to be a static thing. It is to be dynamic. God expects change, growth and movement toward spiritual maturity. Our goal is to be as like Jesus as possible, individually and corporately. He is our Alpha and our Omega, our Source and our Goal.

A key function of the Church, then, is to keep the pressure on its members toward growth. The greatest source of this pressure is the motivation that we internalize as Christians who sincerely want to please our Lord by becoming more like Him. For most of us, though, it helps if there are incentives such as satisfactory relationships with God and other Christians plus benefits such as healing for ourselves and the privilege of working with Jesus to bring about change and growth in others.

Chapter 12

Five Perspectives of Contextually Appropriate Missional Theology

Charles E. Van Engen

Thesis

The search for an "appropriate Christianity" involves the development of a contextually appropriate missional theology that includes elements of at least five different perspectives of contextualization.

Introduction

Elsewhere in this volume Charles H. Kraft has challenged us to search for "appropriate Christianity," by which he means, "a Christian expression . . . that is appropriate to the Scriptures, on the one hand and appropriate to the people in a given culture, on the other." Although such a desire is not new, the recent convergence of a number of perspectives and tools of contextualization offers us a series of steps that may further our search for "appropriate Christianity" in specific contexts. In this chapter, I will summarize five perspectives of contextualization that have developed over the past several centuries of missionary activity. I have called them communication, indigenization, translatability, local theologies and epistemology. In a subsequent chapter, I will offer in outline form a possible methodology for constructing an appropriate contextualized mission theology.

Appropriate Contextualization as Communication

Attempts to construct a contextual theology appropriate to both the Scriptures and to a new receptor culture can be traced as far back as the work of Orthodox missionaries to the Slavic peoples, Cyril (826-869) and Methodius (815-885), and early Roman Catholic missionaries like the Jesuits Robert de Nobili (1577-1656) in India and Matteo Ricci (1552-1620) in China (see Guthrie 2000:694 and Lewis 2000:834.) Beginning with William Carey (1761-1834), whenever Protestant missionaries have encountered a new culture and a new language, like their Orthodox and Roman Catholic counterparts, they have been concerned with communicating the message of the gospel to their receptors in languages and forms acceptable and understandable to the new receptors.

David Hesselgrave and Edward Rommen emphasized the communicational aspect of contextualization, drawing from Eugene Nida's three-culture model (Nida 1960), saying,

> From this point of view, Christian contextualization can be thought of as the attempt to communicate the message of the person, works, Word, and will of God in a way that is faithful to God's revelation, especially as it is put forth in the teachings of Holy Scripture, and that is meaningful to respondents in their respective cultural and existential contexts. Contextualization is both verbal and nonverbal and has to do with theologizing; Bible translation, interpretation, and application; incarnational lifestyle; evangelism; Christian instruction; church planting and growth; church organization; worship style— indeed with all of those activities involved in carrying out the Great Commission (Hesselgrave and Rommen 1989:200).

Even today contextualization as communication continues to be important. It means that the gospel communicator must not only learn the language and culture of the receptor but must also become so steeped in the thought-patterns and deep-level meanings of the receptor as to begin to think and reflect within the receptor's worldview. Thus the Christian missionary who wishes to communicate cross-culturally must learn to do what Kraft has termed "receptor-oriented communication" (Kraft 1991a) which also means "communicating Jesus' way" (Kraft 1999). We must never lose sight nor underestimate the importance of this most fundamental aspect of contextualization. As the Christian cross-cultural missionary communicates the Gospel, faithfulness to the message is paramount.

What I have called a "communication" perspective Stephen Bevans has termed the "translation model" of contextual theology.

> Of the six models we will be considering in this book, the translation model of contextual theology is probably the most commonly employed and usually the one that most people think of when they think of doing theology in context. . . . Practitioners of the translation model also point out that it is possibly the oldest way to take the context of theologizing seriously and that it is found within the Bible itself. . . . In many ways, every model of contextual theology is a model of translation. There is always a content to be adapted or accommodated to a particular culture. What makes this particular model specifically a translation model, however, is its insistence on the message of the gospel as an unchanging message. . . . If there is a key presupposition of the translation model, it is that the essential message of Christianity is supracultural or supracontextual. Practitioners of this model speak of a "gospel core" (Haleblian 1983:101-102). . . . In any case, what is very clear in the minds of people who employ the translation model is that an essential, supracultural message can be separated from a contextually bound mode of expression . . . Another presupposition of the translation

model [is] that of the ancillary or subordinate role of context in the contextualization process. Experience, culture, social location, and social change, of course, are acknowledged as important, but they are never as important as the supracultural, "never changing" gospel message (2002:37-41).

The view of contextualization as communication (or accommodation, or adaptation—whatever word or model one chooses to work with) has had at least one significant weakness. The common assumption has been that the Christian missionary or group of Christians in mission knew and understood all, or at least enough, of what was needed to be known and understood about the gospel they were wanting to communicate. In this perspective, the Gospel communicators did not need to concern themselves about the extent to which their own culture had syncretized, obscured, and possibly contradicted the Gospel. The Gospel communicators did not believe that they themselves needed to learn anything new about the Gospel. Rather, the major methodological task involved a movement from Christians of one cultural context communicating a culturally appropriate Gospel to persons in a new context who had not yet heard or no longer could hear the message of the Bible.

As Paul G. Hiebert rightly pointed out, once this perspective was mixed with an attitude of superiority on the part of Westerners (especially during the era of colonialism) it became essentially a "noncontextual" approach. "This stance," Hiebert wrote,

> was essentially monocultural and monoreligious. Truth was seen as supracultural. Everything had to be seen from the perspective of Western civilization and Christianity, which had shown themselves to be technologically, historically and intellectually superior to other cultures; and so those [receptor] cultures could be discounted as 'uncivilized.' The missionary's culture was 'good,' 'advanced,' and 'normative.' Other cultures were 'bad,' 'backward,' and 'distorted.' Christianity was true, other religions were false (1984:290-291).

Communication was deemed to be important, but the content of the message being communicated went unexamined because the missionary communicators assumed they knew and understood all there was to know and understand about the Gospel they were communicating.

As converts were won throughout the world, new Christians speaking a host of new languages were gathered into churches. This led to a second important perspective on contextualization: indigenization.

Appropriate Contextualization As Indigenization

Wilbert R. Shenk considers the concept of the indigenous church to be "the great theoretical breakthrough of the nineteenth century."

> From its earliest days the modern missionary movement was marked by multiple perspectives. On the one hand, mission

promoters frequently depicted the task to be done as a fairly simple process of presenting the Christian message in a straightforward manner to peoples sunk in darkness and despair, peoples who consequently would respond gladly and quickly. On the other side was the growing group of missionaries in the field who knew firsthand how complicated the process was. As foreigners they had to master a strange language—often before it was written—and try to understand a highly intricate culture with quite another worldview. Learning the new language and culture were requisite to any effective communication of the Christian message. As the complexity of the task became more apparent, mission theorists moved through several stages as they sought to conceptualize the task.

The great theoretical breakthrough in missions thought in the nineteenth century was identification of the indigenous church as the goal of mission. Other theoretical and policy developments were largely embroidering on this basic theme (1999:75).

In his article in the *Evangelical Dictionary of World Mission*, John Mark Terry says,

The term 'indigenous' comes from biology and indicates a plant or animal native to an area. Missiologists adopted the word and used it to refer to churches that reflect the cultural distinctives of their ethnolinguistic group. The missionary effort to establish indigenous churches is an effort to plant churches that fit naturally into their environment and to avoid planting churches that replicate Western patterns (Terry 2000:483).

In *God's Missionary People* I summarized what I then called the "Seven Stages of Emerging within Missionary Congregations."

[When we study mission history, we see] at least seven stages in the emerging of a local and national missionary church—stages that have been repeated time and again in church-planting situations. We might summarize the development of the church in a given context in this way:

1. Pioneer evangelism leads to the conversion of a number of people.
2. Initial church gatherings are led by elders and deacons, along with preachers from outside the infant body.
3. Leadership training programs [select], train, and commission indigenous pastors, supervisors and other ministry leaders.
4. Regional organizations of Christian groups develop structures, committees, youth programs, women's societies, and regional assemblies.
5. National organization, supervision of regions, and relationships with other national churches begin to form.
6. Specialized ministries grow inside and outside the church, with boards, budgets, plans, finances, buildings, and programs.

7. Indigenous missionaries are sent by the daughter church for local, national, and international mission in the world, beginning the pattern all over again (1991:43-44).

These seven steps reflect the development of a new group of disciples of Jesus Christ toward becoming an indigenous church that naturally fits and reflects its local context.

As mission churches (1910s and 1920s) became known as younger churches (1930s and 1940s) and then as national churches (1950s and 1960s), the concept of the indigenous church underwent significant development. British Henry Venn (1796-1873) and American Rufus Anderson (1796-1880) used the word to stress the sustainability of a new group of believers in a new culture. In the late 19th century, indigeneity was predominantly used as an administrative and organizational concept. For a new church to sustain itself apart from external missionary assistance, it needed to become self-supporting financially, self-governing organizationally and self-propagating evangelistically. Fifty years later John Nevius (1829-1893) and Roland Allen (1868-1947) expanded and deepened the concept of indigeneity of the new churches, stressing issues of Bible study, leadership formation, the spontaneous work of the Holy Spirit, the ministry of the members through the exercise of their spiritual gifts and the creation of church structures that could sustain themselves without outside dependence. Building on all four of these, Mel Hodges (1909-1986), American missionary administrator with the Assemblies of God, called for the planting and growth of *The Indigenous Church* (1953), an emphasis that became one of the cornerstones of McGavran's mission theory and of the Church Growth Movement.

Indigeneity had to do with the fit between the forms and life of a church and its surrounding context. In *Verdict Theology in Missionary Theory* (1969), Alan Tippett (1911-1988) expanded the concept of indigeneity to include self-image, self-functioning, self-determining, self-supporting, self-propagating, and self-giving. This was further expanded and deepened by Kraft in *Christianity in Culture* (1979a) to include the concept of "dynamic equivalence churchness." As the churches in Asia, Africa, Latin America and Oceania grew and matured, the concept of indigeneity led to a third perspective of contextualization: translatability.

Appropriate Contextualization as Translatability

A third perspective of contextualization emphasizes the incarnational nature of the Gospel as being infinitely translatable into any and all human cultures—a faith-relationship with God that can be woven into the fabric of any and all worldviews. The Gospel of Jesus Christ can be incarnated, given shape, lived out, in any cultural context—it is infinitely universalizable.

The perspective of appropriate contextualization as translatability draws heavily from the concept of the Incarnation so dominant in the Gospel of John. John tells us that "The Word became flesh and made his dwelling (tabernacled) among us. We have seen his glory, the glory of the One and Only, who came from the Father, full of grace and truth" (Jn. 1:14, NIV).

In *Christianity in Africa*, Kwame Bediako discusses the "translatability" of the faith. "Andrew Walls," Bediako writes, "has taught us to recognize the Christian religion as 'culturally infinitely translatable' (Walls 1981:39). Translatability is also another way of saying universality.   Hence the translatability of the Christian religion signifies its fundamental relevance and accessibility to persons in any culture within which the Christian faith is transmitted and assimilated" (Bediako 1995:109).

The "translatability" of the Christian Gospel and Christian Church entails something broader, deeper and more pervasive than mere communication of a message. This perspective stresses the fact that the Gospel can take on new forms and shapes as it is born in new contexts. Gospel and Church are not foreign plants that have been slightly modified to be able to grow in foreign soil. Rather, this Gospel is a new hybrid seed with new and different characteristics that allow it to sprout, grow and flourish in a new climate. Marc Spindler, along with other Roman Catholic missiologists, has called this "inculturation."

> [Inculturation] implies that in Latin America, Africa, Asia, and other places the new churches can and should understand and express the Christian faith in terms of their respective cultures. Even more, it means that the gospel itself receives its shape in the total culture of the people among whom the church is planted and in the nation of which the church is essentially an integral part.   Successful inculturation may be said to occur when the gospel and the church no longer seem to be foreign imports but are claimed in general as the property of the people (Spindler and Vriend 1995:139-140).

Lamin Sanneh speaks of "mission as translation," a process that creates what Sanneh terms the "vernacular credibility" of the Gospel as it takes new shapes in new cultural settings. It is important to listen to Sanneh at this point.

> Mission as translation makes the bold, fundamental assertion that the recipient culture is the authentic destination of God's salvific promise and, as a consequence, has an honored place under "the kindness of God," with the attendant safeguards against cultural absolutism. . . . Mission as translation affirms the *missio Dei* as the hidden force for its work. It is the *missio Dei* that allowed translation to enlarge the boundaries of the proclamation (1989:31).

> Needless to say, Christian mission did not adhere consistently to the rule of translation, but translation in itself implies far-reaching implications that are worth considering, whatever may be the position of particular missions toward it. . . . Translation is profoundly related to the original conception of the gospel: God, who has not linguistic favorites, has determined that we should all hear the Good News "in our own native tongue." Mission as cultural diffusion conflicts with the gospel in this regard, and historically we

can document the problems, challenges, and prospects that attended Christian expansion across cultures under the consistent rule of translation. . . (1989:174).

Where mission failed to achieve a vernacular credibility it has called forth and deserved every criticism it received, then or in retrospect. Ethnographers and other scholars who have criticized mission for its foreign nature have in a backhanded way conceded the principle that Christianity and vernacular credibility are related (1989:175).

Vernacular translation begins with the effort to equip the gospel with terms of familiarity, and that process brings the missionary enterprise into the context of field experience. . . . There is a radical pluralism implied in vernacular translation wherein all languages and cultures are, in principle, equal in expressing the word of God . . . Two general ideas stem from this analysis. First is the inclusive principle whereby no culture is excluded from the Christian dispensation or even judged solely or ultimately by Western cultural criteria. Second is the ethical principle of change as a check to cultural self-absolutization. . . . This introduces in mission the *logos* concept wherein any and all languages may confidently be adopted for God's word (1989:208-209).[1]

In 1985, C. René Padilla offered three important observations concerning this incarnational view of intercultural communication.

The consciousness of the critical role that culture plays in communication is of special importance for the intercultural communication of the gospel. There are at least three reasons for this.

1. The Incarnation is a basic element in the gospel. Since the Word became man, the only possible communication of the gospel is that in which the gospel becomes incarnate in culture in order to put itself within the reach of man as a cultural being . . .

2. Without a translation that goes beyond the words to break into the raw material of life in the receiving culture, the gospel is a fantasy. The gospel involves the proclamation of Jesus Christ as Lord of the totality of the universe and of human existence. If this proclamation is not directed to specific needs and problems of the hearers, how can they experience the Lordship of Christ in their concrete situation? To contextualize the gospel is so to translate it that the Lordship of Jesus Christ is not an abstract principle or a mere doctrine but the determining factor of life in all its dimensions and the basic criterion in relation to which all the

---

[1] See also Bediako's reflection on Sanneh's proposal in Bediako 1995:119-123.

cultural values that form the very substance of human life are evaluated. . . .

3. In order for the gospel to receive an intelligent response, either positive or negative, there must be effective communication, communication that takes into consideration the point of contact between the message and the culture of the hearers. There can be no true evangelization unless the gospel confronts cultural values and thought patterns (1985:2-93).

This element of "translatability" or "universalizability" that Bediako, Walls, Sanneh, Padilla, Gilliland, Kraft and others have emphasized means that there is a deepening, widening, filling and enriching way Christians live out the Gospel in their context. Ever since Luke listed his "table of nations" in Acts 2, mentioning those who "heard the Gospel in their own language" (Ac. 2:6, 8-11), the truth of the universally-appropriate nature of the Incarnation has been evident throughout mission history. The Gospel is by its very nature native to every culture on earth. All humans were created by the same God, Creator of heaven and earth, the God of Abraham, Isaac and Jacob. Whether one speaks of Natural Theology, General Revelation, Common Grace, Prevenient Grace, "redemptive analogies" (Richardson 2000:812-813), or the lights of God's revelation dispersed amidst all cultures, the implication is the same (though recognizing the profound theological differences between these concepts in many other respects). Together they point to a most fundamental fact: all humans are created by the same God; all are addressed equally by Jesus Christ, the Word made flesh; and the Holy Spirit enables all to hear the Gospel in their own language. "For God so loved the [entire] world . . ." (Jn. 3:16). God speaks and understands all languages. Listen again to Lamin Sanneh.

> Christian life is indelibly marked with the stamp of culture, and faithful stewardship includes uttering the prophetic word in culture, and sometimes even against it. . . . [I]n [the apostle Paul's] view God's purposes are mediated through particular cultural streams.
>
> The mission of the church applied this insight by recognizing all cultures, and the languages in which they are embodied, as lawful in God's eyes, making it possible to render God's word into other languages. Even if in practice Christians wished to stop the translation process, claiming their form of it as final and exclusive, they have not been able to suppress it for all time. It is this phenomenon that the concept of translatability tries to represent. . . . Translatability ensures that the challenge at the heart of the Christian enterprise is . . . kept alive in all cultural contexts . . . (1989:47-48).

This being so, Christians must grapple with the profound implications of the fact that the Christian faith is internally compatible, consistent and coherent with—and can be fully and naturally expressed in—every culture. A realization of the translatability of the Gospel moves contextual mission theology beyond indigenization to Incarnation.[2] The example of the Church in Africa may be helpful at this point. Together with other two-thirds world theologians, Kwame Bediako and John Mbiti have described the struggle to deepen and broaden the African understanding of the Gospel. Bediako's summary of Mbiti's views is instructive.

> Mbiti was early to deplore the lack of sufficient and positive engagement by Western missions with African cultural and religious values. He saw the result of this in an African church which had "come of age *evangelistically*, but not *theologically:*" "a church without theology, without theologians and without theological concern" as he was writing in 1967 and 1969.

> Mbiti, however, soon came to make a distinction between "Christianity" which "results from the encounter of the Gospel with any given local society" and so is always indigenous and culture-bound, on the one hand, and the Gospel, which is "God-given, eternal, and does not change" on the other. In 1970 he wrote: "We can add nothing to the Gospel, for this is an eternal gift of God; but Christianity is always a beggar seeking food and drink, cover and shelter from the cultures it encounters in its never-ending journeys and wanderings" (Bediako 1995 quoting Mbiti 1970:438).

Mbiti rejected the notion of indigenizing Christianity as such on African soil. Bediako cites Mbiti as saying, "To speak of 'indigenizing Christianity' is to give the impression that Christianity is a ready-made commodity which has to be transplanted to a local area. Of course, this has been the assumption followed by many missionaries and local theologians. I do not accept it any more" (1995 quoting Mbiti 1979:68).

In contrast, the Gospel is to be seen as "translatable," taking on fully African deep-level meanings in addition to surface-level cultural forms. "For Mbiti therefore," Bediako writes,

> the Gospel is genuinely at home in Africa, is capable of being apprehended by Africans at the specific level of their religious experience, and in fact has been so received through the missionary transmission of it. . . . The theological principle we see operating in Mbiti's thought is that of translatability—the capacity of the essential impulses of the Christian religion to be transmitted and assimilated in a different culture so that these impulses create dynamically equivalent responses in the course of such a transmission. Given this principle, it is possible to say that the earlier concern to seek an "indigenization" of Christianity in Africa, as though one were dealing with an essentially "Western" and "foreign" religion was, in effect, misguided because the task was conceived as the correlation of two entities thought to be unrelated. . . . The achievement meant

---

[2] See Gilliland, Chapter 28 in this volume.

here is not to be measured in terms of Western missionary transmission, but rather by African assimilation of the Faith. . . . It was therefore misguided to assume that African converts to Christianity assimilated the missionary message in Western terms rather than in terms of their own African religious understanding and background" (1995:118-119).

Thus far we have surveyed three perspectives of contextualization broadly conceived: communication, indigenization and translatability. Together these three deal generally with a one-way movement of Gospel proclamation in word and deed: a movement from those who know God and believe they understand the Gospel to those who do not know, have never heard, or no longer can hear of God's love for them. We have looked at appropriate contextualization in a broad and general sense as involving the search for what elsewhere in this volume Charles Kraft has termed, "appropriate Christianity: a Christian expression of the faith that is appropriate to the Scriptures, on the one hand, and appropriate to the people in a given culture, on the other."

In the rest of this chapter I will survey two additional perspectives of appropriate contextualization that have arisen in missiological reflection during the past thirty years: local theologizing and epistemology. In contrast to the previous three perspectives we have examined, these last two involve an intentional two-way conversation between church and Gospel, on the one hand, and the contextual reality, on the other. Based on these five perspectives, I will proceed in a subsequent chapter to offer a method of mission theologizing whereby the method itself may be constructed to be appropriate both to Scripture and to the people of a context, yielding over time an appropriate understanding of God's revelation in order that people in a given culture may respond and be transformed by the Gospel (in truth, allegiance and power).

Appropriate Contextualization as Local Theologizing

I have entitled this section "local theologizing" as a way to cut through today's confusion surrounding the term contextualization. In this section I am dealing with what many have called contextualization in a narrow sense: that is, as having to do with humanization, with the impact of socio-political, economic, cultural, and other forces in a context on the task of doing theology in that context.

In his dictionary article in the *Evangelical Dictionary of World Missions*, Gilliland discussed how one might define contextualization understood broadly.

> There is no single or broadly accepted definition of contextualization. The goal of contextualization perhaps best defines what it is. That goal is to enable, insofar as it is humanly possible, an understanding of what it means that Jesus Christ the Word, is authentically experienced in each and every human situation. . . . Contextualization in mission is an effort made by a particular church

to experience the gospel for its own life in light of the Word of God (2000a:225).

Contextualization as the development of local theologies was originally catalyzed by the publication, in 1972, of *Ministry in Context* on the part of the Theological Education Fund of the World Council of Churches and is associated with the writings of Shoki Coe in particular.[3]

Ashish Chrispal of Union Biblical Seminary in Pune, India, explains his view of contextualization (conceived as doing theology in context),

> The historical world situation is not merely an exterior condition for the church's mission: rather it ought to be incorporated as a constitutive element into her understanding of mission, her aims and objectives. Like her Lord, the church-in-mission must take sides *for* life and *against* death; *for* justice and *against* oppression. Thus mission as contextualization is an affirmation that God had turned toward the world. . . . Contextualization implies all that is involved in the familiar term indigenization which relates to traditional cultural values, but goes beyond it to take into account very seriously the contemporary factors in cultural change. It deals with the contemporary socio-economic, political issues of class-caste struggles, power politics, riches and poverty, bribery and corruption, privileges and oppression—all factors that constitute society and the relationship between one community and another (1995:1, 3).

Contextualization in this more technical sense of the word involves theologizing as an action rather than theology as a received composite of affirmations: thus the common use of the word theologizing as a verbal form rather than theology as a noun. Tite Tiénou explains:

> The term "contextualization" entered missiological literature in 1972 through the report of the Third Mandate of the Theological Education Fund. . . . At that time, Shoki Coe was director of the Theological Education Fund, an agency sponsored by the World Council of Churches and administered under the auspices of the Commission on World Mission and Evangelism. According to Coe, indigenization is a static concept since it "tends to be used in the sense of responding to the Gospel in terms of traditional culture" whereas contextualization is "more dynamic . . . open to change and . . . future-oriented" [Coe 1976:20-21].

> The word "contextualization" was therefore chosen with the specific purpose of conveying the idea that theology can never be permanently developed. Everywhere and in every culture Christians must be engaged in an ongoing process of relating the gospel to cultures that are constantly changing. As long as the world endures,

---

[3] See e.g., Coe 1976; Norman Thomas 1995:175-176; and Bevans 2002:153 nn 45 and 46.

this process continues. For many people contextualization, not indigenization, is the term that best describes this never-ending process (1993:247).

This dynamic process called contextualization draws from all aspects of human experience in a local context and fosters a conversation between the reality of the context and the church's understanding of the Gospel. "Contextualization," writes Andrew Kirk, "recognizes the reciprocal influence of culture and socio-economic life. In relating Gospel to culture, therefore, it tends to take a more critical (or prophetic) stance towards culture" (1999:91; see Van Engen 1989:97 nn 18-19).

The perspective of contextualization as local theologizing represents a constantly-changing reciprocal interaction between church and context. It is a process of local reflection that begins with an analysis of the historical situation, proceeds to a re-reading of Scripture that in turn leads to interactive theological reflection concerning the context: an act of theologizing that propels the Christian to active engagement with the cultural, socio-economic, and political issues extant in the context. Within this view of contextualization as local theologizing there is a wide spectrum of diverse viewpoints from a nearly total secularization of the process at one end to a heavy emphasis on the transformation of the church at the other end.

Contextualization in this narrow and more technical sense involves not only theologizing as an active process, but also expands the scope of the sources of one's theological reflection to include all appropriate aspects of human experience. This dynamic process of interaction with all aspects of the context was highlighted recently by R. Yesurathnam, professor of Systematic Theology in the Church of South India.

> The term contextualization includes all that is implied in indigenization or inculturation, but seeks also to include the realities of contemporary, secularity, technology, and the struggle for human justice. . . . Contextualization both extends and corrects the older terminology. While indigenization tends to focus on the purely cultural dimension of human experience, contextualization broadens the understanding of culture to include social, political, and economic questions. In this way, culture is understood in more dynamic and flexible ways, and is seen not as closed and self-contained, but as open and able to be enriched by an encounter with other cultures and movements (2000:53).

Stephen Bevans highlights the countercultural and dialogical aspects of local engagement in contextualization.

> Contextualization points to the fact that theology needs to interact and dialogue not only with traditional cultural value, but with social change, new ethnic identities, and the conflicts that are present as the contemporary phenomenon of globalization encounters the various peoples of the world.

> Contextualization, then, [is] the preferred term to describe the theology that takes human experience, social location, culture, and cultural change seriously . . . (2002:27).

Roman Catholic theologians and missiologists have called this process an effort in "constructing local theologies." Nearly twenty years ago, in *Constructing Local Theologies* (1985) Robert Schreiter surveyed the contributions of what he called the "Translation Models," the "Adaptation Models" and the "Contextual Models" for such a construction. Schreiter's thinking on the subject has been furthered by the work of his colleague at the Catholic Theological Union in Chicago, Bevans, in *Models of Contextual Theology* (1992, rev. 2002). In the 2002 edition, Bevans presented six models of contextual theology: what he called Translation, Anthropological, Praxis, Synthetic, Transcendental and Countercultural. Bevans prefaced his survey with an observation about the sources and location of contextual theology.

> Contextual theology's addition of culture and social change to the traditional *loci* of scripture and tradition already marks a revolution in theological method over against traditional ways of doing theology. . . . Both poles—human experience and the Christian tradition—are to be read together dialectically. In addition to this basic shift in theological method, a number of other methodological issues have emerged. When human experience, world events, culture, and cultural change are taken as *loci theologici*, one can ask whether theology is always to be done formally or discursively. What, in other words, is the *form* that theology should take? As theology becomes more of a reflection on ordinary human life in the light of the Christian tradition, one might ask whether ordinary men and women might not, after all, be the best people to theologize (2002:16-17).

Recently Clemens Sedmak of the University of Salzburg, Austria brought together many of the emphases that Schreiter's call for *Constructing Local Theologies* has in common with Bevans' challenge to effectively utilize *Models of Contextual Theology*. In *Doing Local Theology: A Guide for Artisans of a New Humanity*, Sedmak offers a number of theses. Among them, he affirms that,

> Theology is done locally. In order to be honest to the local circumstances theology has to be done as local theology, as theology that takes the particular situation seriously. Local theology can be done with basic theological means. It can be done by the people, and it is done with the people . . . Local theologies recognize that theology takes shape within a particular context. Theologies are developed in response to and within a particular social situation. Understanding the social situation is a necessary condition for understanding the genesis and validity of particular theologies. . . . Theology that tries to do justice to its place in culture and history is contextual. Contextualization literally means, 'weaving together.'. . . Theology is always done within a concrete local social structure that

provides rich resources for constructing local theologies and for developing a local identity as a theologian. The social, historical, cultural, and political context has an impact on the role of the theologian and his or her place in the context (2002:8, 95-96).

Dirkie Smit, Professor of Systematic Theology at the Universities of Western Cape and Stellenbosch in South Africa, points out that, "Contextual theologies . . . have underlined the fact that all theology, all thinking and speaking about God, is contextual, is influenced by the contexts in which the believers live, including the so-called traditional theology of Western Christianity in all its forms" (1994:44; see also Arias 2001:64).

From a Protestant Evangelical standpoint, Stanley Grenz echoes the importance of correlating (he draws the term from Paul Tillich here) the existential human questions posed by the context and the revelatory answers found in the Bible. "The commitment to contextualization . . .," Grenz writes,

> entails an implicit rejection of the older evangelical conception of theology as the construction of truth on the basis of the Bible alone. No longer can the theologian focus merely on Scripture as the one complete theological norm. Instead, the process of contextualization requires a movement between two poles—the Bible as the source of truth and the culture as the source of the categories through which the theologian expresses biblical truth. . . . Contextualization demands that the theologian take seriously the thought-forms and mindset of the culture in which theologizing transpires, in order to explicate the eternal truths of the Scriptures in language that is understandable to contemporary people" (1993:90; see Shenk 1999:77).

Appropriate Contextualization as Epistemology

A fifth perspective of contextualization has to do with an epistemological process of hermeneutical examination and critique of the context and its implications for a missional understanding of the Gospel in that specific context. In the 2002 revised and expanded edition of *Models of Contextual Theology*, Bevans added a model he called the "countercultural model" of contextualization.

> What this model realizes more than any other model is how some contexts are simply antithetical to the gospel and need to be challenged by the gospel's liberating and healing power . . . The countercultural model draws on rich and ample sources in scripture and tradition. . . . More than any other model, . . . it recognizes that the gospel represents an all-encompassing, radically alternate worldview that differs profoundly from human experiences of the world and the culture that humans create. Particularly in contexts that exude a "culture of death," in contexts in which the gospel seems irrelevant or easily ignored, or in those in which the gospel has become "a stained glass version" of a particular worldview, this

model can prove to be a powerful way by which the gospel is able to be communicated with new freshness and genuine engagement (2002:118).[4]

Appropriate contextualization as an epistemological approach to contextualization emphasizes the sense that in each new context, in each new cultural setting, followers of Jesus Christ have an opportunity to learn something about God they had not previously known. Christian knowledge about God is seen as cumulative, enhanced, deepened, broadened and expanded as the Gospel takes new shape in each new culture. This was my thesis in "The New Covenant: Knowing God in Context" (1989, reprinted in 1996:71-89).

In 1979, Bruce Nicholls suggested a distinction between what he called existential contextualization (the type common to World Council of Churches circles) and dogmatic contextualization (one that begins with the biblical text as ultimately the only rule of faith and practice—see Nicholls 1979:24; Stults 1989:151; and Chrispal 1995:5). When contextualization is viewed as an epistemological endeavor in numerous contexts, as a process that searches for a deepening and broadening understanding of God in particular contexts, it does not fit easily into either of Nicholl's categories. Appropriate contextualization as epistemology accepts the contextual (and existential) reality as itself a significant component of its theological (and dogmatic) reflection in which Christians broaden and deepen their understanding and participation in God's mission in a given context.

In his dictionary entry on "Contextualization," Gilliland summarized six models of contextualization: the Critical, Semiotic, Synthetic, Transcendental and Translation models. "The strength of contextualization," wrote Gilliland,

is that if properly carried out, it brings ordinary Christian believers into what is often called the theological process. . . . The objective of contextualization is to bring data from the whole of life to real people and search the Scriptures for a meaningful application of the Word (who) "dwelt among us" (Jn. 1:14). The missiological significance for contextualization is that all nations must understand the Word as clearly and as accurately as did Jesus' own people in his day (2000a:227).

A dozen years earlier, Gilliland had suggested four questions that are of paramount consideration in the task of constructing a contextually appropriate theology:

1. What is the (culture-specific, contextual) general background?
2. What are the presenting problems?
3. What theological questions arise?

---

[4] Bevans quoting Douglas John Hall from "Ecclesia Crucis: The Theologic of Christian Awkwardness" (1996a:199).

4. What appropriate directions should the theology (and missiology) take? (1989b:52).

Theologians and missiologists the world over are now more than ever aware that about two-thirds of all world Christianity is now in Asia, Africa, Latin America, and Oceania. Christianity is no longer a Western religion. This should not surprise us, since the Christian Church did not begin as a Western religion: it began as a Middle Eastern, North African and central Asian religious expression of faith in Jesus Christ. Today there are Christian believers in every political nation and among every major culture, though there yet remain many unreached people groups.

Beginning with Shoki Coe and others related to the World Council of Church's Theological Education Fund initiative, around 1972, the question became one of deriving an understanding of the Gospel that was appropriate to the culture wherever that might be—especially in terms of rejecting the formulations from the West and constructing new understandings that would be more appropriate to Africa, Asia, or Latin America. This epistemological perspective of appropriate mission theology received additional impetus after 1976 when "twenty-two theologians from Africa, Asia, Latin America and representatives of minority groups in North America founded the Ecumenical Association of Third World Theologians (EATWOT) in Dar es Salaam, Tanzania . . . By 2002 EATWOT's membership had grown to over 700 members . . ." (Mbiti 2003). The conferences, papers and published books flowing from EATWOT during the past twenty-five years have provided strong support for an epistemological approach to doing contextually appropriate theology, especially in and from the two-thirds world.

"Contextualization," writes J. Andrew Kirk,

> recognizes the reciprocal influence of culture and socio-economic life. In relating Gospel to culture, therefore, it tends to take a more critical (or prophetic) stance toward culture. The concept . . . is intended to be taken seriously as a theological method which entails particular ideological commitments to transform situations of social injustice, political alienation and the abuse of human rights. José Miguez-Bonino speaks of 'raising up the historical situation to the theological level' and of 'theological reflection in the concrete praxis. . . . The inflexible will to act from the historical situation, analyzed by means of socio-political instruments and adopted in a theological option, identifies . . . the starting point of the theological task' (1999:91).[5]

David Bosch highlighted the importance of this epistemological element in contextualization.

---

[5] Kirk is quoting from Miguez-Bonino 1971:405-407; cited also in Norman Thomas 1995:174 and Bosch 1991:425.

> Contextual theologies claim that they constitute an epistemological break when compared with traditional theologies. Whereas, at least since the time of Constantine, theology was conducted *from above* as an elitist enterprise . . . its main source was *philosophy*, and its main interlocutor the *educated non-believer*, contextual theology is theology *from below*, "from the underside of history," its main source (apart from Scripture and tradition) is the *social sciences*, and its main interlocutor the *poor* or the *culturally marginalized*. . . . Equally important in the new epistemology is the emphasis on the priority of praxis (1991:423).

Bosch goes on to mention five characteristics of this epistemological approach to contextualization:

> First, there is a profound suspicion that not only Western science and Western philosophy, but also Western theology . . . were actually designed to serve the interests of the West, more particularly to legitimize "the world as it now exists.". . .
>
> Second, the new epistemology refuses to endorse the idea of the world as a static object which only has to be *explained*. . . .
>
> Third, (there is) an emphasis on *commitment* as "the first act of theology" (quoting Torres and Fabella 1978:269). . . .
>
> Fourth, in this paradigm the theologian can no longer be "a lonely bird on the rooftop (Barth 1933:40), who surveys and evaluates this world and its agony; he or she can only theologize credibly if it is done *with* those who suffer.
>
> Fifth, then, the emphasis is on *doing* theology. The universal claim of the hermeneutic of language has been challenged by a hermeneutic of the deed, since doing is more important than knowing or speaking (Bosch 1991:424-425). . . . From praxis or experience the hermeneutic circulation proceeds to reflection as a second . . . act of theology. The traditional sequence, in which *theoria* is elevated over praxis, is here turned upside down. This does not, of course, imply a rejection of *theoria*. Ideally, there should be a dialectical relationship between theory and praxis. . . . "Orthopraxis and orthodoxy need one another, and each is adversely affected when sight is lost of the other" (Bosch 1991 quoting Gutierrez 1988:xxxiv).

Bosch cautions us regarding the "ambiguities of contextualization," a discomfort that I share. Bosch affirms that "There can be no doubt that the contextualization project is essentially legitimate, given the situation in which many contextual theologians find themselves. . . . Still, some ambiguities remain, particularly insofar as there is a tendency in contextual theology to overreact (and) to make a clean break with the past and deny continuity with one's theological and ecclesial ancestry" (1991:425-426). Bosch registers his concerns by offering seven affirmations that serve to link contextualization with theology and mission:

1. Mission as contextualization is an affirmation that God has turned toward the world . . . [It is not necessary to dichotomize our God-ward faith relationship from our commitment and involvement in the world. CVE]
2. Mission as contextualization involves the construction of a variety of "local theologies . . ." [But a too-expansive multiplication—or atomization—of "theologies" has profoundly negative implications for relativizing the oneness of the Christian Church's faith in the same Gospel. CVE]
3. There is not only the danger of relativism, where each context forges its own theology, tailor-made for that specific context, but also the danger of absolutism of contextualism. . . .
4. We have to look at this entire issue from yet another angle, that of "reading the signs of the times"; an expression that has invaded contemporary ecclesiastical language. . . .
5. In spite of the undeniably crucial nature and role of the context, then, it is not to be taken as the sole and basic authority for theological reflection. . . .
6. Stackhouse has argued that we are distorting the entire contextualization debate if we interpret it only as a problem of the relationship between praxis and theory. . . .[6]
7. The best models of contextual theology succeed in holding together in creative tension *theoria, praxis* and *poiesis*—or, if one wishes, faith, hope and love. This is another way of defining the missionary nature of the Christian faith, which seeks to combine the three dimensions (Bosch 1991:426-432).

Bosch concludes these remarks by saying, "It goes without saying that not every manifestation of contextual theology is guilty of any or all of the overreaction discussed above. Still, they all remain a constant danger to every (legitimate) attempt at allowing the context to determine the nature and content of theology for that context" (1991:432).

However, with the center of gravity having shifted from the North to the South, from the West to the East, mission in the Twenty-first Century will be from everywhere to everywhere. And all aspects of the reality of each particular context will—and must—have an impact on the content and the method of mission theology in each place. As Andrew Kirk has pointed out, true theology will be—must be—missiological.

> My thesis is that it is impossible to conceive of theology apart from mission. All true theology is, by definition, missionary theology, for it has as its object the study of the way of a God who is by nature missionary and a foundation text written by and for missionaries. . . . Theology should not be pursued as a set of isolated disciplines. It assumes a model of cross-cultural communication, for

---

[6] Bosch cites Max Stackhouse 1988:85.

its subject matter both stand over against culture and relates closely to it. Therefore, it must be interdisciplinary and interactive" (1997:50-51).

"There can be no theology without mission—or, to put it another way, no theology which is not missionary" (Kirk 1999:11).

In the words of David Bosch,

> Just as the church ceases to be church if it is not missionary, theology ceases to be theology if it loses its missionary character. The crucial question, then, is not simply or only or largely what church is or what mission is; it is also what theology is and is about. We are in need of a missiological agenda for theology rather than just a theological agenda for mission; for theology, rightly understood, has not reason to exist other than critically to accompany the *missio Dei*. So mission should be "the theme of all theology" (Gensichen 1971:250). . . . It is not a case of theology occupying itself with the missionary enterprise as and when it seems to it appropriate to do so; it is rather a case of mission being that subject with which theology is to deal. For theology it is a matter of life and death that it should be in direct contact with mission and the missionary enterprise (Bosch 1991:494).

Although he probably would not share the economic and political viewpoints of some of the authors mentioned above, the epistemological slant of the methodology being suggested appears similar to the concept of "critical contextualization" developed by Paul Hiebert (1984). Hiebert called for a "critical contextualization" involving an interactive process that takes the Bible seriously and also interacts constructively with the context.

> Critical contextualization does not operate from a monocultural perspective. Nor is it premised upon the pluralism of incommensurable cultures. It seeks to find metacultural and metatheological frameworks that enable people in one culture to understand messages and ritual practices from another culture with a minimum of distortion. It is based on a critical realist epistemology that sees all human knowledge as a combination of objective and subjective elements, and as partial but increasingly closer approximations of truth. It takes both historical and cultural contexts seriously. And it sees the relationship between form and meaning in symbols such as words and rituals, ranging all the way from an equation of the two to simply arbitrary associations between them. Finally, it sees contextualization as an ongoing process in which the church must constantly engage itself, a process that can lead us to a better understanding of what the Lordship of Christ and the kingdom of God on earth are about (1984:295).

Conclusion

So what is the next step? I believe the next step involves a search for a methodology in contextual mission theology that simultaneously affirms the universality of the Gospel and the particularity of its Incarnation in specific times and places. We need a methodology in mission theology that takes the Scriptures and the Church's historical reflection on them seriously—and at the same time locates it in the environment of the context and the faith pilgrimage of the persons in that context. This is a methodology that, with the Bible in one hand and a newspaper in the other, asks over and over again Gilliland's four questions we mentioned earlier—and then proceeds to discover what God's mission entails in that place at that particular time.

In this chapter, I have summarized five perspectives of appropriate contextualization that build on each other: communication, indigenization, translatability, local theologies, and epistemology. In the next chapter, I will offer a method of mission theologizing whereby the method itself may be constructed to be appropriate both to Scripture and to the people of a context, yielding over time an appropriate understanding of God's revelation in order that people in a given society may respond and be transformed by the Gospel (in truth, allegiance, and power).

Chapter 13

Toward a Contextually Appropriate Methodology in Mission Theology

Charles E. Van Engen

Thesis

In order to give rise to an "appropriate Christianity" in a given context, Christians in that context need to construct a method of mission theologizing in such a way that the method itself is appropriate to Scripture, to the people of that context, and in relation to the world Church, yielding over time a contextually appropriate understanding of God's revelation to which the people of that society may respond and by which they may be transformed (in truth, allegiance and power). This contextually appropriate methodology will need to be integrational, local, Incarnational, praxeological and dialogical.

Introduction

In the preceding chapter, I summarized five perspectives of contextually appropriate mission theology that build on each other: communication, indigenization, translatability, local theologies and epistemology. Drawing a variety of insights from these five perspectives, in this chapter I will offer an outline of a method of mission theologizing whereby the method itself may be constructed to be appropriate both to Scripture and to the people of a context. The method I will outline below consists of twelve steps arranged according to five characteristics of a contextually appropriate mission theology. An appropriate mission theology is characterized by the fact that it is:

1. Integrational: Understanding the Gospel of Jesus Christ.
2. Local: Approaching a New Context Anew.
3. Incarnational: Preparing for New Action.
4. Praxeological: Living out the Gospel in Appropriate Action.
5. Dialogical: Re-shaping our Understanding of the Gospel.

The method outlined below involves an action of hermeneutical spiraling that weaves a web of interaction between Gospel and culture, between Church and context, between what Christians know and understand about God and what Christians experience in living out their faith in the world. As illustrated in Figure 13.1 below, this involves a dynamic interaction over time of theology-from-above with theology-from-below, seeking a deepening wisdom regarding the Church's understanding of God. In chapter four of *Communicating God's Word in a Complex World* (R. Daniel Shaw and Van Engen 2003), I drew from the work of Anthony Thiselton (1980) and Grant Osborne (1991), among others, to describe this theologizing activity as a dynamic, ongoing interaction of four horizons.

The methodology that I will describe below involves just such spiraling. I will describe one revolution of the spiral only. The reader needs to understand that what is being described in the following five steps is a theological and missiological process that needs to be repeated again and again by the people of God in their context in order for them to discover a contextually appropriate mission theology in their particular situation. The first step, then, involves integration.[1]

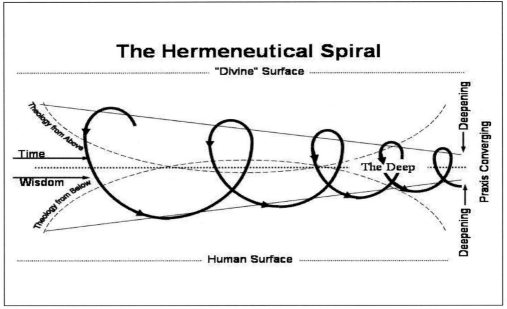

Figure 13.1 The Hermeneutical Spiral

Characteristic 1: An Appropriate Mission Theology is Integrational: Understanding the Gospel of Jesus Christ

The construction of a contextually appropriate mission theology involves a careful and intentional fusing of four sources of data from which the mission theologian draws understanding: the Bible, the context, the Church and one's personal pilgrimage. Over the past three decades, there has been a significant consensus in mission theology on the need to integrate at least three domains of

---

[1] I am indebted to the dedicated, careful and creative work of Shawn Redford in the illustration of many of the diagrams that I developed in this chapter. Figures 13.1, 13.6 and 13.7 were original to Shawn and I am building upon his figures in these cases.

our knowledge in a dynamic, interrelated whole: *Word* (the primacy of the Bible in all contextual theologizing), *world* (the impact of culture, socio-economics, political realities and all other arenas of human life in the reality of a given context) and *church* (the primary agent of God's mission in the world). These three (word, world, church) constitute the basic framework of the missiology that is followed and taught in the School of Intercultural Studies of Fuller Theological Seminary. Some would call this the interaction of text, context and faith community.

At the end of this chapter (Appendix A) there is a preliminary list of missiologists and theologians of the past several decades who have drawn from this tripartite structure. In *Mission on the Way* I described the way these three sources of missiological data impact the development of mission theology (Van Engen 1996:22-26). I also adapted this tripartite understanding of theologizing in mission in *God So Loves the City* as it applies to developing a theology of mission in the city (Van Engen and Tiersma 1994:271-285).

Recently, I began to understand that I was missing a fourth arena that is very important for constructing a contextually appropriate mission theology. I had neglected to include the arena of personal pilgrimage. Once I began working with all four arenas in the construction of my own integration of mission theology I had several of my Methodist and Wesleyan students point out to me that what I was doing looked to them to be similar to what is popularly known as the Wesleyan quadrilateral.

Stanley Grenz explains the quadrilateral in this way.

"The Wesleyan quadrilateral" . . . purports to find its genesis in John Wesley. Theology, proponents declare, appeals to four sources: Scripture (the Bible as properly exegeted), reason (the findings of science and human reasoning), experience (individual and corporate encounters with life) and tradition (the teachings of the church throughout its history) (Grenz 1993:91; see also p. 197 nn 4 and 5.).

This beginning of the process involves self-examination on the part of the mission theologian and the missional church. Jesus referred to this, saying, "First take the plank out of your own eye, and then you will see clearly to remove the speck from your brother's eye" (Mt. 7:5 NIV). This part of the process examines our own knowledge and understanding of God and God's mission as it is informed and shaped by four domains, as follows.

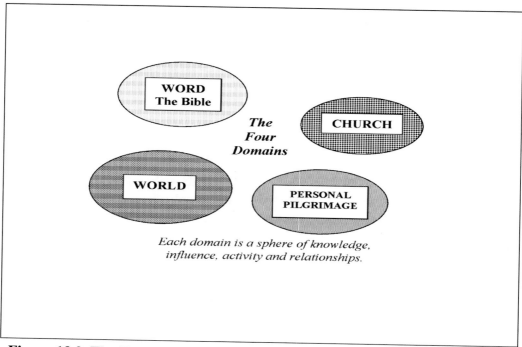

Figure 13.2 The Four Domains

The four-domain approach to contextually-appropriate mission theology includes 1) the Bible as the exclusive source-text of God's mission (similar to the role of the Bible in the Wesleyan quadrilateral), 2) the cultural context (in the place of the quadrilateral's narrower emphasis on reason), 3) personal spiritual and experiential pilgrimage (similar to experience in the quadrilateral), and 4) the church's reflection over time (similar to the role of tradition in the quadrilateral). The reader will see these four domains illustrated in Figure 13.2.

In the following paragraphs I will briefly outline the twelve steps that need to be taken toward an appropriate mission theology. These steps are summarized in Figure 13.9 at the end of the chapter. The first four of these steps involves examining the content of each of the above four domains.

Step 1. The Bible: The exclusive source-text for the process of theologizing in mission is the Bible. The Bible is the missionary manual without equal. It is the revelation of the missionary God. The Bible tells of the in-breaking of God throughout human history. The Bible informs us about the mission of God (the *missio Dei*) and provides the missiological examples to follow Jesus Christ in mission. The Bible informs, shapes and critiques the other three domains. (See, for example, Bosch 1993 and Van Engen 1996:35-43.)

Step 2. The Church's Reflection: The reflection of the church has impacted the lenses (the hermeneutical approaches) that have been used throughout history to understand the Bible, theology, and the mission of the Church. Historical Theology and Systematic Theology are examples of lenses used in the West to read Scripture, reflect theologically, and view mission from a particular viewpoint, too often based on Western assumptions and methodologies.

Churches and Christians in the two-thirds world need especially to reflect on and critique the theology received (usually) from the West, how it does or does not interface with their reality, and how it has impacted their understanding of God in their context.

Step 3. Personal Experience: Those who approach the Bible and examine the story of God's mission bring their own sets of cultural, personal and individual strengths, weaknesses, experiences, and spiritual pilgrimage. These affect the way in which Scripture and mission are understood and perceived— and the ways in which God's mission is incarnated through the life of each person. The Bible, the church, the context, and God's mission are all understood through personal ethnohermeneutical, existential and experiential lenses.

Each person's particular spiritual gifts, natural abilities, experiences, knowledge and personality create a mix that is unique. God's mission is carried out through the life of a particular person in an individualized way that cannot be reproduced or repeated (Rom. 12; Eph. 4; 1 Cor. 12).

Step 4. The Context: In each unique context, mission takes place and shapes the understanding of mission and the process of theologizing in mission. The manifestation of mission and the theologizing process in mission for that context need to be contextually appropriate. All relevant tools of social science need to be brought to bear in one's research and analysis of one's own context. All theologies are local theologies and the impact of the context on one's theological understanding cannot be underestimated.

Each circle in Figure 13.3 below represents a domain of missiology that provides a unique contribution for creating a contextually appropriate mission theology. Each domain is a sphere of knowledge, influence, activity and relationships. The overlap of each circle with another represents a subsequent level of integration and continuity between those two domains. Like-wise the overlap of multiple circles represents an additional level of integration and continuity amid multiple domains. Often conflicting and sometimes contradictory views of God's mission become evident when one compares the perspectives of the various domains.

An overriding theme in all four of the domains is the centrality of Jesus Christ. This centrality is not merely a step but is a pervasive element in all of the steps. For the mission about which we theologize is God's mission, not the Church's or ours. And God's mission is supremely given in Jesus Christ. Jesus Christ must, therefore, be at the center of all the domains of a contextually appropriate mission theology. The church's mission is the mission of Jesus Christ. The disciples of Jesus Christ participate in the *missio Cristi*. "As the Father has sent me, so send I you" (Jn. 20:21; cf. Jn. 17:18).

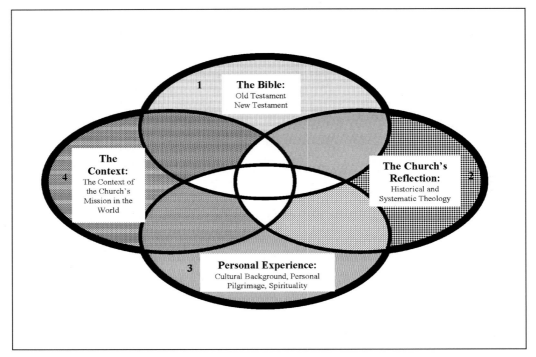

Figure 13.3 Integration of the Four Domains

Step 5: The Integrating Idea. As we proceed, we must recognize the importance of an integrating idea or focus—a conceptual unity wherein all four domains of mission (Bible, Church, Person, and Context) interact and influence each other in relation to our understanding of the mission of Jesus Christ. The integrating idea expresses the over-arching paradigm, the central themes, perceptions, and thinking patterns that draw from the four domains and combine with each other into a cohesive and, at least somewhat, integrated concept of mission in a particular local setting at a particular time.

The integrating idea provides the framework for the creation of a contextually appropriate mission theology and helps the mission theologian gain a deeper understanding of that which will be communicated in word and deed in a new context. Different missiologists and mission groups have built their mission theologies around different centers, held together by different integrating ideas. The integrating idea provides the conceptual framework that serves to hold together and interrelate various levels of integration and continuity between domains.

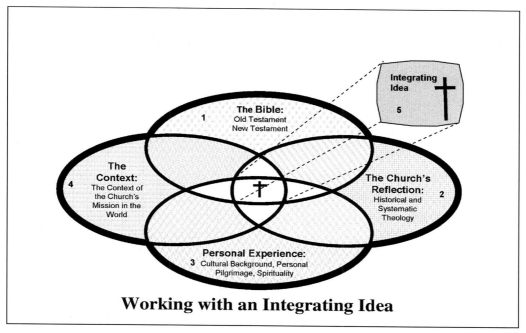

Working with an Integrating Idea

Figure 13.4 Working with an Integrating Idea

Below are a few examples of integrating ideas.

- The integrating ideas for Gisbertus Voetius were:
    The Conversion of the Heathen;
    The Planting of the Church; and
    The Glory of God
- The integrating idea for Orthodox Christianity is The Praise of God
- For William Carey it was The Great Commission
- For Pietism it was The Lostness of Persons
- For Vatican II it was The People of God
- The integrating ideas for David Bosch were:
    The God of Compassion;
    The God of History
    The God Who Values Human Life
- For the WCC Evanston 1954 Assembly it was Ecumenical Unity
- For the WCC Uppsala 1968 Assembly it was Humanization
- For Donald McGavran it was Disciple the Nations

- For Arthur Glasser it was The Kingdom of God and Mission
- For Johannes Verkuyl it was The Role of the Church in Nation-building
- Other examples:

  The Cross: e.g., IMC, Willingen 1952 (Goodall 1953)

  Bearing Witness to the Kingdom

  The Holy Spirit and Mission

  Church Extension -- Ecclesiastics

  Liberation

  The Covenant

Having devoted attention to self-examination concerning the domains of knowledge that have informed our mission theology, we are prepared to take the second step in seeking a contextually appropriate mission theology: we approach anew the local context where our mission action will take place.

Characteristic 2: An Appropriate Mission Theology is Local: Approaching a New Context Anew

The mission theologian is now ready to approach a context in a new way. This context may be a completely different cultural and contextual setting than the mission theologian's own. Or it may be the same culture and same geographic location as that where the mission theologian has been all along. The method we are considering in this chapter is intentionally designed to be useful for constructing an appropriate mission theology in one's "Jerusalem, *and* Judea, *and* Samaria, *and* the ends of the earth" (Ac. 1:8). In any case, after the reflection has been carried out in the first area of consideration as outlined above, mission theologians will encounter even their own context with new understanding and will see it with new eyes.

The second area to deal with in seeking a contextually appropriate mission theology involves an analysis of both the past and the present. One-and-a-half billion persons around the globe claim allegiance to Jesus Christ in some way. Over two-thirds of all world Christianity is now in Asia, Africa, Latin America and Oceania. Christians may now be found in every country, in every city, in every region of the globe. There are still thousands of unreached people groups. But there are no untouched people groups. Even unreached people groups have been impacted by the history of the interaction of the churches and missions with their culture in their context at some point in the recent or distant past. This means that the mission theologian never approaches a context that has never been touched. There is no so-called *tabula rasa* (blank slate) situation left in the world. Thus, when mission theologians approach their context of mission they need to begin by asking historical questions concerning the past interaction of churches and missions with the context—and the impact the context has had on the churches and missions to which it has been related.

Step 6: The Holy Spirit and Prayer. The analysis of the local context must first begin with prayer and recognition of the work of the Holy Spirit. In the Book of Acts, Luke provides us with the historical and theological foundation of our mission theology. We know that Christ's mission is carried out by the work and "in the power of the [Holy] Spirit" (Moltmann 1977). This leads us to ask two questions. 1) What has the Holy Spirit been doing in this context in the distant and recent past? 2) What does the Holy Spirit want to do today and tomorrow in this context? Mission is not ours. It does not belong to the churches or the mission agencies. Churches and missions participate in God's mission (*missio Dei*) (Rosin 1972; Scherer 1987:106-125; Scherer 1993:82-88; John McIntosh 2000: 631-633; J. Verkuyl 1978:197-204), in "Christ's Way" (CWME San Antonio Conference, 1989 – F. Wilson, ed., 1990), guided, propelled, corrected and empowered by the Holy Spirit. Mission in the way of Jesus is always carried out in an atmosphere of the fruit of the Holy Spirit. And the gifts of the Holy Spirit are given for mission (Eph. 4:11-16).

From Pentecost forward, mission is the action of the Holy Spirit through the agency of the Church. The local context is the place where all the theory and action of mission are saturated in the guidance of the Holy Spirit and prayer.

Steps 7 & 8: History. Having recognized the past and present role of the Holy Spirit and prayer in the development of an appropriate mission theology, the mission theologian will proceed to examine three historical aspects having to do with church and mission in the context: 1) the history of mission action by churches and missions in the context (who did what, when); 2) the history of mission theory exhibited by the churches and missions active in the context (their motivations, theoretical constructs, goals and rationale for the methods chosen); and 3) the story of the dynamic two-way interaction of the churches and missions with the people of the context – and the impact of the context on the churches and missions involved.

a. The History of Mission Action/ History of the Church: Everywhere you and I go, there exists a history of the church's interaction with that context. There are both direct and indirect historical factors. The history of mission action in a specific context has too often been ignored in missiology. Throughout history people have tended to first go and do mission and only later have they realized that they needed more complete and intimate knowledge of the history of mission action in that context.

b. The History of Mission Theory: There is also a mission theory associated with the action, and it is this history of mission theory that will help to guide the mission theologian. The particular theological traditions (Ecumenical, Evangelical, Pentecostal/Charismatic, Orthodox, Roman Catholic) have influenced the theoretical framework that has informed mission action.

c. In addition, no one should develop mission theology in a local context without first doing his/her homework concerning the **history of mission activity, mission theory, and missional interaction between the Christian Church and the people in that context.** Whether one thinks of China, Ghana,

Russia, Brazil, Japan, Australia, Saudi Arabia, Thailand, South Africa, Korea, Kenya, Mexico, Germany, the United States, Guatemala, or England, for example, in each place churches and missions—and the local people's view of the churches and missions—have been shaped by the historical and spiritual forces outlined above.

Characteristic 3: An Appropriate Mission Theology is Incarnational: Preparing for New Action

The third characteristic and the ninth step in developing a contextually appropriate mission theology move us from analysis of the past to consideration of the present, on the way to the future. Our examination of the four domains was present-tense. The second step was past-tense. Now we move to considering what an appropriate mission theology should look like in the context where we find ourselves. To stop our reflection at this point yields mission studies but does not lead to active participation in appropriate mission action. This is not satisfactory. As Johannes Verkuyl has said,

> Missiology is the study of the salvation activities of the Father, Son, and Holy Spirit throughout the world geared toward bringing the kingdom of God into existence. Seen in this perspective missiology is the study of the worldwide church's divine mandate to be ready to serve this God who is aiming his saving acts toward this world. In dependence on the Holy Spirit and by word and deed the church is to communicate the total gospel and the total divine law to all (humanity). Missiology's task in every age is to investigate scientifically and critically the presuppositions, motives, structures, methods, patterns of cooperation, and leadership which the churches bring to their mandate. In addition missiology must examine every other type of human activity which combats the various evils to see if it fits the criteria and goals of God's kingdom which has both already come and is yet coming . . . Missiology may never become a substitute for action and participation. God calls for participants and volunteers in his mission. In part, missiology's goal is to become a "service station" along the way. If study does not lead to participation, whether at home or abroad, missiology has lost her humble calling (J. Verkuyl 1978:5-6).

Step 9: The Incarnation is the Heart of Mission Theology. This is the point where we move from the past to the future. This is the critical integrative step. It begins to organize all of the thinking done so far. It transforms and focuses our missiological reflection into issues of mission practice. This is the move from description to prescription. The vertical aspects of God's mission interface with the horizontal categories of human mission action in a complex interweaving of divine and human interaction. To suggest the interactions between the vertical and the horizontal, we can construct a grid with each square of the grid constituting a specific missiological question with a particular emphasis. That grid might look something like Figure 13.5 below.

Aspects of Missional Action	Missio Dei The Mission of God	Missio Homi-num God's Missional Use of Human Instru-ments	Missiones Ecclesi-arum God's Many Missions Through the People of God	Missio Politica Oecu-menica God's Missional Action in Global Civiliza-tion	Missio Christi God's Messianic Mission Through Jesus Christ	Missio Spiritu Sancti God's Mission Through the Holy Spirit	Missio Futurum/ Adventus God's "already/ not yet" Kingdom Mission in Predict-able Future and through Surprising Advent
The Holy Spirit in Mission							
The Context of Mission							
The Agents of Mission							
The Motives of Mission							
The Means of Mission							
The Methods of Mission							
The Goals of Mission							
The Results of Mission							
Hope/ Utopia of Mission							
Prayer in Mission							
Spiritual Power in Mission							
Presence, Procla-mation							
Persuasion, Incorpor-ation							
Structures for Mission							

Figure 13.5 The Theology of Mission – A Working Grid

In the above grid I have sought to represent in a diagrammatic form the interaction of the various theological categories of mission theory with several illustrative aspects of missional action. The interfacing of the mission categories (placed along the horizontal axis) with the aspects of missional action (placed along the vertical axis) yields a host of new questions for mission theology. Each square in the gird constitutes a specific question for appropriate mission theology in a local context.

Characteristic 4: An Appropriate Mission Theology is Praxeological: Living out the Gospel in Appropriate Action

The tenth step in developing an appropriate mission theology has to do with translating the reflection into concrete action. David Bosch, among others, has made a case for the fact that the mission of the Church involves both dimensional and intentional aspects (Bosch 1991:494-496). There are dimensions of the impact of the presence of the disciples of Jesus in a particular context. Their very presence at times may have significant impact on the contextual reality. The dimensions of the presence of the Gospel and of the Church should not be minimized. However, the dimensional aspect is not enough. The Church is also called to active participation in God's mission. The Church is sent into the world by Jesus Christ its head to give concrete shape in specific missional action in each context. This involves the aspect of missional intention. In a given context, what do the churches and missions intend to do? What intentional action steps are called for as the fruit of the reflection carried out in the previous three steps?

Once Christians commit themselves to being involved in missional action, they need to ask careful, sensitive and wise questions that will help to clarify the nature of the task, the action to be taken, the transformation sought, and the results that should be observable as fruit of the action. Each of these in their own right needs to be appropriate to the context.

Step 10: Preparation for Action. Based on the integration offered by the grid, the contextual mission theologian begins to inquire regarding the interrelation of church and context in a specific time and place. In this *new* "here and now" there are specific issues of the church's missional dimension and missional intention vis-à-vis the context. How is the church already engaged in mission in its context? What resources does the church have to carry out mission? What constitutes action that is appropriate both to the mission theory and to the nature of the context?

I define mission as follows:

> God's mission works primarily through the People of God as they intentionally cross barriers from Church to non-church, faith to non-faith to proclaim by word and deed the coming of the Kingdom of God in Jesus Christ, through the Church's participation in God's mission of reconciling people to God, to themselves, to each other,

and to the world, and gathering them into the Church through repentance and faith in Jesus Christ by the work of the Holy Spirit with a view to the transformation of the world as a sign of the coming of the Kingdom in Jesus Christ.

Mission praxis involves a movement from present-oriented reflection and planning to future-directed mission action. As churches and missions engage in missional action it is important that they understand the impact of the action itself on their mission theology. Just as the Jerusalem Council in Acts 15 based its mission decisions on what the Holy Spirit had done in Acts 10, so the churches and missions gain new insight into what is appropriate mission theology in a context precisely through the action of mission itself. The action is itself theological. (For a discussion of how this praxeological method of theologizing plays out in narrative theology, see Van Engen 1996:44-68.)

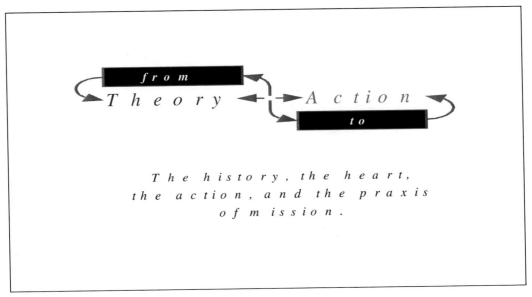

Figure 13.6 Mission Praxis

At this point, reflection leads to action which in turn transforms and informs our reflection, which then leads to new reflection, leading to new action. This dynamic theological interaction of action-reflection-action has been a significant gift that Latin American scholars have offered the world church. Though the notion of praxis is not an exclusively Latin American idea, during the past thirty years Latin Americans have been the dominant voice calling for this approach to doing theology in context. (See Appendix B at the end of this chapter). At this point the contextual mission theologian will translate the reflection into mission action in a particular context, at a specific time, through and with particular people, with specific missional goals in mind.

Step 11: The Missional Action. This is the action itself. The action should be consistent with the foregoing theory (developed in Steps 1 to 4 above). In Figure 13.7 below, a modified version of Hiebert's centered-set perspective is represented graphically depicting the church moving towards Christ and at the same time carrying out mission in the church's context represented by the arrows behind the churches. The one cannot exist without the other. The churches moving away from Christ are not involved in mission.

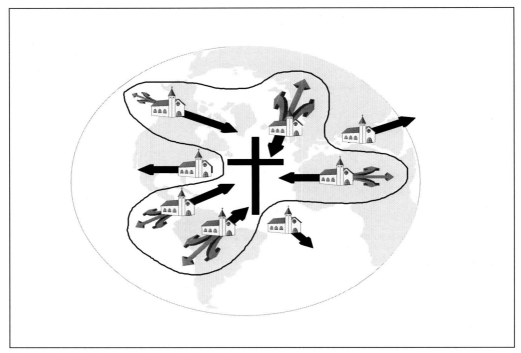

Figure 13.7 Centered Set Perspective

A praxeological approach to contextually appropriate mission theology is made possible when one's theological method is built on what Paul Hiebert has called a "centered-set" approach. In this form of theologizing, the primary concern of the mission theologian is that reflection and action—praxis—be centered and moving toward Jesus Christ in whose mission we participate. In *Anthropological Reflections on Missiological Issues* (1994), Hiebert develops the "characteristics of centered sets." It is instructive for us to listen to Hiebert at this point.

"First," Hiebert says,

> a centered set is created by defining the center or reference point and the relationship of things to that center. Things related to the center belong to the set, and those not related to the center do not . . .

> Second, while centered sets are not created by drawing boundaries, *they do have sharp boundaries* that separate things inside

the set from those outside it—between things related to or moving toward the center and those that are not. Centered sets are well-formed, just like bounded sets. They are formed by defining the center and any relationships to it. The boundary then emerges automatically. Things related to the center naturally separate themselves from things that are not . . .

"Third, there are two variables intrinsic to centered sets. The first is membership. All members of a set are full members and share fully in its functions. There are not second-class members. The second variable is distance from the center. Some things are far from the center and others near to it, but all are moving toward it . . .

Fourth, centered sets have two types of change inherent in their structure. The first has to do with entry into or exit from the set. Things headed away from the center can turn and move toward it . . . The second type of change has to do with movement toward or away from the center. Distant members can move toward the center, and those near can slide back while still herded toward it . . . (1994:123-124).

Hiebert goes on to demonstrate that "Hebrew Culture" was structured as a centered set, based on relationships, especially in terms of a covenantal relationship of the people of Israel to the God of Abraham, Isaac and Jacob.

Hiebert then asks,

What happens to our concept of Christian if we define it in centered-set terms?

First, Christians would be defined as followers of the Jesus Christ of the Bible, as those who make him the center or Lord of their lives . . .

Second, there would be a clear separation between Christians and nonChristians, between those who are followers of Jesus and those who are not. The emphasis, however, would be on exhorting people to follow Christ, rather than on excluding others to preserve the purity of the set . . .

Third, there would be a recognition of variation among Christians . . .

Fourth, two important types of change would be recognized in centered-set thought. First, there is conversion, entering or leaving the set . . .

The second change is movement toward the center, or growth in a relationship. A Christian is not a finished product the moment he or she is converted. Conversion, therefore, is a definite event followed by an ongoing process. Sanctification is not a separate activity, but a process of justification continued throughout life (1994:125-127).

Hiebert then proceeds to look at the Church as a centered set and missions as a centered set, following the four characteristics he mentioned earlier. Hiebert's idea of "centered-set" theological method is an especially important guide in developing contextually appropriate mission theology. It provides a means by which we can be firmly and tightly anchored in truth in Jesus Christ, yet simultaneously be open to differing worldviews, see through different cultural lenses as we read the Scriptures, and interact creatively with differing contexts—all within the same world Church comprised of the disciples of the one Center, Jesus Christ.

Characteristic 5: An Appropriate Mission Theology is Dialogical: Re-shaping our Understanding of the Gospel: Praxis

In the fifth part of the process of searching for a contextually appropriate mission theology, the mission theologian analyzes how the missional action is brought to bear upon the four domains that were examined in the first part of this process.

For the past forty years, Latin Americans have been at the forefront of a particular method in contextual theology having to do with the "hermeneutical circle" as it was articulated and interpreted by people like Juan-Luis Segundo (1976), among others.[2] The hermeneutical circle of Latin American Liberation Theology spearheaded an intentional process whereby one's contextual hermeneutic moved toward a commitment to the preferential option for the poor, which in turn opened one's eyes to re-read the meaning of Scripture for today's situation (a hermeneutics of significance). This provided new lenses through which one could re-read the context of ministry.

Segundo began with the context of a people's reality and developed four decisive moments: 1) a people's plausibility structure (to use Peter Berger's term) leads to a particular agenda or question; 2) a people's agenda, question, or existential concern provides an approach to the biblical text; 3) understanding the text from the point of view of the people's agenda provides a particular application back to the context; and 4) that application leads to a new agenda or question that can be implemented in the context, which starts the cycle all over again. This process leads to a circular movement whereby the present context informs the meaning of the text and maintains the entire circular flow—hence the term "hermeneutical circle."

In Segundo's methodology, certain ideas (Segundo calls them "ideologies") emerge out of a particular context examined by an interpreter with

---

[2] See, for example, Clodovis Boff (1987:63-66; 132-153); Leonardo Boff and Clodovis Boff (1987:32-35); Guillermo Cook (1985:104-126); Samuel Escobar (1987:172-179); Deane Ferm (1986:25-26); Gustavo Gutierrez (1988:13); Roger Haight (1985:46-59); Jose Miguez Bonino (1975:90-104); C. Rene Padilla (1985:83-91); Robert Schreiter (1985:75-94); Juan Luis Segundo (1976:7-38); Gordon Spykman et al. (1988:228-230); Jon Sobrino (1984:1-38); and Raul Vidales (1979:48-51).

eyes that involve a 'hermeneutics of suspicion.'"[3] These concepts are, then, a reflection of the interpreters' perspective, a hermeneutic of that situation that forces questions about the perspectives of the people in those circumstances. Based on the new insights into the context gained in such a re-examination, the interpreters should then re-read the Scriptures. As the interpreters re-read the Scriptures, they see things they did not see before because they are asking new questions that reflect a new understanding derived from the new context. Drawing from the new insights the interpreters have gained from Scripture, they encounter anew their context with new insight derived from their new reading of Scripture. Below is a diagram of this process.

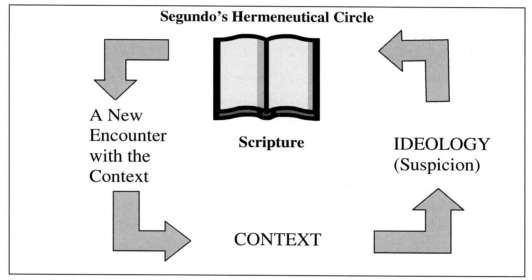

Figure 13.8 Segundo's Hermeneutical Circle
(Juan Luis Segundo 1976:7-38)

---

[3] In Segundo's thought there are four decisive moments or factors influencing the hermeneutical circle:

1. There is our way of experiencing reality that leads us to ideological suspicion. (Mannheim's three elements are involved in Segundo's understanding of this first stage: (a) a concrete evaluational experience of theology; (b) an act of the will on the part of the theologian with respect to his/her theology; and (c) a direction in treating new problems that derives from this act of the will.

2. There is the application of our ideological suspicion to the whole ideological superstructure in general and to theology in particular.

3. There comes a new way of experiencing theological reality that leads us to exegetical suspicion, that is, the suspicion that the prevailing interpretation of the Bible has not taken important pieces of data into account.

4. We have our new hermeneutic, that is, our new way of interpreting the fountainhead of our faith (i.e., Scripture) with the new elements at our disposal (Segundo 1976:7-38).

Following this structure, some theologians have used the term "exegeting the context." to signify a particular perception of reality. This process is extremely important for the development of a contextually appropriate mission theology. The hermeneutical circle seeks to build a dynamic interactivity between the contemporary context and the missiological theory and perspectives of the mission theologian.[4] The hermeneutical circle provides a way to reflect on the missional action of step four.

Step 12: Reflection on the Action. Reflection, re-examination, re-thinking, and re-conceptualizing are needed at this point. Reflection should take place addressing the consistency between the action taken and the initial conceptualization found in the integrating idea. Where there are anomalies, inconsistencies and contradictions between the understanding of the integrating idea and the action taken, we must look more carefully. The place of the anomalies is the place where the reconceptualization begins all over again. This creates a process of action/reflection molded through time.

Looking at the process in its entirety, the reader can image the Integrating Idea flowing clockwise through the entire process (channel) that transforms it from theory into action. In this process, it is evaluated, examined, enhanced, energized, enacted, and finally reintegrated with the four original domains so that reconceptualization can take place leading toward a refinement of mission. Over time, therefore, this becomes an iterative process that is constantly making adjustments in mission theory and practice. The following diagram is intended to show this process in all its complexity.

---

[4] This explanation of the hermeneutical circle as developed by Juan Luis Segundo is an adaptation of a similar section in Chapter 4 of Dan Shaw and Charles Van Engen 2003.

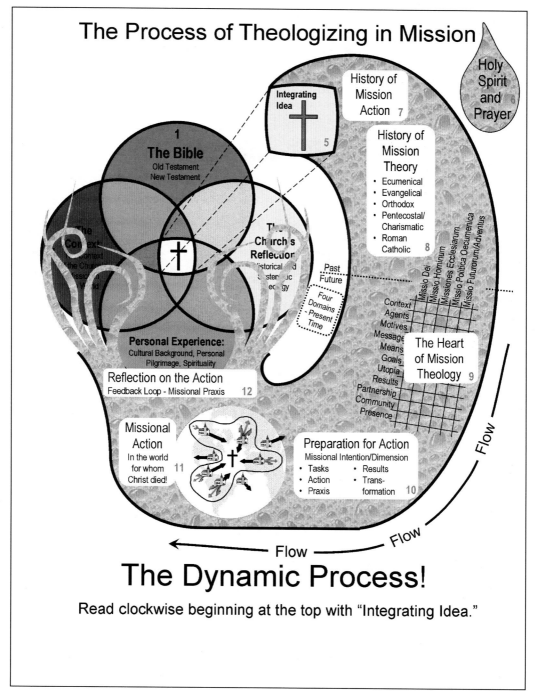

Figure 13.9 The Process of Theologizing in Mission

This brings us back to an awareness of the spiraling process of deepening our knowledge of God and understanding of God's mission. As was said at the beginning of this chapter, the process outlined here is not complete if there is only one cycle. This process needs to be repeated countless times over many years for the mission theologian to begin to grasp "how wide and long and high and deep is the love of Christ" (Eph. 3:18).

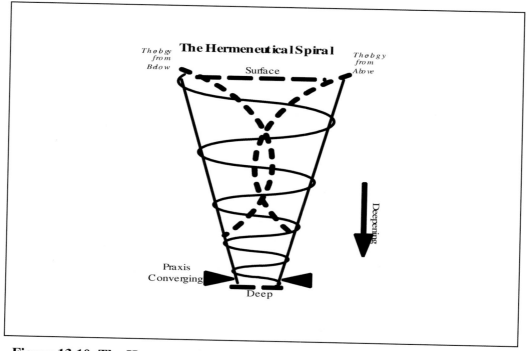

Figure 13.10 The Hermeneutical Spiral

Conclusion

In this chapter I have outlined a method whereby mission theologians might discover a contextually appropriate mission theology for their time and in their context. Our task is as simple as saying to our neighbor in word and deed: "Jesus loves you, this I know for the Bible tells me so." Yet it is also an extremely complex endeavor filled with a host of issues of which we have been given only a glance. In that vein, David Bosch's words seem appropriate as a way to conclude this chapter.

The church-in-mission is, primarily, the *local* church everywhere in the world. This perspective, as well as the supposition that no local church should stand in a position of authority over against another local church, both fundamental to the New Testament (cf. Ac. 13:1-3 and the Pauline letters), was for all practical purposes ignored during much of Christian history. . . .

Mission could no longer be viewed as one-way traffic, from the West to the Third World; every church, everywhere, was understood to be in a state of mission. . . .

The fundamentally innovative feature of the new development was the discovery that the universal church actually finds its true existence in the local churches; that these, and not the universal church, are the pristine expression of church . . . that this was the primary understanding of church in the New Testament . . . ; that the church is the church because of what happens in the local church's *martyria, leitourgia, koinonia,* and *diakonia;* that the church is an event among people rather than an authority addressing them or an institution possessed of the elements of salvation, of doctrines, and offices . . .

At the same time, it has to be said that Catholics tend to appreciate, more clearly than Protestants do, the essential interrelatedness between the universal church and local churches. The church is, really, a *family* of local churches in which each should be open to the needs of the others and to sharing its spiritual and material goods with them. It is through the mutual ministry of *mission* that the church is realized, in communion with and as local concretization of the church universal.

The rediscovery of the local church as the primary agent of mission has led to a fundamentally new interpretation of the purpose and role of missionaries and mission agencies . . .

In the midst of these new circumstances and relationships there is still room for and need of individual missionaries, but only insofar as all recognize that their task is one that pertains to the *whole* church … and insofar as missionaries appreciate that they are sent as ambassadors of one local church to another local church (where such a local church already exists) as witnesses of solidarity and partnership, and as expressions of mutual encounter, exchange, and enrichment.

The new paradigm has led to an abiding tension between two views of the church which appear to be fundamentally irreconcilable. At one end of the spectrum, the church perceives itself to be the sole bearer of a message of salvation on which it has a monopoly, at the other end, the church views itself, at most, as an illustration—in word and deed—of God's involvement with the world (Bosch 1991:378-381).

Appendix A

The Three-Arena Approach to Mission Theologizing

As promised early in this chapter, the following are some of the scholars who have adopted the three-arena approach to mission theologizing.

Bevans, Steven. *Models of Contextual Theology.* Maryknoll, NY: Orbis, 1992; reprinted and expanded 2002.

Bonino, Jose Miguez-. *Doing Theology in a Revolutionary Situation.* Philadelphia, PA: Fortress, 1975.

Branson, Mark and Rene Padilla, edits. *Conflict and Contexts: Hermeneutics in the Americas.* Grand Rapids, MI: Eerdmans, 1986.

Coe, Shoki, "Contextualizing Theology." In *Mission Trends No. 3.* Gerald Anderson and Thomas Stransky, eds. Grand Rapids, MI: Eerdmans, 1976.

Conn, Harvie. "Contextualization: A New Dimension for Cross-Cultural Hermeneutic." *Evangelical Missions Quarterly* XIV: 1 (January, 1978), 39-46.

_____. *Eternal Word and Changing Worlds: Theology, Anthropology and Mission in Trialogue.* Grand Rapids, MI: Zondervan, 1984.

_____. "A Contextual Theology of Mission for the City." In *The Good News of the Kingdom.* Charles Van Engen, Dean Gilliland and Paul Pierson, eds. Maryknoll, NY: Orbis, 1993, 96-106.

_____. "Urban Mission." In *Toward the 21st Century in Christian Mission.* James M. Phillips and Robert Coote, eds. Grand Rapids, MI: Eerdmans, 1993, 318-337

Coote, Robert and John Stott, eds. *Down to Earth: Studies in Christianity and Culture.* Grand Rapids, MI: Eerdmans, 1980.

Dyrness, William A. *Learning About Theology from the Third World.* Grand Rapids, MI: Zondervan, 1990.

Fleming, Bruce. *The Contextualization of Theology.* Pasadena, CA: William Carey Library, 1980.

Gilliland, Dean S. "New Testament Contextualization: Continuity and Particularity in Paul's Theology." In *The Word Among Us: Contextualizing Theology for Mission Today.* Waco, TX: Word, 1989, 52-73.

Glasser, Arthur. "Help from an Unexpected Quarter or, The Old Testament and Contextualization." *Missiology* VII: 4 (Oct., 1979), 401-410.

Grenz, Stanley J. *Revisioning Evangelical Theology: A Fresh Agenda for the 21st Century.* Downers Grove, IL: InterVarsity Press, 1993, 93.

Hesselgrave, David and Edward Rommen. *Contextualization: Meanings, Methods, and Models.* Grand Rapids, MI: Baker, 1989.

Hiebert, Paul. "Conversion, Culture and Cognitive Categories." *Gospel in Context* I.3 (July, 1978), 24-29.

_____. "Critical Contextualization." *International Bulletin of Missionary Research* XI: 3 (July, 1987) 104-111.

_____. "Evangelism, Church, and Kingdom." In *The Good News of the Kingdom.* Charles Van Engen, Dean Gilliland Paul Pierson, eds. Maryknoll, NY: Orbis, 1993, 153-161.

Jacobs, Donald. "Contextualization in Mission." In *Toward the 21st Century in Christian Mission.* James M. Phillips and Robert Coote, eds. Grand Rapids, MI: Eerdmans, 1993, 235-244.

Kraft, Charles. *Christianity in Culture: A Study in Dynamic Biblical Theologizing in Cross-Cultural Perspective.* Maryknoll, NY: Orbis, 1979.

_____. *Communication Theory for Christian Witness.* Maryknoll, NY: Orbis, 1991.

Kraft, Charles and Tom Wisely, eds. *Readings in Dynamic Indigeneity.* Pasadena, CA: William Carey Library, 1979.

Luzbetak, Louis. *The Church and Cultures.* Maryknoll, NY: Orbis, 1988.

Nida, Eugene. *Message and Mission.* New York: Harper, 1960.

Sanneh, Lamin. *Translating the Message: The Missionary Impact on Culture.* Maryknoll, NY: Orbis, 1989.

Schreiter, Robert. *Constructing Local Theologies.* Maryknoll, NY: Orbis, 1985.

Shaw, Daniel. *Transculturation: The Cultural Factor in Translation and Other Communication Tasks.* Pasadena, CA: William Carey Library, 1988.

Shenk, Wilbert, ed. *The Transfiguration of Mission: Biblical, Theological & Historical Foundations.* Scottdale, PA: Herald, 1993, 153-177.

Tiénou, Tite "Forming Indigenous Theologies." In *Toward the Twenty-first Century in Christian Mission.* James M. Phillips and Robert T. Coote, eds. Grand Rapids, MI: Eerdmans, 1993, 249-250.

Tippett, Alan. *Introduction to Missiology.* Pasadena, CA: William Carey Library, 1987.

Van Engen, Charles. *God's Missionary People.* Grand Rapids, MI: Baker, 1991.

Van Engen, Charles, Dean S. Gilliland and Paul Pierson, eds. *The Good News of the Kingdom.* Maryknoll, NY: Orbis, 1993.

(Leonardo Boff, Orlando Costas, David Bosch, Johannes Verkuyl, John V. Taylor, Donald McGavran, Max Warren, Lesslie Newbigin, James Scherer, Gerald Anderson, Carl Braaten, Howard Snyder, Jürgen Moltmann, among others, also utilize a three-arena approach in their theology and missiology, though they may not speak of all three at once in the same place.)

Appendix B

Praxis

The following citations are meant to be an extended footnote which may aid the student of contextually appropriate mission theology to understand the meaning and significance of "praxis."

Bonino, José Míguez-. *Christians and Marxists.* 1976: 91-102.

-------. "Hermeneutics, Truth and Praxis." In *Doing Theology in a Revolutionary Situation*. Philadelphia, PA: Fortress, 1975, 86-105.

Boff, Clodovis. *Theology and Praxis*. 1987: xxi-xxx.

Boff, Leonardo. *Liberating Grace*. 1979: 3.

Boff, Leonardo and Clodovis Boff. *Introducing Liberation Theology*. 1987: 8-9.

Brown, Robert McAfee. *Theology in a New Key.* 1978: 50-51.

-------. *Unexpected News*. 1984.

Cardenal, Ernesto. *Flights of Victory*. 1985: 11-12, 23-25.

Chop, Rebecca. *The Praxis of Suffering*. 1986: 36-37, 115-117, 120-121.

Costas, Orlando. *Theology of the Crossroads*. 1976: 8-9.

Croatto, Severino. *Liberación y Libertad: Pautas Hermeneúticas*. Buenos Aires, Argentina: Ediciones Mundo Nuevo, 1973.

Ferm, Deane. *Third World Theologies: An Introduction*. 1986: 15.

Gutierrez, Gustavo, "Liberation Praxis and Christian Faith." In: Gibellini. *Frontiers*. 1975: 1-33.

-------. *We Drink From Our Own Wells*. 1984a: 19-32.

-------. *The Power of the Poor in History*. 1984b: vii-viii, 50-60

-------. *Theology of Liberation*. 1988: 6-19.

Haight, Roger. *An Alternative Vision*. 1985: 44-48.

Padilla, Rene. *Mission Between the Times*. 1983: 83.

Schreiter, Robert. *Constructing Local Theologies*, 17, 91-93.

Scott, Waldron. *Bring Forth Justice*. 1980: xv.

Spykman, et al. *Let My People Live*. 1988: xiv, 226-231.

Vidales, Raul, "Methodological Issues in Liberation Theology." In: Gibellini. *Frontiers*. 1975: 34-57.

Chapter 14

Appropriate Hermeneutics

Shawn B. Redford

Biblical Theology of Mission is uniquely qualified to provide a missiological critique of the underlying cultural assumptions inherent in Western theology. Largely due to the influence of Western academia, Western theology has generated a hermeneutical process tied to human reasoning, with little room for the Creator of the universe to speak, clarify or guide in understanding the very Scripture that God has created. Meanwhile, new hermeneutical understandings in theology of mission have pointed us to recognizing the missionary nature of the Bible. From this base, the field of Biblical Theology of Mission is able to address the pitfalls of Western hermeneutics while simultaneously validating its strengths. Thus, a more holistic hermeneutical method can be offered to students, missiologists, missionaries and most importantly new Christian believers.

The thesis of this chapter is that hermeneutics in Biblical Theology of Mission must properly critique the culture-boundness of Western hermeneutical method by validating and developing new openness to spiritual dimensions as an equally esteemed part of the total hermeneutical process. This chapter relates to appropriate Christianity by investigating areas where the perspective cross-cultural workers have learned is inappropriate from the start, leading to the exporting of our own misconceptions and infusing them into contextual models of our own making. This chapter, then, seeks to provide a mirror that causes us to examine the very core of the ideas we are attempting to contextualize. One of the flaws of contextualization studies has been a failure to re-examine these ideas. Missionaries advocating contextualization need some sort of critical feedback to balance the human and strongly Western tendencies towards paternalism.

Theological Circles

The focus of this chapter is not on the history of hermeneutics, but some background must be considered in order for missiologists to perceive the "air that we breathe."[1] Three hermeneutical traditions come to mind when looking at

---

[1] I owe this phrase to Wilbert Shenk.

the cultural assumptions of the Western hermeneutical process: that of liberal scholars, that of evangelical scholars and that of Protestant fundamentalists.

In looking at these traditions, my main concern is to address underlying hermeneutical and spiritual assumptions that are made by adherents of these traditions. Unfortunately, proponents of these traditions often claim they make no assumptions at all, and that their perceptions are void of bias. As Newbigin pointed out, however:

> What came to be known as the "historical-critical method" grew to eventually be accepted as the only proper method for interpreting these ancient writings. . . . [T]his move is misunderstood if it is seen as a move to a more objective understanding of the Bible. It is a move from one confessional stance to another, a move from one creed to another. *But it is very hard to persuade the practitioners of the historical-critical method to recognize the creedal character of their approach* (Newbigin 1995b:79-80, emphasis mine).

Insightful theologians and missiologists alike have consistently recognized that no one comes to Scripture in the absence of assumptions (Kirk 1997:9-10, 25; Kraft 2002:30-32; Newbigin 1991:44). In the words of Gordon Fee,

> neither does the exegete come to the text with a clean slate, but also brings his or her agendas to the text, not to mention a whole train load of cultural baggage and biases (Fee 2000:9).

Liberal Method

Liberal methodology has embraced a secular approach to interpretation, assuming that all of the accounts in Scripture should be explained through natural means. The foremost assumption is that Scripture is strictly a historical record. The unstated assumption that follows is that God is *not involved* with humanity in Scripture (Kirk 1997:18-19). It could be characterized as an agnostic hermeneutical approach because God is not part of the process and indeed God need not exist (Newbigin 1995b:69, 100). The burden of proof for any account in Scripture is solely upon humanity (whether good or bad) precisely because an *a priori* decision has been made that God is not at work in human history, including the history set forth in the Bible (cf. Newbigin 1995b:95-96). These assumptions are of course validated in the name of "scientific integrity" (Barth 1962:187-190). Since it is assumed that God is not at work in Scripture, all of God's in-breaking in Scripture must be explained "rationally" (Marshall 2002:12; Gasque 1978:148). Newbigin puts this overall focus in perspective:

> They practice rather the "hermeneutic of suspicion" which leads the student of an ancient record to ask not What is the truth which is here articulated? but What is the interest which is here being advanced? The biblical material is thus interpreted in terms of the various power struggles in Israel and in the church (Newbigin 1995b:83).

Liberal theologians have made many astute observations in understanding the perceptions and values of the biblical writers. This contribution is something that should not be overlooked. However, liberal theologians have limited their understanding of Scripture because they have chosen to severely limit the role of God in Scripture and God's continuity in the development of Scripture (Frei 1974:64). The main thrust of this godless process places humanity in control of nearly ever facet of Scripture, as expressed by Newbigin:

> The gospel challenges liberals' thinking in the sharpest possible way, and perhaps this is the hardest thing for them to accept. It exposes as illusion the liberal picture—the picture of ourselves as sovereign explorers who formulate the real questions in a search for a yet-to-be-discovered reality. The gospel . . . exposes our false pretensions. We are *not* honest and open-minded explorers of reality; we are alienated from reality because we have made ourselves the center of the universe (Newbigin 1995b:104).

Evangelical Theologians

The dividing line between liberal and evangelical hermeneutics is blurred largely because evangelical scholars have largely adopted the historical-critical method from the liberals.[2] However, evangelical scholars have, for the most part, held their conviction that Scripture is the Word of God. The Bible, then, is not seen solely as a historical record. Yet evangelical scholars, by employing historical-critical methodology, have unwittingly sided with liberals in reducing the Bible to mere history.

God is given little capacity to influence the hermeneutical process among evangelicals because of concern that assumptions cannot be made regarding God's involvement in the development of Scripture (which is in itself an assumption). Andrew Kirk notes the paradox that this creates for the scholar who believes in the inspiration of Scripture and is confined to a historical-critical methodology drawing too heavily from the liberals:

> [T]heology has relied so heavily on the renowned historical-critical method. Even where new approaches have arisen that concentrate on the finished text . . . [this] method remains pervasive. . . . The interpreter cannot remain detached from the message of the text, in a kind of cocoon of suspended judgment. For the attempt to remain free from any interaction with the text as communication is already a judgment about one's method and one's relation to the particular configuration of words. As a consequence, I have never understood how it is possible to study the text of the Bible as if it were just another piece of literature from the Ancient Near East, for it manifestly is not . . . (Kirk 1997:9-10).

---

[2] The official name, "the grammatico-historical method," will be used synonymously throughout this chapter.

As a result, God is excluded from the hermeneutical process even though evangelical scholars most often profess faith in God and the inspiration of the Scripture. Few observations are made over the continuity of scriptural themes, since this exists due to God's involvement in developing Scripture. As a result, historical-critical analysis has been prone to fragmentation, and comparatively little work has been done in discourse-level analysis. Themes coursing through Scripture are seen as coincidental to God's nature, but not intended by God and this has made metanarratives suspect in Scripture. Kirk validly claims that "the dominant approach to theology in the West has been rooted in skepticism, rather than in a properly self-critical critical method" (Kirk 1997:48-49).

Additionally, the lack of missionary experience among evangelical theologians (whether at home or abroad) has most often forced Scripture into a pattern of ideas about truth (even when historical-critical method avoids being reductionistic). The hermeneutical ideas that then guide the very Scripture that consistently demonstrates the missionary tragedies and triumphs between God and his people, are most often treated as if they are void of missional questions and categories.

Protestant Fundamentalism

Given the liberal and evangelical scholars' claims of supposed "objectivity" and "neutrality" in their "assumption-less" methods of interpreting Scripture, a reactionary force grew that attempted to force Scripture into another mold of modernity. This approach was typified by a "fundamentalism which seeks to affirm the factual, objective truth of every statement in the Bible and which thinks that if any single factual error were to be admitted, biblical authority would collapse" (Newbigin 1995b:85). Protestant fundamentalism seemed quite different from its liberal "enemy" but it too was built upon a modern worldview that attempted to use reason as the foremost method for interpreting Scripture. Gordon Fee illustrates this reactionary tension by taking on the perspective of the Church:

> Taking Scripture away from the believing community, the exegete made it an object of historical investigation. Armed with the so-called historical-critical method, he thus engaged in an exercise in history, pure and simple, an exercise that appeared all too often to begin from a stance of doubt—indeed, sometimes of historical skepticism with an anti-supernatural bias. Using professional jargon about form, redaction, and rhetorical criticism, the exegete, full of arrogance and assuming a stance of mastery over the text, often seemed to turn the text on its head so that it no longer spoke to the believing community as the powerful word of the living God (Fee 2000:8).

As a result of these uneasy tensions, Christians perceived their only choice was to choose some position along a continuum of "reason," all of which imprisoned Scripture in Western concerns over reason, truth, and inerrancy while missional concerns were given little or no energy at all. The real irony in all of this is that the lack of vision in understanding mission in Scripture among all of these groups has left them in the predicament that they now face.

Examining the Western Lens

Western cultural values have for the most part gone unexamined by theologians, and this is the starting point for addressing our current crisis in hermeneutics. In order to understand the overall focus of the Western worldview as it relates to Scripture, we must consider the assumptions that flow from Western worldview into the historical-critical method. Western theological perceptions have resulted in a polarization in which spiritual or experiential approaches to Scripture are set aside as irrelevant and only reason endorsed.

True, the Bible itself is the focus of these hermeneutical efforts and numerous disciplines assist in various ways of knowing, interpreting, and relating to God's message in Scripture. However, among the disciplines, rational thought has been given the highest precedence because of its perceived superior status over other means of understanding Scripture. Rational thought has been perceived as an objective way of knowing because Western theologians, until recently, have presented the rational hermeneutical method as an unbiased and objective way of reflecting upon Scripture. In contrast, spiritual "disciplines" (for lack of a better term) have been given the least credibility as a means of understanding Scripture. Narrative and experiential ways of knowing hold a higher position than spiritual approaches, but nothing holds the same level of esteem as rational thought. The spiritual areas are most looked down on because of the severely limited way in which these have been perceived in the West. Kirk keenly notes the dichotomy of Western hermeneutical thought as it relates to itself, others and spiritual matters:

> Academic theology's pretensions to being a genuinely critical method are suspect. In traditional academic theology, the historical-critical method has been the bedrock of any work able to claim intellectual rigor and credibility. In accordance with certain Enlightenment emphases, out of which it grew, the method begins with a first principle of doubt (or suspicion). Thus the historical accounts of the biblical narrative are assumed to be guilty of exaggeration or of reconstructing stories to fit a predetermined theological stance, until proved innocent. . . .
>
> In my estimation, in this whole procedure skepticism has been disastrously confused with criticism. For two hundred years or so theological faculties and departments have gone about their work under the illusion that the critical method is an impregnable fortress from which we may sally forth to do battle with all kinds of theological naïveté, fundamentalism, and other forms of strong Christian belief in the accessibility of final truth. . . . It is this

confusion, perhaps more than anything else, that has led to a certain schizophrenia between academic pursuits, on the one hand, and spirituality, mission, and pastoral concerns, on the other (Kirk 1997:15-16).

Current Hermeneutics in Theology of Mission

The good news is that Biblical Theology of Mission has moved beyond many of the limiting cultural assumptions and restrictions of traditional hermeneutics. We have learned to take seriously our assumptions regarding Scripture, historical understanding, cultural perspectives, narrative and community-based theology in mission. As a result, it is important to consider the significant contributions to the hermeneutical process that have taken place. This is not a comprehensive overview, but the areas that follow do represent major shifts from traditional hermeneutics that have come about largely due to a kind of "dialogue" that has emerged between the Bible and mission (Nissen 2002:13-15).

Cultural Lenses of the Missiologist

One of the strengths of missiology has been the tremendous development that has come from understanding culture, modernity and postmodernity. These understandings have helped us to become more aware of our assumptions when approaching Scripture. Missiologists have actively sought to understand the ways in which worldview assumptions affect mission theory and practice. For Western missiologists, the study of modernity and postmodernity has provided even greater depth in revealing Western values ingrained at the worldview level such as individualism, technique/strategy, specialization/fragmentation, time-space separation, rationalism, and working from strength and power (Shenk 1995:56, 62; Shenk 1999:135-137).

This development has helped missiologists and missionaries to realize that they do not operate from an objective position. As a result of this development, alert missionaries *actively attempt to recognize their practical tendencies towards subjectivity.* Missiologists also make assumptions when interpreting Scripture but we work hard at becoming aware of our assumptions and are thus better prepared to understand how our worldview affects our interpretations. These understandings motivate us towards views that validate a broader and more holistic hermeneutical approach—an approach that often enables us to learn from peoples whose worldviews are closer than ours to the authors of Scripture. Besides humbling us, such insights enable us to address the problem of pride in our Western rationalistic and individualistic approaches to Scripture, as if we alone know it all.

Although we probably do not realize most of our assumptions about the nature of Scripture, one positive assumption, drawn from Biblical Theology of Mission, is that God's agenda for mission is imprinted on the pages of Scripture through time. A model of Scripture developed by Charles Van Engen carries this positive assumption. This model is known as the "Tapestry of Scripture." It assumes that God has woven (revealed through time) various threads (themes or motifs) in the many cultural contexts (books or contexts within a book) of Scripture (Van Engen 1996:41; Van Engen and Redford 2002:35). The tapestry was originally developed to avoid the tendency of proof-texting Scripture to support human agendas in mission (Van Engen 1996:42). The model, then, attempts to provide a check on how far an interpretation can vary from God's intent in Scripture. David Bosch points out how subtle this tendency can be:

> [I]t can easily happen that, consciously or unconsciously, *the reader refers only to the biblical data which particularly appeal to him* or provide the 'answers' he is looking for. . . . As a result, it inevitably happens that *a canon develops within the canon*; what is not to the liking of a particular group is simply ignored (Bosch 1980:45-46, emphasis mine).

Van Engen has created a practical application for Kraft's concept of a "tethered distance for proper interpretation" (Kraft 1979a:191-192). Although the tapestry was not based upon Kraft's concept, the tapestry does offer one of the most effective ways for the missiologist to understand God's mission biblically and also to address highly suspect interpretations. Van Engen does not stand alone with this concept. Others include Beeby (1999:32-38, 113), D. Allen (1997:134-135), Horton (1908:183-184), McCartney (2002:3) and McCartney and Clayton (2002:200-206). Larry Caldwell points out that:

> the final authority will not be the individual culture's particular hermeneutical method but the Bible itself and *how each new meaning is consistent with the overall thrust of Scripture*. The Bible must always take precedence over any culture and that culture's particular interpretation, no matter how relevant or receptor-oriented it may be (Caldwell 2000:144, emphasis mine).

The tapestry is a model based on the *assumption* that God has actively and consistently revealed himself throughout the ages. The assumption that God has been involved in the development of scriptural themes is no more or less an assumption than the idea that God has *not* been involved in the development of Scripture. To those who are both faithful to Scripture and value reason above all else, this is a most reasonable assumption concerning the nature of Scripture (Brunner 1931:93-94). If God is not revealed in the Bible then where is God revealed? To those who cry "foul" due to the historical-critical and faithless assumption that God has not been involved in revealing himself in Scripture through the ages, I would continue to point out that their position is also the result of assumptions.

More often than not, these latter assumptions oppose the claims of Scripture regarding God's consistent nature and God's repetitive work in trying to involve the people of God in mission. Furthermore, the idea that God is *absent* in Scripture or the idea that God's will is *absent* in Scripture (a perspective most often built upon scientific agendas that are exclusive of faith) is just as clearly an assumption as the idea that God and God's will are *involved and existent* in Scripture (cf. Newbigin 1995b:101-102). Conversely, the assumptions of the tapestry model are rooted in faith in God and faith in God's concern for humanity.

Some have perceived the tapestry model as simple to follow. It is not.[3] This model requires tremendous integration of biblical concepts and contexts that ultimately require a much broader knowledge of Scripture, but avoids the Western tendency to isolate biblical texts and atomize the whole of Scripture.

History of Mission and Hermeneutics

A great contribution provided by those in the history of mission has been to demonstrate the way in which modern thought has taken missions captive in the present-day missionary movement. Those who come to this discussion primarily as theologians and epistemologists, such as Lesslie Newbigin and David Bosch, and those who come as historians, such as Andrew Walls and Wilbert Shenk, have written extensively on the influence that modernity has had upon mission practice (Bosch 1980, 1991, 1995; Newbigin 1991, 1994, 1995b; Shenk 1993, 1995, 1999; Walls 1996). The ability to see the deficiencies in our understanding has come from investigating the cultural values infused in Western theology through the lenses of mission history. As a result, historical studies of the missionary use of Scripture are one of the most helpful taskmasters in avoiding the tendency to force Scripture to fit a missionary's agenda. As noted by Bosch:

> A study of mission through the ages may, for instance, teach us a lesson in reserve. Churches and missionaries expose themselves to grave danger *whenever they isolate their own missionary activities from the current of nineteen centuries of Church history.* A lack of historical perspective all too easily causes people to draw direct lines from the Bible to their own missionary practice, *oblivious of the degree to which their interpretation of the Bible might be conditioned by their situation.* They then remain blissfully ignorant of the deficiencies of their own enterprise and tend to regard it as the only

---

[3] My personal observation when teaching Biblical Theology of Mission is that many students readily agree to the conceptual ideas of the tapestry but struggle when trying to put this model into practice, primarily because they are not prepared for the complex development of integrative thinking in the Bible (McCartney and Clayton 2002:200).

> correct one, perfectly in harmony with what the Bible teaches (Bosch
> 1980:87, emphasis mine).

Mission historians have also recognized the contextual factors that influence the particular choices of the missiologist in his own time. Much of the critique of hermeneutics offered in this chapter also applies to Western missionary practice. From a hermeneutical standpoint, we need a great deal more historical research to understand the theological assumptions made by various missionaries and the role that these assumptions have played in their understanding of mission.

Missionary Experience

Experience has been excluded from the hermeneutical process for the most part because the "reaction against extreme emotionalism has led many, especially academics, to discount the value of experience in the interpretive process" (Kraft 2002:32; cf. D. Allen 1997:31). This issue has left missiologists timid in defining the role of experience in hermeneutics. "Knowing cannot be severed from living and acting, for we cannot know the truth unless we seek it with love and unless our love commits us to action" (Newbigin 1995b:105).

While introductory texts on hermeneutical method have recognized that various passages require genre-specific insights (e.g., an understanding of Hebrew poetry will help in interpreting poetic passages of the Old Testament), few of these works recognize missionary activity has its own unique genre despite the abundance of mission in the Bible (cf. McCartney and Clayton 2002:223-242; Osborne 1991:149-260; Tate 1997:71-77). Scripture is filled with narratives that include missionary applications, including contextualization (e.g. Mt. 5:46-47 and Lk. 6:33-34), the translation of Christianity (e.g. Ac. 9, 22, 26), cross-cultural tensions (e.g. Ac. 15) and missionary training (e.g. 1 Tim.) to name a few (Walls 1996:25-27, 32-36; Van Engen and Redford 2002:106-107; Redford 2004). The reason for this lack is at least two-fold: there is a lack of experience in mission among theologians, and an assumption that the impact of experience is necessarily negative. However, the Gospels and Acts consistently integrate missionary experience with verbal instruction to transform the understanding of the Apostles.

> Theologians today are afraid of the word 'experience'. . . . But . .
> . the New Testament writers are free from this fear. They recount
> happenings which we would subsume under the head of religious
> experience, and do not hesitate to ascribe them to the mighty power
> of God and to give them right of way in theological argument over
> long-cherished convictions (Newbigin 1953:117-118).

Missionary experience has been one of the most valuable bridges for modern day missionaries in understanding and interpreting the Bible. This has a two-fold benefit. On the one hand, understanding the nature of God's mission in the Bible manifestly guides Christians in application towards appropriate missionary practice.

There are no more reliable grounds than what are given to us in God's revelation. The proper answer to the charge of subjectivity is world mission, but it is world mission not as proselytism but as exegesis . . . The missionary action of the Church is the exegesis of the gospel. (Newbigin 1991:33,35).

On the other hand, missionary experience provides new categories of understanding that allow the biblical interpreter to perceive Scripture in ways that were previously hidden or misunderstood (Brownson 1998:80). The implication of this latter concept is that missionary practice is continually needed in order to gain a proper historical understanding of the strongly missional contexts of the Bible. The dynamic interplay between experience and redeveloping our missional understanding of Scripture is what I have referred to as a reflexive hermeneutic: "Scripture is needed to know God's mission; mission is needed to know God's Scripture" (Van Engen and Redford 2002:25). Missionary experience is crucial in order to properly relate to and interpret the Bible.

Narrative and Mission

Narrative theology has been a topic of great discussion among theologians and missiologists. This brief look at narrative will not attempt to cover that ground (for a missiological overview, see Van Engen 1996:44-68; and Van Engen, Nancy Thomas and Gallagher, eds. 1999:xvii-xxv). However, missionary experience does offer some unique understanding of the use of narrative in Scripture. Narrative approaches are of great benefit in non-receptive Christian contexts or in contexts of extreme persecution. In Jesus' missionary activity, he was addressing a context that was both non-receptive and persecutory.

In non-receptive contexts, narrative teaching such as the parables forces the faithful listeners to take on greater responsibility in *interpreting the message* (Mt. 13:2, 11-12). In Jesus' own ministry, he realized "that when the heart of a people grows dull–that is, unreceptive–direct presentations of truth evoke little or no positive response (Zech. 7:11 and Is. 6:9,10 with Mt. 13:13-17). The only alternative then is to use the language of metaphor, narrative and parable" (Glasser, Van Engen, Gilliland, and Redford 2003: Chapter 12).

Additionally, since narrative is an indirect form of communication, it has the ability to act as a filter for the listeners in various ways. It can provide pace for those needing slow change. For example, the mystery of Jesus' person and the spiritual nature of his Kingdom were so new and revolutionary that he could only disclose these realities gradually, since the Jews were convinced that the Messiah would be an earthly ruler. Narrative can also provide delayed meaning when the ideas are very difficult. For example, some hearers, including the disciples, would have great difficulty initially but would eventually follow Christ and later grasp a more complete understanding of earlier ideas (cf. Jn. 6:60; Mt. 26:26-28).

Finally, narrative can provide no meaning for listeners of hostile intent. Some hostile hearers had no intention of following Jesus, but were searching for statements and activities that would enable them to make accusations. For these hostile listeners, the parables would be no more than "hard sayings" that were thought to be devoid of significance. Faithful believers, however, could interpret and grow from the content of these pictures. As Jesus nears the last week of his ministry, his communication becomes much more direct and hostile hearers attack Jesus based on these direct statements.[4]

Narrative has the overall benefit of forcing its readers to engage in the hermeneutical process themselves. They may succeed or fail, but at least they are involved (Frei 1974:18-19; McCartney and Clayton 2002:178; Van Engen 1996:60). It illustrates that God intended that Scripture be missionally interpreted by everyone, rather than having only professional interpreters carry out the task. Narrative listeners to the New Testament were not trained in hermeneutical method. They inductively learned hermeneutical method based on their interest, causing believers to become relational with Scripture rather than reason-oriented. Narrative is powerful because it develops relationship and ownership in the process of understanding God!

Reason-oriented hermeneutical methods have the danger of allowing the exegete to feel that interpretation is finished when the process is correctly followed. This can result in a divorce between theology and knowing God, which inevitably results in a divorce between theology and mission. Narrative helps the believer to interpret God's actions in Scripture from the standpoint of knowing and discovering the nature of God. This results in a discovery of God's love for all humanity and greater appreciation for God's missionary activity in Scripture.

From a missional perspective, it is more important to involve the listeners in the role of hermeneutical discovery that aids their interest in relating to God, rather than providing the correct interpretation based on correct hermeneutical procedure.

> The apostle asked the converts of Apollos one question: "Did you receive the Holy Spirit when you believed?" and got a plain answer. His modern successors are more inclined to ask . . . "Did you believe exactly what we teach?" (Newbigin 1953:122-123).

Communities of Missiologists

Missionary activity, by its very nature, has always had to deal with a worldwide community and its many ways of understanding the Christian faith. Missiologists have likewise been forced to face this challenge in realizing that there are many ways of perceiving mission. However, alternate perceptions are

---

[4] I owe my thoughts in this paragraph to insights from J. Dudley Woodberry in personal discussions.

crushed at the point when paternalism and cultural hegemony silences the voices of those who stand outside the reigning power structures.

Kirk and Newbigin during the 1990s have led the theological struggle to help missiology to break free from Western hermeneutical control while Van Engen offered new direction in the hermeneutical process (Kirk 1997, 1999; Newbigin 1995b; Van Engen, Gilliland, and Pierson 1993; Van Engen 1996). No other decade has focused so heavily on addressing the issues that deeply affect the way Western missiologists perceive and understand Scripture. However, Shenk appropriately claims that "the control center [is] still in the West" (Shenk 2000:1). Newbigin likewise notes:

> the confessional reader stands within the tradition of the Christian church. . . . It is that community that has put the Bible into their hands and has taught them how to understand it. They read as believers. The difference between this way of reading the Bible and the historical-critical way is not that the latter is neutral or scientific whereas the former is confessional or sectarian; rather, it is the difference between two confessions, two traditions of interpretation developed in two different human communities (Newbigin 1995b:101-102).

Shenk is addressing a fundamental problem in that Western domination in missiology has not given proper attention to nonWestern concepts. I don't believe this has taken place consciously, but it has taken place. Shenk is calling for a level of "affirmative action" in missiology by asking missiologists to intentionally give a voice to the nonWestern world.

> While the churches of the Two Thirds World are eager to have interlocutors representing the church universal, they want conversation partners who truly understand their situation. These they find readily in the first three centuries of Christian history, not in modern Western theology.

> This methodological suggestion has important implications. It encourages the theologian of mission to range over the whole of Christian history rather than being tied to an institutional or ecclesiastical tradition or a particular historical period (Shenk 2000:5-6).

Although missiology has only begun to heed this call, this will have sweeping impact on hermeneutics (Brownson 1998:81). The real challenge for Western missiologists in approaching the nonWestern world is to take a stance as learners and listeners (Shenk 2000:2). Otherwise, missiologists will subconsciously impose their assumptions and leave this issue unchanged.

> [T]here is an urgent need to discover an approach to theology which is a dynamic process of confronting the community of faith with the full range of meaning of the biblical faith without resort to theological systems which become self-regulating. If a church is robbed of this experience in the first generation, by virtue of needing

to accept a second-hand theological system from an alien people and culture, it may be very difficult to change course later on (Shenk 1973:307).

Just as Newbigin called the churches in mission towards repentance over issues of disunity, Shenk is calling for a similar attitude among missiologists to address academic barriers (Newbigin 1961:22, 25). Since missiology is typically not understood beyond the community of missiologists and trained missionaries of the world, few others will call attention to this problem. Consequently, missiologists must pay attention to this concern. Many cross-cultural communities of missiologists can together have the kind of impact that forms a broader community of believers.

Missional hermeneutics can benefit a great deal from understanding the hermeneutical tendencies of peoples who have worldview characteristics similar to those of the Bible. These societies have greater "natural" ability to correctly interpret biblical concepts that are quite distant from 21st century Western thinking (cf. Caldwell 1999:35-36). It is for these same reasons that many missionaries from the West with experience working in traditional societies have offered unique insights into biblical complexities that have sometimes confounded Western theologians.[5]

Examining the Theology of Mission Lens

Following this brief look at the current state of Biblical Theology of Mission, it is helpful to reconsider traditional theological values in light of missiological contributions. Missiologists have reduced the polarization between cognition and experience in theologizing and have addressed the bias of Western rationalism by validating the roles of narrative and experience while broadening the boundaries of the role of community. However, a dark cloud remains over the use of spiritual disciplines in relation to biblical interpretation. The reason for our lack of spiritual understanding is that missiologists, though opening themselves to experience, have, like other Westerners, also succumbed to the dependence on empirical research employed by the "hard sciences" without full awareness that much evidence has been ignored in that process.

Scientific methods, since they depend totally on empirical observation and analysis are ultimately inappropriate for the much more complex relationship found in Scripture between God and humanity. Modern day hermeneutics in Biblical Theology of Mission have existed for the most part as a faithless process because the very source of our understanding, God, has been left out due to a lack of critical assessment of modern hermeneutical methods. Kirk's

---

[5] The *genuine* need for the historical-critical model arises in part from the vast cultural chasm between the biblical writers and those of 21st century western society (Shenk 2000:5). A core value of modernity has been "change" resulting in exponential cultural change that has caused Westerners to have greater need for this method. Societies that have greater cultural similarity to the Bible do not have the same need (Kraft 1979a:132-134).

critique of theology is just as true for missiology; "To take seriously and to be rigorously honest about every kind of bias is the first step toward helping theology in general to be more widely self-critical than it is at present" (Kirk 1997:25). The underlying problem in our hermeneutics stems from an inability to see our own blind spots.

> Missiologists have sometimes raised the cry of syncretism when they have seen churches in Asia or Africa trying to express the gospel in their own cultural forms. The most obvious examples of syncretism, however, are to be found in our Western churches, which have worked so hard to tailor the gospel to fit the so-called requirements of modern thought (Newbigin 1994:130).

The real problem facing missiology today is to ferret out any hermeneutic that has little room for faith and God, and even less room for areas that seek interaction with God for understanding. And as we attempt to deal with our own problem, we need to face the fact that this hermeneutic has been exported into foreign contexts by those theologically trained in the West who are often quite unaware of the severity of the problem (Caldwell 1999:24-27).

Hermeneutics—Foremost a Spiritual Act

Looking forward, I would like to suggest areas of growth that can be made in missiological hermeneutics. Biblical Theology of Mission has pointed us in exciting new directions in hermeneutics. But one important area that remains relatively untouched by missiologists is the role of spiritual disciplines in hermeneutics. Westerners, trained in rational methods, have typically ignored this area.

> One thing clear is that our Western worldview greatly interferes with our attempts to gain insight into the spiritual realities lying behind biblical events. . . . Given our worldview blindness in the spiritual area, however, our instincts are untrustworthy when we try to understand what is going on in that area (Kraft 2002:34-35).

In discussions of hermeneutics, there is little if anything said about the role of the Holy Spirit, prayer, meditation, giftedness and faithfulness. Spiritual disciplines simply are not recommended as part of the hermeneutical process, and this is largely due to the extreme skepticism built into the historical-critical method (D. Allen 1997:5-6; Kirk 1997:15).

> [I]n most theological seminaries, one can take courses in exegesis, but "spirituality," that most slippery of words to pin down, is pretty much left to the individual—and there is seldom any suggestion that the latter has very much to do with the former (Fee 2000:4 cf. Kirk 1997:16).

Recently, however, there has come a greater recognition of the biblical validity of the sovereign role of the Holy Spirit in mission (Gordon 1905; R. Allen 1962; Stronstad 1984; Bevans 1998). Mission fails without the Holy

Spirit and for this reason God's missionary activity is often changing throughout Scripture to produce relational dependence between God and the missionary (Burrows 1996:128). When the People of God uniquely understand their role as God's missionary people, God's leadership is followed in order to understand God's direction in mission (Van Engen 1991:187-188). Such recognition turns us from formulaic understandings of mission that result in human independence that loses sight of the fact that "there is no absolute and mechanical uniformity of the Spirit's working in these matters (Ac. 8:14-17 and Ac. 10:44-48)" (Newbigin 1953:129). Therefore, God's missionary people must interpret their role in God's mission by constantly seeking God's will.

Missiologists must learn to incorporate such facts into their approach to hermeneutics. Western scholars have attempted to define hermeneutics in rigid ways so that there is no place for spiritual insight. This results in a failure to seek spiritual guidance in the interpretational process since the traditional process *assumes* that human rules of interpretation are sufficient. Without denying the importance of human effort and insight, some type of balance must be achieved.

> Let us admit that it is part of the fallen human nature . . . to desire always criteria of judgment which can be used without making too heavy demands upon the delicate faculty of spiritual discernment, clear-cut rules by which we may hope to be saved from making mistakes, or rather from being obviously and personally responsible for the mistakes. We are uncomfortable without definite principles by which we may guide our steps. We fear uncharted country, and the fanatics of all kinds who, upon the alleged authority of the Holy Spirit, summon us with strident cries in all directions simultaneously. . . . But on the other hand let us admit that according to the New Testament we are summoned precisely to the task of 'discerning the spirits'; that it is there taken for granted *both* that the Holy Spirit is free and sovereign, able to work in ways that demand re-thinking of our traditional categories, *and* that He Himself gives to the Church the necessary gifts by which He may be known (e.g. 1 Cor. 12.10) . . . (Newbigin 1953:125-126).

Proper hermeneutics must avoid the tendency to remove God's involvement since our quest is ultimately one of understanding God's intentions for our lives (D. Allen 1997:3-4, 152-153). "Only relatively recently have doctrinal and spiritual theology been pursued in isolation from each other; for most of the history of theology, they interacted richly" (D. Allen 1997:19).

Furthermore, if God is involved as an author in Scripture, then the author's own intent must be sought out by the very criteria of the historical-critical method (LaSor 1978:270). Missiologists cannot consistently call upon the leadership of the Holy Spirit in mission and then adopt hermeneutical methods that reverse this tendency, especially when mission has become known as "the mother of theology" (Kähler cited and translated by Bosch 1980:24, 138).

Scientific methods do have their place, but the Bible is not a scientific book and missiologists are not first of all scientists (Kirk 1997:14-15; LaSor 1978:265). We are believers in Jesus Christ. As such, we should approach the Scripture with methods beyond science, beyond even "method!"

> [Lastly] . . . and most important, hermeneutics when utilized to interpret Scripture is a spiritual act, depending upon the leading of the Holy Spirit. Modern scholars too often ignore the sacred dimension and approach the Bible purely as literature, considering the sacral aspect to be almost a genre (Osborne 1991:5).

I cannot imagine how surprised New Testament writers would have been if they were informed that praying and consulting the Holy Spirit were not allowed in biblical interpretation. Most likely, we would be charged as "false teachers." It must cause God pain for us to request help in so many areas of life, but to absolutely avoid praying for the meaning of ideas that God revealed throughout human history. Considering how often missionaries pray for God's guidance, it seems preposterous that we should adhere to a hermeneutical construct that is any less spiritual.

The interpretation of Scripture is ultimately a process of seeking God's will by understanding God's intentions in the Bible. *Hermeneutic method is foremost a spiritual exercise in relationship with God as the author of Scripture.* It requires spiritually committed believers to enter into the process of interpreting and understanding God's message in Scripture (Fee 2000:7; Wallace 1997:4). I am not advocating a moratorium on reason or the historical-critical method. I am not advocating, as Origin did, that the text should be interpreted *purely* in a "spiritual" way without any regard for the "literal" meaning of the text (cf. McCartney and Clayton 2002:85-89; Fuller 1978:189). I am advocating that spiritual disciplines be given equal credibility with the many hermeneutical areas already discussed, as well as equal attention and development.

Ultimately, I would hope that multiple hermeneutical avenues will lead to similar understandings of Scripture and actually help to build a more integrative and cohesive hermeneutic (McCartney and Clayton 2002:178). Certainly any of these areas can be abused and contorted for the benefit of the interpreter, including reason-based approaches. No solitary method or discipline should stand on its own as the sure-fire hermeneutical pillar, nor should any single discipline have to bear that burden. We must move away from hermeneutical foundationalism and towards mutual integration of multiple means of understanding Scripture.

Spiritual disciplines must be validated and included in hermeneutics if we are to adequately validate the spiritual activity that is hermeneutics. Concern over the potential abuse of spiritual disciplines is not an adequate reason to avoid dealing with this issue. Growing pains over the use of spiritual disciplines will exist along with their benefits over time. Rational thought was refined and given direction (whether rightly or wrongly) for its role in hermeneutics, which gave rise to a certain type of thinking in hermeneutical method that produced greater trust and cohesion in the process (e.g., exegetical method, authorial intent, redaction criticism, etc.).

Spiritual disciplines must be given this same opportunity to be refined, offered proper attention, and placed in practice to bring about a holistic understanding *unencumbered by the fear or ridicule from self-perceived elitist advocates of traditional methods and hard-science approaches.* Spiritual disciplines must be part and parcel to the hermeneutical process because "our concern in coming to the text is to hear from God. No other stance is exegetically in keeping with the text itself" (Fee 2000:14). *Hermeneutics is foremost a spiritual act!*

While I would agree with Fee in claiming that the end-result of the hermeneutical process should result in a deepening of Christian spirituality, I am making a different claim (Fee 2000:4). I am stating that *spirituality should be part of our hermeneutic.* What are the spiritual disciplines that should be included in our hermeneutical process? How do we carry out spiritual disciplines in the hermeneutical process? This chapter will not adequately answer those questions, but the suggestions that follow are an attempt to consider the practical implications of spiritual disciplines within the hermeneutical process.

Hermeneutics Guided by Scripture

Related to the issue of spiritual disciplines is the issue of allowing the Bible to guide believers in the hermeneutical process. Does the Bible offer insights and even examples for its own interpretation? Caldwell, whose focus is ethnohermeneutics, contends that "no one hermeneutical method is inspired; each and every method simply emerges from its own unique hermeneutical milieu [including those in the Bible]" (Caldwell 1999:32). Caldwell is correct in pointing out that there is no way to avoid the hermeneutical tendencies of a particular society, because societies have no other starting point than their own worldview. However, left to their own, this presents the same danger as found in the West—that a people (or some subgroup such as academic theologians) may subconsciously develop a narrow and highly ethnocentric hermeneutical approach that is erroneously propagated as a norm in cross-cultural missionary endeavors.

At the same time, the Bible does not teach a single hermeneutical method that emerges from Scripture (Brownson 1998:44). Specialists dealing with intertextuality, the exegetical use of Old Testament Scripture by New Testament writers, consistently demonstrate multiple hermeneutical avenues within the Bible (Beale 1994; LaSor 1978:274-275; McCartney 2002:8). Since cultural and worldview values do play an important role in the hermeneutical process, we cannot in a wholesale manner claim that hermeneutics in the Bible are normative since there are a multiplicity of cultures, worldviews and hermeneutical models represented in Scripture. If all the hermeneutical models contained within Scripture were adopted together, it would take a lifetime of adopting biblical worldviews just to begin the process of Bible interpretation.

In this final section, I make the assumption that the Bible does teach us ways of interpreting and understanding God's message, and many of those are spiritual ways. The Bible demonstrates a multiplicity of hermeneutical insights that can be synergistically integrated and provide holistic understanding (Marshall 2002:12). For example, the Bible demonstrates a slow (often grudging) process in which Israel learned to respect the ethnic perceptions and epistemologies of other ethnic groups (e.g. Ac. 10, 15, 26). It has also been a slow process for Western hermeneutical method, but this biblical motif is one way that hermeneutics can be informed and shaped.

A great deal of the problem in dealing with hermeneutics is similar to that of missionary practice. Missionaries have to be capable of understanding their own cultural values as they relate to God's message so that the Christian message can be appropriately translated and contextualized in the mission field (e.g,. Walls 1996:112 n. 2). Similarly, the Bible must inform our hermeneutics, and our hermeneutics must be a *translated*-hermeneutics infused with biblical integrity. *There are principles that can be taken from Scripture that should be helpful to guide Christians hermeneutically* (McCartney and Clayton 2002:61-69; D. Allen 1997:135-136).

The Holy Spirit

Throughout the New Testament, missionaries misunderstood God's grace extended to the Gentiles because of predetermined assumptions. These assumptions were most often countered through the work of the Holy Spirit. We should likewise heed this caution in our own time. To assume that the Holy Spirit will *only* act in a certain capacity is to undermine the capacity of the Holy Spirit (cf. D. Allen 1997:10; Fuller 1978:192; McCartney and Clayton 2002:75-77; Osborne 1991:340-341; Wallace 1997:3-4). This assumption quenches the role of the Holy Spirit in leading God's people into mission. To force the Holy Spirit into any prescribed mode of operation is to limit the Spirit. While studying the different ways in which the Holy Spirit has worked may help to understand how He has worked, we should avoid the tendency of generalizing His activity, noting the many biblical instances where God's missionary people missed, or even acted as barriers towards, the mission of the Holy Spirit (cf. Jn. 3). At the same time, we must understand the role of the Spirit in mission.

> [T]he active agent of mission is a power that rules, guides, and goes before the church: the free, sovereign, living power of the Spirit of God. Mission is not just something that the church does; it is something that is done by the Spirit, who is himself the witness, who changes both the world and the church, who always goes before the church in its missionary journey (Newbigin 1995a:56).

While we would agree that the Holy Spirit has a predominant role in mission, how is it that we can think of hermeneutics apart from this same guidance? Theologians addressing the role of the Holy Spirit in hermeneutics have focused on specific texts (predominantly 1 Cor. 2:12-14; 1 Jn. 2:20,27), but this is only a small portion of the biblical witness (cf. Fuller 1978; Wallace 1997). Acts 1:2 points out that instructions were given by the Holy Spirit to the apostolic missionaries. The famous account of the Holy Spirit in Acts 2 comes as a watershed to provide an understanding of God's missionary intentions for the Gentile world.

It was not through the scientific historical-grammatical method in Acts 10 that Peter came to a new understanding of mission through Cornelius' receiving the Holy Spirit. It was through revelation given in a dream on the roof of a tannery. This was coupled with the unmistakable direction of the Holy Spirit (v. 19) and His timing in coming upon the Gentiles (v. 44). This despite ample Old Testament Scripture that consistently demonstrated what Peter (and most Jews) had missed—Israel was to be a missionary nation to the Gentiles! The role of the Holy Spirit was more than a conviction of sin, dealing with prejudice, or mere illumination. The Holy Spirit gave Peter a means of interpreting Scripture. New "data" was imparted to Peter and validated by his missionary experience of the Holy Spirit's interaction with Cornelius. This resulted in Peter's ability to *correctly interpret* the existing body of Scripture (vv. 34-36) and share this new understanding with fellow believers (11:15-18; 15:7-19). This missional reinterpretation of Scripture was something that the larger community of Jewish exegetes had consistently missed or ignored. God did provide a new means of understanding *what had already been revealed and written*; that running throughout Scripture was the backbone of mission to the nations (cf. Kaiser 1996, 2000; Bevans 1998:103).

It was not the scientific historical-grammatical method in Acts 9 that led to Paul's radical change in understanding God and mission. It was through Jesus' appearance on the Damascus road that Paul was transformed in his understanding and thereby given a new theology of mission in his time. Paul was highly trained in the method of his day and one of the most knowledgeable of Scripture. But it was through the activity of the Holy Spirit that Paul's interpretation of existing Scripture was transformed, leading to new insights in his understanding of God and God's will.

Additional examples are found in the activity of the Holy Spirit leading to the *understanding and interpretation of the Scripture* for the Ethiopian eunuch (Ac. 8:30-31) and for the leading of Philip in mission (v. 29). It was through the leading of the Holy Spirit, then, that Paul and Barnabas were sent out to proclaim God's message in the synagogues (Ac. 13:2-5). Again, "The Holy Spirit is party to the decisions of a Church Council" (Ac. 15:8,28) appropriately interpreting the Old Testament for the Gentiles (Newbigin 1953:115). Paul even cites the role of the Holy Spirit in noting that Israel was unwilling to correctly interpret Scripture (Ac. 28:25-28), which is very similar to Stephen's use of

Israel's stubborn missions history in Acts 7. Both passages demonstrate that continued resistance to the Holy Spirit was coupled with resistance to God's mission, showing that the scholars of the day had misinterpreted Scripture (Ac. 7:51; 28:25).

> The gift of the Spirit was a visible, recognisable, unquestionable sign that God had accepted these Gentiles as His own people, and before that fact the most massive and fundamental theological convictions simply had to give way. The Holy Spirit may be the last article of the Creed but in the New Testament it is the first fact of experience. . . . In the New Testament the Holy Spirit appears rather as a sheer fact, God's recognisable witness (e.g., Acts 15.8) to His own presence, and therefore entitled to right of way before all arguments based on an *a priori* reasoning. The repeated use of the word 'witness' in relation to the Spirit is a reminder of just this point: the Holy Spirit's presence is the plain fact by which we know God's mind towards us (Newbigin 1953:114).

The Holy Spirit likewise provided leadership in mission stating that Paul was not to enter Asia (Ac. 16:6-7) as well as offering the prophesy of Agabus (given by the Holy Spirit) regarding Paul's capture (Ac. 21:10-11). *We cannot assume that since the Holy Spirit so easily provides "data" for missionary direction and understanding, that He offers but little when it comes to directing the interpretation of Scripture.* A dichotomy in these two areas is unacceptable because it is simply not biblically defensible. Regardless of how one might evaluate the activity of the New Testament that leads to a proper missional hermeneutic of the Old Testament, it is clear that spiritual activity did exist and that human understanding was guided by spiritual activity. Human reasoning was not an independent and predominant means of interpretation within Scripture.

> Jesus promised his disciples that they would receive the gift of the Holy Spirit, the Spirit of the Father and of the Son, and that the Spirit would interpret to them the meaning of his words and deeds and lead them into the truth as a whole. That promise was fulfilled. This gift of the Spirit, however, did not make the disciples infallible any more than the same gift given to the prophetic writers of the Old Testament made them infallible (Newbigin 1995b:90).

The plain and simple fact is that there are abundant instances in the New Testament in which missionaries were given "new data" in order to understand the nature of God's mission, despite background, knowledge and the existence of Scripture. Therefore, missiologists must avoid the trap of establishing boundaries for the role of the Holy Spirit in hermeneutics.

For those who want to thrust upon Scripture the idea that monumental themes, such as God's mission or the leading of Holy Spirit, are for "that day only," I would simply respond by noting that the ability to eliminate mission and the Holy Spirit on such an unfounded basis will allow anything, even Christ's atonement, to be antiquated and relativized in the same way.

Admittedly, the Holy Spirit is often self-effacing in Scripture, constantly giving glory to the Son in mission, and this makes it very difficult to see all of the ways the Holy Spirit works. However, formulaic conceptions of the Holy Spirit will only diminish our capacity to follow the leading of the Holy Spirit, resulting in a spiritual blindness that continues to misunderstand the Holy Spirit (cf. Jn. 3). Those who address these misconceptions often develop a renewed perspective in following the lead of the Holy Spirit (Archer 2002).

This is quite evident in three modern-day missionaries who have had different ways of seeing the Holy Spirit work in their missionary activity. Roland Allen began his missionary career as an Anglican Missionary in China but eventually wrote the mission classic *The Spontaneous Expansion of the Church* addressing the way in which paternalism and control in mission had crushed any opportunity for the Holy Spirit to move freely among newly developing churches (1962). C. Peter Wagner began as a sociologist and church growth expert but consistently moved toward healing and prayer as a means of missionary activity (1988). Charles Kraft began as an anthropologist and communications expert but consistently moved towards an inner healing and deliverance ministry as an effort towards missional freedom (1989a). The Holy Spirit simply could not be contained or rigidly defined for these missiologists, but the Holy Spirit did change the course of their lives. The influence of the Holy Spirit is evident by the transformation and new understanding given in the midst of God's missionary activity.

Prayer

Without prayer we may never otherwise discern portions of Scripture. If missiology assumes that God is the ultimate source for understanding God's intentions, then prayer has the unique role of allowing missiologists to petition for understanding in Scripture. Prayer has the advantage of enabling us to get beyond simply imitating first century approaches, since God understands that context and has the ability to skillfully speak into our own cultural context. Simply put, God is aware of our cultural background and has the ability to offer insight into biblical contexts through prayer.

Concerning prayer, Newbigin suggests that science is actually a closed system of thought because it relies on itself to validate its own hypotheses (Newbigin 1989:48). Conversely, Newbigin claims that Christianity is not a closed system because Christianity seeks a source beyond humanity—God—to lead and guide Christians in the process of understanding our faith (Newbigin 1991:63). Building upon Newbigin's insight, prayer then allows us to reach beyond our own understanding and engage with God for spiritual understanding. Without prayer, hermeneutics is doomed to become a circular system of human reasoning. Certainly human reasoning has a place in the process, but it cannot be the only place that missiologists look to for meaning. We must recognize that "practically speaking, a Christian does need to ask God to reveal the meaning of a text to him, not in order to avoid the labor of exegesis or to get some guarantee of correctness, but in recognition that all genuine insight comes by God's hand" (McCartney and Clayton 2002:178). Prayer does not avoid research and struggle in order to understand Scripture, but prayer should be central to that struggle (D. Allen 1997:51-52).

Biblical examples of prayerful hermeneutics are abundant. In Jesus' famous prayer in John 17 pleading to the Father for the care of missionaries, Jesus' prayer includes a request for the Father to teach them words of truth (v. 17). The account of Acts 10 begins with Peter praying (v. 9) and this opens the doors for the Holy Spirit and the cross-cultural community of Jews and Gentiles (v. 19, cf. 11:4) allowing Peter to understand the implications of his visions. Hermeneutical insight takes place through the interaction of multiple disciplines that cannot be splintered in real practice. The narrative of Luke 11:5-13 likewise illustrates the integration of prayer, the Holy Spirit and gifting in understanding. This passage cries out for believers to repeatedly pray for understanding. Paul likewise prayed for believers to grow in their understanding and wisdom (Eph. 1:16-19; Phil. 1:9-11), and Paul prayed that this would take place *through spiritual wisdom and understanding* (Col. 1:9-13) (Osborne 1991:340).

In the Orthodox Church, decisions of biblical interpretation are collaborative and reflected in councils through the ages (Stamoolis 1986:15-16,114-115). Given the radical individualism of our day, we must learn from this and integrate the community with prayer.

> Christianity's appeal to the understanding has to be balanced by a reaching out to God in prayer. However natural it is to seek to enlarge our understanding of God through our mind, Christianity is not merely an intellectual option (D. Allen 1997:62).

There are rare cases in Scripture where group decisions were wrong, but these decisions were not rooted in prayer (e.g., Gen. 19, Ex. 32, 1 Cor. 5, Ac. 14).

In the Fall 2002 class of Biblical Foundations of Mission, I informed over eighty students in the class that I expected them to pray together in small groups in order to understand the meaning of the themes that flow through Scripture. I even went so far as to encourage them to cite their understanding from prayer as validly as any footnote they might find from other authors (I was intentionally giving them the opportunity to place their biblical insights through prayer on equal footing with traditional methods of research). Though the students were unaccustomed to citing prayer in their papers (a tragedy in my opinion), many students noted significant breakthroughs in understanding.

A prayer-filled hermeneutical community is in conversation with God to understand Scripture as well as in conversation with one another. There is no separation between the vertical and horizontal. Biblical insights developed through prayer by missiologists should not be independent of others. A community of prayer offers greater protection in addressing individualism and validates the understanding from God through the manifestation of a united effort to seek God. What has already been mentioned about community is critical if prayer is to be given its proper precedence. The process can easily be sabotaged by seeking out others who are in agreement prior to prayer or by remaining within dominating structures. This is one reason why it is beneficial to practice in the classroom because students often come from a variety of backgrounds. This naturally shields against the human tendency toward homogeneity.

Giftedness

Giftedness is an enormous topic that cannot be covered in this brief discussion. However, it would be inconceivable to consider the role of spiritual issues related to hermeneutics and not consider the impact of gifting. Giftedness is naturally given by God and developed through time in Christian maturation. Gifts are often best developed when natural gifts are stretched through continued effort in mission so that gifting is sharpened. However, gifts can be abused, as false prophets did, or those who have real God-given prophetic abilities but refuse to use this gifting for God (e.g., Balaam—Num. 22). Gifts can also be given and taken by God at any time.

Since the area of giftedness is so vast, I can only illustrate the role that gifting plays in hermeneutics through an example of prophetic gifting. Missiologists would rarely consider their roles prophetic because biblical prophets carry a tremendous burden and often tremendous scorn from their audiences. Quite often, the prophets are sent to reform the people of God (e.g., Isaiah, Jeremiah, Ezekiel, Hosea, Joel and Malachi).

Missiologists who focus on ecclesiology are likewise prophetic (though I doubt they would be comfortable with this title). They have called the people of God towards their purpose in following their God-given responsibility in mission. Works focused upon reforming the church for mission include William Carey's *An Enquiry into the Obligations of Christians, to use Means for the Conversion of the Heathens* (1792), John R. Mott's *The Evangelization of the World in This Generation* (1900), Chuck Kraft's *Christianity in Culture* (1979a), Lesslie Newbigin's *Is Christ Divided?* (1961), Chuck Van Engen's *God's Missionary People* (1991) and Wilbert Shenk's *Write the Vision* (1995); (certainly more could be listed). These missiologists have written prophetically to the church calling for reform in the Church's understanding and role of their God-given purpose in mission—much in the same way that Old Testament prophets called Israel to faithfulness in its purpose among the nations.

These missiologists have used their gifting to offer a living hermeneutic that offers greater depth in interpreting Scripture. They offer an example that provides a link to the past so that the role of both Old and New Testament prophets is more prominently understood. It is unlikely that this was their intention. However, it is the natural result of men and women carrying out

God's mission through their gifting that permits the Christian community to re-experience the context and struggle of missionaries in the Bible.

One of the greatest gifts in Scripture is the gift of God's grace. Western society has, however, separated grace from truth in a quest for objective knowledge. In the same way that prophetic gifting offers new interpretation of biblical contexts, the infusing of God's grace is essential for Western Christianity in order to reinterpret the role of truth and theology as it relates to mission (Brownson 1998:82). Newbigin, following Augustine's *"credo ut intellegam"* ("[I] believe in order to understand."), exemplifies the relationship between grace and truth (Edmund Hill 1990:240).

> [T]he great objective reality is God but he is also the supreme subject who wills to make himself known to us not by a power that would cancel out our subjectivity, but by a grace that calls forth and empowers our subjective faculties, our power to grow in knowledge through believing. We believe in order to understand, and our struggle to understand is a response to grace (Newbigin 1991:36).

Scripture in Our Hearts

Hiding Scripture in our hearts may not be on the typical list of spiritual disciplines, but this focus is critical for hermeneutics to be sustained in the life of missionaries. I am not suggesting Scripture memorization for its own sake, although that may be helpful. I am suggesting that we need to have a living account of Scripture in our hearts that allows us to relate our current missionary context to the biblical contexts, which then reshapes our understanding of the Bible in the midst of our missionary journey. Newbigin and D. Allen both vividly illustrate this concept:

> The person who allows the biblical story to be the all-surrounding ambience of daily life and who continually seeks to place all experiences in this context finds that daily life is a continuous conversation with the one whose character is revealed in the biblical story taken as a whole. There is a world of difference between this and a concept of God developed out of reflection on life's experience apart from this story (Newbigin 1995b:88-89).

> Through the meditative reading of the Bible we apply the scriptures to our own moral lives, and eventually this reading shapes us in such a way that we can receive greater knowledge of God through the scriptures. As we allow the knowledge of God gained through the scriptures to guide us, nourishing the heart and mind, we are increasingly formed into the likeness of God. Spiritual growth brings illumination of new and deeper meanings hidden in the Bible (D. Allen 1997:125).

As the witness of Scripture is ingrained in us, meditation upon Scripture follows naturally, leading towards a deeper impact in understanding Scripture. In the midst of this deepening, there is a persistent internalization and integration of God's message since Scripture is at the forefront of missionary thinking. This allows for the reflexive hermeneutic discussed earlier to reinterpret mission through Scripture and reinterpret Scripture through mission.

> It is [possible] . . . to indwell the story as it is told in the Bible so that we are not looking at it, but looking through it to understand our world. That is what Christians did before they were trained in the critical method. It is how millions of Christians still use the Bible (Newbigin 1994:111).

Internalization of Scripture occurs in the midst of meditation and re-reading Scripture so that the biblical witness is ingrained in the essence of who we are becoming as missionaries and missiologists. Therefore,

> we must allow the Bible to provide us with its own account of what it means to speak of the word of God. We have to learn by the actual practice of living with the Bible how and in what ways God speaks. . . . [W]e have to hear, read, mark, and learn and inwardly digest the Bible, taking it wholly into ourselves in a way that shapes the very substance of our thinking and feeling and doing. It is less important to ask a Christian what he or she believes about the Bible than it is to inquire what he or she does with it (Newbigin 1995b:86-87).

Only with Scripture in our hearts can we overcome Western fragmentation and achieve the needed integration that occurs in living the Christian faith with ingrained understandings of Scripture that transform our missionary practice and our interpretation of mission in the Bible.

Faithfulness

As a final focus on spirituality in hermeneutics, the importance of faithfulness must be considered. Faithfulness to God is related to missionary experience, but they are not the same. Faithfulness will lead to some type of missionary experience, but the converse is not necessarily true. Experience, in relation to hermeneutics offers unforeseen perspectives that shed new light upon events in Scripture. As a result, missionary activity infused with our experiences allows those experiences to redevelop our hermeneutical method for understanding Scripture. However, faithfulness relates to Scripture through an ultimate focus upon God and God's will in mission. As a result, faithfulness to God's mission provides a hermeneutical lens for those outside the community of Christian faith that they can use to interpret Scripture.

Faithfulness works in the midst of the world and through Scripture to faithfully seek God in the midst of missionary activity. Our action in the midst of the world results in the practice of biblical motifs and indirectly expresses our understanding of the motifs developed in Scripture. For instance, those who feed the hungry and care for the sick imply (if they are not simply carrying out these functions in a secular way as many do) that the Bible does have a message about God's mission to the sick and the hungry. This lived-out action becomes a faithful expression of our interpretation of God's ideas in Scripture. These actions then function as a lived-out understanding and interpretation of the values we find in Scripture. This actually allows the nonChristian community to interpret the message of Scripture through our lives.

If we live out those actions primarily within the church, then nonChristians will view Scripture as having little to do with mission. If we live out those actions primarily involved in God's missionary activity, then nonChristians will understand that mission is integral to the message of Scripture. For the nations observing Christianity, this means that "the only possible hermeneutic of the gospel is a congregation which believes it" (Newbigin 1989:232). As the nations interpret the Bible through us, their understanding provides feedback regarding our faithful expression of biblical themes, belief and actions. We must prepare to ask "Do the nations have some accurate understanding of God's nature in Scripture through our missionary activity?"

If the answer is "yes," then those seeking God from the nations have indirectly developed a hermeneutic for the Bible. The nations have then begun the process of interpreting Scripture, which means that biblical interpretation is intrinsically missionary in nature. This implication should give missiologists an overwhelming sense of what is at stake in the field of hermeneutics.

A Priority Lens Based in Humility

A final consideration of our hermeneutical assumptions is now in order. Our hermeneutic should be prioritized foremost with God. Other spiritual areas follow along with various human achievements that were initially discussed. Rational methods should be near the bottom. This may seem to be an over-reaction, but proper humility before God demands that caution be exercised when human achievements are involved (Beeby 1999:113; D. Allen 1997:78).

The prioritizing of disciplines is important, but the main difference is that spiritual areas should no longer be ignored (Newbigin 1953:126-127). This does not mean that some sort of objective position has been achieved. Certainly, we will continue to have our blind spots, but we will at least be addressing issues that we can see. It is still the case that we see imperfectly (1 Cor. 13:12), but our vision is more holistic and less filled with prejudice.

Appropriate Hermeneutics

Christian traditions have for some time debated over faith in miraculous healings versus the use of modern medicine. Some have insightfully recognized that the all-knowing God of the universe could manage to work in the miraculous and in modern medicine simultaneously. These Christians faithfully pray for miracles and for God's hand to watch over the practices of modern medicine. Similarly, hermeneutics should never become a polarized discipline in which only one agenda holds priority. Missiologists seeking to interpret

Scripture can pray for God's concerns to be made known through spiritual direction while simultaneously praying for insight in the use of scientific methods. There is no doubt that a long list of additional disciplines could be added, but the main point is for the integration of the spiritual with the rational, the experiential with the faithful, and so on. Faithfulness and experience travel a similar path, but only faith approaches God. Cultural insight and community influence understanding, but only prayer enters into dialogue with the Author of our faith. History and the holism of the tapestry act as guides, but only the Holy Spirit moves pervasively through the interpretive process.

The combination of multiple disciplines integrated synergistically provides an appropriate hermeneutic in Biblical Theology of Mission. This leads to a grace-infused missionary understanding that recognizes valid indigenous ways of understanding, many of which are often more appropriate than what we have provided. This further allows contextualization to be in a process of dialogue with the context in order to seek understanding and feedback that may offer a never-before-seen lens of interpretation, as our missionary hermeneutic is ultimately interpreted by the world. May God transform us as we diligently follow God's missionary nature in Scripture that has so transformed the world.

Chapter 15

Contextualization and Time: Generational Appropriateness

Charles H. Kraft

A previous version of this chapter has been published
in Conn, Ortiz, and S. Baker 2002, pp 132-156.

When we discuss contextualization, we usually ignore the time factor. I have only seen one brief mention of the differences between first and second generation approaches to contextualization in the various studies I have surveyed (R. Daniel Shaw 1995:159). We act as if any group that needs to consider whether or not its Christian expressions are appropriate will need to deal with the same things as any other group might. However, situations differ. And one of the major ways in which contextualization situations differ is in the generation in which they find themselves with respect to their acceptance of Christianity. It is important for us to know where a given people group is in their Christian experience before we can speak knowledgeably about the kinds of things that would be appropriate for them.

We often assume we are working with the first generation of Christians in any given society. But most people are no longer in that generation. So, if we are to be relevant to those who are helping people in the contextualization process, we need to address ourselves to the challenges that face Christians at any point along the way.

In the first generation of a people's Christian commitment, when everything is new and they are just coming out of their preChristian allegiance, the major issues in their minds may not be concerns about relevance and adaptation to their culture. First generation Christians are more likely to be concerned about issues of *separation* and *contrast*. Their attention will most probably be focused on assuring that they are safe from the revenge of the spiritual powers they have renounced (if they have renounced them). Furthermore, they want to discover which customs they are supposed to reject in order to demonstrate their new faith in contrast to the life of those around them who have not converted.

True, it is important that the newly entered faith be experienced as relevant to at least parts of the lives of the converts. But it is probably too much to expect new converts to develop the energy and insight needed to work out the multitude of details involved in changing their way of life, and especially their worldview, to fit their new faith. And the converts should not be criticized if they adopt what may eventually look like too much foreignness in the first generation. There will be much adaptation, to be sure, but we shouldn't be surprised if it is quite incomplete at this point, since imitating the outsiders who brought the good news may in their minds be the only way they can imagine of expressing their faith.

As we see in Acts 15, even those (Jewish Christians) who had known Christ for some time had difficulty imagining that Christian faith could be appropriately expressed in Gentile cultural forms. How much more likely is it that those who come to Christ where the gospel is new have the same difficulty of imagining their own cultural forms as vehicles of the new faith. They, therefore, are usually inclined to simply imitate the cultural forms of the outside witnesses on the assumption (often shared by the outsiders) that those forms are God-ordained.

A major problem, however, is the fact that practices that get started in the first generation tend to get "set in cement" and may not be modified or replaced in succeeding generations with more culturally appropriate practices. It seems to be a well nigh universal tendency for people to regard as absolute, even sacred, most or all of the cultural forms the missionaries brought to them. They see to it, therefore, that the church members carefully imitate and scrupulously pass on these "sacred" traditions to newcomers and new generations.

The first generation problem, on the other hand, is quite different for those who have entered Christianity through a people movement. When large groups come in with their preChristian cultural ways largely intact, they may change their behavior and worldview less than they should. They may simply continue practices that honor their previous gods or that are incongruent with Christian moral standards without even knowing that they should change them. It is more likely to be those who convert one by one or who choose in small groups to go against their previous allegiance who accommodate to the outsiders and change their behavior more than they should.

Either way, there is much contextualizing to be done in succeeding generations. Because of the likelihood of incomplete, inappropriate or otherwise inadequate contextualization, perhaps we should be looking more to the second, third or following generations for most of what we seek in the development of appropriate cultural expressions of biblical faith.

Perceiving Relevance

The essence of contextualization (inculturation, localization or dynamic equivalence), from an evangelical point of view, is the implementation of biblical Christianity in culturally appropriate ways. Ideally this is to be done by the insiders of any given society who perceive the gospel to be relevant and who work out ways to express their new faith in appropriate cultural forms. This process is facilitated by the relevant communication of biblical messages to those insiders. But perceptions of relevance differ from generation to generation. What may be considered very relevant in one generation may be looked at in quite a different way in a later generation. Likewise, structures and other forms of expression of the faith that have been worked out as quite appropriate in one generation may be seen as quite inappropriate at a later time.

Given, say, three generations of Christian witness and experience with Christianity, we can assume that there are reasons why the early converts turned to Christ. We can also assume that there are reasons why those of the second and third generations have continued to follow Christ, and why conversions from the nonChristian populace have continued to happen. But the reasons for each succeeding generation will be different.

I think we can assume that what is appropriate thinking and structuring in the first generation will at best be only partially appropriate for the second, and at worst be totally inappropriate. In addition, whether or not the first Christians did a good job at contextualizing for their time and cultural circumstances, succeeding generations will always have more work to do to "complete" the task. This is true for at least two reasons: 1) the first generation would not have been able to complete the job even for their generation's needs and 2) culture change will have raised some new issues to deal with.

I advocate, therefore, that there be built into the principles on which any group of Christians operate the concept of *continuous contextualization*. What this would involve would be continuous, generation by generation, re-evaluation of church customs and consciously experimenting in one generation with approaches that might well be abandoned in another. This is necessary because the issues are different for each generation, especially in view of the rapid pace of culture change. Even if the contextualization is done right in the first generation, and usually it is not, there will be different issues to deal with in the following generations. We need, therefore, to ask how what might be labeled a "spirit of openness to continual adjustment and change," can be instilled in converts, lest they simply pass on from generation to generation patterns that are culturally and personally dysfunctional.

Dealing with Forms, Meanings, and Empowerment

As anthropologists we have learned to use the label *cultural forms* to designate all of the parts of culture, including customs, material objects and cultural patterns such as words, grammatical patterns, rituals and all of the other elements of culture in terms of which people conduct their daily lives. All of culture, whether surface-level and visible or deep-level (worldview) and invisible, is made up of what we call forms.

People, then, as they use and think about these cultural forms assign meanings to them, usually according to what they have been taught by their parents, peers and teachers. Though the forms are parts of culture, the meanings belong to the people. They are not inherent in the forms themselves. They are attached to the forms on the basis of group agreements. That is, the people of a society, largely because they have been taught by their elders, agree that certain forms will have certain meanings and, therefore, will be used for certain purposes. When outsiders enter a society, they have great difficulty understanding what's going on because they do not know the agreements of the insiders.

But cultural forms can also be empowered with spiritual power. Such things as material objects, buildings and rituals can be dedicated and thus convey the power of God (if dedicated to Him) or of Satan (if dedicated to him). In dedications, blessing and cursing, words are used to convey that power. These words are empowered as they are used in obedience to either God or Satan. When cultural forms are thus empowered, they *convey* (not *contain*) spiritual power.

In the Scriptures we see God empowering such things as the Ark of the Covenant (Josh. 3:14-17), Paul's handkerchiefs and aprons (Ac. 19.12), Jesus' gown (Lk. 8.42-48) and anointing oil (Jas. 5.15-16). But Satan can empower cultural forms also. One passage among many in which it is clear that God recognizes the dangers of satanic empowerment of objects and places is in Joshua 7:11-12. There He commands Joshua to cancel that power by destroying captured objects, tearing down altars to pagan gods and consecrating the land.

Missionary Christianity has been delinquent in dealing with empowerment issues, probably because missionaries didn't know what to do about spiritual power. The fact is, however, that satanic power is usually easy to deal with if it is recognized and handled with understanding and the power of Christ. Material objects that have been dedicated to pagan gods can usually be "cleansed" simply by asserting the authority of Christ to break the power in them. If, however, the object has no other purpose than a religious or occult one, I recommend that it be destroyed as well. Land and buildings can also usually be disempowered relatively easily. All that is necessary is for those in authority over them to assert that authority in the name of Christ to break the power that has been bestowed upon them in the past and in the present.

There are objects and places that need to be *disempowered* before Christian activity can take place unhindered. One of several biblical examples of this principle occurred when King Josiah *purified* the temple (II Ki. 23:4-24) from all the abominations of the worshipers of Baal. Clearly Josiah disempowered the objects and the temple from all evil power. Then by reconsecrating the objects and the place to the Lord, he restored God's empowerment to them.

On several occasions I have heard of or been consulted about mission homes, stations or churches that have been built on land that turned out to be infested with evil spirits. One such story comes from Sierra Leone where about a century ago the village leaders deliberately gave the missionaries rights to a plot called "spirit hill" because they knew it was inhabited by spirits. Missionary after missionary who lived in the homes built on that land were forced to leave the field by such things as illness, marriage problems, accidents and the like until fairly recently when someone who understood how to handle satanic empowerment helped them to break that power. Breaking the power was relatively easy because of the much greater power of Jesus. It was discovering the problem that was the hard part due to the missionaries' ignorance concerning spiritual power. Because of this ignorance, family after family of dedicated missionaries experienced satanic attacks that could have been prevented.

In addition to places that need to be disempowered, power will need to be broken over any objects that have been dedicated to gods and spirits. Not infrequently, missionaries and national church leaders are given or buy art objects or work implements that have been dedicated by their makers or cursed. In many societies, such dedication is routinely done when the object is made. And sometimes a curse is deliberately put on the object by those who wish to thwart God's work. As long as such objects are in homes or churches, there will be enemy interference. Again, such empowerment is usually not difficult to break for those who know what they are doing.

The meaning problem is, however, much more difficult to deal with. For, as pointed out above, meanings exist in people and are attached by people to cultural forms according to group agreements.[1] The introduction of Christianity into a society will, of course, involve both the introduction of new cultural forms and the use of certain traditional forms in new ways. With regard to the latter, there will need to be changes in the meanings attached to them. Converts in the first generation will have to decide what changes to require in the meanings they attach to the traditional forms they retain as well as the approved meanings of the new forms.

Advocates of the new faith (such as missionaries), since they are outsiders, will not be able to guide all of the choices made by the converts, making it probable that the latter will misunderstand at least some of the meanings intended by the advocates. These misunderstood meanings, then, will likely be passed on to the next generation of Christians, creating a problem (whether or not it is recognized) for the second generation.

Since first generation converts usually have a primary concern to dissimulate from their unconverted neighbors, they often borrow too many of the cultural forms of the missionaries, on the assumption that those forms are sacred and a necessary part of Christian faith. Such borrowed forms are almost certain to have mistaken meanings attached to them, especially by the nonChristians who have little or no contact with the missionaries or other advocates of the new faith.

Since people in groups change slowly, even highly motivated Christians may not, at least in the first generation, change the meanings of traditional forms sufficiently to assure that the biblical message is being properly communicated.

---

[1] See Kraft 1991a.

Attempts to "cleanse" words, rituals and other cultural forms of their pagan meanings often take a long time, even under great pressure. And often there is not enough pressure put on such forms to bring about the necessary changes. As an example, Japanese Christians have for several generations used the word *Kami* for God. This word is, however, still far from adequate since it is simply the general word for *spirit* to most people, even to many Christians. Though for many Christians the pressure for change of meaning has been reasonably effective, there has not been nearly enough pressure to measurably affect the meaning in the minds of nonChristians and of many Christians, especially new converts.

Recognizing the fact that it is a very slow process for people to change the meanings of traditional forms, many outside advocates have simply introduced foreign words and rituals. In Latin America, for example, after nearly 500 years of exposure to Christianity, the meanings of many (perhaps most) of the words and rituals introduced by Roman Catholic missionaries are still quite pagan. A case in point is the Spanish word *Dios* which often does not have the same meaning for ordinary people that it had for the Europeans who introduced it. Even after this length of time, *Dios* is usually understood, even by those who call themselves Christians, to be the Sun god, with the name of the Virgin Mary used to label the Moon and the names of Catholic saints attached to lesser traditional gods and ancestors. There has not been nearly enough pressure for change coming from inside or outside of the community of those who call themselves Catholics.

What is usually not built into the first generation concept of Christianity is the need for understandings of Christian things to be continually in process. This process of meaning change needs to be calibrated to the growth of the Christian community in their understandings of Scripture and their experiencing the presence and power of Jesus Christ. Whenever the expectation of such growth and change is not engendered in the first generation, there will be serious hindrances to increasing the inculturation of the Gospel in the second and succeeding generations.

Ideally, the new converts need to learn that whatever cultural forms are adopted, adapted and created in the first generation should be seen as experimental, subject to revision in succeeding generations. Those in the second and succeeding generations, then, should understand that it is incumbent on them to evaluate the first-generation choices in the light of their scriptural understandings and experiences, and to make whatever changes and adjustments seem appropriate.

Since this ideal is seldom realized, Christians of the second and subsequent generations need to be helped to understand the need for them to evaluate and, if necessary, to adjust the cultural forms initiated by the first generation. Even in the occasional cases where the first generation Christians contextualized well, succeeding generations need to adjust their Christian forms and meanings to *their* reality, a reality that will always differ to some extent from that of their predecessors.

Contextualization and Communication

The process of appropriate contextualization is enhanced by communication of biblical messages that receptors perceive as relevant to the realities of their life. Receptors have felt needs. Christianity rightly perceived relates very well to many of the felt needs of a people.

Receptors, however, attach their own meanings to the messages communicated and, therefore, choose how to use Christian messages in relation to their felt needs. So, we who witness cross-culturally do not have as much control as we would like to over what our receptors understand and how they use what we present.

Some people are well-adjusted in their cultural system, others are not. The former are unlikely to want to change their allegiance when the missionary comes to them with the message of the gospel. Unless there is good reason, such as economic gain or political prestige, the well-adjusted members of a society are not likely to embrace the new faith.

Those who are not making it in a society, however, often jump at the chance to adopt an alternative approach to life, or some part of it. Thus, when foreign ideas are introduced, these convert, hoping to achieve the prestige and status in the new system that eluded them in the traditional system. They have learned to move "up" in the world by moving out of their traditions.

There are other, more legitimate felt needs, though often people are not as aware of these as they might be of the desire to escape from their traditional structures. The need for love, the need for meaningfulness, and the need for forgiveness fall into this category. The need for more spiritual power is also usually there and at a more conscious level.

Historically, Christian witnesses have often given or allowed the impression that satisfaction of these deeper needs comes only at the cost of leaving their ancestral traditions. That is, people have perceived that only if they become like the foreigners in many ways will they be eligible for such benefits.

Now, moving away from at least some of a people's traditions may well be required at some point for true Christian commitment. And a primary concern of the first generation is dissimulation (see below). What is unfortunate, though, is that people have usually felt they have to dissimulate more by adopting new surface-level cultural forms, usually from Western sources, than by learning to express their deep-level commitments within their own traditional way of life.

When this happens, it is because something of the essence of Christianity has not been communicated. Converts miss, usually at least partially because the advocates have not emphasized it, that Christianity is a *process*, requiring continual re-evaluation and adjustment as we grow in Christ. Unfortunately, converts often understand their conversion as inducting them into a fairly well-defined and permanent state in which all the rules are set and simply adopted without question, even if the result involves a good bit of poorly understood foreign thinking and behaving.

So, while the messages transmitted may have been relevant, they did not deal adequately with the biblical process of growth. The impression the converts came away with, therefore, was that the cultural forms associated with the first generation are to be forever. These forms are often regarded as sacred, unchangeable, delivered once and for all from heaven to the missionaries and through them to the receiving people. Furthermore, they often feel that these "Christian" forms (including rituals) are *magical,* containing supernatural power made available to those who practice them exactly.

There is an important communication principle involved here. *When cultural (including language) forms that deal with the supernatural are not understood, they will often be perceived as sacred.* People will, therefore, often hold firmly (even fanatically) to these forms as if the *forms* themselves, as opposed to the *meanings* they convey, were God-given. They will assume that these forms are *magical*, containing power in and of themselves. And people are loathe to abandon or change them, lest they lose the blessing or power that these forms supposedly contain.

Missionaries down through the centuries have seldom been aware enough of the dangers inherent in such an adoption of their foreign ways to take steps to prevent it. Indeed, many missionaries have assumed, as have their converts, that the foreign ways of worship, organization, buildings, education and theological thinking are God-ordained and thus worthy of adoption by the converts. Only recently have the small percentage of missionaries who receive training for cross-cultural ministry begun to recognize either the need to help people to resist such, often unconscious, cultural imperialism or the unbiblicalness of the implicit requirement that cultural conversion accompany spiritual conversion.

The adoption of such "sacred" foreign cultural forms is dangerous because it misleads converts into the unbiblical posture of seeing the essence of Christianity in the *forms*, including the rituals, rather than in the *meanings*. Since, then, the foreign forms/rituals are regarded as magical, invested with power, they are felt to be efficacious only if they are carried out exactly.

Resistance to change of such adopted customs is, therefore, based on spiritual misinterpretation as well as on such things as ignorance of the meanings of Christianity and respect for the advocates and their ways. As Darrell Whiteman (Chapter 4 above) points out, this spiritually motivated attachment to Western church customs is probably a greater problem for the first generation than even the common understanding that Christianity requires such customs.

Often, neither the converts nor the missionaries have grasped one of the essential concepts underlying Christianity: that it is the Christian *meanings* that are sacred, not the cultural *forms* used to convey them. Our primary concern, therefore, whether in initial witness or in the continuing practice of the faith, should be that the forms employed be interpreted as conveying the proper meanings. With this in mind, Eugene Nida perceptively contrasts the Islamic concern that Muslims everywhere adopt a large number of "Islamic forms" with the Christian advocacy of what he terms "dynamic obedience" within each cultural context. Nida says,

> While the Koran attempts to fix for all times the behavior of Muslims, the Bible clearly establishes the principle of relative relativism, which permits growth, adaptation and freedom under the Lordship of Jesus Christ. . . . The Christian position is not one of static conformance to dead rules, but of dynamic obedience to a living God (1954:52).

Differences of Concern

By way of illustration of the different concerns of first and second generation Christians, let us take the issue of *baptism*. Though the first generation of believers in New Testament times baptized converts as adults, what were they to do in the second and succeeding generations when children were brought up in Christian homes?

Children brought up by Christian parents are in quite a different situation than people who are being converted "out of the world." Adult converts typically have to turn from their unchristian ways and to adopt a new way of life. Children of Christian parents, though, if they accept their parents' faith, simply affirm the same way of life they were taught as children and continue in it. So, as children of Christian parents they could be seen as children of the covenant their parents had made with God.

Soon after the beginnings of Christianity, then, it occurred to the believers that it would be appropriate to develop an initiation ceremony that would function like Jewish circumcision to label each newborn child as participating in the commitment his/her parents had made with God. Hence, rightly or wrongly, the Church began to practice infant baptism as a contextualization of Christian initiation for those born into Christian families.

In contemporary contexts, we note the concern of the first generation converts to demonstrate their differences from the society around them. But at least by the third generation, we frequently find the Christian community sharing a concern of the nonChristians to "discover their traditional roots." Such sentiments provide fertile ground for discussions of cultural appropriateness, though resistance to change on the part of entrenched leaders often keeps the discussions from accomplishing much in real life.

First Generation Concerns: Separation

In the first generation of Christianity, when the Gospel is new, converts are usually greatly concerned to make a break with their old ways in order to establish their new identity. Unfortunately, the new converts are likely to consider Christianity a religion rather than simply a faith (see Chapter 6) and to assume that they are to borrow and adapt the religious forms of those who brought the message. Thus, leadership and worship patterns, organizational structuring, biblical and theological training and understandings and the like tend to be patterned after foreign models, whether or not the missionaries were recommending them.

Thus, converts in many places have adopted the kind of clothing used by Westerners and a myriad of other surface-level customs, ranging from housing and eating to courtship and marriage patterns, in their attempts to show supposed differences between themselves as Christians and their nonChristian neighbors.

The converts usually feel, then, that the major indication of the separation they seek is largely to be expressed in the different religious forms they adopt. The result is often *differentiation* of cultural forms through adopting and adapting foreign religious forms to replace many of the traditional religious customs, rather than *contextualization* of the faith in the cultural and religious forms of their culture.

First Generation Concerns: Breaking the Power

Many first generation Christians rightly see the need to break from and reject practices that have traditionally served as vehicles of satanic power. Missionaries, especially those from the West, recognizing that there is a problem but not knowing what to do about it, usually push people to reject such customs completely. The concern is right but the way it is usually handled tends to result in what Tippett (1987:200) has called a "cultural void," a situation in which the local customs are condemned but nothing is suggested to replace them.

This void, however, leaves most churches planted by foreign (usually Western or westernized) missionaries with an enormous problem. Since no substitute for preChristian spiritual power has been provided, large numbers of Christians continue to make use of their traditional power sources. Their commitment to Christ may be quite sincere. But when they need such things as healing, blessing, guidance and fertility, things their local shamans, priests and diviners traditionally provide, they feel free to continue their preChristian practice of appealing to these traditional practitioners and to the spirits that provide their power.

Several of the problems related to this practice may be illustrated from an experience our Christian community had while I was in Nigeria. The wife of the village shaman had died quite suddenly. The funeral would, according to custom, last three days with a great deal of crying, followed by dancing and singing. On the second day of the funeral, the Headmaster of our Christian school put the school drum under his arm and led about 90 students to participate in the funeral. This gesture of concern and love by the Christians so impressed the shaman that he started to come to church. He found, however, that the church was filled with his clients, people who, in spite of their commitment to Christ, came to him when they needed blessing or healing. Since, then, he found no power in Christianity, he soon stopped coming to church.

First Generation Concerns: Imitate the Powerful

Few things would be more natural than for a receiving group to imitate those who come with greater power, especially if power is their primary concern. In most missionary situations, the outsiders came with an impressive array of technologically superior machines and implements. Observing such technology, and interpreting it as the result of spiritual power, rather naturally led the receiving groups to assume the superiority of much of the rest of the missionaries' culture. So, those who converted to Christianity gladly accepted the customs, the cultural forms, recommended by the advocates.

Korean and Japanese Christianity are good examples of this fact, as are most of the mission-planted churches of Africa, India, the Philippines and most of the rest of the world. Koreans have developed the art of imitation to such a degree that one worshipping in any of the churches of Seoul could easily imagine him/herself in America, except for the language.

Another example comes from the early days of missionary work in Kenya. We are told that the Kenyans, greatly impressed by the technology of the Europeans, sought to discover the secret behind it and focused on reading. They reasoned, perhaps not too inaccurately, that if they could learn to read, they would have access to the Europeans' power. The only flaw in the Kenyans' reasoning was that they assumed the power they would obtain would be spiritual power. Though that part of their analysis was wrong, this quest for spiritual power became the motivating factor behind the Kenyans' ready acceptance of Western schools.

Perseverance of First-Generation Choices

Such first-generation choices would not be a big problem if people understood the importance of making different choices in the second generation. There is, however, in most parts of the world a pattern of the perseverance into the following generations of the cultural forms adopted in the first generation, whether or not these forms are culturally appropriate. Whatever choices have been made in the first generation tend to determine the forms in which Christianity will be expressed forever after. Thus, if the early converts adopt a Western form of Christianity, that form tends to get "set in cement," with the foreign practices seeming to be sacred, even magical, especially because they are foreign.

A major problem arises for second and third generation Christians who learn that God wants to interact with them in terms of their own cultural forms. When they attempt to make changes in the direction of appropriate contextualization, they find themselves at odds with the older leaders who insist on preserving the foreign forms adopted by the early converts. They often feel that these forms are both right, since the early missionaries were the ones who introduced them, and even that they are sacred and magical. The first generation of Christians tends to assume that the missionaries knew what they were doing when they introduced the forms. I met this kind of attitude in my own ministry in Nigeria. It was felt by Nigerian church leaders and many of the missionaries that I, a young, inexperienced missionary, had no right to question the validity of the recommendations made by the pioneer missionaries who had sacrificed so much to bring the Gospel to them.

The assumption of these early missionaries (as articulated to me by one of my contemporaries) was, "We have had 2,000 years of experience with Christianity. We, therefore, have a right to tell these people how they should understand the Gospel and respond to God." This assumption, then, easily became so basic an assumption of the first generation believers that it never occurred to them to attempt to think things through on their own. So they never expected to be able to interpret the Scriptures from their own points of view, or to use their own music and musical instruments in worship, or to develop their own requirements for church membership or their own ways of training leaders, or to finance their Christian activities in their own ways, or to do anything else that would signal that Christ and His ways were rooted in their soil rather than imported wholesale from abroad. They thought Christianity was *supposed* to look foreign.

The leaders I worked with had more or less willingly given themselves to what they perceived to be a rather totally foreign system. But when some of them learned they could question and adapt the foreign system and, furthermore, that they could adopt customs and perspectives that came from their own cultural roots, I, their missionary, was accused by my missionary colleagues of undermining what the mission was advocating. And a major piece of evidence against me was the fact that our churches were growing so rapidly! When we left, then, the mission leaders assigned a missionary loyal to the organization (the same missionary who had made the comment about our "2,000 years of experience") to come in and bring our leaders back into line with the westernized system of the mission. He failed in his mission, however, because these leaders had tasted the freedom that comes with experiencing Christianity in their own way.

Baptism can again be used as an illustration. Since the Greek word *baptizo* was transliterated rather than translated into English, its meaning can be argued over forever and the significance of the form exaggerated. Likewise with verbal expressions such as "the blood of Christ" and even "in Jesus' Name" or "born again." Such expressions and the form of baptism used, since they are so poorly understood, seem sacred and magical and are so used by many Western Christians, especially the more conservative ones.

The Bible also is for many Westerners a magical thing, invested with power of its own, especially if the language is antique and/or academic and sounds theologically sophisticated. Hence the attachment of many to versions they cannot fully understand that give the impression that God uses a more sacred form of the language than that spoken by people every day. From such attachment comes the extreme resistance of many to Bible translations in contemporary language. This attitude on the part of missionaries often meets with that of nonWestern converts acquainted with sacred books of their traditional religion preserved in antique, "sacred" language (e.g. the Koran, the Gitas, the Vedas) to settle for minimal intelligibility. They, therefore, miss the point that most of the Bible was written in highly communicative, even slangy vernacular language and, therefore, is best represented in translation into that type of language.

So, "anti-contextual" decisions may be made by first generation Christians that often are carried on into the second and following generations even though they are misleading in the practice and communication of Christianity.

Concerns of Second and Following Generations

Though situations will differ from society to society, there are a number of common concerns in the second and following generations, some valid, some to be questioned. Legitimate concerns of these generations relate to any lack of appropriateness either to culture or to Scripture that has been passed down to them from the first generation.

Ideally, second and following generations will give themselves to re-evaluating the cultural forms employed by the first generation converts and making whatever changes might be deemed necessary to bring about more effective understandings of what God wants to do among them and their people. This habit of re-evaluation and the accompanying process of experimenting with new approaches could result in the capturing of more and more of a people's way of life for Christ. Sadly, very few of the inheritors of first generation Christianity understand the need for, and the biblical validity of, such adjustments, preferring to perpetuate both the strengths and the weaknesses of whatever the first generation of converts have developed in their approach to Christianity in their culture.

Leadership

Perhaps the most important of the questionable concerns are those that relate to the transfer of leadership positions to the younger leaders. The motivations of those not yet in power are often somewhat less than biblical. Often those who have prepared to be the next wave of leaders have spent more time in schools than have the older leaders and have developed criticisms of how the first generation leaders have been performing. In addition, they are often impatient to gain for themselves the power the older leaders have been wielding.

Though second generation leaders may be critical of the excessive use of foreign cultural forms by the older leaders, often the training the younger leaders have received is more designed to enable them to work within the foreign system than to critique it. When such is the case, a golden opportunity is missed to move the cultural expression of Christianity in the direction of greater appropriateness.

When, though, there is discussion of the biblically exemplified relationships of Christianity to culture in the training institutions, there is more hope for change. By studying the ways in which the lists of the qualities of leaders in the books of Timothy and Titus relate to their cultural setting, for example, younger leaders can gain insight into the ways in which their cultural leadership ideals can be both incorporated and challenged. Tragically, in many societies the use of schools to train young leaders leading to the appointment of youth to pastoral positions at culturally inappropriate ages has communicated that God is not interested in older men or in working in culturally appropriate ways. Such mistakes can be rectified if training programs seek ways for older and younger leaders to work together so that the younger ones are sponsored by older leaders when they pastor, either alone or in tandem. In many cultural contexts it would be appropriate for every pastorate to involve both an older man without academic qualifications but with prestige in the community and a younger one who may actually do most of the work.

Second and later generation leaders, then, if they develop better cultural and biblical understandings, have a golden opportunity to move things in the right direction.

Relational Aspects of Christianity

Often, though the need for an initial commitment to Christ is communicated quite well, a focus on the need for growth and developing maturity in the relationship with Christ is neglected. We have usually exported the Western custom of leading a person to Christ and from then on assuming that growth in knowledge will automatically be accompanied by growth in intimacy with Christ and closeness to other Christians. Thus, in a family-oriented society such as Japan, Christianity has gotten to be known as primarily a classroom, knowledge-oriented faith.

Christians of the second and following generations would do well to study both the relational aspects of Christianity presented in Scripture (e.g. John 15) and the relational models available in their societies. Having studied these, then, attention should be given to developing practices that produce growth in these areas. What, for example, are appropriate expressions of love in any given society? And what are the culturally appropriate models of family, friendship, fellowship, recreation, intimacy and the like that can be adopted and adapted for use in the churches? What, then, of these aspects of social life in any given society need to be critiqued and abandoned for Scriptural reasons? These are issues often neglected in the first generation that can be worked on by succeeding generations.

Worship music passed down from the first generation is often inappropriate. Frequently, the tunes have been imported and put with translated words by missionaries and/or first generation Christians who, in their attempts to dissimulate from their preChristian cultural forms, simply adopted foreign musical forms. Perhaps no one taught the first generation Christians that God could use their music and that there is nothing sacred about Western musical forms. Second generation Christians ought to be very concerned about such inappropriateness (though they often are not), given the important part music plays in most societies.

In the many societies of the world that speak tone languages (over 50%) and the many more whose music employs a five note scale rather than a Western seven note scale, the use of Western music does great injustice to the cause of Christ. For, both unconsciously and consciously, the message of foreignness is driven home through music with great force, perhaps more than through any other vehicle.

Second generation Christians would do well to recognize this and to develop a new and appropriate hymnody. As Roberta King has discovered in teaching African music in Kenya, young Africans, though usually resistant at first to the use of traditional forms of music in worship, can be freed to appreciate and produce truly African worship music. Year after year, her students would enter her course on African music asking, "Why do we bother with traditional music?" But, by the end the course, their attitude usually changes so that they feel that this was one of the most valuable courses they had ever taken. They discover both the desire of God to reach their people in terms of their own cultural forms and the relevance and usefulness of traditional music in fulfilling this desire of God Himself.[2]

Dependence on Literacy

Similarly damaging are the ways in which missionary Christianity has been taught in the first generation in the great number of societies that had no tradition of literacy. It was natural for the Westerners to introduce such culturally specific forms of education as schools and other educational techniques that are highly dependent on literacy. And there are obvious benefits for those who learn how to read. However, the fact that Christian advocates have largely ignored the rich variety of oral communication forms available in most of the world has again given the wrong impression that God's ways are limited to Western ways. The second and following generations have the opportunity to correct this misimpression by developing the use of oral channels of communication while not ignoring the use and development of literacy.

---

[2] See King's Chapter 18 in this volume for more on this topic.

The United Bible Societies, Wycliffe Bible Translators and other organizations that have seen the need to get beyond literacy have recently started to develop creative approaches to the oral communication of Scripture. One of the discoveries coming out of such experimentation is the fact that oral, non-literacy-based communication is often more appropriate in so-called literate societies as well as in those without a long literary tradition. Second and following generation Christians can bring great profit to the cause of Christ by working their way out of the captivity to literacy that has characterized much of first generation Christianity.

Spiritual Power

Though the first generation may have dealt with some power issues, there are usually many left for the next generations to deal with. This is especially true in the many places where missionary Christianity has largely ignored spiritual power issues and/or simply tried to wean Christians from traditional practices by condemning them. For example, I have heard numerous stories of mission compounds and churches that have been built on land that was infested with satanic power. Those who have lived or worked in these places, then, have experienced various kinds of maladies, from disease to accident to a high level of interpersonal dissention, often without a clue as to where the problems were coming from. Taking the land spiritually is, therefore, an important second generation concern in many parts of the world.

This concern often needs to be brought to the attention of church leaders since, under the influence of Western advocates of Christianity, they have usually become desensitized in this area, at least on the surface. These leaders, like the first generation, would normally have been concerned about issues of spiritual power, as would be true of their nonChristian contemporaries. But, the fact that their Western mentors did not deal with such issues and, in fact, dealt in secular ways with health and emotional problems, led them either to ignore spiritual power or to deal with it underground. I recall vividly a discussion with a pastor serving under a strongly mission controlled church who, when he found I was open to and knowledgeable about demonization, finally confessed that he had a secret ministry of deliverance. Most of his colleagues would either have avoided such ministry or, as he did, keep what they are doing secret from church leaders and outsiders to perpetuate the fiction that demonic problems don't exist in their societies anymore.

A major issue is the problem of dealing effectively with demonization among church members. Following Western custom, the churches in most parts of the world have simply required a testimony of conversion plus some biblical and denominational teaching as entrance requirements. The fact that most, perhaps all of the people coming out of paganism into Christianity are carrying demons has not been in focus. Thus, our churches (both overseas and in America) are full of demonized people and the demons have great opportunity to work from within the churches. Of special concern should be the "cleaning up" of those coming out of nonChristian religions and secret societies. Often, in our ignorance of how demonization works, we assume that conversion gets rid of the demons. I wish that were the case, but it isn't. Christians of the second and following generations need to give major attention to this problem.

Fortunately, some understandings of these issues are coming into training programs both in the sending and the receiving countries. Unfortunately, in many places receiving peoples have developed their own ways to deal with these issues. I am appalled to hear stories both from Korea and from Africa of Christians attempting to free people from demons by beating them. Some demonized people have even died during such attempts at deliverance. Such practices, and many others that create damage while attempting to free people, need to be taught against and those who practice them shown better ways of dealing with demonization.

Other Concerns

Issues such as the cultural appropriateness of church government, how the faith is propagated, how the work of Christ is financed, even in many places what language should be used in worship all ought to be re-examined in the second generation, especially if they have not been handled appropriately in the first. In many situations, there has been some contextualization of these concerns in the first generation but more needs to be done.

Often, the way Christianity was presented and structured in the first generation remains fairly appropriate to one segment of any given population-- the westernizing and, often, more urban segment. More traditional and usually more rural segments of the society, however, often find very little that is culturally appropriate to their way of life in the way Christianity is practiced. A challenge that needs to be faced by the second and subsequent generations, then, is to plant churches that are contextualized within traditional and/or rural culture and that, therefore, differ significantly from the more Western and/or urban varieties.

I wonder how many more Koreans or Japanese or Thai or Nigerians or Indian Americans might come to Christ if they could participate in churches that are more culturally appropriate to their traditional ways than the ones that represent Him in these places today? Not that the churches that are more or less appropriate to the culture of the westernizing segment are to be abandoned but that there need to be in every society other churches, differing in their cultural orientation, aimed at attracting traditional and rural people.

It is likely that biblical standards that require changes in the culture will need to be addressed more fully in the second generation than they were in the first. The application of these standards can have at least two types of thrust: the stiffening of standards that were not strongly applied in the first generation and the relaxing of standards that were too strongly applied or that were applied in a too-Western manner. In many contexts, for example, much attention needs to be given to discovering and applying moral standards that are both culturally and biblically appropriate. ⎟ Often the cultural disruption brought about by westernization (largely outside of the control of the advocates of Christianity) has resulted in major moral problems. On the other hand, culturally insensitive rules against such things as polygamy, non-church weddings, dancing, social drinking of alcoholic beverages and the like need to be re-examined and, often, modified in the second generation, if Christianity is to be appropriately Scriptural. When such re-examination and change is not done, a major negative reaction against Christianity lies in store for the third and following generations. ⎟

Third and Subsequent Generations

The issues mentioned above usually continue to be issues in the third and following generations. As the years go by, however, things not dealt with become more and more entrenched and usually become more difficult to deal with. This is especially true in the many situations where biblical understandings of the relationship of Christianity to culture is minimal. Where, for example, Christianity is treated as merely a religion even by its adherents rather than as a relationship as it is portrayed in Scripture, a deadening nominalism easily takes over at least by the third generation, if not sooner.

The disease of nominalism speaks of the need for renewal. Renewal, then, is often stimulated by new information and new approaches to old problems. Thus, the kind of cultural sensitivity advocated here, when properly linked to Scripture, can become a source of renewal. So can greater experiences of God's power. The latter is transforming Christian experience in Argentina (see Wagner and Deiros 1998). Third generation Christians could well be advised to seek new emphases while praying that these will lead to renewal.

By the third generation, many peoples are expressing nationalistic concerns, especially if they feel they have been held down by colonial political and religious structures. Often, in reaction to Western domination in government, church, economics and most other dimensions of life, the intellectuals begin to influence their followers in glamorizing traditional ways of life they have never really known. Contextualizing in these generations, then, needs to take account of nationalism and to beware of the tendency for people to use Christianity to serve concerns that are more cultural than biblical. Down through the ages, for example, national groups that have emigrated out of their home areas such as Armenians, Eastern Orthodox, Koreans and Irish Catholics who have come to America and Japanese or Korean Christians who live in Brazil have used their Christianity to enhance their ethnic identity. Certain brands of "America first" Christianity fall into this category also.

Nominalism and nationalism, then, are crucial problems that third generation Christians need to deal with. There are usually also many of the earlier problems that have not been resolved. It is important at this stage for believers to not give up on the need to work toward greater biblical and cultural appropriateness.

Conclusion

The concern is for what *meanings* are getting across to the receptors. The question is how to inculturate Christianity in such a way that people attribute scriptural meanings to the cultural forms employed. First generation Christians usually do some things right in this regard but frequently leave much to be done and create much that ought to be redone by later generations.

I have tried to focus on some of the issues I feel are important and to point to the responsibility of the second and following generations to deal with the omissions and commissions of the first generation. Though it is easy to criticize many of the decisions of the first generation converts and of the outsiders who often misled them, we should be sympathetic with their position. They didn't know how to do what needed to be done. We can, therefore, give them the benefit of the doubt and ask those of the second, third and succeeding generations to rectify things.

The sad thing is that these later generations often attain very little more understanding of the relationship of Christianity to culture than their predecessors had. They, therefore, often simply perpetuate the mistakes of the past and even add to them their own mistakes enabling those around them to continue to misunderstand what Christianity is all about.

I wonder, for example, what might happen in Korea or Japan if a truly appropriate Christianity is developed. Many Koreans have, of course, turned to Christ but largely to a Euroamerican Christianity. But there are still about 70% of Koreans who have not come to Christ. Would the 70% respond positively to a truly Koreanized Christianity? And what about Japan? Though it will probably be necessary to break through the satanic power Japan is committed to before anything major can happen there, what kind of Christianity will attract Japanese if the power is broken?

On the other hand, look at what has happened in China. After several generations of missionary contact followed by a generation or two without outside help, and under very uncongenial circumstances, millions of Chinese seem to have discovered great meaningfulness in Christianity. And, though there are still traces of Western influence, they seem to have, at least to some extent, made the Gospel their own culturally as well as spiritually.

I seek in this chapter to alert us to some of the dimensions of the continuing quest toward more appropriateness that needs to be a part of the way Christianity is presented and experienced. All decisions made in one generation concerning the practice of Christianity within any given culture need to be regarded as tentative and experimental, open to re-evaluation and possible change by the next generation. A greater challenge than theorizing this necessity is to get the leaders, both younger and older, of churches to act on the theory.

Chapter 16

Power-Giving Leadership: Transformation for a Missional Church

Sherwood Lingenfelter

Leadership is a crucial issue in any application of the principles of contextualization. Throughout the history of the church Protestant and Catholic missionaries have struggled with the question of empowering new converts to lead newly planted churches. Some have moved rapidly to ordain local leaders, while others have retained mission control for long periods of time. Philip Jenkins reports that the first Jesuit missionaries to China and Japan quickly trained and ordained local Chinese and Japanese Christians to lead a rapidly growing church movement (2002). In the 16th and 17th centuries hundreds of thousands of Japanese and Chinese turned to Christianity through the ministry of these missionaries. Scriptures were translated into both languages and the church seemed to take strong root in these two Asian nations. But, in 1704, the Vatican rejected these translations of Scripture and the ordination of indigenous clergy. The Roman Catholic missions in these lands became once again strictly Latin and European, rejecting contextual leadership. As a consequence of this change in policy, these churches collapsed without strong local leadership, and China and Japan reverted to their preChristian religions.

The Protestant outreach of the 19th and 20th centuries was torn by these same tensions. Some Protestant missionaries such as William Carey, Hudson Taylor and Roland Allen understood the importance of empowering national Christians to carry on the ministry of the church. Others of their colleagues feared a dilution of the gospel and insisted upon retaining the power of leadership in the hands of the European missionaries who planted the churches. Lutherans, Methodists, Anglicans, and Roman Catholics all resisted the ordination of national leaders in Africa and in Latin America. The few nationals who were ordained had become very like Europeans in their expression of faith and their approach to leadership. As missions spread in the context of colonialism, missionaries often held social opinions similar to colonial government officials, seeing their mission as bringing the gospel, the church and the benefits of civilization to primitive peoples.

This chapter rejects the colonial practice of keeping power[1] in mission hands and argues that appropriate leadership for 21st Century mission is power-giving leadership. In the next few pages I will look at two definitions of power, and examine how power is a pervasive part of relationships in society. I will argue that power-seeking is a natural expression of the human psyche and experience, and that relationships in the church usually follow the same pattern as relationships in nonChristian society. I will then seek to show how leaders typically achieve their objectives for ministry through "power exchanges," when in fact the example that Jesus gave was of the Lord and Master giving away His power to others.

I conclude with a detailed discussion of how missionaries can model and teach power-giving leadership. Power-giving leadership begins by embracing "the way of the cross." Denying oneself means releasing control to others and empowering the impotent. I will discuss the difference between exercising power and responsibility, and the importance of accepting the social games of new converts, rather than teaching them ours. Finally I argue that the disciple metaphors of Scripture—cross, servants, friends, word, vine/branches, etc.—contradict the leadership metaphors of our cultures, and when we use them, instead of our cultural metaphors, to define our relationship to Christ and others, we may learn to obey Christ as we make disciples of others.

Power as Control

Control is the basis of power. People who seek to control their circumstances, their jobs, their relationships with others and their effectiveness in their work are all seeking power. Most people do not like to think about themselves as being engaged in power relationships with others. They prefer to reflect and describe their activities as an interest in quality, assuring that things will be done well, protecting those who are unable to protect themselves, or fulfilling one's responsibilities. These activities are not understood as being power-seeking or power-exercising activities. Yet, in fact, they are actions that at the core are intended to control the outcomes of an event in accord with the interests of the person retaining control.

Marguerite Shuster, focusing on the human psyche and power as a dimension of personal identity and action, defines power as "the ability to produce, intended effects in the world" (1987:156-157). As soon as a child is old enough to understand that communication produces intended effects, the child will seek power in his or her relationships. Shuster suggests that a person's existence becomes linked to the kinds of things that one produces. Some find significance in work, others in the multiplicity of relationships and still others in wealth. A person who does not find his or her life leading to at least one significant end feels impotent and even hopeless. Shuster suggests that

---

[1] It should be obvious that the power in focus here is power in social relationships, not the spiritual power discussed elsewhere in this volume (e.g., Chapters 21 and 22).

our meaning and existence are, in a large degree, linked to our sense of power in producing effect in our world.

Richard Adams takes a social and economic approach to power (1975:9-20). He contends that people have power to the extent that they control elements of the environment, material or immaterial, that are sought by others. Adams argues that power differences are an inherent characteristic of all social relationships. For example: a seminary professor controls the grades that students receive for their work in a class; a pastor controls the content and material of a worship service that people wish to attend on a Sunday morning; an employer controls the amount and kind of work and the amount of compensation that an employee is given for his or her labor; the Bible "translator" controls the choice of text, exegesis of meaning and the compensation for a national language "helper" working on Bible translation. In each of these relationships, one person controls concrete aspects of the environment that are valued by others. Adams suggests that "power transactions" are those reciprocal exchanges between persons of unequal power that result in each obtaining some measure of self-interest.

Both Adams and Shuster help us to understand that power has significant implications for one's identity as a person, and for one's interest as one engages in social relationships. Our natural inclination is to seek power to assure that we have meaning and significance in our lives. Further, our personal interests motivate us to engage in reciprocal exchanges with others that satisfy our mutual interests and our need to control events to achieve valued ends.

Power Exchanges and Will

If Adams is right and all social relationships have embedded within them power distinctions, then the normal course of social life results in numerous power exchanges. A *power exchange* occurs when someone who controls something of importance to another, uses that control to obtain compliance or conformity of the other to his/her will. Oftentimes these exchanges are so routine that people do not recognize the implicit issues of control. For example, a pastor tells the music leader the topic of his sermon and assumes that the music leader will select songs that support the topic. The music leader tells the worship team and the organist/pianist what music will be sung and played in the service on the next Sunday and expects them to be prepared to play as instructed. In each of these relationships one person controls some aspect of the environment that is of significance to the others. While the musicians control their skills and performance, the pastor decides what content and even perhaps what selections will be performed. If the music leader rejects the pastor's guidance, the pastor may withdraw support for the music leader and act to remove that person from the worship team. And so it is with each of the other relationships.

While Adams is correct in his assessment of the inherent material basis of power relationships, Shuster helps us understand that our exercising of power in these relationships ultimately focuses on an aspect of our inner person, our will (1987:94-95). The structuring of power relationships as Adams describes them is a normal part of the social structure of society. We can hardly avoid these power differentials, nor should we try to do so. They are an essential part of how we work together in society. Yet, at the same time each of us has a will that we bring to our relationships with one another. Our will emerges from inner motives, often from our personal need to seek power or to avoid impotence.

Shuster suggests that evil is a result of "disruptions of structure and/or will—the Devil spoiling what God has made" (1987:140-151). These disruptions lead people to distort the structures of human relationship and exercise their personal will in the pursuit of power. Perversion of the structures of relationship most often comes from our obsession to achieve a particular good, such as a biblically sound church. In view of that good, we may construct false paths (keeping control in our hands) to achieve the desired end, and make our way the absolute and only way to that end. When we accept the deception of Satan, and will to pursue a good in the wrong way, the end is misery both for us and for the people we seek to serve. The disruptions of will flow from choices of lesser goods (e.g., a sound church instead of obedience to God) and our rigid adherence to our worldview and blindness to and rejection of others.

Each of these distortions—perversion of structure, false paths, lesser goods, rigidity—lead us into destructive patterns of behavior and relationship. When our will is thwarted, we seek to punish others and reassert our control. In our arrogance, we limit options to those we know, and opt for choices we believe are secure, rather than to take the risks that obedience to God demands.

What is Power-Giving Leadership?

Cueing from Shuster, I will first argue that *we must put Jesus "in the place of power as a proper source of healing and will . . ."* (1987:209). We must understand that power cannot be the source of our meaning and significance if we are to be the people of God and leaders who follow Christ. Shuster suggests that "giving all inhumanity power only magnifies their potential for wickedness" (1987:201). Human structures become tyrannical, human will becomes self-serving, and the quest for power leads people to all kinds of temptation and evil.

To be restored in our human psyche and relationships to the will and purpose of God, *Jesus must become the center of who we are and replace our quest for power.* It is only as we are motivated by the Holy Spirit and through the living Word of God that we are able to relate to one another within the structures of human society to accomplish the purpose of God. Yet, Shuster notes that it is impossible for us to make the radical changes to have Word replace the quest for power in our lives (1987:202). The only possible way that this can occur is through the grace of the Lord Jesus Christ. It is precisely this grace and focus on the life changing power of the Holy Spirit and the transforming power of Jesus, the Living Word, that enables us to shift from power-seeking to power-giving leadership.

Walter Wright identifies the second essential principle—*power-giving leadership is in its essence relational, rather than positional (2000:2)*. Instead of focusing on authority and responsibility, the Christian leader works to build relationships that influence others to follow Christ. Jesus demonstrated such leadership, investing His life in a few unlikely disciples, and challenging them with His vision of the Kingdom of God, transforming their Jewish world and culture. Jesus became their friend and mentor; He visited their workplaces and families, and He invited them to join Him in proclaiming good news and healing to the broken. The fruit of the Spirit in His life modeled service *to others* and values that challenged the cultural establishment with its power-seeking leadership.

The centrality of relationship means that *people are more important than authority and control.* This then affects the kind of exchanges that take place between leaders and followers. In the typical power exchange, the leader exercises control in such a way that the will of the leader is done, often at significant cost to the follower. One of my colleagues tells the story of how his mission leader demanded that he do exactly what the leader instructed, and that he do it without question, even at the cost of his personal integrity. In this pattern, the follower is servant, and the leader is served. W. Wright suggests that relational leadership reverses this exchange, and leader is servant, seeking the "growth and nurture of the followers" (2000:13). *Instead of powering outcomes, the relational leader builds trust, and influences followers through integrity of character and depth of relationship.*

In the pages that follow I will present several essential practices for mission and church leaders that place Jesus in the place of power, and give relationship priority over authority and control. Contextual leadership is premised upon the acceptance and empowering of others. To achieve contextual leadership, the missionary, who so often controls resources and knowledge, must intentionally surrender control, and trust Jesus to accomplish His purpose in those he has called to ministry. When we obey his command to love first, then relationship takes priority over control, and contextual leadership becomes possible.

Responsible TO but not Responsible FOR

Many years ago I sat with my family in a group counseling session with a psychologist at Liebenzell Mission USA, where we were contributing to candidate orientation for ministry. As the psychologist explored with me and other members of my family our relationships of power with one another, the psychologist discerned quickly that my daughter and I were emotionally wrestling over power issues. After engaging both of us with some pointed questions he turned to me, "Sherwood, do you feel responsible for your daughter?" I had to confess that indeed, I did feel responsible for her. He then made this statement that I have never forgotten, "Sherwood, you must be responsible TO your daughter, but you cannot be responsible FOR her. She is responsible for her own actions."

Every leader has a certain amount of responsibility. That responsibility comes from the role that the leader must play in reference to structures that are part of the communities in which we live. I have argued elsewhere (1996, 1998) that God has endowed people everywhere both with social structures and with an ability to discern His will that can enable them to use those structures for right relationships in their communities and in the world. These structures include family structures, community, church and working relationships. In all of these structures, power (control over resources) is granted or delegated to persons and groups within that society.

The key for Christians is to understand that appropriate leadership requires that we acknowledge the motivation for power at our emotional core, and that we submit our will and structures in obedience to the Spirit of Christ. The practical outworking of this is that instead of using structural power to accomplish the outcomes we desire, we search to discern how the Word and the Spirit guide us and direct us to act as God's servants in these relationships.

Being responsible *TO* others is an important insight for us. When we act as if we are responsible *FOR*, we take power and we use it to try to accomplish the outcomes that we desire, in effect becoming power seekers. By being responsible *to*, however, we can fulfill the structural role given to us, and yet allow the other persons to take responsibility for their own actions and their obedience to Christ. The act of being responsible *to* involves asking appropriate questions, investing time in the building of relationship and speaking truth in love at times when God directs us to do so.

Two Old Testament leaders, Deborah and Samuel, illustrate "responsible *to*" leadership. When Barak refused to lead the people against Sisera without Deborah (Jud. 4:8), she agreed to accompany him, but told him the credit for the victory would be given to a woman. When Saul chose to offer the sacrifice to God without Samuel (1 Sam. 13:9), Samuel rebuked him, explained how he has violated his responsibility, and informed him of the consequences. After Saul failed in his second opportunity to obey God, sparing Agag and the livestock of the Amalekites in spite of Samuel's clear instructions, Samuel again took limited action (1 Sam. 15:26-31). Samuel's message is one of responsibility *to* Saul, informing him of God's decision to give the kingdom to another, while at the same time accompanying Saul to offer a sacrifice, and thereby upholding Saul's honor among the other leaders in Israel.

These cases illustrate the subtle difference between being a messenger for God and being a supervisor directing a process. Deborah accompanied, but did not direct. After Samuel had anointed Saul to be king over Israel, Samuel completely withdrew from his prior leadership role as the head of all of Israel. From the day of Saul's installation Samuel became a messenger for God and not the one responsible for Israel. Samuel gave up his control over the direction of leadership in Israel, but did not give up his responsibility to be the messenger from God to Saul.

Power-giving leadership, then, is leadership that confers power and responsibility upon others and then releases them to do the work they have been empowered to do. Once one releases control, one does not take it back again. Rather one accepts the successes and failures of the other, is responsible *to* that person, but does not attempt to take back control over the situation that has been given to the other.

While this created much distress for Samuel, (and may also create great distress for many of us), God told Samuel to stop grieving about Saul (1 Sam. 15). God was in charge of leadership in Israel, God had chosen someone to replace Saul, and the new leader would carry out His will in His good time and in accord with His plan and purpose for the people.

Releasing Control

To contextualize leadership, the most essential act in power-giving is to release control. Everything else that we will discuss is based upon this fundamental act. *The leader who wants to be a power-giver must be willing to release control.* For many of us, this is the most difficult act of will. When we release control, we entrust others to act in ways that may not fit with our idea of how they should act. We take the risk that whatever task or responsibility we have released will not be done in accord with our design, and in the worst case, we are willing to accept failure on the part of others with its consequences. By releasing control, we are saying that we will relinquish our right to assure that the desired affects occur, and we do so in faith that God, working through people, will accomplish the divine purpose. That is, we decide to trust both the Holy Spirit and the people He is using.

Releasing control is probably the most difficult thing that Christian leaders must do. The risk of letting go is great. Some may judge us to be inept because we have not controlled outcomes that seem essential to process and progress. We ourselves will feel anxiety and stress because the things that we believe are important may not happen in the way that we desire. The disciplines we think are essential to the successes may not be followed. The outcomes may be disastrous for the group and for the individuals involved.

Releasing control then is a significant act of faith and trust, both in God and in the person(s) released. The leader who decides to give power away is placing trust in that person and in God that the power given will be used to accomplish God's purpose. This is why power-giving is an act of faith and grace; the outcome rests in the power and grace of God. It is only by faith in the power of God, and in the power of the living Word that we can let go of our desire to control and place the responsibility for outcomes in the hands of others and of God. Jesus' act of releasing the leadership of the church to the twelve is the penultimate illustration of this principle. In spite of their failures, before and after His resurrection, Jesus trusted them and so many others, empowered by the Holy Spirit, to do His work, and establish His church.

Empowering the Impotent

The focus of power-giving leadership is to follow Christ, and in so doing, lead others to follow Christ. In the patterns of "normal" cultural life, our power and skills may produce leaders, but probably won't produce followers of Christ. People will certainly imitate us, and if we effectively demonstrate our skills and art to produce socially desired outcomes, they will do the same. The effect, however, is disastrous for the Kingdom of God. The history of the church is littered with the tragic stories of powerful leaders who have not only failed to bring about the kingdom by force, but have caused great damage to the church.

God, working in the people who respond to His call, however, reproduces leaders. As God's servants, we dare not rely upon our skills and training, but, rather, trust the power of God and His Spirit working in men and women to enable them to do God's work. I first experienced this in my relationship with my pastor father. When I was sixteen years old my father one day asked me to come into his study where he invited me to preach the next Sunday evening in our church. He had observed that I had an interest in the Scriptures and was reading the Bible regularly in my devotional life. He suggested that I choose a text from my personal reading of Scripture and then study what others had written on that text from books in his library to understand it more deeply. I accepted his invitation and began the wonderful adventure of studying the Word of God to share it with others. I can no longer remember what happened on that first Sunday evening. But I do remember that it was the beginning, and that I was asked to speak again. Over the next several years I had many opportunities to prepare and preach messages, and each time I was enriched by the experience of studying God's Word and sharing it with others. My father trusted me, empowered me, and gave me an opportunity that launched me into a life-long ministry of preaching and teaching the Word of God.

Understanding, then, that it is God who creates new leaders, we become sowers sowing seed. We, like Jesus, invite men and women who are not well-qualified, who have not had adequate training, who may be just beginning their journey of faith or who may have been on that journey for some time to step out and take on the responsibilities of teaching, preaching, evangelizing, affirming and encouraging others. We look at the least likely people, and see the potential for God to work in them to make them followers of Christ. As we release them to ministry, they will invariably follow us (for good or ill), and by God's grace invite and empower others to join in the journey with them.

The most important aspect of empowerment is releasing people to do the work in their own way. This means allowing them to set their own course and make their own mistakes. Again this is illustrated in Samuel's relationship to Saul. After Saul was anointed king, Samuel did not come back as the judge and leader of Israel. To the best of our knowledge he did not have a long-term internship or training program for Saul. What Samuel did do was communicate the word of God to Saul at appropriate times and then allow Saul to make his own mistakes (1 Sam. 12). Saul did it his way, and we know the story of his mistakes. Samuel confronted him on those occasions, but did not intervene in Saul's leadership.

Resisting the Urge to Offer Help

Because we are by nature power seekers, it is almost impossible for us to resist giving good advice to people that we have empowered for ministry. We see them making mistakes, we feel responsible for them and we intervene by offering helpful direction and advice. But often, and perhaps inevitably, our advice comes across as condemnation. More often than not, we alienate the very person we are trying to help. We push our good things on those we think need them, in hopes of producing our intended effect in the world. That is using our power to bring about the things that will give *us* significance. Power-giving leadership resists the urge to do what Dallas Willard calls "condemnation engineering" (1998:228).

One of my missionary friends made the following statement: "I used to say that I believed in the power of the Word of God to change lives. But in my work on the mission field I discovered that what I really believed in was my power to teach the Word of God and through that teaching to change lives." Once my friend understood the distortion in his own life, he stopped teaching. He realized that his very act of teaching was placing himself and his skill in the place of the Word of God. From that time on he began to help (not direct) those whom he was discipling to study and teach the Word of God themselves.

If we are to truly empower the impotent, we the educated, the experienced, must refuse to use our competence, once we have given the task to another. We must resist even giving advice, unless we are asked by those we are mentoring. And even in the giving of advice we must learn to suggest options—two or three ways of solving a problem—so that they can choose a solution, rather than rely upon our "correct" answer. And when we are asked, we must resist the temptation of doing it for them, or of showing them how by our expert performance. Our expert performance will only discourage the weak, and dismay the novice. Our virtuosity must inspire, but never demoralize. That means that if we are a great teacher, we should teach only in contexts where we are not displacing some lesser teacher. If we are a great organizer, we should limit our organizing to those circumstances where it is our responsibility alone to organize and empower others in their sphere of responsibility. Is this absurd? Should we not use our gifts for the Kingdom of God? Of course. But our primary role should be to encourage, not to dominate. Encouragement is a spiritual gift. Domination is not.

The key lies in the building of relationships that lead to trust, influence and encouragement for the work and purpose of God. If our desire is to truly reproduce followers of Christ, then we must and can give away the power of teaching, the power of organizing and the power of leading to those we are mentoring. When we place Jesus, rather than the quest for power, at the center of our being, then we will look to the Spirit and Word of God to guide us. By setting an example as followers of Christ, we encourage those we mentor to develop their obedience to the Spirit and grow in skills of service as they also follow the Lord Jesus Christ.

I began with the story of my father granting power to me to preach. In so doing he did not tell me how, did not organize my sermon for me, and did not criticize what I had done when I was finished. Instead he encouraged me and gave me more opportunities to serve.

Accepting Alternative Processes and Standards of Performance

The last dimension of power-giving leadership that we will explore here is that of accepting alternative structures, processes and standards for leadership. God has created human beings with a capacity for producing various types of structures. In the study of society, anthropologists have identified four distinctive prototype social games that are a part of human relationships (Douglas 1982, Thompson, Ellis, and Wildavsky, 1990, Lingenfelter 1996, 1998).

Briefly, these "games" can be labeled 1) authoritarian, 2) hierarchist, 3) individualist and 4) egalitarian. When an individualistic American working for a bureaucratic (authoritarian) organization attempts to work in a collective (egalitarian) society, then, we can expect major problems. Unless the American first studies the leadership patterns and expectations of the local community and works hard to adapt his or her approach to that of the receptor society, appropriate leadership will be impossible to achieve. In such a society a power-giving American missionary will affirm and encourage the local leaders to lead according to their familiar patterns under the guidance of the Holy Spirit and the word.

In my first mission consulting assignment, a mission organization working among a tribal people in Brazil invited me to assist a well-meaning missionary who found himself at an impasse in trying to get an airstrip built. He assumed that the tribal leadership game was hierarchist and that all he had to do was to contract with the chief who would arrange for the laborers to do their work and would then pay them with the gifts that he, the missionary, provided. In just a few days of research we discovered that these people were highly individualist (even more than the missionary), not hierarchist, and that the only effective way to engage them was to create individual contracts for each person, utilizing the chief as a coach and advisor. In that context the "chief" functioned more like a cheerleader than like a power broker.

One of the distortions that we as human beings bring to social relationships is the absolutizing of our familiar structure as the only structure that God can use to accomplish His purpose. We then distort the diversity of

God's creation, and reduce the structures for human life to those that are familiar to us. By denying the validity of other structures, we then force people to submit to our standards and structure of relationship to accomplish the work and purpose of God.

Contextualized power-giving leadership is a leadership that understands that the structures that are familiar to one group of people may not be familiar to another. The power-giving leader, then, does not insist upon utilizing his or her structures of relationship to bring about resolution to conflict or to define working relationships with others. Instead the power-giving leader is open to alternative structures and to alternative standards of performance.

In mission contexts this particular openness to other structures and other forms of relationship is especially critical and important. Mission organizations are often engaged in relationships with national churches that have very different structures of society and leadership. When mission and church leaders seek to work together they very often struggle with disagreements about structures and processes. Each group sees their own structure and processes as the right way to do things. As they try to work together they have the tendency to judge one another and condemn one another because of the conflicts in their structures and relationships.

Mission ministries are full of case studies of missionary and local church leaders in conflict because of their disagreements over structure and process. Sometimes these disagreements reach a point where Christians condemn one another, judge one another's spirituality, and ultimately destroy their working relationships together.

In a workshop in 2000 on cross-cultural partnerships, my wife and I invited African church leaders and expatriate mission leaders to meet separately and discuss their ideas of partnership. After each group had spent more than an hour discussing their definition of partnership and their expectations of structures and relationships among partners we brought them back together to share their results with one another. Over the next hour we saw how the ideas about partnership of missionaries and African nationals were radically different. The missionaries said that partnership is not like marriage and the Africans said that partnership is like marriage. The missionaries described partnership as a very task focused and time closed relationship, while the Africans described partnership as a person-focused and lifelong relationship. When asked about the kinds of exchanges that would occur between partners, the missionaries pictured the exchanges as utilitarian and task-directed. The Africans envisioned the exchanges as reciprocal and related to their whole lives. As we continued our discussions over the next two weeks, it became very clear that the fundamental difficulty of both missionaries and nationals was their failure to understand and accept the rules and processes of the others in their attempt to work together as partners.

A leader or group that aspires to be power-giving must accept and work within structures and processes that are different from one's own social game.

We work to understand and employ the structure being empowered, even when we may deem it inefficient or even counterproductive. If we can remember that efficiency and productivity are sought outcomes that come from our own power-seeking, then we can look beyond productivity to Word and Spirit motivated outcomes—outcomes that are part of God's plan for us in our relationships with one another. The commands of Scripture make it clear that the first and most important criterion in our relationship is that we love one another. The Scriptures explain in detail how those relationships will result in patience, compassion, humility, and a whole host of other character attributes that flow from the work of the Holy Spirit in making us like Christ. *As we examine the fruits of the Spirit we will find that none of them focus on efficiency and productivity.* Those are power-seeking goals that arise out of our cultural rules and our need for significance.

Part of our learning to accept others is to accept their decisions even when we believe they may be poor decisions. If we do not accept a decision, we then have no opportunity to dialogue about its context, about its outcomes and about the impact that it may have in terms of the community for which it has been made. The true measure of a decision's effectiveness is whether or not it accomplishes the will and purpose of God. Again, reflecting on the case study of Samuel and Saul, Saul did make poor decisions. In both of the situations recorded in 1 Samuel, Saul's decisions grew out of his desire for power in relationship to people in his own cultural context. Samuel, as the messenger of God, confronted Saul about these decisions and brought God's message to him. Samuel did not change those decisions and accepted the outcomes and the consequences for Saul and for Israel.

Asking for Correction

Over the course of our consulting ministry with mission organizations in Africa and Asia, my wife and I have found that missionary and national leaders are frequently involved in conflict with one another. As we explore more deeply the causes of those conflicts, we find that each group of leaders has proceeded to decisions and action based upon their own understanding of the situation without significant dialogue with others. Both missionary and national church leaders have reached decisions in isolation from one another and oftentimes bring a decision as a finished fact to their colleagues.

For example, a group of church leaders in West Africa informed the mission that they did not want a particular missionary couple to return to their field. They did not explain why, but just said the couple were unacceptable to them. The mission organization responded that they could not make such a decision without bringing the couple back to the field and processing this on the field with them. Both sets of leaders stood in conflict with one another, using their own processes and procedures to defend their actions. Neither took time to ask the other what they were thinking, why they had acted the way they did and what the problems were in the situation. This scenario is a perfect illustration of power-seeking rather than power-giving. Each group of leaders refused to release control over something they valued, each refused to consider the others processes and decisions and each could not understand why the other did not understand them.

The ultimate act of power-giving, even more important than acceptance, is inviting others to critique one's work and decision-making. Because missionaries and mission organizations, controlling key resources, hold a structural power relationship with national churches, they structurally may and often do make decisions that have negative impact on the church without inviting any feedback. When we engage others in such a way as to solicit their reflection, feedback, and interpretation of our decisions, we create an environment of humility, empowering them to help us be more effective in our ministry.

Power-giving leadership invites the other to critique one's work and decisions. By patient listening and intentional hearing what others say, we may correct our own structural rigidity, and thereby become more able to work together for the purposes of the Kingdom of God. The goal is to engage others in such a way that we empathize with their critique, build mutual understanding and commit to community relationship with them. By inviting them to critique our decisions and work, we open the door for greater understanding. By being willing to adjust and change what we do to better minister to them, we in fact create deeper community in Christ and greater capacity to love one another.

The Cross and Culture

According to David Bennett, New Testament metaphors for ministry are quite unlike the power metaphors that we employ in our own societies (1993). In our mission organizations we have CEOs, Vice Presidents, Field Superintendents or Directors, Administrators and other functional hierarchical roles. In our churches we use biblical metaphors, but we add to them the hierarchy of senior, associate and assistant pastor, we add specializations of adults, youth, Sunday school and other kinds of ministries, and we overlay the biblical terms of elder and deacon with cultural roles that are unique to our own cultural settings. Bennett documents how Jesus rejected the *arche* "rule over" metaphors in Greek, using instead metaphors of servant, shepherd, family and friends for his disciples.

Taking my cue from Bennett, I propose three different New Testament metaphors that are essential for power-giving leadership: the cross, servants watching for their master, and witnesses or messengers of the master.

Jesus said "if anyone would come after me, he must deny himself and take up his cross daily and follow me. For whoever wants to save his life will lose it, but whoever loses his life for me will save it" (Lk. 9:23-24). *The cross is intended to overshadow culture*, shaping the life of the church. The essence of this message from Jesus is that we cannot find fulfillment in seeking power or accomplishing specific goals in our lives. North American evangelical literature and leaders focus upon growing our church, planting other churches, teaching more students, making more disciples, gaining more wealth, holding higher positions, and maintaining our health. All in and of themselves are empty pursuits. Once attained, they cannot satisfy us.

Power-giving leaders must begin at the cross. Jesus' death on the cross is the metaphor given for us to follow (1 Pet. 2:21-25): at the cross we lay down our search for meaning and significance apart from Christ! To take up the cross is to let go of our obsessions to belong, to succeed, to excel above others, to be recognized, to find pleasure, to gratify desire, etc. The message of the cross is submission to God and releasing to God every aspect of our lives. We replace the old obsession to control the outcomes of our lives with a new obsession to obey God. By placing control in the hands of God, we are then free by faith to release to others control over things and circumstances that we in our flesh want to control, but in the spirit we know we should relinquish to Christ.

None of the social games of leadership that are available in every culture are in themselves significant. But each is a gift of God to human beings and each is a part of the complex structure that God has given us to live with one another in community. When we obey the call to take up the cross, our obedience and the obedience of others will transform any one of these social games. The command to take up the cross is a call to live in submission to God and His word; to take the path of weakness, rather than power; to engage in repeated acts of forgiveness, rather than condemnation; to submit to and empower others regardless of the social game that we play.

The second metaphor is that of "servants whose master finds them watching." In the gospel of Luke 12:35-48, Jesus describes for his disciples the character of *faithful servants who are ready, prepared and working until their master returns*. The key attribute of a faithful servant is obedience, fulfilling the role assigned by the master, even in circumstances where the master may be absent for long periods of time. Once again reflecting on Shuster's work, the critical issue for faithful service is *will*. In this text, each servant has the same opportunity to exercise will and structure to honor the master. Jesus distinguishes between the servant who wills to follow his master and the one who wills to act in accord with his own interests. The one who is faithful, giving workers "their food allowance in the proper time," is rewarded with even greater responsibility. The contrasting figure in the story, who finds the delay in the master's return an opportunity to seize power to fulfill his own interests and pleasure, in the end loses everything. Do we will to do God's will? Or do we will to accomplish our own purposes and fulfill our own power objectives?

Shuster suggests that we are tempted to pervert the will of God by choosing things that are lesser than God's will for us, or by being deluded by an illusion of progress and achievement. These deceptions, whether of our own design or of demonic influence, lead us to pursue fruits of labor that are different from the fruits of the Spirit that God has intended for us.

Further, Shuster sees our bondage to a particular worldview and social system as another distortion of will (1987:149). When we refuse to see things from the perspective of others and we insist on imposing our standards and our frame of reference upon them, we distort God's purpose and destroy our relationships with those we serve. Like the unfaithful servant, we pursue our interests at the expense of those we have been sent to serve, while we wait for Jesus to come again.

The third metaphor is really a group of metaphors that focus upon the idea of witness or messenger. The most common is the word apostle, sent ones, that is used most often in the New Testament to refer to the twelve apostles, but is also used in reference to messengers to the church in the Pauline epistles. The metaphor of "witness" is used by Jesus and throughout the book of Acts with reference to proclaiming the resurrected Christ to the world. Other metaphors, such as soldier, partner and ambassador, capture the idea of people sent on a mission for the work of the Kingdom of God. The unifying idea of all of these concepts is that of *a people sent by God for His purpose to accomplish His work*. It is not our work, we are not the commanders, we are merely those who are sent by God to accomplish His purpose in His kingdom.

Our role, then, is similar to that of Samuel in his relationship to Saul and David. We are enlisted by God in His service to carry His message. We are sometimes given the privilege and opportunity of anointing a new leader. We occasionally have the opportunity to bring God's message in a distinctive way to challenge, encourage and rebuke those we serve. We may work as partners in relationship with the others that God has anointed to do His work. But the outcome is always in God's hands and in accord with God's purpose. His servants may fail, they may refuse to follow the instructions given through us or others, and they may lose their opportunity to serve as did Saul. Our role is to be obedient to God and to carry God's message to whomever we are sent. As obedient messengers, following the instructions of our Lord, God works in us and through us to accomplish His objectives for the time and place where we are sent.

Conclusion

Appropriate contextualization of Christianity must include approaches to leadership that are appropriate both to Scripture and to the receiving society. We have seen in this chapter how people are inclined to seek control and power in their ministry and leadership roles. Jesus, Samuel and others in Scripture model for us power-giving leadership. But, unlike missionaries, they worked within cultural patterns familiar to them since they worked within their own societies.

Cross-cultural witnesses, however, face the challenge of being power-givers to leaders who practice their leadership in terms of a social game different from that familiar to the missionary. This fact places great responsibility on the missionary to relinquish the power to determine the game that is played, and to study and learn to work with the receptors' social game or an adaptation that they create together. To assist cross-cultural witnesses in this difficult task, I have written two books *Agents of Transformation* (1996) and *Transforming Culture* (1998). I recommend these, plus Walter Wright's *Relational Leadership: A Biblical Model for Leadership and Service* (2000) to those who want to learn to be power-givers.

Part III

Proactive Missiology: The Challenge

Chapter 17

How Appropriate Is the Church Growth Paradigm in Today's Mission Contexts?

Eddie Gibbs

The start of the Church Growth movement is generally dated around 1950 when Donald McGavran was completing the writing of his seminal work *The Bridges of God* (1955, 1981). From the outset it was born in controversy, partly due to the post-World War II and post-Colonial loss of nerve regarding mission that McGavran so vehemently challenged, and partly due to McGavran's resolve to critically analyze the presence of church planting movements around the world. He was determined to clarify the ways of thinking about and reporting the barriers that obscured what was really happening, or not happening, as the case may be, creating a reaction from those who objected to the criteria of effectiveness that McGavran wanted to apply.[1]

Fifty years later many of the issues have changed significantly, to the extent that McGavran's writings will no longer be understood if we simply read him in the context of a new millennium. His theological understanding needs to be challenged or re-stated at a number of points, for McGavran was not primarily a theologian and his writing reflect the limitations of the evangelical missiological thinking of his day (just as ours reflects the limitations of our day). In addition, we face new challenges at this point of time that were not on McGavran's radar screen. Since McGavran wrote the *Bridges of God*, a lot of water has run under those bridges.

At the outset we need to be clear about how McGavran understood church growth, especially as the term has been appropriated and challenged by many individuals who have not in fact read McGavran's works. He himself described rather than defined church growth. It was left to the American Society for Church Growth to provide a formal definition.

> *Church Growth is that discipline which investigates the nature, expansion, planting, multiplication, function and health of Christian churches as they relate to the effective implementation of God's commission to "make disciples of all peoples" (Mt. 28:19-20). Students of Church Growth strive to integrate the eternal theological*

---

[1] See *Understanding Church Growth* (McGavran 1970), Part II Discerning the Outlines, Chapter 4 "A Universal Fog," and Chapter 5 "The Facts Needed."

principles of God's Word concerning the expansion of the Church with the best insights of contemporary social and behavioral sciences, employing as the initial frame of reference, the foundational work done by Donald McGavran. (C. Peter Wagner 1987:114).

My purpose in this review is to reassess the appropriateness of the church growth principles expounded by McGavran, seeking to identify issues of continuing importance–the non-negotiables if you will. Then we will address areas where McGavran's ideas have been modified or refined, both by himself and by later contributors. Then I want to express some concerns in terms of the direction the movement has taken, especially here in the United States. Finally, I will attempt to raise some agenda items as the movement looks to the future.

Issues Of Continuing Importance

1. Misrepresentations of "Church Growth." C. Peter Wagner used to warn his students in the *Foundations of Church Growth* class that he taught at Fuller Seminary from the late 1970s that the logo "church growth" couldn't be copyrighted. Publishers and seminar promoters will take up the title and make it mean whatever they want it to mean, he would say. In class, he illustrated this by showing Xerox newspaper advertisements that declared, "xerox is not a Xerox" and "there is no such thing as a xerox." The Xerox photocopying machine manufacturing company was becoming the victim of its own success and was losing ownership of their own name brand. Whatever make of machine he/she was using they were likely to say, "I will just xerox this for you." The Hoover company had a similar problem with its carpet cleaners in that "to hoover" became a verb meaning to clean the carpet. Some, but by no means all, of the controversy surrounding church growth arose from this purloining of the name, so that McGavran's concerns were soon overlooked or misrepresented.

2. "Church growth" versus "church health." During the past fifty years the term "church growth" has collected so much baggage and garbage that those associated with the Church Growth Movement have debated back and forth whether it has served its time. Should it be dropped or be rehabilitated? As the Donald McGavran Professor of Church Growth at Fuller Seminary, it might appear that I have a vested interest in pursuing the second option. My reasoning is, however, less personally motivated. On balance I would argue for retaining the term "church growth" because it brings together two fields of study that all too often considered in isolation to their mutual impoverishment. Those two fields are ecclesiology and missiology.

A further consideration is that the term "church health" is now widely offered as a preferred alternative. Given the therapeutic culture of the West, I am concerned that this will lead to an introspective emphasis that will result in a loss of mission commitment. A loss of nerve in terms of undertaking missional outreach can lead to an over-indulgence of analysis resulting in procrastination and analysis paralysis. If an alternative is deemed desirable, I would prefer "church vitality," which emphasizes the energy and activity of a healthy body.

3.Reconnecting ecclesiology with missiology. To study the church within the confines of an agenda determined by its internal life will lead to a dormant, even moribund, discipline. This is precisely what has happened in the field of ecclesiology since Hans Küng's magisterial volume entitled *The Church* was published in 1967 in the aftermath of Vatican II (Küng 1967).[2] His volume has a strong section on the church's apostolic calling and of the enabling of the Spirit to fulfill the commission entrusted to it by the ascended Lord. From the Protestant side there has been nothing to parallel that emphasis until the writings of my colleague Charles Van Engen's doctoral dissertation, *The Growth of the True Church* (1981), and his revision of that study in *God's Missionary People* (1991) which explores the missionary dimensions of an appropriate ecclesiology.

One of the unfortunate consequences of academic departmentalization has been a paucity of interaction between theologians and missiologists in the area of ecclesiology. Happily, during the past five years this has begun to be rectified by a series of volumes currently being published by Eerdmans that focus on the the need for mission in North America. The first volume, edited by George R. Hunsberger and Craig Van Gelder, is entitled *The Church Between Gospel and Culture: The Emerging Mission in North America* (1996), and the second edited by Darrell Guder is entitled *Missional Church: A Vision for the Sending of the Church in North America* (1998). In addition, Trinity Press International published a series of twenty-five short books between 1995 and 2000 "to help the church understand its missional responsibility to a culture in crisis".[3] These volumes take up the challenge that Lesslie Newbigin brought to the churches in the United Kingdom and to Europe, namely to recognize that the Western world presented as big a missionary challenge as did major regions in the majority world. This perception has now crossed the Atlantic and the realization that America is once again a mission field is slowly being recognized. Some seminaries have yet to wake up to the implications of this dramatic turn of events for their own futures and for the reshaping of their curricula.

---

[2] See especially his discussion of the Apostolic mission of the church, pp. 344-359.

[3] The following represent some of the titles in the series: Judith Gundry Volf and Miroslav Volf, *A Spacious Heart: Essays on Identity and Belonging* (1997); Lesslie Newbigin, *Truth and Authority in* Modernity (1996); J. Andrew Kirk, *The Mission of Theology and Theology as Mission* (1997); Alan J. Roxburgh, *The Missionary Congregation, Leadership, and* Liminality (1997); Douglas John Hall, *The End of Christendom and the Future of* Christianity (1996b); Lamin Sanneh, *Religion and the Variety of Culture: A Study in Origin and Practice* (1996); Wilbert R. Shenk, *Write the Vision: The Church Renewed* (1995); David J. Bosch, *Believing in the Future, Toward a Mssiology of Western Culture* (1995); Kenneth Cragg, *The Secular Experience of God* (1998); Bert Hoedemaker, *Secularization and Mission: A Theological Essay* (1998); Paul G. Hiebert, *Missiological Implications of Epistemological Shifts* (1999); and Darrell L. Guder, *The Incarnation and the Church's Witness* (1999).

4. Church growth is a mission concept not a marketing concept. Given the entrepreneurial genius of this part of the world, the success-driven and highly competitive nature of the religious "market," pastors caught onto the need for their church to "grow," but in so doing missed McGavran's mission heart-beat for the church to "go" in order to grow. Marketing strategies designed to attract greater numbers to a church with crowd-appeal replaced the need for the church to mobilize its members for their God-given mission in the real world.[4]

It was not only the Church Growth movement that suffered from this come-to-us mentality. Much the same can be said for the charismatic movement with its emphasis on spirit-gifts largely confined to meeting the ministry needs of members within the church, and its ministry emphasis on signs and wonders housed within the sanctuary rather than tested out in the community. Most of the Scripture songs generated by the movement were the language of personal devotion rather than public declaration. This movement faltered because it did not have the nerve for its credibility to be tested in the world.[5]

Academic theologians have, in my view, rightly criticized the marketing approach to ministry that has characterized so much of the evangelical churches in the past two decades. But we seminary professors must also accept some of the responsibility for this unfortunate state of affairs. Faced with a missiological challenge brought about by the marginalizing of the church in society and the emergence of a culture no longer based on Biblical values and metaphors, many pastors found themselves ill-prepared to inform and guide their response to this challenge. Consequently, they adopted the secular marketing language and strategies because they lacked missiological training and insights.

In some respects the churches in Europe have made further progress in thinking through the church's mission in a secular and now religiously pluralistic context than have the churches of North America. Spiritually, Canada is closer to Europe than North America while Australia is probably at the forefront of missional thinking and strategizing in this regard. Australia is highly secularized with a prevailing anti-clericalism and cultural distancing from the church. Such a negative image of the church goes back to the time when Australia was populated as a penal colony when Georgia could no longer be used for that purpose following the American revolutionary war (Robert Hughes 1987). In such a climate, church marketing strategies find few "buyers" so younger leaders are prepared to adopt more radical mission outreach strategies.

---

[4] The main challenges to a marketing approach to ministry are to be found in Os Guinness, *Dining With The Devil: The Megachurch Movement Flirts With Modernity* (1993) and Philip D. Kenneson and James L. Street, *Selling Out The Church–The Dangers of Church Marketing* (1997).

[5] See editorial article, "Has The Wind Dropped?" (1979). This editorial was a text given at the final meeting of the Fountain Trust, a charismatic organization that spanned most of the traditional denominations.

5. Transferability of church growth insights. In the majority world, church growth thinking has been far more extensive, yet intuitively applied, in that the churches tend to have a much larger percentage of first-generation Christians converted out of nonChristian dominant cultures. Church growth principles were initially extrapolated from rapidly growing churches in Africa, Latin America and countries in Asia, principally Korea and Singapore.[6]

The most successful application of church growth insights has been in developing evangelistic and church planting strategies in the majority world. They have also helped in identifying the cultural and historical factors that have prevented people of other faiths from responding to the gospel. It is significant that more Jews have turned to Christ as the long-promised Messiah in the last twenty years than in any other period since the destruction of Jerusalem in the first century of the Christian era. There are movements among Muslims who have come to recognize Jesus as more than a prophet. New understandings of contextualization applied to church growth insights have contributed to these developments. At the same time we must not lose sight of the sovereign acts of the Holy Spirit breaking down human resistance and spiritual strongholds.

However, it is a different story when we try to assess the impact of the Church Growth Movement in Europe, North America, Australia and New Zealand. Church growth insights have proved beneficial to church planters working largely in new suburban areas. They have also contributed significantly to the revitalization of some traditional churches with entrepreneurial leadership. Yet it also has to be admitted that the Church Growth Movement has not made sufficient impact to turn around the tide of decline experienced throughout the Western world. It may have contributed to the reconfiguring of the church-going constituency, attracting a much greater percentage to emerging megachurches. In so doing it may have slowed the slump. But these possibilities have to remain in the realm of conjecture.

On balance I believe that the term "church growth" should be retained, provided that we understand growth, not simply in terms of attracting a crowd, but in terms of the church dispersing throughout the world in order to reproduce "after its own kind." Therein, lies a problem to which we will return later. Furthermore, our understanding of the factors contributing to church growth is far from complete. In light of our experience in the Western world we still have much to learn, as well as some things to unlearn.

---

[6] William R. Read, Victor M. Monterroso, and Harmon A. Johnson, *Latin American Church Growth* (1969); C. Peter Wagner, *Look Out!The Pentecostals Are Coming* (1973), later reissued under the title *Spiritual Power and Church Growth* (1986); Paul Yonggi Cho, *Successful Home Cell Groups* (1981) and *More Than Numbers* (1984); James Wong, *Singapore: The Church in the Midst of Social Change* (1973); and Keith Hinton, *Growing Churches Singapore Style* (1985).

How Church-Growth Thinking Has Developed

1. One of the frequent criticisms directed against church growth is its emphasis on numbers as the dominant measure of success.[7] This criticism is particularly strident from theological thinkers in the majority world who react against Western missionaries who come armed with electronic calculators and formulas and strategies to guarantee results. To the modern mind, a person with the right know-how can solve every problem.

Another strong criticism comes from Western church leaders within declining denominations who take refuge in theological justifications and rationalizations for numerical decline. These criticisms must be taken seriously, but before responding to their concerns we need to hear McGavran within the context that he is seeking to address.

McGavran's insistence on the need to establish an accurate objective database was not as a technique for assuring results and exercising control. In the first place, he was primarily concerned with issues of honesty and integrity.[8] Missionary promotional literature was full of imprecise, slippery terms that concealed the truth behind alleged field success. He was determined to shift the emphasis from *output*, i.e. the amount of the seed of the gospel message that was sown, to the *yield* measured in terms of the spiritual harvest that resulted from all this activity. From the beginning, church growth as conceived by McGavran focused not on crowds who heard, not even with decisions counted, but in the numbers of those who enlisted in Christ's school of discipleship and in communities formed. For this reason he placed great emphasis on the goal of the Great Commission which was to "make disciples," which could not be accomplished without gathering them into communities of believers for nurture, accountability and developing ministry and mission potential.

Again we must bear in mind that McGavran's tradition was within the Disciples of Christ, a church affiliated with the World Council of Churches. During the decade of the 1960s, under the influence of Johannes Hoekendijk (1967), the mission thrust of the World Council of Churches emphasized God's agenda in the world with mission as the bringing about of *shalom* in society

---

[7] See Ralph H. Elliott, *Church Growth that Counts* (1982) and Robert K. Hudnut, *Church Growth is not the Point* (1975).

[8] The great Calvinistic Baptist preacher, Charles Haddon Spurgeon, writing in the previous century, took a similar line to McGavran. He wrote, "I am not among those who decry statistics, nor do I consider that they are productive of all manner of evil; for they do much good if they are accurate, and if men use them lawfully. It is a good thing for people to see the nakedness of the land through statistics of decrease, that they may be driven to their knees before the Lord to seek prosperity; and, on the other hand, it is by no means an evil thing for workers to be encouraged by having some account of results set before them. I should be very sorry if the practice of adding up, and deducting, and giving in the net result were to be abandoned, for it must be right to know our numerical condition." *The Soul Winner* (1895), republished, c1963, pp. 17, 18.

largely through socio/political programs. In pursuing this agenda, the church was largely lost sight of. Herein lies the origin of McGavran's ecclesial focus.

In his seminal work *Understanding Church Growth*, McGavran wrote of church growth as *"a* principal aim of mission," this was later changed in Wagner's revision to *"the* principal aim of mission" (1970:32). Mission thereby became synonymous with church growth, which was an unfortunate development.

Orlando Costas criticized such an ecclesial-centered approach while at the same time preserving McGavran's concern (Costas 1974:Chapters 5-7). He stressed that the growth of the church is a penultimate and not the ultimate goal of mission. The ultimate is the realization of the Kingdom. In other words, the church must always point beyond itself to the Lord it seeks to represent. The church is an anticipatory sign and servant of the Kingdom, but cannot be identified with the Kingdom. McGavran's writing in this regard reflects the confusion of the time in that Church and Kingdom tended to be used interchangeably. I do not know to what extent Donald McGavran and J. Eldon Ladd were talking to each other across their schools as they each dealt in their own ways with the relationship of Church and Kingdom.

A further limitation in McGavran's thinking was his focus on the complex dynamics of the initial turning of individuals-in-community to Christ rather than on the growth of existing churches within a Christianized context. He emphasized that this entailed following Christ as Lord, and their adoption of the Bible as their own book although he did not develop the implications of this in any comprehensive way. It was Orlando Costas who provided a comprehensive taxonomy of growth. He emphasized that growth must be holistic, or organic. In any organism there can be unhealthy as well as healthy growth, such as fat in place of muscle, and cancerous cells feeding on healthy cells. Healthy organic growth is symbiotic and is represented by upward growth in spiritual stature, internal growth in authentic fellowship (*koinonia*), outward growth in service (*diakonia*) and expansion growth through the broadcasting of the message (*kerygma*).

It must be said that McGavran opposed this concept of "holism," concerned that it would dilute emphasis and divert energy from the church reproducing in the world (1970:80). I think his description of the holistic model as the four parallel thrusts expounded by Costas reveals a misunderstanding of the model, in that all four dimensions of growth must be fully integrative. Rather than represent the holistic approach in terms of four parallel emphases, it is more accurate to see the first three in terms of the three essential strands of a rope (i.e growing up, growing together and growing out) that are intertwined, and the fourth (growing more) representing the lengthening of the rope. Without those three strands of maturity, fellowship and service, the rope will eventually fray apart.

2. A second insight of McGavran that has been much criticized is that of the "homogeneous unit principle (HUP)." McGavran understood that "people

build barriers around their own societies and, consequently, people like to become Christians without crossing racial, linguistic or class barriers (1970:198)." While McGavran's point has great validity, the issue is not whether they "like" to cross, but whether they should be "expected" to climb over racial and cultural barriers. The only obstacle the Christian communicator is allowed to retain is the obstacles of the Person of Christ and His unique reconciling mission accomplished on the Cross. The New Testament refers to Jesus as an unavoidable stumbling block who is also the vital cornerstone.

In part this criticism reflects a lack of understanding resulting from a lack of missionary experience. Here in North America, the HUP has been turned into a marketing strategy, failing to recognize that first and foremost it is a missiological insight. It provides an alternative, or sociological, "map" by which to discern the progress of the gospel in any given area, which a geographical map will fail to reveal. It is not a device for attracting "our kind of people" with whom we feel comfortable and among whom we can find our needs met through a custom-tailored gospel. To use the HUP as a rationale for excluding people different from us is a gross misapplication of the principle. Perhaps an illustration will help.

A number of years ago I was visiting a rural area in England for a church growth conference attended by leaders from the twenty-or-so churches serving the village communities. I asked them what tribes lived in these parts. They looked puzzled and then laughed. I asked them who regarded each other as "us" as distinct from "them." Who socialized with whom and who married whom? Within the next few minutes they began to identify the tribes: farm workers, farm owners, successful city-folk who came at the week-ends to play the role of the country-gentry, retirees, commuters who lived in the village but worked in the town. "Any more?" I asked. Then one person said, "We have a lot of truck drivers who take the farm produce to the freezer plants and canning factories?" "Do any of you have truck-drivers or their families attending your church?" Not one was to be found in any of the twenty churches. Here was an unreached people group who would have remained undetected if we simply place pins in a map to identify church members.

I confess that I reacted negatively when I first heard the homogeneous unity principle argued. I was concerned that the church, if it was to be true to the gospel, needed to demonstrate unity through the reconciling power of the gospel. Should not the gospel break down walls of ethnicity, socio-economic status, sexism and generations? Indeed the church must reflect the cultural diversity of the community of which it is a part. But we must then ask what will that "unity" look like in a pluralistic setting. Surely, the church is not to become a blender, to produce some mud-colored concoction.

From the outset, God has created a diverse entity functioning as a complex integrated system. The church is described metaphorically as a body, with many different members. We can apply this to the various ministries within one local congregation. But might it not also be extended to different local congregations having distinctive features but collectively being part of the one body? Can any one church express the full comprehensiveness of the gospel in terms of its inner life and its outwardly directed ministries?

When the HUP is regarded from a missiological perspective it represents the challenge to take seriously the complex mosaic (or more accurately dynamic, every-changing kaleidoscope) of cultures represented by urban societies, and to take the costly steps necessary for a transformative incarnational ministry within each segment. To turn it into a device for niche marketing is to prostitute the principle.

Before concluding our discussion of this issue, a further question needs to be raised, Is it accurate to call it the homogeneous unit *principle*? In certain situations it might be adopted as an operational principle, but it is not a "principle" in the sense of being a theological absolute. In some situations it would be both a denial of the gospel to work on HUP lines, as for instance in situations of tribal exclusivism and ethnocentrism. If by applying the HUP the walls of prejudice are strengthened then it must be denounced.

McGavran's concern was to break down the great commission task in terms of going throughout the world to all peoples. His interpretation of the term *"panta ta ethne"* to mean going to the ethnic groups of the world is anachronistic in that it assumes an understanding of ethnicity that cannot be derived from the Greek. But neither should the term be interpreted according to the translation in most of our English versions as going to the "nations." What is in view are not modern nation states that vary in size and ethnic complexity – from the Peoples' Republic of China on the one hand to Liechtenstein on the other – but to the peoples of the world. Although the term HUP is less in vogue these days – and I side with those in favor of burying it – McGavran's insights, as developed by Ralph Winter at the U.S. Center for World Mission, have led to a people group approach to world evangelization that helps to break down the global task into identifiable units.

3. Another way we need to go beyond McGavran's thinking concerns the relation of the Church and Mission. The bias that comes through in his writing is that the Church is considered as the local congregation or a federation of congregations in an area that has been "colonized," whereas the pioneering work is undertaken by mission agencies. The perception is that these agencies are still largely Western-based, with front-line missionary ranks reinforced by national Christians. Once again, we need to put McGavran's argument in context. In once sense his position can be described as "the last hurrah for Western Mission initiative." But at the time he was writing against a background of a missionary moratorium proposed by some church leaders overseas coupled to a loss of nerve on the part of Western agencies.

Donald McGavran was concerned by the disproportionate amount of resources deployed to shore up existing ecclesial structures in the majority world, to the neglect of continuing mission outreach. He drew attention to the fact that the Christian church in many nations consisted of no more than a bridgehead, sometimes confined to one particular ethnic or socio-economic group. This is another reason why McGavran was an inveterate field-researcher seeking to gauge to what extent the Christian movement had penetrated the various sections of society. In his renowned address that he gave in many parts of the world, "Sunset or Sunrise of World Mission," McGavran challenged the argument that the day of the missionary enterprise was fast drawing to a close now that there was a Christian presence in most of the nations of the world. The clarion call was to make sure that the 4.5 billion yet to hear the gospel should not be betrayed.

Concerns That Need to Be Addressed

1. Church Growth suffered along with much of evangelical scholarship by being impacted by the assumptions of modernity. It was heavily rationalistic, and described as a scientific approach to mission, albeit a soft rather than a hard science. However, the American Society for Church Growth was careful to avoid describing church growth as a "science," preferring the vaguer term "discipline." It's definition balances the tension in integrating "the eternal theological principles of God's Word concerning the expansion of the Church with the best insights of contemporary social and behavioral sciences."[9]

The use of the term "scientific" gave the mistaken impression that Church Growth consisted of a number of principles, which if correctly understood and applied would *guarantee* church growth. Numerous church leaders attended seminars and courses on these foundational principles believing that they would provide the necessary tool kit to remove the obstacles to growth and establish achievable goals. The majority of pastors attending those seminars and courses failed to realize the expectations that were raised through these events. This was partly due to the fact that the teaching provides insights without developing the necessary skills, but, more fundamentally, church growth exponents came to realize that church growth was far more complex then they had been led to suppose.

Yes, we said that we need a Paul to plant and an Apollos to water, but it is only God who gives the growth (1 Cor. 3:6), but our technique-based confidence conveyed a different message. Those church growth principles turned out not to provide tools by which to grow a church but rather communicated insights by which growth-restricting factors could be recognized. The Hartford

---

[9] The full definition as agreed by members of the American Society for Church Growth is as follows: *"Church Growth is that discipline which investigates the nature, expansion, planting, multiplication, function and health of Christian churches as they relate to the effective implementation of God's commission to "make disciples of all peoples" (Mt. 28:19-20). Students of Church Growth strive to integrate the eternal theological principles of God's Word concerning the expansion of the Church with the best insights of contemporary social and behavioral sciences, employing as the initial frame of reference, the foundational work done by Donald McGavran"* (Quoted, C. Peter Wagner, *Strategies for Church Growth* (1987:114).

Consultation in 1979 helpfully distinguished between institutional and contextual factors, local, regional and national (Hoge and Roozen 1979). The methodological approach of focusing on growing churches from which to learn our lessons meant that much greater weight was placed on local institutional factors, identifying strong leadership as a key component. This simply inflated the egos of some ambitious pastors with disastrous consequences.

2. The rise of postmodernity to challenge the arrogant claims of modernity presents a whole new set of issues. On the positive side, it has helped us to question our suppositions and brought a new humility. A rationalistic approach to church growth is doomed to failure. By simply applying church growth principles you may be able to gather a crowd or even expand a movement, but you may not build the Body of Christ.

Two great mysteries in the New Testament are: the mystery of the Gospel of Christ and the mystery of the Body of Christ. About each we can have certain knowledge, but never a comprehensive understanding. Paul cautions the Corinthians who took pride in their knowledge and spiritual insight, that "we see only puzzling reflections in a mirror" (1 Cor. 13:12). Until we gain the perspective of heaven, our view of Christ here on earth is, by comparison, a blurred and limited vision. I believe that similar limitations also apply to the Body of Christ. By our disobedience and stupidity we may be able to frustrate the growth of the church; by our discernment and prayerful-dependence on God we may be able to play a significant role in the growth of the church; but we can never make it happen. As the Scripture reminds us it is the Risen Christ who builds His Church; it is God who makes it grow.

3. Clearly, leadership plays a key role. But the leader is not a controller, still less a dictator, but rather an empowerer of God's people. The senior pastor cannot delegate ministry to others, because we cannot delegate what already rightly belongs to people through the calling and equipping of the Ascended Lord by virtue of being a member of His Body. In this sense, baptism is a rite of ordination as well as a rite of incorporation. As modern theory is also beginning to recognize, leadership emerges at every level of an organization and not simply at the top (Hesselbein, Marshall Goldsmith and Beckhard 1996).[10] Decades of preaching, teaching on spiritual gifts and self-study through spiritual gift inventories has not resulted in the empowering of the laity due to insecurity on the part of pastors, and the damaging consequences of empowering the incompetent. It is perilous to empower without discipling.

In the past two decades C. Peter Wagner has been developing various areas of the spiritual dimension of Church Growth with spiritual gifts, signs and wonders, spiritual warfare, spiritual mapping and most recently, the new apostolic paradigm. It is important that these issues, especially some contemporary expressions of so-called apostolic movements, continue to be

---

[10] "Leadership is no longer positional."

critiqued theologically and researched competently and not simply brushed aside as irrelevant.

4. From leadership we turn to management. The popular distinction between the two was that leadership saw where to go, whereas management worked out how to get there. The acronym for the management tasks was PLOC—plan, lead organize and control. Under the modern paradigm, management became increasingly identified with control, and as systems became more and more complex, that control became an impersonal, oppressive bureaucratization. The consequences were devastating to the human psyche. The advent of postmodernity has changed all that. Western cultures are in the midst of changes of tsunami or seismic proportions.[11]

It is widely accepted that we are now in an era of comprehensive, discontinuous change that is causing institutions, whether political, industrial, medical, military or educational, to redefine and restructure. We can no longer think in terms of long-term strategic planning because we do not know what a single day will bring forth. You may be able to follow a map across firm terrain, but you need a chart and navigational skills to track through a stormy sea in a hurricane force wind. Given our present context, our understanding of management is being redefined in terms of its original meaning, which was to cope or to overcome adversity.

Many churches in North America now have to face this management question, just as have churches in Europe and North America. Some churches will be able to live in denial for a while, living off their endowment or the continuing sacrificial giving of their pre-Boomer generations. But these sources of income are rapidly drying up. The church will have to learn both from the experience of most churches in the majority world, and also from the church of New Testament times until the conversion of Emperor Constantine, how to operate effectively from the margins of society with much reduced material resources. This will not be an easy transition.

5. We cannot think simply in terms of "natural church development," assuming that we can build from where we are (Schwarz 1996). The church will need to face the challenge of the appropriateness of its present structure in a post-Christendom and increasingly neo-pagan cultural and social context. The church will need to experience much breaking and even be prepared to die in order to live the resurrection life.[12] Churches that want to grow must be prepared to pay the price, which may be much higher than we may once have imagined. What this missional church might look like is described by the

---

[11] There have been a number of books addressing the present challenges facing the church that have used the images of tidal waves and seismic shocks. See Leonard Sweet, *FaithQuakes* (1994) and *SoulTsunami* (1999); and C. Peter Wagner, *ChurchQuake!* (1999).

[12] Mike Regele, in *The Death of the Church* (1995), argues that churches in most traditional denominations must be prepared to die in order to live again to face the new missional challenges.

Church and Culture groups and is expounded in the volume edited by Darrell Guder entitled *Missional Church* (1998). Already there is a younger generation of church planters who have gone back to the drawing board in seeking to re-incarnate the church. They recognize that established models are no longer as effective in reaching the unchurched—boomers who are walking away from our churches in increasing numbers, and for many "generation x-ers" who have dismissed the churches as lacking in authenticity and integrity.[13]

Challenges

1. One of the major challenges is to revive the field research focus of Dr. McGavran to discover as much as we can about the progress of the Christian movement around the world, including North America. Much can be learned from the study of growing churches following the case study method, but this is not adequate by itself.

One of the potentially significant contributions in this regard is the study of churches around the world using a standardized format allowing for ready comparison. Christoph Schalk, a German statistician, has developed the measurement and provided the statistical analysis for Christian Schwarz's "Natural Church Development," an agency that takes church growth research beyond the case study method, seeking to establish to what extent non-growing churches have the same qualities as growing churches (Schwarz and Schalk 1998). It also distinguishes between healthy and unhealthy churches. This is important because numerical church growth can occur through a number of factors including abusive, dictatorial leadership or through an editing of the Christian message to make it marketable in such a way that it is seriously distorted. Such methods are inappropriate in terms of a biblical understanding of the nature of the Kingdom and the Church, although all too common in society at large. The methodology has come in for some criticism,[14] the findings need verification and the methodology needs testing to see if it can be reliably applied cross-culturally.

Here in the United States there is little reliable data gathering. We are largely limited to sample polling and overall impressions. Figures are bandied about and gain credibility through mere repetition, while lacking verification. Who really believes that forty percent of Americans are worshipping with a religious community on any given week? Yet that is the percentage claimed in response to specific questions by pollsters.

2. A second area is in regard to ecclesiology. We need deeper insights and a better understanding of the structure, organization and spread of the early church, especially in the period prior to the conversion of Constantine (Stark

---

[13] See Tom Beaudoin, *Virtual Faith* (1998) and Kevin Ford, *Jesus for a New Generation* (1995).

[14] See the critical review of *Natural Church Development* by Daniel E. Simpson (1998) together with the response of Christian A. Schwarz.

1997). We cannot speak of a new apostolic movement, as Wagner does,[15] until we have a better understanding of the Apostolic church in terms of the office of *apostle* and the nature of apostolic mission as it developed from the day of Pentecost onwards.

We need to assess the direction that the traditional denominations will take in the future—those churches that used to be called "mainline" but which have become sidelined in some parts of the Western world. I am not as prepared to write them off as are some observers of churchgoing trends. Although these denominations may be struggling in Europe, North America and Australia, they continue to show amazing resilience in parts of the majority world where they have had a long history and are now in the hands of a new generation of dynamic young leaders who are virtually free from the hang-ups of post-colonialism. Furthermore, some of the most creative responses to the missionary challenge presented by Generation X are being made by churches in traditional denominations whose ministry has broken free from the straightjacket of traditionalism while continuing to draw from the riches of their heritage.

I accept the argument that denominations as we know them are largely a product of modernity and cannot function in the culture of the information age which is replacing bureaucratic hierarchies with relational networks.[16] In the secular world some business organizations are successfully making this transition with impressive results. Why should not this happen within the church? In some ways the church should be in a better position than businesses because it began as a decentralized team-driven, networking movement, if I read the New Testament and the subApostolic period right. Furthermore, businesses are increasingly looking to the non-profit sector to discover leadership that has learned to lead through influence rather than through position and economic sanctions. Again, it is the church that, over the centuries, has demonstrated this dynamic when freed from the shackles of a disempowering and distrustful clericalism.

If we are entering a period of world-history of profound destabilization, then the Church needs to operate on the basis of a daily walk with God, learning to trust Him, and drawing strength from the presence of the Spirit of Christ in our midst. Business enterprises are having to learn to live with a just-in-time leadership and management style, so why should the church be any different? In one sense, the Church moved forward strategically, but it was strategy by-the-skin-of-their-teeth or, even in hindsight, rather than as a result of strategic planning. It was the Holy Spirit who persistently nudged it forward. We have to remember that it took at least fifteen years for the early church to move beyond

---

[15] See C. Peter Wagner, *The New Apostolic Churches* (1998) and *Churchquake!* (1999).

[16] See Lyle Schaller, *Tattered Trust: Is There Hope for Your Denomination* (1996) and *Discontinuity and Hope: Radical Change and the Path to the Future* (1999); and Eddie Gibbs, *ChurchNext* (2000).

Samaria after the Holy Spirit had come upon them and they were ready to witness "to the uttermost parts of the world." Even then there were leaders in Jerusalem who were not convinced.

The Church Growth Movement if it is to remain a movement, must continue to move with the times, clarifying its insights and grappling with the challenge of contemporary missional challenges. We do not honor the founder of a movement by fossilizing his thinking. McGavran didn't get everything right, but the heart of his message is as relevant today as when he first expounded it, namely that the Church as a living organism should be a growing organism. Especially here in the West we need to re-emphasize the church as a missional church. In other words we need a Church *Go* Movement before we can have a significant Church *Growth* Movement! We must move from maintenance to mission if we are to be biblically and culturally appropriate.

Chapter 18

Variations on a Theme of Appropriate Contextualization: Music Lessons from Africa

Roberta R. King

Good news and joy originate out of Africa. It is a continent that knows how to celebrate and express its thoughts and emotions through music. In Africa, as in other areas of the world, music is present in every situation and at every stage of life.

In song and music events we often come to learn of issues deep within the hearts of people. Over the last twenty years, Africa and her music have continually taught me about appropriate contextualization of the Gospel. The people are increasingly appropriating the message of the Good News as their own. As Dean Gilliland says:

> Contextualized theology . . . is the dynamic reflection carried out by the particular church upon its own life in light of the Word of God and historic Christian truth. Guided by the Holy Spirit, the church continually challenges, incorporates, and transforms elements of the cultural milieu, bringing these under the lordship of Christ. As members of the body of Christ interpret the Word, using their own thoughts and employing their own cultural gifts, they are better able to understand the gospel as incarnation (Gilliland 1989a:12-13).

In the local context, Africa is a kaleidoscope of ethnic groups seemingly confined to the rural areas. They function best in their vernacular languages and traditional ways of life. At the same time, there is a rapid movement to the cities. As Samuel Vinay points out, "Context is never static. The globalization of the world economy means that we have to revisit the nature of context. No context can be regarded in isolation, nor as totally unique for every context is now clearly shaped by global drives and trends" (Vinay 1997:1).

In such settings, outsiders easily assume the speaking of an international language, a minimum level of literacy and Western education. Many people come to the city without the education and skills required to bring about their hope of economic improvement. Large numbers of urban dwellers are indeed highly educated and prefer the comforts of a Western lifestyle, yet their thought patterns and values are distinct from those of the West and the so-called *global village*. Urbanization does not automatically change the core of a person's worldview. The plight of the city calls for continued adaptation to new environments and situations. Appropriate contextualization, then, is not limited to rural monocultural situations.

The Rural Context: A Local Perspective

The missionaries to the Senufo people of Ivory Coast, West Africa, translated Western hymns and taught them to the people. Yet, almost every night, a music ensemble composed of three balafons rang out incessantly in a complex mix with two differently-pitched drums. The missionaries were regularly roused from their sleep to the sound of drums.

Music is part and parcel of the life of the animistic Senufo people, to whom the missionaries had come to communicate the Gospel. Given the lukewarm response of the church members, the Western hymns did not fit the context.

Fifty years later, the situation has changed. There is life and vitality in the churches as the people sing their praise to God. Their own instruments, the *balafon* (a 17-21 key xylophone) and the *kaanrigi* (a metal scraper that functions as a rhythm instrument) ring through the villages signaling that the Christians are worshipping. The songs naturally call for participation of the people, with clapping hands and bodily movement, in addition to the singing response. Senufo Christian songs *preach* to the believers and they are hungry for the message (cf. King 1989:270). The non-believers often gather outside the church in order to learn the *catchy* Christian songs.

What has made the difference? Along with translation of the Scriptures, contextualization through the development of appropriately meaningful music communication methods has played a major role in the Senufo's response to the call to Jesus Christ as Lord.

The Urban Context: Global Perspectives

A number of Mercedes, four-wheel drive vehicles and Toyota Corollas jam together in two parking lots and along one of the main arteries into the world-class city of Nairobi, Kenya. Sunday after Sunday, the Nairobi Baptist church is consistently full and overflowing. Everyone knows how to give a good verbal Christian testimony. For many, though, the singing of the hymns is only lukewarm though a few people make the effort to sing wholeheartedly.

With a great hymn tradition brought from England and with many of the members of the church having studied in Western countries, we ask ourselves, Which hymns and songs should be used? It appears that people can worship with the standard *universal* songs found around the world in this day of globalization. Yet, there is a longing for spiritual renewal and revival. Slowly, the use of songs that are from within their heritage draw a deeper response. Is there still a need to contextualize in an urban situation? If so, how?

Principles for Appropriate Contextualization Through Music

These two settings serve as springboards for our discussion. Our purpose is to ask what we can learn about contextualization through music. We will derive some key principles from music in four main areas: 1) the broader musical context; 2) songs and theological development; 3) issues in form and meaning; and 4) music in multicultural contexts.

Principles from the Broader Musical Context

Principle 1: *The role of music in society requires that effective contextualization pursue the integration of the Christian faith into the total lifestyle of a people.*

In Africa, music encompasses all of life. It is one of the most important expressions of life (Bebey 1969:1-16). Most events cannot take place without music, predominantly song. For every major life-cycle event, there is usually song and music. It plays a significant role in not only lending significance to the event but also in teaching its cultural values and norms to the participants.

Funerals, for example, are highly important events in the life of any African community. It is a common feature to have all-night wakes continuously for several nights in a row as a part of the funeral-grieving process. The older the age of the deceased, the more nights of wake are carried out. The ever-present sound of music accompanies and facilitates these all-night events.

Among the Senufo several activities are carried out at these times and many of them deal with the spiritual aspects of the deceased. This includes the sending of the deceased to their proper spiritual abode or *journey down the river* without any known destination (King 1989:191). It is at this very point that the Christian faith provides relevant answers to life's questions. The Senufo people know they are sending their deceased ones somewhere but they are not sure where. The Christians, however, have the promise of heaven.

Although Senufo Christians have songs for worship and evangelism, to my knowledge, they have not yet developed funeral wakes with accompanying songs and balafons. Since nonChristian Senufos spend a great portion of their time dealing with death and its spiritual aspects, Senufo Christians have excellent opportunities to show how the gospel message meets the peoples' concerns and immediate needs at this point.

The integration of all aspects of the Christian life came home to me when I attended the funeral of a church singer in Goma, Zaire (now the Congo). The funeral events included a wake with the playing of bow-harps (*nzenze*) along with the singing of Christian songs in the vernacular language. Here was contextualization of the funeral-grieving process. Besides showing my condolences to the young lady's family, I was enthralled with the music. I went home having participated in the Christian wake as much as possible.

I also attended the burial of the singer. Little did I realize how significant my participation at the funeral was until two years later as I was once again flying into Goma from Nairobi. The immigration officials recognized me immediately. They remembered me from the wake and burial services, commented on it to me, and smoothly allowed me to enter into the country, which is not always the case. Not only does a funeral allow for the singing of answers to life and death from the Christian perspective, but it can also provide a greater witness and impact to the larger community. We can communicate simultaneously on several levels in appropriate incarnational ways.

Unfortunately, we have often compartmentalized Christianity, keeping it out of the rest of a people's lifestyle. Music in Africa serves as a prime example of this. It is well documented that the emissaries of the Western Christian church to Africa "preached against African cultural practices and, . . . adopted a hostile attitude to African music" (Nketia 1975:14). The Christian methodology is in stark contrast to Islam, where "It is not surprising . . . to find extensions of traditional customs or the use of indigenous resources in the musical practice of Islamic-African communities" (Nketia 1975:12-13).

The effects of keeping Christian activities separate from African life at large are still with us today. In attending a rural wedding in Kambaland within Kenya, I was impressed with the striking contrast between the wedding in the church, very formal in the use of only Western hymns, with the celebration back at home. Women were singing and dancing in a circle with great jubilation in their traditional song style. It was as if, having acknowledged God in the small church building, they went home to be *themselves*, almost implying that God could not understand their songs or language, nor could God accept what they were doing. For me, such an experience poses a major question, Do we encourage people to leave God in the church building and not take him home with us? Or, conversely, What are people taking home with them from church?

Principle 2: *Media such as music, its function, use and impact vary from culture to culture. This influences our approaches to contextualization, since significant variants will influence the final product.*

Although music has many similarities in both Africa and the Western world, a number of differences emerge in terms of its function and use. While Western people often focus on music for listening, African music is a major vehicle for involving people in active communal creativity (Bebey 1969).

In Africa, one naturally expects to receive a message through music, whereas Westerners use music predominantly for entertainment or for setting a mood. African music communicates a message, whereas Western music merely entertains. Our next principle derives from this distinction.

Principle 3: *African music is a major means of proclamation or sending a message.*

In Africa, music preaches and carries messages with impact. In Kenya, for example, cassette tapes of songs in vernacular languages are often banned for their political impact. The songs function like editorial commentaries of public opinion.

Likewise, songs communicate and preach in the Church. In East Africa, in both rural and urban areas, it is very common for a person giving a testimony to intersperse it with a song that expresses their deeper feelings. Indeed, even in prayer meetings, prayers are intermingled and offered with songs.

There are, then, alternative forms of communication, such as songs, drama, and storytelling, that carry rhetorical impact, depending on the cultural expectations and norms. In rural settings that are highly dependent on oral communication, songs literally do the work of a sermon often resulting in a person's change of behavior.

One Senufo Christian woman, for example, told me of how she had acted towards other women coming back from the market. She used to swear at them and make negative comments about them. One evening she went to church where they sang a song based on removing the log out of your own eye (Matt. 7:7). She applied the message of that song to her attitude toward the women on her way from the market and went away that evening a changed person.

Principle 4: The definition of music varies from culture to culture. Thus, we must look at all that is included in the music-making process of a culture and make appropriate adjustments toward an appropriate contextualizing of our message.

The majority of African languages do not have a term equivalent to music (Bebey 1969:12). Rather, they talk of the individual parts that form the aggregate we call music. The language equivalents would include *to play the drum, to sing,* and *to dance.*

My interaction with a *griot,* a traditional professional singer in Senegal, is useful here. I visited her and her family in order to learn about the music of the Wolof people. Our goal was to have her set a Christian text to song in a Wolof style for use on a radio program. She had been told that I was a musician. Upon entering into her home I was greeted with the question, "Do you know how to dance?" Throughout the afternoon, the question of the day continued to be whether I knew how to dance in the Wolof dance style of Senegal. They never did ask if I could sing or play a musical instrument. Music and dance for the Wolof are intimately intertwined. Evidently, the dance was more significant than the actual musical sounds at that point.

In general, a song is not complete unless there is clapping, gesturing and dancing (rhythmic bodily movement) that brings the song alive. A Christian Pokot musician, after teaching the melody and text of a Christian song, expressed it this way: "Now, we have to catch the tune." It had to be made complete and brought alive by adding clapping, gestures and movement (dance).

Among the Senufo Christians, *to dance the Christian shuffle* is to give a visual-physical testimony to their faith in Christ. Indeed, if one does not dance, other Senufo believers begin to think that there must be sin in the life of the person. Not to dance indicates a broken relationship between a person and God. Likewise, clapping carries the same significance.

Historically, missionaries found the dance and clapping patterns to be too difficult and foreign to them, so they merely sang without the accompanying physical movements. One wonders how the Senufo people interpreted the missionary pattern of music. The signals they were sending may well have been contrary to their intentions.

Principles from Song for Contextualizing Theology

We turn now to more specific details of music as they contribute to contextualization. The principles come from praxis in doing music contextualization.

Principle 5: What we sing becomes our practical, every-day working theology. Songs shape, influence and impact us at a deep level.

Analyses of Christian song texts from any setting often reveal the spiritual state of a community of Christian believers. James R. Krabill (1995) has done a formidable study of the hymnody of the Harrist Church of Ivory Coast showing how hymns and African music have played a major role in the formation of the church. Indeed, Alan Tippett, in his study of Solomon Island Christianity, shows even further how the frequency of sung hymns reveal the spiritual maturity of the believers. He states that it is his "very carefully considered opinion that . . . Christian hymns have been the dominant formative for popular belief" (Tippett 1967:186).

Briefly, Senufo Christian song texts reveal the people's theological understandings and shape their Christian life. They consider the songs to function like the Word of God in their lives. They claim that the songs are instructional, "they teach to the depths of our hearts, counsel, advise, speak and show the way we should walk," and "teach us new things that we have not yet learned" (King 1989:270).

This is effective teaching of the Christian faith Thus, contextualization through appropriate forms of music communication provides for content-development, not merely the expression of emotions, as crucial as that is.

One of the common complaints about *Kiswahili* choruses sung in Nairobi today (our urban setting) is that they basically say the same thing over and over again. Indeed, I have come to call them *the fruit of the spirit* choruses, since each verse merely replaces a word such as *joy* with *peace*. Yet, the musical style of the choruses is very attractive whereas translated Kiswahili hymns that carry a deeper content, often do not have the rhythmic attractiveness of the choruses. One of the alternatives is to put new musical phrases to the texts of the old hymns. This is being successfully done in Sierra Leone and Ghana. "Pass Me Not O Gentle Savior" has been Africanized by giving it a Ghanaian melody, harmony, and the very popular *high-life* beats of the region. It is an initial partial solution well-received by congregations in both West and East Africa for it brings them closer to home in their self-expression. Yet, one would like to see an authentic verbal expression as well.

Principle 6: Just as faith grows out of our experience with God, so songs come out of experience, revealing our theological understandings. Thus, composing songs provides a forum for doing theology within the faith community.

Moses and the Israelites, after crossing the Red Sea having experienced the deliverance of God in their lives, sang a song of thanksgiving and praise to the God who had delivered them (Ex. 15). The song is full of graphic images of God and the happenings at the Red Sea. The people sing of their experience with God and their theological understandings of Him. Miriam and the other women add a lively choreography to Moses' song with their tambourine and dance. Thus, the Israelites hymnic repertoire was born. We find references to it in the Psalms and other parts of Scripture. It helped to build the theology and faith of the Israelites.

If indeed "the Incarnation is the ultimate contextualization of the Christian message," as Charles Kraft suggests (1989:122), then here we see an incarnational God actively at work in the lives of the Israelites. Song plays a key role in the dialogue between God and His people.

Song composition provides a means for expressing our theological understandings, both correct and incorrect aspects, and also an opportunity to commune with God. In Africa, this was graphically visible among early Senufo Christian songs where the Gospel presentation focused mainly on introducing Jesus Christ to the people. References to Jesus Christ dominated over half of the song texts as opposed to reference to God—sometimes referring to our Father, Jesus Christ. As the people grew in their learning about God, later songs make a distinction between God the Father and Jesus Christ, the Son of God (King 1989:211-212).

Thus, we can say that doing contextualization through composing songs with a faith community provides an opportunity for reflecting on God. It is a form of doing theology at the grass-roots level. This is in great contrast to the philosophical approach as developed in Western/Westernized seminaries. Tite Tiénou rightly suggests that a *prescriptive theology*, which intends to be appropriate to the African context, "has to do with knowing what the needs are and finding the dynamic answers in the Word of God, properly expressed, carefully applied for that particular people and place" (cited in Gilliland 1989a:15).

Song has a major role in doing prescriptive theology, often also serving as a theological thermometer within a given faith community. It reveals what is the next step in the spiritual formation process for meaningful growth in relationship with God.

Principle 7: Theological depth and content increases with the personal growth of the musician: singer-composer. Thus, contextualization is a dynamic process related to people growing in their relationship with God.

As people grow in their relationship with God, they will also grow in the expression of their faith in song. Contextualization, as in song-making, should pursue the goal of a *dynamic expression of Christian experience.*

Early songs in the Senufo Christian repertoire not only had the most simple call-and-response form, but the theological content was limited though still true. When the following song first came out, people thought it was beautiful. It said:

CALL	RESPONSE
Bless my hands	Bless my hands
Bless my feet	Bless my feet
Bless my house	Bless my house
Bless my walk	Bless my walk
Bless my inside	Bless my insides
Bless my spirit..............................	Bless my spirit
	(King 1989:107)

Figure 18.1 Call-and-Response Form

Thus, people understood God's blessing and experienced a new found joy in Him. Yet, with time, the Senufo believers came to understand blessing at a deeper level. A later song said:

SENUFO CHRISTIAN SONG (form #1)
"Every Moment the Hand of Jesus Is on You and Thus All His Blessing"

THEMATIC STATEMENT:
Every moment the hand of Jesus is on you and thus all his blessing.
If we have ever clearly explained our sins,
Every moment the hand of Jesus is on you and thus all his blessing.

DEVELOPMENT/EXEGESIS:
If we have clearly explained our wicked stealing.
If we explain our fetishes made of ox tails to Jesus.
People, stop speaking bad things and pray to Jesus.
People, stop doubting and pray to Jesus.
Let's leave these spiritual discussions in order to pray to Jesus.

THEMATIC STATEMENT:
Every moment the hand of Jesus is on you and thus all his blessing.
If we have ever clearly explained our sins,
Every moment the hand of Jesus is on you and thus all his blessing
(King 1989:306).

Figure 18.2 Senufo Christian Song – Form 1

This song introduces the new concepts of relationship with Jesus, sin, confession, and the receiving blessing as contingent upon acknowledging their sins. There has been theological growth and application to the Senufo's particular context and worldview. Later songs go even further.

From this principle we see that *in the contextualization process, we are called to develop people*, not just discover culturally appropriate forms. Much of our *Christian education* has focused on training pastors in Bible schools often leaving out artists, poets, musicians and women. (In traditional Africa, it is the women who compose the songs while the men are the instrumentalists.) Yet, artists (both men and women) are the very people who could contribute to the development of the Church in significant ways.

In the case of musicians, they should receive training in three major areas: musical skills, personal credibility within a community as a full human being (e.g., a married woman with children) and spiritual development (cf. King 1989:143-149). Sadly, we all too often train people in musical skills and leave the rest to providence. Leadership development and spiritual formation should be a designated objective for developing those who play major roles in the contextualization process.

Principle 8: *Developing appropriate imagery for explaining and describing God through song composing serves as a means to doing meaningful theological contextualization. The song-composing activity provides an appropriate forum for eliciting such imagery.*

If the goal for the development of Christian songs within a particular culture is a *dynamic expression of Christian experience*, then not only does the theological content need to be biblically based, but the imagery of the song texts needs to be drawn from appropriate cultural imagery. Rather than referring to *the lilies of the field* as found in Matthew 6:28-30, the Harrists of Ivory Coast, for whom lilies are next to non-existent have substituted the term *bulrushes* (Krabill 1995:387).

Furthermore, such imagery goes beyond superficial substitution and mere usage of contextual differences such as bulrushes. Rather, more importantly, such imagery seeks to help the singers to understand the significance behind the imagery, from a deeper symbolic level. For example, in composing his song based on Psalm 23, Senyenegatene took the liberty to transform

> the Hebrew concept of shepherd to a more appropriate one within his worldview. . . . For him, the Lord is his nan'anfolo, the one who protects and provides food for his animals. He is totally responsible for their care. At the same time, Senyenegatene also calls out that the Lord is his gboo. Literally, this is the person who carries the growing infant child on her back. The gboo cares for the child, and also raises and educates the child. An intimate bond and relationship develops as a result of their long hours together. This then becomes a lovely picture of the intimate relationship that can mature between

the believer and God, in addition to God's role of protector and provider (King 1989:390).

The act of composing allows the musician time to reflect on God, interact with His Word, and when sensitively encouraged, is the singer is freed up to explain God within his or her own context.

Principles from Music Relating to Form and Meaning

Music, especially songs, are seen as cultural forms that can be adapted for the Gospel. The majority of missiological discussions on form and meaning argue for or against the use of borrowed forms adapted for Christian purposes and the inherent difficulties in doing so (cf. Kraft 1979a:64-69 and Hiebert 1989:101-120). Yet, once a group has agreed to work with cultural forms, there is little guidance on how to shape them for Christian purposes and appropriate communicational impact. What do we do, then, when the church within a given area gives us permission to work within their cultural setting? How do we make the contextualization process more appropriate?

Principle 9: Rather than merely borrowing or adapting forms for the sake of contextualization, we should seek to develop appropriate new forms that arise out of existing cultural norms for effective communication.

In the area of music, song forms are usually referred to as if their form has already found a concrete structure that one would simply borrow, such as a melody, with the mere addition of a Christian text. Indeed, this has been the approach in many early mission situations (cf. *Practical Anthropology* 1962:9). Negative associations with the melody, or more often in Africa, of a particular drum beat, have usually set the scene for total rejection of African music in the communication of the Gospel. However, songs and their song forms, like culture, are dynamic forms of expression and are open to change and development.

There are many styles and forms that a song can take on within any one cultural setting. The majority of world cultures are rich with various song styles that have been developed to *fit* with a particular event.

For example, circumcision songs for Maasai warriors take on a certain musical structure that is appropriate to the context of that particular event. Typical of Maasai warrior singing are several layers of recurring patterns (*ostinatos*) with a solo overlaying of text above the ostinatos. Conversely, Maasai girls at the time of their initiation wear rows of shakers on their legs and sing without the *ostinato* patterns found among the warriors. Although the song forms vary, they each draw on typical Maasai musical idioms and structures (call-and-response forms, scales, rhythms, unison or harmonic singing, vocal tone quality) that are arranged in a way that is appropriate to the occasion and the purpose of the song. A Christian Maasai, therefore, should be free to draw from the Maasai musical heritage creating a song that *sounds like home*, yet developing a form that adequately and persuasively carries the Gospel message and that is worthy of God.

The Senufo Christians of Ivory Coast have excelled at following through on this principle. Borrowing from their storytelling song styles, they have developed a song form that meets their desire to tell the Christian story in an oral form. Characteristic of African song styles, the song is structured around a complex merging of the basic call-and-response form in order to carry a high text load. The form looks as follows:

SENUFO CHRISTIAN SONG (Form #2)		
THEMATIC DEVELOP-MENT	THEMATIC STATEMENT	(EXEGESIS) STATEMENT
SOLOIST: A B A	C C' D A' A' D E	A B A
GROUP RESPONSE: A B A	A A A A A A	A B A
(Key: Each letter represents a verbal statement carried on a musical phrase. Indications such as A' and C' show a variation based on phrases A and C [King 1989:156]).		

Figure 18.3 Senufo Christian Song – Form 2

The song form is dependent on a strong, biblically-knowledgeable and skillful lead singer. The singer is the composer and does not need to train a choir or worship team in order to produce her music. The opening three-phrase thematic statement is sung as a unit with the group singing the full unit back to the lead singer. It has become common practice for the opening set of statements to be volleyed back and forth twice between the lead singer and the group. Thus, the thematic statement is sung a total of four times. This provides for an adequate opportunity to hear the message as the singers pursue a clear presentation of it. The lead singer then develops and exegetes what is meant by the opening statement.

For example, in the Senufo song version of Psalm 23:1-3 the opening, thematic statement claims:

PSALM 23:1-3 OPENING THEMATIC STATEMENT
PHRASE A: The father, Jehovah, is my guide. He takes care of me. PHRASE B: People, David said it in the Psalms. PHRASE A: The father, Jehovah, is my guide. He takes care of me. (King 1989:157)

Figure 18.4 Senufo Christian Song – Opening Thematic Statement

This long textual thematic statement is unique to the Senufo Christian songs.

The song's return to this opening statement as the conclusion of the song is also distinctive of the Christian style. This allows for the main statement to be reiterated showing a heavy emphasis on textual considerations. Thus, we see that a new song form has emerged out of the musical practices of the people. It is distinctively new, both in form and message. Yet it is still distinctively Senufo, allowing non-believers to easily relate to the style and understand what is being said. Meanwhile, believers feel at home, are receptive to the message, and allow it to minister to them. The Senufo believers have developed a song form that allows for high text load and the dissemination of content. It is distinctively Christian and suits the needs of the church.

There are a number of advantages in this method of developing new song forms from within the cultural dictates of music. First, it demonstrates that God accepts people within their culture and a greater understanding of the Gospel message occurs. It also avoids the problem of negative associations such as "does this rhythm have a Satanic background" or "was this tune used for something evil." Each song is composed with the appropriate melody and rhythm for a particular song's message. Most importantly, the Senufo Christian songs are definitely known for being dedicated to Jesus Christ. There are stories of the songs and balafon music functioning as a tool of spiritual warfare. The Christian message at the church resounding throughout the village has stopped Pagan funerals. Local chiefs have asked Christians to stop worshipping so that they can get on with their funeral music that deals with the spirits.

Furthermore, such song development encourages singers to be growing in their understanding of the Gospel and making direct application of Christian teachings and the Scriptures to their lives while church leaders have an opportunity to get feedback on the people's theological understanding or misperceptions.

The disadvantages of this principle include the fact that song development takes time, it is a process. This does not always suit our Western time limitations of reaching a people within *x* number of years or a three-week trip into the *interior*. Rather, it takes time, patience, prayer, a searching of the Scriptures, discussion of believers on what God wants and the working of the Holy Spirit to help people develop an appropriate Christian singing style within their own cultural milieu. Yet, the results of God working in their lives through the music-making process are well worth the struggle of waiting.

Ultimately, the question for us is: Do people within their own contexts have the right to explore and develop new musical idioms that will impact their people for the Kingdom? I believe they do. The benefits of deeper understanding leads to spiritual growth and closer relationship with Jesus Christ.

Principle 10: The development of appropriate music forms is progressive. Song forms become more complex, enriched, and carry deeper content as people take time to experiment with musical idioms and acquire greater theological underpinnings. This development includes learning to discern facets of music that can and cannot be used due to negative implications, demonic associations, or irrelevance to the Christian message.

Missionaries and church leaders have often rejected African traditional musical instruments in an effort to avoid any type of syncretism. Yet, national believers often can distinguish elements that the outsider is unaware of.

The Christian balafon, a frame-xylophone made of wood, cowhide, and calabash gourds, is distinctive from the traditional balafon in that it has seventeen keys rather than twelve keys. The reasoning behind this is that the Christian balafon must be more precise in the sending of its message, the Good News of Jesus Christ. The *master* of the balafon is recognized to be Jesus Christ and decals are put on each key declaring that *Jesus is Lord* and to whom the balafon actually belongs. In addition, over time, the Senufo church has seen growth in the playing of one balafon at a time in worship into the playing of three balafons in the worship service, as more performers develop their skills. Thus, the Senufo Christians have found a way to *redeem* the balafon for the glory of God. They have been able to drop the bad elements, such as sacrifice to the spirits, and have kept the good elements of dynamic Christian communication in a way that people understand and appreciate.

Principles from Music for Multicultural Contexts

The increasing urbanization around the world presents a series of questions regarding appropriate contextualization in the city. With increased globalization and improved electronic devices and marketing systems, urban situations are in danger of returning once again to the incorrect assumption of the old adage that *music is a universal language*. Since the cities look Western, are made up of a supposed majority of *educated* people and hold a large number of Western-type businesses, the assumption easily follows that all peoples will understand the new *global* music. In Nairobi, Kenya this means a growing appreciation for *world music*, a hybrid of musical elements from various cultures especially from the Congo and other parts of Africa.

Admittedly, contemporary Christian music from the West plays a major role in churches all over the world. These kinds of music are valid to a certain extent. However, such validity is true only on a superficial level. While there are larger numbers of people in cities, such as Nairobi, who appreciate Western music, such basic elements as ethnic roots and language communities within the city are merely glossed over. Deep undercurrents of identity and worldview remain hidden and sometimes untouched.

Thus, it is imperative for us to research, know and understand the local, rural, and ethnic contexts before we can understand the complex of needs within the city. If we do not do our homework, our progress will be limited and lend itself to nominalism in the Church, for people are not confronted on deep levels with the reality of God in their lives. In such a case, a foreign group continues to dominate, perhaps more subtly, but in powerful economic and technological ways. In the case of music, with token elements from African traditions blended in, the dominant group still rules with a mere *pili pili* flavoring sprinkled on top to make it *sound* contextualized. Such tokenism runs the risk of the intended appreciation of people groups and their cultural elements degenerating into an insult. One easily interprets it as, "God still doesn't know me as I am." The potential danger is that compartmentalization of the Christian faith continues on, dressed up in new garb with surface commitments to Christ stagnating.

Although the subject of contextualization through music in urban settings is highly complex and worthy of fuller development then allowed in this chapter, it is important to consider a few basic issues. We'll limit our discussion to two principles for reflecting on how we can make the Christian Incarnation appropriate to multicultural settings such as the city.

Principle 11: Multicultural settings call for us to be aware of varying levels of meaning.

In many cities in the nonWestern world, peoples of various backgrounds come together who are not all *urban people*. Indeed, we have come to understand that

> Not all city folk have an urban mentality. Many are peasants who visit or move to the city but keep their small-town attitudes. They join people from their hometown and form small village enclaves in the city where they try to maintain life as they knew it in the countryside. . . . There are also city tribals—people from a tribe who move to the city and live with others from their own people (Hiebert and Meneses 1995:268-269).

This is true of cities both in East and West Africa. People do not automatically change their worldview simply because they have moved to the city. For example, a group of young professionals working in Kampala, Uganda, enjoy getting together for fellowship. They often begin with the music of the city and its westernized forms, yet when they become more open and intimate with one another the cry becomes, "Take me back home!" In other words they are saying, sing in our own language and play our own instruments (the thumb-piano—Akongo).

In practical terms, every ethnic group represented in the faith community should, at some point, have the opportunity to worship in ways that draw from their own heritage. This is in addition to a more international style found to be common to the multicultural group at large. It is not an issue of *either/or* but of *both/and*. Without such inclusion, people are forced to deny certain aspects of themselves. The worshiper who is attempting to worship in spirit and truth (Jn. 4:24) yet does not find ample opportunity to involve his/her whole self in the process, gets frustrated and spiritually discouraged.

Principle 12: Appropriate contextualization in urban, multicultural worship situations must take into account the need for people to worship in languages that are closer to their heart besides the international language of the day.

Although a prestigious nonWestern layperson or highly-trained pastor may enjoy Western hymns, there still remains a part of him/her that is touched when he/she hears a song in his/her mother tongue sung in an appropriate traditional style. This was the case when a former pastor of our church, highly respected for his excellent preaching to an international audience, listened to a song in his mother tongue. Even though he had grown up in a multicultural setting, he could not believe the impact of the song, based on Scripture, as he listened to it. He commented: "That is remarkable. It is touching a part of me, striking a nerve that has never been touched before. Musical needs, then, are for a variety of styles that allow for expression of people's identities with their multiple aspects.

Likewise, the Nairobi Baptist Church has recently been attempting some innovations in worship seeking to develop a prolonged time of singing, which is more appropriate to African singing patterns. In our new format we have included Western hymns, contemporary Christian music and a song in Kiswahili—Kenya's trade language. The response has been very encouraging. To my surprise, the greatest excitement was about the Kiswahili song. One man commented, "That was really good singing today!" I expected him to talk about the contemporary Christian choruses we had included. But he added, ". . . especially the song in Kiswahili." There is still a longing for people to know that God lives in Africa too.

Other comments from the service were even more enlightening: 1) "If you want to reach the 11:30 service, you need to do it through Kiswahili songs" and 2) "I'm already saved, but after singing 'Chakutumaini Sina,' I feel like I want to get saved again." The man knew that he had been touched deeply and that it called for a response of commitment.

Our responsibility propels us to help people to grow in allegiance to Christ beyond the first steps of salvation. Songs with impact can call people forth to love and serve God in ever increasing depths of experience. Inclusion of songs in various languages in a multicultural situation allows for a high level of participation by the members as well as freedom to develop appropriate worship forms. As Gilliland rightly asserts, the New Testament church in Antioch showed a sensitivity to *body life* and thus, "there was a recognition of diversity within the congregation while working for oneness under Christ's rule and teaching" (Gilliland 1989b:54-55). Songs, in various languages, can help us reach an appreciation of God's diversity-and-unity in Christ.

Conclusion

Appropriate contextualization through the development of culturally relevant forms of music offers us more insights than the mere *exotic* sounds that cross-cultural music initially displays. In broad strokes, we have come to recognize four main areas where music helps us to understand what appropriate contextualization entails.

First, just as music is intertwined with life, appropriate contextualization calls for significant integration of the Christian faith into a total lifestyle. In contextualizing theology, for example, we must be careful that it speaks to the basic needs of the people and not compartmentalize it away from every-day life.

Second, appropriate grass-roots theologizing can be effectively accomplished through the song-making process. Contextualization should not be limited to the academic classroom but needs to feature actively in ministry.

Third, musical forms must not become fossilized. Rather, just as each life event has its own musical style, so music can be appropriately developed from within the cultural milieu for the critical needs of the Church. Since music is attached to people; as they grow in their relationship to God, they will also grow in the expression of their faith. When they feel free to participate, committed Christians will learn how to meet the specific needs of the Church in their context. Appropriate contextualization calls for avoiding the mere borrowing of a form. It calls for the creative development of appropriate forms that communicate the Christian message at deep levels.

Fourth, contexts are dynamic and always changing. Globalization is with us. Working with music in multicultural contexts continues to require appropriate contextualization of the Gospel that recognizes people and their culturally specific uniqueness.

Finally, though our discussion has not been exhaustive, we have recognized a major lesson. Appropriate contextualization calls for variations on an unchanging theme: the dynamic reality of our relationship with the living God. Music is one of the main ways in which the people of God can authentically express this relationship.

Chapter 19

Appropriate Relationships

Charles H. Kraft

We have said that contextualization needs to involve asking questions concerning the appropriateness of any given custom both to Scripture and to the culture of the receiving people. The approach I want to take here is to start with scriptural ideals in the extremely important relational area and to ask how these may be expressed in any given society.

Preliminary to our main discussion, it is important that we focus on a series of considerations that need to underlie whatever is recommended. These considerations are as follows:

1. We need to recognize the difference, often a sizeable difference, between scriptural ideals and the place where we and God must start in the process of helping people to grow in their Christian experience. I have mentioned in an earlier chapter the "point plus process" model that I introduced in my 1979 book, *Christianity in Culture*. That model notes from Scripture that God is willing to start with subideal customs and concepts at the start of His working with a people. He then engages the people in a process in which He works with them to move them toward greater and greater approximation to His ideals.

Keeping that model in mind will help us to recognize that any introduction of relational concepts and/or customs presupposes that there will be a process from that starting point in the direction of the scriptural ideal. The main problem, as I have pointed out in Chapter 11, is how to see to it that there is enough press and pull to keep people moving in the right direction.

2. A second consideration is that the culturally ideal form of many customs and concepts of a receiving people may already be quite close to scriptural ideals. Small-scale societies especially are often very relational, thus raising the possibility that a given custom or concept may be fairly acceptable to God as it is.

Often the cultural ideal of the custom is quite close to Scripture but the way the custom is practiced may be quite wide of the mark. For example, a custom that involves parents arranging marriages is intended to assure that the most experienced people in a society decide on behalf of the inexperienced youth who marries whom. This is the ideal. Often, however, greedy parents arrange marriages primarily for economic reasons rather than for the good of the partners.

The ideal is clear and makes sense when measured by scriptural ideals but the actual practice needs transformation by Christian families to come close to those ideals. Note, however, that the transformation needed involves a change in the concept of what must be done. The custom itself may need no change. Christian families, motivated by their desire to please Jesus, can practice this custom in its ideal form, providing for their youth the security that such a custom is intended to bring.

3. Some customs and/or concepts in the relational area, though they may be acceptable by God as starting points, may need radical change as people move closer to Christlikeness. The differential treatment of ingroups as opposed to outgroups in most societies is a case in point. We see in Scripture that God accepts the Jews as His people. He thus identifies with this ingroup. He frequently reminds them, however, that they should treat strangers well for they were once themselves strangers in a foreign land (Deut. 24:17-18). The fact that the Jews became cliquish, disobeying God frequently in this relational area, is cause for a good bit of anguish on God's part.

The point is, God is willing to start with what we have learned to call "The Homogeneous Unit Principle" (see Chapter 17) but He is not willing to endorse such cliquishness as His ideal. Rather, we are to be neighborly and loving even to those we consider enemies (Lk. 10:30-37).

4. The form-meaning principle needs to be kept in mind. It is the meanings attached by people to the customs they practice that should be the primary concern of contextualizers. A relational custom that sees ancestors as a part of the living community, for example, may have a different meaning to the people who practice it than it has for outsiders. And similar customs relating to ancestors may mean one thing in one part of the world and another in a different place.

Though any custom that regards ancestors as still functioning in the society of the living is a candidate for eventual change, whether the attitude of the people is worship or simply honor should make a difference in what is done by the Christian community near the start of the transformation process. In Africa, where most of the peoples believe in a High God, the meaning of what a people do in relation to their ancestors may be more like honor than worship. In Asia, however, where any concept of a High God may be weak at best, the meaning is more likely to be worship.

Whether it is ancestor customs that are in focus, or marriage customs, or funeral customs, or ingroup-outgroup relationships, it is the meanings in the minds of the people, not the customs themselves that need to be the primary concern. The same is true of customs introduced from outside. A lot of damage to the perception of Christianity has been done, for example, through the advocacy of individualistic conversion concepts. In group-oriented societies where major decisions are group matters, one-by-one conversions, especially of young people, convey the wrong meanings about God. So may prohibitions of relational customs such as polygamy, dancing and beer drinking.

God's Major Concern

The Bible is quite clear concerning how God expects people to treat one another. Two major principles are stated and identified as summing up the Law and the Prophets. Mark's version of these two principles is:

1.   You must love the Lord your God with all your heart, all your soul, all your mind, and all your strength (Mk. 12: 30) and

2.   Love your neighbor as yourself (Mk. 12:31).

The supreme relational principle is love. And this love is to be the measure of both our vertical relationship with God and our horizontal relationship with other human beings. Indeed, we are told that "the whole Law of Moses and the teachings of the prophets depend on these two commandments" (Mt. 22:40).

Given the confusion in many people's minds concerning what love is all about, it is good to look at the meaning of the Greek word used for love in this and most other passages in the New Testament. The word is *agape* and it signifies a conscious choice by a person to value and do good to the person loved, no matter what it costs that person who chooses to love. This love involves a commitment, a deliberate choice on the part of the one doing the loving, to be favorable toward the person loved. This love is in no way contingent on the qualities of the person loved, except that it involves a valuing of the *being,* not simply the *doing* of that person.

We are exhorted, then, to make a conscious choice to highly value God and our relationship with Him and, on that basis, to commit ourselves to Him with all our heart, soul, mind and strength (see below).

Contextualization problems arise, however, in the fact that not every people express love in the same way. What may be a perfectly understandable act of love in one cultural context may be interpreted as quite something else in another context. In our mission situation in Nigeria, for example, a major way we sought to express our love to the Nigerians was through out clinics and hospitals. And some of the people got the point. But many, probably most, did not. They saw the fact that our mission charged money for medicine and medical procedures as our primary reason for the medical facilities. Though some of this misinterpretation was probably inevitable, the situation could have been helped considerably if an effort had been made to interpret our medical practices in relation to their traditional medical practices. The fact that we never took their medicine seriously predisposed them to draw their own conclusions concerning ours.

In addition, since their medical customs almost always related sickness and healing to the spirit world, it would have helped enormously if we had been able to perform and interpret our practices so as to connect with their understandings. As it was, our approach was almost entirely secular and, therefore, never really connected with their understandings. Oh, our doctors had prayer before surgery and often went out of their way to develop personal contact with their patients (though more often than not, the doctor did not speak the language well). And this helped the patients to experience a measure of love. But the lack of a pervasive spiritual dimension in our Western medical practices plus the largely impersonal style of dealing with medical problems, often hindered the communication of human love and rather totally obstructed any perception on the part of the receivers that there was a spiritual dimension to the healing that occurred. Thus, the Nigerians missed understanding God's love through their all-encompassing spiritual grid. *The language of the medical procedures may have left them impressed and physically healed but not relationally satisfied through experiencing what they perceived as love.*

Quite different was the ministry of a doctor from another mission who spent half days out with the people, studying their medical practices and attempting to connect what he did in the hospital with where they were culturally. Though he was not very much in tune with the spiritual dimensions of their healing procedures, his witness was great in terms of human relationships. They may not have understood the secular nature of his medicine or may have understood it in more spiritual terms than the doctor did, but they knew he loved them because he spent time with them and took their customs seriously.

Contextualizing a Relationship with God

The principles discussed above for relating to human beings apply also to our relating to God. A small amount of time with God, especially if the time is spent in ritual rather than in very personal interaction, yields a poor and superficial relationship with God. The general principle is the same as with human beings: The more time with God, the better the relationship—depending, of course, on the nature of the interaction that takes place during that time. If, as with humans, the time is spent attempting to manipulate God to do our will, the value of the relationship is diminished. If, however, the time is spent both speaking and sincerely listening, there will be exciting growth in the relationship.

Prayer is the name we ordinarily give to the time spent speaking to God. For many, however, prayer time is like one end of a telephone conversation—we talk, talk, talk, talk and then hang up. If God wants to say anything back to us, all He hears is the dial tone! Learning to listen as well as to talk is something that a lot of us miss. But, again, this takes time.

Cross-culturally we may face other problems. They may be used to spending time in their interactions with the spirit world. But they may see such time as primarily to be spent in rather impersonal rituals. The scriptural ideal of close person-to-person interaction with God, speaking to Him as friend to Friend, may be beyond a people's imagination.

The Jews faced this problem. They believed that if God got close, they would die. Listen to the lament of Isaiah when he says, "There is no hope for me! I am doomed . . . [because] I have seen the King, the Lord Almighty" (Is. 6:5). One important aspect of Jesus' contextualizing of what our relationship with God should look like, then, was to prove to His disciples and to the world that when God gets close, it is good rather than bad news.

Many of the peoples of the world have this same concept of God. They don't want Him close. They have also been deluded into treating Him very mechanistically, assuming that if they do the right rituals they may be able to get Him to do their will. So they spend time, perhaps lots of it, performing rituals, usually designed to fend off dangerous spirits, but sometimes aimed at seeking favor from God. They often see their vertical relationships as primarily with capricious and dangerous spirits rather than with God. Though they may believe that God exists, they tend to ignore Him and to seek on their own to deal with the spirits.

Whatever the specific understandings in this area, it is usually a challenge for contextualizers to guide the Christian community into a more intimate and personal relationship with God than their traditions would allow. Probably most nonWestern peoples need more ritual than most Westerners. The challenge is, however, to help them move from mechanistic manipulation of spirit beings through ritual toward intimate submission to God alone in meaningful ritual. When Abraham began his relationship with God, it was a very personal thing. A major part of the continuing of that relationship, however, involved Abraham learning to use with and for the true God the rituals and customs that he and his father Terah had used in relationship to counterfeit gods. God did not give Abraham new customs. He simply led Abraham to redirect the customs he already had, even reintroducing the custom of circumcision that had apparently been allowed to lapse in Abraham's tribe.

Prayer is intended by God to be a relational thing. So is worship. As Jesus said, we are to abide in Him, in close relationship with Him, obeying Him, asking Him for things, bearing fruit with and for Him, loving Him and experiencing His love, experiencing the joy of close relationship and being known as His friends (Jn. 15:1-17). How this is to be experienced and expressed in any given society is a major challenge for contextualizers. But this is perhaps the most important area we have to deal with if our converts are to really grow in Christ.

We are told in Romans 12:1-2 that our whole lives are to be acts of worship. The intent is that our worship be more than simply ritual. But worship at special times and in special places, including culturally appropriate ritual is certainly to be in view as well. Contextualizers need to discover what worship is in their target society and to aim at capturing traditional worship for Christ. In the Old Testament pagan worship was captured for the true God. When Israel was being faithful, the places of pagan worship (usually high places) were taken over for God. Pagan rituals, including blood sacrifices, were captured for God.

Planting and harvest rituals were captured. Circumcision was reintroduced and, as their history unfolded, new times of worship were introduced to commemorate the Exodus and the rescue of the Jews under Queen Esther.

Great attention needs to be given to the development of appropriate acts of prayer and worship. These are the ways we are to express our love toward God.

With Heart, Soul, Mind and Strength

We are admonished to love God with all our heart, soul, mind and strength. The aim is total commitment and obedience—an all-consuming relationship that starts, as it did with Abraham, with a covenant, a binding agreement and develops into a lifelong and life-giving intimacy. There may be rules for the relationship (e.g. the Law), but the rules are always intended to follow, not precede, to support, not eclipse the covenant. The combination of heart, soul, mind and strength is obviously to indicate a totality of this commitment. But what is each of these parts of a human being intended to contribute to the whole?

The term *heart* stands first in the list. This term is used in the Scriptures to focus on the totality of a person's internal being, including emotion, thought and will. I suspect that here its focus is to be on the will. Jesus' intent here is, of course, that we should love God with the totality of our being. This is the basic relationship for which we were created and there will be no complete satisfaction in life without this total commitment.

How this total commitment is to be expressed, however, is likely to differ from society to society. Implied in the word is that a person is to *will* this kind of relationship. Without pressure to love 100%, people in many societies will settle for fearing God or even ignoring Him. In animistic societies the assumption that since God is good He can be ignored will have to be confronted with the ideal of a much more active approach to relating to God. And in most nonWestern societies, appropriate expression of relationship will tend to be more often a group thing than an individual thing.

For a ritually-oriented people, a major part of this active relating may take the form of group rituals. Care must be taken, however, to assure that the meaning of the rituals is *relationship*, not simply *magic*. There seems to be a human tendency to move toward magical understandings of activities that are repeated over and over—understandings that assume that if the ritual is done correctly, it will automatically bring the favor of God. Even in Western societies, worship ritual plays an important part in the expression of this "total-being" relationship (and with the same danger of it being regarded as magical). The exporting of what is termed "contemporary worship" from western societies to nonWestern societies, though, may not engage the hearts of nonWestern peoples to the same extent that such worship rendered in their own musical idiom would.

The term translated *soul,* though often used with a significance close to that of heart, may in this context refer more to the emotions than to the will. It is important to engage the emotions in our relationship with God. Gratefulness, though primarily an act of the will, should have an important emotional component as well. People who are expressing gratefulness need to feel it as well as to will it.

Appropriate expression of emotion will, however, differ from society to society. Emotional expression in Africa is likely to involve the whole body. In Korea, the movement is likely to be more restrained with even greater restraint of movement in Japan. Contrary to popular stereotypes, though, both Koreans and Japanese are capable of expressing great emotion in worship. For many, including many Westerners, whose emotions have been constricted through cultural conditioning, it is important that we learn to engage our emotions in worship. I myself, though one of those with dampened emotions through cultural conditioning, have been learning to *feel* in my relationship with God as that relationship deepens.

Mind in this context probably refers to understanding, an important ingredient in any form of worship or other expression of relational commitment to God. As usual in Scripture, the mind or perspective is seen as foundational to the ways in which we are to relate to God. We are not to simply express ourselves without understanding what we are doing.

The understanding dimension provides a special challenge to those who seek to help new converts in their relationship with God. For, in animistic societies, the primary relationships tend to be with the intermediate spirits rather than with the High God. Thus, sacrifice and worship ritual directed toward spirits need either to be replaced or captured and invested with new meaning. Though capturing such ritual is not impossible, helping people to understand the changes is extremely important, especially in combating the tendency to understand such ritual as a means of controlling the spirit being to which it is directed, in this case God.

The term translated *strength* probably refers again to God's desire that we pour our whole selves, including our bodies, into this love relationship with Him. Those of us who have worked in Africa have no difficulty in imagining such bodily involvement as we have seen the rather total abandon with which Africans express themselves in dancing. Unrestricted worship, African style, is a total thing, at least at the time of worship. On the other hand, it would be difficult in most societies to imitate the level of total commitment of Japanese Christians as they give their money, their time and all else in expressing their allegiance and gratefulness to God. Though they may not do much with their bodies, the level of their commitment enables many very small churches to support their pastors and their various activities in impressive ways.

Our relationship with God has, of course, both private or personal and public dimensions. Public worship and ritual needs to differ greatly from society to society if it is to be appropriate and maximally meaningful to the worshipers and the nonChristian audience looking on. The tragedy is that there has been so much copying of Western worship styles that there has been a stifling of culturally appropriate ways of expression that would really carry the intended meanings. The work of Roberta King reported in Chapter 18 is a huge step forward in assisting African Christians to publicly express their relationship with God in ways that are meaningful to them and even to their nonChristian neighbors.

Personal and small group worship, then, is another matter. Those Japanese who have learned to give money and time sacrificially may have learned what loving God with their whole being is all about, unless their loyalty is simply duty. Those who learn to express their devotion to God daily, in appropriate ways both in church and outside of it, have learned what Romans 12:1 is recommending. Praying without ceasing, with communication lines between humans and God always open and being used, is always appropriate to Scripture. How this relational praying is to be appropriately implemented in any given society needs to be studied. I'm afraid that Western customs of "personal devotions," centered around reading of Scripture, may not be appropriate for the large number of nonliterate people in the world. The sharing of Bible stories in family groups and individual memorization of biblical stories and texts can be great enhancements to personal and family relationships with God and with each other in many societies.

I'm afraid we need a lot more research as to what total commitment to God means and how it is appropriately expressed in the world's societies. I suspect that if such research is done, we in the West will discover that a lot of creative expression is already going on outside of our limited understandings of how a relationship with God is to be expressed.

Loving Neighbors as Ourselves

In addition to loving God completely, we are to love our neighbors as we love ourselves. And in Luke's version of that command (Lk. 10:25-27), Jesus uses the Parable of the Good Samaritan (Lk. 10:30-37) as His illustration of what loving our neighbors is all about. That parable is in answer to the question, "Who is my neighbor?"

In answering that question, Jesus does two startling things. First, He uses an outcast as His hero. Samaritans were looked down on and hated by the Jews. Thus, a Samaritan was a very unlikely person to be the one to express love toward a Jew. Apparently, though, it is God's ideal that even a hated Samaritan is capable of treating with love a member of a group that hates him. But then, Jesus changed the question. His answer was not focused on who the neighbor is but, rather, on who is acting in a neighborly fashion. Thus the question He wants us to ask is not, Who is my neighbor? Even a Samaritan could answer that question. Instead, Jesus teaches, we are to constantly ask, Are we treating even enemies as neighbors? It is even enemies that we are to love as we love ourselves.

Given the innumerable ethnic divisions in the world, each with its hatreds, the command to love people from other groups as we love ourselves is for many of the peoples of the world a major challenge. Yet, for many, their commitment to Christ enables them to break through this barrier. The Nigerian church leaders I worked with shared with me the fact that they could no longer obey a command of their tribal leaders to go to war with the tribe next door. The reason—they had eaten with members of that tribe. Eating or sharing the Lord's Supper with them meant that they could never again be enemies of that group.

Breaking down such barriers and symbolizing them, however, must be done in culturally appropriate ways. Simply forcing people of different ethnic groups to function as members of a single denomination, as our Mission did, does not do the job. Indeed, it may increase the animosity between groups and, worse, enable the enemies to be more effective in fighting each other. It can simply bring the competitiveness and animosity into a new context—the church context—where vying for power in church politics is added to the variety of ways in which their enmity has traditionally been expressed.

Don Richardson's account of the Peace Child custom among the Sawi and other peoples of Irian Jaya is a good example of a culturally appropriate way of symbolizing reconciliation between former enemies (Richardson 1974).

Though the starting point for God's working with people must always be their acceptance in their traditional groupings (i.e. the so-called Homogeneous Unit Principle), it is not God's intent for His people to continue as cliques. We are to grow in our acceptance of believers from other groups, groups that are often radically different from our own group.

We are, as Jesus commanded us in Luke 6:31, to treat others, even strangers and aliens, as we would like to be treated ourselves—as if they were members of our ingroup. Cross-culturally, however, this "Golden Rule" means that it is the receptor group that defines the treatment, not we ourselves. That is, we are to treat others as we would like to be treated *if we were members of their group*, not as if we are members of our own group. It is *their* definition of love that is to determine our behavior, not our own. Though it is always difficult to hold ourselves to the standards of others, Jesus wants us to do no less in reaching out as He would in our relationships with those we seek to reach for Him.

If the people we go to measure love by the amount of unstructured time we spend with them, that is to be our standard. If they measure love by their standard of kindness, of patience, of never speaking angrily, of always sharing, of always showing hospitality even to the point of sacrifice, or whatever, these are to be our standards among them.

1 Corinthians 13 Is Cross-Culturally Valid

The amazingly precise definition of *agape* love in 1 Corinthians 13:4-7 can provide guidelines for the kind of horizontal relationships God desires His people to practice. Though each of the statements about love needs to be looked at in terms of the sociocultural definitions of the terms, it is likely that most societies will have ideals close to those articulated here, at least in their behavior toward members of the ingroup. The aim of practicing love toward outgroups, however, must always be held out as part of the Christian ideal.

Godly love is patient and kind, we are told. It is likely, then, that the cultural ideals of patience and kindness will provide a good starting point for the Christians of that society in their quest to become more Christlike. So also is there likely to be a negative attitude toward jealousy, conceit, pride, ill-manneredness, selfishness and irritability. But, again, these may only apply with the ingroup. And, though the cultural ideal may be negative toward these things, the actual behavior of the people may fall into one or more of these characteristics. Then, of course, there are societies that seem to foster such characteristics as conceit and pride even though these attitudes are destroyers of good relationships.

When it comes to the kind of love that doesn't keep a record of wrongs, many of the peoples of the world fall far short. Family feuds commonly go on for generations because people do keep such records. On one occasion I was ministering to a citizen of one of the islands of the South Pacific who became very violent as he fought against both a demon and what he had been taught was his own responsibility to retaliate for the murder of his father. His struggle against the demon was much less difficult than his struggle against his own conditioning supported by the expectations of his extended family that he would someday murder a member of the family of the one who killed his father. He finally gave in to what he knew Jesus expected of him, but it was not easy. It can be very difficult for Christians in societies such as his to trade in their society's ideal of revenge in such situations for Jesus' ideal of turning the other cheek (Mt. 5:39).

Love, then, "is not happy with evil, but is happy with the truth" (1 Cor. 13:6 TEV). Again, though the ideals of a society may agree that people should be true to others and not wish or inflict evil on them, the actual behavior may fall far short of such ideals. And the definitions of what is considered evil and what is considered truth can vary widely. In relationships, evil toward outgroups may be allowed or even encouraged. And being true to commitments to outgroup members may not be a high priority. So again, ingroup and outgroup issues emerge.

Ingroup and outgroup issues also emerge when we get to the final characteristic of love—the fact that one who loves never gives up, but always exhibits faith, hope and patience in relationships. These are likely to be considered ingroup ideals but may seldom be found in relationships with outgroups. People may also fall far short of such an ideal between the sexes. Often husbands show little inclination to encourage their wives or even their children.

So, the Scriptures set high standards for Christian behavior in our relationship with others as well as in our relationship with God. Approaching these standards in culturally appropriate ways, then, needs to be a major concern for contextualizers.

Personal Concern

There is a level of human beingness that is deeper than our cultural differences. Love needs to be shown and experienced at that level. In many ways the life experiences of all peoples, no matter what their cultures, develop in very similar ways. Everyone experiences birth, childhood, physical and emotional maturing, adult relationships and responsibilities, difficulties of various kinds and death. As people of different societies go through this universal process, however, cultural differences define things in slightly different ways.

At base, though, we are all human beings and we respond to certain things in very similar ways. One of the things to which people respond in similar ways is personal concern. If, then, we are to relate well across cultural boundaries, we must develop culturally understandable ways of showing personal concern.

Sometimes the occasion for showing personal concern arises when tragedy strikes. I remember well the comment made by the shaman of our village when he was visited during the funeral of his wife by about 90 school children from our mission school. On the second day of the three day funeral, the headmaster of our school tucked the school drum under his arm and led his students to the funeral. They then participated in the drumming and dancing that was appropriate in that situation. The shaman then broke the taboo against coming out of isolation during this part of the ceremony and said to the headmaster, "I never knew you Christians cared about us traditional people." The shaman started to come to church after that.

Showing personal concern may not, however, be as easy as it sounds. What is done needs to be interpreted by the receptors as concern, not as something else. If there is not a trust relationship, it is unlikely that our actions will be properly interpreted. Some of our missionaries learned this when they went to a native dance in native dress and were interpreted as ridiculing the people.

To avoid such misinterpretation, it is important for cross-cultural witnesses to develop a group of disciples to whom they give themselves. These disciples learn to trust the outsider and interpret him/her to the people who are not as close. This was a major function served by Jesus' disciples. They got to know Him intimately and provided communication about Him to the wider populace. They also heard from the people what they were thinking about Jesus.

I remember two occasions, one in Nigeria, and one while working with junior high youth here in the states, on which the closeness I had with a few of those in the group paid off in this way. In Nigeria, we were meeting in a village with the leaders of that village. I was speaking and the leaders seemed to me to be listening intently. My disciples, however, discerned that they really weren't paying attention. Stopping me, they spoke to the village leaders about their relationship with me and turned the whole situation around. They had learned to trust me and to take me seriously and were able to gain for me the trust and attention of the village leaders.

A similar thing happened with the junior high young people. This age group is notoriously difficult to manage and on the occasion I remember, some newcomers were starting to cut up while I was trying to speak seriously to them. At that, a couple of the youth who knew me well interrupted to let the newcomers know that I wasn't like other adults with little to contribute to their lives but, rather, one who had something to say that they needed to hear. The newcomers straightened up right away.

Such can be the important influence on relationships of a group of disciples or trusting friends who also have good contact with the receiving group. Any outsider attempting to reach people on the other side of a cultural boundary needs disciples who will perform this function. There are other good reasons for having disciples as well. But to mediate personal concern is an important one.

Spending Time with People

People of whatever society respond to personal interest. Personal interest, then, usually involves spending time with people. Two difficulties arise, however, for those of us who come from the West. The first is that most of the peoples of the world require more time to develop personal relationships than we do in the West. Often our view of friendship appears superficial to those of more person-oriented societies. We think nothing of calling someone a friend whom we have met two or three times. Other peoples, though, would call such a person a mere acquaintance, reserving the label "friend" for those they see regularly over a longish period of time.

The second problem facing Westerners is that we often see ourselves more as "doers" than as "be-ers." As someone has said, we tend to see ourselves as "human doings" rather than as human beings. I found in Nigeria that even though I attempted to spend what to me was a lot of time with the people, they didn't consider it enough. In addition, I had difficulty spending time with them unless we were scheduled to do something together. And when they came to spend time with me without a specific reason, I tended to get impatient with them. My idea of spending time together was to spend it doing something, not just sitting around chatting. Though my disciples told me I did better than most other missionaries, I don't believe I did very well at contextualizing the relating dimension of appropriate Christianity.

Beneath the cultural differences, then, is the basic human need for spending time together to establish and maintain relationships. But the amount and kind of time expected differs from society to society. However, many in the West are starved for more relational time. This probably means that we in the West are not adequately dealing with an important facet of basic human nature. For example, many of the relational problems that surface in counseling Western adults stem from the lack of time their parents, especially their fathers, spent with them. Spending more time in relating, then, is both contextually and humanly appropriate.

The Fruits of the Spirit

The fruits of the Holy Spirit listed in Galatians 5:22-23 provide another insight into how God wants people to relate to each other. The first fruit listed is, of course, love. Indeed, some would interpret the verses as speaking only of love but breaking it down into many of love's facets. That is, they would interpret the verses as saying that the fruit of the Spirit is LOVE expressed in joy, peace, patience, gentleness, goodness, faith(fulness), meekness and self-control. Since each of these characteristics may be seen as a facet of love, these interpreters would say, the list should be seen as an elaboration of the one quality rather than as a delineation of several parallel qualities.

Whether or not one agrees with this interpretation, it is helpful to see each as important in Christian relationships. Again, however, we must note that each of these characteristics is capable of differing cultural definitions. So we need to ask, How should joy be expressed in such and such a society? And what would it take for an outsider to be seen as patient, gentle or good in such and such a society? And what about meekness and self-control? Faithfulness might be easier to define in horizontal relationships but there is also an important vertical relationship to make explicit in this category as well (see below).

What is it in life that brings joy? Though joy may be thought of as primarily an individual, internal thing, I suspect the primary source of joy for most of the peoples of the world would lie in the quality of their relationships with each other. What a joy it can be for contextualizers to be able to help people experience the joy of Christian love in these relationships. The joy of learning to love and to be loved in a marriage relationship, the joy of bringing children into the world, the joy of watching children learn and develop through the various stages into adulthood—these would probably figure high on any people's list of potential joys. How these relationships are to be expressed among Christians in ways that are appropriate to both culture and Scripture should be of great concern to contextualizers. And feeling and expressing in culturally appropriate ways the joy of being in a proper relationship with the Creator and Sustainer of all of the good things of life should be of equal concern.

Peacefulness, too, has an inner and an outer dimension. Contextualizers need to find culturally appropriate ways of enabling people to relate properly to themselves in the freedom Jesus brings through inner healing (see Kraft 1994). Each people needs to experience the bringing of their heavy burdens, whether internal or external, to Him (Mt. 11:28). How this is appropriately done in each cultural context needs to be discovered. And for many of the world's societies, dealing with internal burdens rather than simply suppressing them may be a completely new experience. How to make peace with enemies may be more familiar to people than seeking inner peace, but getting them to do it may be difficult. And it may be naïve to assume that merely getting people of different groups to worship together will automatically bring peace in their relationships. Cultural appropriateness might require some sort of formal ritual and covenant to signify the ending of long held hostility. How might things have been different in Rwanda if there had been some such ritual? And might some such ritual be appropriate at conversion to signify the termination of hostilities between each convert and God Himself?

I have mentioned the Peace Child ritual above. In our area of northeastern Nigeria, several of the tribal groups had the custom of signifying the desire to end hostilities between individuals by the chewing and spitting out of guinea corn. In some tribes, when a person wants to forgive another person, he chews some guinea corn and spits it on the ground at the person's feet. In other groups, the person spits it on the other person! Perhaps this ritual could be adapted to signify reconciliation between former enemy groups who now choose to covenant together to follow Christ and to relate to each other as brothers and sisters rather than as enemies. Some such ritual could also become a meaningful part of the initiation ceremony of individuals into Christianity to signify their new relationship with God.

Patience is probably considered a virtue in all societies. But, again, how patience is expressed may differ. Likewise with gentleness. Jesus was known for His gentleness and, considering the difficulties He experienced with His disciples, His patience is exemplary also. The challenge, then, is for the people of God to discover how Jesus would have expressed His patience and gentleness in their cultural context. In many societies, their ideal in these areas may already be close to Jesus' behavior. The most difficult thing for contextualizers, then, might be to assure that the motivation is Christian, not simply a matter of conformity to traditional custom.

When we come to goodness we face perhaps the greatest challenge. Jesus said that only God is good (Lk. 18:19). So, learning to be good would again be a matter of imitating God's attitude and behavior within any given society. This would, of course, involve both personal righteousness and treating people as God treats people. God's people need to be seen by the members of their societies as good. Their behavior, then, must be easily interpretable by their people if it is to truly represent the good God. This should put the contextualization of goodness, both personal and relational, high on the list of concerns for those who would be effective in relational contextualization.

Second only to love as a relational aspect of Christianity would be faith. In Scripture, though, the usual meaning of the term "faith," both in Hebrew and in Greek, is "faithfulness"—the characteristic of faithful response to the one related to. We are told in Hebrews 11:6 that without faith(fulness) it is impossible to please God. The contextualization of relationship requires, then, that we help people to discover how to express faithfulness to God within their cultural life.

Humility may be a challenge for many peoples since it is so likely to be interpreted as weakness. But Jesus modeled humility, turning His back on the honor He could have demanded given His credentials. He thus endorsed meekness and humility as Christian virtues, cutting across the grain in His own society and challenging the peoples of the world to motivation and behavior beyond that of their contemporaries.

Self-control, then, is the last of the listed virtues. Like all of the others, this characteristic has both personal and group ramifications. Those who truly love will exercise self-control in their relationships with others. As Christians, the love expressed through self-control is to be exercised both toward the ingroup and toward the members of outgroups. Again, though, a major focus in contextualization of this virtue needs to be the motivation behind the characteristic. Self-control simply as a custom is quite different from self-control motivated by love.

In these and many other ways, Jesus wants His love to be expressed in culturally appropriate motivation and behavior. The challenge for those involved in the contextualization of relationships, then, is to discover and press toward biblically and culturally appropriate expressions of these characteristics.

Relationships Through Institutions?

As a final item in this discussion of relational contextualization, let's look at what has to be a major problem for those who take this area seriously. Since much of missionary effort has become institutionalized, is it possible to talk of contextualization of the relationships between those who operate the institutions and those who are ministered to through them? Some would give up, suggesting that such institutions as schools, hospitals and even churches are too foreign in many societies to foster something as close to the heart of the peoples of the earth as relationships.

I choose not to give up, though the challenge is great, especially among peoples in what have been called "person-to-person" societies. For culturally sensitive people working in institutions can find ways to spend time as learners with people outside of the institutions. I know of a single woman missionary who went to Nigeria as a teacher but spent many weekends living with the families of her students away from the school compound. She became greatly loved by both students and their parents and was very effective in her witness to the families of her students.

I have mentioned the doctor who used his afternoons to conduct research into the medical practices of the people of the villages surrounding the hospital where he worked. Both he and the teacher mentioned above used part of their time to establish and cultivate relationships with the people they came to serve. In this way they learned as much as they could about the people's lives and concerns and sought to contextualize their relationships with them by expressing receptor-oriented love.

Ideally, the institutions we start and continue as means of communicating Christ could be relationally-based. We note that Jesus' training school was relational. Apprenticeship and discipleship are nonformal educational institutions with the relationships between the participants crucial to their effective functioning. If it is our privilege to start a school, why not do it Jesus' way? It was not by accident that He called His disciples together and chose just twelve to enter His school (Mk. 3:13-15)—to first be with Him in close relationship, then to go out and communicate what they have learned, including how to free people from demons. By whittling down the number of followers who would be closest to Him, Jesus was simply recognizing that human limitations don't permit us to relate closely to very many people at a time.

Then, in Jesus' school the focus was on learning to minister, not, as in our educational institutions, simply on learning to *think* about ministry. Jesus and His apostles *did* things together, giving them concrete life experiences to discuss and analyze. In addition, Jesus' apostles were second-career people. They had already learned much about life by participating in secular occupations. This is a factor that we should not miss when we are recruiting disciples.

Many of the societies we go to as witnesses already have an apprenticeship or discipleship structure functioning to train their people for various occupations. Wise contextualizers will seek to find such structures and adapt them for use within and, sometimes in place of, the Western institutions that are so typical of mission-generated Christian communities.

Conclusion

What this is about, then, is a culturally appropriate expression of love toward God and a receptor-oriented love between Christians and both ingroup and outgroups with whom they interact. This is a love that is both sincere at the sender's end and intelligible at the receptor's end. From a missionary's point of view, we need to practice receptor-oriented love toward the people we seek to reach.

To advocate appropriate loving relationships seems easy, to practice them, especially cross-culturally involves a number of complexities brought about by cultural differences. The ideals of Scripture are fairly clear. The application of these ideals in the cultural contexts of the peoples of the world who have not known Christ is considerably more difficult. I hope this discussion helps us to be aware of some of those difficulties and to overcome them in our ministries.

Chapter 20

Contextualizing the Relationship Dimension of the Christian Life

Katie J. Rawson

I was editing my friend Shao-leng's conversion story when an unusual sentence caught my attention: "Hearing the good news for the first time and witnessing the living testimony of Claudia's family was more an admiration than a paradigm shift."

My curiosity was piqued. "Shao-leng, what do you mean when you say that hearing the good news was more an admiration than a paradigm shift?"

Shao-leng had no trouble answering. "I didn't care whether God was my creator or Jesus was the Messiah. I didn't know anything about the Bible. All I knew when I became a Christian was that I wanted a family like [my friend] Claudia's family."

I pressed for deeper understanding. "Since you started out your relationship with God not knowing what He was like or how to relate to Him, what has happened to make you such a mature Christian now?"

Shao-leng, who was born in Taiwan, came to the United States to study at a university on the East Coast in 1981. There she met Claudia, a Christian student. Shao-leng was impressed with Claudia's life and curious about her faith. A weekend with Claudia's family over Thanksgiving sealed Shao-leng's decision to become a Christian. Soon after her initial commitment, Shao-leng became a member of the international Bible study group I was leading at that university, so I was very familiar with her testimony. But this time I was looking for something different.

Having just finished analyzing the conversion accounts of twenty-eight East Asians who came to Christ in the United States, I knew that Shao-leng's decision to follow Christ, though with very little understanding of many aspects of what this involved, was not unusual. All she, and others in my study, understood was that this looked like a relationship worth entering into (Rawson 1999). Unlike certain Americans who convert for theological reasons, the felt need that attracted Shao-leng and many other Asians was the need for a relationship with God and fellow Christians. Having uncovered this fact, my concern was to learn how my colleagues and I could help such a convert grow in her relationship with God.

Shao-leng's story illustrates many of the lessons I have learned about contextualizing relationships. I will, therefore, include parts of her experience here as I discuss the task of facilitating appropriate Christian relationships in cross-cultural contexts.[1]

The Reign of Right Relationships

As Charles Kraft states in Chapter 7, relationship is the most crucial dimension of the Christian life. It is interesting that many physicists now believe that in the quantum world relationships are all there is to reality (Wheatley 1994:32). This scientific support for the primacy of relationship in the universe should not surprise us since, as Christians, we worship a God who is Father, Son and Spirit. In the Son all things hold together (Col. 3:17) and the image of God includes both male and female (Gen. 1:27), each made for relationship with the other. Perhaps it is the Western bias toward knowledge that has kept many Western Christians from seeing the crucial role of relationships both in the Christian life and in the mission to which Jesus has called us.

Mission may be seen as the extension of the Kingdom of God, and the Kingdom of God aims at and is characterized by *shalom*, defined by Dyrness as the rule of right relationships (1983). Mission, therefore, aims at extending relational wholeness, to all peoples, groups as well as individuals.

The *shalom* relationship, according to Viggo Sogaard, consists of five separable relationships: with God, with self, with others, with creation and with the Church (1996:236). Sogaard suggests that mission work may usefully be evaluated by looking at these five relationships.

The three relationships mentioned in the Great Commandments (Matthew 22:37-39) are those with God, others and self. The second commandment assumes that we love ourselves, apparently as a prerequisite to loving others. But it often takes the love of others to help us love ourselves. The phrase in 1 John 4.19, "We love [God] because he first loved us" points to this origination of love outside of us. Loving is apparently a response rather than something we originate ourselves. We need to receive love first before we can appropriately respond to God in love and shower it on others as well as on ourselves.

It is clear from the Scriptures that relationships with God and with others in His Body are mutually dependent; one of the two cannot usually flourish for too long if the other languishes (1 Jn. 4:7-12). When the relationship with God is what it should be, relationships with others, self, Church and creation will eventually become healthy as well. They will be characterized by *shalom,* the peace and wholeness that come from God. In this chapter I will focus on relationships with God and others, assuming that these two relationships will influence the other three in Sogaard's list. As I discuss these relationships I will

---

[1] Shao-leng (not her real name) has given me permission to share her story.

develop a series of key points to assist us in thinking about the contextualization of relationships in the communication of Christianity.

Conveying Truth in Relational Terms

Principle 1: Most of the peoples of the world will respond better to truth conveyed in concrete relational ways rather than in terms of abstract principles. I first realized this truth when considering how best to explain sin to Chinese friends. It was difficult for them to understand sin as violation of a law but much easier for them to see sin as violation of relationship with God. I realized that many East Asians do not respond as well to abstract concepts as they do to relationships. Sin may be appropriately presented to them as covenant-breaking or failure to honor God.

We should think through various aspects of the gospel message and of Christian discipleship and consider how to present them in terms of relationships. What will repentance, faith, growth in grace, forgiveness and holiness look like when we consider them in relational rather than abstract or legal terms? Certainly each of them will lead us deeper into relationship with and cause us to become more like Jesus. Repentance, for example, is the continual process of having our minds renewed so that we have the mind of Christ. Forgiveness is the continual process of receiving grace so that we can give it. Holiness is having Christ's set-apart life imparted to me as I live the reality of Galatians 2:20.

Conveying relational truth is not just a matter of the understanding dimension, however. For people with distant or hurtful earthly fathers like my friend "Benjie" from Japan, work in the freedom and relationship dimensions will be necessary before the truth of the Father's love can be truly grasped. Benjie (and many like him) need for the church to be both family and hospital (a place of healing) as well as classroom.

The Primacy of Partnership

Principle 2: Partnership with national Christians is essential to contextualizing relationships[2]. They are the ones who should be doing most of the evangelism, discipling and leadership. Relationships with them will help us become aware of our cultural lenses; they will usually know what appropriate relationships should look like. There is only one caveat: people who have grown up in churches modeled on Western churches or who have received a Western education may be less in touch with what is really appropriate for their societies.

Many of the suggestions that follow assume that the missionary is doing the work of evangelism and discipling. In pioneering situations that may be

---

[2] I am indebted to my friend Carolynn Hudson for challenging my thinking on the subject of partnership with international students.

true. But as soon as some of the receiving peoples are converted, partnership with them must become a priority. I believe that they should be brought into the decision-making of missionary teams as quickly as possible.

Differences in power distance might make it difficult for new converts to participate with us as equal partners, however. Eric H. F. Law asserts that most white people think in low power distance terms, that is, they perceive themselves as more or less equal to others and believe that inequality should be minimized. Most people of color, on the other hand, accept inequality and feel somewhat powerless in groups dominated by whites (1993:19-25). As with all generalizations, there are many exceptions and qualifications to these statements. But awareness of these tendencies will help missionaries to examine assumptions about cross-cultural relationships.

Law insists that white people learn to practice a spirituality of the cross when participating in multicultural encounters, that we deliberately give up power and choose to listen rather than doing all the talking. And people of color should practice a spirituality of the resurrection, reminding themselves that they are blessed by God and asking for the power of the Holy Spirit to say or do what is needed (1993:41-43). Depending on which side of the power distance equation, they find themselves; cross-cultural workers might find one or the other of these suggestions useful. When we are perceived as powerful in a high power distance culture—a situation that is likely to occur often—we must deny our desires to control things and help new converts to see themselves as gifted and empowered by the Holy Spirit.

We must also learn the communication styles of our partners rather than expecting them to learn ours. For example, if I want East Asians to express their ideas in a group setting, I may have to call on them by name. And if I want opinions on sensitive issues, I may have to talk to people individually in a relaxed setting. I cannot necessarily expect the type of direct communication I would from Americans.

Principle 3: The cross-cultural worker must try to make his or her unconscious assumptions conscious. By becoming aware of our own worldview assumptions in a certain area, we lessen the possibility that we will unknowingly impose those assumptions on the people with whom we are working. How do we make the unconscious conscious? *Figuring Foreigners Out: A Practical Guide* by Craig Storti (1999) is a self-instructional cross-cultural training manual that introduces cultural differences along the individualist-collectivist, and several other, continuums. Direct and indirect communication and differences in power distance are also explored. Although I've been working with international students nineteen years, I found some of the exercises in this book very enlightening. The book is culture-neutral and will be useful to missionaries from any cultural background. But the best way to become aware of our worldview assumptions, of course, is to get into a close relationship with someone who has a different worldview.

Principle 4: *In all our cross-cultural interactions, we must be wary of the assumption of sameness.* Although there are universal human needs and behaviors, it is safer to assume difference in cross-cultural relationships. I once evaluated a number of media tools designed to evangelize or disciple international students (Rawson 1999). Most of these tools did not meet all the spiritual needs of internationals which I had identified in a previous stage of the research. Developers of these materials had made the assumption of sameness—that internationals have essentially the same spiritual needs and questions as Americans. The result was a large number of attractive but inadequate tools.

Interaction Between Horizontal and Vertical Relationships

Principle 5: *Strong relationships with persons who know God are usually necessary to bring about relationship with God. This is true on both the individual and group levels.* Shao-leng came to Christ not because she understood the gospel knowledge-wise, but because of her relationship with Claudia and her family.

The most important task of the cross-cultural worker (on the horizontal level) is to establish trust relationships with members of the target society. Marvin Mayers calls this the prior question of trust. In our witness, he suggests, we should ask ourselves, "Does what I am doing or saying build or undermine trust?" (1974:30). Though trust is "a person thing," rather than a knowledge thing, building trust with members of another society is helped enormously by developing an understanding of their context, their worldview and especially their communication and relationship patterns.

In my work with East Asians, it has become clear that in most cases, relationships with several Christians, not just one, are necessary to bring about the conversion of a non-believer. The most common conversion pattern I have encountered among the students I have interviewed has been conversion to community before conversion to Christ (Rawson 1999). Other researchers have identified a similar pattern among the current North American student generation on college campuses (J. Long 1997).

The example of a loving Christian fellowship is attractive in any setting. This suggests that relationships among missionary team members should have constant monitoring and maintenance. A friend who ministered for years through periodic trips to Eastern Europe from a neighboring country made this comment on relations with other missionaries: "I always thought it was the communist borders that would do me in. I should have known it would be the relationships with other missionaries."

Principle 6: *Interpersonal relationships are also essential in nurturing ongoing relationships with God. Growth in discipleship comes through participation in a community.* Just as for conversion, relationships are necessary in discipling new converts. Being part of a community is not optional; in many cases, a close relationship with a mentor or prayer partner is also needed.

Shao-leng named four persons who were important in her Christian growth process, two Chinese and two Americans. She had also experienced growth through participation in various churches. The biblical pattern seems to be that people need a community in order to experience discipleship (cf. Ac. 2:42-47; 4:32-35; cf. Mk. 3:13-15). That community may be the family, an entire congregation or a smaller group—much depends on the culture and the situation.

Most of the peoples of the world have a better understanding of the need for community than do Caucasian Americans. But postmodern or emerging culture is bringing the need for community to the fore in this country as well. This is a positive development that is helping us become more thoroughly biblical in our evangelism and discipling.

Principle 7: *The cross-cultural worker needs to work at understanding the relationship patterns of the receiving people in order to discover appropriate conversion and growth patterns for the members of that group. Such understanding will help to prevent cultural blunders.* Those working with international students in a Western context must be particularly concerned to seek such understanding since it is easy for them to assume that internationals have adopted our worldview and communication patterns because they seem to be very "at home" in them. In reality, however, the adaptations they have made may be quite superficial.

One of the two most serious problems I uncovered in my conversion research is that indirect communication patterns common in East Asia often keep students from these countries asking the questions about the gospel that are on their minds. They either don't want the Christian Bible study leader to lose face when they raise a difficult question or they simply want to be agreeable. Understanding and adopting the communication patterns of the society one is working in will decrease the risk of misunderstandings. Workers with East Asians should learn to practice anticipatory communication, anticipating the needs and questions of those with whom we are interacting (see Yum 1997:86).

We also need to understand the relationship patterns of the people with whom we are working with whatever has played the role of God among the receiving peoples. What are relationships with local gods and ancestral spirits like? New believers, especially those converted through power encounters with minimal understanding, are likely to relate to the God of the Bible in the ways they related to the old gods. It took quite awhile for many of the East Asian converts I interviewed to understand that relating to the Christian God was not a matter of praying simply to obtain good luck. It is typical for East Asians to simply engage in what Jordan calls "a pantheon exchange" (1993) where the name of the god changes but the way of relating to the god doesn't.

This is what happened to Shao-leng initially. In this situation, our task is to help a person with a pantheon exchange commitment move to a place of heart understanding and dynamic interaction with God. Deepening this type of commitment is essential in order to avoid backsliding, reversion to the previous faith or adoption of another god that appears better able to provide good luck.

Religious practices in the target society may, however, give us clues to effective cross-cultural discipling. A. H. Mathias Zahniser (1997) believes we can learn from other religions how to use symbols and ceremonies in discipling believers from those religions. It is my observation that baptism is much more significant for several of my East Asian informants and their parents than it is for Westerners. For people who do not easily dissociate form from meaning, baptism rather than a conversion decision may be seen as the point of becoming a Christian (unless, of course, baptism is seen as simply magical). Culturally appropriate ceremonies could be very important in discipling such groups.

Understanding relationship patterns in a society is key to effective evangelism and discipling. The outside change agent must be able to identify opinion leaders with whom it is appropriate to build relationships. In 1989 I was able to meet a whole network of Mainland Chinese scholars in the medical field because I became a "conversation partner" with an opinion leader. When his network and my network of Christian volunteers became friends, fruitful ministry and several conversions resulted.

Another reason to examine relationship patterns among the people we're dealing with is that people from group-oriented societies participate in a web of relationships that may be used for sharing the gospel. A Filipina friend shared that after becoming a Christian through a one-to-one gospel presentation by an American, she immediately started spending time with a peer to pass on the good news. But this upset their other friends who were not used to people spending one-to-one time together. They expected her to share her new experiences with the whole group. Such individualizing of communication was insulting to them. She was eager to share the gospel, but, by imitating the one-on-one approach of the American who had led her to Christ, she violated cultural norms. We need to work in terms of existing relational dynamics and to help new converts to do the same. Decisions about baptism, for example, should be made with a view to how it will affect family and friends.

Relationship networks may be used to spread the gospel very effectively. Recently Shao-leng returned to Taiwan and saw fifty family members and old friends. She viewed her vacation as a mission and recruited prayer partners for each day. As a result she had many opportunities to share Christ and was able to lead her niece to the Lord.

Understanding communication and relationship patterns will also help us discover appropriate ways to disciple new converts. The most effective international student ministry I know of functions as an international church where students learn by doing. The founder of this group, a native of Thailand, deliberately uses the fellowship as a means of discipling, although he also meets individually with students to teach them the Scriptures. Aware of the group-oriented nature of the societies most of these students come from, he feels that much of their growth will occur as they participate in community.

It is important to remember that worldview, relationship patterns and communication patterns are usually different for male and female members of the same people group. I have long suspected that East Asian women would speak more freely in Bible discussion groups if there were no men present. A few years ago our fellowship divided into male and female discussion groups. After some months, group leaders realized that the two groups had taken on very different characteristics. We need more research on the relationship and communication patterns within and between the gender groups in different societies.

Principle 8: In working with most of the peoples of the world, we need to think in terms of groups rather than individuals when deciding how to contextualize relationships in appropriate ways. Commenting on Christian growth in strongly group-oriented societies, a friend from Japan observed, "For those peoples, Christian growth is not only a growth of the individual. It is mainly a growth of relationships." In these contexts, one must consider how to disciple the group, not just its individual members. Oral societies are group-oriented. African Independent Churches, for instance, hold long, frequent worship services where both instruction and discipling take place. Jesus apparently took a similar approach especially in his discipling of the twelve (cf. Mt. 11:1; 13:1-2, 10-11, 16-17).

Strengthening Relationship with God

Principle 9: A vision or revelation of the character of God to an individual's heart is a necessary foundation for a growing relationship with God. Proverbs 29:18 says that without vision or revelation from God, the people perish. Paul prayed that the Ephesian Christians would have a spirit of wisdom and revelation to know God better, that eyes of the their hearts would be enlightened to know his incomparably great power and that they would grasp the great magnitude of his love (Eph. 1:17-18; 3:18). The enemy has blinded the minds of unbelievers so that they don't see the light of the knowledge of the glory of God in the face of Christ (2 Cor. 4:4). It has been my experience that this blindness is not always completely removed when a person pledges allegiance to Christ.

As I note below, both family and cultural backgrounds can keep us from really grasping the absolute beauty and superiority of God to all lesser things. One of the most significant ministries we can have to new believers is to pray prayers similar to Paul's (those cited above and Col. 1:9-12; Phil. 1:9-10, among others) for them. I believe that Paul's references to "struggling" and "wrestling" for the churches (Col. 2:1, 4:12) indicate that he and members of his apostolic team wrestled in prayer that these churches would have a vision both of the character of God and of God's will for them. In his excellent book on spiritual formation, *Renovation of the Heart*, Dallas Willard states that a vision of life in the Kingdom of God, the life that God intends for His disciples here and now, is the first step in spiritual formation (2002:86-87). That vision must be accompanied by the intention to undergo spiritual transformation and the use of means (disciplines) to accomplish it (2002:85).

Principle 10: *The key element in nurturing relationship with God is to help the new convert abide in Christ. The discipler should continually work to strengthen that relationship.* As Kraft notes in Chapters 7 and 19, it is the relationship dimension of the Christian life that produces the fruit of the Spirit. In John 15:4-5, Jesus indicates that abiding in Christ is the secret of fruit bearing. Abiding is facilitated by letting his words abide in us (vv. 3, 7) and by obedience, with a commitment to love one another as members of the family of God (vv. 10-12). Jesus' words abide in us as we treasure Scripture in our hearts and apply it in our lives. Obedience, immediate and continual, is necessary to maintain the abiding relationship.

These words of Jesus are true in any cultural context. Jesus emphasizes abiding because he understands the thoroughly sheep-like nature of human beings. We are, as the hymn says, "prone to wander." After years of discipling international students, I have come to the conclusion that praying for them, for protection from the enemy and for strengthening of their bond with God, is prerequisite to anything else I might do. It is essential to help new converts learn to discern what God is saying to them and to make obedience a daily habit. The Holy Spirit will develop the converts' relationship with God as they obey Him and as we intercede.

It is crucial that new converts be given understanding about the Holy Spirit and His roles and be trained in discerning the voice of the Spirit. I once developed a "Listening Prayer" seminar, complete with guidelines for discernment and practical exercises, for new international converts. This type of training is essential for people from shamanistic backgrounds to help them develop a functional substitute for shamanistic practices formerly used in decision-making. Two books that have helped me understand and grow in hearing from God are *The Joy of Listening to God* by Joyce Huggett (1986) and *Hearing God: Developing a Conversational Relationship with God* by Dallas Willard (1999).

Jesus' relationship with His Father, as described in the Gospel of John, serves as a model for our relationship with the Father. Jesus said He saw what His Father was doing, participated with the Father (Jn. 5:19-20) and heard from the Father (Jn. 8:40). New converts should be taught to expect the same kind of intimate walk with God that Jesus had. They should also be involved in ministry as soon as possible.

Participation in God's work and discovery of spiritual gifts will greatly strengthen bonding with God. How are spiritual gifts discerned and expressed in various cultural contexts? Western inventories to discover gifts might not be appropriate in group-oriented societies. It seems more natural for the members of a Christian body to discern an individual's gifts as they observe that individual in ministry. And appropriate contexts and ways in which to express gifts should be determined by relationship patterns in the society.

Principle 11: Relationship with God is strengthened in the vicissitudes of daily life, good times and bad, if we continue to abide in Christ. One of the events that strengthened Shao-leng the most was a serious traffic accident in which she fractured her sternum and a vertebra. As she continued to seek God in the midst of that experience and her Christian community provided the support she needed, she found that her faith deepened. She also experienced comfort from the words of Scripture.

One of the most difficult lessons for many converts to learn is that God will not always protect us from trials. The Scriptures command us, in fact, to consider trials an occasion for joy, since they produce endurance and maturity in us (Jas. 1:2-4). Dallas Willard, citing James and Romans 5:1-5, insists that it is in the everyday events of life, particularly trials, that we develop Christlikeness (1998:348-350). For Christians to respond to trials in a way that strengthens their relationship with God, they need a good deal of freedom and understanding and strong relationships with other Christians.

In the understanding dimension it is important to present an accurate picture of Christian growth so that trials do not take young disciples by surprise. J. Long suggests that in the past Westerners have seen faith development as a linear process, but that the appropriate model for a postmodern world is faith development as a journey (1997:175). Another possible model would be the spiral (see Wheatley 1994:89). By presenting the spiral as a model of Christian growth, one acknowledges that certain issues will be revisited in the growth process, circling back for greater depth (Samaan 1990:157). The journey image, because it focuses on the process rather than the product, is useful to convey the true nature of Christian growth. Using this metaphor, what we need for the journey are companions, not just a map (J. Long 1997:174). There is a great difference between an individual alone with a map and a group of companions. For most of the cultures of the world and for the emerging culture in this country, the second picture is the most helpful for ongoing discipleship.

Principle 12: The Holy Spirit is the One who contextualizes relationships. The discipler's role is to facilitate both understanding and freedom by giving the Holy Spirit opportunities to work in the lives of those involved. There came a point in Shao-leng's life when she sensed a spiritual attack. By that time we were both living in California, and she was partnering with me in ministry. When she shared about the attack, I invited her to a prayer retreat where we addressed issues of ancestral sin and idolatry. Shao-leng's relatives had been Buddhist priests and nuns, and she had routinely performed rituals to appease various spirits. We looked at the Ten Commandments and allowed everyone present to repent for our own sins and renounce the sins of our ancestors. There was a struggle, but Shao-leng was set free from spiritual bondage that day and never again sensed this kind of attack. It took a second meeting about a year later to uncover a family stronghold in her thought patterns, the belief that every woman in her family would die early. After these two occasions Shao-leng sensed a deeper intimacy with God and began to discover new spiritual gifts.

Here we see how the three crucial dimensions of the Christian life interact. The freedom dimension brought greater heart understanding of God's love and thus deeper relationship with God for Shao-leng. The role of the discipler in this situation resembles that of a gardener. Weeding, through facilitating freedom and understanding, gets anything that hinders the work of the Holy Spirit out of the way. Fertilizing, which often involves providing proper understanding, deepens and enriches relationship with God. Modeling relationship with God and others is an essential fertilizer as well. One of the people who influenced Shao-leng the most was her pastor. He did not mentor her, but he modeled relational skills and discernment as he interacted with a leadership team on which she served. As we weed and fertilize, we must trust the Holy Spirit. In faith we can look forward to what God is going to do. Our expectations will often spur those we disciple on to greater growth (Elliston 1992:121).

Dallas Willard suggests two primary objectives for a curriculum in Christlikeness: first, "to bring apprentices to the point where they dearly love and constantly delight in that 'heavenly Father' made real to earth in Jesus" and, secondly, "to free the apprentices of domination, of 'enslavement' (Jn. 8:34; Rom. 6:6), to their old habitual patterns of thought, feeling and action" (Willard 1998:321-322). In his first objective, Willard is actually referring to both the understanding and relationship dimensions. Although he does not mention evil spirits, his second objective corresponds to Kraft's freedom dimension.

Diverse Ways of Relating to God

Principle 13: The cross-cultural worker should provide understanding and practice in the spiritual disciplines—the many diverse ways the people of God have used to strengthen their relationship with Him. Spiritual disciplines are activities in which disciples engage in order to be able to replace their dependence on the merely human or natural (the flesh) with an appropriate dependence on God (Willard 1998:353). They include disciplines of abstinence such as solitude, silence, fasting and sacrifice and disciplines of engagement such as study, worship, service, prayer, fellowship and confession (1998:418). Some of these disciplines, such as prayer and study of Scripture, may occur in diverse ways, either individually or in groups. The cross-cultural worker who is acquainted with these disciplines may find that some are more appropriate to the target people than others.

Perhaps the place to begin is to experiment with several of the ways of worship found in the Bible. A study of the words and postures used for worship and praise would be a good place to start. In Scripture we see people kneeling, standing, prostrating themselves or dancing before the Lord. People may shout, clap, sing or play various instruments or be silent in God's presence. We in InterVarsity are used to teaching students how to have a quiet time; as if this were the only way to experience the Lord. But the appropriate approach to communion with the Lord in many societies might better be a joyful noise time than a quiet time. Sharing the variety of biblically acceptable approaches to worship with new converts may provide fertilizer for the Holy Spirit, who can help them find what are appropriate ways of worship for themselves and their people. The same should be done with prayer. After teaching the many ways of relating to God that we find in the Bible, we may inform new converts about various streams of spirituality throughout Christian history. Richard Foster's *Streams of Living Water* (1998) is an excellent introduction to six of those traditions.

Cultural Strengths and Weaknesses

Principle 14: Cultural and family backgrounds give us unique strengths in our relationships with God. But strengths may become weaknesses. Shao-leng noted that from an early age Chinese people learn the value of sacrifice for others and they quickly develop a strong sense of obligation to those who have sacrificed for them. Speaking from the Asian-American experience, Greg Jao described such strengths this way:

> Many of us, for example, come from faith communities that modeled the Confucian values of duty, community and altruistic self sacrifice. Our churches, therefore, often reveal great faithfulness, deep sacrifice, committed prayer, obedience to Scripture. . . . And our actions are powered by a keen sense of the holiness of God, the cost of Christ's death on the cross, and an awareness of our dependence on the Holy Spirit (Jao 1998:129).

But Shao-leng has observed that if people push such strengths too far, they may become weaknesses. She has seen Chinese missionaries with such a sense of obligation to Christ that they live overly ascetic lifestyles and miss some of the joy God intends for them. In the same way, Korean-American prayer is full of faith and passion but is often shaped by shamanistic magical attitudes (Jao 1998:130). With some prayerful reflection, Christians of every society should be able to discover how cultural influences have both strengthened and weakened their discipleship.

For example, in accordance with the worldview assumptions of her society, Shao-leng spent most of her life before becoming a Christian afraid of the gods, trying to avoid making them angry. Her mother had died young and she feared this was her destiny too. This view of the gods as easily angered clearly affected her ability to believe in the love of her heavenly Father. It took both teaching and horizontal relationships with other Christians for her to begin to sense God's love.

Confucian thinking, reinforced by family experience that places fathers at a distance in a hierarchical family system, makes it difficult for people from Confucian societies to experience intimacy with God the Father (Jao 1998:130-131). Since cultural influences cause them to see the Father as all-important, however, Asian Americans may emphasize that relationship, even though they see the Father as distant. This emphasis is detrimental to their relationship with Jesus. Desiring something more in the emotional realm than what their parents have given them, they may go overboard in seeking emotional experiences with the Holy Spirit. even to the point of misunderstanding the Person of the Spirit (Jao 1998:134-139).

Members of the current Japanese student generation are used to absentee fathers. Some Chinese women have been made to feel unwanted by both parents because they were not the desired sons who could maintain the family name. These were two of the situations I encountered regularly in interviewing East Asian converts. Under these conditions, Jesus may be the most approachable Person of the Trinity. When I first met Benjie from Japan he assured me that he wasn't a Christian but that Jesus was his hero. He eventually invited Jesus into his life but is still struggling with trusting men. He needs more work in the freedom and understanding dimensions before he can experience God as Father and men as friends.

These examples from Asian Americans and East Asians exemplify the strong influence our family and cultural backgrounds have on our relationships with each Person of the Trinity and with other people. Sometimes a perceptive outsider can see these influences better than an insider. Cross-cultural workers may serve Christians from other societies by sensitively pointing out negative family and cultural influences.

Relationships in the Body of Christ

Principle 15: Cross-cultural workers should try to move as soon as possible to the roles of brother or sister, especially if their initial roles were more those of parent or benefactor. In 1983 Shao-leng moved to the Los Angeles area. So when I enrolled in Fuller Seminary to take a short summer course in 1984, I took the opportunity to visit her. She showed me Hollywood and the Olympic venue and even took me grocery shopping. At the time we laughed because she was doing for me what I normally did for international students on the East Coast. I remember feeling great satisfaction with the role reversal. Looking back on it now, I realize that it was that summer that I stopped being Shao-leng's discipler and became her friend. Her observation was, "By becoming a friend, you opened yourself up to having a more powerful influence on me than you had as a discipler. The distance between us was removed."

Westerners tend to enjoy the positions of spiritual leader or benefactor and not relinquish them soon enough when interacting with new converts and young churches. This tendency has produced the universal problem of dependency on missionaries. Glenn Schwartz believes that the Western understanding of the evangelistic mandate has caused Westerners to go out with a form of authority that sows the seeds of dependency. He insists that Western missiology needs a shift in attitude from "Thus says the Lord" to "I beseech you therefore brethren" (1998:20).[3]

Dean Gilliland notes that the apostle Paul trusted the Holy Spirit in the lives of new believers and churches and insists, "Because we doubt that the new Christian can sense the Spirit's presence, the missionaries become the presence" (1983:127). We need to trust the Holy Spirit and seek to root out all attitudes and mindsets in ourselves that would promote dependency on the part of new converts. Faith in God, rather than fear of what might happen if we give up control, must characterize our decisions. International student workers are not immune to the problem of over-control. If anything, letting the students run the fellowships is more difficult for us because the majority of Christian internationals we work with are new converts.

Responsibly moving from the role of spiritual parent to that of brother or sister is a great challenge. Worldview and other cultural traits may make that move more difficult for many. Reflecting the respect for elders and teachers that their societies engender, some women in our international Bible study group still insisted on referring to me as "our teacher," even after I deliberately turned over most of the leadership of the Bible discussions to the women themselves.

Bringing about a role reversal such as the one I experienced with Shao-leng is extremely useful. And helping new converts discover their spiritual gifts also helps to equalize relationships. We need to carefully plan actual leadership transitions so that those taking the baton from us will feel confident and well prepared for their new tasks and responsibilities.

Principle 16: *Members of every society need the insights of the worldwide Body of Christ in order to develop a more well-rounded understanding and practice of our relationship with God.* Commenting on her experiences of discipleship in both American and Chinese contexts, Shao-leng felt that Americans (in keeping with things our society does best) had helped her to understand the grace of God and the freedom of the Christian life. As already noted, our cultural backgrounds predispose us to understand certain characteristics of God very well but not to really internalize others. That is why we need contact with Christians from other societies. People from societies different from our own can help us see our cultural blind spots concerning discipleship, to get the logs out of our eyes (Mt. 7:3-5). Once the logs are removed from our eyes, then we are better able to point out the cultural blind spots of others. For example, just this week, some Korean friends told me that American Christians tend to fear three things: death, persecution and poverty. I was able to prayerfully identify two of those fears in myself. Now that we have looked at weaknesses in my cultural background, I feel the freedom to gently point out what appear to be some Confucian influences on my friends.

---

[3] Perhaps a third step in the relationship would be for the missionaries to echo the words of the apostle Paul to the Christian church in Rome: "that you and I may be mutually encouraged by each other's faith" (Rom. 1:12).

When relating with members of another society, we would do well to ask ourselves the question, "What unique aspect of God's desires for human beings do the people of this society reflect?" Once God has shown the answer, we can share it with them. For example, I have learned much about the caring community God wants the church to be from my Chinese brothers and sisters. After sharing the lessons we have learned from them, then we may share aspects of discipleship that they may have missed.

Principle 17: *The "one another" commands in the Bible give us clear directions concerning relationships in the Body of Christ.* God commands us to love one another, forgive one another, submit to one another, bear one another's burdens, offer hospitality to one another, clothe ourselves with humility in dealing with one another and so on (Jn. 13:34; Eph. 4:32, 5:21; Gal. 6:2; 1 Pet. 4:9, 5:5).

As missionaries, we need to be especially attentive to these commands in our relationships both with other missionaries and with those we serve. When we remember the definition of love in 1 Corinthians 13, these commands seem even more challenging. It is sometimes extremely difficult never to be resentful or irritable, and to always bear all things and hope all things.

It is also often difficult for missionaries to admit they have made mistakes. Repenting to those we are called to lead is not something that comes easy to most people. Kraft tells the story of a time when, as a missionary in northern Nigeria, he apologized in public for a mistake he had made. The people were amazed and embarrassed. His leaders told him after the event that they had never heard a missionary apologize before. They were aware that missionaries frequently made mistakes but thought they were either unaware of them or too proud to admit them.

Given the fact that in many societies people are embarrassed if a prestigious person admits a mistake, it is both Scriptural and relationship-building to carefully press through the cultural resistance to social leveling-off that ensues on such sharing. It is, however, important to learn how to make such admissions in culturally approved ways, lest the embarrassment of the hearers cause a greater problem than the original mistake. It is important, then, to have close friends within the society who will tell you when you make a mistake and then help you to decide what to do about it.

The command to forgive one another is probably one of the most difficult to obey for persons of any society. But people from religious backgrounds where karma is paramount, Hindus and Buddhists, and from religions that seek to earn entrance to heaven by good works, may find grace either unfair or unbelievable. And if grace makes no sense, then forgiveness—either receiving it or giving it—may seem impossible. I will never forget a Mainland Chinese scholar friend telling me, "Forgiveness seems crazy to us." For converts with this kind of mindset, learning to live by grace rather than trying to earn God's love and learning to forgive from the heart may take years.

Lewis Smedes has examined the relationship between shame and grace from a Western perspective (1993). There is a need to examine the role of shame in keeping people from internalizing grace and the role of grace in healing shame in other societies. This would be especially helpful in societies where "face" is all-important, such as those in East Asia.

Spiritual Formation for Missionaries

Principle 18: In order to facilitate spiritual growth cross-culturally, the missionary's own relationships with God and others must be healthy. The character, faith, spiritual sensitivity and humility required to carry out the above recommendations do not come easily. Yet most Western training programs for missionaries do not pay nearly enough attention to the spiritual formation and relational skills of cross-cultural workers, assuming that these needs have already been addressed by their churches. The nearly exclusive focus on knowledge in our training does not allow us to give the time and attention we should to the development of spirituality and relational abilities.

The truth is that spiritual formation—or cooperation with God to enable the character of Christ to be formed in us (Gal. 4.19) —is never finished, and it cannot be assumed that enough has taken place earlier in a missionary's training program. Mid-career missionaries probably need to focus on spiritual formation as much as do missionary candidates. Each stage in life has its own unique tests, tests that will bring us closer to God if we are sufficiently prepared to meet them.

It is easy to become discouraged when considering even a few of the character traits needed for godly cross-cultural relationships. Willingness to give up control, humility and a realistic view of suffering, for example, are often developed through trials. And the very characteristics that allow us to pioneer a ministry may become detriments when we attempt to hand over leadership of the ministry to others. Because I have strong leadership gifts, it was not too difficult for me to start an international student fellowship at North Carolina State University. But when it came time to turn over leadership to a student team, the leaders asked me not to attend their meetings so I wouldn't influence them too much. For two long years I could only use my strongest gift in indirect ways. But the fellowship flourished, and the leadership team eventually came to the point where they felt that my presence in the meetings would not be harmful.

Having to die to self in even minor ways reminds us that Christ's Incarnation is our model. Jesus was the ultimate cross-cultural Messenger. He worked with His disciples until He could call them friends rather than servants and He anticipated that they would do greater works than He had done (Jn. 14:12, 15:15). As we begin to experience the reality of Galatians 2:19-20, "I have been crucified with Christ, and it is no longer I who live but it is Christ who lives in me . . ." we are enabled to give up control and empower others.

Paul used several metaphors for his missionary role: farmer, builder, servant and parent, among others (1 Cor. 3:5-9, 1 Thess. 2:9,12). I believe that one of the most helpful is that of midwife (cf. Gal. 4.19). Although the spiritual parent image is a biblical one, it is too easy for many who see themselves as spiritual parents to become paternalistic. The image of midwife suggests participation in the travail of childbirth, a travail experienced by many in intercessory prayer (cf. Col. 2:1). Intercession keeps us dependent on God and reminds us that it is God who gives spiritual birth. And it is the Holy Spirit who produces the fruit, not the missionary. Seeing ourselves as midwives rather than parents might prevent both undue paternalism on our part and dependency on the part of those we have helped come into the Kingdom.

Principle 19: *We should periodically evaluate our Christian relationships and teach others to do the same.* In addition to evaluating their own spiritual formation, missionaries should from time to time also evaluate the Christlikeness of the groups they serve.

James Bryan Smith offers a simple grid for considering relationships. He sees the Christian life in terms of receiving God's acceptance, forgiveness and care and giving acceptance, forgiveness and care to self and others (1995). Accepting, forgiving and caring are all essential blocks for building relationships. As we help our disciples to experience and share these Christians character traits, they will probably need to work in both Kraft's freedom and understanding dimensions in a conscious, deliberate manner. Evaluating relationships will help us see what areas need further development and what may be the strategic starting points for intentional growth.

Shao-leng and I finally became members of the same small group, a group that provided mutual accountability, encouragement and support. It is a joy to be in a friendship relationship after having been a discipler. Shao-leng has engaged in evangelism in ways I never could because she is an insider in Chinese culture. And God has used means I would never have dreamed of to bring her to maturity and to enable her to help others. But relationships with God and with the Christian community, according to her definitions of relationship, have been constants throughout the process. Continually strengthening these relationships is critical for growth in Christ.

Jimmy Long has suggested that the Great Commandments ought to replace the Great Commission as the mandate for Christians in a postmodern world. The Great Commission is centered on truth (teachings) and self (disciples) and implies human progress. The Great Commandments center on relationships and community and imply human weakness, with people needing a loving environment in which to develop their potential in Christ (1997:196-197). There are elements of truth in both perspectives, of course. But most of the peoples of the world are more group-oriented than Westerners, and postmodern Westerners now yearn for community and integration as well. Therefore, it seems beneficial to keep the Great Commandments in mind alongside the Great Commission when we think about our calling. When we strive to obey the Great

Commandments, we line ourselves up with God's intentions for all of creation and cooperate with God in bringing about shalom, the reign of right relationships, in appropriate ways.

Reflection/Application Questions

In concluding this chapter, it might be helpful to focus on some questions that a cross-cultural witnesses might seek to answer in order to work toward better contextualization of the relational dimension of Christianity.

1. What are the major assumptions about appropriate relationships in this society? About proper behavior among people of various roles, statuses and genders? How do they differ from my assumptions?

2. What are the relationship and communication patterns in this society? How are these patterns different from those in my society? (These patterns would include kinship structures, dominant dyads and use of verbal and nonverbal communication among others.)

3. How can I build trust? What words, actions and attitudes may undermine trust?

4. How can I demonstrate *agape* love without being misunderstood? How can I express unconditional acceptance?

5. How should I appropriately show affection to different members of the society (including people of both genders)?

6. How should I express care, concern or sympathy?

7. How should I confront people and resolve personal conflicts? (How can Christians obey Matthew 18 in this society, especially if it is a society that allows only indirect ways of confrontation?)

8. How should I express gratitude?

9.   How are conflicts resolved?

10. How should I express forgiveness?

11. How can I express servant leadership? (What if there is no such concept in the society?)

12. What are the relationship patterns with God (and/or with spiritual beings)? Are there different patterns for different religious groups?

When considering evangelism and discipling in another society:

13. What networks and relationship webs can be used to spread the gospel? What is the appropriate way for such news to be shared in these networks?

14. What do these relationship patterns, both among humans and with supernatural beings, suggest about appropriate evangelism and discipling?

15. Should we be thinking in terms of groups rather than individuals when considering conversion and growth among these people?

16. What can we do to strengthen the bonds between new converts and God? Could any initiation ceremonies and symbols help, in addition to baptism?

17. What are some of the ways you have heard from God? In what other ways has God communicated in the Bible? What means of communication might God be likely to use with the receiving people?

18. What spiritual gifts are most honored and desired in your society? Which ones might be overlooked? What about in the culture in which you work?

19. What influences from your own cultural context promote and hinder relationship with each Person of the Trinity? What about the receiving people?

When evaluating one's spiritual formation and preparation for ministry:

20. Why is it easy for cross-cultural workers to develop paternalistic attitudes? How can we avoid doing so?

21. What character traits do you need to develop in order to model Christlikeness more completely in your relationships?

22. In which of the following relationship skills do you need to grow? Listening, expressing needs, apologizing, giving and receiving constructive criticism, encouraging/affirming, expressing empathy, questioning?

23. How would the communication acts listed above be appropriately expressed among your receiving people?

24. How can the image of midwife apply to your ministry relationships?

25. Using J. B. Smith's criteria for considering relationships, how would you evaluate your relationship with God, self and others? How about relationships within the group you serve?

Chapter 21

Spiritual Power: A Missiological Issue

Charles H. Kraft

Most of the world is heavily involved in enslavement to and manipulation of spiritual powers. In addition, once one is attuned to this fact, even a casual observation of the world Christian scene leads to a recognition that a large percentage of the world's Christians participate in what I have called "dual allegiance." That is, since they find within Christianity little or none of the spiritual power they crave for the meeting of their needs for healing, blessing, guidance, even deliverance from demons, they continue their preChristian practice of going to shamans, priests, diviners, temples, shrines and the like for spiritual power. They may attend church faithfully and be truly committed to Christ on Sundays. But, if they wake up ill on Monday, off they go to the shaman, since they know there's no healing in the church and the hospital is too slow and expensive.

This being so, it seems strange that we find virtually no discussion of spiritual power in publications concerning contextualization. Missionaries, development workers and others who seek to help cross-culturally, since they come largely from the West, have ignored this facet of biblical teaching and social concern. Perhaps the same Western worldview blindness that dominated missionaries working in areas saturated with consciousness of the spirit world has affected our theorizing about contextualization. And just as that blindness kept the missionaries from ever learning to deal adequately with the problems raised, so it keeps us from addressing them in our theoretical treatments. Nor do we give the attention we should to the great need to help Christian converts to deal with spirit world problems in ways that are both biblically and culturally appropriate.

Where are the discussions concerning biblically legitimate and culturally appropriate approaches to such areas of Christian experience as warfare prayer, deliverance from demons, healing, blessing and cursing, dedications, visions, dreams, concepts of the territoriality of spirits, angels, demons and the like? Shouldn't we be discussing the contextualizing of a Christian approach to spiritual warfare? What are the scriptural principles applicable to every cultural situation and what are the cultural variables in this important area? Something as important to nonWestern and, increasingly, to Western Christians needs to be discussed and dealt with.

The Biblical Validity of Dealing with Spiritual Power

Though the concept has been questioned by ivory tower theoreticians, spiritual warfare is an important biblical reality and, for those of us who are practitioners, a continual existential reality (see Guelich 1991). Jesus treated Satan and demonic forces as real foes, frequently casting out demons and thus setting free people he called "captives" and "oppressed" (Lk. 4:18). Such language is warfare language. Furthermore, He calls Satan "the ruler of this world" (Jn. 14:30). In a similar vein, Paul refers to Satan as "the evil god of this world" who blinds people to God's Good News (2 Cor. 4:4) and John says, "the whole world is under the rule of the Evil One" (1 Jn. 5:19).

Like most of the world today, biblical peoples saw the world as populated by enemy spirits that could cause trouble if they were not properly dealt with. Unfortunately, through most of its history, the people of Israel chose to deal with these spirits as the animistic peoples around them did rather than as God commanded them to. So God is constantly warning His people against worshiping the gods (= demons) of the nations around them and punishing them when they disobey. We know that our God is a patient God. He has demonstrated this countless times in his dealings with human beings. But there are areas of life, especially those dealing with the counterfeiting of His power-oriented activities in which He has made it clear that there is to be no compromise. This has to be factored in at every point in any discussion of contextualization in relation to spiritual power.

Note, as one of many examples, what God said to Solomon in 1 Kings 11 (esp. vv. 9-13) concerning the penalty he would have to pay because he disobeyed God by turning to other gods. God was angry with Solomon and took the kingdom away from his son because of his idolatry. In Acts 5, then, Peter asks Ananias why he "let Satan take control" of him (v. 3) that he should lie to the Holy Spirit about the price of the property he had sold. And in 1 Corinthians 10:20-21 we are warned against eating what has been offered to demons. This warning, then, is given even more sternly in Revelation 2:14 and 20.

But Jesus came "to destroy what the Devil had done" (1 Jn. 3:8) and gives His followers "power and authority to drive out all demons and to cure diseases" (Lk. 9:1) and to do the works that he himself did while on earth (Jn. 14:12). We can't be either biblical or relevant to most of the peoples of the world without a solid approach to spiritual power.

A Personal Failure

"What can we do about evil spirits?" This was a burning question for the Nigerian leaders I was attempting to guide. But I, their missionary, knew virtually nothing about the subject. My three volume seminary theology textbook only had two references to Satan and none to demons. And that's about all I had learned about the enemy kingdom and its activities, in spite of the prominence of that subject in Scripture. So my Nigerian friends were on their own. I couldn't help them.

But now, forty years later, God has led me into regular and frequent open conflict with demonic "rats" with the aim of setting captives free. I deeply regret that I didn't know in the late 1950s what I know now. In that setting, I contributed to the growth of a dual allegiance church. That memory plus my present experience has led me to commit myself to raise this issue wherever possible in missiological circles in hopes that coming generations will be better able to deal with spiritual power than I was.

Spiritual Power in Balance

In any discussion of contextualization in relation to spiritual power, we need to keep our focus balanced. We have spoken in a previous chapter of the need for contextualizers to do their work in three crucial dimensions. As pointed out there, these dimensions are 1) our allegiance/ relationship to Christ with all the love and obedience that entails, 2) the understanding that comes from continually experiencing His truth and 3) the spiritual power Jesus gives us to use as He used it to express His love and bring freedom to others.

For spiritual power in Scripture, though prominent, is never an end in and of itself. It must always be balanced by concern for our relationship with God and for God's truth. When Jesus' followers came back from a power-filled excursion into the towns and villages of Galilee reporting with excitement that "even the demons obeyed us when we gave them a command in your name" (Lk. 10:17), Jesus cautioned them and pointed them to something more important. That more important thing is our *relationship* with the God who provides the power. This relationship, resulting in our names being written in heaven (Lk. 10:20), is, according to Jesus, to be a greater cause of rejoicing than even our power over demons.

So, as crucial as the power issue is both scripturally and contextually, the relationship issue is even more important. As evangelicals, of course, we've recognized the importance of emphasizing the need of a commitment to Christ resulting in a freeing and saving relationship with Him. In focusing on spiritual power, we must be careful not to de-emphasize or neglect all the love and other fruits of the Spirit that that relationship entails (see Chapter 17).

Nor dare we neglect the issue of truth. Jesus spent most of His time teaching, demonstrating and leading His followers into truth. In keeping with the implications of the Greek word for truth, this is to be an experienced truth, not simply intellectual truth. That continual experiencing of the truth, then, leads to ever deepening understanding both of the truth dimension of Christianity and also of the power and relationship dimensions.

For this experienced truth dimension is, according to John 8:31-2, based on obedience to Jesus within the relationship. And all bearing of fruit, including the fruit of spiritual power, is dependent, according to John 15:1-17, on our abiding in Christ. We are, then, to encounter people and the enemy in contextually appropriate ways with a balance of allegiance, truth and power encounters (see Kraft 1991b). Any approach to Christianity that neglects or ignores any of these three dimensions is an incomplete and unbalanced Christianity.

Though, as mentioned, evangelical Christianity has usually been deficient in dealing with spiritual power, it has been strong on the truth dimension. And it has focused to some extent on allegiance and relationship, though in practice this dimension has often been treated largely as a byproduct of truth and knowledge. Pentecostal and charismatic Christianity have often been more relevant to the peoples of the nonWestern world through their emphasis on spiritual power, but have often compromised their strength through overemphasis on tongues and emotion and/or a negative attitude toward the cultures of the receptor peoples.

When we look at these three dimensions in relation to Western evangelical missionary work, we come up with a chart such as the following:

	ALLEGIANCE	**TRUTH**	**POWER**
TRADITIONAL RELIGION	Wrong Allegiance	Counterfeit Truth	Satanic Power
WESTERN CHRISTIANITY	True Allegiance	God's Truth	
BIBLICAL CHRISTIANITY	True Allegiance	God's Truth	God's Power

Figure 21.1 Three Crucial Dimensions

Since the power dimension has not been dealt with by the advocates of (Western) Christianity, the people continue to go to their traditional sources of power, even though they have pledged allegiance to Christ and are learning biblical truth. Any attempt to rectify this situation must apply biblical emphasis and guidelines to the missing dimension.

Secularization or a Bridge from Power to Power?

Western witness, having largely ignored spiritual power issues, has tended to unwittingly recommend secularization as the antidote to traditional approaches to obtaining spiritual power. Western secular medicine and hospitals, for example, are offered as the answer to health problems, secularizing schools as the right way to deal with what Westerners perceived as ignorance, secular agricultural techniques, even secular approaches to church management and leadership, not to mention insights into culture and communication that largely leave out the activity of the Holy Spirit.

With this approach, is it any wonder that mission-planted churches around the world are deeply involved in secularizing their members? I believe it was

Lesslie Newbigin who said that Christian missions have been the greatest secularizing force in all of history. Without intending it, then, our strategy has been to secularize in order to christianize.

What this approach has produced, is secular churches (like most of those we have in the home countries), that depend almost entirely on the power of secular techniques and structures to replace traditional methods of blessing, healing, teaching and organizing. There is, of course, a certain amount of power in these techniques. But it is stronger on human and/or naturalistic power than on spiritual power, even though it often replaces what people have traditionally sought in spiritual ways. For example, for most of the traditional peoples of the world, healing was/is a spiritual matter, not a secular one. So is agriculture and human and animal fertility. In the West, however, we have secularized each of these matters.

Pennoyer (1990) suggests that secularization can assist Christian evangelization by breaking the domination of spiritual power in people's lives. Though this may be true in some cases, I'm afraid secularization has for many peoples clouded rather than assisted much of what a scriptural approach to conversion should engender. For it has changed the subject from what ought to have been a change from one spiritual power source to another (e.g. from satanic power to that of Jesus), to a change from spiritual answers to secular answers for problems that traditional peoples have always regarded as spiritual.

Simply moving from a pagan power source to the true God as the Source is, I believe, the shortest bridge for power-oriented people since it involves little or no conversion from spiritual power to secular power. The conversion is, rather, from one power source (Satan) to another power Source (God), as it was for Abraham. The cultural results of an approach that focuses on such change of power source are likely to be forms of Christianity that look very similar to their pagan predecessors but with a different power Source. The Christian practitioners would look very like native shamans and other healers, but would work only in ways appropriate to biblical Christianity and only under the power of the true God. The places of worship and the ways in which worship and other rituals are conducted would look as much like their pagan predecessors as the places and rituals Abraham captured for the true God looked like their predecessors.

As with Israel, the practices and personnel would undoubtedly change over time to be less like their pagan models, especially where these God-exalting practices prohibited such God-condemned activities as divination. But they would have started at points familiar to the people rather than with foreign practices that give the impression that God's whole system has to be imported. And when prohibited practices in the spiritual power area are substituted for, let the substitution be a spiritual power substitution, not a secular one.

I will speak more specifically in the following chapter about such substitutions.

Relationship Between Spirit and Human Worlds

In dealing with spiritual power cross-culturally, there are a variety of basic principles to be made explicit. Among them is the scriptural fact that there is a close relationship between what goes on in human life and what goes on in the spirit realm. We learn from the discussion between God and Satan in Job 1 and again from Jesus' statement that Satan wanted to sift the apostles like wheat (Lk. 22:31-32) that Satan is anxious to assert himself to disrupt our lives. We learn from Daniel 10:13 (an answer to prayer delayed by a demonic being) and 2 Corinthians 4:4 (Satan blinding unbelievers) that the enemy can sometimes be successful in thwarting God's plans. And we learn from the ministries of Jesus and His disciples that we can thwart at least some of the enemy's plans by casting demons out of people. In addition, the angels and, presumably demons as well, are watching us as we carry out our activities (Eph. 3:10;1 Tim. 5:21; 1 Pet. 1:12).

Satan, the Contextualizer

Satan is an excellent contextualizer. He does an expert job at meeting people at the point of their felt needs in culturally appropriate ways. The fact that he often does so through deceit is not usually recognized. I am told that there's a Japanese volcano where people have erected signs imploring the spirits not to allow it to erupt again. There are also shrines and a temple there at which visitors can add their petitions to those of decades' worth of earlier visitors. Satan's ability to deceive in Japan in contextually appropriate ways is enhanced by the fact that the language shows no adequate distinction between ordinary spirits and a high God. All are called *kami* and generally considered to be of the same nature and capriciousness. Attempting to appease the *kami* of the volcanic mountain is, therefore, not seen as essentially different from what Christians do on Sundays, except by the handful of Christians who have gone deeply enough into biblical Christianity to understand the difference.

In addition, our enemy has duped a large percentage of the world's population into believing that ancestors continue to participate in human affairs. All he needs to do now to be culturally relevant is to assign demons to impersonate those who have died. With regard to reincarnation, likewise, he has long since convinced people of the logic of the recycling of persons. All he has to do in this matter is to assign demons to recount for people the details of the lives of real people who lived in the past, as if these lives were their former lives. Very convincing, and very contextualized. And, since people have such a felt need for spiritual power, how better to gain control of them than by giving certain of them (e.g., shamans) that power. Shamans, however, know that in repayment for the use of that power during their lifetimes they will die a horrible death. But they consider it worth the cost for the power and prestige they have been given.

In addition to these larger areas of satanic contextualization, demonic beings are quite skilled at providing for "smaller" felt needs for such things as money, position, fame, control, revenge, even security and wantedness. But all with an eventual price tag attached. I read a letter once from a woman who made a pact with the Devil, bargaining for power, prestige and wealth. She promised him in writing that if he would give her these things, she would give him her first son and every first son from then on in the families of her descendents. The report I heard was that it can be shown now, about three generations later, that each of the first sons in her family have suffered major problems of one sort or another—problems of the kind that lead one to suspect that the lady's pact with the Devil is in effect.

Satan's Predictability

A principle that becomes apparent when we study the enemy is that the ways in which he works are quite predictable. I believe we can deduce from Scripture that angels are sterile and uncreative. So, instead of originating things or ideas, Satan and his hosts spend their time counterfeiting and damaging those things that God has brought into existence. They can, however, influence people who are creative and thus, through deceit, gain some ability to originate. Whatever creativity Satan has, therefore, comes from the humans he deceives.

Though he depends on this stealing of human talents, his activities tend to be easily recognizable by those who understand the ways in which he works. For example, I have often been able to figure out how a demon has been functioning by simply asking myself the question, "If I were a demon (or Satan), what would I do in this situation?"

Perhaps this is what Paul was getting at in 2 Corinthians 2:11 when he stated that "we know what [Satan's] plans [or devices or schemes] are." It is fairly obvious, for example, that he works in terms of human constants such as pride and the desire for prestige, position and power. He is active in promising such things, allowing good to happen for a time and then "closing in" on people, making them pay for whatever he has given them. It is predictable that he will deceive people into believing his promises and accepting his gifts. He does this more often by telling partial and twisted truths than by lying. His gifts, however, counterfeit the things God gives, since he has nothing of his own making to give. Thus, he counterfeits healing gifts (even deliverance) and gifts of prophecy, knowledge, wisdom, even tongues.

He counterfeits spiritual reality by producing religious systems (biblical faith is not intended to be a religion—see Chapter 6) that are quite logical once people believe the basic lie or deceit underlying them. What is more logical than to believe that people get recycled through reincarnation once one has accepted ideas such as that one life is not enough to accomplish all that we're meant to accomplish or that because baby looks like dead grandpa, he is a reincarnation of grandpa? And how logical it is to worship something inside or outside of human beings, once one has concluded that whatever lies beyond the grave is unknowable. It is also logical to assume that negative things that happen today are the result of revenge taken by dissatisfied ancestors, once one has believed that ancestors remain a part of the living community after death. We note, however, how predictable it is that our enemy will always in some way direct attention to humans, spirits or created objects under his control as the objects of worship, never to the Creator of all (see Rom. 1:16-25).

And doctrinally, the counterfeit systems of faith are disturbingly similar to what God has revealed in Judeo-Christianity. Advocating righteousness, truth, peace, gentleness, the Ten Commandments and other admirable virtues seems so much like what Jesus taught. How can those systems be wrong merely because they leave out the need for a relationship with Jesus? And what, many people ask, is the difference between the Christian belief that God became one of us in Incarnation and the similar concept in Hinduism? Just about every Christian doctrine and ritual has its parallels in the religions of the world, making sense to the people who practice them and imitating God's truth. And animistic systems are amazingly similar worldwide, leading us to suspect that there is a single mind behind them.

Since Satan's objective is to counter God and disrupt His creation, it is predictable that he will attempt to turn good things into bad (or at least unattractive), make bad things worse and get people who insist on pursuing good things to go after them in exaggerated ways. In tempting, then, he seldom simply opposes things, choosing rather to raise questions about rightness, fairness and the like, as he did in the Garden of Eden. He prefers to work in terms of deceit rather than with outright lies.

Another satanic predictability, playing off a human vulnerability, is that, once he has planted a deceit or a lie, he seems to "train" humans to perpetuate that untruth themselves. Thus, the deceit on which reincarnation and ancestor cults are based gets perpetuated within the human community generation after generation, probably without much help from satanic beings themselves. And, since meanings are difficult to change (see below), the staying power of such lies is great.

So, in looking at Satan's activities cross-culturally, we need to look for many quite predictable things. We need to recognize, however, that these predictabilities will be in terms of the ways of thinking and behaving of the receptor society, whether or not they fit our logic. That is, Satan contextualizes his deceit. In Western societies, for example, where people are quite unaware of spiritual reality, Satan likes to capture people through apparently innocent games such as Dungeons and Dragons, through membership in apparently constructive organizations such as Freemasonry, through philosophical or psychological ideas that appear erudite and innocent. In nonWestern, family-oriented societies what could be more logical than the satanic lie that one's ancestors are still alive and participating in the lives of their descendents? Or that it would be better to be with my ancestors when I die, even if they are in hell, than to go to heaven? Or that people reincarnate after they die?

Cross-Cultural Constants

As in all of life, beyond the differences in cultural understandings and expression, there are basic things that are the same cross-culturally. In working for God there are basics such as obedience to Him, preceded by listening to Him and following His leading whether in life in general or in bringing freedom to captives. With regard to Satan's kingdom, there are basics relating to how Satan attracts people, how he influences and/or enters them and the kind of strategies he uses to keep them under his influence. In addition to these basics concerning God and Satan, there are certain basics of human beingness relating to such things as how we use our wills, our capability for relating to the spirit world, our vulnerability to temptation and deceit and the like.

That both God and Satan work in partnership with people in terms of their culture is a constant we can expect to find in every cultural context. Underlying this fact is the fact that both God and Satan have plans for any given people and their culture and work with human will to seek to accomplish those plans. Though it is apparent that Satan is having great influence on the human scene, we learn from Scripture, especially the events surrounding Jesus' life, death and resurrection, that God is working out His own purposes in the background and that Satan's ultimate defeat is certain. We, therefore, can expect to find both Satan and God working in every cultural context. Satan, of course, has his human representatives working hard to expand his kingdom. We believe, however, that God is not inactive in any cultural situation. According to Romans 1:16-2:16, God is working in conscience and culture so that, whatever excuses those who choose Satan's way may give, they are accountable to God for their disobedience.

Person and Culture

In dealing with culture, it is always important to distinguish cultural structure from the persons who operate that structuring. Contextualization studies usually focus on the structuring, leaving implicit the fact that it is people who produce and operate that structuring. Culture does not run itself. Culture simply lies there, like the roads we drive on or, to change the metaphor, like the script of a play, memorized but regularly altered by the actors for a variety of reasons, some good, some bad.

In dealing with spiritual reality, it is important to recognize that we have both human persons and spirit beings involved in the way cultural structuring is used. Most cultural structuring is capable of being used either for good or for evil. Such things as status and prestige, for example, provided by a society on the basis of birth and/or achievement, can be used by those who have them either to help others or to hurt them. The fact that given people have status and the power that goes with it is not in and of itself a bad thing. Satan, however, entices people to use their status to hurt others while God gently prods His people to use their status and the authority and power that goes with it to assist the powerless.

But in each case, the spiritual being (God or Satan) works with people, and in terms of the cultural structuring in which the people are involved. In dealing with spiritual warfare, as with all studies of contextualization, our focus needs to be on *people* within culture, not simply on culture itself.

The important place of human habit must, however, be recognized. Culture seems to have power over people because people follow cultural guidelines through force of habit. That is, the apparent power of culture is in reality the power of human habit. Thus, any attempts to change culture are really attempts to change human habits. The structuring is a function of the script produced by and followed, for the most part, fairly closely by the actors out of habit (once they have memorized it). It is, however, often creatively changed by them, either because they forgot, or because something didn't go as planned, or simply because they chose to be creative. When we find enemy influence contextualized within sociocultural patterns and habitually followed, we appeal for people to change their habits so that they use either their present cultural patterns or changed ones for godly purposes. The point is, our appeal is always to *people* to change habits, with or without a change in structure. We cannot appeal to an impersonal thing like a cultural structure or pattern.

Forms, Meanings, and Empowerment

A very important issue in any discussion of contextualization is the difference between cultural forms and their meanings. By "forms" we mean all of the customs and structures, visible and invisible that make up a culture. By "meanings" we mean the personal interpretations that yield a people's understandings of these forms. The forms are the parts of culture. The meanings exist, not in the forms themselves, but in the people who use the forms. Meanings are attached by people, according to the agreements of their group concerning what the forms signify.

By virtue of the fact that people participating in the same sociocultural group agree with each other what significance to attach to each cultural form, they can communicate with each other. If they did not agree, they could not communicate. This is the problem with people who speak different languages. Though the members of each language group use essentially the same sounds, they organize them differently. Members of another language group, then, cannot even interpret accurately words that sound familiar to them, since they are not in on the agreements of the speakers of the first language. Though they have been taught to agree with the members of their language group what particular combinations of sounds mean, they do not know what the agreements of the other group are unless they learn that language. Language learning, like all culture learning, is a matter of learning the agreements concerning meanings that the new group habitually attaches to the sound forms they use in speaking to each other.

A major problem in contextualization is the problem of changing the meanings of familiar forms. In seeking to assist people to accept and practice Christianity in terms of their own cultural forms, we are assisting them to use those forms for new purposes and, therefore, to attach new or modified meanings to them. When John the Baptist began to use baptism within the Jewish community to initiate people into his renewal movement, he was reinterpreting a form that was well known as a way of initiating Gentile converts into Judaism. This cultural form was also used by Greek mystery religions as an initiation ceremony. When the Church decided to use it to signify initiation into the Church, they were largely following John's lead, since the early Christians assumed that Christianity was to remain within Judaism. When the Church used baptism in Gentile territory, then, the meaning was more in keeping with that signified by its use in the initiation of Gentiles into Judaism. In either case the meaning was in part the same as that of previous practice and in part a modification of that meaning. Jesus, then, took the Jewish Passover meal and reinterpreted it into what we call the Lord's Supper. In addition to these cultural forms, the Early Church reinterpreted words such as *theos* (God), *ekklesia* (church), *kurios* (Lord), *agape* (love) and a host of other Greek words.

But cultural forms can also be *empowered* by spirit beings. God regularly flows his power through words such as "in Jesus' Name" and the commands we give to demons. When such words are conveying God's power, we call them "empowered language forms." James recommends that we use anointing oil to bring healing to the sick (Jas. 5:14). But if the oil is to be effective, it needs to be dedicated in the name of Jesus and thus empowered. The elements used in the Lord's Supper can (and should) also be dedicated for specific purposes such as blessing and healing and thus empowered. Paul's handkerchiefs and aprons were empowered so that people received healing through them (Ac. 19:12). Likewise, with Jesus' robe (Lk. 8:43-48).

In many nonChristian societies, it is the usual thing for at least certain people to dedicate the things they make to spirits or gods, especially if those things are to be used for religious purposes or in dangerous pursuits. In the South Pacific, for example, those who made the large canoes used for fishing and/or for warfare regularly dedicated them to their gods. I suspect they still do, even if they call themselves Christians. When such things are dedicated to satanic spirits, they are empowered by those spirits. Many a missionary and traveler who bought dedicated things and took them home has experienced difficulties related to the fact that by putting those objects in his home, he has unwittingly invited enemy spirits into the home.

Nevertheless, breaking the power of such objects is usually not difficult. Since we have infinitely more power in Jesus Christ than such objects can contain, we simply have to claim his power to break the enemy's power in the object. After claiming the power of Jesus to break enemy power in such objects, then, I usually go on to bless the object in the name of Jesus. The problem with satanic empowerment is not whether we have the power to break it but overcoming our ignorance so that we know when it is there and what to do to break it.

In contextualizing the power of Christ, it is important to disempower whatever has been empowered with satanic power before attempting to use it. Satanic power can, however, be broken over rituals, buildings, carvings, songs and almost any other custom or artifact a people wants to capture for God's use. Despite the fact that many counsel us to refuse to use whatever the enemy has used, I believe we are to *capture* cultural forms, not reject them merely because our enemy has been using them. But we shouldn't try to use them until the power is broken. That would be unwise in the extreme.

The bigger problem is, however, the meaning problem. It may take two or three generations before the preChristian meanings associated in people's minds with a given object can be fully replaced. People often want to throw away every vestige of their culture that reminds them of their old involvement with shamans, rituals and evil spirits. In their place, however, they tend to borrow foreign stuff to which they often attach dubious meanings (such as sacredness simply because it is not understood) and which signals that God wants them to be foreigners in their own country rather than to capture their traditions for Christ. But, since we Westerners have so poorly understood the spiritual power dimensions of our movement, we have often gone along with and even encouraged the people's desire to dissimulate. And this has enabled them to produce a Christianity that is as powerless as ours in the West and, thus, unattractive to most of the people of their lands except as it has provided such things as human status, prestige and power.

We should not, however, give up, especially since the danger posed by secularization is so great. Though we have not, perhaps, learned very well how to build the short bridge between animism and Christianity, we should have learned by now that a secularized Christianity (the usual form in most missionized lands) is a long way from the Bible in the area of spiritual power. When people have learned to depend on secular medicine without the power of God, rather than either medicine as a gift from God or direct healing through prayer, they have moved away from the spirituality of the Scriptures and it is difficult to reindoctrinate them.

Levels of Warfare

Spiritual warfare has to be waged on at least two levels. The lower level is what I call "ground-level warfare." The upper level, then, is ordinarily known as "cosmic-level warfare" (called "strategic-level warfare" by Wagner). Ground-level warfare involves dealing with spirits (demons) that inhabit persons. My experience would suggest that personal spirits or demons are of at least three kinds: family, occult and "ordinary."

Ground-Level Spirits (living in people)		
1.	**Family Spirits** (resulting from dedications to family gods)	
2.	**Occult Spirits** (resulting from occult allegiances)	
3.	**"Ordinary" Spirits** (attached to sinful attitudes and emotions)	

Figure 21.2 Ground-Level Spirits

Family and occult demons usually seem to be stronger than the "ordinary" demons, but dealing with them is essentially the same as dealing with ordinary demons. Family and occult spirits (including the spirits of nonChristian religions) gain their power through conscious or unconscious dedication to them. They, then, are passed down from generation to generation even after the practice of dedication has ceased (e.g., because a person has become a Christian). "Ordinary" spirits are those that empower emotions such as fear, shame and anger, plus problems such as lust, suicide, rebellion and many others. In each case, demons can only inhabit people by legal right. Rights are given through such means as dedications and wallowing in sinful emotions. In each case there is a human cause that gives the spirits access.

At cosmic level we are dealing with at least five kinds of higher-level spirits that I have labeled territorial, institutional, vice, nature and ancestral.

Cosmic-Level Spirits (in the air, Eph. 2:2)
1. **Territorial Spirits** such as those over nations mentioned in Daniel 10:13 and 21 (called "Prince of Persia" and "Prince of Greece"), spirits over regions and spirits over cities
2. **Institutional Spirits** such as those assigned to churches, governments, educational institutions, occult organizations (e.g., Scientology, Freemasonry, Mormonism), nonChristian religions (e.g., the gods of Hinduism, Buddhism, animism), temples, shrines
3. **Vice Spirits** such as those assigned to oversee and encourage special functions including vices such as prostitution, abortion, homosexuality, gambling, pornography, war, music, cults and the like
4. **Nature, Household and Cultural Item Spirits** such as those residing in trees, rivers, homes and cultural items such as dedicated work implements, music, rituals, artifacts used in religious worship and the like
5. **Ancestor Spirits**, believed by many peoples to be their physically dead ancestors who still participate in the activities of the living community

Figure 21.3 Cosmic-Level Spirits

Cosmic-level spirits are apparently in charge of ground-level spirits, assigning them to people and supervising them as they carry out their assignments in people or do their tempting and harassing of people from outside of them.

Jesus, of course, frequently encountered and cast out ground-level demons. The evidence that He dealt with higher level spirits is, however, slim except in his encounter with Satan himself (Lk. 4:1-13). I suspect, though, that in confronting and defeating Satan in his own territory (i.e., the wilderness was considered the property of Satan) at this time, Jesus broke much of Satan's power over at least that part of Palestine. And some have suggested that the demons afflicting the Gerasene demoniac (Lk. 8:26-33) were territorial spirits. If so, they were concentrated in one man, like ground-level demons and dealt with in the same way Jesus dealt with those whose assignment was purely ground level.

Discussions of the contextualization of biblical understandings of the spirit world and spiritual warfare need to take into account these levels of spirits and what to do about them. See the following chapter.

Conclusion

We have surveyed some of the aspects of spiritual power that need to be carefully but effectively dealt with in any consideration of appropriate Christianity. It is unfortunate that, in most situations missionized from the West, these issues have not been taken seriously. Or, if they were taken seriously, the whole culture was condemned as if the evil were in the customs of the people rather than in Satan working behind the scenes. Since spiritual power was not dealt with properly, then, converts have often moved into an allegiance to Christ without fully giving up their previous allegiances to traditional spirits and gods. This and many other problems that have arisen because of the lack of attention to the contextualization of spiritual power desperately need to be faced and worked through to discover answers that are both scripturally and culturally appropriate.

Chapter 22

Appropriate Contextualization of Spiritual Power

Charles H. Kraft

In the preceding chapter I have asked, Where are the discussions concerning biblically legitimate and culturally appropriate approaches to spiritual power? It should be an important part of Missiology to deal with cross-cultural issues such as the activities of demons, blessing and cursing, dedications, visions, dreams, concepts of the territoriality of spirits, angels, demons, warfare prayer and the like. Given the prominence of such subjects in Scripture, we should be seeking scriptural principles concerning the treatment of such issues in the societies into which Christianity is being introduced.

It is a sad fact of the Western missionary effort that these topics have usually been overlooked, leaving people to fend for themselves in dealing with the evil spiritual realities that surround them. Most of the peoples to whom we go as missionaries are very aware of the strong influence of evil spirits in their life and that of their neighbors. But new Christians. and many who have been following Christ for some time, need the help of outsiders who have both studied the Scriptures and had experience with the evil spirit world themselves. Unfortunately, there are too few of such people around.

But things are changing a bit. There now are several of us teaching courses on spiritual warfare, writing on the subject and doing the works that Jesus promised we would do in relation to the evil spirit world (Jn. 14:12, 20:21; Lk. 9:1-2). From such activities, then, we can at least point to ways in which we can explore the contextualization of a Christian approach to spiritual power.

The Danger of Overcontextualization

We start with a warning. We will be taking spiritual warfare seriously, for there is both a need for such activity and scriptural precedent for it. But there are plenty of examples of people "going off the deep end" in this area. Whether out of unfamiliarity with the spirit world or the uncritical adopting of preChristian ways of dealing with spirit world problems or for some other reason, many have fallen into unacceptable practices—practices that don't fit into scriptural guidelines and, often, don't even measure up to common sense.

I use the term "overcontextualization" to signify situations in which people have come to practice at least parts of their Christianity, and in this case techniques relating to spiritual power, in ways that fit in with the surrounding culture but fail to measure up to biblical standards.   Appropriate Christianity balances cultural appropriateness with scriptural appropriateness.   An overcontextualized Christianity loses that appropriateness at the scriptural end, though it may serve well the culturally inculcated desires of any given society.

Though it is of great importance to see the use of spiritual power contextualized, it is also of great importance not to overdo it.   By this I mean that there are several ways in which people have gotten into spiritual power and carried their emphasis too far.   One of the perversions that is widespread in America is the so-called "Name it, claim it" or "Word faith" heresy.   Advocates of this approach teach that if we generate enough faith and with it claim anything we might happen to want, we can manipulate God into doing our will. We can thus gain material things, healing or whatever strikes our fancy.   God wants us to be prosperous, they say, so all we have to do is to produce the faith and He will grant us our desires.   This is overcontextualization because it makes God captive to the American ideal of prosperity for everyone and seeks to use His power for our ends.

Another perversion is the one that holds that since God *can* heal without the use of medicine, we should not use medicine.   There are, unfortunately, several deaths every year in the United States as a result of people denying themselves or their children medical assistance on this premise.   They fail to see that it is God who heals through medicine and doctors as well as apart from them.   And when we demand that God do the healing in the way we prescribe for Him, we are really guilty of trying to manipulate God to do our will in our way.

The opposite is also an overcontextualization.   Many Christians have so secularized their understandings of healing that they place all their faith in medicine and doctors and little or none in God.   If someone is ill or experiencing emotional problems, their only thought is to get them to medical or psychological help, perhaps with a perfunctory prayer that God will lead the secular professional.   If they pray at all in earnest concerning healing it is only after all secular means have failed.

In many societies, Christian healers use the methods of shamans rather uncritically.   In Korea, Africa, India and other places, for example, an unfortunately large number of pastors who seek to bring about physical healing and deliverance, do so by using violence, loudness and other very unChristlike dramatic techniques in their ministries.   Both in Korea and in Africa I have heard of people being beaten in attempts to free them from demons.   Certain American healers are also given to dramatic displays that make good drama but are quite unlikely to be methods Jesus would endorse.

Such methods are overcontextualizations since they may be appropriate to at least subgroups within any given society but they are not appropriate to

Scripture. That is, they are manipulative and do not manifest the love, faith and good sense that we see in scriptural personages such as Jesus and Paul.

Animism vs. God-Given Authority

Most of the world, including most of the adherents of so-called "world religions," practice what anthropologists and missiologists call "animism." This is the belief, and the practices that go with it, that the world is full of spirits that can hurt us unless we are careful to appease them. Animists may or may not believe in a high god. When they do, he is usually seen as benign and thus in need of little if any attention. Animists agree, however, that the spirits need to be watched and kept happy, lest the spirits hurt them. In addition, animists believe that evil spirits can inhabit material objects and places such as certain mountains (e.g., Old Testament high places), trees, statues (e.g., idols), rocks (e.g., the Ka'aba in Mecca), rivers (e.g. the Ganges), territories, fetishes, charms and any other thing or place that is dedicated to the spirits. Animists also believe in magic and the ability of at least certain people to convey power via curses, blessings, spells and the like.

What the Bible teaches concerning spiritual power both recognizes the validity of the power and the power techniques practiced by animists and teaches us to use similar techniques based on similar principles but with the true God as our Source of power. The deceptive thing is that much of what God does and endorses looks on the surface like what animists do. There is a reason why this is true and I deal with this below. But those without experience and understanding of what's going on in the interaction between the spirit world and the human world can easily miss it.

The reason why animism and Christianity look so similar is that the basic difference between them and us is not at the surface level. It is in the source of power. In areas such as healing, dedicating and blessing, for example, we and animists do essentially the same things but the source of their power is Satan, the Source of ours is God. We learn both from Scripture and from practical experience that many, if not all, of the rules that apply to God's interactions with humans also apply to the ways the enemy interacts with us (see Kraft, ed. 1994, Chapter 2). For example, obedience to God in prayer, worship, sacrifice and service enables Him to carry out His purposes in the world. On the other side, when people obey Satan in these same ways, he is enabled to accomplish his purposes. The importance of obedience and the fact that this is a warfare issue are thus underlined.

For example, animists believe that objects such as idols or implements used in religious rituals may be dedicated to gods or spirits and thus *contain* spiritual power. The Bible shows that objects can be dedicated to our God and thus *convey* His power (e.g., Paul's handkerchiefs, the Ark of the Covenant). On the surface, containing and conveying power look the same, especially since what animists believe to be power *contained* in objects is in reality satanic power *conveyed* by them.

For another example, animist diviners, shamans, priests, etc., can heal with the power of Satan. So can God. The fact that satanic healing leads sooner or later to captivity and misery is not immediately apparent to the one healed. More immediately obvious is the fact that God's healing leads to freedom and peace. But at first, both types of healing look the same and people who seek healing rather than the Healer are easily deceived, especially since demons seem often to work faster than God does.

Our authority as Christians versus the authority Satan can give his followers is an important issue at this point. Those who don't know the difference between God-given authority to work in spiritual power and what animists do, accuse those of us who are working in God's power of practicing "Christian animism" (e.g., Priest, T. Campbell, and Mullen 1995). But when we exercise the power and authority Jesus gives us to do things animists do, such as healing, casting out demons, blessing people and objects, dedicating buildings, praying for rain or against floods, we are not animists because we are working in God's power, not Satan's. We are simply exercising the authority Jesus gave His disciples (Lk. 9:1) and told them to teach to their followers (Mt. 28:19).

We may summarize some of the major issues in this discussion by means of Figure 22.1 designed to show many of the contrasts between animism and God-given authority. Note again that the primary expressions of each of these areas will look very similar at the surface level. It is in the underlying power and motivations that they differ.

Satan is very good at protecting himself from what he knows to be a power much greater than his. He knows that God has infinitely more power than he has and that Jesus passed this power on to us. His primary strategy, therefore, is to keep God's people ignorant and deceived so that we cannot use God's power against him.

A very important first step in contextualizing spiritual power, therefore, is to help people to know who they are scripturally and how this is to be expressed culturally. Scripturally, we are the children of God, made in His image, redeemed by Jesus Christ to be heirs of God and joint heirs with Him (Rom. 8:17). This gives us all the power and authority Jesus gave His followers to cast out demons and cure diseases (Lk. 9:1), to do the works Jesus Himself did (Jn. 14:12), to be in the world what Jesus was (Jn. 20:21) and to crush the enemy under our feet (Rom. 16:20). Scripturally, then, we need to follow Jesus' example, always using His power to show His love.

Christians in other societies, like we in the West, then, will be accountable to God to resist traditional cultural models for the exercise of power. We need, rather to discover or create models that will be interpreted by cultural insiders as consonant with Scripture. But what are appropriate ways of exercising power in love in their cultural contexts may look quite different from the appropriate expressions in Western societies. For many Euroamericans set a poor example of scriptural contextualization in this area. Instead, we often show captivity to our home cultural models in our approaches rather than working out scripturally appropriate use (capture) of traditional customs, with or without modification.

	ANIMISM	*GOD-GIVEN AUTHORITY*
POWER	Believed to be *contained in* people and objects	God *conveys* His power *through* people and objects
NEED (in order to utilize spiritual power)	Felt need to learn how to manipulate spirit power through magic or authority over spirits	We are to submit to God & learn to work with Him in the exercise of power and authority from Him
ONTOLOGY (what is really going on)	Power from Satan: He is the one who manipulates	Power from God: He empowers and uses us
GOD	God is good but distant, therefore ignore Him	God is good, therefore relate to Him. He is close and involved with us
SPIRITS	Fearful and can hurt us, therefore appease them	They are defeated, therefore assert God's authority over them
PEOPLE	Victims of capricious spirits who never escape from being victims	They are captives, but we can assert Jesus' authority to free them
COST	Those who receive power from Satan suffer great tragedy later	Those who work with God experience love and power throughout life and eternity
HOPE	No hope	We win

Figure 22.1 Contrasts between Animism and God-given Authority

Demonization

An important issue to deal with in every society is ground-level demonization. There will always be a high percentage of people (unfortunately, including many Christians,) who are hosting demons, especially in societies where babies are dedicated to spirits or gods. In such societies, we can expect the percentage of demonized people to be nearly 100 percent, since such dedication invites the demons to inhabit the children. How demons behave in any given society, and how what they do and don't do differs from society to society, are fitting subjects for research in this area.

At ground-level, the casting out of demons by the authority of Jesus Christ appears to be cross-culturally valid. Though I have seldom been able to simply command demons out as easily as the Gospels seem to show Jesus doing, I have been successful in confronting and defeating them in Jesus' name in several different cultural contexts.

My experience in ministering to demonized people of other societies leads me to conclude that the basic principle of "dual causation" is cross-culturally valid. This principle holds that demons can live in a person only if there are problems within that person that give them a legal right. The dual causation, then, is to recognize that there is both a human cause (the internal problem to which the demons are attached) and a spirit problem (the demons themselves). Dealing with demons in people of other societies requires us to deal with the internal problems as well, just as it does with Westerners.

The analogy I use is to say that demons are like rats and rats live where there is garbage. Demonic "rats" gain their rights and their strength from the human spiritual, mental and emotional "garbage" in the life of the persons they inhabit. That garbage may be spiritual, such as dedication to spirits. Or it may be mental, such as believing lies. Or it may be emotional, such as wallowing in fear, anger, shame, hatred, lust or the like. It is when a person is carrying such garbage that gives demons entrance, allows them to stay and gives them power.

Whether in the West or cross-culturally, therefore, dealing with the garbage in people is the most important aspect of the process of fighting demons at ground level. Demons must have legal rights to inhabit people. Those rights are a function of the garbage. The garbage, therefore, is much more important to deal with than the demons, though, if the person is to get well, both problems must be dealt with. When the garbage is dealt with first, the demons are weakened and go quietly when they are challenged (see Kraft 1992b). They seldom, if ever, leave on their own, though—they usually need to be cast out. We will see below that this rats and garbage principle also applies to cosmic-level spirits.

As mentioned in the preceding chapter, our enemy is good at contextualizing. He will adapt his approach to the problems and concerns most prominent in any given society. A major part of his strategy is, however, to be able to do his work without being noticed, especially in areas where there might be Christians who know how to combat demonization. The practice of making negative things worse and getting people to go overboard on positive things is another of his preferred ways of working. Yet the things he pushes in each society will differ for maximum effectiveness in Satan's attempts to deceive and disrupt.

In Asian societies, for example, where the relationship between mother-in-law and daughter-in-law is a difficult one, demons will often be active in pushing mothers-in-law to be oppressive and daughters-in-law to hate them. In African societies where fear of the unknown is endemic, demons will push all the buttons they can to increase the fear and the practice of going to diviners (where demonic influence is increased) for relief. In Latin America, Asia and Europe, where male domination of women and children is culturally inculcated, the enemy kingdom is very active in increasing the abuse and the pain felt by women and children. And we can speak of satanic enhancement of racism and social class oppression in many parts of the world. The thing that all such examples have in common is that the seed from which Satan works to produce harmful fruit is always culturally appropriate.

With regard to techniques people use for dealing with demons, then, the enemy is also active in seeing to it that culturally appropriate excesses are regular occurrences. In Korea and Africa, for example, it is common to hear of deliverance sessions that involve beating the demonized person to get the demons out. Such attempts at deliverance may thus be orchestrated by Satan himself. I know of two situations in which demonized Koreans were killed as a result of such beatings, thus fulfilling a demon's intent to destroy those he inhabits.

The appropriate and proper approach to getting people free from demons in any society seems, then, to always be the same: deal with the spiritual and emotional garbage to weaken the demons, then kick them out. Fighting physically with them is never a good idea. And even when it is necessary to physically restrain a demonized person, it is God's power wielded through words, not that wielded through physical force, that gets the demons out.

Though I have found this approach to be cross-culturally valid, there can be problems. Asians and persons of many other societies, for example, often find it very difficult to admit things that they have done or said that have given rights to the demons. There often is a worldview value that holds that if a problem is hidden or denied, it will simply go away if one waits long enough. This is, of course, not true. In fact, the longer people hold onto deep problems, the more such problems can fester deep inside of them and affect their present lives.

Since God is a God of truth, no matter what the culture, people have to "come clean" and be willing to deal with the things they have done and that have been done to them, if they are to be healed. And this is true no matter how culturally strange it might for people to admit these disagreeable things and to forgive those who have hurt them. As in the West, it is especially the reactions to things done to them that must be dealt with, in order that the heavy emotional loads (Mt. 11:28) such reactions produce may be brought to Christ and laid at his feet. The hurtful events cannot be changed. What happened happened. But, with the help of Jesus, reactions such as anger, bitterness, fear and especially unforgiveness can be given to Jesus, bringing emotional healing. When, then, such things are brought to Christ, the demons have nothing more to cling to and are easily banished.

Dealing with Family Spirits or Occult Spirits

Several years ago I was working to bring "inner healing," including freedom from some demons, to a 50ish Chinese Christian woman missionary. In addition to the fairly "normal" problems to which demons were attached, such as hate and anger, she was carrying "family" demons that she had inherited from her parents. These, then, had been strengthened at times when her parents dedicated her at a temple soon after her birth and when they took her to a temple as a child for healing. She was also carrying demons who entered when she was involved in practicing Chinese martial arts under a "master" who, without her awareness, dedicated all he did to demonic spirits. But she had no idea that these things that had happened long ago could be responsible for the daily (and nightly) torment she experienced. She believed in demons but had until recently been believing the lie that demons could not live in Christians (especially dedicated ones such as those who served as missionaries).

Fortunately, unlike others who had tried to deliver her, I have worked with enough Chinese (and Koreans and Japanese) to know that just about every Chinese child born into nonChristian families and even many born into Christian families are dedicated by mother, grandmother or some other close relative. Such dedications both empower the inherited family spirits and add spirits. The name and exact date of the baby's birth (even, often, the time of day) is written down and taken to a priest to be registered with the gods of the temple. Though many Chinese families claim not to believe in spirits anymore, often this is done "just in case."

It is usually easy to break the power even of long standing family demons, since the power of Jesus is so great. We simply claim Jesus' authority over the vows, curses, dedications, sins and any other ways in which rights have been given to demons by ancestors. This I have done numerous times. The issues that remain, then, relate to the canceling of all permission the person him or herself or anyone in authority over the person has given in any of the same ways during his/her lifetime. This usually involves dealing with demons attached to emotional reactions such as anger, hatred, unforgiveness, fear and the like. Once each of the areas of such permission has been dealt with, the demons go quietly at our command.

We can count on finding family spirits in anyone who is within three or four generations of the routine dedications to gods or spirits and/or who have received healing from such gods or spirits. This means that we can expect family spirits in nearly all Asians, Africans, Latin Americans, South Pacific islanders, American Indians and many Euroamericans. Anyone within three or four generations of conversion from Hinduism, Buddhism, Islam, Shinto, animism or any occult organization such as Mormonism, Freemasonry, Scientology, Jehovah's Witnesses and the like are likely to be carrying family and/or occult spirits.

Occult spirits are dealt with in the same way as family spirits. We look for the curses, dedications, etc., that give the demons rights and break their power, then cast the demons out. Unfortunately, occult spirits, like family spirits, can be inherited down to at least the third or fourth generation and probably longer in some cases. So, if a person has had a father or grandfather who was a Freemason or a mother or grandmother who was into Christian Science, we can expect demons from those sources to be living in the person we are working with even though that person, himself or herself, has had no involvement in these occult organizations.

Cosmic-Level Spirits

Most of the world believes there are specific spirits attached to nations, regions, mountains, rivers and other geographical features. We find this understanding in the Old Testament, where the Baal gods were considered to have control of the plains while Yahweh was supposed to be merely a mountain god. In the events recorded in 1 Kings 20:23-30, we see Yahweh angered at this belief on the part of the Syrians and, therefore, giving Israel a victory on the plains.

One of the spinoffs of the belief in territorial spirits is the understanding that when a person enters the territory of a given god, he needs to show respect to that god. In the Old Testament we continually find Israel honored the Baals and other gods when they were in territory they believed to belong to these gods. See, for example, Hosea 2:8 where Israel attributed their prosperity in the area in which they lived to the Baal gods. Solomon, then, in order to cement relationships with the surrounding countries, both married wives from Ammon, Moab, Edom and other places and erected altars to their gods to show honor to their countries. In this way he kept peace with these countries by keeping the wives and their relatives happy (1 Ki. 11:1-10). But he sacrificed the favor of Yahweh.

Westerners tend to feel that such beliefs need not be taken seriously since, we believe, these so-called gods are not gods at all but imaginary beings empowered only by superstition. The Bible, however, shows God and His people taking such spirits seriously, though we are warned against giving them honor or fearing them, since the true God is greater and more powerful than these servants of Satan. And, if we are properly related to the true God, we have the authority to protect ourselves from other gods and to confront and defeat them when necessary.

It is my position, though, that people who have been under the sway of territorial spirits for generations have a great deal of understanding of what territory the spirits have influence over and what are the results of this influence. Any approach to Christianity in such areas, therefore, will need to recognize the reality of the spirits over the area and gain understanding of their assignments. We will then have to deal with them by taking away their rights as we work with the true God to retake territory that is rightfully His. See Wagner (1991) for case studies dealing with territorial spirits.

Experiments going on in Argentina and elsewhere in the world suggest that a direct approach to warring against cosmic-level spirits can be successful. Just as with ground-level warfare, however, it is most important to deal with the spiritual "garbage." Thus, issues of confession of sin, repentance, reconciliation and unity ("corporate garbage") are the first order of business if our praying against territorial bondage is to be successful. The chapter in my book *Behind Enemy Lines* (Kraft ed. 1994) by Ed Silvoso (1994) reports on the success of such an approach in Resistencia, Argentina where he led a three year comprehensive spiritual attack aimed at breaking the power of the territorial spirits over the city and opening the people up for evangelism. That approach involved getting the pastors (the spiritual "gatekeepers") to repent of their sins and their disunity and to unite, training pastors and lay church leaders in spiritual warfare praying, repentance, reconciliation and prayer marching and, after two years of such preparation, all-out evangelism. The results have been spectacular.

Some have criticized such efforts to wage war at the cosmic level, pointing out that Jesus never seemed to concern himself with any level above ground level. Could it be, though, that the Holy Spirit is simply leading us in our day (the last days?) into some more of the "all truth" that Jesus promised in John 16:13? And might it be that by cleaning up so much of the ground level garbage and praying as much as he did in private, as well as in John 17, Jesus was contributing greatly to the breaking of satanic power at cosmic level? It seems clear, from what those engaged in cosmic-level warfare are discovering, that most of what it takes to effectively confront higher level spirits takes place at ground level. I am referring to such things as confession of sin, repentance, reconciliation and the need for spiritual gatekeepers to work in unity.

Whether or not strategies to confront cosmic-level spirits are Scriptural, we cannot argue against the scripturalness of such things as repentance, unity and intercessory prayer that are felt to provide the key to breaking the power of higher level spirits. Disunity, lack of repentance and failure to fast and pray may be seen as the cosmic-level "garbage" on which cosmic-level "rats" feed.

An important technique developed by spiritual warfare activists such as George Otis, Jr. (1993, 1999), John Dawson (1989), Ed Silvoso (1994), C. Peter Wagner, ed. (1993) and others is called "Spiritual Mapping." This is an approach to discerning and identifying the cosmic spirits that are over the areas charted in the preceding chapter as a step toward developing strategies to oppose and defeat them.

Spiritual mapping is much like what God told Moses to do when he commanded him to send spies into the Promised Land to discover what the situation was that Israel would face as they attempted to take the land. Such spying is a regular feature in warfare and provides a major component of the development of the strategies for attacking the enemy. It should certainly be a part of any attempt to contextualize spiritual warfare.

Gods, Idols and Divination

Our efforts to contextualize spiritual power concerns must take into account the strong negative tone of God's pronouncements concerning compromise with regard to other gods and spirits and the ways in which their power is engaged. I want to point to several of the prohibited areas and then to discuss what may be done about them.

God's ideals in this area are quite clear from Scripture. The Old Testament, especially, is an excellent source from which today's peoples can learn what is and is not allowable. Most of today's peoples share with the peoples of biblical times the understanding that the world is populated by evil spirits and that higher level spirits are in charge of territory (see Dan. 10:13, 21). God never counters that belief.

However, God is very much against His people honoring these spirits when it is assumed, as it is both in biblical times and in most present societies, that when we enter the territory of any given spirit, we should be polite and recognize that spirit's right to control the territory. Indeed, God got quite angry and taught the people a lesson when it was assumed that he was only powerful in the mountains but not on the plains (1 Kgs. 20:23-30).

The Bible, both Old and New Testaments, is clear that the worship of any god but the true God is not permitted. We are to "worship no god but me [Yahweh]" (Ex. 20:3). There are, then, to be no idols made or worshipped because "I am the Lord your God and I tolerate no rivals" (Ex. 20:5). And among the warnings in the New Testament is the command at the end of 1 John, "My children, keep yourselves safe from false gods!" (1 Jn. 5:21).

Perhaps the clearest indication of what God feels about his people having relationships with other gods is found in the story of the people of Israel at Peor in Numbers 25. God became very angry at the Israelite leaders who attended feasts with Moabite women "where the god of Moab was worshipped" and where "the Israelites ate the food and worshipped the god Baal of Peor" (vv. 2-3). God was so angry at them that he commanded that those who had participated in that worship should be killed publicly (v. 4). Then, when an Israelite man openly challenged the prohibition by taking a Midianite woman into his tent, God commended Phinehas, Aaron's grandson, for killing both the man and the woman saying, "Because of what Phinehas has done, I am no longer angry with the people of Israel. . . . [and] . . . He and his descendants are permanently established as priests, because he did not tolerate any rivals to me and brought about forgiveness for the people's sin" (vv. 11, 13). Contextualization of idolatry, then, is impossible for Christians.

Several other practices are also forbidden to God's people and labeled as the reasons why God gave his people the right to drive out the inhabitants of Palestine. In Deuteronomy 18:9-13 several of these things are listed and labeled "disgusting practices." The practices listed there are, sacrificing children, divination, looking for omens, using spells or charms and consulting spirits of the dead. The text says, "God hates people who do these disgusting things, and that is why he is driving those nations out of the land as you advance" (v. 12).

So it is clear that many common pagan practices involving spiritual power are forbidden. God does not tolerate appeasing pagan gods or spirits or seeking information, health, wealth or blessing from them. His answer to the quest for these things is to relate to Him and allow Him to take care of the opposing spirits and to provide the blessings we need.

What such total condemnation says to today's "dual allegiance" Christians is frightening. It is probable that the majority of Christians in nonWestern, and many in Western contexts, find so little spiritual power in Christianity that they regularly seek help from nonChristian power sources. In most of the world the kind of Christianity they have received has been strong on the intellectual and spiritual distinctives of Western evangelical Christianity but virtually powerless in areas such as healing, deliverance, blessing and the other areas traditionally covered by pagan shamans and priests. So, failing to find these needs met within Christianity, the Christians (including many pastors and other church leaders) have continued to go to traditional power brokers.

If, as these Scriptures say, God tolerates no rivals, the situation is serious if going to these other gods and spirits constitutes worship. I trust, though, that God takes the ignorance of such people and their missionaries into account. We find in 2 Kings 5 that God does take pagan authority relationships into account. After Naaman was healed and committed himself to the God of Israel, he asked the prophet Elisha how he should now behave when he is required by his master to accompany him to a pagan temple. Naaman says, "I hope that the Lord will forgive me when I accompany my king to the temple of Rimmon, the god of Syria, and worship him" (v. 18). Elisha simply says, "Go in peace" (v. 19), indicating that God will understand and not hold it against Naaman.

In attempting to see biblical Christianity contextualized, then, we recognize that God allows no rivals. Though he allowed Israel's belief in many gods to continue for some time, he insisted that there be no compromise with regard to allegiance—no rivals. And no contacting spirits or dead people. Places of worship and even rituals and transition rites such as circumcision and baptism previously used for pagan purposes can, however, be captured, disempowered, purified and used to honor the true God. This is what Israel did with pagan worship rituals and ceremonies, the use of high places as places of worship, even blood sacrifices.

The customs used by the early Israelites nearly all came from their pagan background and were "captured" for Yahweh. In the New Testament, then, baptism had pagan roots as did the requirements for church leaders listed in 1 Timothy 3:1-13 and Titus 1:6-9. So did words such as those translated lord, church, grace and most of the other important words used for important Christian concepts.

Ancestors

As mentioned in Chapter 21, I believe ancestor cults to be satanic contextualizations carried out through demonic deception. Probably everyone, especially those in societies that are strongly family-oriented, are greatly concerned over what happens to their loved ones when they die. What a stroke of genius on the part of Satan to convince people that their loved ones are still alive (true) and that they continue to actively participate in human life (false)! By so doing, demons are able to work freely, disguised as ancestors. And since they already know everything about that ancestor, they can do an excellent job of impersonation and, in the process, exert a great amount of control over the people. Demons, posing as ancestors, can give and they can take away. And by so doing, they can bind people to false beliefs and the rituals that go with them in a most impressive way.

Given the appropriateness of such contextualization from Satan's point of view, the question to be raised is what we can do about it. Most of the peoples of the world have long since bought the lie that it is really their loved ones who are receiving and responding to their attentions. And it is not easy to get them to understand that what they have been believing for generations is a lie. Nor is it easy to get the academics who, with no experience with the demonic world themselves, argue interminably on the basis of pure theory about whether or not ancestors, demons or Satan are real. Our enemy has done a good job of deluding, or at least confusing, them also. Unfortunately, then, the academics' lack of agreement affects the practitioners and would-be practitioners, causing doubt and uncertainty in their efforts to preach and teach and in their attempts to wage war against evil spiritual forces operating at the ancestor level.

Among the arguments advanced suggesting that ancestors are really conscious of what is going on in human life and are present to influence it, is the interpretation of the passage concerning King Saul's excursion to the medium in Endor (1 Sam. 28:3-19). This account, however, and the fact that at the Transfiguration Moses and Elijah appeared to Jesus (Lk. 9:28-31), are best interpreted as specific times when God allowed deceased people to return for specific purposes. They have nothing to do with the possibility that ancestors are conscious of, and interacting with, human life. More to the point is the statement in Hebrews 12:1 that "we have this large crowd of witnesses round us." But, though this verse may mean that the deceased are able to watch us, it gives no indication that they can participate in human life.

So, we are left scripturally with no encouragement to believe that the dead interact with the living. And, in fact, we are warned sternly not to attempt to contact the dead (Lev. 19:31; Deut. 18:11). The practice of diviners seeking information about this life, and especially about the future, from the deceased is well-known, both in Scripture and in contemporary societies. It is a form of divination called "necromancy." God's attitude toward this practice is stated in the strongest terms in Deuteronomy 18:12, "The Lord your God hates people who do these disgusting things, and that is why he is driving those nations out of the land as you advance."

When ancestors are regarded as participants in the living community, then, people are in actuality being deceived. But how can we tell them that and still expect them to listen to our message? And when people have for generations offered sacrifices and done other acts of worship to these supposed ancestors, the problem of how to present Christianity to them is compounded greatly. "Where are my ancestors now," they ask, often adding that they want to be with them for eternity even if they are in hell. With regard to where they are, I believe God's words to Abraham apply when He asked, Will not the God of all the universe do right? (Gen. 18:25). And Jesus helps us (and them) greatly when He tells the story of the rich man and his servant Lazarus (Lk. 16:19-31). For, if any of our ancestors are in hell, according to that story, they desperately want us, the living, to be able to avoid going where they are.

To free people spiritually from satanic deception in ancestral matters, we will have to deal with demonization early on. For such commitment to enemy spirits is an invitation for them to live inside. And since this commitment has been going on for generations, with accompanying dedications of each newborn to the spirits, what we are dealing with are ancestral, family spirits inherited from a person's parents. These need to be banished. So do the spirits inhabiting the ancestral tablets and/or other paraphernalia associated with the reverence and/or worship accorded them.

The difficulties involved in dealing with change of meaning, however, are another matter. Will people agree to speak to Jesus, asking Him to convey any messages He chooses to the ancestors? Will they, then, replace the pictures of ancestors with that of Jesus, or place His in the center and the others in secondary places? And if they do that, are the meanings in their minds changed enough? Are the experiments in Papua New Guinea designed to present Jesus as the Great Ancestor working? And are they theologically valid? We need to hear of more experiments in this area.

Reincarnation

I asked a demon once if reincarnation was one of the things they did to deceive people. He answered something like, "Of course. We know people's lives in detail. It's easy for us to simply tell people someone else's life as if it was their own past life." This is how they fool Westerners into believing something that is new in the West. It's even easier to fool Hindus who have philosophized the recycling of lives. As in many of Satan's activities, he has trained them to perpetuate his deceit themselves, without much, if any, of his help.

The Scripture is clear that "everyone must die once, and after that be judged by God" (Heb. 9:27). There is, therefore, no scriptural allowance for anyone to be reborn into another earthly existence. God has created each of us unique and eternal. This belief, therefore, like idolatry and divination, cannot be contextualized. Dealing with the demons of reincarnation may, however, be the first step toward freeing people from this lie.

It is important that we recognize Satan's ability to heal and bless those who come to places dedicated to him. For too long Christians have tried to ignore Satan's counterfeiting and the attraction it has for many who seek enough spiritual power to enable them to live their lives reasonably well.

I stood with a Japanese friend at a Shinto shrine one day. As people entered and poured water over the statue there, we asked them what it was they sought. They said blessings for marriage and for school examinations, healing of various ailments and relationships, fertility for themselves or loved ones and other such things. As I stood there, I thought, Jesus is concerned about all of these things. How great it would be if the churches sponsored shrines where people could receive prayer in Jesus' Name for such requests. For Japanese people are used to going to places of power at times convenient to them rather than at set times such as Sunday morning. So, even if such needs are prayed for in church (and they often are not), Christian shrines would be more appropriate places to deal with them.

Such shrines would, of course, differ in several respects from normal Shinto shrines. For one thing, the land on which they stand would be spiritually cleansed of satanic power and dedicated to God. In addition, such shrines would involve people who would pray for those who come, not simply a statue to pour water over. And it would be recommended at these shrines that those with further interest attend regular meetings (Sundays and other days) sponsored by the church. There would be literature there as well and the shrines would be advertised, as other shrines are, on the trains. And those who pray for people could be young people, thus providing for the youth a kind of ministry for which they would usually have to wait several years.

These shrines, therefore, would look to Japanese like places where their power needs can be met. They would not look like foreign incursions into Japanese life where knowledge about a foreign religion is dispensed but the power people seek in religious activity missing.

Such an approach might be suggested for other areas of the world as well. Many of the world's peoples are accustomed to frequenting shrines to satisfy their quest for spiritual power. In some Muslim countries, it is customary for people to seek spiritual power at the tombs of saints (even Hindu saints!). Might some adaptation of that custom for Christian witness be appealing to the people of those areas?

Wherever such an approach is attempted, of course, the land and any buildings taken over will have to be spiritually cleansed and then blessed with the power of Jesus. Traditional customs for dedicating buildings and property are likely to be adaptable for such purposes, but the power behind the dedications would be that of the true God, not of the traditional gods or spirits.

What to Do About Forbidden Customs

Understanding which customs God is against is the easy part of our consideration. It is much more difficult to work out how to handle such customs in contemporary situations in a way that is loving and does not distract from the main message of Christianity. We have learned, for example, that simply condemning customs such as polygamy and the drinking of native alcoholic beverages has in many places given Christianity a very disagreeable reputation. Unfortunately, such rules have kept many out of the Kingdom because they were focused on secondary cultural changes, supposedly required by God, rather than on the centrality of a relationship with Christ.

The Old Testament shows how strongly God is against such customs as the worship of other gods and divination. But the messages that make these points are directed to Jewish people—people whom God calls "His people." It is not surprising that God would want to warn His people concerning falling into pagan practices and attitudes. But is God's attitude on such matters the same toward those just coming out of paganism who may still believe and practice some of the things from their preChristian lives? Can God be patient with subChristian beliefs and practices in the spiritual power area, just as He is with subideal practices (e.g., polygamy, common law marriage) in other cultural areas?

The account of Naaman the Syrian whom God healed of leprosy through Elisha (2 Kgs. 5) is possibly relevant here. As Naaman was about to return to his country after being healed, he requested

> two mule-loads of earth to take home with me, because from now on I will not offer sacrifices or burnt offerings to any god except the Lord. So I hope that the Lord will forgive me when I accompany my king to the temple of Rimmon, the god of Syria, and worship him. Surely the Lord will forgive me! (vv. 17-18).

The prophet Elisha responded "Go in peace," presumably indicating that God would allow such a concession.

Given that God requires primary allegiance to Himself (Ex. 20:3), can we assume from the fact that Israel accepted the existence of many gods for some time, that God will allow this today? I believe we can. But the other gods and allegiances (e.g. family) have to be seen as secondary. Only the true God can be a Christian's primary allegiance. It might not be too difficult, however, for many people who believe in many gods to add Yahweh to their pantheon and to put Him in first place. Perhaps even those who worship their ancestors would be willing to put God over them, as Israel did when they used the phrase, "The God of Abraham, Isaac and Jacob." The Israelites, like many animistic peoples would gladly have worshipped Abraham, Isaac and Jacob. But, to keep that from happening, they learned to focus on the God of these revered ancestors rather than on the ancestors themselves as objects of worship.

As with all conversion and cultural transformation, then, the crucial thing is the pressure for continued movement in the right direction once people have decided to adopt a new custom (see Chapter 10). The point of a people's choice to make Yahweh or Jesus number one needs to be followed by the process of greater and greater insight into and acceptance of God's ideals if the personal or cultural transformation is to continue in the right direction. And often this requires someone or something to keep the pressure on. If the people are highly motivated, that motivation coming from inside of them is often sufficient pressure. If strong motivation is not there, however, outside persons or agencies are often needed. Failing the growth, pressure or not, though, the result will not be appropriate Christianity.

Perhaps an illustration from language learning will help make the concept of point plus process clearer. In the first few weeks of a person's attempt to learn another language, he/she may not pronounce the words very well and will make numerous grammatical mistakes. But those helping the person will encourage that person by complimenting that person on how well he/she is doing, even though there are many mistakes. If, though, after five or ten years that person is making the same mistakes, the judgment will be different. The language learner is expected in the early stages to be bold and to try to speak, even if he/she makes many mistakes. But the person is expected to grow and improve in ability as time goes on by practice assisted by the internal pressure of the motivation to make him or herself understood plus or minus pressure put on by others who may be helping in the language learning process. So it is for group and individual converts—they are expected to grow in their ability to practice their new faith but, like the language learner, will need the internal plus or minus external pressure to keep them growing.

For, as I have written in *Christianity in Culture* (1979a), conversion is a directional thing. To be a Christian is to be one who is growing toward greater Christlikeness, not simply one who appears to live like a Christian or who calls him/herself a Christian. It is not so much the position that one is in that makes one a Christian but the direction in which one is headed. Thus, the thief on the cross, in response to Jesus, turned and headed toward Him. And he was saved. The Pharisees, on the other hand, who believed most of what Jesus taught and practiced conscientiously, the commands of the Old Testament, because their motivation was not right, were headed in the wrong direction. And they were lost.

So, in this all important area (as in all other areas), I believe God is willing for those who have not known Him to start with nothing more than a commitment to Him, making Him their primary allegiance. From that, then, is to flow the growth in understanding of what that commitment means concerning the changes that need to be made in a person or group's secondary allegiances and cultural practices. Such practices as ancestor worship, a belief in reincarnation, seeking healing from shamans, divination in all of its many forms and the like, are to be turned away from as soon as possible, but not as preconditions for salvation. There is only one precondition—faith commitment to God through Jesus Christ.

Are the rules different for those who have been recipients of God's revelation, such as the Hebrews, than for those who have not received such an advantage? I believe they certainly are. Though the faith requirement— commitment to Jesus—is the same, the knowledge available to converts makes a big difference in what is expected of them behaviorally. Though all are expected to change over time, the amount and kind of change will depend on where a person or group starts in that process. The thief on the cross started at a very long distance from ideal Christian belief and behavior, with only one qualification for salvation—faith in Jesus. The believing Pharisees, and there were many, started their life of faith in Jesus with much of the expected behavior already habituated. And both the believing thief and the believing Pharisees were saved on the basis of their faith allegiance to Jesus—a faith allegiance that started them moving in a Christward direction that meant salvation for them.

Developing Functional Substitutes

Once faith in Jesus is pledged, though, a lot of the ensuing growth may depend on whether or not other customs are developed to replace the customs that are judged to be inappropriate for Christians. It is a sad fact of much missionary work that customs were condemned with nothing developed to take their place by serving the function previously served by the preChristian custom. With regard to the power customs, this has usually resulted in people continuing to practice their preChristian customs, often in secret from missionaries and/or other outsiders. And in places such as Latin America, such pagan customs take place quite openly—even in the church buildings.

The first and most important custom to be replaced is, of course, the primary faith commitment to gods, spirits, family, ideas, movements or whatever else was the primary allegiance of the person or group. For it is this commitment that creates the dividing line between Christian and nonChristian. There are, however, other customs related to this that have to be replaced as well. The custom of seeking assistance from a pagan shaman or priest is one. New converts need to learn how to appeal to the true God instead of to false gods for their needs.

And this is where missionary Christianity has often failed badly by not providing functional substitutes to replace the customs of the receiving peoples in this area. Often the habit of going to shamans has been condemned but all that has been put in its place is a weak appeal to God in prayer or simply the use of a secular Western technique such as medicine or fertilizer—no ritual, no authoritative use of the power of Christ to heal or bring fertility, no blessing of fields or animals or of couples seeking children. Not that we should ignore secular techniques. But we should honor God by appealing to Him first, before using medical, agricultural or other techniques that He has led people to discover.

We should recognize that for most of the peoples of the world, healing, fertility, protection from misfortune and the like are spiritual things, not simply the human manipulation of physical substances, as we see them in the West. And any such manipulation, if it is to adequately function as a substitute for their pagan custom needs to be conducted with primary concern for the spiritual nature of the problem and wrapped in meaningful ritual. If this is not done, the people are left with a void in their experience that they will probably seek to fill by returning to their preChristian practices.

A specific example of this problem would be the way funerals are conducted in areas where Christian missionaries have worked. Pagan funerals, of course, usually involve a great deal of interaction with the spirit world. When such activity has been forbidden to Christian converts, they or their families typically satisfy themselves by doing much of that activity in secret. How different things could be if a study were to be made of the pagan funerals and functional substitutes developed for each part of the activity so that the felt needs of the people are met rather than ignored. The traditional concern over the involvement of the spirit world in death needs to be taken seriously and Christian answers worked out in culturally appropriate rituals that satisfy people that the spiritual dimensions of life that death brings to the fore are adequately taken care of. If this is not done, people will often expect retribution from the spirits or gods that have not been properly satisfied.

When the understandings of the people are that ancestors are involved in funeral exercises, this belief needs to be taken seriously and substitute understandings and rituals need to be developed. As mentioned above, I believe it is possible to honor the ancestors in culturally appropriate ways just as long as God is recognized as primary. When the ancestors are not given what the people believe is their due, if misfortune strikes the family, the people are all too ready to blame the lack of attention to what are perceived to be the ancestors' desires as the reason for the misfortune.

An example of dealing with the spiritual dimensions of conversion in culturally appropriate ways can be found in the Issan region of northeastern Thailand. The churches there, under the wise guidance of Covenant missionaries, have captured a custom used by the people to show their allegiance to spirits. The custom involves tying a string around the wrist as a symbol of several things including dedication to spirits and friendship commitment to other people. This custom is now used by the Christians to symbolize conversion and love for one another. The traditional cultural felt need for such a ritual is thereby satisfied, though the meaning of the ritual has been changed for Christians. This capturing of a traditional ritual is reminiscent of the way God led Abraham to capture the ritual of circumcision and to change its meaning.

When it comes to divination, the problem of finding a functional substitute is made more difficult by the fact that God condemns the practice out of hand. We are forbidden to use any of the forms of divination to discern the future (see Deut. 18:10-13). However, God Himself gives the spiritual gifts of prophecy, words of knowledge and spiritual discernment (1 Cor. 12:4-11). Christians can be taught to seek these gifts, to practice them and to use them as God leads. And some will discover that God has gifted them in these areas and that they are able for the sake of the Christian community to function in many of the ways the diviners function, and with greater accuracy. Some may even find themselves regularly consulted, as diviners are, when something lost needs to be found or special advice from God is desired.

Dealing with magic and magical expectations can be another troublesome area. The essence of magic is to expect that if certain things are said or done, the desired result will be automatic. The great temptation is for people (Westerners as well as others) to try to control God through words or rituals that people regard as efficacious in getting Him to do our will. The key change here is to help people recognize that the Christian life is to be a life of submission to God, not of controlling Him. A part of this submission to Him, however, involves the authority He gives us in ministry. And this, though not magic, can be even more powerful that magic. A part of the instruction people need on this subject is the fact that when people think they are able to control things through magic, what is really happening is that they are submitting unconsciously to satanic power.

What I am suggesting, then, is that solid attention be given to developing "Christian" functional substitutes for the customs traditional people practice in the exercise of spiritual power. Many of the churches in missionized areas are, of course, already secularized in these matters—at least on the surface. We ran into a situation on the island of Chuuk, however, that is likely typical of such churches worldwide. My wife asked a group of about 50 pastors' wives if there is any use of traditional power in their churches. Without hesitation they said, "Yes, of course." In fact, they told my wife that they themselves regularly go to traditional spirits when they feel they need a quick answer to their problems. "God is too slow," they said!

I would suggest, then, that we look even in westernized churches for the ways in which spiritual power is sought and seek, if necessary, to assist even westernized Christians to deal with their power needs in ways that are more appropriate to the Bible. Many, of course, have been secularized and are not expecting God to work in power. They need to become more Scriptural. Many others, however, have been meeting their power needs underground in traditional ways. These need to be helped to discover that the powerful God of Scripture is still alive and doing powerful things in the present.

And, if the witness of Christ that we desire is to have the impact on the world's power-oriented peoples, we need to be presenting a Christianity with power. Jesus, working with a power-oriented people used signs and wonders as a major part of His strategy. And He has passed this power on to us (Jn. 14:12). Let's learn to do His work in His way—to move out of any infection we have received from secular, powerless Christianity into biblical Christianity which is always three dimensional. Neglecting the power dimension of our faith has, I believe, cost us millions of converts. Let's not let that continue to happen.

Conclusion

I have tried in this chapter to discuss several aspects of the spiritual power dimension of our Christian faith. This is by far the most neglected of the three dimensions by those of us who have gone out from the West as cross-cultural witnesses. Though it is in many respects a very difficult area to deal with, we should not continue to neglect it. Ours is a faith that can flow through the forms of any culture, even those considered "religious." The contextualization of the spiritual power dimension needs to be thought through so that the power customs that people are into as well as the other areas of their lives can be captured for Christ.

Chapter 23

Appropriate Approaches in Muslim Contexts

John Travis and Anna Travis

Much has been written over the past twenty-five years on the application of contextualization in ministry among Muslims. In 1998, I (John), wrote an article for *Evangelical Missions Quarterly (EMQ)* in which I presented a model for comparing six different types of *ekklesia* or congregations (which I refer to as "Christ-centered communities") found in the Muslim world today (Travis 1998b). These six types of Christ-centered communities are differentiated in terms of three factors: language, cultural forms and religious identity. This model, referred to as the C1-C6 spectrum (or continuum), has generated much discussion, especially around the issue of fellowships of "Muslim followers of Jesus" (the C5 position on the scale). Parshall (1998), an advocate of contextualization, feels that C5 crosses the line and falls into dangerous syncretism. In subsequent writings many of Parshall's concerns have been addressed (see Massey 2000, Gilliland 1998, Winter 1999, Travis 1998b and 2000). *Yet in spite of concerns that some may have on this issue, the fact remains that in a number of countries today, there are groups of Muslims who have genuinely come to faith in Jesus Christ, yet have remained legally and socio-religiously within the local Muslim community.* The purpose of this chapter is to note some key literature on contextualization among Muslims, describe and discuss the C1-C6 Continuum, and focus on key theoretical and practical dynamics of C5 "insider movements" within Islam. We will close the chapter with a brief look at insider movements presently taking place in contexts other than Islam.

Throughout this chapter we will not be contending that C5 is the best or only thing God is doing in the Muslim world today; indeed God is bringing Muslims to Himself in a great diversity of ways, some of which we may only understand in eternity. What we will argue, however, is that one way God is moving at this point in salvation history, is by sovereignly drawing Muslims to Himself, revolutionizing them spiritually, yet calling them to remain as salt and light in the religious community of their birth.

Relevant Literature

Recent literature applying contextualization theory to outreach among Muslims began to appear in the 1970s. Early important articles came from

J. Anderson (1976), Wilder (1977), Kraft (1979b), and Conn (1979). Four landmark books concerning contextualization among Muslims came out prior to 1990: *The Gospel and Islam* (ed. McCurry 1979), *New Paths in Muslim Evangelism* (Parshall 1980), *Beyond the Mosque* (Parshall 1985) and *Muslims and Christians on the Emmaus Road* (ed. Woodberry 1989). These books and articles, along with the advent of new classes and seminars taught at colleges and churches, meant that by the 1990s, cross-cultural sensitivity and some level of contextualization was fairly widely accepted with regard to outreach to Muslims.

Toward the mid-1990s, much of the discussion involving contextualization among Muslims focused on the issue of what many today refer to as "insider movements" (C5 on the continuum). The concept of insider movements, however, had already been broached earlier by J. Anderson, Wilder, Kraft and Conn (see articles mentioned above). A landmark paper by Woodberry (1989) pushed our thinking ahead in this area by showing that most Islamic religious forms, even those involving the Five Pillars, are actually borrowed from the practices of seventh century Middle Eastern Jews and Christians. Woodberry's message is that when we contextualize to so-called "Islamic forms" we are actually "reusing" many of the forms formerly found in the faith of our antecessors. This article also gives an excellent case study of a C5 movement in one predominately Muslim nation. As mentioned above, articles on the C1-C6 continuum in *Evangelical Missions Quarterly* (Parshall 1998; Gilliland 1998; Travis 1998a) brought the discussion on C5 to a wider audience, and helped prompt the publishing of an entire edition of the *International Journal of Frontier Missions* (Weerstra 2000) devoted to the C5 question. While missiologists and field workers continue to discuss this phenomenon, in a number of locations around the world there are thousands of Muslims who have put their faith in Christ, yet have seen their path clear to remain legally and culturally Muslim. We will now turn to how the C1–C6 Continuum was developed.

The C1-C6 Continuum

When we first arrived in the Muslim world fifteen years ago, our goal was to plant contextualized churches. We had read most of the above mentioned literature, and our aim was to declare "Al-Masih (Christ) only and Him crucified" (1 Cor. 2:2), stripping the Gospel of its foreign veneer and elements as best we could.

During our first three months on the field, we lived with two different Muslim families: one in a city and one in a village. We attempted to see the world through their eyes. Living under Muslim roofs, we were struck with how far their world was from the Christian world. During early discussions about Christianity we heard the same answers repeatedly: "There are many roads to the capital city" (in other words, "All religions are the same".) "Your religion for you; mine for me" (in other words, "Don't expect me to change my religion.") "Our people group is a Muslim people group" (in other words, "Christianity is not welcome here.")

After these months living with families, we rented our own home in a close-knit middle class Muslim neighborhood. Here we raised our children and experienced warm and close relationships with our neighbors. Yet we picked up even stronger messages concerning the local Christian minority (made up almost entirely of people from non-Muslim ethnic groups.) According to our neighbors, Christians dressed immodestly, ate forbidden food that turned their stomachs, liked to get drunk on Christmas, were impolite and worshipped statues, among other offenses. To encourage a member of the neighborhood to consider Christianity was an evil act.

Like many Muslim countries around the world, ours has a longstanding minority Christian population with its own particular subculture in terms of language, music, architecture, etc.—all forms that largely came from or are identified with the "Christian West." In light of our neighbors' sentiments, we assessed what options existed for Muslims who would decide to follow Jesus. The first was to simply join one of the traditional national churches. In our city, we saw two types of such churches: the first used the national *lingua franca* of the area; the second (the minority by far) used the ethnic language of the surrounding Muslim population (in this area Muslims are bilingual; for most, their "heart language" is the ethnic language).

There was another type of fellowship emerging as well—one where a number of principles of contextualization were being applied. This type, meeting either in a home or church fellowship hall (not the sanctuary), incorporated into worship not just the ethnic language of the surrounding Muslim population, but local non-Islamic music and cultural forms as well. They incorporated ways of greeting, congregating and discipling more in keeping with the local culture than ways used by traditional national churches.

If seen on a continuum moving in a contextualized direction, each of these types of Christ-centered communities could be placed at a given point. We labeled the national church using the *lingua franca* or a foreign language as "C1" (i.e., Christ-centered Community type 1). The national church using an ethnic language we labeled "C2." The contextualized fellowship using non-Islamic ethnic forms we labeled "C3". The whole continuum, then, looks like this:

C1	C2	C3	C4	C5	C6
Traditional church using a language different from the mother tongue of the local Muslim community	Traditional church using the mother tongue of the local Muslim community	Context-ualized Christ-centered community using the mother tongue and some non-Muslim local cultural forms	Context-ualized Christ-centered community using the mother tongue and biblically acceptable socio-religious Islamic forms	Com-munity of Muslims who follow Jesus yet remain culturally and officially Muslim	Secret or under-ground Muslim followers of Jesus with little or no com-munity

Figure 23.1 C1-C6 Continuum

Moving beyond these first three types (C1-C3), we, along with a number of national and expatriate coworkers, felt compelled to apply contextualization theory further. We looked for religious forms commonly used by local Muslims which were either expressly Biblical, or at least neutral, so that Muslims coming to Christ would need to change outward forms as little as possible. When we actually analyzed Muslim religious forms and practices, we saw much that was usable (this is partially due to the heavy influence of early Christianity and Judaism on Islamic socio-religious forms as Woodberry has pointed out). Along with a group of national Christians burdened for lost Muslims, some of whom were Muslim Background Believers (MBBs), we experimented with "Islamic" forms of dress, terminology and prayer forms, in sharing the Gospel with Muslim friends and relatives. Other groups were carrying on similar experiments in nearby areas. What developed over time was a contextualized expression of faith in Christ, in which the believers called themselves "followers of Isa" rather than "Christians" (the term "Christian" bears much unnecessary, mostly Western, baggage). Within a few years there were several hundred believers. The communities of faith they formed are at the "C4" point on the continuum and closely resemble the types of congregations described and commended by Parshall (1980).

This C4 lifestyle greatly helped the new follower of Christ remain a part of his family and neighborhood. Yet in time (usually about three months to one year), the community would realize the C4 believers were in fact no longer Muslims. Although they would still keep the fast, wear Islamic clothing, use Islamic terminology, keep Muslim dietary practices, and not change their names, they would generally not pray in the mosque and no longer referred to themselves as Muslims. Rejection would eventually come (though it was postponed and less severe), and the flow of the Gospel stopped. Gradually the distance between C4 believers and their Muslim communities widened.

However there was strength in these C4 communities: since outward forms were similar to what was familiar to the community, Muslim friends were forced to look beyond forms to meanings. Some from the community realized this new faith was not just a change of religion, but rather a change of heart. This was especially evident when God healed the sick in the Messiah's name, when impoverished believers began to find better work (due to new Biblical character traits as well as answered prayer), and when those oppressed by demons were set free in Isa's name.

Incidentally, over a period of several years now, the C4 expression of faith in Christ has been found to be very fitting for Christian Background Believers (CBBs) who reach out to and live among Muslims. The C4 lifestyle requires sacrifice, rigorous changes and the adoption of some Muslim forms on the part of the CBB, but does not involve identifying oneself as a Muslim.

During the time we were beginning C4 experiments (the late 1980s) we also began hearing about some cases of Muslims, many of them leaders, who had come to faith in Isa (both in our area and in other countries) and who chose to remain in the Muslim community, much like Jews of today's Messianic Jewish movement remain culturally and officially Jewish. Whereas some Muslims upon salvation want to get as far away from anything Islamic as possible, some feel just the opposite. They say something like this: "My father is a Muslim, my mother is a Muslim. The foreign and/or minority Christians near me are not my people. I have now made Isa my Lord and Savior, yet I desire to remain with my own people." These Muslim believers are able to set aside certain Islamic beliefs, interpretations and practices, yet remain a part of the Islamic community as they follow Isa. They do not change their name or legal religious affiliation. They continue to identify with the religion of their birth and participate in things Islamic insofar as their conscience and growing sensitivity to Scripture allows. This point on the continuum—a community of Muslims who follow Christ yet remain culturally and officially Muslim—is referred to as C5. Others refer to emerging networks of C5 congregations as "insider movements", since the evangelism, discipling, congregating and organizing of C5 believers happens within the Muslim community, by Muslims with Muslims.

In recent years we have had the privilege of meeting a number of C5 Muslims, and although our religious backgrounds and forms of worship are quite different, we have experienced sweet fellowship in Isa the Messiah. There is no question in our minds that these C5 Muslims are born again members of the Kingdom of God, called to live out the Gospel inside the religious borders of their birth. As we have continued to see the limits of C4 in our context, and as our burden for lost Muslims only grows heavier, we have become convinced that a C5 expression of faith could actually be viable for our precious Muslim neighbors and probably large blocks of the Muslim world. We ourselves, being CBBs, maintain a C4 lifestyle, but we believe God has called us to help "birth a C5 movement" in our context (this will be discussed later in this chapter).

The final point on the continuum, C6, is in one way quite different from the other five points—these Muslim believers in Jesus have no regular fellowship with other believers. C6 believers often come to the Messiah through a miracle (dream, vision or healing), a radio broadcast, reading Christian literature, or through the witness of a Christian they may have known at some point in their lives. Either due to social pressure, fear of death and persecution, geographical isolation, or simply not wanting to be expelled from their community, these believers, for at least the time being, worship God and intercede for their lost family members alone and are generally silent about their faith. (As Wilder points out, there are many such believers scattered throughout Muslim lands.) We have met a few C6 believers, and heard of many more. We have included C6 in the continuum because these MBBs are born again, and are part of the Body of Christ.

We close this section with a perspective on C5 movements. We have attended many Muslim funerals. We grieve every time we see another Muslim friend buried, having passed into eternity without salvation in Christ. As we have seen the resistance toward changing religions and the huge gap between the Muslim and Christian communities, we feel that fighting the religion-changing battle is the wrong battle. We have little hope in our lifetime to believe for a major enough cultural, political and religious change to occur in our context such that Muslims would become open to entering Christianity on a wide scale. But we do have great hope, as great as the promises of God, to believe that an "insider movement" could get off the ground—that vast numbers could discover that salvation in Isa the Messiah is waiting for every Muslim who will believe. We sense the desire of Jesus Himself to take the "yeast" of His Gospel to the inner chambers of Muslim communities, calling men, women and children to walk with Him as Lord and Savior, remaining vital members of their families and Muslim communities. The following section will deal with some of the theological and theoretical dimensions of C5.

Theoretical and Theological Issues Regarding C5

The purpose of this section will be to look at C5, or insider movements, from a number of theoretical and theological perspectives. The intent is not to *prove* if C5 *can* happen, as case studies already indicate that it *is* happening. Rather, we hope to help build a framework from which to understand this phenomenon and to answer some of the questions that have arisen such as: From a Biblical perspective can a person be truly saved and continue to be a Muslim? Doesn't a follower of Christ need to identify himself as a Christian and officially join the Christian faith? Can a Muslim follower of Christ retain all Muslims practices, in particular praying in the mosque toward Mecca and continuing to repeat the Muslim creed? This section will be framed around ten premises.

Premise 1: For Muslims, culture, politics and religion are nearly inseparable, making changing religions a total break with society. Our discussion of C5 must begin here. Martin Goldsmith states:

> Islam is within the whole warp and woof of society—in the family, in politics, in social relationships. To leave the Muslim faith is to break with one's whole society. Many a modern educated Muslim in not all that religiously minded; but he must, nevertheless, remain a Muslim for social reasons, and also because it is the basis for his political belief. This makes it almost unthinkable for most Muslims even to consider the possibility of becoming a follower of some other religion (1976:318).

This fact is at the heart of our discussion: in a Muslim society, changing religions is not just a spiritual rebirth. It is generally a clean break with family, culture and society as a whole. Contextualization is the attempt to maintain continuity between a people's culture and their faith in Christ. But what are we to do when religion has become an inseparable, permeating fixture of the culture? One logical conclusion would be to do what Kraft suggests: view religion as an integral part of one's culture, allowing God to work through it rather than against it (1996:210-214). Although elements of Islam (like culture) must be evaluated in light of the Word of God (see Premise 8 below), we work through the totality of who Muslims are, focusing on issues of the heart and allegiance to Christ rather than social, religious or cultural changes.

Premise 2: Salvation is by grace alone through relationship/allegiance to Jesus Christ. Changing religions is not a prerequisite for nor a guarantee of salvation. The New Testament teaches clearly that salvation is found only through Christ alone (e.g., Jn. 17:3; Ac. 4:12, 15:11, 16:31). It is not through membership in a church nor affiliation with a particular religious group. In the words of Grudem, "Saving faith is trust in Jesus Christ as a living person for forgiveness of sins and for eternal life with God" (Grudem 1994:710). Kraft uses the terms "allegiance" and "commitment" in describing this saving relationship we have in Jesus: "With respect to allegiance, we must maintain that people are saved or lost on the basis of whether or not their primary commitment is to the true God in Christ" (1996:210). Kraft goes on to explain that since our salvation is through Christ and not religion, a nonChristian could be saved through relationship with Jesus while still being a part of his original nonChristian religious community of birth.

Premise 3: Jesus' primary concern was the establishment of the Kingdom of God, not the founding a new religion. The predominant theme of the teaching and ministry of Jesus was the Kingdom of God (Mt. 4:23). His parables describe the Kingdom (Mt. 13, 18, 20, 25; Mk. 4; Lk. 13) and when He healed, Jesus said, "the Kingdom of God is near you" (Lk. 10:9). The Twelve were instructed to "preach the Kingdom of God" (Lk. 9: 2), and throughout Acts we find the early believers following in their Master's footsteps, preaching the good news of God's Kingdom (Ac. 8:12; 19:8; 20:25; 28:23,31).

Toward religion, Jesus had primarily words of criticism. His constant concern was for issues of the heart rather than outward religious categories and rituals (Mt. 23:22-28). With the woman at the well in John 4, we see it was the condition of her heart, not the inadequacies of her syncretized Samaritan religion, that concerned Jesus. Throughout the New Testament we find that being clean or unclean is a matter of relationship with Jesus rather than following a particular brand of religion (Mk. 3:23-27, 7:1-8, 14-23; Jn. 4:19-26; Ac. 10:28-29, 44-48; Heb. 9:12-14).

This emphasis on the heart and the Kingdom, rather than religion, has led some to ask if Jesus came to earth with the intention of establishing a new religion. Theologian David Bosch made the bold assertion that "Jesus had no intention of founding a new religion." He contended that the early "Jesus community" was intended to be a "movement" rather than an "institution" (a religion) – a movement that would cross frontiers, emphasize new "life" rather than ontological doctrines and serve as a model of submission to the reign of God for all peoples to emulate. Bosch points out that over time the "Jesus community simply became a new religion" (1991:50). Yet it is important to bear in mind that religion *per se* was not a part of the core message of Jesus. One implication of Bosch's paradigm (movement versus religion, life versus doctrine, and modeling of the Kingdom of God), is that evangelism to unreached peoples should aim to plant the seed of the Gospel in the very heart of another's religion, allowing it to permeate the whole as yeast, rather than simply "winning converts" who leave their former religion and join Christianity. In the words of J. Anderson (1976:288), by pulling new believers out of the "culture in which God has placed them" we are in effect "robbing Islam" of one of the few ways its members will ever experience the Kingdom, namely though intimate interaction with their own people who have tasted of new life in Christ.

Premise 4: *The very term "Christian" is often misleading—not all called Christian are in Christ and not all in Christ are called Christian.* When an evangelical asks if someone is a Christian, he is using the term in a *spiritual* sense (i.e., Is the person "born again," "converted," or "saved"?). For many European "state church" people, the term has a *religious* or *ethnic* connotation, referring to one's community rather than personal faith, whereas for the Muslim the term often refers to Europeans and/or attitudes and practices associated with "the West." The term Christian can be misleading and not helpful.

It is instructive to note that the earliest followers of Christ did not refer to themselves as "Christians" (Greek: *christianos*) but rather as followers of "the Way" (Ac. 9:2; 24:15). Muslim followers of Christ likewise should not feel under compulsion to refer to themselves as "Christians" due to the negative baggage of Western culture (not to mention the crusades!) associated with that term. We say this, however, with the following understanding: while a Muslim follower of Jesus may with integrity deny being a "Christian convert", neither he nor any true believer may ever deny being a follower of Christ (Lk. 12:8-9; Mt. 26:69-75).

Premise 5: Often gaps exist between what people actually believe and what their religion or group officially teaches. Many Westerners refer to themselves as "Christian" yet adhere to personal beliefs akin to Hinduism, Buddhism, secular humanism or even atheism (see Gibbs 1989 on Western Christians). Likewise many Muslims hold to personal beliefs religiously at odds with Islam (see Bowen 1998:21-27, 38-40; Massey 2000:11-12; Bernard 2000:18-19). Referring to the world's largest Muslim nation, Indonesia, Marantika, estimates that thirty percent of the nation's Muslim community observes "the rituals of Islam, but are not personally committed to its teachings" (1989:218). This gap between personal commitment and official theology is one of the things that allows for some Muslims to remain a part of their community and still follow Jesus as Lord and Savior.

Wilder states that Christian workers often encounter such Muslim followers of Christ (1976:306). He mentions two Muslim men he has known personally who speak openly of their faith in Jesus, considering themselves to be "true believers in Christ and at the same time members of the Muslim community." From the Turkish context, Wilder reports on "self-sustaining groups of followers of Jesus remaining within the fold of Islam" (1976:306). In 1976 these Turkish groups had been in existence for forty-five years and were meeting in two or three different cities. Teeter, working among Arabs, has seen the same phenomenon of "Muslim followers of Jesus" (1990) A more recent example comes from the United States National Prayer Breakfast, held in February, 2002, where a Muslim follower of Jesus from the Middle East actually shared publicly. Below is an excerpt of his testimony:

> This is an actual conversation between a friend and myself. My friend asked me, "What is your religion?" I said, "I am a Muslim and a follower of Jesus." He asked, "How can that be when you are not a Christian?" I answered, "Jesus did not come to save only the Christians . . . He came for all the world." My friend asked, "Is this written in your book?" I said, "Of course. . . . All the stories and teaching of the Old Testament are written in the Qur'an with the same content from Abraham, Ishmael, Isaac, Jacob, Moses, etc." The Qur'an confirms much of what is written in the New Testament about Jesus' life and mission. His immaculate conception is beautifully described in the Qur'an: . . . "'Behold!' The angels said, 'Oh Mary! God gives you glad tidings of a Word from Him: His name will be Messiah Jesus . . . '" (3:45). He also performed many miracles in God's name, for example: " . . . I heal those born blind, and the lepers, and I quicken the dead, by God's leave" (3:49). The Qur'an confirms that Jesus preached the Gospel [*Injil*], confirming the Law of Moses which preceded him: " . . . We sent Jesus, the son of Mary, confirming the Law that had come before him. We sent him the Gospel: therein was guidance and light, and confirmation of the Law that had come before him; a guidance and admonition to those who fear God" (5:46).

I read about Jesus and I love what I learned of him, and I wanted to know more of Him. So I read the New Testament, which according to the Qur'an, is a holy book that I have to read and respect as a Muslim. I love His principles, His teachings, His way of life. I came to love Him more and more and I decided to put Him in my heart and to follow Him. My friend said, "So you are a good Christian now." I said, "That is your point of view. From my point of view, I am a good Muslim because I surrender to one God and because I follow Jesus." He asked, "What did you like in Jesus?" I said, "Everything."

Premise 6: *Some Islamic beliefs and practices are in keeping with the Word of God; some are not.* Wilder states that "probably eighty percent of Muslim doctrine and ethics, and sixty percent of Muslim prayer and worship is parallel to or compatible with Christian doctrine and worship" (1977:314). Woodberry explains one of the reasons why so many parallels exist between Muslim and Christian beliefs and practices:

> Islam may be viewed as originally a contextualization for the Arabs of the monotheism inherited directly from the Jews and Christians, or indirectly through Arab monotheists…[t]he pillars of faith along with associated vocabulary were largely the precious possessions of Jews and Christians. Any reusing of them then is but the repossession of what originally belonged to these communities (1989:285-286).

Muslims, like Christians, therefore, are monotheists who trace their spiritual heritage through Abraham. They recognize as Scripture the Torah (*Taurat*), the Psalms (*Zabur*) and the New Testament (*Injil*); they believe in the divine birth and ministry of Jesus and the role of His disciples (the *Hawariyun*); they acknowledge as prophets most of the major Biblical figures (including John the Baptist!) and they believe in the Day of Judgment and the second coming of Christ. Yet in spite of many similarities, there are also fundamental differences. Although Jesus is referred to as the Word of God (*Kalimat Allah*), the Spirit of God (*Ruh Allah*) and the Messiah (*Al-Masih*), Muslim theology proper teaches that Jesus is not divine nor the Savior of humanity. Islamic doctrine allows for a man to have up to four wives and for Muslims to engage in Holy War (*jihad*). For issues such as these, where Muslim doctrine contradicts the clear teachings of Scripture (particularly the New Testament), we need a Biblically and culturally informed framework with which to evaluate these doctrines in light of God's Word.

Hiebert's model of *critical contextualization* (1987) offers such a framework. This model calls for a careful examination of the practices and beliefs of the "context" (i.e. religion or culture), combined with a fresh study of corresponding Biblical beliefs and practices, in order to see what aspects of the context under study can be maintained, what elements need to be modified and what parts need to be rejected outright. Often in ministry with C4 and C5 believers, we have applied Heibert's model in order to understand and evaluate local Islamic beliefs and practices in light of Scripture. Our tentative conclusion is that most Islamic forms are Biblically sound, that several ceremonies can be modified, and that a number of Islamic teachings must be rejected in order to avoid harmful syncretism.

Kraft states (as mentioned above) that although salvation comes about through having a "primary allegiance" to Christ as Lord, one could still have a number of "secondary" allegiances, rituals, beliefs, and practices that would not necessarily interfere with their primary allegiance to Jesus (1996:210). C5 believers are likely to have a number of these secondary factors such as the *ritual* of praying five times a day and the *practice* of keeping the annual fast of *Ramadan.* They will also have an allegiance to their Muslim family and community that C1-C4 believers would likely not have. What secondary allegiances, rituals and practices are permissible for C5 believers would depend upon the leading of the Holy Spirit on a case by case basis as the new believers apply the principles of critical contextualization described.

Some C5 Muslims we have known still pray in the mosque facing Mecca; some do not. This brings to mind what the Lord spoke to Naaman through Elisha, granting him permission to follow his master even into a pagan temple (2 Kgs. 5:17-19), though Naaman declared he would never make a sacrifice to other gods. Recalling that Jesus focuses on the heart and personal relationship with His followers, it seems that from a Biblical standpoint it matters little *where* or *how* one prays (Jn. 4:21). What matters is that the prayer is to the Father through virtue of one's relationship with Jesus (Lk. 10; Jn. 4:23-24). As we see in Romans 14:1-6, on disputable matters, God deals with us as individuals. Only He knows the heart motives of Muslim believers who still pray in the mosque.

Some C5 believers still repeat the creed ("there is no god but God and Muhammad is His prophet"); some do not. Others have modified it to exalt the name of Jesus. We have heard some C5 believers say that they can accept Mohammed as a "prophet" in that he pointed his people to the one true God and spoke highly of Jesus in the Qur'an. They are quick to add, however, that Muhammad is neither divine nor a savior.

In our work, what seems to most hinder the new Muslim believer's relationship with Christ is not so much wrong theology or even allegiance to Muhammad, but instead it is bondage due to former occult involvement and heart wounds. From these he must be freed and healed (see Premise 8 below).

Premise 7: *Salvation involves a process. Often the exact point of transfer from the kingdom of darkness to the Kingdom of Light is not known.* Direction and process are crucial dynamics in understanding C5 or other insider movements. Models by Kraft and Hiebert are helpful in illustrating these dynamics.

In the *starting-point-plus-process* model, Kraft states that "God starts working with human beings where they are, solely on the basis of their faith commitment to Him" (Kraft 1979b:239). The only unacceptable starting point in the process of growth toward Christ is a primary allegiance to a god or spirit other than the God of the Bible. Like the thief on the cross and the Philippian jailer, when people call out to Jesus, they are saved. That means that the newly born again Muslim, the recently born again Jew, the just born again Methodist or Catholic and the just saved agnostic, are all now in the Kingdom, beginning the process of sanctification. As they follow Christ day by day, they are being transformed into His likeness with ever-increasing glory (II Cor. 3:18), though this fact may not be immediately apparent to the outside observer who would have trouble differentiating the "wheat" from the "tares" (Mat. 13:24-29).

Related to Kraft's model is Hiebert's model of "bounded" and "centered" sets (1994). A "bounded" set is one that has clear cut, black and white boundaries. One is either inside or outside the set (e.g. one is either a Christian or a nonChristian). On the other hand, a centered set is one where *direction* is more important than *current position*. A center point is pictured with arrows scattered around it. Some arrows near the center (Jesus) are pointed away from it; others far from the center are pointed toward it. A person with little Biblical knowledge yet pointed and moving toward Christ may be closer to the Kingdom than one with correct theology yet pointed and moving away from Christ (e.g. a Muslim seeker of Christ may be closer to Him than a person who was born and raised to know correct theology yet who does not pursue a personal relationship with Jesus). In a centered set view, we let God worry about exactly when our Muslim friend enters the Kingdom of Christ, and we focus instead on encouraging him to keep heading toward Christ.

Premise 8: *A follower of Christ needs to be set free by Jesus from spiritual bondages in order to thrive in his/her life with Him.* An estimated seventy percent of the world's Muslims are what many call "Folk Muslims" (Parshall 1983:16). Cutting across Islamic sects and divisions, this type of Muslim is one who incorporates magic, animism, shamanism and other such practices into his daily spiritual experience. Due to the overtly demonic nature of most of these folk Islamic practices, unless a new believer renounces them and is set free by Jesus, he is likely to fall back into the occult, becoming hamstrung in his spiritual growth.

In our field experience, the need for deliverance from occult bondage was obvious from the start. We have watched with joy as new believers destroy occult objects, renounce (and lose) former occult abilities, and receive deliverance from demons invited in by repeated occult rituals. However, we were puzzled by an ongoing lack of joy in their walk with the Lord, especially in their relationships with others. Misunderstandings and hurt feelings between believers and others caused some to fall away from the faith. In recent years we have begun to discover the role of healing prayer for heart issues in the discipleship of new Muslim believers. In an atmosphere of prayer, the Holy Spirit reminds the new believer of a particular heart wound, usually caused by childhood experiences. The believer is encouraged to pour out all his pain to the

Lord, instead of attempting to forget and deny it. We have been amazed at how Jesus makes Himself very real in these moments, and removes the sting of childhood rejection, sexual abuse, and deep shame. It often naturally follows to order out any demons that have found their home in these heart wounds. The fruit of Jesus' heart healing is tangible. Conflict in marriages, friendships between believers, and relationships between believers and others is reduced, and the ability to obey the commands of Scripture is increased. We have become convinced that a mix of Scripture study and healing prayer is necessary over a period of time to see a new disciple become grounded in the love of Christ, able to survive in his Muslim community and thrive in his walk with Christ. It is very helpful to have a simple method for healing prayer that can be easily passed on to new believers as they rely on Jesus Himself to heal and deliver.

It is also likely that there are powers and principalities inherent in aspects of Islam as well. While we do not know to what extent powers over whole institutions can be bound as they are in individuals, we must at least give careful attention to seeing each new believer personally set free from demonic strongholds that affect his group. This is especially important in the case of C5, since the believer will continue to have close contact with the community that is still bound by these powers. We have seen first hand in recent years that as the believer is set free in these three areas: occult involvement, heart wounds, and Islamic bondage, he is able to remain a part of the Muslim community of his birth without giving the enemy a place in his life (Jn. 8:14).

Premise 9: *Due to the lack of Church structure and organization, C5 movements must have an exceptionally high reliance on the Spirit and the Word as their primary source of instruction.* There is no substitute for reliance upon both the Spirit and the Word in the life of a believer. However, in one sense, this reliance is perhaps more obviously needed in a C5 movement than it is in the normal C1 or C2 church. The rather isolated C5 believers must rely upon personal or small group Bible study with very direct guidance by the Spirit of Truth. They don't have churches with Sunday schools, worship services, seminars, Bible studies, Bible colleges and prayer meetings to facilitate the growth of the believer. Two things are implied here. First, C5 believers must have access to comprehensible translations of the Bible that incorporate religious vocabulary appropriate for Muslim readers. Second, the simple home-based C5 fellowships must be able to hear the voice of the Holy Spirit in a manner reminiscent of New Testament narratives (Ac. 10:19-20, 13:2, 16:6-10). This would mean wide use of New Testament gifts (*charisma*) as well.

Premise 10: *A contextual theology can only properly be developed through a dynamic interaction of actual ministry experience, the specific leading of the Spirit and the study of the Word of God.* It is instructive to see in Acts 15 how the early church determined God's will regarding Gentile believers and what they must do in order to "be saved" (Ac. 15:1). One group of born-again Pharisees, based upon their interpretation of Scripture, contended that Gentiles "must be circumcised and required to obey the law of Moses" (Ac. 15:5). By describing the events leading up to the council as well as its actual proceedings, Luke informs us as to how the early church settled this most crucial matter. As we shall see, it was an interaction based upon experiences from the field, the leading of the Spirit and an understanding of Scripture.

Note that as the delegation of Paul and Barnabas traveled through Phoenicia and Samaria on the way to Jerusalem, they told the believers along the way "how the Gentiles had been converted" (Ac. 15:3). Their case studies/testimonies of God's work among the Gentiles made all the believers "very glad". Upon arrival in Jerusalem, the case studies continued as Paul and Barnabas told the elders "everything God had done through them" in their Gentile ministry (Ac. 15:4). Next to speak was Peter, who offered his case study of Gentile work (Ac. 10). Peter related how, to the utter astonishment of his born-again Jewish companions, the Holy Spirit was "poured out" in front of them upon Gentiles who began "speaking in tongues and praising God" (Ac. 10:46). This, along with the vision he had received from God (Ac. 10:9-16), was all the apostle Peter needed to declare, "Can anyone keep these people from being baptized with water?" (Ac. 10:47).

At this point in the Acts narrative, the entire Jerusalem council became quiet as the floor was handed back to Paul and Barnabas to offer more case studies on the "miraculous signs and wonders God had done among the Gentiles" through their ministry (Ac. 15:12). Only at this point does the council leader James arise, affirm the value of case studies, and state that what has miraculously already *happened* experientially on the field among Gentiles is, in fact, *supported* by Old Testament Scripture (Ac. 15:13-18). The Scriptural basis was there all along for the acceptance of Gentiles, but it took first hand experience, and the unmistakable work of the Holy Spirit, for the early church to properly interpret Scripture in light of their present day context.

In the first century Paul and the early church sought God for a contextual theology to undergird and understand the ministry God was thrusting them into among the Gentiles (Ac. 15:19-29; Gal. 2:2; 1 Cor. 9:19-23; Rom. 3:28-30; Eph. 3:6). Initially many could not conceive of how a Gentile could be saved or of how certain theological positions would have to be scrapped in order to be obedient to the new thing God was doing. We are presently in a similar situation today as we attempt to bring the love of Jesus in an incarnational manner to the world's one billion Muslims. We desperately need a contextual theology of ministry and church to apply in today's Islamic milieu (Gilliland 1989a on contextual theologies). In order to not miss what God wants to do (as the Jerusalem church could have done), our theology for Muslim ministry must be Biblically-based, Spirit-led and informed by real life case studies from the field.

As stated earlier, God is already producing a C5-type church. The question is whether or not we will agree to it.

A Look Beyond the Islamic Milieau

As of the year 2000, Christianity in all of its many branches and expressions, is by far the world's largest faith (see Johnstone 1993:20). Yet one of the most striking features of this phenomenal growth is that in 2000 years, the Gospel *has only been established among animistic and certain polytheist peoples!* Whether among preChristian pagan Greeks and Europeans, or African and Asian tribal peoples, the Gospel has only taken root in social environments where "ethnic" or "folk" or "national" religions are embraced (what anthropologists often pejoratively call "low" or "primitive" religions). Of the world's "mega" faiths, that is the numerically huge, ancient, international religions – primarily Islam, Hinduism and Buddhism – the Gospel has yet to find a home (Buddhist Korea in the 20th century being an exception). What is the reason for this? Why has this wonderful news of the Gospel been stopped outside the gates of each of these "mega" religions?

Using the term "high" religion for what we are calling "mega" faiths, and "primitive" religions for the smaller animistic and tribal faiths, Church historian Kenneth Latourette discusses what happened when medieval Christian Europe was attacked by peoples that followed a "high" religion and peoples that followed a "primitive" religion:

> In contrast with the East where the major incursion, that of the Moslem Arabs, brought with it a "high" religion, Islam, all invasions of the West were either by "barbarians" who were already in part converts of Christianity or who had more nearly "primitive" religions. *It is a generalization borne out by universal human experience that a "primitive" religion yields more readily to "high" religion than does a "high" religion to another "high" religion.* Christianity won back none of the ground lost by it in the East to Islam, but, in contrast, it not only regained all of the territory in the West which it lost but pressed out beyond its former frontiers and gathered into its fold pagan peoples of "primitive" faiths and cultures (1975:328, author's emphasis).

What is it in these "high" or "mega" religions that makes them so much less open to the Gospel than the animistic or local religions? One reason is the increased group sense of "we must be right" due to sheer numbers ("How could one billion people and all my ancestors be wrong?"). A second reason is an increased sense of power and prestige that the mega-faiths have due to social, political and economic clout in the world arena. A third reason is the presence in the mega-faiths of formalized clergy, holidays, theologies, pilgrimages, Holy Books, places of worship, training centers, etc., all of which give a sense of permanence and at least outward forms of holiness. But perhaps the chief reason is simply the high fusion that seems to exist in ethnic groups where mega-faiths are followed, making the separation of culture and religion nearly impossible. Our understanding of the place of culture and religion will inform the type of contextualization we engage in as we approach people of mega-faith backgrounds.

Most of us have observed that an individual's spiritual experience and convictions are often, to varying degrees, different from the standard theologies of their religion or denomination. Many mainline Protestants have had a "born again" or a "charismatic" experience, something that may not be endorsed by their church or pastor. Yet, for social and familial reasons, they often stay within their church or denomination, augmenting their spiritual life with outside Bible study and fellowship. This is certainly the case as well with many "evangelical" or "charismatic" Catholics who stay in the church yet do not believe all the church's official teachings on certain issues such as the role of Mary in a believer's life. The amazing phenomenon of Messianic Judaism, a movement where Jews have come to recognize Jesus as the Messiah, yet have no interest in joining "Christianity" per se is another case in point. Lastly, as we have discussed elsewhere in this chapter, there are now thousands of Muslims around the world who either in private (C6) or in small groups (C5) acknowledge Jesus as their Lord and Savior and yet have stayed within the community of Islam. In most of these cases involving Christianity, Judaism and Islam, these Jesus followers highly esteem the religion or denomination of their birth, yet have also given full allegiance to Jesus of the Bible. Perhaps one of the reasons this can work in a mainline Protestant church, the Catholic church, a Jewish synagogue, or a mosque, is the fact that all these faiths are monotheistic and trace their lineage through Abraham. But what of other mega-faiths that are not necessarily monotheistic or do not trace their roots and holy books back to Abraham and other Jewish, Christian and Muslim prophets such as Noah, Moses, Jonah, David and Solomon? Could any form of insider movement occur within the fold of Hinduism or Buddhism?

An amazing book has just been republished by William Carey Library entitled *Churchless Christianity* (Hoefer 2001). The author, while formerly teaching at a seminary in India, began hearing stories of Hindus who in fact where worshipping and following Jesus in the privacy of their own homes. Knowing that there are many Hindus who have high regard for Jesus as a teacher, he set out to find out if indeed they had accepted Him as Lord and Savior or only as an enlightened guru. His quest became the basis of a doctoral dissertation in which he interviewed eighty such Hindu and Muslim families in the area of Madras India. His conclusion is that a large number of these families, though having never been baptized or joined churches, indeed have a true relationship with Christ and pray and study His Word fervently. Hoefer says that most want baptism, but have never seen a baptism which is not one in the same with becoming an official member of a particular church. His conclusion after a very extensive process of interviews and statistical analysis is that in Madras there are 200,000 Hindus and Muslims who worship Jesus—an amount equal to the total number of Christians in that city!

It is instructive to note that 200 years ago, William Carey referred to Hindu followers of Jesus as "Christian Hindoos." Apparently this was due to the strong linkage in the minds of the Indians (and presumably William Carey) between being Hindu and being Indian (etymologically the word India comes from Hindia which means the land of the Hindus). Rather than Hinduism being close to monotheistic faiths, it is just the opposite: adherents can worship any number of gods and goddesses. It appears that this openness allows room to exclusively worship the God of the Bible as the one true God (note the words of Joshua in Joshua 24:14-15).

In the early 1900s, Indian evangelist Sadhu Sundar Singh ran into hidden groups of Jesus followers among Hindus. As he preached the Gospel in Benares, his listeners told him of a Hindu holy man who had been preaching the same message. Sadhu spent the night at the man's home and heard his claim that his Hindu order had been founded long ago by the apostle Thomas, and now had up to 40,000 members. Sadhu later observed their services (including worship, prayer, baptism and communion) which were held in places that looked exactly like Hindu shrines and temples, minus the idols. "When Sundar tried to persuade them that they should openly declare themselves as Christians, they assured him that they were doing a more effective work as secret disciples, accepted as ordinary *sadhus,* but drawing men's minds toward the true faith in readiness for the day when open discipleship became possible" (Davey 1950:80).

Recently, we met a man doing outreach among Buddhists where there is an extremely high fusion of culture and religion. To my surprise he had taken the C1-C6 Continuum and adapted it to a Buddhist context. Though it appears impossible for the Gospel to thrive inside Buddhism, might there not be millions of Buddhists who are nominal believers and who are only Buddhist due to birth and nationality? As Kraft has stated (1996:212-213), once this principle of true spiritual allegiance versus formal religion is grasped, "we begin to discover exciting possibilities for working within, say, Jewish or Islamic or Hindu or Buddhist or animistic cultures to reach people who will be culturally Jewish or Muslim or Hindu or animist to the end of their days but Christian in their faith allegiance." (Note the capital "C" on Christian in this quote. Kraft defines Christian with a capital "C" as a true follower of Christ verses christian with a small "c" as referring to those merely attached to the religious institution by that name).

What is all of this leading to? Is there not blatant idolatry in traditional Hinduism? Yes, but not among those Hindu followers of Christ described by Hoefer and Davey. Is there not a denial by most Muslims that Jesus died on the cross? Yes, but not by those Muslims we have known who have put their faith in Christ. Is it not true that Jews teach the Messiah is yet to come? Yes, but thousands of Jews go to Messianic synagogues and believe, as did thousands of Jews in the first century, that Yeshua is indeed the long awaited Son of David.

We are tentatively coming to the conviction that God is doing a new thing to reach these remaining sociocultural groups dominated by mega-faiths. If Bosch had it right that faith in Christ wasn't meant to be a religion, could it be that we are witnessing some of the first fruits of vast movements where Jesus is causing the Gospel to break out of the confines of what has been known as "Christianity"? Could it be that God wants those who know Jesus to remain as a sweet fragrance inside the culture, including the religion of their birth, and eventually the number of born again adherents grows so large that a reform movement from inside that religion is birthed? The process may be theologically messy, but we see no other alternative. If we view both culture and religion as a person's own skin, we can look beyond it to the millions of human hearts longing for God yet longing to remain in community with their own people. This is in no way universalism (the belief that in the end all will be saved). Rather this is a call to take much more seriously Christ's final words to go into all the world—Hindu, Buddhist, Muslim, Christian—and make disciples of all nations.

Chapter 24

A Typology of Approaches to Thai Folk Buddhists

Paul H. DeNeui

Is it possible for Buddhists to remain within their cultural context and faithfully follow Jesus Christ? In many Buddhist countries national identity is closely linked with religious identity; good citizenship is equated with being a Buddhist. This religious patriotism seems problematic for the cause of the gospel of Christ. As a result, cross-cultural missionaries have often viewed Buddhism as the enemy of evangelism and have sought ways to counter it with Christianity. This approach has not only served to alienate people socially, but has also reinforced the misunderstanding that Jesus is a foreigner, the leader of a foreign religion. For too long, Christ has been presented in the Buddhist world, in the words of Thomas Wisley, as "more Western than Christian" (1985:128).

In addition to viewing it as the enemy of Christianity, many cross-cultural missionaries seek to deal with Buddhism as if it is a pure elite religion. They strategize by studying orthodox Buddhist doctrines such as Dharma, the Four Noble Truths and the Eight-fold Path in hopes that they can convince Buddhists that Christianity is better. My experience living in Thailand for fourteen years, however, is that what is called Buddhism is more animism than orthodox Buddhism. This "folk Buddhism" seems perfectly acceptable to all but a handful of elite Buddhist monks. But it puzzles the majority of Christian missionaries who find their favorite approaches to Buddhists falling on deaf ears. Appropriate approaches to folk Buddhists have, by and large, not been developed. It is time to recognize this reality and to consider that a diversity of approaches is needed. Existing models that focus on countering elite Buddhism with Christianity on the intellectual level have a role to play in reaching those few who are truly followers of an elite form of Buddhism. But new approaches will need to be developed to reach the majority who are folk Buddhists and will not be attracted by arguments focused on doctrine.

Biblical and Historical Precedent

From the beginning of recorded Scripture, God was calling a people out of animism. Joshua 24:2,3 records God's words,

Long ago your forefathers, including Terah the father of Abraham and Nahor, lived beyond the River and worshipped other gods. But I took your father Abraham from the land beyond the River and led him throughout Canaan and gave him many descendants (NIV).

Two generations later, Jacob's wife insisted upon stealing her father's household gods (Gen. 31:19) to take with her for protection as she traveled (Barker 1995:52). In the Exodus account, God specifically states that the final plague was a judgment upon the Egyptian gods, an act and a calling-out to be celebrated by generations to come (Ex. 12:12,17). God's first commandment, "You shall have no other gods" significantly ends with the words "before me" (Ex. 20:3 NIV) or "in hostility towards me."[1] God acknowledged the existence of other gods (after Him) in the lives of his people but instead of demanding their immediate repudiation allowed time for the transformation of their allegiances (Kraft 1996:210).

Certainly, the history of the Israelites, an animistic people in the midst of other animistic societies, shows the disastrous results of confusing secondary with primary allegiances.[2] Even God's prophet Elisha's approval to Naaman in 2 Kings 5:15-19 seems to indicate that God understands when social obligations require certain actions that might appear compromising to faith. For God, the condition of the heart always has priority over the external ritual. God rejects rituals, even those he once commanded, when offered out of hypocrisy of the heart (Amos 5:21-24).

It is often noted how Paul used animistic Greek images and forms to speak to Greeks (Ac. 17:16-23; I Co. 9:19-23). It was the actual inclusion of non-Jewish animistic Gentile believers into the family of faith that brought about the most revolutionary transformation of the church. To the hearers of its day the term "Gentile believer" was an oxymoron. "Being Gentile surely carried implications of religious consequence, deeply ingrained in the psyche of every Jew and Judaizer who objected to their inclusion in the church without first converting to Judaism" (Massey 1999). To say "Gentile believer" was akin to our saying "Buddhist Follower of Jesus", "Muslim Believer," or even "NonChristian Christian." The term "Christian" was never required of the followers of the Way; all three usages found in the Bible are pejorative (Ac. 11:26; 26:28; I Pe. 4:16). And nowhere in Scripture is there any indication of an agenda to erase the distinctives of the various peoples gathered into the family of God (Roxburgh 2002). Instead, every nation, tribe, people and language will ultimately be represented and somehow miraculously joined together in a gloriously comprehensible tribute of praise to the Lamb (Rev. 7:9).

---

[1] This Hebrew word is translated "in hostility toward" in Gen. 16:12, 25:18 (Barker 1995:114).

[2] Gods with a small "g" are mentioned 221 times in the Old Testament.

Believers in the first centuries of the church had to come to an understanding about their animistic heritage. Who were they if they were not Jewish?

> Early Gentile Christianity went through a period of amnesia. It was not so critical for first-generation converts: they responded to a clear choice, turned from idols to serve the living God, accepted the assurance that they had been grafted into Israel. It was the second and third generations of Christians who felt the strain more. What was their relation to the Greek past? (Walls 2000:13-14).

Greek theologians would borrow from their animistic tradition in order to communicate the gospel in ways to which their people could relate and respond:

> They used the Greek epics; they used the Homeric myths, and also Stoic and Epicurean philosophy when it suited them. We even find Clement of Rome, after arguing for the reasonableness of the resurrection from the fact that seeds die and come to life again in new flowers, laying enormous stress on the phoenix. This Eastern (mythological) bird was said by the poets to die and be reborn from its own ashes every 500 years. Clement really believed this! It is the climax of his argument. He was in this respect as others a child of his age. Even so, it was not the phoenix he was interested in, but Christ. Anything in Greek thought that would help his listeners to lay hold of the wonder and the reality of the resurrection was good enough for Clement. And this is the characteristic aim which the Greek exponents of the gospel set themselves: to embody biblical doctrine in cultural forms which would be acceptable in their society. Not to remove the scandal of the gospel, but so to present their message in terms acceptable to their hearers, that the real scandal of the gospel could be perceived and its challenge faced (M. Green 1970:142).

The earliest missionaries to the pagan animist inhabitants of the British Isles in the early sixth century questioned their own interaction with the animistic context. What from animism, if anything, could be used for the gospel, and what must be rejected? They received the following response from Pope Gregory I:

> The heathen temples of these people need not be destroyed, only the idols which are to be found in them. . . . If the temples are well built, it is a good idea to detach them from the service of the devil, and to adapt them for the worship of the true God. . . . And since the people are accustomed, when they assemble for sacrifice, to kill many oxen in sacrifice to the devils, it seems reasonable to appoint a festival for the people by way of exchange. The people must learn to slay their cattle not in honour of the devil, but in honour of God and for their own food; when they have eaten and are full, then they must render thanks to the giver of all good things. If we allow them these outward joys, they are more likely to find their way to the true inner

joy. . . . It is doubtless impossible to cut off all abuses at once from rough hearts, just as the man who sets out to climb a high mountain does not advance by leaps and bounds, but goes upward step by step and pace by pace (Norman E. Thomas 1998:22).

Numerous examples, possibly from every continent and society, could be given to illustrate the historical interaction between a politically dominant Christianity and animism that attempted to eradicate animism but merely drove it underground. Religious-oriented evolutionary thought gave rise to the notion that animism would eventually die out to the higher religions, preferably Christianity. As recently as 1973 missions anthropologist Alan Tippett wrote, "I give [folk religion] ten years, at the very utmost twenty" to disappear (1973:9). Many Christian missionaries admit that this is unrealistic but continue to act as if it were true. In fact, folk religions have had a recent resurgence (Van Rheenen 2002), particularly in modern urban contexts (Hard 1989:45-46).

It was not required of early believers that they attend "Jewish" classes in order to become full-fledged church members. Why are we requiring the same thing from people coming from other religious and cultural backgrounds? Bruce Heckman describes this from the Muslim perspective in which he worked:

> Muslim believers need a community which is distinct from the Christian community. Their community cannot be simply a "new believer" class which is attached to an existing church, nor a temporary arrangement which hopes to eventually bridge them into the Christian community. The Muslim believers' community will need the freedom to critically examine their Islamic background and decide upon the inclusion, exclusion or alteration of old religious and social forms. The style, location and scheduling of meetings needs to be a result of their communal choice rather than based upon Christian patterns (Arab or expatriate) (1988:128).

In an effort to address these issues, John Travis has developed the C1 to C6 Spectrum "to assist church planters and Muslim background believers to ascertain which type of Christ-centered communities may draw the most people from the target group to Christ and best fit in a given context" (Travis 1998a:407). The spectrum has been a helpful and highly debated tool among mission groups working within a Muslim context. I believe that this spectrum, with modification, has application for those working in the folk Buddhist context as well.

One Mission, Many Types of Response

The C1 to C6 spectrum presents six types of churches and Christ-centered communities that exist in the Muslim world. These same types also exist in the folk Buddhist world. The spectrum is not intended to judge one type of church as more valid than another but simply to describe the cultural types that exist. It is unfortunate that it has been described as a continuum with movement up and down from one cultural type to another. In fact, there is no particular "up" or "down." Such terminology tends towards negative categorization and a great deal of ambiguity about direction. A typology suggests ways of discussing, with some degree of comparative understanding, approaches that differ from each other in certain ways. Such comparisons of Christ-centered communities suggest that all types of "church" can be equally valid but that all not all types are as culturally relevant as we believe God would want them to those who attend. Lateral movement from one position on the scale to another is possible either towards cultural relevancy or away from it. It is hoped that the people worshiping in any of the types are in the process of transformation and meaningful spiritual growth.

Application of C1 to C6 to a Thai Folk Buddhist Context

What follows is an expanded description of the six church types found on the C1 to C6 spectrum as it has been adapted for a folk Buddhist context primarily in Thailand. With further research, it is hoped that this scale will become a tool with application throughout the broader folk Buddhist world. In each description, leadership styles, meaning and identification for the members, and engagement with the local society are illustrated by examples and a brief evaluation of strengths and weaknesses.

C1	C2	C3	C4	C5	C6
Intentional transplant church using dominant national language, con-sciously alien to local culture and religion	Intentional transplant church using local language, overtly alien to local culture and religion	Local language church, overtly alien, but able to incorporate religiously neutral cultural forms	Local language Christ-centered community using cultural, biblically permissible folk Buddhist forms	Christ-centered community of Buddhist followers of Jesus	Secret groups of under-ground believers

Figure 24.1 C1 to C6 Spectrum Adapted for Folk Buddhist Context
(With acknowledgment to John and Anna Travis)

C1 Intentional Transplant/Dominant Language Church

The advocates of a C1 church type deliberately attempt to transplant forms and structures of Christianity from another culture (usually Western) to the folk Buddhist receptor culture. Travis defines the resulting churches as traditional Western churches using a language different from that of the local community (see Chapter 23). Such churches will use the dominant national language of the host society, but otherwise will be consciously alien culturally and openly, aggressively anti-Buddhist and anti-local culture. If the dominant national language happens to be the language of the members, it becomes for them a C2 church (described below). C1 churches appeal to those who, for a variety of reasons, desire to identify with forms that are primarily Western. C1 believers call themselves "Christians" who practice Christianity and understand it to be an imported religion.

The leader of a C1 church will usually be a native of the target culture who has been trained in a Bible school, college or seminary that has a Western-based curriculum. The language of instruction may be the dominant national language or an outside language (e.g. English). He or she will identify with the communication methods, theologies and organizational structures of Western Christianity and will be taught to incorporate them into the life of the local congregation.

Though the members of such foreign looking and acting churches may be quite sincere, they are often those already marginalized by their society who see the possibility of greater personal advancement by linking with a missionary or a foreign religion. Others may seek status, cultural or career advancement, or genuine freedom from spiritual enslavement and feel a strong desire to reject anything having to do with Buddhism and related cultural expressions.

Many who follow Christ in a C1 approach make significant personal sacrifices, and are often cut off socially from their communities. They develop strong allegiances to forms and practices, even relationships, consciously alien to their original society and its religion. As a result, C1 churches have limited interaction with local nonChristian communities. Some may invite members of their communities to special celebrations (e.g. at Christmas time). But the forms used in such events will remain firmly outside of the local language and customs.

A subcategory of C1 is the English-speaking international church type such as those found in Bangkok and Chiang Mai. This church type deliberately attempts to replicate Christian forms and styles as they exist in the West, primarily to be a "home away from home" for expatriates located away from their home culture. It will not attract many local people.

Examples of C1:

The First Gospel Church of Thailand (GCT) in Khon Kaen, in the center of northeast Thailand is an example of a C1 church. Started by American missionaries in the 1930s, it uses the Central Thai language and employs foreign organizational structures and forms. Although it is in the heart of the Lao-speaking northeast Thai region, known as Isaan, members almost visibly shed their identities at the door. This is true throughout the breadth of Isaan and is also true of some churches in the *kammüang*-speaking churches of Thailand's northern region. Very few churches in Thailand employ anything other than the national language (Central Thai), in spite of the fact that over half of the Thai population speak a different mother tongue (Smalley 1994:1).

Strengths

In type C1, the separation from local culture is very distinct. The intentional use of foreign forms and outsider language are probably the most important distinctives of these churches. This is what builds the cultural framework that makes the worship and the congregational experience appealing to the target group. C1 churches attempt to build a new psychological and spiritual identity to support those separated from their traditional community. Some have established programs that help their new members through the initial painful periods when unbelieving family and friends reject them (Caleb Project 1988:56).

Weaknesses

Due to the large cultural chasm, social rejection is high. Those who get involved in a C1 church may be viewed with suspicion by family, or may be encouraged to get involved for ulterior motives. Locals who are not fluent in the dominant language may be hesitant to get involved. C1 churches often contribute to feelings of ethnic inferiority by exclusively promoting a national language and foreign culture when the majority of the members speak a different language and practice a very different culture at home. Another weakness of C1 churches is that they attract social outcasts and misfits. Such individuals are, however, often willing to sacrifice whatever remains of their cultural and/or religious identification because they see the former ways as having already failed them (Keyes 1993:271).

C2 Church Transplant Using Local Language

C2 is essentially the same as C1 except for the use of the local language and a subtle degree of mellowing. Though insider language is used, religious vocabulary, ritual, structures and forms would still be nonBuddhist and foreign, easily identified by C1 believers as distinctively "Christian." Few churches originate as C2; most were started as C1. However, over time, the cultural and religious alienation wears down to where the ethos, although still overtly alien, becomes a degree more tolerant, at least towards local language usage. Leaders may come from folk Buddhist backgrounds, or from Christian family backgrounds, but most would have been trained in forms familiar to the C1 approach. They would use C1 terminology and likely use a Western denominational label to refer to themselves. Though they may or may not be familiar with the Western "church forms" before they joined the church, they want to learn them because they assume them to be required. When referring to themselves C2 believers willingly call themselves "Christians" who practice Christianity.

In spite of using the local language, the cultural separation between the surrounding folk Buddhist community and the C2 church is still distinct. Interaction with people in the local context is limited similarly to C1.

Examples of C2:

It might be assumed that in a city like Bangkok, located in central Thailand where the heart language is Central Thai, that most church members would be Central Thai speakers which would then make the churches C2. This was not the case. One survey indicated that of forty-seven Bangkok churches contacted, none had purely Central Thai members; most were a mixture of Chinese-Thai and members from the north, the south, and the northeast regions. Less than twenty percent of any church was made up of members from Bangkok or central Thailand[3] (Caleb Project 1988:53).

The Mahaporn church, born originally out of the Christian and Missionary Alliance (C&MA) C1 English-language Evangelical Church on Sukhumvit Soi 10 in Bangkok, is one of the best examples of a C2 church. This congregation has given birth to several other Thai-language C2 congregations in the greater Bangkok area and has sent Thai church planters from the mother church to begin a (C1) church in Thep Satit district in the northeast province of Chayaphum.

Strengths

People are attracted to C2 churches for a wide variety of reasons. These may range from a strong feeling of disillusionment with their Buddhist past to a strong desire for freedom from spiritual bondage in animistic practices. Some have experienced physical healing. For many of these people a definite sense of separation from their nonChristian past is critically important. Their new sense of loyalty is to Christ and His Church and they are eager to embrace this relationship. As in the case of C1, the sense of a Christian identity is clear-cut in C2 churches. Separation from local culture, while often painful, is distinctly clear. C2 eagerly identifies with the larger global Western church in form. Expatriate visitors can be deeply moved hearing their own songs sung in a foreign language. Uniformity is an important strength.

Weaknesses

As in C1, C2 can result in cultural ostracism of members. Members have little opportunity to interact freely with community and family members[4], as well as social (and sometimes physical) martyrdom[5]. A C2 church can often feel

---

[3] The average proportion of the churches was Chinese 22%, Thai-Chinese 35.2%, Isaan 7.9%, Northern 8.3%, Southern 7.4% and Bangkok 18.5% (Caleb Project 1988:53).

[4] Southern Baptist pastor-trainer, Sinchai Chaochareonrhat was so motivated by his own personal experience of familial rejection that he wrote a book, "Christians on the Thai Path" calling for a more culturally-interactive approach. Mejudhon and Bharati also plead for less aggressive methodologies.

[5] A vivid description of the painful torture and martyrdom of the first two Thai

as if it is on the defensive culturally and may develop a preservationist attitude (not unique to Thailand). If missionary leadership was involved in starting the church, the transition to local leadership can be difficult. Sometimes the initial forms that the missionaries introduced in order to get things started become sacred. As Paul Hiebert has said, "The scaffolding somehow got built into the structure itself."[6] Diversity is viewed with suspicion, preservation is key. Formal similarity is important.

> Missionary Christianity planted within the Thai church a Western-style dualism deeply concerned with protecting Christian purity from any defilement by "heathen practices." The Thai church has especially emphasized refraining from participation in Buddhist-animist ritual and ceremony as a key way of protecting its purity, and one finds Thai Protestant Christians constantly worrying over the question of idolatrous behavior in situations in which they are faced with having to join in Buddhist rituals—such as funerals, opening exercises in schools, and community events. The general rule has been to take a hard-line approach, one that adheres to as strict a definition of the boundaries between Christianity and Buddhism as possible (Swanson 2001:14).

Forms used in C2 churches can be confusing initially to outsiders who are trying to understand what Christianity is all about. Thai believers tell numerous stories on themselves about their first encounters with Christianity. Here is one from missionary observer Thomas Wisley reporting on a church experience in northeast Thailand:

> The elder stood before his congregation directing the twenty-five or so men and women as they sang one of their favorite hymns, *Phralohit Phrayesu* (Nothing But the Blood of Jesus). On one side of the *sala* (open air chapel) a young new convert perched on the backless bench and looked quizzically at the open hymn book in his hands. Obviously he was having a difficult time reading the words and following the music. . . . Because of the addition of Western musical notes to the indigenous Thai tonal pattern a strange new language had been created thus complicating even more this Thai attempt to worship God. . . . The leader was using his hands to beat out the time directing the song as he had been taught to do in the Bible school. But instead of directing 4/4 time as the song was written, he was beating 3/4 pattern that did not match the timing of the song. . . . I began to wonder whether Christianity in Thailand might be more Western than it was Christian (1985:127-128).

Christians in Chiang Mai is included in Alex Smith's volume, *Siamese Gold* (1982:68).

[6] Recollection by Charles H. Kraft in class lecture November 2002.

C3 Local Language Churches Using Religiously Neutral Cultural Forms

C3 churches attempt to reduce the cultural chasm between the church and the surrounding folk Buddhist community. This is done by including in the life of the church local forms from which Buddhist or animistic elements have been filtered out in an attempt to retain only nonreligious cultural elements. Meeting facilities may be in Western-style churches, local buildings, or homes. Religiously neutral forms may include some local music (whenever appropriate), culturally neutral combinations of local and Western instruments, use of artifacts, time, space, artwork, architecture, furniture (or lack of) and local communication methods. Folk Buddhist elements (where present) are filtered out so as to use purely nonreligious cultural forms. The aim is to reduce foreignness of the gospel and the church by incorporating what the leaders consider to be biblically permissible cultural forms. The members would come from a folk Buddhist background and most would not be familiar with Christianity but would be learning about it.

Leaders may have come from folk Buddhist backgrounds, or from Christian family backgrounds, but most would have been trained in Central Thai, using forms familiar to the C1 approach. Forms of Bible teaching may be preaching or Bible discussion. They would use C1 terminology when referring to themselves and to most aspects of their Christian experience, with some differences stemming from their particular denominational and church polity.

C3 church members would strongly identify with C1 and C2 Christianity. However, the issues of separation so dominant in the first generation may be somewhat softened in succeeding generations. While identification with worldwide Western Christianity is strong, there is a willingness to consider what it means to integrate some Thai forms into the Christian walk and into the life of the church. Members and leaders may have a C1 or C2 background but find meaning in the filtered cultural forms from the folk Buddhist community. C3 believers would still refer to themselves as "Christians."

Like C2, a C3 church is in process. It is distinguished from C1 or C2 in that it is beginning to attempt to consider ways in which it can interact with its local society while remaining loyal to its faith in Jesus Christ. It recognizes some of the barriers either of forms or attitudes inherent in their practice of Western Christianity and is beginning to contemplate ways in which these barriers can be addressed or removed without compromising Christian commitment. Unlike C1 and C2, C3 churches view cultural forms as potential points of connection with outsiders.

Examples of C3:

A good example of a C3 church in the folk Buddhist world exists in the capital city of a neighboring country to Thailand.[7]   Here a well-established

---

[7] The name is omitted for security reasons to the leadership and members of that

church, started by missionaries nearly eighty years ago, decided to transition into a more local-friendly approach. For them, this has meant taking out all of the Western style pews from inside the structure and replacing them with the familiar woven straw mats upon which everyone is seated when they enter. No longer are shoes worn within the church but are kept on racks outside. Other than this, the church has basically maintained its C2 approach but in this one area it is attempting to transition into C3.

Another example of C3 is the Suwanduangrit Church described by Herbert R. Swanson, an expatriate member and employee of the Church of Christ in Thailand (CCT). This church is in the community of Ban Dok Daeng located twenty kilometers east of Chiang Mai in northern Thailand. This church was originally started by American Presbyterian missionaries in 1880 using a C1 approach that gradually became C2. Over the years it developing into a fairly strong Christian minority located in its own segment of the village:

> Like other Thai Protestant churches, the Suwanduangrit Church has generally stood apart from the communal life of its village in spite of the facts that there were several inter-faith nuclear families and that most of the Christians have Buddhist relatives. Christians took no part in *wat* (Buddhist temple) activities other than to help with cooking at temple festivities when called upon to do so. Christians would attend those festivals and other events, such as funerals, but strictly as visitors. In this atmosphere of mutual distrust, the church lived largely for itself and took no thought as to how it might act as a witness to the love of God in Christ or carry out peacemaking activities. Its neighbors, in any event, would have treated any form of community involvement with suspicion, based on their general perception of Christians as being soul winning "head hunters" (2002:61).

When, in 1996, the local Buddhist temple built a new *phraviharn* (main ritual building in any Thai Buddhist *wat*), representatives from the temple committee contacted the church to find out how it would participate in the dedication festivities. "They made it clear that the usual policy of silence by the church was unacceptable to the larger community" (Swanson 2002:62). The resulting crisis that faced the church caused the members to struggle with the reality of the cultural chasm between themselves and their community that had existed for over one hundred years.

In spite of the heated discussions that ensued, the church eventually followed the temple's suggestion and participated in the *wat* festivities by donating a *tonkuatan,* known as a money tree, which is a bamboo frame upon which currency and other small items are hung. These money trees are then paraded through the streets and into the temple with loud music, drums and gongs, cheering and "well-oiled" dancing. Although this is a very typical sight

fellowship.

in much of Thailand, "what was new was the Christians, straggling along at the back—but *in* the procession" (Swanson 2002:7). This was seen as a major breakthrough by the community (2002:75).

While this one-time event may seem of little significance, it set in motion a new relationship between the Christians and their Buddhist community that was not forgotten. Five years later when the Suwanduangrit Church was close to completing its new multipurpose hall, members of the temple committee asked if they could donate a money tree to the church and sparked a second processional celebration. This time the church invited a Christian music group that contextualizes local music in worship to provide the music and during the procession of the money trees church members were seen dancing as well. "Being a Christian or with Christians, for once, was fun" (Swanson 2002:68).

The final event recorded by Swanson in this on-going transition occurred the following year, 2001, when the Buddhist temple was going to dedicate its own multipurpose building. At this point the church not only donated a money tree but also set up a booth at the temple festival, brought their own drums and gongs, and were seen as part of the community. It was agreed by the members and "even the leading elder of the 'separatist' group (that) the ceremony was 'really' only a traditional Thai one and not essentially religious" (2002:72). Through this process they were able to engage in a "redefinition of religious boundaries, a key issue for Thai local theology" (2002:72).

Strengths

When Christians borrow and incorporate popular forms from the local culture it can facilitate greater dialogue with the surrounding community members. It indicates that a church is struggling to chart its own course within the culture. This process, although sometimes quite painful, can promote deep spiritual growth. C3 Christianity is usually a sign of a church in transition desiring to become more culturally relevant with its local community.

Weaknesses

Not all secular forms, even if they are not strictly religious, can be assumed to be value-neutral. The so-called filtering process assumes a distinction between culture and religion that is not a reality for most of the Buddhist world. A C3 approach downplays the reality that so-called religiously neutral forms may carry strong cultural and faith values that are questionable from a biblical perspective. Some Buddhist, and even animistic, forms contain biblical truth and therefore may not necessarily require elimination (example: five major precepts of Buddhism) but their use may at the same time provide a strong pull back into Buddhism or animism. Because C3 attempts to transition from a completely outsider perspective to an integration with local perspectives, it will be attacked by C1 and C2 as compromising and yet viewed as Western by those in C4 or C5. Buddhists may resent the attempt to "filter out" elements of their practices. Additionally, in the process of "filtering" the question remains as to what is then substituted for the removed element. Unless it is initiated and accomplished internally, the transition in C3 from a Western orientation in form or attitude towards a new substitute can be imposed with paternalistic fervor equal to that of the original culturally-alienating approach. As William Smalley has written with regard to Western attempts to lead or force churches to support, lead and propagate themselves

> I strongly suspect that the "three selfs" are really projections of our American value systems into the idealization of the church, that they are in their very nature Western concepts based upon Western ideas of individualism and power. By focusing them on other people we may at times have been making it impossible for a truly indigenous pattern to develop. We have been westernizing with all our talk about indigenizing (Smalley 1958:51,55).

C4 Local Language Christ-Centered Communities Using Cultural and Biblically Permissible Folk Buddhist Forms

C4 adds to C3 biblically permissible folk Buddhist forms and practices that the members find acceptable and meaningful. C4 communities are comprised almost entirely of folk Buddhism background believers who may recognize C1-3 forms as representing the same Christianity of which they are a part, but find biblically permissible local forms most meaningful. They know little of Western forms of Christianity and are not learning about them or adopting them. Western cultural forms as found in C1 and C2 are avoided. Meetings are not held in Western-style church buildings but generally in homes, shops or public meeting areas.

Leadership of C4 groups are almost always those who have not been so removed from their folk Buddhist culture as to be unable to relate naturally to it. Believers raised in folk Buddhism, trained in a C1 approach and later attempting to minister in C4 work have rarely been successful.[8] Personal conflicts within the individual quickly surface and any lack of genuineness becomes obvious. Equipping leaders for a C4 approach is a challenging new direction that Bible schools, colleges and seminaries in the Buddhist context have yet to fully develop.

Members of C4 congregations are hesitant to use Christian terminology when it builds a barrier between themselves and those of their social context. They recognize areas of conflict between their Buddhism and their faith in Christ and try to bring new meaning to forms that may not have been familiar but can be learned as functional substitutes. Their identity would be as followers of Jesus but also part of the Buddhist community, engaging in some cultural forms that do not conflict with Scripture. C4 believers would identify themselves as "Followers of Jesus," "Children of God" or similar terms, and

---

[8] The experience of the author is that few leaders who have studied abroad could return to the same level of ministry and entry into the culture they previously had. Many could not condone the use of local instruments or ceremonies in their churches.

avoid the term "Christian" because of its Western associations. C4 believers, though highly integrated into the surrounding community, are usually not seen as Buddhist by folk Buddhists.

Examples of C4:

An example of one church that successfully transitioned to using biblically permissible cultural forms is the Christian Church of Thailand (CCT) congregation in the Sakorn Nakorn province of northeast Thailand. Originally a C1 missionary plant, the church, under new missionary leadership, began to incorporate the *wai* (palms together) during prayer, using rice for communion, using local music and dance in worship, and sometimes even saying "*Satoo*" (*pali* for "so be it") at the end of prayer. This is a word that is used in Buddhist prayers. The Catholic church in Thailand has moved towards a C4 approach as well:

> Indigenization of the Catholic church has entailed adapting the Christian message to the local cultures, including to existing religious traditions insofar as this is possible without compromising fundamental Christian dogmas. In Thailand the church has adopted many Thai Buddhist terms for Christian concepts and has adapted Buddhist temple architecture for Catholic churches (Keyes 1993:273).

Strengths

The cultural chasm between C4 and the community is significantly reduced from that of C3. The biblical distinctives of Jesus' followers are more clearly identifiable than in C5 (see Figure 24.1 above). When appropriating local customs for use in the Christ-centered community the church will address issues of spiritual power that are deeply significant in the folk religious context. C4 is an attempt at a dynamically-equivalent church using local forms that communicate as much as possible. If the first generation is planted this way many of the mistakes of C1 and C2 can be avoided. If successful, the worshipping community will be able to manage the local ministry and carry on outreach within the confines of its own resources and giftedness. Overhead costs for a church structure are not necessary and leadership can be voluntary.

Weaknesses

C4 groups will be under pressure to conform to the already established C1 and C2 churches. Practices of C4 will be called into question by C1 and C2 congregations. In some cases the national government may insist upon a certain Western orientation and restrict movement by Christian groups beyond C3.[9]

---

[9] The Burmese government's attempts to eradicate all churches less than one hundred years old is one example. Buildings constructed more recently were being destroyed. Also, at one time, the Kampuchean government, in an effort to restore some cultural forms lost during the Khmer Rouge regime, required all music played on public radio to be traditional

Local formal Western-trained leadership coming from C1 and C2 backgrounds will have difficulty transitioning into a C4 mode and may be unwilling or unable to change. Local leadership will need to be trained from the grass roots in ways that are nontraditional.

Because of the emphasis on dynamic equivalency, nonChristians will notice and there may be negative reactions. "Indigenization of the Catholic Church in Thailand prompted a reaction by some conservative Buddhists who perceived a threat from a Christianity that was no longer clearly 'foreign'" (Keyes 1993:273). If clear communication is not established from the beginning the results can actually be damaging.

It appears that at least one difficulty in the overall communication of Christian meanings in this situation had to do with the alleged failure of Roman Catholics to observe the appropriate beginning levels of communication before going to a more advanced level that required greater degrees of confidence. The Roman Catholics assumed that the community would feel more comfortable with indigenous architectural roof design. This may have been true for the Christians in the community. Due to a lack of trust at the preliminary level a total breakdown in the community image took place (Wisley 1985:170-171).

C5 Christ-Centered Communities of Buddhist Followers of Jesus

C5 believers remain socially within their folk Buddhist context. Aspects of folk Buddhism that are incompatible with the Bible are rejected or reinterpreted if possible. This would include issues related to idolatry, merit-making, reincarnation, and others. C5 members celebrate their new life in Christ in ways that are familiar and meaningful to them, including location and forms of gatherings, communication styles, organizational structures, and methods of leadership and discipleship. Meetings are not held in Western-style church buildings but generally in homes, shops, or public meeting areas. C5 believer communities are comprised entirely of believers who come from folk Buddhist backgrounds, know little about Western forms of Christianity, and are not learning about them, or adopting them.

A question that might be raised with regard to C5 communities is whether a Christian leader of a C5 Christ-centered community can fulfill the ritual role of the monks. Without wearing a robe, many secular leaders already do. And anyway, in most of the Buddhist world, the impersonation of a Buddhist priest is a crime punishable by law. The understanding that a dynamically-equivalent church leader in C5 must look like a Buddhist monk is a false formal-equivalency. The function must have priority over the form. C5 leaders do not necessarily have academic training but their status in the community is one that

---

style and some of this entered into the church. Today this has been relaxed.

must be earned rather than achieved through formal Bible training or the earning of degrees.

Members of C5 groups would not use the terms "Christian" or "Christianity" to describe themselves. Their identification would primarily be as Buddhist followers of Jesus. They would not claim to be accepting, following or practicing "Christianity" but following Jesus Christ. C5 believers claim primary allegiance to the one true God and are viewed as "Buddhists who have Jesus" by the Buddhist community. They refer to themselves as "Children of God" or a similar name that would not build barriers between them and their communities.

C5 groups desire to engage closely with their people. They understand that there are certain aspects of folk Buddhism that are incompatible with following Jesus. However, they try to use culture as a bridge to reaching out, rather than focusing on the issues that separate. Folk Buddhists may view C5 believers as not being true Buddhists because they do not seek means of making merit or appeasing spirits as other folk Buddhists do. Participation by C5 believers in some Buddhist and animist functions varies from person to person and group to group. C5 believers do, however, participate in some of the folk Buddhist functions in the name of Jesus.

Examples of C5:

A group known as the "Church of the Grace of God," found in northeast Thailand, Chiang Mai, and Bangkok, Thailand, would, by most definitions, fit the description of C5. They meet in homes or other neutral meeting areas, some with merely a sign that states, "The Meeting Location of the Worshipping Community of (Village Name)." They employ local musical forms, song, dance and instruments. When they celebrate communion they use the local staff of life to represent the body of Christ (rice). Some members of the community have participated in giving food to monks in the name of Jesus. Others participate in a variety of community festivals. The group has developed a number of its own ceremonial practices that are functional substitutes for those found within folk Buddhism including funerals, weddings, house dedications, baby dedications, and a number of others (Institute for Sustainable Development 1993). Many of these ceremonies, involve the use of string-tying, a long tradition in Lao society that comes from animistic practices, but is redefined to visualize the invisible concept of the love of Christ. Careful explanation is given beforehand that the strings have no magical power. For those who participate, this signifies a new understanding of the power found in relationship with Jesus Christ. Many have stated it is the first time they feel they could follow Jesus and still remain a Thai. Other examples of C5 are found in some villages in the Det Udom district of Ubol Ratchatani, Thailand as well as in neighboring Buddhist countries.[10]

---

[10] Not listed for security reasons to members there.

Strengths

C5 is attractive to rural folk Buddhists. Gatherings that celebrate Christmas and Easter can attract many of the village communities. Communication of meaning is high, participation is high, local ownership, due to local leadership, is high. C5 focuses on transformation, not separation. Issues of spiritual power are clearly discussed, biblically addressed and relevant rituals are incorporated into the life of the community.

Weaknesses

C1-C2 groups may view C5 as unfaithful, syncretistic, or pagan. Opportunities to enrich one another between typologies through dialogue and interaction become difficult because of any number of reasons including mutual misunderstandings, fear, jealousy, or name-calling.[11] This may result in C5 churches moving towards isolationism or, even worse, a superior attitude, that views other typologies as less than effective. According to Massey, one weakness of C5 is to:

> Accuse brothers down the spectrum of obstructing the flow of the gospel with a culturally insensitive, extractionist approach. Pride can easily develop in those who are early adopters of God's unpredictable ways, as if they are on the cutting edge of a movement of God due to some personal ability of their own. Many fall into a trap of believing the approach God has called them to is the approach for everyone (1999).

Another potential weakness is that meaning of forms can revert to the original definitions and thereby reinforce a movement away from Christ towards syncretism.

C6 Secret Groups of Underground Believers

C6 describes persecuted believers who, due to fear, isolation, threat of extreme government repression, or social restriction, cannot or do not confess their faith in Christ openly. When C6 believers worship it is in secret meetings and they may use any form from C1 to C5. C6 is not actually a typology but it is a real situation of which all believers need to be made aware. God desires His people to witness and to have regular fellowship. Nevertheless, C6 believers are part of the family of Christ. Though God may call some to a life of suffering, imprisonment, or martyrdom, he may be pleased to have some worship him in secret, at least for a time. C6 believers would privately claim Christ as their Lord but would be perceived as Buddhists by their folk Buddhist community and would identify themselves as Buddhists.

Leaders for C6 communities can be of many types. Some are former leaders from other types of approaches (from C1 to C5) that have gone

---

[11] Some workers with the described movement in northeast Thailand were labeled "satanic" and their teachings heresy (Gustafson 1983).

underground and avoided detection. Others are gifted lay people. Leadership structures are sometimes intentionally ill-defined.

Due to intimately personal situations, the goal of C6 believers is to appear as one of the crowd as much as possible. There is no desire to confront traditional society or engage it in witness for Christ. At the same time, these brothers and sisters do bear a silent witness for Christ, with occasional verbal opportunities as well.

Examples of C6

C6 believers, while not evident in Thailand at present, probably exist in some form in every Buddhist country. Few Thai Christians seem aware of the fact that there are documented cases of their spiritual brothers and sisters imprisoned only a few kilometers away in the neighboring countries of Laos, Myanmar, Vietnam, and farther away, Sri Lanka, due primarily to religious persecution. Christian Aid Mission reports:

> Christians in Laos are facing cruel forms of physical and psychological abuse as authorities appear to be working to wipe out Christianity in the country. A confidential source said last week that since the country's new religious laws came into effect in July, Lao authorities are using new forms of persecution against churches in Laos. These methods are called "forced labour" and "community vocal shame." In the forced labour penalty, Christians are taken to a remote area to perform hard labour without pay for an extended period. They are told if they deny Christ, they will be returned to their home village and never taken away again. "Community vocal shame" involves putting believers on display before a large crowd of people in a village. Then, one by one, the villagers shout shameful words of abuse at the believers (2002).

Strengths

From the position of religious freedom, it is too easy to stand in judgment upon members of the family of Christ who live under repressive religious persecution and do not openly witness about their faith. There may be times in which God is pleased to allow His children to remain silent witnesses in order, for example, to stay at home as a provider or caregiver for the family, rather than suffer separation or physical harm. There is much to learn from those whose faith has been purified with the fire of persecution.

Weaknesses

God created His people for fellowship and witness. Believers who feel they must remain underground are in need of a special measure of God's grace and the uplifting prayers of the other members of the family of God.

The whole continuum for the Thai folk Buddhist context would look like this:

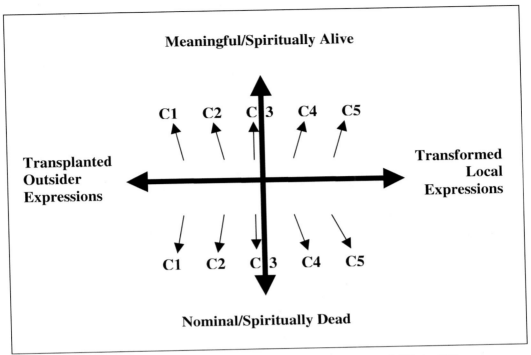

Figure 24.2 Grid for Viewing Directions of Movement of C1 to C6

Missiological Considerations

Viewing C1-C6 in Many Dimensions:

Critics of the C1-C6 spectrum have been quick to note that the spectrum primarily evaluates behavioral forms and virtually ignores the deeper cognitive (knowledge) and affective (feelings) domains (Søgaard 2002; Visser 2002). The accusation is valid since this is the major function of such a tool. Yet for animistic societies, where forms are the means by which people perceive and apply significance to content, the focus on forms is important. Just as communication is culturally oriented, so also all theological and biblical understanding comes wrapped in cultural forms of expression. However, there is a need to look beyond behavioral forms and address the question of meaning at another level. Even critically-contextualized, dynamically-equivalent, biblically-transformed churches can become nominal or even worse, revert to previous allegiances. Yet a strict separatistic approach that relies solely upon transplanted forms does not guarantee an avoidance of syncretism either.

The C1 to C5 spectrum can be plotted as a horizontal axis ranging from C1, transplanted outsider expressions, to C5, transformed local expressions. Across this horizontal line can be overlaid a vertical axis that measures meaning and nominality. On this resulting grid, it is possible to plot the position of any of the C1 to C5 types of church planting with regard to both form and function. This provides an evaluative model that begins to plot the affective and cognitive dimensions as well as the behavioral dimension, and provides a more rounded picture of the particular church type. Note that in Figure 24.2, examples of C1-5 are shown above the horizontal axis indicating movement towards deeper meaning as well as below the line towards nominalism. Any faith group can go in either direction but it is the direction in which the group is moving that is most important. Since C6 can be anywhere on the typology spectrum it is not shown.

It is important to note that in all approaches, from C1 to C6, it is possible for a believer to find significant spiritual meaning and to pursue continued spiritual growth toward Christ. It is also possible for syncretism to thrive at every level. No particular paradigm sets an absolute standard for the church, though one has historically tended to dominate. Given the complex nature of the folk Buddhist world, and the vast creativity of God, it is time to begin to consider types such as C4 and C5 and to recognize that these are also valid ways in which Buddhists are coming to Christ.

A Need For Diversity

As previously stated, most missionaries and church-planters in the Buddhist context focus primarily on seeking conversions from elite Buddhism. In spite of thousands of Christian groups already present, I would venture to say that most approaches used in the Buddhist world today are not yet diverse enough to allow the gospel to reach folk Buddhists in ways to which they can appropriately respond. J. Davis writes about Asia:

> [Churches] should be *first* dynamically equivalent and *second* culturally appropriate (if that is possible without compromise). This means that there will not be some sort of predictable structures for all cultures. Various decision making procedures, types of leadership (plural!), methods of discipline, ways of worship will all be different, determined by the cultural matrix. There will be no doubt that on occasions a new church will have to break out from traditional forms and structures (1998:260-261, author's emphasis).

The Role of Background:

Evaluating the C1 to C6 scale for Muslims, Massey raises the issue of the importance of the background of those working in a C5 type of ministry:

> Every C5 worker I know sees a huge difference between someone from a Christian background taking a C5 identity and someone from a Muslim background becoming a C5 believer. In fact, one pro-C5 team I know has a country-wide policy disallowing anyone from a Christian background from becoming C5; their identity can go no further than C4. If someone from a Christian background goes around calling himself a Muslim, all they'll do (according to popular C5 opinion) is either look like a total phony, or mislead Muslims into thinking they converted to Islam (1999).

Many significant differences exist between the Muslim and Buddhist contexts, but there are significant similarities regarding the role of the background of those who minister effectively within a C5 context. Most Buddhists who come to Christ in a C1 or C2 church are taught to separate from all things animistic and Buddhist. The resulting social disruption is well-documented (Chaochareonrhat 1998:8; Keyes 1993:259-283; Komin 1991:10; Phrommedda and Wechkama 2001:76). The high social cost paid by these believers includes leaving their former religious identity and establishing another entirely new one. It is unrealistic to expect persons who have experienced this pain to have any desire or ability to move to a C4 or C5 type of ministry without feeling as if they are compromising their faith. These forms of Christian expression would not be appropriate for them. For them, this is partaking of meat offered to idols (1 Cor. 8) and they should not. It is a C1 or C2 ministry that is appropriate for them.

Very few examples of intentional C4 or C5 ministry exist within the folk Buddhist context. However, in those cases where these approaches have been used, it is evident by the worldview exhibited that those best involved in the frontline leadership of these ministries come from this background and have never left it. This would include missionaries, both local and expatriate. It has been extremely difficult for those trained in a C1 or C2 approach to transition beyond C3. Based on personal interactions, I observe that some of the most gifted and well-educated staff involved in the C5 movement described above continually struggle internally with C1 training methods that they had previously received. Some had to resign because it became obvious that their heart did not resonate with a C5 methodology and everyone could tell. One gifted Asian Christian leader, raised in the folk Buddhist culture but trained in a C1 context, told me, "I feel closest to God when I pray in English." A woman such as herself would never feel comfortable nor could she come across with any degree of genuineness in a C5 type of work.

The Role of Missionaries Beyond C3:

Many missionaries would like to see their ministry go as far as C4 but their national leadership is unwilling. In this regard, missionaries can be both an extreme help and a potential hindrance. The presence of a foreigner in almost any Christian work in Asia will often lead to deference to the missionary—particularly if that person is paying the salaries! Missionaries, who have built up a level of trust from leadership within the local context, can continue to provide motivation and encouragement to those on the front lines to remain engaged with the cultural issues of the society at hand. There are few resources that encourage churches in C1 to C2 to move in the direction of C3 or farther. But missionaries with spiritual sensitivity and tact, missionaries who are able to learn from unwesternized insiders and to avoid paternalism, can greatly enable C3 to C5 Christianity.

Among Christian missionaries, there has been a widespread buying into the Asian cultural value that harmony equals consensus. But Biblically, unity in Christ does not mean that we all need to look and act the same but rather that we are all headed towards Jesus Christ. Biblical Christianity involves culturally appropriate growth toward Christlikeness. It is a "directional" faith (Kraft 1979a), that can be contextualized in any culture or subculture, not a "positional" religion that has to have a particular cultural form and that, therefore, can only be adapted to cultures other than the one in which it originated.

Chapter 25

Renewal, Revival, and Contextualization

Paul E. Pierson

It is clear from the study of history that mission normally, if not always, flows out of movements of renewal and revival. I believe it is also true that while there are normally generic elements in such movements, they also lead to a significant degree of recontextualization of the Church and its message in the new historical situation. Even churches that were appropriate to both culture and Bible in their beginnings, (and many churches were not,) tend to get out of synchronization with either or both as they move from generation to generation. After a few generations, therefore, they are in need of both spiritual and social renewal to restore appropriateness.

Such renewal and the recontextualization that accompanies it usually involves new ways of communicating the Gospel, new forms of the Church and new, less elitist, methods of selecting and training leaders as the giftedness of all believers is recognized. Just as with contextualization, the process of recontextualization asks four questions regarding the communication of the Gospel. They are: Who, How, Where, and To Whom? Nearly always in renewal movements, new, unexpected persons, with little or no status in the institutional church, have communicated the message. Usually new methods and styles of communication are used. This normally takes place outside the four walls of the traditional church, and reaches people thought to be undesirable or outside the reach of the Gospel.

Revival and Renewal

In thinking about revival it is important to note that no movement is ever perfect nor does it ever affect the entire church, much less its society. We live in a fallen world and the Church is still made up of sinners. Thus it is clear that every movement is disorderly around the edges and sometimes at the center, among its adherents, and even among its leaders. So there will always be criticisms of renewal movements, some justified, others unfair. Thus we want to avoid two unhistorical views. Advocates and participants in movements often fail to be self-critical, ignoring their exaggerations and blind spots. On the other hand, opponents often look only at the imperfections and fail to see the very real accomplishments, refusing to recognize the sovereign grace and power of God working in and through unexpected people and imperfect movements.

Now for some definitions. Packer defines revival as

> a work of God by his Spirit through his word bringing the
> spiritually dead to living faith in Christ, and renewing the inner life
> of Christians who have grown slack and sleepy. In revival God
> makes old things new, giving new power to law and Gospel and new
> spiritual awareness to those whose hearts and consciences had been
> blind, hard, and cold (1990:36).

Davies proposes the following;

> A revival is a sovereign outpouring of the Holy Spirit upon a
> group of Christians resulting in their spiritual reviving and
> quickening, and issuing in the awakening of spiritual concern to
> outsiders or formal church members; an immediate or, at other times,
> a more long-term effect will be efforts to extend the influence of the
> Kingdom of God both intensively in the society in which the Church
> is placed, and extensively in the spread of the gospel to more remote
> parts if the world (1992:15).

I suggest four rubrics as a helpful way to understand such movements.
The first is *renewal*, in which an individual or small group seeking a deeper and
more authentic life with God receives a profound experience of His power and
presence. This leads them to pray for and seek the next stage, *revival* in the
church as a whole, in which multitudes of believers are quickened in their faith.
The third stage occurs as the new life spills over into the society outside the
church, resulting in an *awakening*. Wider and more innovative evangelism,
ministries of compassion, often with the marginalized, and attempts at social
transformation result. In the fourth stage the revived church is motivated to *take
the Gospel* to those of other societies, often in geographically distant areas.

This is not to imply that every such movement has followed these steps in
this order. Some have been limited to a relatively small segment of the church
so that stage three never happened although stage four may result. Others have
been cut short by contextual factors and persecution or by the limited
understanding of their leaders. But the fact that this pattern can be seen in many
movements throughout history suggests that it can provide a model that we are
called to follow. And it is clear that Puritanism, Pietism, Moravianism, and the
evangelical awakenings of the 18th century, out of which the Protestant
missionary movement developed, each exhibited the characteristics mentioned
above.

Richard Lovelace helpfully describes for us the generic elements in
renewal. He suggests two preconditions of renewal, two conditions that prepare
people to hear the Gospel with new power. The first is the awareness of the
holiness of God, both His justice and His love. The second is the awareness of
the depth of sin, both in our personal lives and in our community.

He then lists what he calls the "primary elements of renewal." These are
first, justification—the fact that we are accepted in Christ. Secondly comes
sanctification—the recognition that in Christ we are free from the bondage of sin

and called to exhibit this in daily life. Thirdly, we are not alone because in Christ we have the indwelling Spirit. And finally, through Him we have authority in spiritual conflict (Lovelace 1979:75).

Again, I am not suggesting that every movement follows this order exactly, but in each one we find all of these important elements. For example, Peter Waldo, in the twelfth century, was concerned about what he perceived to be his sin of usury, forbidden by the medieval Church. This led him to sell his goods, give to the poor, and seek to follow Christ fully. The result was a movement that swept hundreds of thousands into the Kingdom during the next century, despite severe persecution. Its remnant became one of the streams that merged with the Hussites and became the nucleus of the Moravians in the 18th century.

Luther's spiritual struggle was centered on the question, "How can I find a gracious God?" Finding that frequent confession and ascetic exercises brought no satisfaction, he discovered justification by faith in his study of Romans. John Wesley was zealously seeking to serve God. He wrote in his journal that he went to North America as a missionary in the hope of saving his soul. But at the Aldersgate street meeting he discovered grace, proclaiming in now famous words, "I felt my heart strangely warmed, I felt that I did trust in Christ, Christ alone, for salvation; and an assurance was given me that He had taken away my sins, even mine, and delivered me from the law of sin and death" (Latourette 1975:1025). And the primary focus in the preaching of Jonathan Edwards, the major figure in the Great Awakening in colonial North America, was justification by faith alone.

Lovelace lists five additional elements that he calls "secondary" although I would rather call them essential *results* of renewal. The first is mission—following Christ into the world, presenting the Gospel in proclamation and in social demonstration. The second is prayer—expressing dependence on the power of His Spirit, individually and corporately. The third is community—being in union with His Body, both in small groups and in the broader Church. The fourth is what he calls disinculturation—being freed from destructive and protective attitudes toward one's own culture. And the last is theological integration—having the mind of Christ toward revealed truth and toward our cultures (Lovelace 1979:75).

Clearly the freedom and creativity of the Holy Spirit have led the Church in the past into recontextualization as believers have discovered new ways of communicating the message, structuring the Christian community and its leadership, and thinking biblically about the Gospel and culture as it has moved into new contexts. *My thesis is that this is typical of movements of renewal and revival and that as we seek to be faithful today, we have much to learn from such movements.*

Pentecost and Following

The Pentecost event has often been considered a paradigm of revival and it illustrates many aspects of this thesis. It began with united prayer by the tiny group of disciples, followed by unique manifestations of the Holy Spirit. Both the Christian community and those watching could see that something very unusual, foreign to their normal categories of religious experience, had occurred. Among those in attendance there were two reactions. The skepticism on the part of many must have been heightened by the fact that those who spoke were Galileans, outsiders, a group generally denigrated in Jerusalem. (It is important to recognize that most renewal movements have begun among those considered to be outsiders.) But some of the hearers were open and even eager to discover the meaning of the event and the new thing God seemed to be doing. Many of these would become part of the infant church.

It is essential to note that the message began with the mighty acts of God centered in redemptive history, focusing on the Incarnation, the cross, and the resurrection of the Messiah. Based on these events came the call to repentance and the conversions that resulted. A new community was formed with a great sense of *koinonia*, intense worship and eagerness to hear the teaching of the apostles. This was accompanied by signs and wonders.

But problems soon arose. One concerned an important ministry of the church, the care of widows. Consequently a group was named to supervise their care, and a new structure was created, appropriate to the context. Out of this group new leadership emerged, primarily Stephen and Philip. At this point the young church saw itself correctly, as the new Israel. But it also seems to have believed that its message was only for the Jews, failing yet to understand the universal dimensions of the faith and its mission. It was these new younger leaders who soon pushed out the edges of the understanding and actions of the infant church. The fact that they were bicultural, Greek speakers raised in the *diaspora*, no doubt helped them begin to see the universal purpose of God more clearly.

First Stephen began a process of theological reformulation, presenting a view of history that put the sovereign saving activity of God at the center. He demonstrated from Scripture that God's power and presence were not limited to any particular place, challenging the traditional theological paradigm of the Jews. And although he did not say so, he seemed to imply that God's saving purpose was not limited to a particular people. Thus he began to lay the theological foundation for the future mission to the Gentiles. These concepts enraged the bystanders and led to his death. But one of them, Saul of Tarsus, would later take the theology of Stephen to its logical conclusion that the Gospel was for all.

As persecution scattered the church, Philip took the message first to the despised Samaritans, then was led to the Ethiopian. But the beginning of the greatest theological and missiological breakthrough came when Peter was told to go to Cornelius. That was clearly a sovereign act of God, as the Spirit spoke to both men simultaneously. The radical nature of this step is shown by the fact that Peter took witnesses with him and had to defend his actions back in Jerusalem (Ac. 9:1-10:18). Cornelius could have been considered an exceptional case by the infant church, but now a group of unnamed "laypersons," also Hellenistic Jewish believers, took the message to Gentiles in Antioch (Ac. 11:19ff). This was the most important missiological breakthrough in history, and from Antioch the formal mission to the Gentiles would soon begin.

Paul's encounter with the risen Christ and his call to mission to the Gentiles forced him to integrate these events into his theology, the first example of theological contextualization. No doubt the address of Stephen had initiated the process in his mind. Now the former Pharisee had to reread the Scriptures and reformulate his theology in light of what he saw God doing in history. That was painful for the church. It led to division as some, the "Judaizers," wanted the new Israel to remain within Judaism. Another reason might have been resentment over the leadership of Paul, seeing him as a rival to the original apostles.

It is clear from these events at the very beginning of the Church's life, that God is constantly leading His people to push out the edges (Ac. 1:8), taking the Gospel to groups and places often considered beyond the possibility of salvation. Furthermore, God has often used unexpected people like Paul, Stephen and Phillip, coming from the periphery rather than the center of the Church, to do so. "Peripheral people" have often been at the center of renewals and revivals. In this analysis of Acts, then, we see all five of Lovelace's "secondary elements" of renewal: mission, prayer, community, disinculturation and theological integration. Now we will see how recontextualization has been an essential characteristic in revival movements throughout history.

Recontextualization

First, it is important to examine the context in which such movements occurred and discover how specific aspects of the Gospel addressed issues within each situation and became the trigger of revival. The 12th century Waldensian movement arose at a time of great distance between the church hierarchy and the common people, with little or no preaching, and formal church life that seemed to hide rather than communicate the Gospel. The passion of the founder, Peter Waldo, was simply to live out and communicate the basic Christian message that he discovered through reading the New Testament in the vernacular. For the Waldensians this message called them to simple faith in Christ and a lifestyle commensurate with that faith. Lay preachers, both men and women spread the movement, and eventually hundreds of thousands responded, despite persecution. Often, in revivals, social distance decreases. That is, the reality of Christ coming to dwell with us becomes clearer, distinctions between clergy and laity, between social and ethnic groups, and even between men and women lessens. Much later, at Azusa Street, in 1906 during a period of great racial division, it was said that the color line was washed away by the blood of the cross (Cox 1995:58).

The 18th century Moravians began with a small remnant of an underground church, the Unitas Fratrum, heirs of both the Hussites and Waldensians. As religious refugees of other backgrounds joined their community, Herrnhut, dissention arose and there was danger of division. At this point Zinzendorf led the group in a study of 1 John, with fasting and prayer, focusing on the need for unity. This triggered the "Moravian Pentecost" of 1827 that soon led them into mission to twenty-eight countries in as many years and made them the major catalyst of the Protestant missionary movement.

The first major figure in the Korean revival of 1903-1907 was a medical missionary, R. A. Hardie, who had devoted himself to evangelism. As he led a small group of missionaries who were seeking renewal in 1903, he began to confess his own sin, including pride, hardness of heart, and an attitude of paternalism and feelings of superiority toward the Koreans. From that group the movement of revival spread. This led to reconciliation between missionaries and Korean leaders, and by 1906 leadership of the movement had passed to Koreans.

We see something similar in the East African revival. In the Anglican mission in Uganda and Rwanda, many European missionaries kept themselves apart from the Africans. There were rivalries in the mission between hospital and church, and there was famine and starvation. Many were being baptized but much of the Christian life was superficial. Joe Church, a Cambridge educated physician, wrote, "I was beginning to see that I needed more victory and the love of God to carry me though the situation" (Church 1981:49). A year later, in 1929, Church met Simon Nsibambi, an African hospital worker, in a prayer meeting and the two were united as they shared an experience of the "power of Pentecost." The revival soon spread from that encounter. The first letter of John, with its emphasis on the unity of the church and walking in the light, was also important in this movement. Later, during the Mau Mau movement in Kenya, when its leaders urged a return to traditional religion in which goats were sacrificed, the revivalists insisted that the blood of Jesus, not the blood of goats, was necessary. And in that violent movement in which many were killed, those involved in the revival, both black and white, were able to maintain their unity in Christ (Smoker 1994:36ff.)

Thus among the Moravians, in East Africa and in Korea, the power of the Holy Spirit was released as reconciliation came between different groups and races. And in East Africa, as in Korea, the leadership of the revival soon passed out of the hands of Europeans and into the hands of the receiving people.

The Pentecostal movement arose primarily among the poor at a time when Baptists and Methodists who had earlier been marginal people themselves, had become quite respectable in most cities. Some Methodist churches even charged pew rents, a far cry from Wesley's classes and societies among the poor. And while many felt a deep need to experience God's presence and healing power, the older churches appeared to deny its reality. The growing liberalism doubted that miraculous activity had ever taken place, while Princeton orthodoxy and dispensationalist fundamentalism taught that all miracles had ceased after the age of the apostles. The early Pentecostal movement spoke directly to this issue, insisting on the possibility of a direct experience of God and the availability of His power today. And it is no coincidence that Pentecostal renewal arose primarily among the newly arrived urban masses who did not feel welcome in the traditional churches, just as it has done since then in Latin America.

It would be helpful to study the contexts of other movements, asking how specific aspects of the Gospel addressed important questions in the church and society. Such an analysis might help guide our thinking and praying today as we seek to discover the crucial questions in the contexts where we are in ministry.

Now we will examine a number of movements, hoping to discover that they carried out their mission in ways that went significantly beyond the parameters of their contemporaries. Both new vision and new methodologies came out of revivals. These have resulted in considerable recontextualization in each of the five areas pointed to by Lovelace: communication, prayer, community, disinculturation and theological integration.

A. The Communication of the Message

When we look at renewal, we find recontextualization in four crucial aspects of the communication of the message. First, those who take center stage tend not to be those already in church leadership. There is usually a recontextualization of those who communicate the message. Secondly, there tends to be recontextualization with regard to how the Christian message is communicated. New methods are discovered and pressed into service. Thirdly, there is recontextualization as to where the communication takes place. Christians move out of their church ghettos to where the people are. And, fourth, there is recontextualization with regard to whom the message is communicated. New audiences are sought and found.

1. Who? A powerful, new experience of the Holy Spirit compels men and women, often those with little or no status in the church, to proclaim the message. We saw this in Acts as new leaders arose and unnamed men took the message to Gentiles in Antioch. This factor, plus the needs of growing movements, have led to new, more flexible, less elitist patterns of leadership selection and training. In Acts 2:17-21 Peter quoted the prophet Joel concerning God's plan to pour out His Spirit on all flesh, on old and young, men and women, slaves and free. This becomes a new reality in revival movements.

The early Waldensians have already been mentioned in this regard. Nearly all the early Moravian missionaries were laypersons, and women as well as men served as elders. Both men and women served as class leaders in the early Methodist movement, and it began to grow rapidly in England and later in

North America only after John Wesley and then Francis Asbury began to appoint lay preachers who had demonstrated their call and gifts in local ministries. This was the opposite of the elitist university model of leadership training in the established churches of the time. It was not that the preachers were to be without training. Rather, an alternative, noninstitutional method was used. Wesley wrote books of instruction and expected the workers to study them.

Even in a group more wedded to institutional preparation of pastors we see that the Presbyterian phase of the first Great Awakening in North America owed much of its leadership to men trained in the "log colleges." These were established as an alternative to the colleges in New England and Scotland. Their purpose was to prepare pastor/evangelists in their own context. And the revival that began in the United States in 1857 was led primarily by laypersons. Jeremiah Lamphier, a layman, converted through the ministry of the evangelist Charles Finney, who himself had not been formally trained in theology, was the key figure. The 1886 conference which initiated the Student Volunteer Movement, was convened by the lay evangelist D. L. Moody. and with one exception, all of major the speakers were laymen.

Perhaps the most striking example of a nontraditional leader used in a remarkable way was William Seymour, a one-eyed African-American preacher with no formal instruction. He was the major figure in the Azusa Street meetings in 1906, generally seen as the beginning of the Pentecostal movement. This continues to be the most rapidly growing form of the Christian faith in many parts of the world, especially among the urban masses. Women also played a key role in its early missionary outreach. And while Pentecostal leadership training has become more institutionalized in the United States, in much of the world the movement is still spread primarily by laypersons with little or no formal training.

Prior to the East African revival, the Anglican church in East Africa gave little encouragement to Africans in leadership, let alone to lay ministry. The revival began to change this, however, as Africans took an active role and both men and women were involved in lay witness teams that became an important feature of the movement. Festo Kivengere, a future Anglican bishop was brought to faith through the testimony of a former drinking companion.

An even more striking example may be found in the house churches of China. Their amazing growth in the midst of persecution is without parallel in history. With Christian institutions of higher education closed by the government and many church leaders imprisoned, the house churches have been led almost completely by laypersons. And it is reported that three-fourths of the leaders are women, in a society that has traditionally seen women as inferior. Now there are a number of programs to give ongoing training to house church leaders, some originating within the country, some from outside.

Another example comes from a movement in India that has seen half a million "dalits," or untouchables, come to Christ in twenty years. The leader of the group, a former untouchable himself, trained in an American seminary, recognizes the need for leadership appropriate to the context. So lay couples are selected, given three months of training, and sent out into the villages to plant and pastor churches. The plan is to increase the training to six months, but the movement is growing so rapidly that it is difficult to do so.

There are two major points here. First we are called to recognize that God often works through surprising people, not necessarily those whom the institutional church would choose. The other is that it is essential that the methods of selecting and training leaders be appropriate to the context. Today, when the church is growing so rapidly in many parts of Asia, Africa and Latin America, it is essential to construct training models for grassroots pastors. These are not to take the place of further training and the careful reflection that can take place in traditional institutions. But if the latter is the only kind of training that is recognized, the whole church will suffer and millions of new believers will have little or no pastoral care and instruction.

2. How? New methods of communication are usually a characteristic of such movements. They often include a recontextualization of music. Music that is new to Christian contexts is often borrowed from secular contexts or created after secular patterns. The hymns of Charles Wesley were as important to the early Methodist movement as the preaching and organizational genius of John. The Moravians were known for their music, using it especially to teach children. The early Pentecostal movement soon produced its own music. I once was invited to preach in a large Assemblies of God church in Northeast Brazil on a festive occasion. During the service, groups of men and women, most from the surrounding sugar cane fields, sang and played their music on homemade instruments. While the music might not have been appropriate in a middle class church, even in Brazil, it was the authentic music of these poor farm workers. They had written it and applied biblical themes to their lives.

The movement among the dalits in India has also produced its own unique music. One of the songs of these people, who have been terribly oppressed for centuries, insists they will no longer be treated like monkeys on a pole. And a feature of the revival among Mizos in Northeast India in the 1920s was new music that used modified traditional Mizo songs accompanied by drums and dancing, instead of the Western hymns used previously.

The "Jesus people" movement among the "hippies" in the 1960s is another example. Many of its young leaders expressed a fresh and firsthand Christian experience through literature, art, music and other modern media. Their music, in which guitars replaced organs and pianos was an essential feature of the movement and has had a major impact on worship in the older churches in the United States and elsewhere.

William and Catherine Booth, founders of the Salvation Army, exemplified all of the characteristics in focus here. They adopted the principle that people were best reached by those of their own socio/economic class. So they used laymen and women, new converts to communicate the Gospel, using new music in their "hallelujah bands," and meeting in circus tents and hired halls. They went to the worst slums, to prostitutes, the poor and drunkards with "soup, soap, and salvation." This indicated their realism regarding human need, as well as their compassion.

Preaching styles often changed and became much more personal, and less abstract. George Whitefield, the 18th century evangelist who took part in the awakenings on both sides of the Atlantic, has been called "the Divine Dramatist" (Stout 1991). In one of his best known sermons he engaged in a conversation with Father Abraham, asking him who was in heaven. He replied that it was not members of this or that church, only those who had been washed in the blood of the lamb!

3. Where? A simple communication principle is that the Gospel must be communicated to people where they are, without expecting them to enter a traditional church building. Often they feel intimidated, unwelcome, or even antagonistic to the church. Consequently revivals often take the message to people where they are. This is a recontextualization in that it returns the message to the marketplace where it started in Acts 2.

John Wesley said that, at first, he could scarcely imagine anyone being saved outside the four walls of an Anglican church building. But encouraged by Whitefield, he became well known for his preaching in the streets and fields, and used private homes for his class meetings and hired halls for the Methodist societies. Whitefield was also well known for his outdoor meetings, where he spoke to crowds of up to 30,000.

During the Korean revival new believers were brought together in the countryside for intensive Bible study, several weeks at a time. They lived in temporary shelters that they constructed. The camp meetings on the American frontier in the early 19th century contributed greatly to the ongoing revivals. And the annual conventions that brought together thousands, were an important feature in East Africa.

The movement in China initiated by Watchman Nee, known as the "Little Flock," began by meeting in private homes. It became one of the major streams contributing to the remarkable house church movement in that country. There were similar movements in Ethiopia during the Communist regime, and currently they are flourishing in Cuba. In each case there has been significant church growth and lay leadership has been a characteristic.

4. To whom? If we believe that God is constantly seeking to push out the edges of His Church, to bring in the marginalized, and those of other races and social classes, we should expect any genuine movement of the Holy Spirit to reach out to those whom the Church has neglected. The early Wesleyan movement that spread primarily among the poor, was criticized by members of the nobility who accused it of attempting to do away with class distinctions. The Korean revival soon reached a number of butchers, considered an inferior class, and they organized their own church and insisted on being recognized. And the Korean women! They were not expected to have any role outside the home except in shamanistic religion. But many not only received the Good News joyfully, they became zealous evangelists, Bible teachers and small group leaders.

The Pentecostal movement has been a most striking example. The earliest congregations were composed of domestic servants, washerwomen and janitors, mostly African Americans. Soon whites, Asians, and Mexicans joined them. And worldwide, the first generation that has flocked to Pentecostal churches has been composed almost totally of the poor (Cox 1995).

The original constituencies of the Salvation Army, the Jesus people churches, the dalits of India and the movement in China have already been mentioned.

B. Prayer

Prayer has normally been both a precursor and a result of revival. The focus on prayer can be classified as a recontextualization by virtue of the fact that is it often engaged in as a kind of discovery of what the Bible teaches. Prayer, then, becomes an appropriate contextualization of Scripture and a return to what God intended His Church to be. Before a people turn to prayer, the church members have usually grown lax in their concern for and practice of prayer. Often in desperation, then, they turn to beseeching the Lord to bring renewal, following God's injunction to Solomon that "If my people who are called by my name will humble themselves and pray and seek my face and turn from their wicked ways, I will hear from heaven and will forgive their sins and heal their land" (2 Chron. 7:14).

Over fifty years before the Wesleyan movement began, Anton Horneck, a German pietist, began to organize societies for prayer and Bible study in England. By the time the Wesleyan movement began, there were a hundred such groups meeting regularly in London. The early morning prayer meetings in Korea began in 1906 during the revival. The revival that began in New York in 1857, led by Jeremiah Lamphier, was primarily a movement of prayer. Daily meetings for prayer were held in nearly every city, church membership grew by twenty percent within two years, and many were encouraged to enter missionary service.

The Korean revival seems to have been answer to the prayers of two Methodist women serving as missionaries. That led to a conference on prayer among the missionaries at which Dr. Hardie took leadership. From there it spread among the Koreans.

When Pandita Ramabai, the remarkable Indian Christian leader, heard of the Welsh revival in early 1905, she formed a prayer circle in which 250 were soon meeting twice daily. The result was a movement in which 1200 came to faith in a two-week period in June of that year, wrote her friend Minnie Abrams, the wife of Methodist missionary Willis Hoover, in Chile (Cairns 1986:184, 199). That was an important factor in the Pentecostal revival in that nation which began in 1910 and led to extraordinary growth of the church among the poor.

On the other hand, prayer as a result of revival can also be seen. Immediately after the Moravian "Pentecost," a twenty-four hour prayer watch was initiated that lasted for one hundred years. This both motivated and undergirded their remarkable missionary activity. And the concerts of prayer, through which Carey was called to mission, resulted from the 18th century awakening.

C. Reshaping the Christian Community

Rarely if ever have the old wineskins of the traditional church been able to contain the new wine of the movements we have described. Soon new structures, recontextualizations, are needed for nurture and encouragement, and give greater scope for laypersons to become more active in ministry. And without such alternative structures, movements do not usually last long. Often those that are formed remain as a part of the larger church, frequently in tension with it. At other times new denominations are the result.

We have already seen that a heightened sense of *koinonia* is one result of revivals, providing more intimate fellowship than is possible in a larger group. In addition, the newly formed groups provide nurture for new believers and often become the source of new outreach. The Puritan conventicles, the Pietist small groups (the little church within the church), the Moravian bands and choirs and the Methodist classes, are all examples. In most cases these groups met at times different from regular worship in order to avoid competitiveness.

In East Africa the groups for fellowship and witness had positive cultural elements. They were similar to kinship groups in the traditional society. They were more egalitarian than the churches had become and encouraged the ministry of the laity, both men and women. In addition, they were large enough to overcome individualism but small enough to be flexible and creative. Thus the revival was spread principally by those from the fellowship groups and the conventions, rather than through the regular worship of the church.

And such groups have existed in very different contexts. Whether it was a Moravian band, a Pentecostal prayer meeting, or a student group on a college campus, they have encouraged participants to go deeper in their faith and seek to be serious disciples wherever that might lead them. Hence it is no coincidence that new ventures in mission, both in proclamation and in ministries of compassion, have usually come from such groups.

Paradoxically, while revivals have often been a unifying factor across denominational and racial divisions as in East Africa, at other times they have led to schism and the formation of new churchly structures or even whole denominations. Often the parent body has refused to recognize or allow the new movement and give it the flexibility it needs if it was to be responsive to the Spirit. The Waldensian and Methodist movements are examples, even though their founders had no desire to leave the established Church. Some, in the early Moravian movement, wished to be part of the established Lutheran Church. Others did not. But it is clear that in all three of these movements the greater flexibility in forms of ministry and mission enabled them to make contributions to the Christian movement of their time and beyond that would not have been possible if they had been limited to traditional structures.

This is even more striking when we examine the modern Pentecostal movement in all its dimensions. The older churches, some of which had their origins in movements similar to Pentecostalism (Baptists, Methodists, and Nazarenes) immediately repudiated the movement. But however untidy it was, Pentecostalism grew in an extraordinary fashion at the grass roots level. Brazil is a good example. The first Presbyterian, Baptist and Methodist missionaries arrived in the 1850s and 60s. Today the churches that resulted from their efforts number around two million adult believers. The first Pentecostals arrived in 1910, and today their total is at least twenty million. While the movement may exhibit dangers of superficiality and emotionalism, there can be no doubt that millions of people, especially the poor, have embraced Christ in Pentecostal churches and as a result, have rejected destructive patterns of life. And today, in some areas of Latin America, Pentecostal churches are initiating significant ministries of social concern (cf. D. Peterson 1996).

Our dilemma is that while we insist on the unity of the Body of Christ, frequently the traditional church leadership and structures are unwilling to find room for the new initiatives of the Spirit. Thus we are called to hold in tension our concern for the unity of the Body of Christ while affirming the surprises of the Spirit, which often lead to new forms of the church.

D. Disinculturation

This is a less familiar concept. There are at least three important aspects of it to note. The first is, as Lovelace suggests, that it involves a process in which the cultural limitations of a particular group are "transcended by a clear separation of the absolute Christian message from its relative cultural incarnations" (Lovelace 1979:79). The early church had to begin that process as the Gospel was taken to the Gentiles. The need to do so is accentuated whenever new cultural groups are reached. For these newly reached groups, the issue is to disentangle the Christian message from the culture of the advocates and to contextualize it for and with the receivers. For the sending churches that have drifted away from contextually appropriate forms, renewal can and should bring a new concern for appropriateness and recontextualization as they see the responses of those for whom the Gospel is new.

A second aspect of disinculturation is described by Andrew Walls who helpfully goes beyond Lovelace to describe the tension between what he calls the "indigenizing principle," and the "pilgrim principle" (Walls 1996:7-8). The former speaks to the desire "to live as a Christian and yet as a member of one's own society . . . to make the church . . . a place to feel at home" (1996:7). Thus new believers should be able to enter the Church without crossing major sociological or cultural barriers. The latter principle recognizes that while God in Christ accepts people as they are, "He takes them in order to transform them into what he wants them to be," and that to be faithful to Christ the believer "will be out of step with his own society" (1996:8).

A third aspect of disinculturation is the need for Christians to discover their primary identity, not as members of a particular cultural group, but as citizens of the Kingdom of God. This often leads them to embrace the Abrahamic paradigm, the willingness to go out in response to the call of God, without knowing where it will lead. It also makes it possible for them to relate positively to believers of other races and cultures, in the recognition that their common citizenship in the Kingdom takes precedence over membership in a particular cultural group.

All three of these aspects may be seen in many revivals. The creation of new music, styles of worship, methods of leadership selection and preparation, and restructuring the church, all represent the indigenizing principle. Often some practices of the preChristian religious practices are accepted. For example, the early morning prayer meetings and prayer mountains seem to have been features of Korean shamanistic religion before the advent of Christianity. And most of the leaders, or Mudangs, were women. That seems to have been the only role allowed to women outside the home. This helps us understand how the "Bible women," were accepted as evangelists.

The "pilgrim principle" has operated as participants in revivals have sought to minister to marginalized persons ignored by their societies, and even go beyond that in attempts to change destructive customs and unjust laws. The schools for the poor established by Puritans and Pietists, the manner in which Moravians treated Blacks in South Africa and Native Americans in North America are examples. The issue of "female circumcision" in Africa divided the church but the "saved ones" in the East African revival began to speak against the practice. And an early characteristic of the Azusa Street meetings was the acceptance of those of different races. Indeed, Cox asserts that for Seymour, that was the surest sign of the filling of the Holy Spirit (Cox 1995:63). The anti-slavery movement and other laws for social reform that came out of the 18th and 19th century awakenings are well known.

However, we must be honest and note that often this countercultural aspect of revivals is soon lost as those in the movement begin to conform increasingly to their surrounding culture. Wesley was strongly opposed to slavery and would not allow a slaveholder to hold office in the Methodist church. But by the early 19th century in the United States, many Methodist leaders had slaves. And the interracial aspect of early Pentecostalism was soon lost as two major denominations were formed, one white, the other, black. A number of groups that emerged from the late 19th century revivals in the United States included women in ministry. But today that has been reversed (cf. Hassey, Janette, No Time for Silence 1986).

As participants in revivals have discovered their identity more as citizens of the Kingdom of God than as members of their own nation or culture, they have been more apt to hear the call to mission far beyond what they have thought to be the normal parameters of their lives. This has certainly been one factor, although not the only one, in the close relationship between revivals and mission.

E. Theological Integration

It is tragic that so often revival movements have exhibited an anti-intellectual bias. There seem to be two reasons. One is a reaction against the disdain or rejection of such movements by church leaders and theologians who may fear loss of control of movements they do not lead or understand. The other is probably due to the fact that so often the leaders of such movements come from the periphery of the Church, sometimes with little or no formal theological study. There are exceptions of course, including the Puritans, Pietists and the 18th century awakenings. But even those movements were rejected by most of the church leadership. And many of the 19th and 20th century revivals were led by laypersons which probably helped lead the fundamentalism which developed from them, into superficial theology concerned only with the saving of souls.

The early church was forced by events and led by Paul to recognize what God was doing among the Gentiles and thus reformulate its theology. And throughout history, as the Holy Spirit has initiated movements taking the church to new frontiers, it has been challenged to learn from Scripture and events and integrate the new insights into its theology.

In this chapter I can only point to examples I have already given, hoping they will suggest further reflection. Going back to Pentecost we see two themes that have often been forgotten and resurfaced in revivals. One is the sovereign activity and power of the Holy Spirit, the other, related to this, is the giftedness of every believer. Another recurring observation is the need of intentional groups for prayer, fellowship, nurture and challenge if the Church is to be vital and healthy. Most traditional theological systems pay scant lip service to these needs. And even movements that have come out of revivals have often forgotten them as they have become more institutionalized.

In some institutions doing theological/missiological education there are attempts to incorporate some of the issues mentioned above. One is the recognition of the importance of the ministry of the laity, both in traditional churches and in the role of nonprofessional missionaries in places such as China and other countries of restricted access. This really goes back to a New Testament phenomenon A second is the examination of the issue of spiritual power, first examined in academic circles by Alan Tippett and now continued and expanded by Charles Kraft. A third is the focus on alternative ways of communication, through music, drama and art, so important in most nonWestern cultures and increasingly important in our own. A fourth is a new approach to the study of the history of the Church as the people of God. This focuses less on the development of the ecclesiastical institution in the West and more on the spiritual and social dynamics that have motivated the penetration of the Gospel into a myriad of cultures and areas once ignored or written off by traditional churches.

We need to go further. This study suggests that we are always called to leave space for the Holy Spirit to work in unexpected ways through unexpected people, and somehow to incorporate that into our theology and our structures. That will include the encouragement of every believer to use his or her gifts in ministry, to dream dreams, to take new initiatives. And as we come to the end of the era of Christendom in the West, it is all the more important to be open to the reshaping of the Church and its mission. I strongly suspect that much of the impetus for this process will come from churches in Asia, Africa, and Latin America which have frequently been forced to struggle with the issues described here far more than traditional churches in the West.

Conclusion

We can sum up much of our discussion by noting that we should expect to be surprised by the Holy Spirit! He is the Spirit of creativity and mission as well as power. Following the model of Pentecost, He is constantly leading His people to enlarge the tent, to push out the edges, by taking the Gospel to those who are outside. This will continue to involve an endless process of discovering how the message is to be communicated and lived out, and how the Christian community is to be structured in each context. And as we do so, we will discover that we have much to learn about contextualization and recontextualization from special movements of the Spirit in the past.

Chapter 26

Appropriate Witness to Postmoderns: Re-Incarnating the Way of Jesus in 21st Century Western Culture

Jonathan Campbell

The Emerging Spiritual Revolution

I believe deeply that we must find, all of us together, a new spirituality.

— The Dalai Lama[1]

A new spiritual revolution is sweeping across Western societies.

While riding the ferry home from Seattle late one evening, I visited with Chris, a senior technology consultant and friend. We had one of those conversations that went quickly to the heart. After sharing a bit of our personal stories, Chris said, "I'm Buddhist. . . . I believe in God and Jesus, but Buddha gives me a way of life." He dismissed church as an option for its lack of holism and its feeble spirituality. Chris represents many of my friends who are part of a spiritual renaissance in the West. These eclectic seekers believe in God (or a supreme being), enjoy the contemplative lifestyle of Eastern practices and have little tolerance for institutionalized religion.

Many believed modernity was going to bring an end to religion—that science would ultimately triumph over faith. According to Friedrich Nietzsche, God died and the church was marginalized by modern culture. Knowledge and reason suppressed intuition and spirit. By the end of the twentieth century, however, all over the Western world we are seeing signs of disenchantment with modernity. Interest in the spiritual and transcendent is surging. In many ways, these new spiritual seekers are reacting against Christendom and the modern forms of religion. David Elkins, former Christian minister and author of *Beyond Religion*, summarizes this new spirituality:

> As we move into the postmodern age, we can no longer afford the luxury of tribal gods and narrow spiritual views. We simply must see that God is everywhere, that artesian wells of spirituality exist across the land. We must recognize that spirituality is universal and that the spiritual blood, as it were, that flows in our own veins is no

---

[1] From an interview with the Dalai Lama by J. C. Carriere (1995:18-23).

different from that which flows in the veins of every other man and woman. To develop a new, universal vision of spirituality, we must be willing to open our hearts and let go of narrow religious views. We must be willing to join hands with others and work toward a common faith (1998:36).

The demise of modernity leaves a spiritual void in the cultures and hearts of the West. The words of Pascal are as true today as they were four centuries ago, "There's a god-shaped vacuum in every man." Every society also has its own unique spiritual longings—the spiritual-religious dimension that wrestles with such fundamental questions as "Who are we?", "What is the source and meaning of life?", "How can we live in peace?" and "What happens after death?" During times of mass social change, spiritual hunger intensifies.

With new-found courage, people are open to acknowledge they are essentially spiritual beings. But as one psychiatrist friend of mine confessed, "I know I'm spiritual, but I don't know *why*." Though many don't know why or what to do about it, they are recognizing the metaphysical dimensions of life. Bill Moyers asked the venerated mythologist Joseph Campbell shortly before his death if he still believed "that we are at this moment participating in one of the very greatest leaps of the human spirit to a knowledge not only of outside nature but also of our own deep inward mystery." Joseph Campbell thought for a moment, then replied, "The greatest ever" (Joseph Campbell 1988:xix). Now fifteen years later, the spiritual longings continue to deepen and broaden across a diversity of generational, socioeconomic, geographic and educational profiles.

These new spiritual seekers are no longer looking either to the Western church or to secular humanism for fulfillment. They are looking *everywhere*. And unlike anything before, postmodern societies nurture an eclectic spiritual blend of premodern, modern and postmodern themes. Though there is no monolithic force nor clear boundaries for this spiritual revolution, various streams of Eastern philosophies and neo-paganism are converging upon the Western landscape. The result is neither Eastern nor Western, but an often paradoxical mix of the two. Figure 26.1 illustrates the current shifts in how postmoderns approach spirituality:

From . . . **MODERN SPIRITUALITY** **Rooted in Western Religion**	*To . . .* **POSTMODERN SPIRITUALITY** **Rooted in Eastern Philosophy**
Greco-Roman / Eurocentric	Hindu / Asian
North American	Native American
Traditional Institutions	Spiritual Relationships
Disenchantment / Objectivity	Re-Enchantment / Mystification
Atheism / Secular Humanism	Panentheism / Pantheism
Humanity above Nature	Humanity merged with Nature
"Is there a God?" / "God is Dead"	"Which god (or gods)?" / "We are god"
"Jesus is THE way to God"	"There are many paths to god (or God)"
Propositional Truth	Personal Beliefs
Evidence / Apologetic	Experience / Incarnational
Dualism (Sacred-Secular Split)	Holism (Unification)
Individualized / Private	Interconnected / Community
Orthodoxy / Dogmatism	Paradox / Pluralism
Preaching / Tracts	Narrative / Testimony

Figure 26.1 Shifts in Spiritual Perspectives

Shifts in Spiritual Perspectives

In contrast to the fragmentation and individualism of modernity, much postmodern spirituality is characteristically mystical, holistic, pluralistic and eclectic. There are also varying degrees of synthesis with mythology, astrology, the occult, animism, Gaia, alternative healing, Wicca, deep ecology, parapsychology and the mystical influences of Hinduism, Buddhism and Taoism.

The emerging spirituality is not grounded on a set of propositional truths, but rather on an eclectic collection of personal beliefs and practices. People are pursuing an experiential reality, regardless of how paradoxical or ambiguous it may seem.[2] The question is no longer, "Do you believe in God?" but "Which

---

[2] In fact, for some, the more mysterious the better. "Life is not a problem to be solved but a mystery to be lived" (Peck 1987:99). This is not far from the New Testament idea of mystery (cf. Eph. 3:2-12, 5:32, 6:19; Col. 1:25-29, 2:2-3, 4:3-4) and the wisdom literature of

god (or gods) do you believe in?" Their reluctance to commit to any one religious tradition leads to a permanent search for the next new thing—a sort of "serial spirituality." As my friend Howard who is Jewish and now a "Buddhist at heart" said, "I have been on a very intentional spiritual quest which started through alternative healing practices . . . I have yet to realize healing or wholeness . . . I have come to accept that it may not be on this side." This endless wandering leads many to a lonely desperation from which they yearn for a spiritual center or unifying truth, transformational power and loving community.

Once considered "Christian," Western culture is now clearly post-Christian, and, in some areas, anti-Christian. Modern societies may have been "Christianized" or "Christened" by the religious structures of Christendom, but a majority of people remain unaffected by the authentic, life-transforming Gospel of Jesus. While postmoderns object to institutionalized religion, they are not necessarily anti-God. They are reacting in many ways against the modern forms of religion—the human-made systems for understanding God, the lack of genuine community and anemic spirituality. They are anti-institutional spiritual seekers.

The Marginalization of the Modern Church

With the curtain of modernity pushed aside, the new light of postmodernity is revealing the hollowness of the Christendom church and westernized gospel. Throughout Christendom the church has been willingly squeezed and redefined by modernity. Os Guinness submits a poignant explication of secularized evangelicalism: "Compared with the past, faith today influences culture less. Compared with the past, culture today influences faith more" (1993:16). The modern church is now a subculture on the fringes of postmodern culture(s).

This Christendom paradigm was initiated by Constantine, affirmed by the Protestant Reformation and reinforced by modernity. Church as a missional movement with a distinct lifestyle was sacrificed on the foundation of institutionalism. The Western gospel and corresponding ecclesial institutions are in stark contrast with the simple[3] Way of Jesus and the early church: religious institutions have dominated the modern missionary movement; radical individualism displaced spiritual community; gnosticism supplanted experiential

---

the Old Testament practically grappling with the paradox of how to live wisely and righteously and authentically, surrounded by a hostile world of pain, suffering, pleasure and joy (cf. Esther, Job, Daniel, Lamentations, Ecclesiastes, Proverbs and Psalms.)

[3] I use the word "simple" not as "easy" or "simplistic," but to describe that which is not mixed, compounded or complicated. To follow Jesus in loving obedience is simple, but not easy or without its costs (cf. 2 Cor. 11:3). There is a direct correlation between simplicity and mobility—with increased simplicity, comes and increased capacity for mobility.

faith;[4] and professional clerics superseded the priesthood of all believers (Jonathan Campbell 1999). Once a way of living, modern "Christianity" is now almost entirely confined to dedicated buildings, worship services and structured programs. The problem with the church is not that it's out of touch with the culture, but out of touch (i.e., conformity) with Christ. Our powerless ecclesiology reflects our powerless Christology.

The church is no longer faithful to the nature of the gospel, nor is it redemptively engaging culture. The church sacrificed its integrity for relevance, resulting in a syncretism of modernity and Christianity.[5] The problem is we have defined the gospel one way (i.e., scripturally and spiritually), then have established structures and practices that are contradictory (i.e., institutional, individualistic, pragmatic and political).[6] As Wilbert Shenk asserts, "The church in modern culture has succumbed to syncretism in pursuit of evangelization by its uncritical appropriation of the assumptions and methodologies offered by modern culture" (1995:56). Generations of uncritical enculturation have left us with a diluted, nominal and impotent church.

The Blessings of the Postmodern Crisis

The Chinese characters of "danger" and "opportunity" are combined to communicate the idea of "crisis." A crisis is perceived to be a "turning point"—a type of crossroads with potential for both positive and negative opportunities. The postmodern era is indeed a time of crisis that holds "dangerous opportunities" for mission. Crisis is part of being the people of God. Crisis is

---

[4] Gnosticism rests upon a "metaphysical dualism" between the spiritual and material, between soul and body, between metaphysical truth and phenomenal representation, and ultimately between faith and practice. Modern Christianity is built on gnosticism's high regard for information with no necessary connection with loving obedience to Jesus. (See Senneh 1989:17 and Jones 1992.)

[5] Because the Western church has been the dominating missionary influence until recently, the effects of syncretism can be seen worldwide. "This should not surprise us, since the model and practice of church taken to Asia, Africa, and Latin America was that of Christendom, and nominality has cropped up wherever Western missions have gone" (Shenk 1997:154). For example, my friend, Kasereka Kasomo observed the effects of missionaries who brought more than the gospel to the Wanande people of eastern Zaire: "I discovered that what we had been calling 'orthodox Christianity' was 'Western syncretistic Christianity.'" He concludes, "our Christianity was doubly syncretistic. Doubly syncretistic, as the Nande Church struggles to be 'orthodox,' while really trying to be a Western church" (1994:13). See also W. A. Visser 't Hooft *In No Other Name: The Choice Between Syncretism and Christian Universalism* (1963) and also "Evangelism in the Neo-Pagan Situation," in *International Review of Mission* (1976:83); Nida (1960:184-188); Vander Veer (1994:197).

[6] Even the popular American psychiatrist, M. Scott Peck observes, "It has become apparent to me that the vast majority of churchgoing Christians in America are heretics. The leading—indeed, traditional—heresy of the day I call pseudodocetism. It is this predominant heresy that intellectually allows the Church to fail to teach its followers to follow Jesus" (1987:297).

part of life. To deny the cultural-ecclesial crisis (as many churches still do) is a dangerous delusion.

Christendom not only must end; it is ending. The breakdown of modernity and the demise of the modern church are setting the stage for God to do a new thing. "The rapid erosion of the old structures of Christendom over the past three centuries may be a necessary—but nonetheless painful—stage in rehabilitating the church" (Shenk 1995:3). Indeed, postmodernity is at once one of the greatest challenges to Christian mission and also one of the greatest opportunities for mission expansion.

Postmodernity may be an instrument of God's sovereignty to cause his people to reclaim their identity as a missionary community. As postmoderns reject modern, institutionalized Christianity, they become more open to fresh expressions of the gospel that are free of modern values and structures. What opportunities does this cultural-spiritual crisis provide for incarnating the gospel and community?

Responding to the Postmodern Crisis

The issue at hand is not whether the church will respond, but rather *how* the church will respond to meet the postmodern challenge with integrity and power. A critical question for developing mission strategy in Western contexts is, On what basis (or authority) do we make decisions regarding contextualization? Having been gradually marginalized, the churches and mission organizations are now reacting primarily in one of two ways: primitivism or Church Growth. Although not as popular, there is a third approach we will discuss—the translational or incarnational approach.[7] These options represent three distinct paradigms for missional engagement.

Primitive Paradigm

The primitive paradigm emerges from a restorationist position. The objective here is to restore church to a particular cultural expression or idealized form in history. Richard Hughes explains, "Restorationism involves the attempt to recover some important belief or practice from the time of pure beginnings that believers are convinced has been lost, defiled, or corrupted" (1995:x). Primitivists appeal to past tradition as the authority for adjudicating changes in

---

[7] Others have made similar distinctions: Lamin Sanneh's "cultural attitudes:" Quarantine – the self-sufficient attitude nurtured in isolation, sometimes even in defiance of the world; Accommodation—attitudes of compromise predominate over those of defiance; and Prophetic Reform—a critical selectiveness determines the attitude toward the world (1989:47-48). Rodney Clapp's Retrenchment, Relinquishment (sentimental capitulation), and Radicalization (1996:32). J. Christiaan Beker proposes three choices for the church to interpret and adapt Paul for today: 1) Traditional adaptation, 2) Adaptation that acknowledges the burden of the tradition, and 3) Wholesale neglect and deconstruction of the tradition (1991:115-116). Wilbert Shenk's five alternatives for renewal (cf. 1997:157-158).

their contemporary context. They often fail to distinguish between what is intended to be temporary and what is to be normative.

Primitivists are prone to read Scripture as rigidly prescriptive and fail to take into account cultural differences between the first century and today. Historically such groups as the Mennonites, Amish, Campbellites, Church of Christ, Pietists, Swiss Brethren and some Baptists have been considered restorationists. Previously held tradition is simply imposed upon contemporary times as if there was no intervening history or cultural progression. Primitivism has the potential of sliding into premodern superstitions where the adherents gain power through performing prescribed rituals and fear the consequences of ignoring or changing such traditions.

As cultural fundamentalists, they reminisce about the "good old days" in their own past or project their understanding of the apostolic church directly upon today: "If it was good enough for the apostles, it is good enough for me" or "What would our founders say?" Tradition is the authority. Loyalty to the past is superimposed on listening and obeying the Spirit. Seeking to preserve its own heritage and structures, primitivism leads to separatism which is evidenced by isolation from society as well as division from the greater body of Christ.

Church Growth Paradigm

Currently the most popular approach to contextualization is the Church Growth paradigm. This is an approach developed by Donald McGavran and his disciple C. Peter Wagner, both of whom taught for many years in the School of World Mission, (now School of Intercultural Studies,) Fuller Seminary. This approach was framed as a reaction on the one hand against Liberalism and, on the other, against the primitivist attempt to simply impose their cultural and denominational forms on people of other societies. In opposition to Liberalism, McGavran fought to make central the Bible and conversion to Christ leading to enfolding in spiritually alive churches. In opposition to the primitivists, he insisted that followers of Christ needed to follow Christ *within* rather than *against* their cultures.

To accomplish such church growth, McGavran and Wagner spoke of being "fiercely pragmatic." By this they meant that people ought to be able to come to Christ with what McGavran called "a minimum of social dislocation" and to form churches that do not simply mimic the home churches of the missionaries. They recommended, then, that in order for churches to grow rapidly and well that they be formed of people who are comfortable with each other, people of the same social class. Such groupings of people were called "homogeneous units." It was recognized, though seldom mentioned, that such groupings could become cliquish and, therefore, would need eventually to become more inclusive. McGavran was, however, so focused on winning the lost that the need for dealing with such cliquishness was little dealt with. Nor was the possibility that pragmatism without biblical-cultural considerations could be dangerous.

Within Fuller's School of World Mission the understandings of the relationships between Biblical Christianity and the cultures of humankind served to balance to some extent the more dangerous aspects of Church Growth theory. Unfortunately, the teaching of Fuller professors Alan Tippett and Charles Kraft, whose works support the translational approach, had little influence on the American Church Growth movement. American pastors and church growth specialists simply took the pragmatic emphases, with little cultural or theological sensitivity, and ran with them.

The result was a mix of American pragmatism, uncritical accommodation to people's preferences and American entrepreneurship. In the hands of American pragmatists, with little cultural sensitivity, the approach moved from McGavran's intense desire to follow Paul in becoming a Jew to Jews and a Gentile to Gentiles *in order by whatever means to win the lost* (1 Cor. 9:19-22) to seeing Church Growth simply as a way to grow big congregations. Characterized by the increasing emphasis on relevance, creativity, entrepreneurship and excellence, the primary criterion for evaluation became quantifiable results. Adaptation to the concerns of whatever group was to be appealed to (usually middle and upper class Anglo-Americans) came to be emphasized over biblical considerations.

Though some, especially those working in cross-cultural contexts, have worked with the principles of Church Growth in ways that approximate the translational approach (see below), some, especially in the American context, have devolved into blatant pragmatism. For the latter, the tendency has been to assume, "If it works, it must be right" or "If it is successful, it must be of God." Wagner represents this position well in a chapter entitled, "Consecrated Pragmatism":

> The approach of consecrated pragmatism recommends the option which most effectively and efficiently accomplishes the goal. In that sense, but only in that sense, *the end is the only thing that can possibly justify the means.* A means that fails to accomplish the goal is not, by anyone's measurement, a justifiable means (1981:75, emphasis added).

Good intentions and, more importantly, results become the standard for guiding belief and practice.[8] Therefore, we live as if Christianity were true, not because it is true, but because it *works* for us.[9] Social measures of "success" become the authority for church and mission practices.[10]

---

[8] Ramseyer states, "The church growth strategy is pragmatic and utilitarian with only one criterion for evaluation—usefulness in gathering visible countable people into visible countable congregations" (1979:67). For more related to this discussion, see also Shenk, ed. (1973) and Guinness (1993).

[9] See also Isaiah 1:10-18, Proverbs 21:27, Matthew 5:23-24 and especially 1 Corinthians 13.

[10] This relates to Wagner's view that the "cultural mandate" forms a pair with the

This approach fails to appreciate not only what God is doing, but how He moves in and through cultures. And contrary to popular belief, much of Church Growth practice does not truly respect culture, but rather "uses" dimensions of culture for its own institutional purposes.[11] Relying on human creativity, their strategies fail to engage people in a way that produces genuine transformation and people movements (something McGavran was strong on). A pragmatic perspective is ill prepared to appreciate *kairos* moments, spiritual revelation, human suffering, religious persecution and other "distractions" that deter the plans of leaders.[12] Perhaps it was in recognition of this that Wagner has turned largely to dealing with spiritual factors in preference to the more secular techniques of Church Growth.

Even with the rising awareness of postmodernity, most Christian leaders continue to perpetuate the Church Growth paradigm. The primary question today has become, How do we start "postmodern" churches? In his book, *Reinventing Your Church* (1998), Brian McLaren builds on this thesis in another way by asking, What kind of church would *we* want if *we* had to start from scratch? (emphasis added).[13] The idea of reinventing the church reflects the height of arrogance and independence—it's up to us to decide how we fulfill the Great Commission.[14] To think that we could create or re-engineer the church is the ultimate evidence of humanism and modernity's influence in shaping the church. And by the time the church reinvents itself it will again be irrelevant and behind the times.

Mission is reduced to social science or business theory. It is no wonder Western leaders are enamored with business gurus such as Peter Drucker, Jim Collins, Margaret Wheatley, Stephen Covey, Warren Bennis and Peter Senge.[15]

"evangelistic mandate" (1981:12-14; 50-54). This explains Wagner's comment, "Whereas, some theologians suggest that sound theology precedes fruitful ministry, the opposite is usually the case" (Wagner 1994:56). Cf. Wagner (1979:2-5; 86-93 and 1981:83).

[11] For example, the "seeker-friendly" (or seeker-driven) paradigm popularized by Willow Creek Community Church of the Chicago suburbs and Saddleback Church of California's south Orange County attempts to attract or entertain people into the Kingdom.

[12] The apostle Paul writes, "If any one of you thinks he is wise by the standards of this age, he should become a 'fool' so that he may become wise" (1 Cor. 3:18-19; cf. Isa. 55:9).

[13] Though the book was revised and re-published in 2000 with a new title, *The Church on the Other Side*, the thesis remains the same and is indicative of current mission efforts in the West.

[14] The individualism characteristic of Western culture manifests corporately as well as individually (e.g., the phrases "Your church" or "My church" as if each is distinctly owned. In contrast, Jesus says, "I will build MY church" (Mt. 16:18); He calls us to join him in His work (Jn. 5:19-20; 15:7-17).

[15] My point is not to criticize these fine leaders for I have benefited both personally and professionally from each one. Instead, my admonition is directed to Christian leaders for disregarding the organic nature of church by embracing the institutional business paradigm.

Church is big business.[16] Corporate consultants have become the theologians and missiologists of the contemporary Western church. Grounded in an institutional paradigm of church, this approach advances the modern assumptions of human reason, the idealization of knowledge and inevitable progress.

Pragmatism most often yields a culture-bound model of church that constantly needs to be re-engineered and tweaked. It fails to appreciate the Church as a living organism capable of dynamic engagement with culture. So leaders are always chasing and experimenting with new (and not so new) programs, experts and techniques that will foster the institutional change and growth they long for. This unrestrained pursuit of relevance turns to relativism. Ironically, the openness to relativism reinforces a rigid pragmatism—where rightness is measured by human standards of institutional success. Though the Church Growth movement is diverse and evolving in many ways, this pragmatic paradigm remains the *modus operandi* of a large percentage of Christian leaders, especially in America.

Translational Paradigm

The translational paradigm holds that there are transcultural principles that can (and should) be applied in all cultures. Like primitivism, the translational approach has a strong orientation toward beginnings. The difference lies in being flexibly authoritative to incarnate the gospel in new contexts with the goal of indigenous movements.[17]

The translational paradigm is the viable choice for the current cultural-ecclesial crisis because the objective is not self-preservation (i.e. the Christendom agenda), but the church being *born again* or re-incarnated in each new context and culture. Kraft described this approach in the 1970s with his theory of dynamic-equivalence: "What we seek is a Christianity equivalent in its dynamics to that displayed in the pages of the New Testament" (1979a:382; see also Bevans 1992). The New Testament is both descriptive and prescriptive, providing a norm for what is authentically Christian. All the apostolic patterns are perfectly represented in the life and teachings of Jesus Christ, are embodied in the early church and have the capacity to be translated in any cultural-historical

---

[16] Barna advertises his book, *Church Marketing*, with "How to run the business side of your church without compromising your spiritual integrity" (1992). My question is, when in the life of the early church did it have a business side, how many "sides" does a church have? See also David Wells' critique of the church as "Big Business" (1994:72-77).

[17] This is the distinguishing difference between the two main streams of Protestantism: the reformation and the radical reformation. The radical reformers wanted to go back, before Constantine, to the church's New Testament roots. Although not as strong a theme today as it once was, several groups throughout history have upheld the existence of normative patterns, including Anabaptists, Mennonites, Friends and some baptist groups. There have always been those who have sought to follow the New Testament patterns even when it meant persecution or scorn. See also R. Baker (1954:9-10) and Richard Hughes (1995).

context. The translational paradigm rides on the edge of primitivism and pragmatism. When the church does not fully appropriate the life and work of Jesus Christ, it may fall into one of three errors: 1) *syncretism*, where we engage culture without critically exegeting Scripture, 2) *dogmatism (hypocrisy)*, where we may exegete Scripture, but never engage the culture and 3) *isolationism*, where neither the Scriptures nor the culture is effectively engaged.

This process of engaging people both redemptively and incarnationally is ongoing because cultures are always in some state of flux. "For a static religion poorly serves a dynamic culture" (Kraft 1979a:383).[18] In his summation of theology of mission as 1990, David Bosch asserts, "A crucial task for the church today is to test continually whether its understanding of Christ corresponds with that of the first witnesses" (1991:22). To affirm a translational approach is not simply observing the practices of the early church and making direct application to today. Translation is a dynamic process that maintains the continuity of patterns of both faith *and* practice amid the discontinuities of historical and cultural change.

	Primitive	Church Growth (Pragmatic)	Translational
Object-ives	*Restore / Preserve* Escape from Culture Reinstate / Retrench Controlled Growth	*Reform / Re-engineer* Embrace the Culture Improve / Adapt Programmed Growth	*Translate / Incarnate* Engage the Culture Rebirth / Reinterpret Spontaneous Reproduction
View of Church Values	Religious Institution Forms of Church Tradition / Heritage Bible as Prescriptive Stability / Survival Practices Restoration	Flexible Organization Functions and Models Human Creativity Bible as Descriptive Success / Results Progress Relevance	Organic Community Lifestyle and Movement Innovation[19] / Incarnation Descriptive *and* Prescriptive Authenticity / Integrity Patterns (faith & practice) Revelation
Approach to Culture	Quarantine *Retrenchment* Myopic View of Past Little Adaptation	Accommodation *Relinquishment* Myopic View of Present Full Freedom to Adapt	Prophetic Reform *Radicalization* Bi-Focal / Ancient & Future Freedom with Limits Idealization
Potential Dangers	Legalism / Elitism Isolationism / Separatism Reduce theology to a code of conduct	Relativism / Liberalism Syncretism / Humanism Contextualize with few theological boundaries	Alienation by Christendom Movement and leaders beyond ability to manage or control
Questions	"We never did it that way before" "How can we keep what we had?"	"What do we think will work?" "If it works, it must be of God"	"What example did Jesus give us?" "How do we continue in the Way of Jesus?"

Figure 26.2 Paradigms for Missional Contextualization

---

[18] "The Christian position is not one of static conformance to dead rules, but of dynamic obedience to a living God" (Nida 1954:52).

[19] Innovation is fundamentally different from creativity. Innovation is an organic term derived from the Latin, innovare, which means to renew or modify. It originally referred to a shoot that arises at or near the apex of the stem of a moss plant, usually after the reproductive organs have completed their development; the formation of such a shoot.

A Translatable Gospel

The Gospel is Jesus and Jesus knows no cultural boundaries. The gospel is not Eastern or Western, Jew or Gentile, but is the "power of God for the salvation of everyone who believes" (Rom. 1:16-17; cf. Eph. 3:8-9). To every spiritual and relational yearning, the gospel of Jesus is indeed good news. But when the Gospel becomes acculturated or overcontextualized, it becomes less than the good news and thereby hinders the natural progression across cultures.

In my experience with believers from both Western and nonWestern contexts, I have seen the gospel embodied in a variety of ways—from Seattle, Washington to Ulaanbaatar, Mongolia.[20] And the more I experience the power of God at work in diverse settings, the more I appreciate the power and simplicity of the Gospel. The following beliefs and assumptions have emerged from our journey:

- The Gospel is culturally translatable
- There is no such thing as a cultureless Gospel
- The Gospel is often held captive by cultural ideologies, traditions and structures
- In order for the Gospel to spread across cultures, the Gospel must be free from the control of any single society
- The Gospel of Jesus answers the spiritual *and* relational longings of all peoples (specifically the needs for identity, love, truth and power)
- Western fields are becoming increasingly ripe for harvest

A Call to Repentance

The postmodern crisis calls for nothing less than complete repentance (*metanoia*)—a transformation of the mind, a change of heart and a new way of living. But before significant change can occur, the people of God must realize how far we have followed modernity away from the Way of Jesus and patterns of the early church. Renewal is not enough.[21] The New Testament reveals a gospel far more radical, transformational and even revolutionary than we see in the common church of our day. One thing is certain, the church cannot make a difference *in* the world unless it is different *from* the world. We need

---

[20] I say "our" journey, because I would never have experienced this by myself. I am indebted to bands of brothers and sisters who have courageously loved Jesus and me. I'm especially grateful to Jennifer Campbell (my companion of over fifteen years), Ted and Julie Leung, and Paul and Colleen Ziakin for their faithful prayer and input in this paper.

[21] Hoekendijk observes, "When we casually use this big word, "renewal," we usually think of little more than some new furnishings and a few revisions in the inner architectural structure—a little shifting to the left and a little modernizing to the right. It is as if we have come to a mutual agreement that renewal may never amount to a radical change: to make different that which exists" (1966:69-70).

revolutionary changes. And nothing less than a radical reorientation is needed for the church to break free from the modern influences.

To repent from its modern influences and turn back to the simple ways of Jesus will be costly—even painful. To the extent that the church repents of modernity's influence, the church will be positioned to be reborn as a new spiritual reality in postmodern contexts.

We all need to go through a conversion something like the apostle Peter experienced in Acts 10 and 11. Peter's conversion from an ethnocentric Jew to an advocate for Gentile missions was one of the most significant paradigm shifts in the history of the church.[22] Likewise today, the church must repent of any cultural tradition that hinders the movement of the gospel across cultures— whether modern, postmodern or premodern. Just as Gentiles can now receive salvation free of Jewish tradition, so all peoples have a right to be followers of Jesus without having to become Western or to become institutionalized. Every people group is entitled to experience "The Way" of Jesus in their own culture.

New Wineskins for a New (Postmodern) World

No one pours new wine into old wineskins. If he does, the new wine will burst the skins, the wine will run out and the wineskins will be ruined. No, new wine must be poured into new wineskins. And no one after drinking old wine wants the new, for he says, "The old is better" – Luke 5:37-39

The radical nature of postmodernity compels us to re-examine the radical nature of the New Testament. And the more we wrestle with both the Scriptures and our culture, we realize we need new wineskins for every new culture. Jesus warned against trying to re-use the old. We face three choices: 1) Maintain the modern church, "The old is good enough"; 2) Change the Modern Church, "Pour new wine into old wineskins"; or 3) Start radically new churches, "New Wineskins." For the church to recover her missional integrity in any culture will require nothing less than a radical transformation resulting in new wineskin churches.

Through our journey, we have come to realize that the way of Jesus *is* the wineskin. In Him we experience new wine *and* new wineskins. Jesus is the way *to* life and He is the way *of* life. He never wrote a book, nor built a building, nor initiated an institution, but He did gather a new community of believers, lived with them, and commissioned them to carry on His mission in the same way (cf. Jn. 13-17, 20:21-23). The greatest challenge facing the church in the postmodern era is to rediscover what it means to live the way of Jesus in community (*ekklesia*) and mission (*apostolos*) in the world.

Jesus is not modern. Jesus is not postmodern. And His body (the Church) is neither modern nor postmodern; neither Eastern nor Western. His community

---

[22] Note however, Peter's ongoing struggle in Gal. 2:11-16.

is a *way of life*. The new focus of church must be on discipling people to become faithful followers of Jesus without having to become "modern" Christians or be initiated into modern religious institutions. Postmodernity calls the church to undergo a systemic paradigm shift that goes to the root of ecclesiology—one that questions all the assumptions of the Christendom model.

In Acts 15:19, James said, "It is my judgment, therefore, that we should not make it difficult for the Gentiles who are turning to God." In the same way, we should not make it difficult for *postmoderns* (or any other group) who are turning to God.

Re-Incarnation as Missional Process

Flesh gives birth to flesh, but the Spirit gives birth to spirit. – John 3:6

In the Kingdom of God, death precedes life. We cannot faithfully incarnate Jesus until we die to ourselves. Unless we lay aside our rights, comforts, traditions, politics and other self-interests, we will inevitably transplant our own culturally-conditioned traditions instead of the powerfully simple Gospel of Jesus. As Jesus said, "I tell you the truth, unless a kernel of wheat falls to the ground and dies, it remains only a single seed. But if it dies, it produces many seeds" (Jn. 12:24). The journey toward fruitfulness begins with death.[23]

Just as God became flesh and dwelt among us, so now we as the Body of Christ are to carry on the mission of Jesus and be incarnate among the peoples of the earth. Jesus set the pattern for us to follow. The most powerful message for postmoderns is not an ecclesial institution, but a living, breathing missional community. For this to happen, church as we know it must die (i.e., the Christendom and modern paradigm).

Ecclesial translation is intrinsically spiritual. Only the Holy Spirit can bring new life. At work in both the church and in the culture, the Holy Spirit freely gives wisdom, guidance and power to embody the gospel in its surrounding environment. This requires keen discernment between the exotic (i.e., modern or culturally-specific) and the essentials (i.e. transmodern or culturally-translatable). In every culture where the gospel seed is planted the church must be re-incarnated.[24]

The process of translation is symbiotic or bi-directional. It requires a continuous and mutual exchange between the gospel and the culture. Bosch

---

[23] The idea of death and rebirth is a central theme throughout the Bible. Cf. 1 Sam. 17; Jer. 1:10; Lk. 8:14, 9:23; Eph. 4:22-24; and Heb. 12:1.

[24] I purposely hyphenate "re-incarnate" to set apart the missiological process of ecclesial translation from the Eastern religious understanding of "reincarnation" (e.g., the Hindu concept of rebirth of a soul in a new human body). I use this word for both its technical and "spiritual" connotations. Technically, reincarnation is derived from the Latin meaning "taking on flesh again." It refers to a fresh embodiment or the rebirth in new bodies or forms of life.

writes, "Inculturation suggests a *double movement*: there is at once inculturation of Christianity and Christianization of culture. The Gospel must remain Good News while becoming, up to a certain point, a cultural phenomenon" (1991:454, emphasis author's). The challenge is to relate to people free of cultural trappings that are foreign to the context (i.e., not to "transfer" one's own native customs into a new culture). Incarnation represents a way of life that can be summarized by the following process and questions:

1.Deconstruct our cultural-bound paradigm of the Gospel and church: How have we been shaped by our culture(s)? What do we need to abandon or repent of?

2.Recover the culturally-translatable Gospel and patterns of church: What is the Way of Jesus? What are the essentials of Gospel and church?

3.Embody the Gospel in new cultures: How will we live the Way of Jesus in new cultures? How is the Spirit moving in this context?

1. Deconstruct our Cultural-Bound Paradigm

I tell you the truth, unless a kernel of wheat falls to the ground
and dies, it remains only a single seed. But if it dies, it produces
many seeds. – John 12:24

Early in our church planting experience, we realized the real challenges are not methodological or structural as much as they are theological and spiritual. This journey has not been easy for most of us. As we have exegeted our culture and the Scriptures, we have realized that *we* are a lot more worldly (i.e. modern) than we think we are (cf. Rom. 12:1-2). We must continue to critically determine what traditions have evolved during modernity and be ready to let them go.

The modern ecclesial paradigm is incapable of renewal for two reasons: First, it is a model that has become entwined with a particular culture and historical period (i.e., modernity). Without a radical paradigm shift, the modern church's only hope is to "convert" postmoderns to a syncretized form of Christo-modernism. This is essentially what the Judaizers did, for which they were soundly condemned for preaching a false gospel.[25] Second, it has abandoned its organic nature as a missional community and turned to non-living, mechanistic functions. This brings to mind the warning in Revelation 3:1, ". . . I know your deeds; you have a reputation of being alive, but you are dead." Only as the church dies to itself, will it have the opportunity to be organically reborn as the body of Christ—a missional community in new and different cultural realities.

For change to occur, the Western church must come to realize that we are substantially more modern, even syncretistic, than we realize. Ecclesial translation, therefore, must begin with evaluating how we have been shaped by

---

[25] Cf. Acts 15 and Galatians.

cultural influences (e.g. educational, religious, family, political, economic), so that we can sift out whatever portions of our worldview and methodologies are incompatible with apostolic patterns.

Only as the church is different *from* the culture can it make a difference *in* the culture. Deconstruction calls for the all-out abandonment of the modern constructs of church that will enable the people of God to rediscover the radical nature of the church to embody the Gospel in new cultures. It calls for the complete conceptual, liturgical, and institutional disengagement from modernity and the purging of *any* modern trappings that prevent the church from functioning as a living organism. Everything that has become a modern necessity for church must be challenged: financial dependencies, dedicated buildings,[26] imported programs, hierarchical professionals, suprachurch agencies and any other institutional expectations.[27] Question everything. Make no concessions.[28] We must clear away anything that hinders the body from functioning and reproducing—anything that is heavy, complicated and cultural-bound.[29]

To the extent that the church disengages from the assumptions, images and structures of Christendom, the church avails itself to be reborn out of the rubble of modernity and reproduced beyond modern cultures. Of all the world faiths, Christianity is the one that can and must die only to be reborn again. Only through intentionally dying to the rigid structures of modernity will the church be capable of genuine spiritual renewal and missional movement. The painful process of deconstructing requires genuine humility. Our attitude should be the same as that of Christ Jesus:

> Who, being in very nature God, did not consider equality with God something to be grasped, but *made himself nothing, taking the very nature of a servant*, being made in human likeness. And being found in appearance as a man, he *humbled himself and became obedient to death*—even death on a cross! (Phil. 2:5-8).

---

[26] With regard to church buildings, Charles Olsen writes: "The church's utter dependence on a place reveals an adolescent behavior pattern. When the church comes to a mature understanding of the gospel, valuing life together and mission to the world, it can be weaned from this dependency. Then the edifice complex will no longer rob the church of its vital energy and resources" (1973:145).

[27] All of these factors were absent in the development of the early church. Today they have become the building blocks of church.

[28] In face of the church crisis, Hoekendijk asks the question, "What then shall we do?" "It seems to me that we have to cultivate a healthy skepticism toward all traditional forms and procedures; we must prevent ourselves being hypnotized by familiarity. Therefore, we must put the fundamental questions: not begin halfway with the question 'How shall we continue to do in the future what we used to do in Egypt?' The question is not how, but whether we should do it or not" (1966:178).

[29] Cf. 1 Cor. 6:12; 8:13; 10:23-33; Heb. 12:1-3.

2. Recover the Culturally-Translatable Gospel and Patterns

*I am sending to you Timothy, my son whom I love, who is
faithful in the Lord. He will remind you of my way of life in
Christ Jesus, which agrees with what I teach everywhere in
every church. –*
1 Corinthians 4:17

After years of struggle, we now believe the Gospel calls for one way of being church (i.e., the way of Jesus), but this way has the inherent ability to be embodied in a countless number of cultures (i.e., one way, many expressions). The translatability of the Gospel enables the indigenous expression and reproduction of churches in any context.

The key questions for recovering the radical nature of the church are, "What is the Gospel?" "What is the way of Jesus?" and "What are the essential patterns of faith and practice that can then be incarnated in this context?[30] These are not merely pragmatic questions. Rather, they constitute questions of profound theological and missiological significance.

In Jesus we discover not only *what* to believe, but also *how* to live—to know Him and follow His way of life. Jesus is good news for postmoderns. Through His Incarnation and life, Jesus provides a living example that He expects us to continue to live through community.[31] His life now continues in a Spirit-empowered community. The Gospel is neither an abstract idea nor an institutional structure. The Gospel is a living reality. Jesus is the way *to* life and the way *of* life.

The challenge is how to rediscover the basic necessities of church and mission—to discern between essentials and non-essentials or "contextuals" (see Figure 26.3). These "patterns" are not structures or methodology, but represent a *modus vivendi*—a distinct way of living.

---

[30] Here is a simple exercise: Take a blank sheet of paper and fold it down the middle. On one side put the heading, "Essentials for Church." Name the other column "Non-essentials for Church." See what you come up with. There are actually very few essentials that are as important as Jesus, His Word, His Spirit and His Community. But the church is filled with so many non-essentials like dedicated buildings, budgets, Robert's Rules of Order, constitutions, choirs, Sunday School, Christian books, curriculum, sound systems, marketing, budgets, paid staff and mission boards, etc., etc.

[31] Cf. Jn. 13:15, 20:21; Ac. 2:38-39, 4:12, 33, 5:17, 42, 8:5, 25, 35, 9:20-22, 10:34-43, 12:16-40, 17; 18:5; Rom. 10:9-10; 1 Pet. 2:21; 1 Jn. 2:6.

| **Essentials** | **Contextuals** |
Culturally-Translatable Patterns	*Culturally-Specific Practices*
Grounded in Translation / Incarnation	Grounded in Pragmatism
Bible as Prescriptive (and Descriptive)	Bible as Descriptive
Normative	Creative
Based on Revelation	Based on Cultural Relevance
Received (Revelation)	Conceived (Perception)
Non-Negotiable	Negotiable
Fixed	Flexible
Genotype[32]	Phenotype[33]

Figure 26.3 Tensions of Contextualization

As we read the Bible we see patterns emerge that are rooted in the life of Jesus, are manifest throughout the New Testament record and can be lived out in a variety of cultural contexts throughout history. Here are three basic filters for determining normative patterns:

1. Jesus: Are these patterns seen in the life and teachings of Jesus Christ?

2. Apostolic Church: Are the patterns evident in the expansion of the first-century church?

3. Culture: Can the patterns be incarnated across a variety of cultural-historical contexts? Can they be readily translated in new cultures?

Every New Testament apostolic pattern will reflect the simplicity and purity of Christ. Patterns reflect Kingdom values which often differ from the prevailing culture. They are not organizational, religious or secular—they are of Christ.[34]

These essential patterns are observable in various cultural and church settings throughout the New Testament record.[35] They are affirmed by Luke

---

[32] Gen·o·type: The genetic makeup, as distinguished from the physical appearance, of an organism or a group of organisms.

[33] Phe·no·type: The observable physical or biochemical characteristics of an organism, as determined by both genetic makeup and environmental influences.

[34] For more discussion on the character of the patterns based on the person of Jesus Christ, see Jonathan Campbell (1999), Kraybill (1978) and Yoder (1972; 1992).

[35] Raymond Brown's Sprunt Lectures in 1980 were published under the title, *The Churches the Apostles Left Behind* (1984). He compares and contrasts the different church traditions of the late first century as they are reflected in the New Testament. See also Birkey (1988) and Branick (1989).

(Ac. 1:1-5), Paul (Rom. 15:5; 1 Cor. 4:16-17, 11:1; Phil. 2:5, 3:16-17; 2 Thess. 2:15, 3:4-7; 2 Tim. 1:13-14, 2:1-2), Peter (1 Pet. 2:21), the author of Hebrews (Heb. 2:3-4) and John (1 Jn. 2:6, 3:16).

The strength and effectiveness of patterns rest in their inherent simplicity and cultural flexibility. They are not culture-specific. True patterns can be lived out in any mission context. William Dillon asserts, "If *one* of these principles [or patterns] can be practiced successfully in *one* part of the world, they can *all* be practiced successfully in *all* parts of the world" (1957:11, emphasis author's). They are so simple, flexible, mobile and culturally transferable that Paul could simply tell his readers to remember how he lived and what he taught.[36]

3. Embody the Way in New Cultures

Though I am free and belong to no man, I make myself a slave to everyone, to win as many as possible. . . . I have become all things to all men so that by all possible means I might save some. I do all this for the sake of the gospel, that I may share in its blessings. – 1 Corinthians 9:19, 22-23

If the Apostle Paul were living in the West, he might well claim, "To the postmoderns, I became like a postmodern (though I myself live by God's metanarrative revealed in the way of Jesus), so as to win those postmoderns."[37] In the same way, to effectively translate the Gospel requires us to embody "The Way" of Jesus in "ways" that can be understood by receptor societies. The guiding questions are "How can we pass on the way of Jesus in a way that will lead to a movement of indigenous churches?" and "How is the Spirit moving in this context?"

When we talk about translating the church in postmodern cultures, we are not proposing establishing a "postmodern church."[38] We don't want the church to be shaped by postmodern culture any more than by modern culture. The challenge is to be the church *in* postmodern culture without being *of* postmodern culture.

We aim to bring to every people group an indigenous faith that is true to the life of Jesus without Christendom's culture-bound faith. An indigenous

---

[36] Cf. 1 Cor. 4:16-17, 11:1-2; Phil. 3:16-17; 1 Thess. 1:4-7. Paul warned churches from straying from these simple patterns and from their devotion to Christ (cf. Rom. 12:1-2; 2 Cor. 11:3; Col. 2:6-10; Gal. 1:6-9; see Deut. 8:6; 2 Kgs. 17:13; Isa. 42:24; Ezek. 33:11).

[37] In Acts 15, we see Paul fight for freedom from the customs of Moses for the Gentiles. He wrote, "Do not cause anyone to stumble, whether Jews, Greeks or the church of God—even as I try to please everybody in every way. For I am not seeking my own good but the good of many, so that they may be saved (1 Cor. 10:32-33). Paul exhorted others to follow this pattern (cf. 1 Cor. 4:16-17; Phil. 3:16-17).

[38] We should not start "postmodern" churches any more than we should start "black" churches, "Vietnamese" churches, "Anglo" churches, "Gen X" churches or "house" churches. We start churches. Our identity is first in Jesus, not in our ethnicity or culture or generation or style (cf. Gal. 3:28).

church is one in which new believers feel that their church is an original work within their own culture. Indigeneity is not about structures, though structures will emerge in every culture. They don't have to become an American or modernist in order to follow Jesus. For the church to be indigenous means that it is not dependent upon any "artificial life support" (i.e., anything that is culturally foreign or non-essential, especially money, buildings and professional clergy). It is free from exotic (foreign) influences that would impede the organic inclination to grow *and* reproduce in the natural environment.[39]

Only as the Gospel becomes a way of life in the culture of the people will it be capable of ongoing adaptation and reproduction to a changing environment. The objective of our mission in any context is to plant the simple seed of the Gospel in such a way that it will take root, grow and reproduce throughout new fields (1 Cor. 3:5-9). This involves incarnating the Way of Jesus in the Power of Jesus—the fullness of both Word and Spirit.

As Roland Allen reminds us, "The spontaneous expansion of the church reduced to its elements is a very simple thing" (1962:156). The very nature of the church as a living system calls us to plant the seed (the essential DNA)—nothing more and nothing less. Then let the seed grow! Put no structural expectations based on modern values (i.e. greatness of buildings, size of budgets or number of bodies)—only organic expectations that it be healthy, growing, bearing fruit and reproducing in the soil of the culture.

Church as Incarnation and Witness of Christ

The Gospel is fully realized in *and* through community. Contrary to modern individualism, the most profound spiritual experience we can have is not in isolation but in community.[40] The Church "proves" the Gospel in her very existence by providing a tangible expression of God's love and reality. Through the living Body of Christ, the Word is again "made flesh."

The Gospel and community were inseparable to the early church. To believe in Jesus is to be part of His body.[41] The good news of God was present in Jesus' life, teachings, atoning death and resurrection. These early believers embodied the life-giving reign of God—founded in eternity past, experienced in the present and yet to be fulfilled in the future.

The body image illustrates the diversity, fellowship and interdependence of believers under the headship of Christ.[42] As we examine the life of the early church, we see the mutual nature of such a community—like a healthy family where people are committed to each other because of their common bond. Thus,

---

[39] The opposite of indigenous is exotic. Exotic is that which is foreign to the context. Anything that is imported violates indigeneity to some degree.

[40] Cf. Mt. 18:15-20; Eph. 4:1-16; Phil. 2:1-11; Col. 3:15-17.

[41] Cf. Rom. 7:4; 1 Cor. 10:16, 12:27; Eph. 1:23, 4:4, 12; Col. 1:24.

[42] Cf. 1 Cor. 11:3; Eph. 1:10, 22, 4:15-16, 5:23; Col. 1:18, 2:10, 19·

churches are personal, intimate, committed and small enough to facilitate healthy relationships. Jesus' life and mission now continue through his Spirit-empowered community.

Before postmoderns will consider the truths of Jesus, they must see *and* feel (both spiritually and physically) these truths. As my friend Paul Ingram, a church planter in Seattle, explains, "A postmodern will only have as much faith in God as they have in you." This reflects the promise in Luke 10 where Jesus says, "He who listens to you listens to Me; he who rejects you rejects Me; but he who rejects Me rejects Him who sent Me." Christian community is *the* postmodern apologetic.

The mission of the church grows out of the relational heart of God. We are the living Body of Christ where people are drawn into right relationship with God and into right relationship with one another. In the midst of our current cultural-ecclesial crisis, the most powerful demonstration of the reality of the Gospel is a community embodying the *way*, the *truth* and the *life* of Jesus—nothing more and nothing less.

"Peace be with you! As the Father has sent me, I am sending you."
And with that he breathed on them and said, "Receive the Holy
Spirit..."
John 20:21-22

Chapter 27

Reciprocal Contextualization

Frecia C. Johnson

All of us who have worked cross-culturally return home as changed people. We have lived in what to us is a new world, with new rules of behavior based on assumptions we often don't understand. To the extent that we were able to adjust to that new world, then, we became bicultural. We became more than we were before we went into that other world and we were forever changed.

As we became accustomed to that other world, we often began to assimilate some of the assumptions of the people among whom we worked and began to look at things from their point of view. Kraft speaks of how he gained new insight into many biblical passages through attempting to look at them through the eyes of the Kamwe people of Nigeria among whom he worked (Kraft 1979a, 1996). There were, for example, severe limitations when dealing with the account of Noah and the ark among a people who have never seen a body of water bigger than a river that swells to 1/4 mile in width during the rainy season and goes virtually dry during the dry season. The fact that these people had never seen a boat larger than a canoe strongly affected their ability to accept the biblical account of Noah.

On the other hand, the Kamwe people, unlike most Americans, were immediately able to understand why the woman at the well of John 4 was full of shame as she met Jesus that day. For in their own culture, as in first century Palestinian culture, only a woman who was barren would have attracted five husbands. Far from being an immoral woman, she was a desperate woman and not to be condemned because she had given up on her ability to prove her fertility and thus to live a normal life.

The sociocultural perspective from which we interpret the Scriptures, therefore, will sometimes limit our ability to understand, as with the Kamwe and the story of Noah or with Anglo-Americans who assume the Samaritan woman was a harlot. Or that perspective may enhance our ability, as it does for the Kamwe when they hear of the Samaritan woman. We can be certain, though, that our understanding (like those of other peoples) will be affected for better or worse by our cultural conditioning. It will also be affected by the conditioning of any other cultural perspective(s) we may have picked up and by a variety of other life experiences that may have come our way.

My Kazakhstan Experience

Having helped my husband plant a church in Kazakhstan that was attended by Kazakhs, Tartars, Russians, South Africans, Germans, Americans and other nationalities who were Muslims, Jews, Orthodox, Anglican and evangelical Christians, I was immersed in a sea of conflicting cross-cultural perspectives. What heartened us most was to see people, who attended the church merely to learn English, turn to the Lord and be received into His arms as His children. As their questions became more frequent and probed more deeply, their viewpoints brought a range of fresh, often insightful perspectives that were new to us. It was impossible not to continually re-evaluate and refine what we believed as we engaged in biblical discussions with these babes in Christ who were so eager not only to learn, but to have us seriously engage in dialogue with them.

Because I was the first Western woman many of them had been exposed to, the discussions often centered on issues like the role of women in the church or whether a woman should divorce a husband who seriously physically abused both her and their children, but was unwilling to change. The discussions were inevitably long, deep and lively. At first, the Kazakhstanis yielded to our opinions as if they were "capital T" truth. After all, we were successful Americans in the midst of a society that was virtually bankrupt financially, structurally, socially, morally and spiritually.

But once we had achieved a deeper level of familiarity, they voiced concern about a certain rigidity they perceived in our thinking. For example, having been an executive in two major corporations, as well as a leader in other areas, I encouraged several women to volunteer as members of the church board we were founding. One of the male members, Sasha[1] however, was outraged because he was convinced that Paul did not approve of women as leaders. It was then my turn to step back and examine my position, particularly in his context.

The Kazakhstan society had been very male dominated under the communist regime, therefore it was easy for Sasha to read a few passages from Paul's letters and condemn women as church leaders in light of his own communist experience. I took his challenges to heart and reviewed Scripture and the commentaries on the subject and quickly realized that he had not considered the Scriptures on women in Paul's context, nor in the context of either Paul's or Jesus' attitude toward all of God's children, including women. I cannot say that Sasha was convinced by my interpretation, which was quite different from his. While I returned to something close to my previously held position, it was from a new, more critical perspective. In the process, I gained a greater understanding of his worldview and the needs of his society—as well as my own. As a result, while at Fuller Seminary, I intentionally attended Dr. Dean

---

[1] A fictitious name to protect his privacy.

Gilliland's course on the Apostle Paul's theology in order to become more deeply immersed and enlightened by this critical subject.

In Kazakhstan, similar discussions took place between the church members and the missionaries on other issues as well, with an important result. It affirmed to Sasha and the other Kazakhstanis that we were willing to seriously question our own understandings in light of their perspectives. Even when we did not significantly change our beliefs as a result of this process, we found ourselves fine-tuning them and seeing the Lord in a new light. As each one who developed a more personal relationship with Christ shared insights, joy and delight, we found ourselves seeking and achieving more intimacy with each other and with Christ as well.

The Benefits at Home and Abroad

Upon returning home and sharing with our own people the insights that we had developed, we discovered that we had changed in radically new and exciting ways that often startled those who sent us. We reasoned that the ability to look at the Scriptures and life from another perspective had been good for us and, therefore, it would be appreciated by the people at home. If it is good for the people of Kazakstan to contextualize Christianity in their cultural context, should not the lessons learned there have an impact on the sending churches, especially those that have become mired in their own ethnocentrisim, as well as traditions that have little relevance today?

But it was our turn to be startled. We were now looked at as strange by our home churches and affected by what they considered to be alien influences. The people in these churches often did not know where we were coming from and why we should be so concerned with issues they felt were irrelevant to their lives. We found a disturbing lack of understanding and concern even among those churches that supported forward-looking, relevant missionary efforts.

For example, many churches have for years supported Bible translation teams whose efforts as part of the broader contextualization movement have resulted in better translations for tribal peoples than the ones the sending churches are using back home. And though such churches are very mission-minded, it is distressing to find that they have not learned what they could have from the Bible translators they have been supporting.

While by now there are several good dynamic equivalence translations in English, many mission-minded churches hold fast to literal translations such as the New King James or New American Standard versions that give a very poor impression of God's willingness to use the language of ordinary people—a willingness He showed by putting His Word in ordinary Greek and Hebrew.

The home church traditions, then, give the wrong impression concerning God's attitude toward culture. In contrast, the people on foreign fields are using translations that vividly teach and demonstrate that God can speak their languages and use their cultures. In time, the people are simultaneously affirmed in who they are and see Jesus as their God.

What is missing in the method used by the home churches and the Bible schools and seminaries in which the pastors receive their training? And what is missing in the way those of us in cross-cultural mission engage with those in the home churches? How good it would be for the contextualization movement to also affect the home churches and the Bible schools and seminaries in which the pastors receive their training.

The Missing Ingredient

An often missing ingredient in this whole discussion is respect for the Christians of other societies and the ways in which they think about and practice the faith. Our habit has been to regard them as children, immature in the faith and so having nothing or little to contribute to those of us who see ourselves as proprietors of the faith. Since the Gospel came to us first, we seem to think we own it. Such lack of respect is felt keenly by many of those in mission lands, especially when they come to America for schooling and find that they are not taken seriously unless they accommodate to our ideas and approaches.

The experience of many of us, plus the studies we have been able to do in the area of contextualization have, however, demonstrated beyond doubt that people of other societies can think helpfully about Christian faith and can effectively witness to it. With this in mind, Kraft has called for a "more broadly based, multiculturally applicable theological perspective" (1979a:12). He further states, *"Theologizing by those of nonwestern cultures (if within scriptural limits) can both enrich the rest of us and alert us to deficiencies in our commonly held interpretations"* (1979a:304, emphasis author's).

Who are the recipients of mission and what is their response to Western mission today? Many are no longer tolerating Western disrespect. In reaction, Latin American scholars proposed Liberation Theology a number of years ago—an approach that, though deeply flawed in some respects, needed to be taken seriously as a backlash against Western paternalism and the tendency of conservative evangelicals to ignore the needs of the poor and politically oppressed.

The African Independent Church movement is another example of a reaction against a largely intellectual Christianity that disrespects and seeks to eliminate African culture. As Africans study the Scriptures and find that God is strongly into both relationship and power, but also learn that the Western Gospel seems to neglect these things, many turn to independency from the Western church. While that may be quite healthy, would it not be better if we learned theology from these Africans in light of their reaction to our Lord's transcultural Gospel and allow our own theologies to be challenged?

From such reactions and similar feedback from a variety of societies globally, we need to recognize that many nonWestern churches and their leaders have matured in the last few generations to the point that they have earned the right to enter into theological conversation with Westerners as equals. We from the sending countries need to recognize this and change our view of ourselves from simply taking the Gospel to the unsaved (though we should continue this) to also engaging with the young Christians in serious communication and mutual learning. Theologian Robert Schreiter notes that:

> The churches in Latin America, Africa, Asia and Oceania are not satisfied to repeat the tradition as it has come to them, in rote fashion. They are anxious to take their place alongside the churches of older origin in contributing their response to the gospel to the great stream of Christian tradition (Schreiter 1997:xi).

Contextualization studies make it clear that Western missiologists have made great strides in understanding how the Gospel should relate to the culture of the receptors. Missiologists have moved from approaches centered on the transplanting of theological insights forged in the West to recognizing the need for new forms of theology and practice to appropriately convey Biblical Christian meanings in the context of the receptors' cultures.

But a certain reticence continues in our home churches and training institutions toward accepting insights from the receiving churches. This sending/recipient relationship would be similar to that of a student of a professor who has attained a Ph.D. and is hired as a colleague, but is never recognized by his/her former professor as of equal status. Many in our home churches and training institutions enjoy having those from mission lands come for visits, but seldom accept them as having anything to offer to the home society's expressions of Christian experience, thinking and theology. The tendency in our home churches and training institutions is to resist sincerely allowing their experiences and conclusions to touch our own beliefs and practices.

The missionary who supervised our volunteer group to Kazakhstan is an example of one who attempted to shut down our incarnational approach to mission. Among other things, he ordered the group not to live among the locals, but to live in the compound that he controlled. His attempts to censor and structure when, where and how the Gospel was presented severely limited our witness, as well as any opportunity to be touched by the Kazakhstanis or to engage in reciprocity. As a result, the volunteers resigned as a group from the sending agency, but stayed in Kazakhstan, continued the mission and encouraged a level of reciprocity with the Kazakhstanis that resulted in respectful, often humorous and always insightful, debates in which each of us had to re-evaluate our positions.

Though we rejoice with receiving peoples when Jesus becomes their Lord, speaking their language and using their cultural forms, what are we learning from them that we can apply in our home contexts? As we missionaries who have gone to the ends of the earth and have deeply engaged other societies, and touched and been taught by the Holy Spirit through the people we serve, so our home churches and training institutions need to be touched and taught. Our concern, then, needs to go beyond contextualization in the receiving churches to their impact upon the sending churches and training institutions. This is what I mean by Reciprocal Contextualization.

While mission literature often touches on something akin to reciprocity, it is usually addressed in a casual or circumspect way. For example, in 1990 William Dyrness proposed an Interactional Model that involves the missionary opening Scripture to a people, followed by a dialogue between Scripture and the perspectives of the people. Dyrness briefly, but rightly, proposes that the West needs to learn from the Third World so that we may "reflect more deeply on our setting, to the end that our witness there may be more effective" (1990:286).

In 1992, Dyrness discussed the importance of developing local theologies and said briefly "we must be able to learn from each other" (1992:168). Though he suggests in both books that we learn from other peoples, much of what he has written here continues to reflect a Western approach. He does not complete the process by proposing a serious re-evaluation of the perspectives of the missionary and his/her home constituency as a result of that encounter and what that might mean to both participants. There is, however, literature that has attempted to go beyond previous approaches, but has usually fallen short of true reciprocity.

Another example would be Leslie Newbigin who proposes a similar concept among the religions in his 1995 book, *The Open Secret*.

> [O]bedient witness to Christ means that whenever we come with another person (Christian or not) into the presence of the cross, we are prepared to receive judgment and correction . . . . The dialogue with people of other religions will certainly lead to reconsideration and reformulation of Christian doctrines formulated in other circumstances. . . . We participate in the dialogue believing and expecting that the Holy Spirit can and will use this dialogue to do his own sovereign work, to glorify Jesus by converting to him both the partners in the dialogue (1995a:182-86).

It is unfortunate that Newbigin does not apply this concept to mission in context as well.

One notable exception is Kortright Davis's brilliant 1986 article entitled, "Bilateral Dialogue and Contextualization." K. Davis, an associate professor of theology at Howard University Divinity School, calls for a mutual search through bilateral dialogue: "[I]f context is to be understood as the dynamic totality of reality, no section of the human family can claim exception from the need to be transformed by the sovereign appeal of the Word of God" (1986:388).

K. Davis uses a self-expanded definition of the term "bilateral" and states that, "bilateralism consists more in a mutuality of learning and listening than in bargaining and contracting" (1986:391). For instance, in discussing missiology, K. Davis asks the question, "When we look at other faiths and denominations, what do we see in ourselves?" (1986:396), to which I would add, "and are we willing to re-evaluate our beliefs based on what we see?"

While I affirm the value of dialogue[2] between those equally committed to Christ, I go even further and ask how that dialogue impacts not only our own beliefs and theology, but those of our sending church and sending agency. By common definition, dialogue as used by K. Davis involves an interchange between two or more persons and is, therefore, inherently bilateral. It contrasts with mere conversation in which there may be an interchange of thought, but there is no guarantee that either participant will be touched by the process. I suggest that the term "Reciprocal" comes closer to what K. Davis is describing.

Reciprocity in dialogue involves something that is given and felt by each in return. It is mutual and equivalent, denoting mutual sharing—touching and being touched—without the need to agree on a single interpretation, but giving each participant the opportunity to learn how things look from the other's point of view. Going beyond mere intellectual handling of interpretations, reciprocity denotes an interaction resulting in mutuality and respect.

While the literature has been sparse on the issue of reciprocity, it is imperative that mission seriously consider Reciprocal Contextualization as an important core aspect of mission.

Reciprocal Focus Defined

Here I propose an expanded focus for those of us involved in the effort to see Christianity contextualized in the societies to which we take the Gospel. It is a focus on what happens to the cross-cultural witnesses and, beyond them, to their sending churches when the message of Jesus' love is looked at and internalized from a cultural perspective, i.e., a perspective other than that of the missionaries themselves and their home constituencies. This is what I am calling Reciprocal Contextualization.

The purpose of such reciprocity is to create respect for and recognition in the home churches and training institutions of the value of the perspectives of the receiving peoples. Though our focus has rightly been on seeing the message appropriately contextualized in the receptor society, we can ask, What have the missionaries and their home constituencies learned about God and His works from the receiving peoples? We, therefore, go a step further than our previous focus by reevaluating our own theology and praxis in the light of what field missionaries have been learning from Christians of other societies. We who have worked cross-culturally need to take the recipients' influences on our own theology and praxis home to our own sending agencies and especially to our

[2] I am aware that the concept of dialogue is used by Liberals in a way that implies that the Christian way is but one way among many and that, therefore, we are only to dialogue with people of other faiths without trying to convert them. By suggesting that we dialogue with mission planted churches I am in no way buying into that liberal error. My aim is dialogue "between those equally committed to Christ."

training institutions. We should be agents to engage them in dialogue with the receiving society, to respectfully see the sending church's theology as potentially as valid as our own. As the churches in the receiving society become missionary sending agencies themselves, they would have learned from us to engage in the same process. Following this pattern, all societies ultimately engage in a mutually inclusive dialogue leading to additional insight and spiritual growth for everyone.

Diagramatically, we may picture the contrast as follows:

1. The normal focus is:

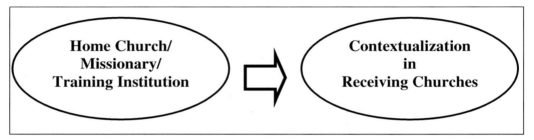

Figure 27.1 Normal Focus

2. This focus has the arrows going both ways:

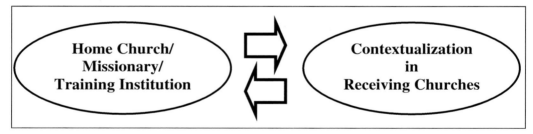

Figure 27.2 Reciprocal Focus

This process basically represents a communicational interaction between a giver and a receiver so that both give and both receive. Giving without receiving creates an imbalance—a dependency on the giver as the power source and an obligation or debt on the part of the receiver. When the process is not reciprocated, the imbalance continues and can lead to antagonism, resentment, resistance and even alienation, not to mention an inappropriately Western theology and praxis.

Communication of the Gospel by Westerners to nonWestern peoples has often resulted in a kind of theological imperialism, as if we alone are able to hear God clearly. Through Reciprocal Contextualization, we who had the privilege of hearing the Gospel first can learn to hear it anew through the lives and thinking of our receptors. In this way we can learn to hear Christ with new ears and to see Him through new eyes so that we add a new dynamic and vitality to our own faith. Just as God spoke to them through us, so He desires to speak to us through them. In this way, God's Word will be revealed to us more clearly and with greater personal meaning.

A statement by Dr. Jacob Loewen, a retired American and United Bible Societies consultant, comes to mind. He has said something like, "Until we are able to enter into the interpretations of the Bible embodied in the translations of the Bible into every language and culture of the world, we will not have experienced all of the riches of God's Word." What God wants to communicate to us is so vast, so rich and so varied that none of us can expect to comprehend it all through our own native perspectives alone. We can grow spiritually as we enter into the interpretations of other peoples and learn from their perspectives what we could never have learned within the limitations of our own.

One strength of this focus is that it respects the receptors and their ability to hear from the Holy Spirit. Another is that we allow ourselves to become aware of the fact that the Holy Spirit is working in their midst just as He is working in ours. Still another is the increase in our understanding of God and His works. In the end, it reaffirms and visibly demonstrates our genuine commitment to our often stated belief in the doctrine of the Priesthood of the Believer.

But this focus should not end with merely a greater intellectual understanding of Christianity. It should also lead to appropriate reciprocal understandings of both the relational and the spiritual power dimensions of the Gospel (see Chapter 7 of this book). Through entering into the total Christian experience of our receptors, those in direct contact with them can experience renewal in every aspect of our Christian experience. Through mutual sharing of our hearts as the Holy Spirit engages us, both their joy and faith and ours can be renewed, leading to a broadening of our perspective that is more empathetic and more transformed.

The greatest difficulty, however, is not the development of such renewing and broadening in the life of those who are interacting with those in the younger churches. It is helping people at home to share such enrichment. For them, the tendency is to not fully respect those who have received from us and to not value the new perspectives they can gain from the perspectives of those who have only recently come to faith in Christ. Though they may be curious about how these people are responding to the Gospel, those in the homelands may be so entrenched in their familiar ways of believing and doing that they are not very open to perspectives coming from people culturally distant from themselves. Often, when missionaries make presentations in the home churches and training institutions, the attitude of both leaders and congregations/students is simply mild interest and toleration of the new things that are described. The idea that such new perspectives and approaches to Christianity should be allowed to affect the way Christ is thought of, taught and worshipped will usually be far from their thinking.

As an example, many of us returning from the field with stories of healing and deliverance have been "stonewalled" when we have suggested that God's power is still available today even in the homeland. Our stories are treated as if those are the kinds of things God wants to do overseas but not here. There are even theologies that have infected pastors in the homeland that contend that God uses miracles to get the church started, but ceases to do them when the church has matured and "no longer needs them."

Something similar occurs when we hear of conversions in other societies taking place in family groupings. Our American individualism continues to drive us to advocate one-by-one conversions, even among young family members without their parents' permission. Shouldn't we learn from more family-oriented societies to advise young prospective converts to attempt to win their parents before we accept them for baptism and church membership? How much more likely that a young person will continue in his/her commitment to Christ if there is a supportive family. Though it may not be possible to win them, it would be good to delay formal recognition of the conversion of a young person until it is obvious that family members are not going to join him/her.

One of the young women in our Kazakhstan church, Tatiana[3], struggled with her commitment because her grandmother, who had a Muslim background but was not a practicing Muslim, had threatened never to speak to her granddaughter again if she became a Christian. Rather than baptize Tatiana right away, we helped her to mature in Christ and share her faith with her parents as she grew. Her father and sister began to attend church, followed by her mother, and the entire family eventually committed themselves to Christ. Although Tatiana's grandmother never did join the church, she eventually accepted the situation because the entire nuclear family had made their choice. In sharing the results of Tatiana's commitment and testimony to people at home and the effect it had on us, many hearts at home became more receptive to hearing the Gospel as well.

With regard to biblical interpretation, we at home have much to learn from the perspectives of believers whose cultures are much closer to biblical cultures than are Western cultures. Respect for the Old Testament and God's constant battle with idolatry recorded there would be a case in point. So would the greater understanding of covenants and the seriousness with which God takes them as portrayed in the Old Testament. Insight into the meaning of the phrase "Son of Man," Jesus' favorite name for Himself, is gained from God's constant use of that term to mean "Human Being" in Ezekiel. Kraft speaks of having learned this from his experience with the Hausa language of northern Nigeria.

The challenge of reciprocal learning may be greater for those deeply into theological theory (e.g., theologians) than for those whose primary concern is application (e.g., ministry-oriented persons), especially if that application is

---

[3] A fictitious name to protect her privacy.

cross-cultural. It is the frequent experience of those of us serving in training institutions that those who have invested much of their time and energy in the study of Western theology have so committed themselves to those perspectives that they are often loathe to take seriously new insights coming from Christians of nonWestern societies. But both theologians and ministry-oriented people can be guilty of ignoring the value of reciprocity and both can benefit from it. As the dialogue continues in new understandings and applications, a continual process of upwardly spiraling learning can occur that will hopefully bring all of us closer to a broader grasp of God's truths.

A major goal of reciprocity is the hope that Westerners acknowledge the receptors' beliefs by allowing ourselves to re-evaluate our own beliefs in response to the perspectives of other societies, recognizing that we have much to learn. As Kraft has said in advocating such openness, "...*any monocultural perspective* on truth is no more complete than the single perspective of any given individual" (Kraft 1979a:292).

Reciprocal Contextualization does not replace the better parts of the processes involved in the models of contextualization proposed by Bevans. As one example, the action process of praxis would continue to be valid, but would take place within the giving culture as well as in the receiving culture. "Rather than truth being worked out apart from life, praxis thinking holds that truth can only be grasped in a dialogue with life as it is actually lived, suffered through, and celebrated" (Bevans 2002:73).

I would add the words "through and with our global neighbors" to his comment. We are all interrelated in one way or another. Reciprocal Contextualization, then, goes to the next step in thinking, relating and evaluating.

Concerns

While reciprocity may, in theory and in practice, bring greater rewards, there are also potential concerns that must be addressed. First, we run the risk of our witness turning, as it has often done for those engaged in Liberal Theology, into mere dialogue that dilutes Scripture. Individuals and denominations have sometimes learned to respect other perspectives to the extent that they have relativized the Gospel. This could lead, as it already has for groups like the World Council of Churches, to a Christianity that is seen as just one religion among many with no greater claim to absolute truth than any other religion. Dialogue is a good means to discovery of new understandings only if there is a solid foundation from which to work. If any and all ideas are as good as any and all others, there is no place to stand and there are no meaningful conclusions to be reached. Liberals have often taken a worthy means and made it an end.

Dialoguing about the possibility of new interpretations of Scripture and new practices allowed by Scripture is quite a different thing from dialogue that considers Scripture as just one of many equally valid approaches to reaching

God. With both approaches to dialogue there is exciting learning. But one brings us closer to God while the other leaves us lost in a morass of ideas that may be fascinating, but provides no solid foundation for life and no meaningful relationship with the Source of life.

A second risk, more feared than real, is that Westerners might make so many changes in their theology that it would be impractical in the homeland. Such a condition is, however, only likely to occur if the Western person or group is either ungrounded in Scripture or already into impractical theology. If the grounding in Scripture is weak, people may simply be looking for intriguing ideas and may easily get so caught up in them that they go off the tracks. If they are into "head trip" theology they may simply add new ideas coming from other societies to the impractical ideas they already have. Actually, such a risk is quite small since most of what is there to learn is more on the practical side than the theoretical.

Third, some might allow the concept of reciprocity to lead them to a diminishing of missionary commitment. They might mistakenly think that we are contending that all cultural perspectives are as good as each other and, therefore, that people don't really need Christ to be saved. This is not what is being said here. Though Reciprocal Contextualization is advocating respect for every cultural point of view, it is not suggesting that every approach to God is correct. On the contrary, there is only one way to God according to Scripture. There are, however, many helpful perceptions that we Westerners could learn from people, especially Christian people, who for cultural reasons see things differently than we do.

This approach is certainly not advocating that missionaries turn from evangelistic work. What it is saying is that we need to listen to and learn from those who have responded. They can often tell us how best to reach their people and point to scriptural precedents for their suggestions. They can also often help us to better understand how our faith is to be expressed in new, more culturally relevant ways, both in their contexts and ours.

Fourth, it is feared that our willingness to engage in reciprocity could lead to greater tolerance of aberrant cultural practices at home. Recent generations of missionaries who have learned that God takes culture seriously, for example, have often been accused of advocating subChristian customs. I know of a missionary who, because he advocated the baptism of believing polygamists, was accused by his colleagues of advocating polygamy as God's ideal and even of wanting a second wife himself. Those who criticized this missionary's culture-sensitive approach had no understanding of God's willingness, as seen in Scripture, to accept at the start people's subideal customs in non-essential areas and then to patiently work for change. Their assumption was that advocating patience with any custom among new converts could only mean that this missionary was advocating that custom for everyone in all cultures—including polygamy in American culture.

Yet when there are customs such as idolatry, adultery and misuse of power that God regularly speaks out against, we should be no more patient than God is. We need to recognize that there is a big difference between something we see God being patient with in Scripture, such as polygamy, and something He categorically condemns and shows no patience with.

Although, in imitation of God's approach, we can be gentle and loving toward those who fall into sin by mistake, God shows no patience toward those who defy His commands. Uncritical, unscriptural tolerance is not of God. With God, we love the sinner but loathe the sin. In loving sinners, however, we dare not allow ourselves to become desensitized to the fact that sinful humanity needs to constantly be made aware of God's standards as well as of His love. Though the customs and perspectives of all peoples are to be taken seriously, all are also sooner or later to be judged and many changed according to God's standards as set forth in Scripture.

Desirable Effects

Regardless of our proper concern for the potential misunderstandings and misuse of reciprocity, the benefits far outweigh such potential problems. Some of these benefits are addressed above. They could be summarized and elaborated upon as follows.

First, the receptors are validated by the process. Seeking reciprocity is respectful and loving. It honors the receptors and invites them into a genuine give-and-take relationship. It fights our inborn tendency to be imperialistic and paternalistic. It puts us in the position of being willing to engage in meaningful interaction and mutual growth based on a greater depth of relationship, more respect between the participants and, therefore, more receptivity by the receptors.

Second, the missionary is put into a position to grow in Christ rather than simply to win and disciple others. As advocates, we missionaries can come to appreciate God's working in us through those we seek to serve, as well as God's working in them as we serve them. We are not always to be the source and they always the receptors. We, whom God is still working on, are to be receptors as well, with the receptors of our message being an important source God uses to work in our lives. God is bigger than any one cultural perspective can handle. It is, therefore, reasonable to expect that the more perspectives we allow to touch us and influence our thinking, the greater opportunity we have to open the door to sincere and relevant maturity.

Third, reciprocity fosters humility. In that regard, our attitude is governed by our expectations. If we expect to only give, never to receive, we will miss a great deal. If, however, we recognize that God has been at work with the people we are called to even before we arrived there, in humility we can be on the lookout for what He has for us as well as for what He wants to communicate through us to them. With this recognition, the work of the missionary should begin with the *expectation* of reciprocity, including the expectation that both the missionary and the receptors are to be transformed as they relate to one another. The relationship between communicator and receptor will then be changed from one of parent-to-child or teacher-to-student to one of learner-to-learner.

Fourth, the home constituency can learn from insights gained from the cross-cultural work it supports and, as a result, deal more effectively with people of other societies both at home and abroad. This is especially important in our own increasingly pluralistic society. Any attitude of superiority or paternalism toward people of other languages and cultures can be confronted and overcome if the lessons of reciprocity are learned. People at home, both in our churches and in our training institutions, can learn that those who think differently are not to be looked down on, but to be interacted with and learned from.

Fifth, the home constituency that is willing to engage in reciprocity is likely to become more committed to cross-cultural mission, both abroad and at home. Though evangelism would still be in focus, such a church can develop a healthy expectation of growing through the sharing of Christian experience by those coming from differing cultural perspectives. A church or training institution that is inquisitive and inclusive is more likely to experience satisfaction and growth than one that is closed and exclusive. This is already being realized as one of the benefits of short-term, church-sponsored missions.

Sixth, the home church's understanding and implementation of evangelism can be helpfully broadened. Although the possible loss of evangelistic zeal was mentioned as a danger, the opposite is actually more likely to happen. The broadening of a church's understanding of how to do evangelism in culturally appropriate ways can be a great gain. Such broadening could result in the church becoming more successful in reaching people of other cultural backgrounds living in the area or even in reaching today's youth who have learned to respect cultural differences. Hopefully, then, those with such respectful and open attitudes can be attracted to missionary service.

Seventh, the theology of the sending churches and training institutions should become stronger rather than weaker. As monocultural theological perspectives are replaced by cross-cultural understandings of God and His works, theological insights are broadened and become more in tune with Scripture. For the Bible is a cross-cultural book, written by people of other times and other cultures. Coming to it with perspectives developed in societies with cultures closer to the Bible than ours, then, contributes to a strengthening of the relationship between theological insight and the Bible.

Eighth, the churches and institutions in the homeland gain the potential for developing a meaning-based, rather than a form-based approach to evangelism. Rather than focusing on the details of the cultural forms in terms of which we in our traditions respond to God, dialogue would center upon scriptural understandings, meanings and interpretations through the eyes and ears of differing peoples. In doing so, Western Christians may well learn that the meanings originally expressed through certain cultural forms (e.g. of worship and doctrine) have been lost or changed to the point that they are no longer relevant or valuable either abroad or at home.

Finally, and most importantly, Reciprocal Contextualization would enable all of those who seek the truth of Scripture to move together toward greater maturity in their understandings of God's Word. As said above, a single cultural perspective on truth is incomplete. A multiperspective approach is much to be desired. While we must be cautious lest we go to the extreme of the prevailing Western relativism that accepts everything as truth, we must also be open to the infinite possibilities that may have previously eluded us.

Having said that, I hasten to add that while it is true that Western understandings are not inviolate, it is also true that they have been developed thoughtfully by very capable people over lifetimes of study and are not to be simply discarded. Though our Western understandings and interpretations are not the last word on truth and so must not be absolutized, they ought not to be ignored either.

Summary

Reciprocal Contextualization must become a part of the core teachings of Christian mission. Through a reciprocal focus in contextualization we stand to gain greater understanding, coupled with more respect from unbelievers as well as from believers, more receptivity to the Gospel, and a strengthening of our own beliefs. The Christian identity of each of us may well struggle for understanding, redemption and transformation as individuals, but the identity of Christianity as a whole cannot help but be transformed through humble reciprocity. Just as God has been patient with us as we have struggled over the centuries in attempting to learn who He is, so we must be patient with each other, including rather than discriminating, receiving rather than simply imparting and reciprocating rather than imposing.

In this world of globalization in which the majority peoples of the world have been reached by the Gospel message, and where many in other societies have moved a long way toward spiritual maturity, it is time that we stop thinking only in terms of being culturally sensitive to the implementation of the Gospel. It is time that we engage in meaningful interaction and communication with all peoples in such a way that we allow ourselves to be touched by the people to whom we have taken the Gospel.

As Western mission continues to take the Gospel to others, it is time for it to also engage in a mission of discovery, recognizing the potential for profitable influences by the receptors on the West, incorporating those influences into Western thinking, squaring them with Scripture and carrying those influences on theology and praxis to our churches and training institutions. We may well find that the discoveries we make are as appropriate at home as they are on the field.

We may also come closer to discovering who we are and who God is.

Part IV

Final Word

Chapter 28

The Incarnation as Matrix for Appropriate Theologies

Dean S. Gilliland

The title of this many-faceted volume is *Appropriate Christianity*. After journeying across variegated terrain and multiple roadways we are now ready for the last mile. These chapters have shown again the all-embracing and profoundly diverse applications of contextualization theory. Everything that has been written is committed to making clear the first and final statement of Christian faith: Jesus came into the world to be at home with all people in every place. Therefore, they can welcome Him, knowing that that He belongs with them and they with Him. Without this fundamental Word, there is no way to speak of appropriate Christianity. Through the Incarnation, God personally and intimately entered into the world of His own creation. Never can anything be more contextually appropriate! In closing this volume, we shall ponder the mystery of the Incarnation for mission and contextualization even though, humanly speaking, we can never reproduce it.

When my wife and I were missionaries in Africa we not only learned a lot about ourselves but also about other missionaries. The Africans talked freely about the habits of missionaries. One of the most interesting topics was how well or how poorly some missionaries connected with the Africans as people. Some rarely went into the villages or took the time to visit them in their homes. One doctor was well known for his isolation. The Africans would-comment, "Our own native doctors can help us because they know our secrets. This mission doctor does not know us. When we need help we have to go to him at his place." Then, pointing to the hospital they would say, "He is in our country but not in our house." His work was to bring healing in the name of Jesus but there was very little about his work that could be called incarnational mission. It took place during the era of "British West Africa." In addition to colonial attitudes, the sophistication of treatment and foreignness of the hospital had no connection with or use for African traditional healing. The mission practitioner kept himself at long distance from the people. He scarcely knew the language and while he was a fine Western technician, he cared little about African realities. In fact, he was a mysterious figure who offered only foreign medicine for those who could travel to him and could bring the required fees. In a radically different paradigm, the Incarnation of Jesus Christ brings God into "our house" in a way that sets the Christian faith apart from any other. Through the Incarnation, the door is open wide for all human beings to have a close and personal relationship with God.

There is simplicity about the Incarnation that even a child can grasp; yet, it is an enigma that is always beyond us. Throughout history, the greatest of minds have tried to help believers understand how a transcendent God could "become flesh and live among us." Ironically, these well-meaning attempts to explain the mystery led the early church into serious controversy and heresies.[1] While the idea of *logos* carried a wide range of meanings in speech and literature the overall meaning was that thought and idea can be transformed into language and discourse.[2] In this way, *communication* was at the very center of what was meant by *logos*. John the Apostle went beyond what was usually associated with the term when he spoke of *logos* as Word, making the association with Jesus (John 1:1-14). In a three-step sequence, he declared that the living Word was with God, the Word was actually God and that the Word (God) became flesh and lived among us. With this, John uses the *logos* idea in a contextually, dynamic way never known before.

Attempting to Understand the Incarnation

Theologians, both ancient and modern, have resorted to analogies to help ordinary humans grasp this ineffable mystery of Incarnation. In the 4th Century, Athanasius explained that the Incarnation was like a great king who journeyed to one of the villages of his kingdom to deliberately live as one among the ordinary people. Such action would bring that village honor above all others and would give profound dignity to all the residents. With the king physically present, it would be unlikely that enemies would harass or violate the citizenry.[3] As late as the last century, still searching for a way to understand the Incarnation, Kierkegaard again used the analogy of a king. This time the king desired to marry a girl from among the common folk of his kingdom. In order to romance her he had to lay aside his royal robes and he, himself, went into the village to

---

[1] For example, in the 3rd Century Clement and Origen tended to emphasize the divine character of the Word, although both realized the Savior had to be human if there was to be any true connection to people By the 4th Century Arias promoted the Word as human but not divine. He did this to meet the problem raised by Jesus being different from all human persons. Arianism, however, raised the greater problem of how to save humanity from sin. In the 5th Century, Nestorius taught that Jesus was both divine and human but in separate entities and these combined somehow into a third entity (Christ). This debate centered on Mary, the mother of Jesus. G. Ettlinger (1997:567-568).

[2] In Jewish thought, God's word is more than verbal communication but has a dynamic and substantive existence of its own. e.g. Psalm 33:6-9 the agent of the word is creation. Isaiah 55:11 God's word is the prophetic word. In Greek thought *logos* is better translated as "reason" or "rational principle" yet having a divine or at least a semi-divine origin and, on occasion, it was identified with God *(theos)*. D. Winslow (1977:687-690).

[3] Athanasius: "Introduction to the Treatise on the Incarnation of the Word" (1953:41).

request her hand from the family, as would any commoner. He could not overwhelm the humble girl with an entourage nor could he send a messenger to speak for him. Kierkegaard had such a high view of the meaning of the Incarnation that he was reluctant even to speak of it in ways that are analogous to human experience. Yet, he concluded "love is exultant when it unites equals, but it is triumphant when it makes that which is unequal equal in love."[4]

To understand the Incarnation fully is beyond the reach of the human mind. Because it is at the highest level of divine revelations it may seem presumptive, even irreverent, to speak of the Incarnation as a "model" for contextualization. In this chapter, we deal with this issue. Throughout this volume we have been speaking of contextualization as "appropriate Christianity." When this supernatural truth of God in Jesus Christ is put alongside any human attempt to reproduce it even the term "appropriate" seems quite superficial. Yet, by speaking this way, the idea and objectives of contextualization are made more accessible. The most appropriate way of approaching every man and woman, wherever they are, is in the spirit of what transpired through this event, -God's self-expression to human persons.

Incarnation as *logos*: John 1:14

Through the Incarnation, God opens the way to receive the truth that men and women of every culture and nation are created in God's image (Genesis 1:26, 27; 5:3, 9:6). However, we ask, "If we are created in God's image how can we know what God is like and what we were meant to be?" The Good News is that by seeing Jesus we see God (John 14:8-11) and by seeing God through Jesus, we have confidence that the image can be restored. What more profound revelation could there be or how could there be a clearer communication about God's intention? "The Word (God's expression) became flesh *(en sarki)*." This *en sarki* of John 1:14 is the astonishing declaration that changed everything after creation. By this testimony, and other scriptural witnesses, we are assured that Jesus, a truly human and complete person, became the new Adam (I Cor. 15:22, 45, 47), providing a way of redemption for a fallen creation. Jesus actually lived with us, on our ground and in our space. When we look at Jesus, we know that God is truly with us. By seeing Jesus, finite men and women can understand what it meant to be created in God's image.

Incarnational theology, therefore, tells us that God desires to be visible in every people and community. It means that God is touching and interacting with every area of life in tangible and concrete ways. Isaiah prophesied that God would be with us in a special kind of way when he spoke of the Messiah as *Immanuel* (Is. 7:14, Matt. 1:23). "God with us" means that there is no human

---

[4] Robert W. Brethald, ed. (1946:165). In relating the analogy, Kierkegaard adds that a courtier remarked to the king, "Your majesty is about to confer a favor upon the maiden for which she can never sufficiently grateful her whole life long." Kierkegaard's comment was, "So it is with the incarnation."

need that is beyond the reach of Jesus Christ, the Word. This message is good news, indeed, because the presence and power of God comes into the life of people where they are. The task of contextualization is to help everyone, regardless of race, religion or life situation, to know that God can be "at home" with him or her.

Incarnation as *kenosis* (Philippians 2:6-11)

The sublime *kenosis* passage of Philippians 2:6-11 is parallel, in certain ways, to the prologue of John's Gospel. The striking similarity between these two passages lays in the way the mind and purpose of God is revealed through the Incarnation. Philippians 2:5, the verse that immediately precedes the Christological passage (5:6-11), can be taken as an introduction to the Christ-hymn. In saying this, we are pointing to Paul's exhortation that Jesus' followers are to have "the mind" of Christ. This "mind" should characterize all who would follow Jesus' example. The *Word Biblical Commentary* translates the Greek as; "This way of thinking must be adopted by you which was also the way of thinking adopted by Christ Jesus."(G. Hawthorne 1983:75) The N.R.S.V. says, "Let the same mind be in you that was in Christ Jesus." However, the Greek (*proneistho*) has been translated in various ways, for example, "the same mind" or "this way of thinking," or "this frame of mind." However, the emphasis is squarely on the fact that in their relationship to all people, and certainly to each other, Christians are expected to demonstrate the same attitude, the same spirit, as was manifest by the Incarnation.[6] In addition, what was this attitude or mind that compels the believer? It is this: Christ Jesus, "being in the very nature of God, did not consider equality with God something to be grasped, but made himself nothing, taking the very nature of a servant, being made in human likeness. (NIV)."

While verses 2:5-11 are unparalleled as a Christological statement, they were meant to show the spirit or attitude that should underlie what Christians are to be and do. Paul frequently called upon Christians to take Christ Jesus as their example (Romans 15:1-7; I Cor.10: 3-11: 1; II Cor.8: 6 -9). This spirit of self-sacrifice and humility that serves "the other" in love is what Jesus had "in mind (2:5)" when, as the Word, He became flesh and lived among us."

It is my intention in this final chapter to show that the Incarnation is the locus within which and through which all thinking about appropriate Christianity must be carried out. In this sense, the Incarnation as the ultimate expression of God's person to humankind is irreproducible. It is for this reason

---

[6] There are unclear and numerous ideas about the source of the hymn (Greek, Old Testament, Iranian and others) however the lack of single-source clarity does contribute to the hymn's universality as its meaning can be applied far and wide, that is, self-sacrificing service on behalf of another. "Although this hymn is unquestionably a Christological gem unparalleled in the NT....John's object is not to give instruction in doctrine but to reinforce...Christ a the ultimate model for moral action." See G. Hawthorne (1983:79).

that the Incarnation, strictly speaking, it is not itself a model but is the frame or matrix within which a variety of contextualization models are formed. We will show, therefore, that the value and usefulness of any model is determined by the way or extent to which it can be defined by the Incarnation.

The remainder of the chapter will be a discussion of this idea by showing (1) why Incarnation is matrix rather than model, followed (2) by a discussion of three biblical principles of *logos* and *kenosis* that are essential to the matrix. Then, (3) I will show how six contextualization models fit into the Incarnation matrix and (4) conclude the chapter with a review of ways in which the authors in this volume have contributed to the Incarnation idea as contextual mission theology.

The Incarnation as Matrix

It is common to speak about the Incarnation as a way to understand contextualization; yet, the nature of the Incarnation is such that it is impossible to construct an Incarnation model. Definitions of models are so varied and kinds of models so diverse that the best way to describe models is by what they are intended to do. I. G. Barbour, the classic source for understanding models, would classify the type of model we are using in contextualization as a theoretical model.[7] A model of this kind, he says, is "a symbolic representation of selected aspects of the behavior of a complex system for particular purposes."[8] Expressed in this way, the key idea is that a model is not the reality itself; rather, models represent certain selected features of that reality. Further, the objectives of all models are predetermined, that is, the originator of the model has certain purposes or goals in mind that shape the model. Speaking more crudely, contextualization models, when taken together, are a kind of toolbox for communicating and applying the message in diversified situations. The particular task in this or that context must be carefully thought out, the end product kept in mind and the right tool (model) selected. Doing this work will usually require a combination of these tools and often a new tool must be fabricated to match the particularities of a given task. Avery Dulles has this in mind when he says that a model is, "a relatively simple, artificially constructed case, which is found to be useful and illuminating for dealing with realities that are more complex and differentiated."[9]

In this brief summarization, we are not saying that models are not useful in contextualization. On the contrary, models are the most practical method, if not the only method, for working in a concrete way with images and abstractions,

---

[7] Barbour discusses models as four types, experimental, logical, mathematical and theoretical. I. G. Barbour, *Myths, Models and Paradigms, A Comparative Study in Science and Religion* (1974:29-30), quoted in S. B. Bevans, *Models of Contextual Theology* (1992:24).

[8] Barbour (1974:7).

[9] A. Dulles (1983, 1992:30).

Bevans speaks of models in striking way: "Even though models are not, so to speak, the axe, they can function as a kind of wedge; even though they cannot bring the whole picture into focus they can provide and angle of vision."[10] Therefore, in contextualizing the Christian faith for diverse peoples, models are the best tools we have for shaping a product that is fitting and relevant to each situation.

However, our problem is that what we know about the Incarnation cannot be contained in or defined by models. Models fall short as a way to think about the Incarnation of Jesus Christ. Following is a summary of the differences between human models and divine Incarnation:

	Human Models	*Divine Incarnation*
Origin:	finite constructions	divine revelation
Nature:	symbolic representation of reality	absolute reality
Scope:	partial vision of the whole	complete, final disclosure
Purpose:	natural means to comprehend the event	the supernatural event
Method:	limited by subjectivity	unrestricted objectivity

Figure 28.1 Human Models Versus Divine Incarnation

The Incarnation as the final and complete revelation of God must be good news for all people, regardless of race or religion. The task of communicating the message and of designing ways to apply the message in these complex situations can never be equated with the divine event of salvation grace through the birth and life Jesus Christ. Contextualization models, therefore, must be constructed with the Incarnation as the all-embracing reality to which all models conform and from which all models derive intention, spirit and method.

I choose, therefore, to speak of the Incarnation as a matrix into which models are fitted. This Incarnation matrix is the entity or locus in which the model is conceived; it is where the objective and method develops. The intentionality of any given model, the slant or vision it provides and the bias of the originator must be subject to the Incarnation. As we proceed with this way of thinking about models, I will take the matrix-idea a step further to say that the metaphor (matrix) will be identified as the supernatural Word who took human form and is, therefore, a symbolic way of speaking about Jesus Christ.

Principles of Incarnation as Matrix (Jesus)

To simply reflect on the meaning of Incarnation is not enough. We must ask how the Incarnation of Jesus Christ can guide us in our search for appropriate Christianity. How can the Incarnation, as attitude and spirit, be translated into action? What steps can be taken to bring these ideals into real life,

---

[10] Bevans (1992:25).

so that God touches and changes people where they are? Missionaries, for example, need to know if they are working in the way and manner of the Incarnation. What is required of the mind and spirit of the messenger and what kind of actions will convey these intentions? Let us think about some of the implications of the Incarnation as matrix and set out three guidelines for what is required when we think and act in Incarnational ways. There are three things required by the truth of the *logos* and *kenosis* passages if we are to apply the Incarnation to both contextual theology and appropriate forms of Christianity.

Bring self-inclinations under control.

Imposing an "outsider's" worldview on others, forcing foreign ways of thinking and behaving, and expecting alien standards of behavior has caused much offense in the history of missions. While contextualization is an attempt to correct this, it is often done in ways that patronize and dominate people who are attempting to shape their own theologies and find answers to their own problems. Appropriate Christianity is a Christianity that grows out of the very soil where the seed has been planted. Whether this will or will not take place begins with the mindset of the messenger. God must "become flesh" among every people, tribe or nation. This means that the messenger must lay aside his/her own prejudices and attachments, his or her hardened biases and even certain personal notions about behavior and life style. The Incarnational hymn in Philippians 2:7,8 begins with a profound statement that binds us all to this first step in the model. The magnificent words are that "(Christ Jesus) . . . *emptied* himself . . . he *humbled* himself and became *obedient* . . ."

We have already taken note of the fact that the Incarnation of Jesus Christ is divine revelation of the highest order, making it presumptuous, even preposterous, for humans to clone, as it were, Jesus' Incarnation. We can only attempt, on the human level, what God accomplished at the divine level through Jesus the Word. The inimitability of the Incarnation, however, does not preclude our right, or our responsibility to act on this first principle: we must divest ourselves from the prideful restrictions of our own world in order to understand and enter into the world of "the other."

The extent to which persons can divest themselves from whom they are has been a long and debatable question.[11] Of course, the identity of any person is shaped by his or her birth and environment, by family and society, by the influences of associates and church. To suspend or put aside one's own up-bringing or tradition, in the ultimate sense, would be a denial of one's personhood. As communicators, we have various strengths and weaknesses. In

---

[11] Phenomenologists speak of necessity for the *epoche* which is the "bracketing of (personal) experience in order to understand the giveness of the data to the observer." Charles Long (1967:80) in *The History of Religions* edited by Joseph Kitagawa. Yet, in the same volume, Kees Bolle says that if *epoche* means, "suspending one's own tradition," it is "an impossibility and a hermeneutical hoax." (Bolle 1967:101)

reaching out to others, the greatest gift we can give is sincerity and authenticity. Our communication to others flows through the person that we are. Still, the attempt to deal firmly with one's own presuppositions and to study carefully the habits of one's own dogmatism opens the way to see others more objectively and understand them without being judgmental.

I remember something that happened to me during my first year as a missionary. I was teaching African men who were to become pastors. I had recently graduated from seminary and I felt the best thing I could give these men was what I had learned. I felt my logic and scheme of study was what they needed if they were going to be properly fitted for the ministry. I was just a beginner in the language. This handicap was further complicated by the fact that I felt they should hear what I learned in seminary. The way to begin any systematic theology course is to ask questions about the existence of God. In my mind, how could anyone do anything in theology if God's existence was in question? I had learned five philosophical proofs for God and proceeded to go through these, one by one. There were no African language equivalents for the five English terms used to prove God's existence. Among them were the anthropological proof, the teleological, the cosmological and ontological proof and another that I cannot now remember. Not far into the explanation, one of the men, much older than I, raised his hand with a question. He asked me in all honesty if I, the teacher, had a problem about the existence of God. If so, he said I should get that sorted out for myself because no one in the class had any need for proofs of God's existence. Properly corrected, I asked the class what they would rather study and their answer was that they wanted to study the Book of Revelation. I was surprised and embarrassed because Revelation was a Book that I did not understand enough to teach. Revelation was close to their own experiences because there they read about dreams, visions, symbols, mysteries and prophecies. This was not what I wanted to do. It was not comfortable for me to think that my ideas about what they ought to learn did not correspond to what they wanted or needed. I did teach them Revelation. It was painful for me even though they were enthusiastic about it. In the process, however, I learned invaluable things about African culture and the way God speaks to Africans. In fact, Africans helped me see that biblical culture and African culture had much more in common with the Bible (especially the Old Testament) than did my American experience.

Of course, the Christian witness does demand a commitment to the essentials of the Gospel. At the same time, contextual theology requires that no prefabricated system of the messenger be forced upon people of another faith or culture. The biblical message of God's grace and forgiveness through Jesus Christ is for all peoples. This means that theological biases that the messenger holds will have to be carefully examined in light of the context. Issues of truth, the choice and ordering of themes, as well as styles of approach, all must fit the particular people and place. Having said this, we are not implying a compromise of the Light that enlightens everyone (John 1:9). We are saying, however, that in order to bring our personal inclinations under control, personal preferences must be carefully scrutinized in light of the context. This is not easy because, as we have said, nearly everyone who ministers in the name of Christ is bound to such things as denominational doctrines and personal convictions. To suppress personal inclination demands disciplined changes in thinking and behavior on the part of the missionary. Why? Because the Incarnation requires the same emptying-out of the self in obedience as was modeled by Jesus. With a commitment to the Word, ours is to observe, listen, learn and wait for the patient work of the Spirit. In this way, the Word can become flesh and can fully live among the people, wherever they are and whoever they may be.

Connect to the deepest needs of people

We have been looking at the implications of what it means to be guided by the first stage of the Incarnation-the discipline of setting aside natural inclinations to think and do things in our own way. A second step is to follow Jesus by living as Jesus did in a special way with the people he came to save. John 1:14 says simply that, "The Word became flesh *and lived among us.*" This was not some kind of casual or disinterested living relationship. The manner in which Jesus lived with people was of an intimate kind. It is probable that John carefully chose the Greek word. *eskenosen* (1:14) to help us understand this closeness. *Eskenosen is* built upon *skene,* the word for "tent." In turn, we are reminded of the tabernacle-presence of Jehovah which was at the very center of his needy people in the wilderness (Exodus 25:8; 40:34) Even more striking was the pillar of cloud hovering over and at the door of the tabernacle signifying the immanent and visible presence of the Lord (Exodus 33:9,10).[12] Jesus, the God-man, literally "pitched His tent" in a place where He was constantly and intimately connected to His people. However "theologically straight" or "doctrinally correct" our teaching may be, the gospel is not good news if it does not provide answers to the felt needs of the people. This requires that the messenger be in close and constant contact with people in order to know as deeply as possible their needs, their pain, their hopes and the injustices they feel. This kind of knowledge comes only by living in purposeful identity with them, while studying their problems and searching for ways to meet problems once we know what they are. We have written about how difficult it is to live in close identity with people when one is from the "outside." However, while this handicap can never be completely overcome, it can be minimized by accepting the ideals of the Incarnation as a challenge that has to be faced on a daily basis

---

[12] In the condition of human weakness God "pitched his tent (*skene*)" among us to reveal his glory and give assurance of his presence (c.f. *shekinah,* having the same consonants as the Greek *skene.* "The Exodus associations are intentional and are part of the theme of revelation and redemption of the Logos-Christ...." G. R. Beasley-Murray (1987:14).

During the 1970's, I was doing research among what are often called African Independent Churches. The thesis behind the research was that these churches are much closer to the real needs of the African people than are the traditional mission-type churches. Further, the way in which they meet these needs are directly connected to the way Africans solve their own problems, that is, through means available to them from their culture. This was an especially important study since conversions to the way of Jesus from Islam have been so few and so ineffective in the mission churches. However, many from among the Yoruba people have turned from Islam to Jesus Christ in the Christ Apostolic Church. I also knew that the C.A.C. church has tried to keep the Bible and Jesus Christ at the center of their church life and worship. My research focused on this Church in several cities to see what can be learned about ways of attracting Muslim men and women into fellowship with Christians.

When I talked to the pastor of one of the C.A.C. churches in the city of Ilorin about the purpose of my research he was so interested that he invited me to observe a prayer service for a Muslim woman who had come to the Prayer House on that day. This day of the week was set-aside for women who needed healing from various illnesses. On this occasion, a Muslim woman had arrived on the church grounds in a taxi. She had been childless and was in deep trouble with her husband since causes for barrenness are always laid upon the women. I was able to stand at the back of the large room to observe the ritual. Only women were allowed to participate in the healing service. The Muslim wife sat on a stool in the center of the room. With hands upraised each woman present prayed a loud prayer while all responded with affirmations. Following this, another woman began beating a drum while the entire group of eight formed a circle around the Muslim woman who sat motionless on the stool. Then dancing began in a tight circle round and round the woman along with singing and shouting God's name and the name of Jesus repeatedly. During the ritual, some would put their hand on the woman's head while others stopped dancing and prayed with hands placed on her abdomen,

I have recited this because it shows how the physical need of a Muslim person was enough to bring God's people around her. Without requiring belief or answers to questions of faith, this ministry gave a needy woman the assurance of God's power to meet her need. Over a year later, I was in touch with the pastor who told me that she gave birth to a baby boy and she had confessed Jesus as her Lord. As a result, the resistance of her Muslim husband to Christians and the church was broken down.

Connecting with felt needs is at the very core of the Incarnation. No one can know what these deepest needs are without cultivating close relationships. One must then be willing to innovate to meet these needs through the power of the gospel. The problem with the illustration I have just recounted is that those who ministered to the Muslim woman were not "outsiders." It can be argued, therefore, that they would naturally know what to do and how to do it. The point is that missionaries who minister from a strict "truth" or knowledge paradigm often do not want to focus on the physical needs as a way to access salvation in Christ nor would the emotional approach shown by the C.A.C. church come easily for them. Usually the church-trained missionary would have objected to praying publicly about barrenness and would not like the African style of calling on God to meet the woman's need. To truly live with people, as Jesus did, that is. to truly, "pitch one's tent," as it were, in the midst of those we want to love and win to Christ, calls us to meet deep needs in appropriate ways. This is the secret of the Incarnate Word, this Christ, who first emptied himself and then lived as one with us.

It is beyond the human mind to ponder what was required of the Eternal Word in becoming flesh to live intimately among us. To do this at the human level requires great effort. However, our cultural limitations and our ties to cognitive truths are not impossible barriers. In this volume Kraft has written about three crucial dimensions in contextualization (allegiance, truth and power) and of his own "personal failure" to see the power dimension at work during his missionary days. For myself, I cannot emphasize enough how much I learned from spending time with African indigenous churches, as in the case above. It was through them that I learned the secret of connecting to people with power at the point of their greatest need. Without this Incarnational dimension, men and women cannot understand or trust the truth.

Reach into every aspect of life

In saying that the Word became flesh and lives intimately among us means that no facet of life is untouched by the claims or challenges of the gospel. When speaking about the Word taking up residence at the very center of life, we mean that every compartment of human experience is subject to the authority of the Lord Jesus. The prologue of John's gospel speaks eloquently about the absolute ownership of creation by the Word. "All things came into being by him and without him not one thing came into being (1:3)." The Incarnational hymn of Philippians carries the same note of God's sovereignty over all people and, by inference, all things. Ultimately, "every knee should bend . . . and every tongue should confess that Jesus Christ is Lord (Phil. 2:10.11)." When we think about the comprehensive nature of the Incarnation we also confess that the all-embracing, ubiquitous Holy Spirit is the continuing presence of Jesus Christ among us. Biblical Incarnation is multidimensional. "The Word that saves" means that the gospel must be communicated in ways that people are not only attracted to it but they and the society in which they live are changed.

Therefore, the first dimension of an incarnational mission paradigm is evangelism. The aim is to communicate the Word to men and women in such a way that they turn from idols, as Paul says, to serve the true and living God (I Thess. 1:9). Conversion is the personal experience of faith that begins from a place that is deep within the individual life. Circumstances and events that bring about an awareness of need for conversion are different for each person. Awakening to the need for Jesus Christ, therefore is intensely personal. We who have been engaged in evangelistic ministries in other cultures can recite case after case of situations that brought persons to a point where they readily accepted Jesus as Lord. Obviously, the content of the message as well as the style in which it is delivered needs to fit the culture and idiom of the place. This sensitivity in evangelism requires knowledge of the context that grows from intimate and respectful relationships with people.

A second dimension of an incarnational mission paradigm is nurturing or teaching. Not only does the great commission speak about discipling in terms of initial belief or conversion, it also speaks a about the obligation to teach faithfully and comprehensively all those things that Jesus commanded. The nurturing dimension of contextualization is extremely important for the up building of new converts and appropriate expressions of Christian belief and practice from place to place. Teaching incarnationally means that the Bible must be communicated in ways that are readily understood and taught so that believers understand and accept what following Jesus requires of them. Biblical teaching is incarnational when it is grounded in the daily lives of people and leads them to understand their faith through idioms of their everyday life. Jesus taught this way. There is both a conversion and nurturing dimension of the Great Commission. (I)"Make disciples of all nations (people)(by) baptizing them. . . (2) and teaching them to obey everything that I have commanded you (Matt. 28:19,20). Conversion must be followed by long-term, appropriate teaching.

The third dimension of an incarnational mission paradigm is social action. Christians have to care for God's creation and to work with God to put right the wrongs that degrade and destroy life. Wherever he went, Jesus healed the sick, restored respect to the marginalized, and the socially rejected. He lifted the honor of women; upset the status quo, exposed sins of religious and political leaders, criticized tradition, and laid out terms for peace and justice in the new Kingdom. Incarnational Christianity moves beyond personal conversion to stand with Jesus when he declared himself to be the one who was to "bring good new to the poor . . . to proclaim release to the captives . . . recovery of sight to the blind (and) to let the oppressed go free (Matt. 3:18)."

In thinking about the Incarnation matrix the following graphic illustrates the way in which these three principles from the *logos* and *kenosis* passages define the principles of the Incarnation matrix.

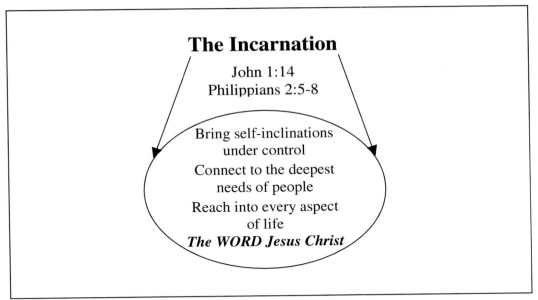

Figure 28.2 The Incarnation Matrix

Fitting Models into the Matrix

Since models are ways to approach the variables in human situations, we want to show that the Incarnation must characterize both intention and attitude in the contextualization process. Our argument is that the Incarnation itself cannot be configured as a model, because the Incarnation is the context (matrix) of divine self-expression of God in Jesus Christ. Rather, it is within this irreproducible context that models are constructed and it is from this matrix that the objectives or ideals of models can be worked out.

How appropriate any model is will be determined by the results. Appropriate Christianity requires answers for two important questions: (1) Do people understand the gospel as good news and (2) does accepting the good news bring about changes that are relevant to human needs in particular situations? In reviewing models to show how they reflect the Incarnation, we do not imply a kind of sanctity for models, since they are all human constructions. Nor do we mean that the originators of all these models were intentionally or consciously centered on Jesus the incarnate Word. Some models were generated to deal primarily with socio-political realities while others show greater dependence on biblical sources and church tradition. While models have their differences, they also share several features in common. We must take note when models are consistent with and reflect the ideals and spirit of the Incarnation-when Jesus, the Word, becomes real among people and when Jesus is honored as the way redemptive changes take place. Let us review six of the models to see how they reflect the Incarnation matrix. There are additional models and most are known by more than one name. I have chosen these because they are generally the best known and have bearing on the Incarnation theme.[13]

The Adaptation Model: *If anyone hears my voice:* Revelation 3:20

Not only is *adaptation* the place to begin alphabetically, it is also one of the earliest approaches to contextualization. When "adaptation" was in vogue as language in missiology, the term contextualization was unknown. This was the era when most conversation about appropriate Christianity centered on the concepts of "indigenous" and "indigeneity." This was still the colonial era when Western churches and governments dominated mission efforts. Out of that context, *adaptation* addressed the foreignness of mission churches as Western norms influenced these Christians to think and act in Western paradigms.

One of the most influential mission scholars of this period was Hendrik Kraemer. The awareness of the need for *adaptation* grew out of what Kraemer saw as the need to express Christian truth "against the background of, and in conflict with, the moral and religious context of the non-Christian religions."[14] As long ago as 1938, he saw the alien characteristics of mission churches and lamented the fact that Christians in both Asia and Africa did not seem concerned about this foreignness. His observation was that, "(Indigenous Christians) do not trouble much about it because in most cases they already cherish the forms in which they received Christianity from the Western missionaries as a precious tradition and a symbol of social prestige." In a time of ecumenical controversy between modernism and fundamentalism, Kraemer had a deep commitment to Jesus Christ and the Bible. His emphasis on *adaptation* was greatly needed, but the new way of thinking was approached with caution because, as he said, Biblical realism (his term) would be revolutionary and would mean "a total rupture with one's religious past, because it presupposes conversion in the deepest sense of the word." Even so, he saw clearly that because, "Asiatic and African settings are natural and legitimate, . . . Christianity must find in its various environments an intellectual, emotional and institutional expression . . . and not (be) an impediment or inhibition."[15] Because this was controversial in mission thinking fifty years ago, the importance of beginning this process toward contextualization cannot be minimized. Attention, however, was given

---

[13] See my summaries in two sources: *The Evangelical Dictionary of World Missions* (Gilliland 2000a:225-227), and *The Word Among Us, Contextualizing Theology for Mission Today,* (Gilliland, 2002:313-317).

[14] Hendrik Kraemer (1963:308).

[15] Kraemer (1963:313). *Adaptation*, in the Protestant tradition, had a close parallel among Catholic missiologists developed somewhat later, for which they preferred the term, "accommodation." Louis J. Luzbetak gives the definition of "accommodation" as "the respectful, prudent scientifically and theologically sound adjustment of the Church to the native culture in attitude, outward behavior and practical apostolic approach." *The Church and Cultures, An Applied Anthropology for Christian Workers* (1970:341).

primarily to terminology and external forms without touching the deeper levels of culture or ways of theologizing.

The inadequacies of this approach are obvious to us now. Yet, thankfully, there was recognition of the problem. It was becoming clear that if the receiving peoples are to be genuinely Christian, Euro American concepts and approaches would need to be at least somewhat adapted to the receiving peoples' cultural perspectives. There is something incarnational about the struggle with foreignness that began with these *adaptation* ideas. They represent the first serious attempts by "outsiders" to understand a particular people in their own milieu with the objective of setting aside or modifying irrelevant dogma and forms. This led to a new kind of humility and introspection in mission that was not known before. Here was a search to understand what expressing Jesus Christ should mean for every person, regardless of religion or culture.

The Anthropological Model: The Word became flesh: John 1:14

The birth of the Word, Jesus, is, at once, a transcendent and exquisite human event. Nothing could be more culturally profound than the circumstances that brought Joseph and Mary to Bethlehem, -the crowded city, the manger and curiosity of shepherds. Reverently, we can say the Incarnation was, indeed, an anthropological event. It was so because humankind is at the very center of why Jesus was born and God's love for all nations of people is shown openly through everyday, earthly life. The anthropological model seeks for evidence of truth expressed through cultural thinking and behavior that commends Christ to people. The truth of Incarnation is not only revelation from above; it is grounded, as well, in the life-ways of people. Anthropology provides the tools for understanding values and truth expressions of people. In his introduction to John Taylor's book, *The Primal Vision*, Max Warren speaks about the way God witnesses to the Word through culture.

> Our first task in approaching another people, another culture, another religion is to take off our shoes, for the place we are approaching is holy. Else, we may find ourselves treading on men's dreams. More serious still, we may forget that God was here before our arrival.[16]

Because of the secular nature of anthropology as a behavioral science, there was opposition to the idea of culture as a source for truth. This came especially from certain mission theologians who had negative ideas about culture and felt that culture rather than revelation was becoming the source of truth. Kraft's work, *Christianity in Culture,* allayed the fear about culture for many, while provoking controversy among others. His position of God-above-

---

[16]M. A. C. Warren, Introduction to John V. Taylor, *The Primal Vision: Christian Presence Amid African Religion,* (J. Taylor 1963:10). Bevans says these words "express more clearly than any I know the central and guiding insight of the anthropological model." (Bevans 1992:49).

culture[17] holds to the absolute transcendence of God as distinct from culture. However, alongside is culture, "the milieu in which all encounters with or between human beings take place and in terms of which all human understanding and maturation occur." Culture, apart from how it is used by humans, is neither evil nor good but neutral-in essence-the means appropriated by human beings to "get people where they need to go." Kraft says. "God chooses the cultural milieu in which humans are immersed as the arena of his interaction with people."[18]

The anthropological model seeks to identify symbols and ideas that are precious to people and can serve to articulate and confirm God's truth. The transcendence of God was manifest to human persons through human birth and the human aspect of the Incarnation can be celebrated through the Incarnation model. Justin Martyr's ancient reference to *spermatikos logos* lifts up the idea that the seeds of the gospel of Jesus Christ are already there in cultures and religions.[19] If evangelists take the time to listen and learn from culture they will find confirmation of the biblical message, much as did Paul when he declared in Lystra that, "(God) has not left himself without a witness (Acts 14:17)."

I once asked the elders in our Nigerian church if they might to show how they could express their faith in a symbolic way by creating something for the communion table at the front of the church. After two weeks of deliberation they placed a Bible on the table, opened at John 3:16. Next to the Bible and covering part of it, they placed a hand-made hoe. These men were all simple farmers. Everyone had a hoe. It was often carried as part of their dress, hooked over the left shoulder. Surprised by this symbolism I began to see how close the planting and harvesting of seed was to the gift of eternal life in Jesus. People recognize truth when it arises from the home of the soul. The contribution of the *anthropological* model to the matrix is that we can mine-out this truth and bring it to enlightenment through the Word.

The Critical Model: The true light that enlightens: John 1:9

The Incarnation is beyond human reason because by faith Christians accept a rationally irreconcilable statement: the incarnate Word, Jesus, is both human and divine. Yet, it is in this critical integration between humanity and divinity that Jesus Christ opens the way for human salvation. The human and divine aspects are also engaged in doing critical contextualization as cultural forms and meanings, precious to Christian believers of every culture, are placed alongside serious interaction with the Bible. The approach of critical

---

[17] H. Richard Niebuhr (1951).

[18] Charles H. Kraft (1979a:113-114).

[19] Aylward Shorter contends that the idea of the seed-bearing Word is the one original contribution that Justin Martyr made to Christian theology, holding that seeds of the Word "had been planted in every human culture since all things were created through him and with him." (Shorter 1988:75-76)

contextualization, developed by Paul Hiebert, confronts the risk of allowing either too much permissiveness for cultural forms that have no correspondence in scripture or rejecting as unchristian traditional belief and practice. The one will lead to unacceptable syncretism while the other denies the incarnational character of the Word and leads to foreign rather than appropriate Christianity.[20]

Traditions, rituals, stories, songs, etc. are sacred to every people. The institutions that define and authenticate life must be respected by the messenger. Beyond this, they must be utilized as widely as possible for communication and for working out appropriate theologies. On one hand, if after turning to Christ, these precious institutions of a culture are ignored or denigrated the people will continue to practice, sometimes secretly, what is trusted and natural for them. On the other hand, after professing faith in Jesus Christ, if these cultural institutions are accepted uncritically, that is, without concern for biblical corroboration, distortion and syncretism will result. Critical contextualization calls us to take seriously these deep level beliefs and practices and to understand the meanings they convey. The idea then, is to apply these familiar or modified forms to Christian living, worship and theology. When engaging the critical process, modifications of old forms are found and, hopefully, new forms will result. Appropriate Christianity is the expression of this critical process. When maximizing the use of forms that are precious to a people, these forms must also convey Christian meanings with minimum distortion to the message of the Bible. The incarnate Jesus Christ was constantly calling into question traditions and practices of the Jews when comparing old ways with the new. While, as an insider, he could speak with authority about tradition, it was Jesus' often repeated words, "but I say unto you." that distinguished his teaching from that of the scribes and Pharisees.

Critical contextualization is, perhaps, not a model in the narrower sense of the term. Rather, in bringing forward the "old ways," so to speak, in order to understand them in light of the "new Way" we are speaking about the intention and spirit that guides all contextualization. It reflects what the critical presence of Jesus meant as he lived among his own people, confronting traditional beliefs and practices. The historical and cultural context, reflected in religious forms, human needs and social issues must be evaluated alongside biblical norms. This work is a continuing process, as believers in each context seek to integrate cultural gifts with their confession that Jesus is Lord.

The Praxis Model: Be doers of the Word: **James 1:22**

When properly understood, the ideas imbedded in the term praxis actually lie very close to what God did in the Incarnation of Jesus Christ. Saying this, however, may sound strange to some who know how praxis has been used in theological method. For years, thinking about praxis was so closely associated

---

[20] See Paul G. Hiebert, "Critical Contextualization" (1987:104-112).

with Latin American liberation theology that it was resisted by most evangelicals. Reasons for these negative attitudes were/are based on what they saw as restrictive, even naïve ways that liberation theologians appropriate the Bible for predetermined objectives, their tendency to identify salvation with social action, their reductionistic view of sin and use of theoretical Marxism.

A more recent understanding of praxis has to do with corporate reflection on issues followed by action. Praxis is best understood in the reciprocity between thinking critically about real problems and making decisions to bring about constructive change. Bevans describes praxis as "a way of doing theology that is formed by knowledge at its most intense level– the level of reflective action." He goes on to say that the praxis model has a "rough precedent in Christian tradition," by referring to the prophets who contended for action and the New Testament mandate that Christians are not only to be hearers of the word but also doers (Jas. 1:22).[21]

With care and without presumption I want to say that with the Incarnation we are describing the praxis of God. Salvation history throughout the Bible is the record of a God who knows fully the dilemma sin has brought into perfect creation and who intervenes into history to redeem and effect change. With reference to Jesus, God made provision for our rescue from the "futile ways entrenched from (our) fathers even before the foundation of the world (I Peter 1:20)." This is a thinking, reflective God who took redemptive action at just the right time (Rom. 5:6).

The praxis approach does not have to focus only on social and political liberation. It is conceptualized in such a way that it reflects three important points that connect to the Incarnation. First, the intersection of problems in a given society must be thoroughly understood. Deciding what action needs to take place for change follows this analysis. After reaching a consensus about issues, there must be the resolve to correct them. Our God is a God who acts. The Incarnation is God's intervention into human history to put right what was spoiled by sin and the enemy. A third feature of the praxis model is that the action must be on-going. Once the action is taken, there is reflection on the outcome and this may call for correction and further action. Sadly, the misreading of the Scriptures and Marxist-type thinking by liberation theologians often misled people into revolution and violence. The Bible, especially the Old Testament, is a story of God taking action time and time again to deal with the disobedience and rebellion of his people. The Incarnation of Jesus Christ is the divine praxis of God, the final answer to the human dilemma if sin and the need for peace and salvation.

---

[21] Bevans (1992:71-72).

When bringing a word like "synthetic" to the Incarnation one feels a negative response. The popular association with "synthetic" is that something has been artificially produced or is a substitute for the original. How unlike the Incarnation! However, in contextualization, the idea of synthesis means that components of the totality of life are brought together into wholeness and ways are found so that these values and insights from one place can be shared with believers in other contexts. In this, we are very close to one meaning of the Incarnation, that is, through the Incarnation, the way is open for diverse nations to share in the one body of Christ. These expressions that can be shared between peoples of Christian faith are possible because Jesus Christ is, "the first-born of all creation, . . . and in him all things hold together (Col. 1:16,17)."

The first dimension of the synthetic model, therefore, is that the realities of any given place or people, such as history, culture, religion or society communicate truth about that people. Each of these domains of truth provides paths for understanding the particular situation and the needs of that people, place and time. Through the Incarnation Jesus Christ became intimately associated with the full range of human experience.[22] The lifestyle God expected of the Jews can be gathered up in one word-"Shalom." Spiritual issues cannot be treated as though they are unconnected to other compartments of life. Jesus' teachings had authority because personal piety, politics, social relationships, religious habits and ethics were critical to his message. The synthesis, therefore, embraces all aspects of life. Questions need to be answered. What ideas about Christianity are already present; what insights are available from the culture; what social problems need to be dealt with what are the indicators of change? The content of the gospel will be conditioned by the way these aspects are brought together. Culture, tradition and change contribute insights that interact in a dialogical way to show how the message of Jesus can have maximum impact on the particular place and people.

A second dimension of the synthetic model is that Christian people in one place are connected to all others who have different history, different culture, religion and society. These differences need not separate or alienate people from each other once the Incarnation is understood. The synthesis, therefore, requires understanding the truth domains of the local situation and then moves out to find areas of belief and practice that are common or different from others. In this way, experiencing both the particularity and universality of revelation is possible. The revelation of God through Jesus Christ opens up continuity among people of faith. What God has done through the written word of Scripture and through the incarnate Word, is a once-for-all norm. The Incarnation is

---

[22] The lifestyle God expected of the Jews can be gathered up in one word: Shalom, Shalom is the harmony intended between people and God and involves all facets of human relationships. Even while living in an alien culture during the exile, God commanded his people to "seek the shalom of the city (Babylon)" Jeremiah 29:7.

revelational ground that binds together all believers, bridging the discontinuities of history and culture. Common bonds of faith in the common Lord calls for dialogue and appreciation for differing insights into faith. To understand which truths are special to one people and which can be shared with others is something that must be continually studied and celebrated.[23]

The Translation Model: Hear and understand. Matt.15:10

Two of the most fundamental questions in communication are: What is the message and how should the message be presented? If the message about Jesus is for all people (as we know it is), then all people must hear what they need and when they hear they must understand. The translation model is the best known and most widely employed of all models for communicating the essential message in appropriate ways.[24] The essence of the Christian message is about a supernatural event but it is men, women and children in their natural, everyday world that have to hear and understand. Until this connection between supernatural and natural is made, we cannot speak of the incarnate word as "good news" for anyone. At the birth of Jesus, the pastoral world of the shepherds was radically different from the mystic world of the wise men, yet the infinite communicator, God, reached both with the same supernatural message.

The translation model is built, first, on the fact that the supernatural message is also supracultural; that is, the unchanging message can be separated from contextually bound modes of expression. All who hear the message should be able to grasp the meaning as clearly in their own life context as did those who heard Jesus in his day. To make this happen the translation principle of "dynamic equivalence" is the way supra cultural truth is conveyed to culture-bound men and women. I refer again to Chuck Kraft's seminal work, *Christianity in Culture.*

> For today's receptors, Jesus needs to walk their paths, eat in their homes. The receptor's need to live and learn, as the original disciples did, in Jesus presence today. For this they need dynamic witness, living and speaking a dynamically equivalent message in terms of the receptor's perceptive grids.[26]

In the translation model "form" is carefully scrutinized to assure that the forms being employed express as accurately as possible the biblical message. In translation, articulation of the biblical message is always the primary task,

---

[23] Bevans sees this as most important in this model when he speaks of the historicity and commonality of biblical revelation, "Revelation is both something finished, once and for all, of a particular place –and something ongoing and present, operative in all cultures." S. B. Bevans in *Models of Contextual Theology* (Revised and expanded edition 2002:91).

[24] Bevans says the translation model "is the one most commonly employed" *Models of Contextual Theology* (2002:37) and Robert Schreiter speaks of it as "the most common model for local theology" *Constructing Local Theologies* (1985:6).

[26] Kraft (1979a:276).

however, cultural expressions (forms) that are specific to the biblical context can inadequately (even erroneously) express these meanings in particular situations. This led Nida and Taber to say that, "to preserve the content of the message the forms must be changed."[25] Dynamic equivalence is the appropriate use of local forms in order to convey the intended meanings. The issue of form-change is not unlike the Incarnation of Jesus, God's self revelation in a form that is immediately, fully understood by humankind, having, of course, special "equivalence" to Jesus' own people, the Jews.

Contextualization is committed to finding appropriate forms because imprecise forms, whether language, symbols, customs, myths, etc. will misrepresent the message. Kraft says, "If an equivalent meaning is to be conveyed, the forms employed must be as appropriate for expressing those meanings in the receptor culture as the source forms are in the source culture.[26] The translation model fits into the Incarnation matrix because it demonstrates God's self expression in ways that are accessible and understandable to people. God is pure and infinite Spirit. The Word who became flesh, is God "speaking" his loving desire for relationship with, finite and temporal human beings Through the Incarnation there is a form we can grasp; it is the humanization of Spirit.

Incarnation as the Matrix for Contextualization Models

The Incarnation stands, as it were, above all models as the divine metamodel. We can speak of an appropriate model for any given context as one that is conceptualized within the "Incarnation matrix.' All that we have written about the implications that Incarnation has for contextualization must be carefully evaluated when choosing a model or creating new models. The spirit, intention and meanings that lie within the Incarnation, as we have reviewed them, must be reflected in the spirit, intention and meaning of the way contextualization for a given people and place is done. The absolute irreproducibility of the Incarnation event must be held sacred. Compared to the Incarnation (God's Ultimate Act of Contextualization), our best human efforts are flawed and finite imitations. In seeking appropriate pathways to Christianity, the Incarnation is the guide and conscience of contextualization.

We conclude, therefore, that while the Incarnation is not, of itself, a model, it is the all-embracing, transcendent paradigm from which and within which all approaches to contextualization are conceptualized. The Incarnation is not the model but is the matrix in which varieties of models are constructed. The matrix as Incarnation is, as we have said throughout, Jesus Christ who, along with the principles of Incarnation that we have covered above, is the locus for all

---

[25] E. A. Nida and C. R. Taber, *The Theory and Practice of Translation* (1969:3-8), quoted in Kraft (1979a:273).

[26] Kraft (1979a:273).

models The relationship of human models to the Divine Model can be illustrated by the following figure:

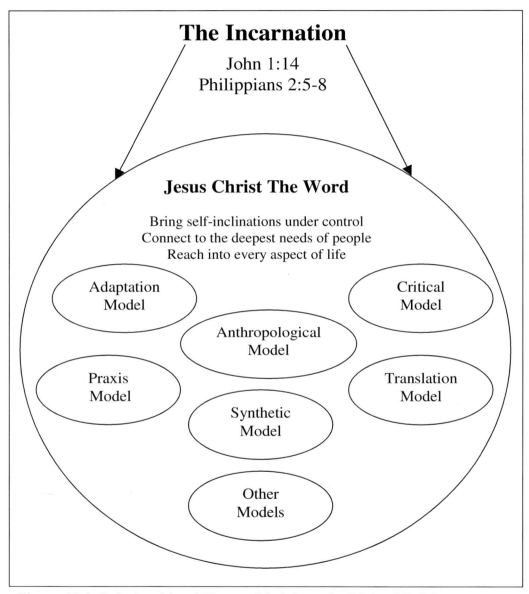

Figure 28.3 Relationship of Human Models to the Divine Model

The illustration might be criticized for projecting the idea that all features of these models are valid and fit, as they are, into the Incarnation paradigm. The history of models is that they are constructed in the pursuit of mission and have relevance for the believing community and society. Therefore, if assumptions of any model do not correspond to the spirit of the Incarnation or reflect ideas that are alien to the Incarnation, that model or parts of it must be reckoned as inappropriate. Models cannot be built on sources that are incompatible with the

Bible or ignore boundaries between inappropriate cultural practice and Christianity. In teaching contextualization I have encouraged students from many cultures to work out their own models, taking into account the problems, values, needs and ambiguities that have grown up with their churches, many of missionary origin. In doing so, I always emphasize that models must be brought to the scriptures for validation and be tested within the crucible of the Incarnation.

Insights to Incarnation in This Volume

Before ending this volume, we want to show how the Incarnation has been featured in many ways throughout the chapters. While the actual term, Incarnation, is rarely used, it is the Incarnation idea that underlies all that can be said about "appropriate Christianity." As our colleagues have been writing, we have been reminded repeatedly of the incarnational basis for contextual Christian witness.

Chuck Kraft speaks about Incarnation when he emphasizes the need for "localization" of the message. Kraft speaks about Alan Tippett, mentor to several of us. Tippett often spoke of the need for all people to, "see the Lord as their own and not as a foreign Christ." Kraft, himself, puts his strongest emphasis on *people* and, accordingly, he has reminded us that the message is intended for *people,* not for organizations or institutions. Receptor-oriented communication is incarnational communication. Kraft continues, "The messages (that people hear) will be those that they construct largely from the materials in their own words, with or without much understanding of where we (the outsider) are coming from." Obedience to the Incarnation means being sensitive to the needs of persons in their own local situation, living intensely with others, interacting with their deep needs and sharing their hopes. This is the Jesus model. Kraft asks us to imagine what it would have been like if the "cultural shock" Jesus experienced in taking on human flesh had influenced him to revert to the heavenly culture. The implication is that often contextualization requires such radical adjustment that the missionary refuses to separate from his or her own "home culture." Incarnation as the model for contextualization would not allow that to happen. This is a reminder, Kraft says, that contextualization calls for the human effort to imagine, as best as we humans can, what Jesus' behavior would be in any given society.

Eddie Gibbs insists that the younger generation is taking the initiative to re-incarnate the church. This is their attempt to bring the Word into their world so it can speak to them where they are. Sadly, traditional models (of church) are not meeting the postmodern mindset. "Boomers" are "walking away from the church," says Gibbs, while the "X-ers" dismiss the church as "lacking in authenticity and integrity." This situation exposes the failure of the church to be an incarnational church. Roberta King, through communicating music in culturally appropriate ways, is directly concerned with "integrating the Christian faith into the total life of a people." Quoting Kraft, she reminds readers, "the incarnation is the ultimate contextualization of the Christian message."

Katie Rawson's entire chapter about relationship deals with the central issue of the Incarnation. The Incarnation is the very essence of relational activity. The great need is for a God who is "up there" to connect in real experience with young people who are "down here." This is an eloquent call for a re-enactment of the Incarnation. as the Word becomes flesh *among us* who are in *this* place at *this* time. Rawson asks, how could it be otherwise, since the Trinitarian God is by nature an interpersonal, communal God. It is this relational Father-God that people come to know through Jesus, the Son.

In a similar way Robert Gallagher shows how the covenant, before anything else, is a drama of God's relationship with his people. The covenant needs to be appreciated as a visible instrument God put in place to explain his intimate connection to Israel. Wilbert Shenk is speaking openly about the Incarnation when he says that missionaries, "as outsiders, can engage particular cultural contexts with the same seriousness that God modeled in the sending of Jesus Christ into the world in a particular time, to a particular people and a particular culture." Paul Pierson has shown that a dynamic feature of renewal in the church is "disinculturation." This term stands for a kind of reversal of those forms that have led the church into alien expressions of the Christian life. Through disinculturation believers are released from inappropriate, ill-fitting garments of faith to freedom and joy, as the Spirit flows into and from believers who "feel at home" with their faith.

Hiebert and Tienou have shown that there are three types of law that parallel, in many ways, three types of theology. The problem before us is: How can law and theology bridge the gap between cognitive, universal truth and the empirical everyday needs of people? They draw out parallels between "missional theology" and "modern law" because in both there is an emphasis on finding truth from individual cases. This means that while there is a place for universal theory, both systematic theology and statutory law (representing universal approaches) are not conceptualized from the "here and now." Because of this, they fail to apply to situations and events taking place in specific, human situations. However, just as the modern approach to law deals with applied theory in particular cases, so missional theology communicates the gospel in real contexts where men and women live. Another name for this approach to theology could well have been "Incarnational theology." To engage in missional theology is seeking to understand a particular world in the same way that the people of 'that world" understand it and finding solutions to issues raised by that world.

What is the key to power-giving leadership? Lingenfelter has made the case that "releasing control" and handing leadership to others is probably the most difficult thing that leaders have to do. The possibilities that open up to the powerless when well-trained, highly advantaged leaders trust others with power leads us to the Incarnation. Christ Jesus "did not regard equality with God as something to be exploited but emptied himself . . . " This was the spirit of obedience that brought him finally to the cross. It was for the powerless that Jesus gave his life. In Jesus' own day, not all, by any means, accepted the challenge to surrender status and personal reputation to lift up others. The powerful Messianic expectation contrasted with Jesus self-effacing spirit caused Jesus own people to turn away from him. "But to all who received him, who believed in his name, he gave power to become children of God (John 1:12)."

Chuck Van Engen's chapters are comprehensively centered on how to construct mission theology for today. Written quite independently of this chapter, he also sees that the Incarnation provides the integrating idea for appropriate theology. Why? "Because God's mission is supremely given in Jesus Christ, Jesus Christ must be at the center of all the domains of a contextually appropriate missiology." The Bible, the particular context, the Church's reflection and personal experience are the dimensions contribute to mission theology, with each gathering meaning from and around the Center. When Van Engen speaks about Incarnation as the third step in a methodology for appropriate theology he is calling for "new action." By speaking this way, he shows that praxis and Incarnation are related through Jesus Christ. Even as this divine action broke into human history, so mission theologians are forced to go beyond sterile theory. Thinking and reflecting on mission is never enough; it is participating with God in the mission of Jesus, which is the very heart of mission. Van Engen contends that modeling mission theology after the Incarnation will require change; it is the dynamic step beyond indigenization. He says that, "the Christian faith is internally compatible, consistent and coherent with–and can be fully and naturally–expressed in very culture." This way of speaking goes to the very core of what Incarnation means. The Incarnation of Jesus was historically and culturally precise, so it is totally inadequate, even erroneous, to propagate the Christian faith among diverse cultures as a "ready-made commodity."

By turning to the field of hermeneutics, Shawn Redford has helped us see that the Word is for all the people of God rather than the few who are trained in exegesis. The critical formulaic approach too often becomes a static, academic exercise that leads to rigid dogma and elitist controversy. Redford reminds us that as the Word drives the church to mission, as it should, fresh insights and new meanings open up to the interpreter that are not comprehensible to the technical scholar. Because we believe the Holy Spirit speaks to believers through the Word, hermeneutics is not a one-way inquiry, but a spiritual exercise, a heart-to-heart conversation, as it were, with the Spirit of the Word. We know that textual ambiguities are further complicated by the interpreter's biases as well as various factors present in the receiving culture. Referring to Van Engen, Redford emphasizes that scripture is a "tapestry" rather than a flat, monochromatic picture. The Bible, the individual believer and the believing community are the basic resources for understanding what God is saying. In reality, very few church leaders, worldwide, have resources for critical study. I know from my Africa years that most pastors read only the Bible and perhaps one or two other simple books. Therefore, Redford sees hermeneutics as a spiritual exercise as meanings of the Biblical text are illuminated through fellowship with those who know their own life situation. With Bible in hand, guided by prayer and the Holy Spirit, believers can ask of each other, "What does this passage mean for us at this time?" (Rev. 2:29).

Two chapters (Travis and DeNeui) have dealt with the C-1 through C-6 models for churches among Muslims and Buddhists. These ideas put the contextualization of worship and church life on a on a continuum from traditional (westernized) mission forms to various degrees of acculturated forms. How saddened we ought to be when DeNeui writes that cross-cultural missionaries have often viewed Buddhism as the enemy of evangelism and have sought ways to counter it with Christianity. This approach has not only served to alienate people socially but has reinforced the misunderstanding that Jesus is a foreigner, the leader of the foreigner's religion. Buddhism, Hinduism and Islam are religions that have presented some of the greatest challenges for contextualization. This is because along with Christianity, these religions represent the greatest numbers of people in the world and are primarily religions of culture. This means they are religions of birth and are integrated with tradition and worldview in such a way that life is a single bundle, making religion and culture inseparable. In discussing the merits and problems associated with the C- I through C-6 paradigms, DeNeui laments the way Christianity, as practiced by missionary converts, has separated believers from families and friends because there seems to be no way to preach or teach Jesus Christ except in forms that are familiar only to foreigners. While admitting the risks that arise when introducing Buddhist forms and symbols, DeNeui and Travis hope that C-3 and even C-4 levels of the continuum can become a reality, which they are not at present. Here the churches would at least be "attempting transition from what is completely the outsider's perspective to an integration with local perspectives (DeNeui)." Were this possible, Western cultural forms and terminologies would be avoided along with other practices that build barriers between the believers and their indigenous social context.

To this I have to add from my own missionary years that it would have been easier just to continue doing what is foreign, that is, remain non-incarnational. Ironically, long-practiced Western forms in mission-planted churches are usually not considered as foreign to local believers. This is because they were introduced from Europe and America when very little was understood about Incarnation as the way to evangelize. Held as sacred, churches feel these imported forms guard the church from syncretism and provide differentiation from non-Christians. Yet the fact is, relatively few are coming to Christ from religions such as Islam and Buddhism and many from among those who do make the turn toward Jesus, afterwards revert to the old ways.

Appropriate Christianity calls for courage to minister with innovations that risk misunderstanding even disapproval from those who are entrenched in older mission styles and methods. The Incarnation of Jesus was a radical, totally unconventional event; it did not connect with the long-held tradition of the Jews about how the Messiah would appear. The sad result was, "He came to what was his own and his own people did not accept him (Jn. 1:11)."

We have now reached the end of this volume. That Jesus entered the world to be with us is the secret to bringing his good news to the world. Dan Benuska has written about the meaning of Jesus' birth which brings God into the deepest of relationships with all people. I close with what he wrote about Dr. John Rosen, a psychiatrist in New York City. Dr. Rosen is known for his work with catatonic schizophrenic patients.

> Normally doctors remain separate and aloof from their patients. Dr. Rosen moves into the ward with them. He places his bed among their beds. He lives the life they must live. Day to day, he shares it. He loves them. If they don't talk he doesn't talk either. It is as if he understands what is happening. His being there, being with them, communicates something they haven't experienced in years – somebody understands.

> But then he does something else. He puts his arms around them and hugs them . . . and loves them back into life. Often the first words they speak are simply, "thank you,"[26]

This is what God did for us when Jesus came into our world. He moved into the ward with us. He placed his bed among our beds. Today, all who see him, touch him and are, in turn, touched by him, find life and will eternally say, "Thank you!" This is the appropriate Christianity about which we have written.

---

[26] Dan Benuska in *Sermon Illustrations for Gospel Lessons*, (1982:69).

Vita
of Dean S. Gilliland

PRESENT POSITION

Senior Professor of Contextualized Theology and African Studies, School of Intercultural Studies, Fuller Theological Seminary, Pasadena, CA

PERSONAL DATA

Birth:	Born May 13, 1928 in Akron, Ohio
Family:	Married to Lois M. (Harris) Gilliland
	Five children: Dean II, David, Dale, Barbara Jo, Douglas
Residence:	550 Mayflower Rd., Claremont, CA 91711
Denomination:	United Methodist, Ordained in 1954 (E.U.B.)

EDUCATION

B.D. (Missions)	Evangelical Theological Seminary, Naperville, IL, 1954
Th.M. (New Testament)	Princeton Theological Seminary, Princeton, NJ, 1960
Ph.D. (Religions)	Hartford Seminary Foundation, Hartford, CN, 1971

PROFESSIONAL EXPERIENCE

1948	Preaching License, (Ohio Conference, Evangelical United Brethren)
1948-50	Pastor: Warsaw and East Orangeville (NY) E.U.B. churches
1950-54	Pastor: Trinity Evangelical United Brethren Church, Clinton, IA
1954	Ordained as Elder, Ohio Conference, Evangelical United Brethren Church

1954-55	Assistant Pastor and Minister of Music: Calvary E.U.B. Church, Akron, OH
1955	Commissioned as Ordained Missionary to Nigeria, Board of Missions, E.U.B. Church, Dayton, OH
1955-76	Missionary to Nigeria in a variety of ministries as follows:

	1956-58	Pastor, Bambur (Muri Church) Nigeria
	1956-59	Principal: Evangelists' Training School, Banyam, Nigeria
	1960-63	Principal: Pastors' Training School, Banyam, Nigeria
	1962-67	Field Secretary, E.U.B. Mission, Nigeria
	1966-68	Field Secretary, Sudan United Mission, Nigeria
	1970-76	Professor: Theological College of Northern Nigeria
	1971-76	Principal: Theological College of Northern Nigeria
		Pastors training institution for seven Nigerian denominations
	1972-76	Sudan United Mission, International Committee
	1974	Co-founder: West African Association of Theological Institutions

1977-83	Assistant professor of contextualized theology and African Studies, School of World Mission, Fuller Theological Seminary
1983-92	Associate professor of contextualized theology and African Studies, School of World Mission, Fuller Theological Seminary
1992-99	Professor of contextualized theology and African Studies, School of World Mission, Fuller Theological Seminary
2000-	Senior professor of contextualized theology and African Studies, School of Intercultural Studies, Fuller Theological Seminary

POSITIONS HELD

Board Chair:	Zwemer Institute of Muslim Studies,
Board Member:	Mission Society for United Methodists
Board member:	Missions International, Nashville, TN
Consultant:	Advance Renewal Ministries, St. Louis, MO
Consultant:	West African Association of Theological Institutions

Secretary for U.S.A.:	Rural Development Counselors for Christian Churches in Africa
Membership:	African Studies Association
Membership:	Association of Professors of Mission
Membership:	American Society of Missiology
Membership:	Theological Task Force for Mission (BOGM) United Methodist
President:	American Society of Missiology, 1995-96.
Secretary/Treasurer:	Western Association of Professors of Mission

PUBLICATIONS:	See separate listing of books, chapters and articles.

Bibliography
of Dean S. Gilliland

Books:

Pauline Theology and Mission Practice, Grand Rapids, MI: Baker, 1983. Reprint, Eugene, OR:Wipf & Stock, 1998.

African Religion Meets Islam: Religious Change in Northern Nigeria, Lanham, MD: University Press of America, 1986.

The Word Among Us: Contextualizing Theology for Mission Today, ed., Waco, TX: Word Books, 1989. Reprint, Eugene, OR: Wipf & Stock, 2001.

The World Forever Our Parish, ed., Lexington, KY: Bristol Book House, 1991.

The Good News of the Kingdom; Mission for the Third Millenium, co-edited with Charles Van Engen and Paul Pierson, Maryknoll, NY: Orbis, 1993.

Announcing the Kingdom: The Story of God's Mission in the Bible, by Arthur F. Glasser, co-edited with Charles Van Engen, Grand Rapids, MI: Baker Academic, 2003.

Chapters in Books

"Integration Is More than Method." In *Nishkamakarma*, John Finch, ed. Pasadena, CA: Integration House, 1982.

"Priests, Kings and Chiefs in Religious Change." In *Religion and Society in Nigeria*, T.Falola, ed., Ile-Ife, Nigeria: Owolowo University Press, 1987.

"West African Church." In *Case Studies in Missions*, Paul G. & Frances F. Hiebert, eds., Grand Rapids, MI: Baker Academic, 1987.

"Introduction to Contextualization." In *The Word Among Us: Contextualizing Theology for Mission Today*, D.S. Gilliland, ed., Waco, TX: Word Books, 1989.

"Contextual Theology as Incarnational Mission." In *The Word Among Us: Contextualizing Theology for Mission Today*, Waco, TX: Word Books, 1989.

"Contextualization in the New Testament: Continuity and Particularity in Paul's Theology." In *The Word Among Us: Contextualizing Theology for Mission Today*, Waco, TX: Word Books, 1989.

"Models for Contextualization." In *The Word Among Us: Contextualizing Theology for Mission Today*, Waco, TX: Word Books, 1989.

'The Making of a Declaration." *In The World Forever Our Parish*, D.S. Gilliland, ed., Lexington KY: Bristol Books, 1991.

"Kings, Priests and Religion in Northern Nigeria." In *Religion and Society in Nigeria*, Olupona and Falola, eds., Ibadan, Nigeria: Spectrum Books, 1992.

"Introductions to Parts 1-5." In *The Good News of the Kingdom: Mission Theology for the Third Millennium*, Van Engen, Gilliland and Pierson eds., Maryknoll, NY: Orbis.

"Bibliography of Arthur F. Glasser's Works (1946-1993)." In *The Good News of the Kingdom*, Maryknoll, NY: Orbis, 1993.

"Evangelism and Music from a Wesleyan Perspective." In *Evangelization, the Heart of Mission*, S. T. Kimbrough, Jr. ed., New York: Board of Global Ministries, 1995.

"Paul Pierson: Mission Educator Par Excellence." In *Missiological Education for the 21st Century*, J. D. Woodberry, C. E. Van Engen and E. Elliston, eds., Maryknoll, NY: Orbis, 1996.

"For Missionaries and Leaders: Paul's Farewell to the Ephesian Elders." In *Mission in Acts*, Robert Gallagher and Paul Hertig, eds., Maryknoll, NY: Orbis, 2004.

"The Incarnation as Model for Appropriate Theologies." In *Appropriate Christianity*, Charles Kraft, ed., Pasadena, CA, William Carey Library, 2005.

Articles

"Don't Pity the Missionary." *Church and Home* (July, 1965), Dayton, OH: 14-16.

"The Indigenous Concept in Africa." *Missiology*, (July, 1973): 343-376.

"In Nigeria Religious Maturity Grows." *New World Outlook* (January, 1977): 19-22.

"Religious Change Among the Hausa 1000-1800." *Journal of Asian and African Studies*, 14- 3 (July-October, 1979): 242-257.

"Phenomenology as Mission Method." *Missiology*, 7 (October, 1979): 451-459.

"Relief Organizations as Prophetic Movements." *Together* (Oct-Dec., 1985): 29-31.

"How Christian Are African Independent Churches?" *Missiology*, 15-3 (July, 1986).

"Encounters in History." *Fuller Theological Seminary, Theology News and Notes*, 35-4 (December, 1988): 9, 12, 26.

"Superstition." *Dictionary of Pastoral Care and Counseling*, Rodney Hunter et. al., eds. (Nashville: Abingdon), 1990: 1239.

"Sacrifice." *Dictionary of Pastoral Care and Counseling*, Rodney Hunter, et. al., eds. (Nashville:Abingdon), 1990: 1110-1111.

"First Conversion and Second Conversion in Nigeria." *Mission Studies*, 7 (2) (Hamburg), 1990 :131-150.

"First Conversion and Second Conversion in Nigeria." *Journal of Asian and African Studies* 26 (3), (July-Oct., 1991): 237-252.

"Turning of the Tide in Nigeria." *Fuller Theological Seminary, Theology News and Notes*, 38, (March, 1992): 6-7.

"Muslims and Jesus." *Mission Advocate*, Spring, 1993.

"Principles of the Christian Approach to an African-Based Islamic Society." *Missiology*, 1997, 25 (1): 1-13.

"Revival and United Methodists." *Challenge to Evangelism*, 1998, 31-(1): 6, 11.

"Sweeping Evangelism and Church Growth in Asia, Africa and Latin America." *Challenge in Evangelism*, 1998, 31 (2): 8, 10.

"Context is Critical." *Evangelical Missions Quarterly*, 1998, 34 (4): 415-417.

"My Pilgrimage in Mission." *International Bulletin for Missionary Research*, 2000, 24 (3):119-122.

"Modeling the Incarnation for Muslim Peoples." *Missiology*, 2000, 38 (3): 329-338.

"Methodist Missions." *Evangelical Dictionary of World Missions*, A Scott Moreau, Harold Netland and Charles Van Engen, eds., (Grand Rapids, MI: Baker) 2000: 618-619.

"Contextualization." *Evangelical Dictionary of World Missions*, A. Scott Moreau, Harold Netland and Charles Van Engen, eds., (Grand Rapids, MI: Baker) 2000: 225-228.

"Kwebulaya, Apolo." *Evangelical Dictionary of World Missions*, A Scott Moreau, Harold Netland and Charles Van Engen, eds., (Grand Rapids, MI: Baker) 2000: 543.

"Mills, Samuel John, Jr." *Evangelical Dictionary of World Missions*, A Scott Moreau, Harold Netland and Charles Van Engen, eds., (Grand Rapids, MI: Baker) 2000: 628.

"Whitefield, George." *Evangelical Dictionary of World Missions*, A. Scott Moreau, Harold Netland and Charles Van Engen, eds., (Grand Rapids, MI: Baker) 2000: 1015.

List of Students
of Dean S. Gilliland

Year	Student	Degree	Thesis Title
1978	Lenning, Larry G.	M.A.	*Needs Assessment in Theological Education in Africa*
1978	Ebhomielen, Paul	Th.M.	*History and Growth of Nigerian Baptist Convention Mission*
1978	Youssef, Michael	M.A.	*Theology and Method for Muslim Evangelization in Egypt*
1979	Haleblian, Krikor	Th.M.	*Worldview and Evangelization: Case Study on Arab Peoples*
1979	Lenning, Larry G.	D.Miss.	*The Concept of Blessing and Its Application to Mission in Islamic West Africa*
1979	Musk, Bill	Th.M.	*Turkey: Towards a Harvest Strategy*
1979	Parreno, Jonathan	Th.M.	*A Critique of Philippine Values: Implications for Evangelism and Church Growth*
1979	Watney, Paul B.	D.Miss.	*Ministry Gifts: God's Provision for Effective Mission*
1980	Dollar, Harold	D.Miss.	*A Cross-Cultural Theology of Healing*
1980	Weber, Steve	M.A.	*The Relationship of Various Types of Relief and Development Philosophies to the Growth of the Church in Haiti*
1981	De Waard, Hendrick	D.Miss.	*The Spiritual Experience of Al-Ghazzali: A Christian Response*
1981	Downey, Raymur	Th.M.	*Old Testament Patterns of Leadership Training: Prophets, Priests and Kings*
1981	Iroezi, Chukwuma J.	D.Miss.	*Igbo Worldview and the Communication of the Gospel*
1981	Nelson, Ronald	Th.M.	*Fulbe Cultural Elements as Contact Points for the Gospel*
1982	Mfiwilwakanda, N.	Th.M.	*The Mandate for a Missionary Church in Africa*
1982	Zijlstra, Folkert	Th.M.	*The Poor and Poverty in God's Economy*

1983	Persons, David N.	Th.M.	*Discipling Through Teaching: Implications of Matthew 28:20 for the Methodist Church in Zaire*
1984	Aigbe, Sunday A.	M.A.	*The Phenomenon of Prayer in African Traditional Religion*
1984	Tienou, Tite	Ph.D.	*The Problem of Methodology in African Christian Theologies*
1985	Chishak, Luther	M.A.	*Relationships Between Church and State as They Affect the Church of Christ in Nigeria*
1985	Downey, Raymur	Ph.D.	*Ministerial Formation in Africa: Implications of the Experiential Component for Training Zairian Alliance Church Leadership*
1985	Gehman, Richard	D.Miss.	*Ancestor Relations Among Three African Societies in Biblical Perspective*
1985	Hansen, Carl	Th.M.	*Planting the Church in the Islamic Horn: A Strategy for Penetration*
1985	Huffard, Evertt W.	Ph.D.	*Thematic Dissonance in the Muslim-Christian Encounter: A Contextualized Theology of Honor*
1985	Jones, Kaleli	Ph.D.	*Theoretical Foundations of African and Western Worldviews and Their Relationship to Christian Theologizing: An Akamba Case Study*
1986	Groseclose, David	Th.M.	*A Plan for Discipling a Believer of Israeli Muslim Arab Background*
1987	Green, Stanley W.	M.A.	*A Liberating Hermeneutic (South Africa)*
1987	Hutchins, Paul	M.A.	*Continuity and Change Among the Maasai People*
1987	Ndonye, Johnson	M.A.	*Akamba Worldview and Leadership: The Need for a Dynamic Theological and Hermeneutical Method for Africa*
1988	Foster, K. Neill	Ph.D.	*Discernment, The Powers and Spirit Speaking*
1988	Kim, Sung-Tae	Th.M.	*Shamanic Influences over the Theology of the Korean Church in Presbyterian Perspective*
1988	Mdaka, Jonguxlo M.	M.A.	*The Search for a Relevant Ministry to Black Youth in South Africa*
1988	Mulumba, Mukundi	Ph.D.	*Witchcraft Among the Kasaian People of Zaire: Challenge and Response*

1989	Aigbe, Sunday A.	Ph.D.	*The Prophetic Role of a Church in a Developing Economy*
1989	Joseph, Pottiayyathu	Th.M.	*Covenant to Commission: Old Testament Covenants, Their Transition to the New Testament Commission and Relevance to the Work Among Tribals in Kerala, India*
1990	Persons, David	Ph.D.	*Contextualization of Basanga Puberty Rites in the United Methodist Church (Zaire)*
1990	Rees, O.	D.Miss.	*The Role of Baptism in Pauline Theology of Conversion*
1990	Mussa, Mohammed	M.A.	*Oromo Worldview and Contextualization of the Gospel*
1991	Fisk, Thomas	Th.M.	*Lakota Culture and Christianity: Worlds Apart or One in Christ?*
1991	Jonsson, Kjartan	Th.M.	*Worldview and the Gospel among Pokot Males*
1991	Kim, Sung-Tae	Ph.D.	*Contextualization and the Presbyterian Church in Korea*
1991	Sumarto, Wagiyono	D.Miss.	*Aspects of Islam in Indonesia*
1992	Amuzie, Charles C.	Th.M.	*Formulating a Theology of Mission for the Anglican Church in Nigeria: Echoes from the Twelfth Lambeth Conference*
1992	Ko, Changwan	Th.M.	*Pauline Principles of Contextualization to Motivate Korean Churches and Missionaries for Asian Mission*
1992	Koe, Joong W.	D.Miss.	*Church Growth Insights in the Ministry of John Wesley and the Korean Methodist Church*
1992	Mbuva, James M.	M.A.	*Witchcraft Among the Akamba and Africa Inland Church*
1992	Nwosu, Roland, C.	Th.M.	*Major Barriers Affecting Muslim Evangelism in Nigeria*
1993	Lundell, In-Gyeong	D.Miss.	*The Contextualization of he Korean Church of the Nazarene in Southern California*
1994	Kang, Il Jun	Th.M.	*Theology of Stewardship for Korean Missionary Leadership*
1995	Pottiayyathu, Joseph	D.Miss.	*Tribals in Kerala, India with Special Reference to Muthuvans and Mannans In Idukki District*
1995	Kim, Caleb Chul Soo	Th.M.	*Missiological Understanding of the Swahili Muslims in Zanzibar*

1995	Kim Yong Shik	Th.M.	*Contextualizing a Mission Theology for Korean Diaspora in Brazil*
1995	Lundstrom, Klas	Th.M.	*Contextualizing Theology in Relation to Traditional Ancestor Beliefs In Southern Tanzania*
1995	Nwosu, Roland C.	D.Miss.	*The Seventh Day Adventists Philosophy of Wholeness within the African (Igbo) Wholistic Context*
1995	Park, Ki Tae	Th.M.	*A Missiological Study on the Image of God in Humankind from a Redemptive and Eschatological Perspective*
1995	Park, Myon Ki	Th.M.	*Toward a Theology of Land Reform (Division): A Theological Study of Joshua*
1996	An, Seung Oh	Th.M.	*The Kingdom of God as a Paradigm for Renewal in the Presbyterian Church of Korea*
1996	Byrne, Frances Michael	D.Miss.	*The Biblical Motif of the Servant: A Theology for Mission*
1996	Jin, Hee Keun	D.Miss.	*Preaching in the Korean Presbyterian Church with Insights from a Shamanistic Worldview*
1996	Mutunga, Mutinda wa	D.Miss.	*Akamba Theology and the Ecology of Marriage and Family*
1997	Bernhard, Wendy Lee	Th.M.	*Bundu dia Kongo: A New Non-Christian Religious Movement in Zaire*
1997	Nwankpa, Vincent O.	Ph.D.	*The World and World in Africa: Contextualization Among the Igbo of Nigeria*
1997	Park, Ki Tae	D.Miss.	*A Missiological Study of Imago Dei in Humankind from the Perspective of the Kingdom of God*
1997	Young, John William	Th.M.	*Making the Presbyterian Ministry to the Dagomba People More Effective*
1998	An, Seung Oh Paul	Ph.D.	*Toward Witness-Oriented Worship in the Presbyterian Church of Korea*
1998	Baik, Jong-Ahn	Th.M.	*Contextualizing the Korean Missionary and the Presbyterian Church in the Philippines*
1998	Diesto, Genaro	Ph.D.	*The Effects of Colonial Mentality on the Religious Consciousness of Filipinos*

1999	DomNwachukwu Chinaka S.	Ph.D.	*Spiritual Power in Africa: Insights from Culture and the African Independent Churches of Lagos*
1999	Popadic, Dimitrije	Ph.D.	*Krisna Slava Among the Serbs: A Case for Contextualized Reinterpretation*
2000	Kantiok, James Bakut	Ph.D.	*Muslims and Christians in Northern Nigeria: Political and Cultural Implications for Evangelism*
2000	Owdenburg, Mdegella	Th.M.	*Leading a Confessional Church to Renewal: Affirming the Priesthood of Believers in the Tanzanian Lutheran Context*
2000	Park, Daniel Jinkoo	Ph.D.	*The Chinese Concept of Beol Se as the Basis for Incarnational Mission: With Special Reference to Singapore*
2001	Jun, David Chul-Han	D.Miss.	*An Historical and Contextual Mission Approach to Seafarers by Korean Churches: With Special Reference to Muslim Seafarers*
2001	Kim Caleb Chul-Soo	Ph.D.	*Supernaturalism in Swahili Islam: With Special Reference to the Therapeutic Cults of Jinn Possession*
2001	Lasisi, Lawrence Adeniyi	Ph.D.	*Bridging from African Indigenous Churches to Muslims in Southwestern Nigeria*
2001	Park, Myonki J.	Ph.D.	*Toward a Contextual Approach to Land Reform for Post-Reunification Korea*
2002	Moo, Saw Hay	D.Miss.	*Doing Theology in the Karen Church: The Gospel as Incarnation (John 1:1-14) Within the Karen Ywa (God) Tradition*
2003	Olam, Belay	D.Miss.	*Contextualizing the Church Among the Muslim Oromo*
2004	Komolafe, Sunday Babajide	Ph.D.	*Christian Intellectuals in Church Leadership of the Methodist Church in Kenya*
2004	Mwiti, Gershon	D.Miss.	*Christian Intellectuals in Church Leadership of the Methodist Church in Kenya*
2005	Kim, Sung Hwan	Ph.D.	*Imitatio Christi: Towards a Pauline Mission*
2005	Newman, Daniel	Ph.D.	*Uri as Contextual Theology for the Korean Church and Its Mission*

References Cited

Adams, Richard Newbold
  1975   *Energy and Structure: A Theory of Social Power.* Austin, TX:
          University of Texas Press.

Allen, Diogenes
  1997   *Spiritual Theology: The Theology of Yesterday for Spiritual Help
          Today.* Cambridge, MA: Cowley Pub.

Allen, Roland
  1912   *Missionary Methods, St. Paul's or Ours: A Study of the Church in the
          Four Provinces.* London: R. Scott.

  1927   *The Spontaneous Expansion of the Church.* London: World
          Dominion Press. (1st American edition: 1962 Grand Rapids, MI:
          Eerdmans.)

  1962   *The Spontaneous Expansion of the Church: And the Causes Which
          Hinder It.* 1st American edition. Grand Rapids, MI: Eerdmans. (1st
          edition: 1927 London: World Dominion Press.)

Anderson, Allan H.
  2001a   "A 'Falure in Love'? Western Missionaries and the Emergence of
          African Initiated Churches in the Twentieth Century." *Missiology*
          29:275-286.

  2001b   *African Reformation: African Initiated Christianity in the 20th
          Century.* Trenton, NJ: Africa World Press.

Anderson, Gerald H., ed.
  1976   *Asian Voices in Christian Theology.* Maryknoll, NY: Orbis Books.

  1994   *Mission Legacies: Biographical Studies of Leaders of the Modern
          Missionary Movement.* Maryknoll, NY: Orbis Books.

  1998   *Biographical Dictionary of Christian Missions.* New York:
          Macmillan.

Anderson, Gerald H., and Thomas F. Stransky, eds.
  1976   *Mission Trends No. 3.* Grand Rapids, MI: Eerdmans.

Anderson, John D. C.
  1976   "Missionary Approach to Islam: Christian or 'Cultic.'" *Missiology*
          4:285-300.

Anderson, Rufus
        See: Beaver, R. Pierce, ed.

Arbuckle, Gerald A.
    1985   "Inculturation and Evangelisation: Realism or Romanticism." In
            Missionaries, Anthropologists and Cultural Change. See: Darrell L.
            Whiteman, ed. Pp. 171-214.

    1990   *Earthing the Gospel: An Inculturation Handbook for Pastoral
            Workers*. Maryknoll, NY: Orbis Books.

Archer, Kenneth J.
    2002   "Pentecostal Hermeneutics and a Critique of the Evangelical
            Historical-Critical Method." Paper presented on at the 2002 Annual
            Meeting of the Society for Pentecostal Studies (SPS), held at
            Southeastern College, March 14-16, 2002. Lakeland, FL. (Paper
            presented on March 15, 2002, and made available from the author via
            e-mail at karcher@cogts.edu.)

Arias, Mortimer
    2001   "Global and Local: A Critical View of Mission Models." In *Global
            Good News: Mission in a New Context*. See: Howard A. Snyder, ed.
            Pp. 55-64.

Armerding, Carl Edwin, ed.
    1977   *Evangelicals and Liberation*. Grand Rapids, MI: Baker Book House;
            Nutley, NJ: Presbyterian and Reformed Pub. Company.

Arulefela, Joseph O.
    1977   "The Covenant in the Old Testament and Yoruba Culture." M.A.
            thesis, Fuller Theological Seminary, Pasadena, CA.

Athanasius
    1953   "Introduction to the Treatise on the Incarnation of the Word." In *St.
            Athanasius*. A Select Library of the Nicene and Post-Nicene Fathers
            of the Christian Church, Second Series, Vol. 4. See: Philip Schaff
            and Henry Wace, eds. P. 41.

Augsburger, David W.
    1986   *Pastoral Counseling across Cultures*. Philadelphia, PA: Westminster
            Press.

Axenfeld, Karl
    1910   Discussion. See: World Missionary Conference, Pp. 421-423.

Baker, Robert A.
    1954   *The Baptist March in History*. Nashville, TN: Broadman Press.

References Cited 537

Barbour, Ian G.
> 1974   *Myths, Models and Paradigms: A Comparative Study in Science and Religion.* New York: Harper and Row.

Barker, Kenneth
> 1995   *The NIV Study Bible.* Grand Rapids, MI: Zondervan.

Barna, George
> 1992   *Church Marketing: Breaking Ground for the Harvest.* Ventura, CA: Regal Books.

Barrett, David B.
> 1968   *Schism and Renewal in Africa: An Analysis of Six Thousand Contemporary Religious Movements.* Nairobi, Kenya: Oxford University Press.

Barth, Karl
> 1933   *Theologische Existenz Heute!* Munich, Germany: Chr. Kaiser Verlag.

> 1962   *Credo.* New York: Charles Scribner's Sons.

Beale, Gregory K., ed.
> 1994   *The Right Doctrine from the Wrong Texts? Essays on the Use of the Old Testament in the New.* Grand Rapids, MI: Baker Books.

Beasley-Murray, George. R.
> 1987   *John.* Word Biblical Commentary, Vol. 36. Waco, TX: Word Books.

Beaudoin, Tom
> 1998   *Virtual Faith: The Irreverent Spiritual Quest of Generation X.* San Francisco, CA: Jossey-Bass.

Beaver, R. Pierce, ed.
> 1967   *To Advance the Gospel: Selections From The Writings of Rufus Anderson.* Grand Rapids, MI: Eerdmans.

Bebey, Francis
> 1969   *African Music: A People's Art.* New York: Lawrence Hill.

Bediako, Kwame
> 1992   *Theology and Identity: The Impact of Culture upon Christian Thought in the 2nd Century and Modern Africa.* Oxford: Regnum Books.

> 1995   *Christianity in Africa: The Renewal of the Non-Western Religion.* Maryknoll, NY: Orbis Books.

Beeby, H. Dan
> 1999   *Canon and Mission.* Harrisburg, PA: Trinity Press International.

Beker, J. Christiaan
    1991   *Heirs of Paul: Paul's Legacy in the New Testament and in the Church Today.* Minneapolis, MN: Fortress Press.

Bennett, David W.
    1993   *Metaphors of Ministry: Biblical Images for Leaders and Followers.* Grand Rapids, MI: Baker Books.

Benuska, Dan
    1982   *Sermon Illustrations for Gospel Lessons.* St. Louis, MO: Concordia Publishing House.

Berlo, David K.
    1960   *The Process of Communication.* New York: Holt, Rinehart and Winston.

Bernard, Dutch
    2000   "Should Muslims Become 'Christians'?" *International Journal of Frontier Missions* 17:15-24.

Bevans, Stephen B.
    1992, 2002 *Models of Contextual Theology.* Maryknoll, NY: Orbis Books. (Revised and expanded: 2002 *Models of Contextual Theology: Revised and Expanded Edition.* Reprinted: 2004.)

    1998   "God Inside Out: Toward a Missionary Theology of the Holy Spirit." *International Bulletin of Missionary Research* 22:102-105. Available online at: http://www.sedos.org/english/Bevans.html.

Bevans, Stephen B., and Norman E. Thomas
    1991   "Selected Annotated Bibliography on Missiology: Contextualization/ Inculturation/Indigenization." *Missiology* 19:105-108.

Birkey, Del
    1988   *The House Church: A Model for Renewing the Church.* Scottdale, PA: Herald Press.

Boff, Clodovis
    1987   *Theology and Praxis: Epistemological Foundations.* Maryknoll, NY: Orbis Books.

Boff, Leonardo, and Clodovis Boff
    1987   *Introducing Liberation Theology.* Maryknoll, NY: Orbis Books.

Bosch, David J.
    1980   *Witness to the World: The Christian Mission in Theological Perspective.* Atlanta, GA: John Knox Press.

    1991   *Transforming Mission: Paradigm Shifts in Theology of Mission.* Maryknoll, NY: Orbis Books.

References Cited 539

1993   "Reflections on Biblical Models of Mission." In *Toward the Twenty-First Century in Christian Mission.* See: James M. Phillips and Robert T. Coote, eds. Pp. 175-192.

1995   *Believing in the Future: Toward a Missiology of Western Culture.* Valley Forge, PA: Trinity Press International.

Bowden, Henry W. and James P. Ronda, eds.
1938   *England: Before and After Wesley; The Evangelical Revival and Social Reform.* London: Hodder and Stoughton.

Bowen, John R.
1998   *Religions in Practice: An Approach to the Anthropology of Religion.* Boston, MA: Allyn and Bacon.

Branick, Vincent
1989   *The House Church in the Writings of Paul.* Wilmington, DE: Michael Glazier.

Bready, J. Wesley
1980   *John Eliot's Indian Dialogues: A Study in Cultural Interaction.* Westport, CT: Greenwood Press.

Bretall, Robert W., ed.
1946   *A Kierkegaard Anthology.* Princeton, NJ: Princeton University Press. (Reprinted: 1973.)

Bright, John
1953   *The Kingdom of God: The Biblical Concept and Its Meaning for the Church.* Nashville, TN: Abingdon-Cokesbury Press.

1976   *Covenant and Promise: The Prophetic Understanding of the Future in Pre-exilic Israel.* Philadelphia, PA: Westminster Press.

Brown, Raymond E.
1984   *The Churches the Apostles Left Behind.* Raymond, NJ: Paulist Press.

Brownson, James V.
1998   *Speaking the Truth in Love: New Testament Resources for a Missional Hermeneutic.* Harrisburg, PA: Trinity Press International.

Brunner, Emil
1931   *The Word and the World.* New York: Charles Scribner's Sons.

Bühlmann, Walburt
1978   *The Coming of the Third Church: An Analysis of the Present and Future of the Church.* Maryknoll, NY: Orbis Books.

Bulatao, Jaime
1966 *Split-Level Christianity*. Manila, Philippines: Ateneo de Manila University.

Burrows, William R.
1996 "A Seventh Paradigm: Catholics and Radical Inculturation. In *Mission in Bold Humility*. See: Willem A. Saayman and Klippies Kritzinger, eds. Pp. 121-138.

Buswell, James O. III
1978 "Contextualization: Is It Only a New Word For Indigenization?" *Evangelical Missions Quarterly* 14:13-20.

Cairns, Earle E.
1986 *An Endless Line of Splendor*. Wheaton, IL: Tyndale.

Caldwell, Larry W.
1999 "Towards the New Discipline of Ethnohermeneutics: Questioning the Relevancy of Western Hermeneutical Methods in the Asian Context." *Journal of Asian Mission* 1:21-43.

2000 "Ethnohermeneutics: The Author Responds Further." *Journal of Asian Mission* 2:135-145.

Caleb Project
1988 *Reaching the Peoples of Bangkok*. Littleton, CO: Caleb Project.

Campbell, Jonathan S.
1999 "The Translatability of Christian Community: An Ecclesiology for Postmodern Cultures and Beyond." Ph.D. dissertation, Fuller Theological Seminary, Pasadena, CA.

Campbell, John
1822 *Travels in South Africa*. London: F. Westley.

1840 *Maritime Discovery and Christian Missions*. London: J. Snow.

Campbell, Joseph
1988 *The Power of Myth*. Bill Moyers (contributor) and Betty Sue Flowers (editor). New York: Anchor Books.

Carey, William
1792 *An Enquiry into the Obligations of Christians, to Use Means for the Conversion of the Heathens*. Leicester, England: Ann Ireland, etc.

Carriere, J. C.
1995 "Beyond Religion." *Shambola Sun*. (November) Pp. 18-23.

References Cited

Casino, Tereso C.
1996 "The Text in Context: An Evangelical Approach to the Foundations of Contextualization." Ph.D. dissertation, Asia Center for Theological Studies and Mission, Seoul, Korea.

Chao, Samuel H.
1988 "John L. Nevius (1829-1893) and the Contextualization of the Gospel in 19th Century China: A Case Study." *Asian Journal of Theology* 2:294-311.

Chaochareonrhat, Sinchai
1998 *Khristachon Bon Witii Thai* (Christians on the Thai Path – Thai Language.) Bangkok, Thailand: Baptist Christian Education Thailand.

Childs, Brevard S.
1974 *The Book of Exodus: A Critical, Theological Commentary.* Philadelphia, PA: Westminster Press.

Cho, Yong-gi
1981 *Successful Home Cell Groups.* Plainfield, NJ: Logos International.

1984 *More than Numbers.* Waco, TX: Word Books.

Chrispal, Ashish
1995 "Contextualization." In *Doing Mission in Context.* See: Sunand Sumithra and F. Hrangkuma, eds. Pp. 1-15.

Christian Aid Mission
2002 "Persecution of Christians in Laos." October 3, 2002 newsletter.

Church, J. E.
1981 *Quest for the Highest.* Greenwood, SC: Attic Press.

Clapp, Rodney
1996 *A Peculiar People: The Church as Culture in a Post-Christian Society.* Downers Grove, IL: InterVarsity Press.

Clark, Sidney J. W.
1928 *The Indigenous Church.* London; New York: World Dominion Press.

Clooney, Francis X.
1990 "Roberto de Nobili, Adaptation and the Reasonable Interpretation of Religion." *Missiology* 18:25-36.

Coe, Shoki
1976 "Contextualizing Theology." In *Mission Trends No. 3.* See: Gerald H. Anderson and Thomas F. Stransky, eds. Pp. 19-24. (Originally published: 1973. "In Search of Renewal in Theological Education." *Theological Education* 9:233-243.)

Cone, James H.
  1969 *Black Theology and Power.* New York: Seabury Press.

Conference on Missions held at Liverpool
  1860 London: J. Nisbet.

Conn, Harvie M.
  1977a "Contextualization: Where Do We Begin?" In *Evangelicals and Liberation.* See: Carl E. Armerding, ed. Pp. 90-119.

  1977b "Mission of the Church." In *Evangelicals and Liberation.* See: Carl E. Armerding, ed. Pp. 60-89.

  1978 "Contextualization: A New Dimension for Cross-Cultural Hermeneutic." *Evangelical Missions Quarterly* 14(1):29-46.

  1979 "The Muslim Convert and His Culture." In *The Gospel and Islam: A 1978 Compendium.* See: Don M. McCurry, ed. Pp. 97-111.

  1984 *Eternal Word and Changing Worlds: Theology, Anthropology, and Mission in Trialogue.* Grand Rapids, MI: Zondervan.

Conn, Harvie M., Manual Ortiz, and Susan S. Baker, eds.
  2002 *The Urban Face of Mission: Ministering the Gospel in a Diverse and Changing World.* Phillipsburg, NJ: P and R Publications.

Cook, Guillermo
  1985 *The Expectation of the Poor: Latin American Base Ecclesial Communities in Protestant Perspective.* Maryknoll, NY: Orbis Books.

Coote, Robert T., and John R. W. Stott, eds.
  1980 *Down to Earth: Studies in Christianity and Culture.* Grand Rapids, MI: Eerdmans.

Costas, Orlando E.
  1974 *The Church and its Mission.* Wheaton, IL: Tyndale House.

Cox, Harvey
  1995 *Fire from Heaven.* New York: Addison-Wesley Publishing.

Cragg, Kenneth
  1998 *The Secular Experience of God.* Harrisburg, PA: Trinity Press International.

Crollius, Ary A.
        See: Ary A. Roest Crollius.

References Cited

Curtin, Philip D.
  1960 "Scientific Racism and the British Theory of Empire." *Journal of the Historical Society of Nigeria* 2:40-51.

Daneel, M. L.
  1971-1988 *Old and New in Southern Shona Independent Churches.* 2 Vols. The Hague: Mouton. (Note: Vol. 3 is published by: Gweru, Zimbabwe: Mambor Press.)

Daneel, M. L., Charles E. Van Engen, and H. M. Vroom, eds.
  2003 *Fullness of Life for All: Challenges for Mission in Early 21st Century.* Amersterdam; New York: Rodopi.

Davey, Cyril J.
  1950 *Sadhu Sundar Singh.* Kent, UK: STL Books.

Davidson, Randall T.
  1889 *The Lambeth Conferences of 1867, 1878, and 1888: With the Official Reports and Resolutions together with the Sermons Preached at the Conferences.* London: SPCK; New York: E. and J. Young and Company.

Davies, Ron
  1992 *I Will Pour Out My Spirit.* Trumbridge Wells, England: Monarch.

Davis, John R.
  1998 *Poles Apart: Contextualizing the Gospel in Asia.* Bangalore, India: Asia Theological Association.

Davis, Kortright
  1986 "Bilateral Dialogue and Contextualization." *Journal of Ecumenical Studies* 23:386-399.

Dawson, John
  1989 *Taking Our Cities for God: How to Break Spiritual Strongholds.* Lake Mary, FL: Creation House.

de Gruchy, John W., and C. Villa-Vicencio, eds.
  1994 *Doing Theology in Context.* Maryknoll, NY: Orbis Books.

Deere, Jack
  1988 "Being Right Isn't Enough." In *Power Encounters among Christians in the Western World.* See: Kevin Springer, ed. Pp. 101-115.

Dennis, James S.
  1897 *Christian Missions and Social Progress: A Sociological Study of Foreign Missions.* 3 vols. New York: Revell.

Dillon, William S.
  1957 *God's Work in God's Way.* River Grove, IL: Voice of Melody.

Douglas, Mary
   1982   "Cultural Bias." In *In the Active Voice*. Pp. 183-254. London: Routledge and Kegan Paul.

Dulles, Avery R.
   1983, 1992 *Models of Revelation*. New York: Doubleday. (Reprinted: 1992 Maryknoll, NY: Orbis Books.)

Dye, T. Wayne
   1976   "Toward a Cross-Cultural Definition of Sin." *Missiology* 4:27-41.

Dyrness, William A.
   1983   *Let the Earth Rejoice!: A Biblical Theology of Holistic Mission*. Pasadena, CA: Fuller Seminary Press.

   1990   *Learning about Theology from the Third World*. Grand Rapids, MI: Zondervan.

   1992   *Invitation to Cross-Cultural Theology: Case Studies in Vernacular Theologies*. Grand Rapids, MI: Zondervan.

Ebeling, Gerhard
   1963   *Word and Faith*. Philadelphia: Fortress Press; London: SCM Press.

Eighmy, John L.
   1987   *Churches in Cultural Captivity: A History of the Social Attitudes of Southern Baptists*. Knoxville, TN: University of Tennessee Press.

Elkins, David N.
   1998   *Beyond Religion: A Personal Program for Building a Spiritual Life Outside the Walls of Traditional Religion*. Wheaton, IL: Quest Books.

Elliott, Ralph H.
   1982   *Church Growth that Counts*. Valley Forge, PA: Judson Press.

Elliston, Edgar J.
   1992   *Home Grown Leaders*. Pasadena, CA: William Carey Library.

Elwell, Walter A.
   1988   "Covenant." In *Baker Encyclopedia of the Bible*. See: Walter A. Elwell, ed. Vol. 1. Pp. 530-536.

Elwell, Walter A., ed.
   1988   *Baker Encyclopedia of the Bible*. 2 vols. Grand Rapids, MI: Baker Book House.

Elwood, Douglas J.
   1980   *Asian Christian Theology: Emerging Themes*. Philadelphia, PA: Westminster Press.

References Cited

Erickson, Millard J.
  1983-1985 *Christian Theology.* 3 vols. Grand Rapids, MI: Baker Book
      House.

Escobar, Samuel
  1987 *La Fe Evangelica y las Teologias del la Liberacion.* El Paso, TX:
      Casa Bautista de Publicaciones.

Ettlinger, Gerard H.
  1997 "Incarnation." In *The Encyclopedia of Early Christianity.* Vol. 1.
      2nd ed. See Everett Ferguson, Michael P. McHugh, and Frederick W.
      Norris, eds. Pp. 567-567.

Evans, Gillian R., Alister E. McGrath, and Allan D. Galloway
  1986 *The Science of Theology.* Grand Rapids, MI: Eerdmans.

Fee, Gordon D.
  2000 *Listening to the Spirit in the Text.* Grand Rapids, MI: Eerdmans.

Fee, Gordon D., and Douglas K. Stuart
  2002 *How to Read the Bible Book by Book.* Grand Rapids, MI: Zondervan.

Ferguson, Everett, Michael P. McHugh, and Frederick W. Norris, eds.
  1997 *The Encyclopedia of Early Christianity.* 2 vols. New York: Garland
      Pub.

Ferm, Deane W.
  1986 *Third World Liberation Theologies: An Introductory Survey.*
      Maryknoll, NY: Orbis Books.

Finger, Thomas N.
  1985 *Christian Theology: An Eschatological Approach.* Vol. 1. Nashville,
      TN: Thomas Nelson. (Reprinted as part of 2 vols.: 1987-1989
      Scottdale, PA: Herald Press.)

First Plenary Assembly of the Federation of Asian Bishops' Conference
      (Taipei, 22-27 April 1974)
  1976 *His Gospel to Our Peoples* Vol. 2. Manila, Philippines: Cardinal Bea
      Institute.

Fleming, Bruce C. E.
  1980 *Contextualization of Theology: An Evangelical Assessment.*
      Pasadena, CA: William Carey Library.

Ford, Kevin G.
  1995 *Jesus For a New Generation: Putting the Gospel in the Language of
      Xers.* Downers Grove, IL: InterVarsity Press.

Foster, Richard J.
   1998   *Streams of Living Water: Celebrating the Great Traditions of Christian Faith*. San Francisco, CA: HarperSanFrancisco.

Freedman, David Noel, ed.
   1992   *The Anchor Bible Dictionary*. Vol. 1. New York: Doubleday.

Frei, Hans W.
   1974   *The Eclipse of Biblical Narrative: A Study in Eighteenth and Nineteenth Century Hermeneutics*. New Haven, CT: Yale University Press.

Fuller, Daniel P.
   1978   "The Holy Spirit's Role in Biblical Interpretation." In *Scripture, Tradition, and Interpretation*. See: W. Ward Gasque and William S. LaSor, eds. Pp. 189-198.

Gallagher, Robert L., and Paul Hertig, eds.
   2004   *Mission in Acts: Ancient Narratives in Contemporary Context*. Maryknoll, NY: Orbis Books.

Gasque, W. Ward
   1978   "Nineteenth-Century Roots of Contemporary New Testament Criticism." In *Scripture, Tradition, and Interpretation*. See: W. Ward Gasque and William S. LaSor, eds. Pp. 146-156.

Gasque, W. Ward, and William S. LaSor, eds.
   1978   *Scripture, Tradition, and Interpretation*. Grand Rapids, MI: Eerdmans.

Gensichen, Hans Werner
   1971   *Glaube fur die Welt: Theologische Aspekte der Mission*. Gutersloh, Germany: Gerd Mohn.

Gibbs, Eddie
   1989   "Contextual Considerations in Responding to Nominality." In *The Word among Us: Contextualizing Theology for Mission Today*. See: Dean S. Gilliland, ed. Pp. 239-261.

   2000   *ChurchNext: Quantum Changes in How We Do Ministry*. Downers Grove, IL: InterVarsity Press.

Gibellini, Rosino, ed.
   1979   *Frontiers of Theology in Latin America*. Maryknoll, NY: Orbis Books.

Gilliland, Dean S.
   1983   *Pauline Theology and Mission Practice*. Grand Rapids, MI: Baker Book House.

1986   *African Religion Meets Islam: Religious Change in Northern Nigeria.*
        Lanham, MD: University Press of America.

1989a   "Context Theology as Incarnational Mission." In *The Word Among
        Us: Contextualizing Theology for Mission Today.* See: Dean S.
        Gilliland, ed. Pp. 9-31.

1989b   "New Testament Contextualization: Continuity and Particularity in
        Paul's Theology." In *The Word Among Us: Contextualizing
        Theology for Mission Today.* See: Dean S. Gilliland, ed. Pp. 52-73.

1998   "Context is Critical in 'Islampur' Case." *Evangelical Missions
        Quarterly* 34:415-417.

2000a   "Contextualization." In *Evangelical Dictionary of World Missions.*
        See: A. Scott Moreau, Harold A. Netland, Charles E. Van Engen, eds.
        Pp. 225-228.

2000b   "Modeling the Incarnation for Muslim People: A Response to Sam
        Schlorff." *Missiology* 28:329-338.

2002   "Contextualization Models." In *The Word Among Us:
        Contextualizing Theology for Mission Today.* See: Dean S. Gilliland,
        ed. Pp. 313-317.

Gilliland, Dean S., ed.
    1989, 2002 *The Word Among Us: Contextualizing Theology for Mission
        Today.* Dallas: Word Publishing. (Reprinted: 2002 Eugene, OR:
        Wipf and Stock Publishers.)

Glasser, Arthur F., with Charles E. Van Engen, Dean S. Gilliland, and Shawn B.
        Redford
    2003   *Announcing the Kingdom: The Story of God's Mission in the Bible.*
        Grand Rapids, MI: Baker Books.

Gödel, Kurt
    1992   *On Formally Undecidable Propositions of Principia Mathematica
        and Related Systems.* New York: Dover Publications.

Goldschmidt, Walter Rochs
    1966   *Comparative Functionalism: An Essay in Anthropological Theory.*
        Berkeley, CA: University of California Press.

Goldsmith, Martin
    1976   "Community and Controversy: Key Causes of Muslim Resistance."
        Missiology 4:317-323.

Goodall, Norman, ed.
    1953   *Missions under the Cross.* London: Edinburgh House.

Gordon, Adoniram J.
  1905   *The Holy Spirit and Missions.* 4th edition. London: Hodder and
         Stoughton. (1st edition: 1893 Hodder and Stoughton.)

Green, Joel, ed.
  2004   *What about the Soul? Neuroscience and Christian Anthropology.*
         Nashville, TN: Abingdon Press.

Green, Michael
  1970   *Evangelism in the Early Church.* Grand Rapids, MI: Eerdmans.

Grenz, Stanley J.
  1993   *Revisioning Evangelical Theology: A Fresh Agenda for the 21st
         Century.* Downers Grove, IL: InterVarsity Press.

Grudem, Wayne A.
  1994   *Systematic Theology: An Introduction to Biblical Doctrine.* Leicester,
         England: InterVarsity Press; Grand Rapids, MI: Zondervan.

Guder, Darrell L.
  1999   *The Incarnation and the Church's Witness.* Harrisburg, PA: Trinity
         Press International.

Guder, Darrell L., ed.
  1998   *Missional Church: A Vision for the Sending of the Church in North
         America.* Grand Rapids, MI: Eerdmans.

Guelich, Robert A.
  1991   "Spiritual Warfare: Jesus, Paul and Peretti." *Pneuma* 13:33-64.

Guinness, Os
  1993   *Dining with the Devil: The Megachurch Movement Flirts with
         Modernity.* Grand Rapids, MI: Baker Book House.

Gundry Volf, Judith M., and Miroslav Volf
  1997   *A Spacious Heart: Essays on Identity and Belonging.* Valley Forge,
         PA: Trinity Press International.

Gustafson, James W.
  1983   "The Historical Development of the Center for Church Planting and
         Church Growth in Northeast Thailand." Paper given for World Relief
         Phase III workshop, held February 14 – March 4, 1983. Udon Thani,
         Thailand. Unpublished manuscript.

Guthrie, Stanley M.
  2000   "Nobili, Robert de." In *Evangelical Dictionary of World Missions.*
         See: A. Scott Moreau, Harold A. Netland, Charles E. Van Engen, eds.
         P. 694.

Gutierrez, Gustavo
  1973, 1988 *A Theology of Liberation: History, Politics and Salvation.*
        Maryknoll, NY: Orbis Books. (Reprinted as a Fifteenth Anniversary
        edition: 1988.)

Haight, Roger
  1985 *An Alternative Vision: An Interpretation of Liberation Theology.*
        New York: Paulist Press.

Haleblian, Krikor
  1983 "The Problem of Contextualization." *Missiology* 11:100-105.

Hall, Douglas John
  1996a "Ecclesia Crucis: The Theologic of Christian Awkwardness." In
        *Church between Gospel and Culture: The Emerging Mission in North
        America.* See: George R. Hunsberger and Craig Van Gelder, eds. Pp.
        198-213.

  1996b *The End of Christendom and the Future of Christianity.* Valley
        Forge, PA: Trinity Press International. (Reprinted: 1997 Harrisburg,
        PA: Trinity Press International; 2002 Eugene, OR: Wipf and Stock
        Publishers.)

Hamilton, Kenneth
  1977a "Liberation Theology: An Overview." In *Evangelicals and
        Liberation.* See: Carl E. Armerding, ed. Pp. 1-9.

  1977b "Liberation Theology: Lessons Positive and Negative." In
        Evangelicals and Liberation. See: Carl E. Armerding, ed. Pp. 120-
        127.

Hanciles, Jehu J.
  2001 "Anatomy of an Experiment: The Sierra Leone Native Pastorate."
        Missiology 29:63-82.

  2002 *Euthanasia of a Mission: African Church Autonomy in a Colonial
        Context.* Westport, CT: Praeger.

Hard, Theodore
  1989 "Does Animism Die in the City?" *Urban Mission* 6:45-46.

Harris, Paul William
  1999 *Nothing but Christ: Rufus Anderson and the Ideology of Protestant
        Foreign Missions.* New York: Oxford University Press.

"Has the Wind Dropped?"
  1979 *Renewal* 80. (April/May 1979). Editorial article. Esher Surrey, UK:
        Fountain Trust.

Hassey, Janette
    1986   *No Time for Silence.* Grand Rapids, MI: Academie Books.

Hawthorne, Gerald F.
    1983   *Philippians.* Word Biblical Commentary, Vol. 43. Waco, TX: Word
            Books.

Heckman, Bruce
    1988   "Arab Christian Reactions to Contextualization in the Middle East."
            Fuller Theological Seminary, Pasadena, CA. Unpublished
            manuscript.

Hefner, Robert W., ed.
    1993   *Conversion to Christianity: Historical and Anthropological
            Perspectives on a Great Transformation.* Berkeley, CA: University
            of California Press.

Herion, Gary A., and George E. Mendenhall
    1992   "Covenant." In *The Anchor Bible Dictionary.* See: David Noel
            Freedman, ed. Pp. 1179-1202.

Hesselbein, Frances, Marshall Goldsmith, and Richard Beckhard, eds.
    1996   *The Leader of the Future: New Visions, Strategies, and Practices for
            the Next Era.* San Francisco, CA: Jossey-Bass.

Hesselgrave, David J., and Edward Rommen
    1989   *Contextualization: Meanings, Methods, and Models.* Grand Rapids,
            MI: Baker Book House.

Hiebert, Paul G.
    1978   "Missions and Anthropology: A Love/Hate Relationship."
            Missiology 6:166-171.

    1984, 1987 "Critical Contextualization." *Missiology* 12:287-296.
            (Reprinted: 1987 *International Bulletin of Missionary Research*
            11:104-112. Also reprinted: 1994 in *Anthropological Reflections on
            Missiological Issues.*)

    1989   "Form and Meaning in the Contextualization of the Gospel." In *The
            Word among Us: Contextualizing Theology for Mission Today.* See:
            Dean S. Gilliland, ed. Pp. 101-120.

    1994   *Anthropological Reflections on Missiological Issues.* Grand Rapids,
            MI: Baker Books.

    1999   *The Missiological Implications of Epistemological Shifts: Affirming
            Truth in a Modern/Postmodern World.* Harrisburg, PA: Trinity Press
            International.

References Cited

Hiebert, Paul G., and Eloise Hiebert Meneses
> 1995 *Incarnational Ministry: Planting Churches in Band, Tribal, Peasant, and Urban Societies.* Grand Rapids, MI: Baker Books.

Hiebert, Paul G., R. Daniel Shaw, and Tite Tienou
> 1999 *Understanding Folk Religion: A Christian Response to Popular Beliefs and Practices.* Grand Rapids, MI: Baker Books.

Hill, Edmund, ed.
> 1990 *The Works of Saint Augustine: A Translation for the 21 Century.* Part III, Vol. 2 Sermons 20-50. Brooklyn, NY: New City Press. Sermon 43. Pp. 238-243. (Original: Migne, Jacques-Paul, ed. [1800-1875] *Sermon 43, 7, 9: Patrologiae Cursus Completus, Series Latina.* 38, 257-258, Paris.)

Hill, Eugene
> 1987 "Inculturation." In *The New Dictionary of Theology.* See: Joseph A. Komonchak, Mary Collins, and Dermot A. Lane, eds. Pp. 510-513.

Hillers, Delbert R.
> 1969 *Covenant: The History of a Biblical Idea.* Baltimore, MD: Johns Hopkins Press.

Hillgarth, J. N., ed.
> 1969 *Christianity and Paganism, 350-750: The Conversion of Western Europe.* Philadelphia, PA: University of Pennsylvania Press. (Reprinted: 1986.)

Hinton, Keith W.
> 1985 *Growing Churches Singapore Style: Ministry in an Urban Context.* Singapore: Overseas Missionary Fellowship.

Hodges, Melvin L.
> 1953 *The Indigenous Church.* Springfield, MO: Gospel Publishing House.

Hoedemaker, Bert
> 1998 *Secularization and Mission: A Theological Essay.* Harrisburg, PA: Trinity Press International.

Hoefer, Herbert E.
> 2001 *Churchless Christianity.* Pasadena, CA: William Carey Library.

Hoekendijk, Johannes Christiaan
> 1967 *The Church Inside Out.* London: SCM Press; Philadelphia, PA: Westminster Press.

Hoge, Dean R., and David A. Roozen, eds.
> 1979 *Understanding Church Growth and Decline: 1950-1978.* New York: Pilgrim Press.

Horton, Robert
   1908   *The Bible: A Missionary Book.* Edinburgh; London: Oliphant,
           Anderson and Ferrier.

Hudnut, Robert K.
   1975   *Church Growth Is Not the Point.* San Francisco, CA: Harper and
           Row.

Huggett, Joyce
   1986   *The Joy of Listening to God: Hearing the Many Ways God Speaks to
           Us.* Downers Grove, IL: InterVarsity Press.

Hughes, Richard T., ed.
   1995   *The Primitive Church in the Modern World.* Urbana, IL: University
           of Illinois.

Hughes, Robert
   1987   *The Fatal Shore: A History of the Transportation of Convicts to
           Australia, 1787-1868.* London; Sydney: Collins Harvill.

Hunsberger, George R., and Craig Van Gelder, eds.
   1996   *Church between Gospel and Culture: The Emerging Mission in North
           America.* Grand Rapids, MI: Eerdmans.

Hunt, Everett N., Jr.
   1994   "John L. Nevius, 1829-1893." In *Mission Legacies.* See: Gerald H.
           Anderson, ed. Pp. 190-196.

Hunter, George G., III
   1996   *Church for the Unchurched.* Nashville, TN: Abingdon Press.

Hwang, C. H. [Shoki Coe]
   1962   "A Rethinking of Theological Training for the Ministry in the
           Younger Churches Today." *South East Asia Journal of Theology*
           4:87-34.

Hynson, Leon O.
   1984   *To Reform the Nation: Theological Foundations of Wesley's Ethics.*
           Grand Rapids, MI: Francis Asbury Press.

Inch, Morris A.
   1982   *Doing Theology across Cultures.* Grand Rapids, MI: Baker Book
           House.

Institute for Contextual Theology
   1991-? *Challenge: Church and People.* Johannesburg, South Africa:
           Contextual Publications.

References Cited

Institute for Sustainable Development
> 1993   *Kho Phrakamphi Somrap Phitii Dtang Dtang Leh Rabiep Kanprakob Phitii* (Scriptures for Use in Various Ceremonies and Order of Ceremonies – Thai Language.) Udon Thani, Thailand: ISD Printing.

Jao, Greg
> 1998   "Spiritual Growth." In *Following Jesus Without Dishonoring Your Parents: Asian-American Discipleship.* See: Jeanette Yep, ed. Pp. 129-144.

Jeganathan, W. S. Milton, ed.
> 2000   *Mission Paradigm in the New Millennium.* Delhi, India: ISPCK.

Jenkins, Philip
> 2002   *The Next Christendom: The Coming of Global Christianity.* Oxford; New York: Oxford University Press.

Johnstone, Patrick
> 1993   *Operation World.* Carlisle, UK: OM Publishing.

Jones, Peter
> 1992   *The Gnostic Empire Strikes Back.* Phillipsburg, NJ: Presbyterian and Reformed.

Jongeneel, Jan A. B., ed.
> 1992   *Pentecost, Mission and Ecumenism: Essays on Intercultural Theology.* Frankfurt; New York: Peter Lang.

Jordan, David K.
> 1993   "The Glyphomancy Factor: Observations on Chinese Conversion." In *Conversion to Christianity: Historical and Anthropological Perspectives on a Great Transformation.* See: Robert W. Hefner, ed. Pp. 285-303.

Kaiser, Walter C.
> 1996   "The Great Commission in the Old Testament." *International Journal of Frontier Missions* 13:3-7.

> 2000   *Mission in the Old Testament.* Grand Rapids, MI: Baker Books.

Kalluveettil, Paul
> 1982   *Declaration and Covenant: A Comprehensive Review of Covenant Formulae from the Old Testament and the Ancient Near East.* Rome: Biblical Institute Press.

Kasomo, Kasereka
> 1994   "Nande Culture: A Solid Ground for Theologizing In!" M.A. thesis, Fuller Theological Seminary, Pasadena, CA.

Kato, Byang H.
   1975   *Theological Pitfalls in Africa.* Kisumu, Kenya: Evangelical Pub.
          House.

Kenneson, Philip D., and James L. Street
   1997   *Selling Out the Church: The Dangers of Church Marketing.*
          Nashville, TN: Abingdon Press. (Reprinted: 2003 Eugene, OR: Wipf
          and Stock Publications.)

Keyes, Charles F.
   1993   "Why the Thai Are Not Christians: Buddhist and Christian
          Conversion in Thailand." In *Conversion to Christianity: Historical
          and Anthropological Perspectives on a Great Transformation.* See:
          Robert W. Hefner, ed. Pp. 259-284.

Kierkegaard, Soren
          See: Robert W. Bretall, ed.

King, Roberta R.
   1989   "Pathways in Christian Music Communication: The Case of the
          Senufo of Cote d'Ivoire." Ph.D. dissertation: Fuller Theological
          Seminary, Pasadena, CA. University Microfilms: Ann Arbor, MI.

Kinsler, F. Ross
   1978   "Mission and Context: The Current Debate about Contextualization."
          Evangelical Missions Quarterly 14:23-29.

Kirk, J. Andrew
   1997   *The Mission of Theology and Theology as Mission.* Valley Forge,
          PA: Trinity Press International.

   1999   *What is Mission? Theological Explorations.* London: Darton,
          Longman and Todd.

Kitagawa, Joseph, ed.
   1967   *The History of Religions: Essays on the Problem of Understanding.*
          Essays in Divinity, Vol. 1. Chicago, IL: University of Chicago Press.

Klein, William W.
   1990   *The New Chosen People: A Corporate View of Election.* Grand
          Rapids, MI: Academie; Zondervan.

Knapp, Stephen C.
   1977   "Preliminary Dialogue with Gutierrez' A Theology of Liberation." In
          Evangelicals and Liberation. See: Carl E. Armerding, ed. Pp. 10-42.

Komin, Suntaree
   1991   *Psychology of the Thai People: Values and Behavioral Patterns.*
          Bangkok, Thailand: National Institute of Development
          Administration.

References Cited

Komonchak, Joseph A., Mary Collins, and Dermot A. Lane, eds.
1987   *The New Dictionary of Theology.* Wilmington, DE: Michael Glazier.

Koyama, Kosuke
1974   *Waterbuffalo Theology.* Maryknoll, NY: Orbis Books.

1977   *No Handle on the Cross: An Asian Meditation on the Crucified Mind.* Maryknoll, NY: Orbis Books.

Krabill, James R.
1995   *The Hymnody of the Harrist Church among the Dida of South-Central Ivory Coast (1913-1949): A Historico-Religious Study.* Frankfurt am Main, Germany: Peter Lang.

Kraemer, Hendrik
1963   *The Christian Message in a Non-Christian World.* 3rd edition. Grand Rapids, MI: Kregel Publications.

Kraft, Charles H.
1978   "The Contextualization of Theology." *Evangelical Missions Quarterly* 14:31-36.

1979a   *Christianity in Culture: A Study in Dynamic Biblical Theologizing in Cross-Cultural Perspective.* Maryknoll, NY: Orbis Books. (Revised 25th Anniversary edition published 2005.)

1979b   "Dynamic Equivalence Churches in Muslim Society." In *The Gospel and Islam: A 1978 Compendium.* See: Don M. McCurry, ed. Pp. 114-124.

1980   "The Church in Culture: A Dynamic Equivalence Model." In *Down to Earth: Studies in Christianity and Culture.* See: Robert T. Coote and John R. W. Stott, eds. Pp. 211-230.

1989   "Contextualizing Communication." In *The Word Among Us: Contextualizing Theology for Mission Today.* See: Dean S. Gilliland, ed. Pp. 121-138.

1991a   *Communication Theory for Christian Witness.* Maryknoll, NY: Orbis Books.

1991b   "What Kind of Encounters Do We Need in Our Christian Witness." *Evangelical Missions Quarterly* 27:258-265.

1992a   "Allegiance, Truth and Power Encounters in Christian Witness." In *Pentecost, Mission and Ecumenism: Essays on Intercultural Theology.* See Jan A. B. Jongeneel, ed. Pp. 215-230.

1992b   *Defeating Dark Angels: Breaking Demonic Oppression in the Believer's Life.* Ann Arbor, MI: Vine Books.

1994   *Deep Wounds, Deep Healing.* Ann Arbor, MI: Servant Publications.

1996   *Anthropology for Christian Witness.* Maryknoll, NY: Orbis Books.

1999   *Communicating Jesus' Way.* Pasadena, CA: William Carey Library.

2002   *Confronting Powerless Christianity: Evangelicals and the Missing Dimension.* Grand Rapids, MI: Chosen; Baker Books.

Kraft, Charles H., ed.
1994   *Behind Enemy Lines: An Advanced Guide to Spiritual Warfare.* Ann Arbor, MI: Vine Books. (Reprinted: 2000 Pasadena, CA: Wipf and Stock.)

Kraft, Charles H., and Thomas N. Wisley, eds.
1979   *Readings in Dynamic Indigeneity.* Pasadena, CA: William Carey Library.

Kraus, C. Norman, ed.
1980   *Missions, Evangelism, and Church Growth.* Scottsdale, PA: Herald Press.

Kraybill, Donald B.
1978   *The Upside-Down Kingdom.* Scottdale, PA: Herald Press.

Kroeber, A. L., and Clyde Kluckhohn
1952   *Culture: A Critical Review of Concepts and Definitions.* New York: Vintage Books.

Küng, Hans
1967   *The Church.* New York: Sheen and Ward.

Kuper, Adam
1988   *The Invention of Primitive Society: Transformations of an Illusion.* London: Routledge.

Lambeth Conference, 1888.
        See: Randall T. Davidson.

LaSor, William S.
1978   "The Sensus Plenior and Biblical Interpretation. In *Scripture, Tradition, and Interpretation.* See: W. Ward Gasque and William S. LaSor, eds. Pp. 260-277.

Latourette, Kenneth Scott
1975   *A History of Christianity: Volume 1 to A.D. 1500.* San Francisco, CA: HarperSanFrancisco.

References Cited

Laudan, Larry

1977   *Progress and Its Problems: Toward a Theory of Scientific Growth.*
        Berkeley, CA: University of California Press.

Law, Eric H. F.

1993   *The Wolf Shall Dwell with the Lamb: A Spirituality for Leadership in
        a Multicultural Community.* St. Louis, MO: Chalice Press.

Lee, Hyun Mo

1992   "A Missiological Appraisal of the Korean Church in Light of
        Theological Contextualization." Ph.D. dissertation, Southwestern
        Baptist Theological Seminary, Ft. Worth, TX.

Lewis, James A.

2000   "Ricci, Matteo." In *Evangelical Dictionary of World Missions.* See:
        A. Scott Moreau, Harold A. Netland, Charles E. Van Engen, eds. P.
        834.

Lingenfelter, Sherwood

1996   *Agents of Transformation: A Guide for Effective Cross-Cultural
        Ministry.* Grand Rapids, MI: Baker Books.

1998   *Transforming Culture: A Challenge for Christian Mission.* Grand
        Rapids, MI: Baker Books.

Long, Charles H.

1967   "Archaism and Hermeneutics." In *The History of Religions: Essays
        on the Problem of Understanding.* See: Joseph Kitagawa, ed. Pp. 67-
        87.

Long, Jimmy

1997   *Generating Hope: A Strategy for Reaching the Postmodern
        Generation.* Downers Grove, IL: InterVarsity Press.

Lovelace, Richard F.

1979   *Dynamics of a Spiritual Life: An Evangelical Theology of Renewal.*
        Downers Grove, IL: InterVarsity Press.

Luzbetak, Louis J.

1963, 1970 *The Church and Cultures: An Applied Anthropology for the
        Religious Worker.* Techny, IL: Divine Word Publications.
        (Reprinted: 1970, 1975 Pasadena, CA: William Carey Library.
        Revised and expanded: 1988 *The Church and Cultures: New
        Perspectives in Missiological Anthropology.*)

1981   "Signs of Progress in Contextual Methodology." *Verbum* 22:39-57.

1988   *The Church and Cultures: New Perspectives in Missiological
        Anthropology.* Maryknoll, NY: Orbis Books. (Note: Some portions
        of this book were originally published: 1963, reprinted: 1970 and

1975 *The Church and Cultures: An Applied Anthropology for the Religious Worker.*)

Marantika, Chris
  1989   "In the Indonesian Context." In *Muslims and Christians on the Emmaus Road.* See: J. Dudley Woodberry, ed. Pp. 214-218.

Marshall, I. Howard
  2002   "Developing a Biblical Hermeneutic for a Developing Theology." Paper presented at the 2002 Institute of Biblical Research (IBR), held at the Regal Constellation Hotel, November 22-23, 2002. Toronto, Ontario, Canada. Available via e-mail at: http://www.zondervanchurchsource.com/clip/convention/ibrschedule.htm.

Massey, Joshua
  1999   "His Ways Are Not Our Ways." *Evangelical Missions Quarterly* 35:188-197.

  2000   "God's Amazing Diversity in Drawing Muslims to Christ." *International Journal of Frontier Missions* 17:5-14.

Mayers, Marvin K.
  1974   *Christianity Confronts Culture: A Strategy for Cross-Cultural Evangelism.* Grand Rapids, MI: Zondervan.

Mbiti, John S.
  1970   "Christianity and Traditional Religions in Africa." *International Review of Mission* 59:430-440.

  1971   *New Testament Eschatology in an African Background: A Study of the Encounter between New Testament Theology and African Traditional Concepts.* London: Oxford University Press.

  1979   "Response to the Article of John Kinney." *Occasional Bulletin of Missionary Research* 3:68.

  2003   "Dialogue between EATWOT and Western Theologians: A Comment on the 6th EATWOT Conference in Geneva 1983." In *Fullness of Life for All: Challenges for Mission in Early 21st Century.* See: M. L. Daneel, Charles E. Van Engen, and H. M. Vroom, eds.

McCarthy, Dennis J.
  1972   *Old Testament Covenant: A Survey of Current Opinions.* Richmond, VA: John Knox Press; Oxford: Basil Blackwell.

  1978   *Treaty and Covenant: A Study in Form in the Ancient Oriental Documents and in the Old Testament.* Rome: Biblical Institute Press.

McCartney, Dan G.
  2002 "Should We Employ the Hermeneutics of the New Testament
        Writers?" Also titled: "Can We Reproduce the Exegesis of the New
        Testament?" Paper presented at the 2002 Annual Meeting of the
        Evangelical Theological Society (ETS), held at the Regal
        Constellation Hotel, November 20-22, 2002. Toronto, Ontario,
        Canada. Available via e-mail at:
        http://www.zondervanchurchsource.com/clip/convention/ibrschedule.
        htm.

McCartney, Dan G., and Charles Clayton
  2002 *Let the Reader Understand: A Guide to Interpreting and Applying the
        Bible.* 2nd edition. Phillipsburg, NJ: Presbyterian and Reformed.
        (1st edition: 1994 Wheaton, IL: Victor Books.)

McCurry, Don M., ed.
  1979 *The Gospel and Islam: A 1978 Compendium.* Monrovia, CA:
        MARC.

McGavran, Donald A.
  1955, 1981 *The Bridges of God: A Study in the Strategy of Missions.* New
        York: Friendship Press. Revised and enlarged edition: 1981.

  1970 *Understanding Church Growth.* Grand Rapids, MI: Eerdmans.

McGee, Gary B.
  1986 *This Gospel Shall Be Preached.* Vol. 1. Springfield, MO: Gospel
        Publishing House.

McIntosh, G. Stewart
  1995 "The Legacy of John Ritchie." *International Bulletin of Missionary
        Research* 19:26-30.

McIntosh, John A.
  2000 "Missio Dei." In *Evangelical Dictionary of World Missions.* See: A.
        Scott Moreau, Harold A. Netland, and Charles E. Van Engen, eds.
        Pp. 631-633.

McKenzie, Steven L.
  2000 *Covenant.* St. Louis, MO: Chalice Press.

McLaren, Brian
  1998 *Reinventing Your Church.* Grand Rapids, MI: Zondervan. (Revised
        and republished: 2000 *The Church on the Other Side.*)

  2000 *The Church on the Other Side.* Grand Rapids, MI: Zondervan.
        (Revision of: 1998 *Reinventing Your Church.*)

Mendenhall, George E.
  1954   "Covenant Forms in Israelite Tradition." *The Biblical Archaeologist* 17:50-76.

Miguez-Bonino, Jose
  1971   "New Theological Perspectives." *Religious Education* 66:403-411.

  1975   *Doing Theology in a Revolutionary Situation.* Philadelphia, PA: Fortress Press.

Moffat, Robert
  1842   *Missionary Labours and Scenes in Southern Africa.* London: J. Snow. (Reprinted: 1969 New York; London: Johnson Reprints.)

Moltmann, Jurgen
  1977   *The Church in the Power of the Spirit.* Translated by Margaret Kohl. New York: Harper and Row.

Moreau, A. Scott, Harold A. Netland, and Charles E. Van Engen, eds.
  2000   *Evangelical Dictionary of World Missions.* Grand Rapids, MI: Baker Books.

Mott, John R.
  1900   *The Evangelization of the World in This Generation.* New York: Student Volunteer Movement for Foreign Missions.

Nabofa, N. Y.
  1985   "Blood Symbolism in African Religion." *Religious Studies* 21:389-405.

Nevius, John L.
  1886   *Methods of Mission Work.* Shanghai: American Presbyterian Mission Press. (Republished: 1899 *Planting and Development of Missionary Churches.* New York: Revell. Reprinted: 1956 Presbyterian and Reformed.)

Newbigin, Lesslie
  1953   *The Household of God.* London: SCM Press.

  1961   *Is Christ Divided?: A Plea for Christian Unity in a Revolutionary Age.* Grand Rapids, MI: Eerdmans.

  1989   *The Gospel in a Pluralist Society.* Grand Rapids, MI: Eerdmans.

  1991   *Truth to Tell: The Gospel as Public Truth.* Grand Rapids, MI: Eerdmans.

  1994   *A Word in Season: Perspectives on Christian World Missions.* Grand Rapids, MI: Eerdmans.

1995a *The Open Secret: An Introduction to the Theology of Mission.*
Revised edition. Grand Rapids, MI: Eerdmans. (1st edition: 1978:
Eerdmans.)

1995b *Proper Confidence: Faith, Doubt, and Certainty in Christian
Discipleship.* Grand Rapids, MI: Eerdmans.

1996 *Truth and Authority in Modernity.* Valley Forge, PA: Trinity Press
International.

Nicholls, Bruce J.
1979 *Contextualization: A Theology of Gospel and Culture.* Downers
Grove, IL: InterVarsity Press.

Nicholson, E. W.
1982 "The Covenant Ritual in Exodus 24:3-8." *Vetus Testamentum* 32:74-
86.

Nida, Eugene A.
1954 *Customs and Cultures: Anthropology for Christian Mission.* New
York: Harper.

1960 *Message and Mission: The Communication of the Christian Faith.*
New York: Harper.

Nida, Eugene A., and Charles R. Taber
1969 *The Theory and Practice of Translation.* Leiden, Netherlands: Brill.

Niebuhr, H. Richard
1951 *Christ and Culture.* New York: Harper. (Reprinted in paperback
edition: 1975 New York: Harper and Row.)

Nissen, Johannes
2002 *New Testament and Mission: Historical and Hermeneutical
Perspectives.* New York: Peter Lang. (1st edition: 1999 New York:
Peter Lang based on the Danish version, 1996 *Ordet tog bolig iblandt
os* Copenhagen: Forlaget ANIS.)

Nketia, J. H. Kwabena
1975 *The Music of Africa.* London: Gollancz.

Olsen, Charles M.
1973 *The Base Church.* Atlanta, GA: Forum House.

Osborne, Grant R.
1991 *The Hermeneutical Spiral: A Comprehensive Introduction to Biblical
Interpretation.* Downers Grove, IL: InterVarsity Press.

Otis, George, Jr.
  1993   "An Overview of Spiritual Mapping." In *Breaking Strongholds in Your City*. See: C. Peter Wagner, ed. Pp. 29-47.

  1999   *Informed Intercession*. Ventura, CA: Renew.

Packer, J. I.
  1990   *A Quest for Godliness: The Puritan Vision of the Christian Life*. Wheaton, IL: Crossway Books.

Padilla, C. Rene
  1985   *Mission between the Times: Essays on the Kingdom*. Grand Rapids, MI: Eerdmans.

Pannenberg, Wolfhart, ed.
  1968   *Revelation as History*. New York: Macmillan.

Parshall, Phil
  1980   *New Paths in Muslim Evangelism: Evangelical Approaches to Contextualization*. Grand Rapids, MI: Baker Book House.

  1983   *Bridges to Islam: A Christian Perspective on Folk Islam*. Grand Rapids, MI: Baker Book House.

  1985   *Beyond the Mosque: Christians within the Muslim Community*. Grand Rapids, MI: Baker Book House.

  1998   "Danger! New Directions in Contextualization." *Evangelical Missions Quarterly* 34:404-406, 409-410.

Peck, M. Scott
  1987   *The Different Drum: Community-Making and Peace*. New York: Simon and Shuster.

Pennoyer, F. Douglas
  1990   "In Dark Dungeons of Collective Captivity." In *Wrestling with Dark Angels*. See: C. Peter Wagner and F. Douglas Pennoyer, eds. Pp. 249-279.

Peterson, Douglas
  1996   *Not by Might Nor by Power*. Oxford: Regnum.

Peterson, Eugene
  1997   *Leap Over a Wall: Earthy Spirituality for Everyday Christians*. San Francisco, CA: HarperSanFrancisco.

Phillips, J. B.
  1960   *The New Testament in Modern English*. New York: Macmillan.

Phillips, James M., and Robert T. Coote, eds.
  1993 *Toward the Twenty-First Century in Christian Mission*. Grand
        Rapids, MI: Eerdmans.

Phrommedda, Tongpan and Banpote Wechkama
  2001 *Voices from Asia: Communicating Contextualization through Story*.
        December 2001. Translated by Paul H. DeNeui. Fuller Theological
        Seminary, Pasadena, CA. Unpublished manuscript.

Pinnock, Clark H.
  1977 "Call For the Liberation of North American Christians." In
        Evangelicals and Liberation. See: Carl E. Armerding, ed. Pp. 128-
        136.

Pobee, John. S.
  1979 *Toward an African Theology*. Nashville, TN: Abingdon Press.

Pontificia Univ Urbaniana, ed.
  1993 *Dizionario di Missiologia*. Bologna, Italy: Dehoniane.

Priest, Robert J., Thomas Campbell, and Bradford A. Mullen
  1995 "Missiological Syncretism: The New Anamistic Paradigm." In
        Spiritual Power and Missions. See: Edward Rommen, ed. Pp. 9-87.

Ramseyer, Robert L., ed.
  1979 *Mission and the Peace Witness: The Gospel and Christian
        Discipleship*. Scottdale, PA: Herald Press.

Rawson, Katie J.
  1999 "Evangelizing East Asian Students in the United States with Special
        Reference to Media Tools." D.Miss. dissertation, Fuller Theological
        Seminary, Pasadena, CA.

Read, William R., Victor M. Monterroso, and Harmon A. Johnson
  1969 *Latin American Church Growth*. Grand Rapids, MI: Eerdmans.

Redford, Shawn B.
  2004 "The Contextualization and Translation of Christianity: Acts 9:1-9,
        22:3-33, 26:2-23." In *Mission in Acts: Ancient Narratives in
        Contemporary Context*. See: Robert L. Gallagher and Paul Hertig,
        eds. Pp. 283-296.

Regele, Mark
  1995 *Death of the Church*. Grand Rapids, IL: Zondervan.

Richardson, Don
  1974 *Peace Child*. Glendale, CA: Regal Books.

  1981 *Eternity in Their Hearts*. Ventura, CA: Regal Books.

2000   "Redemptive Analogies." In *Evangelical Dictionary of World Missions*. See: A. Scott Moreau, Harold A. Netland, and Charles E. Van Engen, eds. Pp. 812-813.

Ritchie, John
1946   *Indigenous Church Principles in Theory and Practice*. New York: Revell.

Roche, Garry
1989   "Moka and Covenant." *Catalyst* 19:163-181.

Roest Crollius, Ary A.,
1978   "What Is So New about Inculturation: A Concept and Its Implications." *Gregorianum* 59:721-738.

1993   Article on Inculturation. In *Dizionario di Missiologia*. See: Pontificia Univ Urbaniana, ed. Pp. 281-286.

Roest Crollius, Ary A., ed.
1984   *Inculturation: Working Papers on Living Faith and Cultures*, 2 Vols. Rome: Pontificia Univ Gregoriana.

Romantz, David S., and Kathleen Elliott Vinson
1998   *Legal Analysis: The Fundamental Skill*. Durham, NC: Carolina Academic Press.

Rommen, Edward, ed.
1995   *Spiritual Power and Missions: Raising the Issues*. Pasadena, CA: William Carey Library.

Rooy, Sidney H.
1965   *The Theology of Missions in the Puritan Tradition*. Grand Rapids, MI: Eerdmans.

Rosin, H. H.
1972   *Missio Dei: An Examination of the Origin, Contents and Function of the Term in Protestant Missiological Discussion*. Leiden, Netherlands: Interuniversity Institute for Missiological and Ecumenical Research.

Ross, Andrew C.
1994   *A Vision Betrayed: The Jesuits in Japan and China, 1542-1742*. Maryknoll, NY: Orbis Books.

1998   "Moffat, Robert." In *Biographical Dictionary of Christian Missions*. See: Gerald H. Anderson, ed. Pp. 464-465.

Roxburgh, Alan J.
1997   *The Missionary Congregation, Leadership and Liminality*. Harrisburg, PA: Trinity Press International.

2002   "Shaping the Journey: Reforming the Church in North America." *Missiological Lectures*, November 13-14, 2002. Fuller Theological Seminary, Pasadena, CA.

Ruganda, John
  1973   *Covenants with Death*. Nairobi, Kenya: East African Publishing House.

Rynkiewich, Michael A.
  2004   "What About the Dust? Missiological Musings on Anthropology." In *What about the Soul? Neuroscience and Christian Anthropology*. See: Joel Green, ed. Pp. 133-144.

Saayman, Willem A., and Klippies Kritzinger, eds.
  1996   *Mission in Bold Humility*. Maryknoll, NY: Orbis Books.

Samaan, Lynn Elizabeth
  1990   "Images of Missionary Spirituality: A Study of Spiritual Formation." M.A. thesis, Fuller Theological Seminary, Pasadena, CA.

Samovar, Larry A., and Richard E. Porter, eds.
  1997   *Intercultural Communication: A Reader*. 8th edition. Belmont, CA: Wadsworth.

Sanneh, Lamin O.
  1989   *Translating the Message: The Missionary Impact on Culture*. Maryknoll, NY: Orbis Books.

  1996   *Religion and the Variety of Culture: A Study in Origin and Practice*. Valley Forge, PA: Trinity Press International.

Schacter, Daniel L.
  1996   *Searching for Memory: The Brain, the Mind, and the Past*. New York: BasicBooks.

Schaff, Philip, and Henry Wace, eds.
  1953   *St. Athenasius*. A Select Library of the Nicene and Post-Nicene Fathers of the Christian Church, Second Series, Vol. 4. Grand Rapids, MI: Eerdmans. (Reprinted: 1978.)

Schaller, Lyle E.
  1996   *Tattered Trust: Is There Hope for Your Denomination?* Nashville, TN: Abingdon Press.

  1999   *Discontinuity and Hope: Radical Change and the Path to the Future*. Nashville, TN: Abingdon Press.

Scherer, James A.
  1987   *Gospel, Church, and Kingdom: Comparative Studies in World Mission Theology*. Minneapolis, MN: Augsburg Publishing.

1993   "Church, Kingdom and Missio Dei." In *The Good News of the Kingdom*. See: Charles E. Van Engen, Dean S. Gilliland, and Paul E. Pierson, eds. Pp. 82-88.

Schineller, Peter
1990   *A Handbook on Inculturation*. New York: Paulist Press.

Schreiter, Robert J.
1985   *Constructing Local Theologies*. Maryknoll, NY: Orbis Books.

1997   *The New Catholicity: Theology between the Global and the Local*. Maryknoll, NY: Orbis Books.

Schwartz, Glen
1998   "How Missionary Attitudes Can Create Dependency." *Mission Frontiers* 20:20-24.

Schwarz, Christian A.
1996   *Natural Church Development: A Guide to Eight Essential Qualities of Healthy Churches*. Carol Stream, IL: ChurchSmart Resources.

Schwarz, Christian A., and Christopher Schalk
1998   *Implementation Guide to Natural Church Development*. Carol Stream, IL: ChurchSmart Resources.

Scott, W. Richard
1987   *Organizations: Rational, Natural, and Open Systems*. Englewood Cliffs, NJ: Prentice Hall.

Sedmak, Clemens
2002   *Doing Local Theology: A Guide for Artisans of a New Humanity*. Maryknoll, NY: Orbis Books.

Segundo, Juan Luis
1975   *Liberacion de la Teologia*. Buenos Aires, Argentina: Ediciones C. Lohle.

1976   *Liberation of Theology*. Maryknoll, NY: Orbis Books.

Shaw, R. Daniel
1995   "Contextualizing the Power and the Glory." *International Journal of Frontier Missions* 12:155-160.

Shaw, R. Daniel, and Charles E. Van Engen
2003   *Communicating God's Word in a Complex World: God's Truth or Hocus Pocus?* Lanham, MD: Rowman and Littlefield Publishers.

Shenk, Wilbert R.
1973   "Theology and the Missionary Task." *Missiology* 1:295-310.

1980 "The Changing Role of the Missionary: From Civilization to Contextualization." In *Missions, Evangelism, and Church Growth.* See: C. Norman Kraus, ed. Pp. 33-58.

1995 *Write the Vision: The Church Renewed.* Valley Forge, PA: Trinity Press International. (Reprinted: 2001 Eugene, OR: Wipf and Stock Publishers.

1997 "Mission, Renewal, and the Future of the Church." *International Bulletin of Missionary Research* 21:154-159.

1999 *Changing Frontiers of Mission.* Maryknoll, NY: Orbis Books.

2000 "Developments in the Theology of Mission since 1990." Paper presented at the School of World Mission Faculty Luncheon on October 31, 2000, Fuller Theological Seminary. Pasadena, CA.

Shenk, Wilbert R., ed.
1973 *The Challenge of Church Growth.* Scottdale, PA: Herald Press.

1983 *Exploring Church Growth.* Grand Rapids, MI: Eerdmans.

1993 *The Transfiguration of Mission: Biblical, Theological and Historical Foundations.* Scottdale, PA: Herald Press.

Shorter, Aylward
1988 *Toward a Theology of Inculturation.* Maryknoll, NY: Orbis Books.

Shuster, Marguerite
1987 *Power, Pathology, Paradox: The Dynamics of Evil and Good.* Grand Rapids, MI: Zondervan.

Silvoso, Edgardo
1994 "Argentina – Evangelizing in a Context of Spiritual Warfare." In *Behind Enemy Lines.* See: Charles H. Kraft, ed. Pp. 263-283.

Simpson, Daniel E.
1998 "Natural Church Development: A Guide to Eight Essential Qualities of Healthy Churches." Review of: *Natural Church Development: A Guide to Eight Essential Qualities of Healthy Churches* by Christian A. Schwarz. Reviewed in: *Journal of the American Society for Church Growth* 9:57-70.

Smalley, William A.
1958 "Cultural Implications of an Indigenous Church." *Practical Anthropology* 5:51-65. (Reprinted: 1979. In *Readings in Dynamic Indigeneity.* See Kraft and Wisley, eds. Pp. 31-51.)

1994 *Linguistic Diversity and National Unity: Language Ecology in Thailand.* Chicago, IL: University of Chicago Press.

Smedes, Lewis B.
1993   *Shame and Grace: Healing the Shame We Don't Deserve.* San
         Francisco, CA: HarperSanFrancisco.

Smit, Dirkie
1994   "The Self-Disclosure of God." In *Doing Theology in Context.* See:
         John W. de Gruchy and C. Villa-Vicencio, eds. Pp. 42-54.

Smith, Alexander G.
1982   *A History of Church Growth in Thailand: An Interpretive Analysis
         1816-1980.* Bangkok, Thailand: Kanok Bannasan (OMF Publishers).

Smith, James Bryan
1995   *Embracing the Love of God: The Path and Promise of Christian Life.*
         San Francisco, CA: HarperSanFrancisco.

Smoker, Dorothy
1994   *Ambushed by Love: God's Triumph in Kenya's Terror.* Ft.
         Washington, PA: Christian Literature Crusade.

Snyder, Howard A., ed.
2001   *Global Good News: Mission in a New Context.* Nashville, TN:
         Abingdon Press.

Sobrino, Jon
1984   *The True Church and the Poor.* Maryknoll, NY: Orbis Books.

Sogaard, Viggo B.
1996   *Research in Church and Mission.* Pasadena, CA: William Carey
         Library.

2002   Personal Correspondence. November 11, 2002.

Song, Choan-Seng
1979   *Third-eye Theology: Theology in Formation in Asian Settings.*
         Maryknoll, NY: Orbis Books.

Spencer, Aida Besancon, and William David Spencer, eds.
1998   *The Global God: Multicultural Evangelical Views of God.* Grand
         Rapids, MI: Baker Book House.

Spindler, Marc R., and John Vriend
1995   "The Biblical Grounding and Orientation of Mission." In *Missiology:
         An Ecumenical Introduction: Text and Context of Global Christianity.*
         See: Frans J. Verstraelen, Arnulf Camps, L. A. Hoedemaker, and
         Marc R. Spindler, eds. Pp. 123-143.

Springer, Kevin, ed.
1988   *Power Encounters among Christians in the Western World.* San
         Francisco, CA: Harper and Row.

References Cited

569

Spurgeon, Charles H.
1895, 1963 *The Soul-Winner: How to Lead Sinners to the Savior.* Originally Published: 1895 New York; Chicago: Fleming H. Revell Co. Republished: 1963 Grand Rapids, MI: Eerdmans.

Spykman, Gordon J., et al.
1988 *Let My People Live: Faith and Struggle in Central America.* Grand Rapids, MI: Eerdmans.

Stackhouse, Max L.
1988 *Apologia: Contextualization, Globalization, and Mission in Theological Education.* Grand Rapids, MI: Eerdmans.

Stamoolis, James J.
1986 *Eastern Orthodox Mission Theology Today.* Maryknoll, NY: Orbis Books.

Stark, Rodney
1997 *The Rise of Christianity: How the Obscure, Marginal Jesus Movement became the Dominant Religious Force in the Western World in a Few Centuries.* San Francisco, CA: HarperSanFrancisco.

Stewart, Charles, and Rosalind Shaw, eds.
1994 *Syncretism/Anti-Syncretism: The Politics of Religious Synthesis.* London; New York: Routledge.

Stock, Eugene
1899 *History of the Church Missionary Society.* 3 vols. London: CMS.

Storti, Craig
1999 *Figuring Foreigners Out: A Practical Guide.* Yarmouth, ME: Intercultural Press.

Stronstad, Roger
1984 *The Charismatic Theology of Luke.* Peabody, MA: Hendrickson Publishers.

Stults, Donald LeRoy
1989 *Developing an Asian Evangelical Theology.* Metro Manila, Philippines: OMF Literature.

Sumithra, Sunand, and F. Hrangkuma, eds.
1995 *Doing Mission in Context.* Bangalore, India: Theological Book Trust.

Swanson, Herbert R.
2002 "Dancing to the Temple, Dancing in the Church: Reflections on Thai Local Theology." *Journal of Theologies and Cultures in Asia* 1:59-78.

Sweet, Leonard I.

1994 *FaithQuakes*. Nashville, TN: Abingdon Press.

1999 *SoulTsunami: Sink or Swim in New Millennium Culture*. Grand Rapids, MI: Zondervan.

Taber, Charles R.

1978a "Is There More Than One Way to Do Theology?" *Gospel in Context* 1:4-10. (Reprinted: 1993 *Didaskalia* 5:3-18.)

1978b "Limits of Indigenization in Theology." *Missiology* 6:53-79. (Reprinted: 1979. In *Readings in Dynamic Indigeneity*. See Kraft and Wisley, eds. Pp. 372-399.)

1979 "Contextualization: Indigenation and/or Transformation." In *The Gospel and Islam*. See: Don M. McCurry, ed. Pp. 143-150.

1983 "Contextualization." In *Exploring Church Growth*. See: Wilbert R. Shenk, ed. Pp. 117-131.

1991 *The World Is Too Much With Us: Culture in Modern Protestant Missions*. Macon, GA: Mercer University Press.

Tate, W. Randolph

1997 *Biblical Interpretation: An Integrated Approach*. Revised edition. Peabody, MA: Hendrickson Publishers. (1st edition: 1991 Hendrickson Publishers.)

Taylor, John Vernon

1963 *The Primal Vision: Christian Presence amid African Religion*. Philadelphia, PA: Fortress Press. Introduction by M. A. C. Warren.

Taylor, William M.

1879 *Pauline Methods of Missionary Work*. Philadelphia, PA: National Pub. Association for the Promotion of Holiness.

Teeter, David

1990 "Dynamic Equivalent Conversion for Tentative Muslim Believers." *Missiology* 18:305-313.

Terry, John Mark

2000 "Indigenous Churches." In *Evangelical Dictionary of World Mission*. See: A. Scott Moreau, Harold A. Netland, and Charles E. Van Engen, eds. Pp. 483-485.

Thiselton, Anthony C.

1980 *The Two Horizons: New Testament Hermeneutics and Philosophical Description with Special Reference to Heidegger, Bultmann, Gadamer, and Wittgenstein*. Grand Rapids, MI: Eerdmans.

Thomas, Norman E., ed.
    1995, 1998 *Classic Texts in Mission and World Christianity*. Maryknoll,
        NY: Orbis Books. (Reprinted: 1998.)

Thompson, Michael, Richard Ellis, and Aaron Wildavsky
    1990   *Cultural Theory*. Boulder, CO: Westview Press.

Tiénou, Tite
    1993   "Forming Indigenous Theologies." In *Toward the Twenty-First
        Century in Christian Missions*. See: James M. Phillips and Robert T.
        Coote, eds. Pp. 245-252.

Tippett, Alan Richard
    1967   *Solomon Islands Christianity*. Pasadena, CA: William Carey Library.

    1969, 1973 *Verdict Theology in Missionary Theory*. Lincoln, IL: Lincoln
        Christian College Press. (Reprinted: 1973 Pasadena, CA: William
        Carey Library.)

    1971   *People Movements in Southern Polynesia: Studies in the Dynamics of
        Church-planting and growth in Tahiti, New Zealand, Tonga, and
        Samoa*. Chicago, IL: Moody Press.

    1987   *Introduction to Missiology*. Pasadena, CA: William Carey Library.

Torres, Sergio, and Virginia Fabella, eds.
    1978   *The Emergent Gospel: Theology from the Developing World*.
        London: Geoffrey Chapman.

Travis, John
    1998a   "The C1 to C6 Spectrum" *Evangelical Missions Quarterly* 34:407-
        408.

    1998b   "Must all Muslims Leave Islam to Follow Jesus?" *Evangelical
        Missions Quarterly* 34:411-415.

    2000   "Messianic Muslim Followers of Isa: A Closer Look at C5 Believers
        and Congregations." *International Journal of Frontier Missions*
        17:53-59.

Tucker, Gene M.
    1965   "Covenant Forms and Contract Forms." *Vetus Testamentum* 15:487-
        503.

Turner, Harold W.
    1967   *History of an African Independent Church: Church of the Lord
        (Aladura)*. 2 Vols. Oxford: Clarendon Press.

    1977   *Bibliography of New Religious Movements in Primal Societies, Vol.
        1: Black Africa*. Boston, MA: G. K. Hall.

Ukpong, Justin S.
    1987a "Contextualization: A Historical Survey." *African Ecclesial Review* 29:278-286.

    1987b "What is Contextualization?" *Neue Zeitschrift fur Missionswissenschaft* 43:161-168.

Van Engen, Charles E.
    1981 *The Growth of the True Church: An Analysis of the Ecclesiology of Church Growth Theory.* Amsterdam, Netherlands: Rodopi.

    1989 "The New Covenant: Knowing God in Context." In *The Word Among Us: Contextualizing Theology for Mission Today.* See: Dean S. Gilliland, ed. Pp. 74-100. (Reprinted: 1996. In *Mission on the Way: Issues in Mission Theology.* Pp. 71-89.)

    1991 *God's Missionary People.* Grand Rapids, MI: Baker Book House.

    1996 *Mission on the Way: Issues in Mission Theology.* Grand Rapids, MI: Baker Books.

Van Engen, Charles E., Dean S. Gilliland, and Paul E. Pierson, eds.
    1993 *The Good News of the Kingdom.* Maryknoll, NY: Orbis Books.

Van Engen, Charles E., and Shawn B. Redford
    2002 MT520/MT620 class syllabus. Pasadena, CA: Fuller Theological Seminary, School of World Mission.

Van Engen, Charles E., Nancy Thomas, and Robert Gallagher, eds.
    1999 *Footprints of God: A Narrative Theology of Mission.* Monrovia, CA: MARC.

Van Engen, Charles E., and Jude Tiersma, eds.
    1994 *God So Loves the City: Seeking a Theology for Urban Mission.* Monrovia, CA: MARC.

Van Rheenen, Gailyn
    2002 "Evangelizing Folk Religionists." *Monthly Missiological Reflections* 23. Dated March 12, 2002. http://www.missiology.org. Accessed March 12, 2002.

Vander Veer, Peter
    1994 "Syncretism, Multiculturalism, and the Discourse of Tolerance." In *Syncretism/Anti-Syncretism: The Politics of Religious Synthesis.* See: Charles Stewart and Rosalind Shaw, eds. Pp. 196-211.

Venn, Henry
    1856 "Instructions to Missionaries." *Church Missionary Re*gister 27:153.

1868   "Instructions to Missionaries." *Church Missionary Intelligencer* NS
         4:316.

Verkuyl, Johannes
    1978   *Contemporary Missiology: An Introduction.* Grand Rapids, MI:
             Eerdmans.

Verstraelen, Frans J., Arnulf Camps, L. A. Hoedemaker, and Marc R. Spindler,
         eds.
    1995   *Missiology: An Ecumenical Introduction: Text and Context of Global
             Christianity.* Grand Rapids, MI: Eerdmans.

Vidales, Raul
    1979   "Methodological Issues in Liberation Theology." In *Frontiers of
             Theology in Latin America.* See: Rosino Gibellini, ed. Pp. 34-57.

Vinay, Samuel
    1997   "The Contextualization of Jesus." Paper prepared for the Lausanne
             Consultation on Gospel Contextualization. Haslev, Denmark.

Visser, Marten
    2002   Personal Correspondence. November 3, 2002.

Visser 't Hooft, Willem Adolph
    1963   *No Other Name: The Choice Between Syncretism and Christian
             Universalism.* London, England: SCM Press.

    1976   "Evangelism in the Neo-Pagan Situation." *International Review of
             Mission* 65:81-86.

von Allmen, Daniel
    1975   "Birth of Theology: Contextualization as the Dynamic Element in the
             Formation of New Testament Theology." *International Review of
             Mission* 64:37-52.

von Rad, Gerhard
    1961   *Genesis: A Commentary.* Translated by John H. Marks. London:
             SCM Press.

Vos, Geerhardus
    1948   *Biblical Theology: Old and New Testaments.* Grand Rapids, MI:
             Eerdmans.

Wagner, C. Peter
    1973   *Look Out! The Pentecostals Are Coming.* Carol Stream, IL: Creation
             House. (Reissued: 1986 *Spiritual Power and Church Growth.*)

    1979   *Our Kind of People: The Ethical Dimensions of Church Growth in
             America.* Atlanta, CA: John Knox.

1981   *Church Growth and the Whole Gospel: A Biblical Mandate.* San Francisco, CA: Harper and Row.

1986   *Spiritual Power and Church Growth: Lessons from the Amazing Growth of Pentecostal Churches in Latin America.* Altamonte Springs, FL: Strang Communications Center. (Reissue of: 1973 *Look Out! The Pentecostals Are Coming.*)

1987   *Strategies for Church Growth: Tools for Effective Mission and Evangelism.* Ventura, CA: Regal Books.

1988   *How to Have a Healing Ministry without Making Your Church Sick.* Ventura, CA: Regal Books.

1994   *Spreading the Fire: Book 1, Acts 1-8.* Ventura, CA: Regal Books.

1999   *ChurchQuake!: How the New Apostolic Reformation Is Shaking Up the Church as We Know It.* Ventura, CA: Regal Books.

Wagner, C. Peter, ed.
1993   *Breaking Strongholds in Your City.* Ventura, CA: Regal Books.

1998   *The New Apostolic Churches.* Ventura, CA: Regal Books.

Wagner, C. Peter, and Pablo Alberto Deiros, eds.
1998   *The Rising Revival: Firsthand Accounts of the Incredible Argentine Revival – and How It Can Be Spread throughout the World.* Ventura, CA: Renew; Gospel Light.

Wagner, C. Peter, and F. Douglas Pennoyer, eds.
1990   *Wrestling with Dark Angels: Toward a Deeper Understanding of the Supernatural Forces in Spiritual Warfare.* Ventura, CA: Regal Books.

Wallace, Daniel B.
1997   "The Holy Spirit and Hermeneutics." Biblical Studies Press. Available via download at: http://www.bible.org/docs/soapbox/hermhs.htm.

Walls, Andrew F.
1981, 1982   "The Gospel As the Prisoner and Liberator of Culture." *Faith and Thought* 108:39-52. Also published: 1982 *Missionalia* 10:93-105.

1996, 2000   *The Missionary Movement in Christian History: Studies in the Transmission of Faith.* Maryknoll, NY: Orbis Books.

Walton, John H.
1994   *Covenant: God's Purpose, God's Plan.* Grand Rapids, MI: Zondervan.

References Cited

Weerstra, H. M., ed.
  2000   *International Journal of Frontier Missions* 17.

Wells, David
  1994   *God in the Wasteland: The Reality of Truth in a World of Fading Dreams.* Grand Rapids, MI: Eerdmans.

Wheatley, Margaret J.
  1994   *Leadership and the New Science: Learning about Organization from an Orderly Universe.* 2nd edition. San Francisco, CA: Berrett-Koehler Publishers.

Wheeler, Ray
  2002   "The Legacy of Shoki Coe." *International Bulletin of Missionary Research* 26:77-80.

Whiteman, Darrell L.
  1997   "Contextualization: The Theory, the Gap, the Challenge." *International Bulletin of Missionary Research* 21:2-7.

Whiteman, Darrell L., ed.
  1985   *Missionaries, Anthropologists and Cultural Change.* (Studies in Third World Societies No. 25.) Williamsburg, VA: Dept. of Anthropology, College of William and Mary.

Wilder, John W.
  1977   "Some Reflections on Possibilities for People Movements among Muslims." *Missiology* 5:301-320.

Willard, Dallas
  1998   *The Divine Conspiracy: Rediscovering Our Hidden Life in God.* San Francisco, CA: Harper.

  1999   *Hearing God: Developing a Conversational Relationship with God.* Downers Grove, IL: InterVarsity Press.

  2002   *Renovation of the Heart: Putting on the Character of Christ.* Colorado Springs, CO: NavPress.

Williams, C. Peter
  1990   *The Ideal of the Self-Governing Church: A Study in Victorian Missionary Strategy.* Leiden, Netherlands: E. J. Brill.

Wilson, Frederick, ed.
  1990   *The San Antonio Report – Your Will Be Done: Mission in Christ's Way.* Geneva: WCC.

Winslow, Donald F.
    1977   "Logos." *The Encyclopedia of Early Christianity.* Vol. 1. 2nd ed.
            See: Everett Ferguson, Michael P. McHugh, and Frederick W. Norris,
            eds. Pp. 687-690.

Winslow, Ola Elizabeth
    1968   *John Eliot: Apostle to the Indians.* Boston, MA: Houghton Mifflin.

Winter, Ralph D.
    1999   "Going Far Enough? Taking Some Tips from the Historical Record."
            In *Perspectives on the World Christian Movement.* See: Ralph D.
            Winter and Steven C. Hawthorne, eds.

Winter, Ralph D., and Steven C. Hawthorne, eds.
    1999   *Perspectives on the World Christian Movement.* Pasadena, CA:
            William Carey Library.

Wisley, Thomas N.
    1985   "Dynamic Biblical Christianity in the Buddhist/Marxist Context:
            Northeast Thailand." Thesis, Fuller Theological Seminary, Pasadena,
            CA.

Wong, James Y. K.
    1973   *Singapore: The Church in the Midst of Social Change.* Singapore:
            Church Growth Study Centre.

Woodberry, J. Dudley
    1989   "Contextualization among Muslims: Reusing Common Pillars." In
            The Word among Us: Contextualizing Theology for Mission Today.
            See: Dean S. Gilliland, ed. Pp. 282-312.

Woodberry, J. Dudley, ed.
    1989   *Muslims and Christians on the Emmaus Road.* Monrovia, CA:
            MARC.

World Missionary Conference
    1910   *Report of Commission I: Carrying the Gospel to All the Non-
            Christian World.* Edinburgh; London: Oliphant, Anderson, and
            Ferrier.

Wright, G. Ernest
    1950   *The Old Testament against Its Environment.* Chicago, IL: Henry
            Regnery Company.

Wright, Walter
    2000   *Relational Leadership: A Biblical Model for Influence and Service.*
            Waynesboro, GA: Paternoster Press.

References Cited

Yep, Jeanette, ed.
 1998 *Following Jesus Without Dishonoring Your Parents: Asian-American Discipleship.* Downers Grove, IL: InterVarsity Press.

Yesurathnam, R.
 2000 "Contextualizing in Mission." In *Mission Paradigm in the New Millennium.* See: W. S. Milton Jeganathan, ed. Pp. 44-57.

Yoder, John H.
 1972 *The Politics of Jesus.* Grand Rapids, MI: Eerdmans.

 1992 *Body Politics: Five Practices of Christian Community before the Watching World.* Nashville, TN: Discipleship Resources.

Young, B. W.
 1998 *Religion and Enlightenment in 18th-century England: Theological Debate from Locke to Burke.* Oxford: Clarendon Press.

Yum, June Ock
 1997 "The Impact of Confucianism on Interpersonal Relationships and Communication Patterns in East Asia." In *Intercultural Communication: A Reader.* 8th edition. See: Larry A. Samovar and Richard E. Porter, eds. Pp. 78-88.

Zadeh, Lofti Asker
 1965 "Fuzzy Sets." *Information and Control* 8:338-353.

Zahniser, A. H. Mathias
 1997 Symbol and Ceremony: Making Disciples across Cultures. Monrovia, CA: MARC.

Scripture Index

Author Index

General Index

A priori, 26, 122, 228, 246, 344
Abortion, 373
Academia/Academic, ix-x, xvii, 32,
  39, 43, 45, 53, 68-69, 72, 89-90,
  102-103, 122, 124, 133, 227,
  231-232, 235, 239, 243, 266, 268,
  295-296, 324, 387, 429, 451, 517,
  525, 564
Acculturated, 464, 518
Accurate/Accuracy, 120, 197, 252,
  298-299, 301, 350, 370, 394, 512
Activist, 384
Acultural, 120
Adapt/Adaptation, 10, 19, 29, 33,
  38, 40, 51, 60, 68, 83, 85-87, 89-
  91, 96-97, 114, 137, 170, 172,
  184-185, 195, 205, 220, 255-256,
  260, 263-264, 266, 268, 284, 290,
  310, 318, 338, 340, 346, 380,
  389, 413, 417, 419, 428, 436,
  458, 460, 463, 472, 506-507, 541
Administrate/Administrator, xvi, 32,
  69-70, 117, 129, 187, 193, 287
Admission, 17, 32, 69, 102, 129-
  130, 133, 139, 230, 241, 247,
  297, 321, 355, 381, 418, 518
Adultery, 487
Advent, 166, 213, 304, 398, 450
Advise/Advice/Advisor, 35, 64, 73,
  77, 145, 272, 283-284, 314, 394,
  484
Advocate/Advocacy, 3-4, 7-8, 10,
  13, 17-18, 20, 34, 38, 69-70, 72,
  76, 105, 113, 123, 159, 167-168,
  180, 227, 242-243, 257, 259-263,
  265-266, 269-270, 272, 326, 340,
  364, 368, 376, 397, 419, 437,
  449, 465, 484-487, 527
Africa/African, ix-x, xvi-xvii, 9, 22-
  23, 29, 34, 36, 39-42, 57-58, 60-
61, 71, 73-75, 79, 95, 123, 125,
  130, 152-153, 160, 180, 187-188,
  191, 196, 198, 210, 212, 240,
  265, 269, 271, 275, 285-286, 297,
  309-315, 317-319, 321-323, 326,
  331-332, 348, 376, 380-382, 411,
  442, 444-448, 450, 452, 457, 476,
  478-479, 493, 500, 502-503, 506-
  507, 518, 521-523, 525-527, 529-
  533, 535, 537, 540, 547, 549,
  552, 554, 558, 560-561, 563, 565,
  570-572
Agape, 327, 333, 358, 371
Age, 37, 131, 156, 191, 212, 306,
  311, 336, 352, 417, 443, 453, 461
Agency, 42, 64, 72, 125, 133, 193,
  211, 223, 301, 305, 391, 468,
  479, 481
Agenda, 47, 52, 59, 157, 172, 201,
  218, 224, 228, 233-234, 252,
  294-295, 298, 416, 462, 548
Agent, 45, 57, 175, 205, 213, 223,
  244, 290, 347, 482, 494, 557
Agnostic, 228, 408
Ahistorical, 120
Aid, 226, 237, 432, 541
Ailments, 389
Aim, 9, 18, 22, 42, 46, 84-85, 94,
  106, 110, 168, 170-171, 178,
  180-181, 193, 212, 271, 299,
  329-330, 334, 342, 363, 384, 398,
  404, 417, 424, 471, 481, 503
Akongo, 322
Akron, 521-522
Aldersgate, 439
Algonquian, 37
Algorithmic, 120-121
Alien/Alienate, 27, 55, 144, 198,
  229, 239, 283, 333, 415, 419-421,

597

Cohesion/Cohesive, 208, 242-243

College, ix, xv, 18, 40, 46, 70, 72-
73, 92, 102-103, 107, 151, 345,
398, 409, 420, 427, 444, 448,
522, 536, 571, 575

Colony/Colonialism, 36, 41, 46, 61,
185, 272, 275-276, 296, 301, 439,
493, 506, 532, 549

Commandment/Command, 63, 92,
143, 148, 177-178, 258, 286, 327,
342, 350, 355, 357, 368, 371,
391, 409, 416, 487

Commission, ix, 40, 42, 63, 149,
177, 184, 186, 193, 209, 273,
293, 295, 298, 301-302, 357, 461,
465, 504, 522, 531, 553, 576

Commitment, 6, 8-9, 13, 19, 30, 33-
34, 40, 68, 72-73, 75-76, 83, 87-
90, 93-94, 97, 99-100, 104, 106,
110, 112, 151-152, 157, 159, 161,
169-170, 172, 177, 196, 198-200,
218, 255, 261, 263-264, 268, 294,
322-323, 327, 330-334, 341, 346,
349, 363, 388, 391-393, 403, 405,
408, 424, 483-484, 486, 500, 506

Common/Commoner, 11, 14, 44,
56, 63-64, 95, 122, 125, 127-128,
139-140, 152, 155, 178, 184-185,
190, 193, 195, 197, 262, 267,
289, 305, 311, 313-314, 319, 322,
334, 345-346, 375, 381, 385, 390,
400, 441, 450, 454, 464, 472,
478, 481, 494, 497, 500, 505,
511-512, 576

Communicate, xiii, 4, 10, 15, 24,
47-51, 53, 58, 64, 68, 74, 103,
106, 111, 119, 124-125, 129,
136-137, 139, 147, 152-153, 156,
159, 163-164, 168, 173, 179,
183-185, 197, 204, 208, 212, 259,
261, 268, 283, 302, 310, 312-313,
324, 340, 359, 370, 417, 428,
437, 439, 441, 443, 445-446, 452,
457, 483, 487, 497-498, 503-504,
511-512, 515-516, 519, 556, 563,
566

Communication, xvi, 7, 18, 25, 30-
31, 46-47, 53, 68, 73, 76-77, 84,
87, 91, 99, 127, 137, 156-159,
162-165, 167-168, 178-179, 183-
186, 188-190, 192, 200, 202-203,
225, 229, 236-237, 247, 256,
261-262, 267, 269-270, 276, 310,
313-314, 318, 321, 328, 332, 335,
343-348, 358-359, 364, 420, 424,
429, 431, 433, 437, 443, 445-446,
451, 479, 482, 489, 494-495, 500,
509, 512, 515, 529, 538, 554-555,
561, 565, 577

Communicator, 157-159, 163-165,
184-185, 300, 488, 499, 512

Communion, 87, 135, 153-154, 173,
223, 351, 413, 428, 430, 508

Communism/Communist, 89, 345,
446, 476

Community, xv, 12, 18, 20, 24, 46,
53, 56-60, 64, 77, 100-101, 117-
118, 122, 124, 128, 136, 139,
161, 163, 166, 169-170, 173,
178-180, 193, 205, 230, 232,
237-239, 245, 248, 250-253, 260,
263-264, 268, 280, 284, 286-288,
296, 298, 300, 305, 311-312,
314-315, 317, 321-322, 326, 329,
340, 345-347, 350, 352, 355, 357,
368, 371, 373, 387, 394, 397,
399-407, 409, 412, 414, 418-432,
438-443, 448, 452, 455-456, 458,
461, 463, 465-467, 469, 472-473,
495, 514, 517, 540, 542, 547,
557, 562, 577

Companion/Companionship, 51,
131, 350, 410, 444, 464

Compartmentalize, 312, 322, 324,
503, 511

Compassion, 16, 132, 171, 174,
209, 286, 438, 446, 448

Compatible, 190, 406, 517

Competition, 76, 83-86, 94-97, 117,
157, 296, 333, 448

Complaint, 61, 314

Complexity, 4, 28, 30, 39, 54, 119,
138, 169, 186, 204, 212, 220,

Shepherd, 287, 317, 507, 512

Shinto, 171, 382, 389

Shrine, 161, 172, 361, 366, 373, 389, 413

Sierra Leone, 39-40, 42, 258, 314, 549

SIL, xvi

Sin, 19, 30, 39, 50, 55, 57, 64, 77, 101, 123, 125, 131-132, 166, 174, 245, 313, 316-317, 343, 350, 373, 382-385, 403, 437-439, 442, 447, 487, 494, 504, 510, 544

Sinai, 146-149

Singapore, 13, 34, 74, 297, 533, 551, 576

Singing, ix, 180-181, 247, 264, 310-315, 317-320, 322-323, 351, 428, 439, 502

SIS, x

Slavery, 39-40, 51, 64, 131, 147, 443, 450, 471

Slavic, 183

Social, 4, 12-13, 27-28, 37, 39, 42-44, 46, 55-56, 59-60, 62, 78, 89, 125, 128, 131, 137, 140-141, 143, 148, 162-163, 166, 170, 185, 194-195, 198-199, 207, 268, 272, 275-278, 280, 284-285, 288-289, 294, 297, 302, 304, 355, 361, 381, 402-403, 411-412, 416, 418, 421-422, 427, 431, 435, 437-439, 441, 446, 449-450, 452, 454, 459-461, 504, 506, 509-511, 518, 535, 539, 543-544, 576

Society, x, xv, 5-6, 8-12, 14-15, 18-20, 24, 27, 30, 34, 39-46, 52-53, 55-57, 61-62, 64, 72-75, 77, 79, 84-86, 88-91, 93, 96-97, 99, 104, 111-115, 121-123, 125, 131-133, 139, 149, 152-153, 155-157, 161, 166, 168-173, 175-177, 186, 191, 193, 202-203, 239, 243, 250, 255-256, 258-259, 261, 263, 267-271, 276, 278, 280, 284-285, 287, 289, 293, 296, 298, 300-302, 304-305, 311, 325-326, 329-332, 334-340, 343, 345-349, 351-356,

358-359, 368-369, 371, 375-376, 378-381, 385-387, 403, 416-420, 424, 430, 432-433, 435, 437-438, 442-444, 446-450, 453-454, 456, 459, 464, 471, 476, 478-479, 481, 483-486, 488-489, 499, 503, 510-511, 514-515, 522-523, 525-527, 530, 536, 541, 543, 551, 555-556, 559-560, 567, 569, 571, 575

Sociocultural, 5-6, 8, 10-13, 27, 68, 111, 121, 125, 127-128, 131, 155, 157, 334, 370, 414, 475

Socioeconomic, 193-194, 198, 205, 300, 302, 454

Sociology, 37, 39, 43-44, 247, 300, 450

Sociopolitical, 192, 198, 505

Socioreligious, 397, 400

Song, 23-24, 277, 296, 309-320, 323-324, 372, 422-423, 430, 445, 509, 568

Soul, 36, 142, 166, 298, 327, 330-331, 425, 439, 451, 457, 466, 508, 548, 565

Sovereignty, 137, 147, 229, 240-241, 244, 297, 397, 437-438, 440-441, 451, 458, 480, 503

Sowing, 282, 298, 353

Spain/Spanish, 23, 36, 119, 178, 260

Specialization, x, 18, 165, 186, 232, 243, 287, 460

Spirit, 5-6, 8, 10, 20, 24-25, 30, 33-34, 38-39, 44-45, 48, 50-51, 56-57, 62-65, 68, 73, 76-77, 85, 87-91, 96, 100-101, 103, 106-108, 110, 112-114, 123, 129, 137, 142, 150-151, 160, 166, 168-169, 171, 173, 179, 181, 187, 190, 210-213, 215, 237, 240-242, 244-248, 253, 257-260, 264, 278-282, 284, 286, 288, 295-297, 306, 309, 314, 316, 320-322, 327-329, 331, 337, 342, 344, 346, 348-354, 357, 361-364, 366, 368-369, 371-375, 377, 379-386, 388-389, 392-394, 406-410, 430, 438-443, 446, 448-454, 459,

Appropriate Christianity